D1477459

BRICK BUILDING IN ENGLAND

For C. H. Wight, M.C., M.R.C.S., L.R.C.P., my father

Wednesday, 22 January, 1941:

'As I was passing Reydon Hall this morning a Dornier 17 came out of a cloud and opened up on me with his machine guns. The bullets hit the road just behind the car. Called to a shocking accident near the Brampton Dog Cross Rds' . . .

Thomas Martin ('the historian of Thetford') (1697–1771) describes the demolition of the Tudor brick Hall at Westhorpe, Suffolk, with its terracotta ornaments:

'I went to see the dismal ruins of Westhorpe Hall, formerly the seat of Charles Brandon, Duke of Suffolk. The workmen are now pulling it down as fast as may be, in a very careless and injudicious manner. The coping bricks, battlements, and many other ornamental pieces are made of earth, and burnt hard, and as fresh as when first built. They might, with care, have been taken down whole, but all the fine chimnies and ornaments were pulled down with ropes, and crushed to pieces, in a most shameful manner. There was a monstrous figure of Hercules sitting cross legged with his club, and a lion beside him, but all shattered to pieces.'

Quoted by JOHN WODDERSPOON, in *The Historic Sites of Suffolk*, 1841.

BRICK BUILDING IN ENGLAND

FROM THE MIDDLE AGES TO 1550

Jane A. Wight

4, 5 & 6 Soho Square, London

First published in 1972 by
JOHN BAKER (PUBLISHERS) LTD
4, 5 & 6 Soho Square
London W1V 6AD

ISBN 0 212 98400 4

Printed in Great Britain by
W & J MACKAY LIMITED, CHATHAM

Contents

Illustrations

PLATES

FIGURES

Permission to reproduce the plates was kindly granted by *Hallam Ashley*, pls. 8, 11, 12, 13, 19, 21, 22, 51, 52; *Laurence H. James*, jacket illustration; *Arthur Mackenzie*, pl. 49; *Edwin Smith*, pls. 23, 24, 48; *Margaret Wood*, pl. 16; *Aerofilms Ltd*, pl. 25; *The British Museum*, pls. 1, 9, 10; *The Guardian*, pl. 63; *Essex County Record Office*, pl. 4; *Norman May's Studio Ltd*, pl. 25; The photographic library of the then-*Ministry of Public Building and Works* supplied pls. 7, 14, 15, 16, 20, 26, 27 and the *National Monuments Record* supplied pls. 3, 5, 42, 43, 46, 47, 50, 75, all of which are *Crown Copyright*. Plate 33 is reproduced *By Courtesy of the Ashmolean Museum*, Oxford. All other photographs were supplied by Elaine Barrault and were specially taken for this book.

The maps and details of figures 1, 2, 6, 7, 8, 9, 11, 12, 15-19 were drawn by Cecil Bacon.

Acknowledgements

I have received from friends and strangers reassuring kindness, encouragement, information and material assistance, especially over photographs. Curators and librarians have helped me beyond the needs of duty. Craftsmen have considered and answered unexpected or anachronistic questions. I am grateful for the help of rectors and of houseowners. I have written without introduction to experts on particular subjects or areas and have received generous and detailed information. I have also, gratefully, been able to work in the British Museum Reading Room and the Library of the Royal Institute of British Architects. The resources of the National Monuments Record, Westminster, and the kindness of the staff there have been vital.

I must particularly thank reference librarians at Westminster, St Albans (including Mr A. R. Threadgill, now County Reference Librarian at Bedford), Norwich, Great Yarmouth and also Miss D. M. White of the Ipswich Central Library. Of the experts who have answered queries I owe special debts to: Canon P. Binnall, for help over Lincoln buildings; John Harvey, author of *The British Mediaeval Architect*, for information about Andrew Ogard's house at Emneth and his Rye House; K. W. E. Gravett for information about early brick in Kent and Sussex; John Newman for extra notes on entries in his two Penguins on Kent; S. E. Rigold, of the Ministry of Public Building and Works, for details of Bishop's Waltham Palace and of brick in the South-East generally. I hope these people will forgive my errors. Margaret Wood, author of *The English Mediaeval House*, has kindly allowed me to use her photograph of Little Wenham Hall. Arthur Mackenzie drove a long distance to take photographs of the terracotta tombs at Oxborough, Norfolk. Hallam Ashley has let me have new photographs of Norwich buildings and of Caister Castle, Norfolk.

I would like to make particular thanks to the owner of Leez Priory. My cousin Miss M. Wight, photographer, has helped me over Worcestershire buildings. Adrian Bell gave me details of the moulded brick or terracotta tomb-chest at Barsham in Suffolk. Timothy Matthews kindly showed me his brickworks near Tring. I would like to thank Professor L. H. Butler of St Andrews University for giving me a lasting interest in fifteenth-century English society, of which this book is a distant by-product. To Rachel Young, of the Norwich Museums, my obligation is manifold, and I thank her especially for information about Norfolk buildings and for her encouragement. Among other friends who have helped in many—and sometimes expensive ways, with cars and cameras,—are Merrie and Robin Cave ; Michael and Frances Gotch; Mary L. Lloyd; the Ebert family; Bill and Daphne

Mellors; Stanley and Bernadette Robertson; Bill Cooke; Ilse Rolfe; the Rev. A. H. and Mrs Waller, Laurie and Pat Jones. The Bank Manager has been an ally. In the later stages of publication Geoffrey Hines, disinterestedly prompted by his enthusiasm for brick, provided valuable help and publicity.

This list must have its omissions, for which I apologize. My overriding debts, however, are clear. I thank K. M. Dowdall for transport, for typing so much of the final version,—for constant necessary encouragement and warmth. I thank Elaine Barrault (from Paris) for a season of perceptive company and for dozens of photographs confirming or revealing what I had come to expect in early brickwork and was unable to describe. I thank, also inadequately, John Baker, publisher (who died on 26 November 1971), and Donald Kidd.

Introduction

THE general plan of the book is that the chapters deal with themes and that the Select Gazetteer lists and details important English buildings of, or using, brick of before 1550. Chapter I outlines the development of brickwork, its regional basis and the shaping of dressings. At the end of this chapter is a section on 'Early Brick Vocabulary', showing how brick was described, often ambiguously, in mediaeval documents. Chapter II deals with the expansion of brick building from the mid fifteenth century, expressed in the building and ornamentation of manor-houses, with chimneys as an architectural feature. Chapter III deals with defended and semi-defended buildings and with historical and cultural influences on them. Chapters IV and V deal with ecclesiastical buildings, including the monastic buildings and the effects of the Reformation on these. Chapter VI deals with the terracotta work of Henry VIII's reign, especially in domestic settings. Hampton Court Palace, the largest Early Tudor brick building, has its own chapter (VII). Apart from Hampton Court and the four castles described at the end of Chapter III, the information on individual buildings is concentrated in the Select Gazetteer, following the text. Overwhelmingly the most important counties for old brick are Norfolk and Essex, followed by Suffolk.

This study has involved me, with increasing intensity, for ten years. It has provided the justification for meeting many people and visiting places and, latterly, has cost me nearly two-thirds of accustomed income as the price of a fairly free timetable and of research. It has thus been a matter of love and not of sensible economics. Such absorption was certainly not intended when I first became aware of the existence, then the interest and often the beauty of the East Coast's mediaeval brickwork—like the Greyfriars' lantern at King's Lynn and the high tower of Caister Castle, Norfolk. My study has not been a scholarly process and, because it would be artificial and insincere to try to present it as such, I am using this introduction chiefly for explanations and questions. It was a good challenge and proof of a certain originality to be told that one's subject of mediaeval brick did not exist. The corollary, though, was the near-complete absence of straightforward literature on early brick and, even, on Tudor brick, whose existence is accepted and even famous. I have found generally that the rôle of materials has been underplayed, as against the architectural style and social history of buildings. As my subject logically extended itself to take in a longer period, a wider geographical area and various historical themes, I discovered more literature, but much of it scattered and scrappy. I have been over-dependent on printed matter, especially for the gazetteer, but have also found it inadequate for my needs—even, surprisingly, on Hampton Court Palace, which is visited by half a million people a year. Brick building, even with the rough date limit of 1550, is a good subject and a big subject and I still want information. I hope people will alert me to facts and buildings that I have failed to find myself. In particular, I would like to know more about the technical factors of early brick-making and building, although I have in this book concentrated on the description and cultural placing of surviving buildings.

The invariable question addressed to me has been, how did I first become interested in the subject. This was as the unintended consequence of an interest in social unrest, immigrant workers and foreign-influenced new trades in the fifteenth century. Some of the most revealing documents for the study of social change at this period are the *Paston Letters.* These and much of the brick belong to East Anglia, which was my home country. It at first appeared that brick-making was a new trade, but, in fact, what happened in the fifteenth century was only the acceleration of an existing trade, that acceleration including the recruitment of Flemish and German workers—such as Baldwin Ducheman, the Tattershall Castle brick-maker in the 1450s. The question of foreign influences and of imports is still not settled, but the work that was done was too extensive and too sophisticated for any theory of complete dependence on the Continent to hold up. The old idea that the first bricks came in accidentally, as ballast, is obviously nonsense as cargo space would not have been wasted in any scale, though there seem to be some fourteenth-century imported bricks in Kent and there is a record of materials brought by sea in the mid fifteenth century for the lost brick house of Andrew Ogard at Emneth, Norfolk. I soon learned that bricks were made at Little Coggeshall in Essex for the Abbey at the turn of the twelfth century and that Kingston-upon-Hull was a brick-built town from its establishment at the end of the thirteenth century. (Hull is described in section 2 of this chapter.) The legend that there was no brick-building in England from the Romans to the fifteenth century began to look progressively odder. It apparently dated back to the archaeologically-minded Bishop Lyttleton of Carlisle at the end of the eighteenth century, living at a period when the exteriors of mediaeval buildings had often been stuccoed over and interiors heavily plastered and when far fewer documents were known. Lyttleton did read that the Church of Holy Trinity at Hull was brick-built: he conscientiously went to look at the church and saw no brick, because the fabric was then all rendered. In the nineteenth century Thorold Rogers had reinforced the legend by always reading the, in fact, ambiguous 'tegulae' of mediaeval documents as 'tiles'. The beliefs of Lyttleton and Rogers so long ago, however, can scarcely explain the persistence of the legend in general books today, which still tend to present Tudor brick as devoid of parents, a stage god out of a machine. It began to look as if the most valuable work I could do, besides finding out more about the lost buildings of Hull, was to start counting surviving early brick buildings.

The oldest bricks in this country, the large square bricks or tiles of the Roman Empire, belonged to another culture and seemed worth citing only in particularly important re-uses, as at St Botolph's Priory in Colchester and in the tower of St Albans Abbey, following the Norman Conquest. Our proper starting date is the end of the twelfth century, with the bricks of Polstead Church in Suffolk and of Little Coggeshall Abbey. The 1550 finishing date needs more explanation. The reasons for it are partly historical and partly architectural. The Early Tudor period, from the winning of the throne by Henry VII to the reign of Mary I, sees the climax of several themes. Though still limited to the areas where it could be made locally, brick was accepted as the fashionable material, chosen by Henry VII, Henry VIII and Cardinal Wolsey. It was established and had also become fairly common. It typified and to some extent expressed the domestication of great buildings, the needs of warmth, comfort and housekeeping overriding old concerns for defensibility. The increasing effectiveness, through centralization, of government made the undefended mansions and new middle class homes practical.

Brick had a part in the enlargement of old churches, and sometimes religious houses, till the Reformation put a stop to new work, as each type of eclesiastical institution was threatened or threatened and destroyed in turn. Elizabeth I had to legislate to repair or preserve from further harm parish churches that had suffered from the destruction of their figured glass in the Edwardian iconoclasm. The religious orders had been abolished and by her reign their buildings were either in ruins or converted (or superseded). Thus the middle of the sixteenth century is a natural historical break. Our period takes us from brick in minor rôles to completely brick buildings, such as Faulkbourne Hall (Essex) in the mid fifteenth century and various Essex church towers and porches of the early sixteenth century. The bricks were now a rough uniform size, even if roofing tiles were not. The moulding of dressings and decoration had reached a peak, the final, most flamboyant examples being the terracotta work and the chimneys of Henry VIII's reign: in the Elizabethan and Jacobean periods dressings and any elaborate work was usually done in stone, as earlier at Hampton Court Palace, or in wood. This was so even if the fabric material was brick. Brick decoration apparently reasserted itself only with the brick festoons and swags of the eighteenth century and then the heavier Victorian work.

CHAPTER I

The development of building in brick

BRICK was revived in England in the Later Middle Ages, largely to fill a lack in nature in the prosperous, relatively highly-populated Eastern Counties, where good stone was absent. Brick was the most strongly man-ordained of the mediaeval building materials. Since it was an artifact, its use represented a choice and involved an act of creation, though not necessarily dramatic or ambitious. One should thus be aware, as the material was developed, of its cultural background. At first this awareness is very vague, because of the absence of early documentation. As more sophisticated work was done, though, it coincided with the making of records that have survived. The later cultural, even sociological, background is partly known and some of that knowledge is sharp. For all the gaps—especially technical or technological gaps—in the information about Sir John Fastolf and the building of Caister Castle in the 1430s and about Thomas Wolsey and the building of Hampton Court from about 1514, an incredible amount is known about these patrons, their careers and their incomes and the buildings. Three years' accounts for the Caister works survive and nearly complete accounts for Wolsey's Hampton Court—followed by massive volumes of accounts kept for Henry VIII. It is also possible to trace the careers, foreign visits, family connections with other brick builders and the financial sources of many men of lower status and income. Although ecclesiastical building was dominant and demanding, less usually is known about those who financed church or monastery brickwork. Unfortunately, too, almost nothing is known about the makers and bricklayers—at least not till the late fifteenth century, when we begin to find names and contracts.

The making and use of brick were activities quite different from the shaping, however elaborate and even painful, of existing materials such as wood, clunch, limestone or granite. Without brick, the builder's role would have been limited to shaping and placing the natural materials, which were of varying cost and durability. The choice would usually have been limited to what was available locally, though, for example, for great buildings Caen stone was imported from Normandy and Purbeck marble was transported far beyond its source in Dorset. Sometimes the adaptation of materials must have meant incredible expenditure on tools and labour: in the High Middle Ages the body of Launceston Church, Cornwall, was rebuilt of granite, the exterior being carved from ground to eaves with continuous motifs simple or complex. At the other end of the financial scale, sun-dried clay was used for wattle-and-daub, which made for mere shelter or, combined with a good timber frame, for unambitious, vernacular architecture. There were great advantages in brick. In contrast with stone it was cheap, because of the saving on the carvers' wages and because it was lighter, which reduced the costs of transport and equipment. It was adaptable and could usefully be combined with other materials. With half-timber, for instance, it provided a stronger infilling than even lath-bonded plaster. For flint rubble, as the Romans had demonstrated, it could provide bonding courses.

Besides the fabric bricks, dressing bricks could be specially moulded for making up archways, windows and other special uses, though this was much more skilled work. After the Conquest the greatest funds were spent on castle, abbeys and churches, usually of stone or stone and flint. The growth in brick building in eastern England is associated with the fifteenth-century increase in sheep-farming, weaving and other 'industrial' developments, some foreign in origin. The expansion of the towns, through manufactures and marketing, and the consequent appearance of the middle class stimulated building. Large houses and institutional buildings—like the early fifteenth century brick guildhalls at Lynn and Boston—were erected, as well as houses for the friars and new charitable or educational structures. Brick was as much used for these new town purposes as for the demesne-sited halls of lords and other landowners. With rather more delay, it was adopted for church building. The very largest buildings in brick were to be the Early Tudor royal palaces and Wolsey's palaces, when one may deduce that brick now allowed big projects to be carried out fairly quickly and with relatively small quotas of skilled workers.

Handmade until modern times, the units of brickwork were shaped for handling and this surely conditions our response to brick fabric. Though the walls of buildings were much thicker, a mere boundary wall need be little more than one brick deep—the English bond giving alternate courses of stretchers and headers. Then as now, the fabric brick was in length about twice its width. In weight substantial but not really heavy, it was large enough to justify course-making but practicable enough not to fatigue the workers. We may contrast mediaeval bricks with large masonry blocks, which had to be moved by pulleys. Brick's associations are with sturdiness, practicality, warmth. The steps of construction are normally visible and comprehensible, whereas the awe stimulated in me by stone building is probably a polite disguise for lack of understanding. In brick's early engineering roles, in fabric of other materials, you can see what it does for each structure—whether the reused Roman bricks of Colchester or the earliest native bricks, those of Little Coggeshall Abbey and of the Polstead Church arches.

Brick is domesticated, built up on an acceptably human scale, even when it is used for the eleven feet thick defensive walls of the Norwich Cow Tower of 1380. It is domesticated when used for the gatehouses as well as the courtyard ranges of the grandest Early Tudor mansions, that were built to express power and status. The material impresses you with its reliability, despite the rough or pitted texture, the sand-creases, the pebbles, the half-puddled clay mixes of early brick. The superb colours—in part products of uneven firing and of weathering—come as an undeserved bonus. The human element seems always present, and the sense of filling needs. Initially, brick provided a good and adaptable reinforcement or fabric material in areas without satisfactory stone—and with estuarine clay or inland clay deposits fairly near the surface. Finally, at the Early Tudor climax, brick was able to provide upper crust decoration, occasionally supplemented by extravagant Renaissance terracotta. The major brick-built structures, the vaulting of ceiling or stairs and the subtler mouldings are all products of assertive and cultivated choices. In the literal sense fabric and pre-shaped bricks were usually the products of local or on-site firing, so a manufacturing and a construction industry were organized together, until the building was finished. The use of brick, however, made for less elaborate architectural lines than were fashionable in the Perpendicular period's stonework. This simplification of design is seen in towers and turrets and in grand house façades, but it is also well demonstrated by some church arcades and panel-tracery windows, these erected not long before the Dissolution. (See Chapter V, section 1.)

The strict beginning of the story for us is with the Romans, who used thick squarish tiles for small structures like houses and shops and for bonding courses in the flint or rubble walls of their forts and garrison towns in South-East England. Roman walls of flint with some brick are found, for example, at St Albans (Verulamium), Colchester (Camulodunum) and at Richborough (in Kent), and Dover has a Roman 'pharos', or lighthouse, constructed in this way. A particularly impressive example of this foreign building practice is the

Roman fort known as 'Burgh Castle', which has a riverside site inland from Great Yarmouth and the walls of which now surround a cornfield. In Roman defences the big tile-like bricks were used for an engineering bond, with two courses at intervals of about four feet. The Roman bricks are standard, measuring 18 × 12 inches and an inch thick. The Romans finally abandoned the country in A.D. 410 and the Dark Ages peoples avoided the strategic Roman sites, that had been defended 'by nature as well as by art'. That the amount of brick used by the Romans was considerable is suggested by a descriptive sentence in the 'Historia Britonum' (or 'Deeds of the Britons'), compiled by Nennius in the mid ninth century. This chronicle is known from later manuscripts, the twelfth-century 'Harleian MS.' version being published by Joseph Stevenson in 1838. Nennius said of Britain: 'In ea sunt viginti octo civitates, et innumerabilia promontoria cum innumeris castellis ex lapidibus et latere fabricatis',—'In it are twenty-eight cities and uncountable headlands, with numberless forts built out of stones and brick'. Another version had the plural, 'ex lapidibus et lateribus fabricatis', 'from stones and bricks'. 'Lateres', as explained in the early brick glossary, means literally 'walling' or 'building blocks', but the term is *usually* employed for bricks, not masonry, and in the Nennius context 'stone' has already been used.

In the more sophisticated generations before the Norman Conquest Roman towns were revived, but only after the Conquest was their military potential again realized. The Normans used the Roman towns, but concentrated their defences on a central castle on a hill or artificial mound. Later, if Roman walls were lacking, new town walls were built. The post-Conquest revival of Colchester as a military stronghold produced in Colchester Castle a Norman building that has Roman elements. The Norman policy of replacing Saxon lords by motte-and-bailey castle-dwelling Normans proceeded often in a guerilla atmosphere: the whole community was fined if any Norman was murdered, and any unexplained corpse was presumed by law to be a Norman unless proved otherwise. The Norman castle were regular forts. Colchester Castle is a 155 × 113 foot keep of flint rubble, with large numbers of reused Roman bricks. These are employed for bonding in the Roman style and, with squarish stone blocks, for quoins and jambs: in addition to the more regular bonding courses, though, there are irregular patches of Roman bricks laid vertically or in herringbone courses. Roman Colchester was used as both quarry and building site in the Middle Ages. Since, however, much of the Roman wall survives, 'constructed of concrete with cut stone faces and bonding courses of brick' (Pevsner), we can compare the original use and the reuse, in several buildings, of Roman brick. At St Albans, though the medieval town was built to the north-east of Verulamium, the Roman town was gradually destroyed for its materials and only fragments of the walls remain.

E. M. Jope has found reused Roman brick at Saxon levels in excavations at Oxford Castle, a secular site. Above ground, though, Roman bricks reused by the *Saxons* are seemingly limited to churches. The reuse reached the spectacular in the marvellous deep round arches of Brixworth Church in Northamptonshire, where Roman tiles also are laid flat for pier capitals. Brixworth is basically of the late seventh century, though possibly rebuilt in the tenth century. Other late Saxon churches with reused Roman brick are St Martin's at Canterbury, St Mary-in-Castro at Dover and Holy Trinity at Colchester. The most extensive and finest reuses of Roman brick are post-Conquest, these being the ruined St Botolph's Priory Church at Colchester and the magnificent square tower of St Albans Abbey. The Abbey chronicler recorded that about 900 the eighth abbot (Ealdred) first collected bricks and stones from the Roman town, intended for building the abbey church. Paul, abbot from 1077 to 1093, was credited with having built in 'opere lateritio' (brickwork) the whole church in eleven years. The central tower, though, which alone remains, is apparently early twelfth-century. It should be admitted that these structures were originally plastered over and the texture of the bricks thus obscured and evened out. From the Dissolution until it was ruined by bombardment during the 1648 siege of Colchester by Parliamentary forces St Botolph's was preserved as the town's main church. It had been built in the late eleventh century for an Augustinian house. It retains the 108 feet long brick-dressed nave, with a magnificent round-arcaded west front of Roman brick. A newel stair constructed of Roman brick survives. The façade is matched only by Norman stonework elsewhere: for brick it is unique, though originally rendered. Essex has much more reused Roman brick than any other county has, though there is a fair amount in Kent and Sussex. The main ways in which it was reused led naturally into some of the early engineering uses of new brick in East Anglian churches, where this provided arches, voussoirs, quoins, jambs and stairs in flint rubble fabric. The old parish churches of Colchester, Great Tey Church and the church at Bradwell-on-Sea (St Peter-in-the-Wall) are noted for their Roman brick, but the Essex Record Office has calculated that there are at least 102 Essex churches with reused Roman materials. The reused brick at Colchester Castle, of a decade after the Conquest, shows some continuity with Roman practice, but Roman brick does not feature in other mediaeval defended buildings in England. Colchester Castle's fabric—though scarcely jerry-built—is a mess in which we cannot read the future of brick, except to say that it is chiefly employed for its engineering properties.

The date for the first appearance of new or native brick has been, partly through greater knowledge of documents, pushed back to the twelfth century. The list of surviving buildings with brickwork of before 1450 covers a wide range of structural uses and types of building, but ecclesiastical contexts predominate. Some of the bricks may have been imported, including perhaps the small yellow bricks of Horne's Place Chapel (1366). Nathaniel Lloyd identified among the bricks of the fifteenth-century Hurtsmonceux Castle in Sussex some small bricks imported from Flanders. Sometimes foreign workers, especially brickmakers, were employed—as William Vesey, probably a 'Ducheman' (Fleming or German) was employed by the Crown in the 1430s and 1440s and Baldwin 'Ducheman' by Lord Treasurer Cromwell in the 1450s. A very early use of the word 'brick' appears in 1416–17 with the Flemings who were working on the manor at Stonor in Oxfordshire. Yet, the records from 1303 onwards show that Hull had a municipal brickyard staffed by men with English names, though the bricks were called 'tegulae' (tiles) till 1353. From the 1330s the great abbey of Ely was using bricks made at Ely or brought there from Wisbech and elsewhere in the Fenland. Sometimes bricks may be positively identified as being made of the local clay. It is impossible to assess the strength of foreign influences and the proportion of foreign labour involved, but these have probably been overemphasized, while the amount of early brickwork itself has definitely been underestimated. In the twentieth century the accepted date for brick's reappearance has been inched back, through the study of the records of lost and surviving buildings and their fittings, but early brick is still undervalued in cold print. I am told that eleventh-century flooring bricks have been found at Norwich Cathedral, and there is certainly a long history for fired floor tiles. Surviving brick of before the fourteenth century *is* very rare, the most extensive use being at Little Wenham Hall in Suffolk (1270/80), but the list of surviving buildings of before 1450 (printed at the beginning of the Gazetteer) shows that there is a considerable amount of fourteenth-century brick extant, normally subordinated to other materials and not used for main fabrics. The earlier exceptions, with brick used for the fabric, are Holy Trinity Church at Hull (1320 on), Sutton Church (1346) and the clerestory of Roos Church (mid fourteenth century), all in Yorkshire. Sutton in Holderness, close to Hull, was a collegiate church and presumably the lost college buildings were of brick too. In the south the first extant all-brick building is the Norwich Cow Tower (1380).

The influential Lyttleton and Rogers both took as the date for the reappearance of brick-making the last years of the fourteenth century. Charles Lyttleton (1714–68) was an antiquary and latterly Bishop of Carlisle. He contributed to the first three volumes of the periodical *Archaeologia*. His article in the first volume, published in 1757, was 'The Antiquity of Brick Buildings in England posterior to the time of the Romans', is apparently the first statement of the dearth of post-Roman brick-making. Lyttleton fastened on the reign of Richard II as the earliest date for the revival, and for this his source was what he read about Hull in John Leland's 'Itinerary', which had been printed for the first time in 1710–12 at Oxford by Thomas Hearne in nine volumes, but Leland's notes had already been used by William Camden and John Stow, Elizabethan antiquaries. The 'Itinerary' consisted of notes for a proposed survey of England which he never completed, for he was insane in his last years. He was chaplain and librarian to Henry VIII, and in 1533 was made 'King's Antiquary'. These notes he made between 1534 and 1543 on journeys about the country. Fortunately he was interested in building materials as well as in great buildings. He wrote in especial detail about Hull and was obviously impressed by the brickwork there, which he said dated back in the main to the expansion of the town in Richard II's reign, when Michael de la Pole was Chancellor. This was a simplification of the town's history and he apparently knew nothing of the founding of the town and the earliest brick buildings. Lyttleton accepted that the brick town walls had been built in the late fourteenth century. Leland had also noted that there was much brick in the fabric of Holy Trinity Church, but when, in November 1756, Bishop Lyttleton visited the church his finding was that 'there does not appear a single brick in or about the whole fabric'. This is evidently explained by the exterior's having at some date been rendered with 'compo' or stucco, which is mentioned by a later historian, Allen; only in the early nineteenth century, when the fabric was in poor condition, with the rendering flaking off, was the brickwork rediscovered. (The tower is of stone.) The interior was plastered, of course, as in mediaeval times. Thorold Rogers' work was the *History of Agriculture and Prices in England*, covering the years 1259–1793, published in seven volumes between 1886 and 1902. Speaking generally of the period 1259 to 1400, this Victorian heavyweight pronounced 'bricks never appear to have been used', but he believed bricks were used from just before the beginning of the fifteenth century, although 'tegulae' (tiles) were used earlier.

Interior brick had usually been obscured by lime plaster from its mediaeval origin, even such finely detailed work as the mid fifteenth-century passage vaulting at Tattershall Castle (Lincolnshire). Interiors were plastered for warmth, and in successive centuries in churches in particular fresh coats were added during repairs. Thus fabric brick was not revealed. The Polstead arches, which probably just predate the earliest fragments of brickwork at Little Coggeshall Abbey, were stripped only in this century. Exterior brickwork was sometimes rendered at the time of building. This was done by the Normans to the reused Roman brick fabric of St Botolph's Priory and of the tower of St Albans Abbey, evidently to be more impressive: we may compare the Conqueror's White Tower at the Tower of London, which took its name from the plaster rendering. There are stray later mediaeval records which show that exteriors were sometimes rendered as imitation masonry or ashlar-facing. The fourteenth-century chapel of Gonville College, Cambridge, was of brick-faced clunch, but the brick itself was rendered: the plaster was scored with 'masonry' lines. This is reminiscent of the late mediaeval practice of painting the outlines of masonry blocks, sometimes each decorated with a small stencilled cinquefoil, on interior plaster.

Somewhat perversely—when one thinks of the rather earlier extensive brick façades of his Greenwich, Richmond, Oatlands and Hampton Court Palaces—the new house erected for Henry VIII at the Dartford Priory site (Kent) was rendered and painted with ochre lines in the 1540s. In the 1530s, however, Henry's Nonsuch Palace in Surrey had already been tricked up with all sorts of facings, including gilded slate carvings. The Early Tudor norm for grand building in the brick areas other than East Anglia was brick with stone quoins, copings, doors and windows (or some of these). A notable earlier and royally patronized example of the combination is Queens' College, Cambridge. Arms planels were practically invariably carved in stone, despite the flamboyant cut brick beasts—heraldic supporters—of East Barsham, Norfolk. What was done at the diapered brick Lovell's Gateway to Lincoln's Inn in London is particularly interesting in our present context: there the archways were made of moulded brick, which was rendered to imitate stone; this was discovered during the recent reconstruction. Lovell's Gateway shows just how strong a disguise of basic fabric was plaster or mortar (in the pre-cement ages). The restorers, incidentally, maintained the contrast of colour by replacing the archway dressings with stone. The bricks for Lincoln's Inn were made in Lincoln's Inn Fields, and the rendering was obviously an economy over stone, though stone was used for the special work of heraldic decoration of Lovell's Gateway. Probably more often than is now apparent brick detail was rendered, and stone detail 'whitened', as the parapets of the new lodgings for the Queen at Hampton Court were whitened in 1536. Late Perpendicular examples of brick structures which had their main face, only, ashlared at the period of building are the South Gate of King's Lynn (Norfolk) and the surviving priory gateway at Great Malvern (Worcestershire). In the eighteenth and nineteenth centuries mediaeval exteriors were often given as ashlar facing or were stuccoed over, just as new country houses had at least their grand front stuccoed, the sides and rear showing their brick. These practices contributed to the 'disappearance' of mediaeval brick. At Cambridge particularly, where damp-prone clunch had been used by the mediaeval builders, eighteenth-century restorers went in for wholesale ashlaring—and the Early Tudor brick buildings of Lady Margaret Beaufort's Christchurch College still have their eighteenth-century ashlar facings.

Thus, interior brick was normally plastered anyway and, from the eighteenth century, exterior brick tended to vanish under stucco or cement or ashlar. Where brick was found in buildings of before 1400 it could still, however, be explained away by the 'ballast theory', according to which bricks came to England by accident, or by the belief that all must have been imported. That later argument and the discovery of real evidence against these generalizations have so lacked impact on ordinary textbooks and outlines of architectural history—outside specialist literature—is rather surprising. The casual extension of the myth of no brick till the Tudor period suggests, perhaps, that tidy categorization and a necessary blank in knowledge have proved psychologically attractive. Nathaniel Lloyd's *History of Brickwork* contradicted the myth, but the book has long been unavailable.

Though it was not then preserved the kiln where bricks for Little Coggeshall Abbey were made was found and excavated as long ago as 1845. Wasters were found which corresponded with shaped bricks at the Abbey. Lloyd, who traced at the Abbey a recurring fault from a defective mould, does not mention the discovery of the kiln, but emphasizes that the bricks had been purpose-moulded for their buildings. The surviving St Nicholas's Chapel away from the main site is dated early thirteenth century, and there are twelfth-century bricks among the remains of the Abbey itself. The dating for the earliest of these has been pushed back, by the study of documents, to about 1160. Most of the shaping was done by moulding, but sometimes—as in the hollow chamfer of the Chapel's East window (strictly, three lancets)—carving exposed the dark, less well-fired core of the bricks. The abbey bricks are vital to the buildings, providing windows, doors, jambs, quoins and vaulting. The plain bricks are large, $12 \times 6 \times 1\frac{3}{4}$ inches. The shaped bricks are singular for their date, unmatched by dressings of any elaboration till the mid fifteenth century. The lack of any stone dressings is also very unusual. Little Coggeshall does, though, exemplify the use of brick for structural detail in flint rubble, typical especially of East Anglia. The shapes include segmental bricks for round columns, lobed bricks for roll mouldings, chamfered bricks and diamonds. The texture of these reddish bricks is fine, and the Firmans have suggested that extra sand was added for the purpose-shaped bricks. At the Belgian Cistercian Abbey of Coxyde are similar shaped bricks. The conclusion must be that Cistercians from the Continent, where brick was already established and where the Order had originated (at Citeaux in France), carried out or at least supervised the brick-making here. Possibly brick was used at other Cistercian houses in England, now lost, by foreign craftsmen who could have trained English lay workers—like those for whom St Nicholas's Chapel was provided.

Until the Hull accounts begin in 1303 Little Coggeshall provides the best *proof* of mediaeval brick *manufacture* in this country. Although, however, this Essex brickwork fits with our themes of the early combination of brick with other materials and its development in the clay areas, the mouldings have a sophistication that seems altogether late mediaeval. Other early mediaeval shaping of brick amounts to little more than chamfering, as of the vaulting ribs of the undercroft of St Olave's Priory, Herringfleet. Ornamental shaping of more complexity apparently comes only with the fifteenth-century increase in the use of brick and—this is the key point—when combined with fabric brick. The first known records, made at the time of their use, of the use of fabric bricks or tiles are of 'Flanders tiles' imported in 1278 and 1283. The Exchequer in 1278 recorded the purchase of 202,500 tiles imported from Yprès for work at the Tower of London: they cost £20. 4*s*. and their sea-carriage £32. 5*s*. In 1283 101,350 more, costing £23. 3*s*. 5*d*., were bought for the wall between the Tower of London and the City. In his *Survey of London* (1598) Stow stated that Flanders tiles were imported in 1215 for use in London. Stow's account is that, during the wars between King John and his barons Geoffrey de Mandeville, Earl of Essex, and other barons repaired Aldgate, Ludgate and others of the City gatehouses. This de Mandeville was descended (through the female line) from his anarchic namesake, builder of adulterine castles in the reign of Stephen. The political background to these repairs was that the barons had now renounced their allegiance to John and, under Robert Fitzwalter, had marched their forces to London, where they were joined by both London citizens and royal officials. They repaired the defences against expected attack by the King and his foreign mercenaries. These activities led up to the 'Magna Carta', whereby the King acknowledged the rights of the propertied classes at least. London's defences were then a mixture of the Roman and the mediaeval, the landward walls complete. Stow found information that the tiles had been employed in the stone masonry in the Norman manner. (Some of the stone had been removed from the houses of Jews, who could be safely exploited in the regular climate of distrust and hostility: all the Jews, their property confiscated, were to be expelled by Edward I in 1290.) It sounds as if the tiles were used for strengthening, perhaps as the Norman leader Eudo Dapifer had used Roman tiles in Colchester.

The mediaeval documentary picture is rather confused because the unqualified term 'tile' (Latin 'tegula') is used for stone or for fired roof tiles, for tiles or bricks for walls and for floor tiles. The word 'walltile' for brick is first used at Ely monastery in 1307, at Hull in 1353 and at York Minster in 1404, but 'brick' itself appears regularly only in the fifteenth century. Apart from the 1340 record of a stair and dungeon constructed 'in petris et brikis' (in stone and brick) at Windsor Castle, the first known reference to brick building is at Stonor in 1416–17. Tiles for roofs or floors were common earlier than brick, and the London authorities in 1189 were able to rule that roofs—to stop the spread of fire from burning thatch—should be tiled or slated. As brick building and tiling increased so sources of regular supply developed, in contrast to imports or the making of bricks for isolated projects. The Hull Chamberlains' rolls from 1303 record the activities of the corporation brickyards, with the 'tegulae' selling at 3*s.* 1½*d.* and 3*s.* a thousand in 1303 and 1304. Towards the end of the fourteenth century their capacity was evidently sufficient to rewall the town, with four main gates and numerous towers incorporated in those walls. At the same time new brick houses were being erected in Hull. Now, the only product remaining of all this enterprise is the brickwork of Holy Trinity Church. Accounts for 1330–80 survive from the Battle Abbey tilery in Kent, and this was commercially organized even if the main buyers were other religious houses. In the 1450s Ralph Lord Cromwell was selling large numbers of bricks from his kilns at Boston (Lincolnshire), besides making bricks at Edlington Moor for his own castle, the school and other work at Tattershall. A royal employer, Henry VI, could institute brickmaking on a very considerable scale for his own projects. William Vesey's appointment in 1437 was to search for earth suitable for making tiles ('tegulae') called 'brike' and to arrange with the landowner to dig such earth for the royal manors: the yard Vesey set up at Slough that year served Windsor Castle and then Eton College. Even so, in the 1440s bricks were also imported from Calais for the King's works.

Commercialization was still not complete. Where castles or great houses in the countryside were concerned it was quite normal for a claypit to be worked and clamps or kilns set up at the site, and the bricks made just for that one building and its ancillary structures. These examples are interesting because their claypits can still be located. In the marshes near Caister the source of the earliest bricks used for Sir John Fastolf's castle has been found. The pits used for Tattershall Castle in the 1450s were ten miles away at Edlington Moor: it is even thought that a brick house surviving there, at Halstead, was that of Baldwin Ducheman, the brickmaker. The claypits for the great, now ruined Bradgate House near Leicester are traceable in the park: the house was built in the 1470s. The pits for the early sixteenth century Hales Place (Norfolk), now lost, are also traceable. Kilns for decorated floor tiles have been found in quitea large number of places, including: Malvern, Repton, Droitwich, Coventry, Nottingham, the Chiltern region, Chertsey and at Bawsey in Norfolk.

Despite the confusion of names and meanings over 'tile', which can cover burnt clay for floors, walls and roofs, the crafts seem to have been very specialized and exclusive. Regulation of the workers and standardization of materials was attempted, prompted by the results of economic growth. In 1477 a statute of Edward IV attempted to standardize tile sizes, with important requirements on the preparation of the clay. The 1571 Tudor 'standard' brick was to be $9 \times 4\frac{1}{2} \times 2$ inches, an informal standardization more influential than the earlier attempts and in tune with the times, when symmetry became much more of an ideal in architecture. An interesting document from 1425–6 gives some details of local procedure: it is a ruling from Quarter Sessions held at Chelmsford, Essex, that a standard 'form' or mould should be kept at the Moot Hall in Colchester, where there had been complaints about the irregularity of brick sizes—which made repairs and additions difficult. It cites 'diverse formes . . . to noissance and harming of the said people . . . No Tyle maker (was to) make no manner of tyle but all after a fourme . . . in Moothalle of said Towne, upon payne of XXs.' 'Tile' here means 'brick'. Twenty shillings was a very steep fine, enough to pay for 4,000 bricks perhaps. From the earliest times brick sizes had varied much, but the so-called 'Great Brick' of up to 20 inches long scarcely persisted into the Later Middle Ages. Very small bricks were also used in the early days, so no real tendency can be discerned.

The different craftsmen making or using tiles or bricks kept apart in their organization. Only in 1568 did the London Tilers and Brickmakers come together in one company and were granted a coat of arms. In 1598 in Hull the Bricklayers, Tilers, Wallers, Plasterers and Paviour (layers of paved floors) formed one company, whose ordinances began both democratically and with a fine and pious pun about materials: 'All men are by nature equal, made by one workman of like mire.'

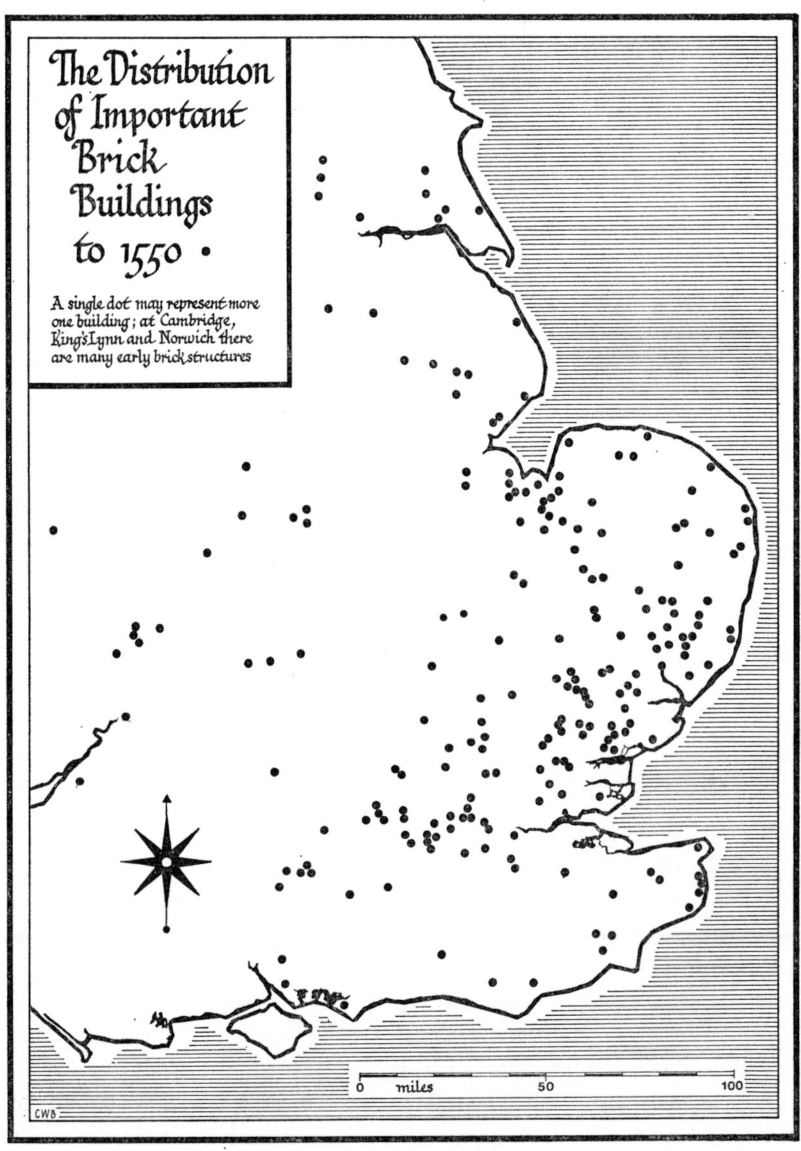
The Distribution of Important Brick Buildings to 1550 •
A single dot may represent more one building; at Cambridge, King's Lynn and Norwich there are many early brick structures
0 miles 50 100
CWB

I. THE DISTRIBUTION OF IMPORTANT BRICK BUILDINGS TO 1550.

1. Manufacture and regions

There is a rough correspondence between these regions: the geologists' 'Lowland Britain' of softer, younger stones, flints and clays and also of woodland; the region—south and east of a line from York to Exeter—with the highest population density and therefore political importance in mediaeval times; the mediaeval wheat-growing region, to some extent overlapping with and competed for by sheep-farming; the areas where baked clay roof tiles were used. This large region includes the mediaeval brick-building areas. Round its coastland or just inland on the estuaries were the chief ports, also the most important towns: York, Hull (founded in 1290), Boston, Lynn, Great Yarmouth, Norwich, Ipswich, London, Southampton—where Leland in the sixteenth century saw brick buildings, now lost—and also Bristol. These were supplemented by smaller ports, such as the South Coast 'Cinque Ports', some of which in the Later Middle Ages suffered from shifts in the coast and from foreign attacks; Brightlingsea in Essex; internecine little Suffolk ports, like Orford, Blythburgh and Walberswick. The operations of the English Staple, which had a monopoly over the wool trade at the price of paying over customs duties to the Crown, and the largely German Hansa helped increase and consoldiate trade through the big ports. The Hansa had offices at York, Hull, Boston, Lynn, Yarmouth, London and Bristol. York and Bristol were stone-built, though York has a little later mediaeval brick, but the others are important in the early history of brick and the Hansa has been credited with influence on this, with a renewed wave of influence after 1474, when a treaty was made between the Hansa and England after a period of conflict. The Lynn Hanseatic office was set up in 1271, but the premises surviving there date from about 1475 and are of brick and timber.

Some tiles and bricks were brought to these places from the Continent, especially from the province of Flanders—which belonged to the Duchy of Burgundy from the mid fourteenth century to the death of Charles the Bold in 1477. To them, too, came a number of immigrant brickmakers and designers. The strength of these foreign elements cannot be assessed, just guessed at, but the transients and settlers were responding to economic growth and helped its expression in new houses and institutional buildings and in the rebuilding or additions to churches. It was sensible economics to employ foreign craftsmen. Sea transport costs and the price of a cargo of bricks or tiles might be equal. Even the Channel crossing was expensive, for it might take a week or ten days. Trade, especially with North Europe, was too regular and intensive for there to be wasted space on the return journey to be filled with bricks as ballast. The bricks would anyway have had to be purchased, for even broken bricks, known as 'brickends' and used for foundations and coring, had their price. The idea of odd batches of bricks being used for ballast and then being used in England for building seems implausible, whereas speculative or ordered cargoes of bricks do not. In the early days Flanders tiles were brought in for royal works in London. There are some small yellow bricks, said to be imported, in Kent. The small bricks, 'imported from Holland', that Nathaniel Lloyd found at Hurstmonceux Castle can have had no purpose except as extra supplies. It was as part of the exceptionally extravagant building programme of Henry VI that the bricks from Calais—where they were currently being used in renewing this garrison town's defences—were imported in 1440 for use at Richmond Palace, just when bricks for local use were being made at Slough by Vesey, King's serjeant, surveyor of the beerbrewers and probably a 'Ducheman'.

At the same date a private citizen, the naturalized Dane Sir Andrew Ogard, probably imported the bricks for a lost mansion at Emneth in the Norfolk Marshland: thirty years later William of Worcester, previously secretary of Sir John Fastolf of Caister, noted down that the construction of this house had cost about £1,400 (the manor itself cost (£1,000) and that timber and the bricks were brought 'from beyond the County of Lincoln'. Surely this was not a weirdly circumlocutious way of referring to Yorkshire, but means the bricks were imported? They could have come from Flanders, but possibly Ogard renewed contacts with his native Denmark (which had its outstanding much earlier churches at Sjaelland and Roskilde). His Rye House gatehouse of about 1443 in Hertfordshire, built apparently of local brick like the house of his colleague and neighbour at Hunsdon, has unusually fine and early mouldings to the oriel windows and the passage vault; this must have been of Continental inspiration or work. The Emneth imports may be explained by a dearth of brickmakers: suitable clay was available locally, as is shown by the Early Tudor brick structures at the nearby villages of Fincham, Upwell and Outwell, to look no further.

In the south and east were the active or development areas, with the highest populations (minute by modern standards) in the Holland area of Lincolnshire and in Norfolk, whose chief town of Norwich gained its mayor in 1403 and had greatly increased in size by the end of the Middle Ages. Lincolnshire has some important mediaeval brick, as does Kent in the south, but the great brick counties are Norfolk and Essex, followed by Suffolk. Population and development demands for building materials were satisfied chiefly according to the geological basis, for it was rare for materials to be carried more than ten or twelve miles at most. Bricks were usually made only when clay or brickearth was available if the natural materials were inadequate in some way. Royal and other exceptional projects might, however, bring materials from far away. Fastolf at Caister in the 1430s had some materials brought from France. The distribution of surviving brick buildings—probably not very different from the mediaeval distribution—is, therefore, composed of special, irregular groupings inside 'Lowland Britain'. Away from the East Anglian concentration the distribution is fragmented. There are only a few brick buildings in the true stone-building areas, while the farthest outliers, like Thornbury Castle in Gloucestershire and Sollershope Court Farm in Herefordshire, have only decorated brick chimneys. The terminal date of 1550 is taken partly for historical reasons, but also because brick seems to me to have reached then a plateau in scale of production and in inventiveness of mouldings. Concentrating on load-bearing brick and stopping in the Tudor period means that we are mainly concerned with grand buildings or at least those erected by people or organizations with means and which, therefore, have a certain cultural unity. Vernacular buildings of brick, such as small town houses, cottages, agricultural structures are uncommon till the eighteenth century. Small timber-framed buildings very much earlier in date with brick nogging are *not* uncommon, though examination may show us that the brick is a replacement of withy- or lath-bonded daub or plaster. Dating brick nogging—horizontal or herringbone in the early period—is not easy, but replacement may be detected by the bricks being comparatively thick and short (and therefore modern) or by the auger-made holes in the timbers, provided for the panel rods of the original in-filling. Sometimes the replacements were too heavy for the timbers, causing sagging and the entry of damp. The use of roof tiles instead of thatch, though, and of a limited amount of brick for chimney flues evidently spread to vernacular buildings. As noted of London this was officially promoted in towns as a precautionary measure against the spread of fire.

Roof tiles, tile or brick chimneys and bricks used for engineering roles in rubble buildings were all well established before brick was commonly used for the panels of timber-framed buildings and I believe brick-building proper was also established as the coming choice before brick was used for panels. This view may be coloured by the accidents of survival, but brick nogging seems to belong to the end of the fifteenth century or the Tudor age—when Tilbury-juxta-Clare Church in Essex has a wall painting showing, in the background, a brick-nogged house. Alec Clifton-Taylor has suggested that the practice was stimulated by a dearth of good plasterers—perhaps only a relative dearth, for the demand for new building had obviously increased. The weavers' houses of Lavenham and Sudbury in Suffolk and elsewhere, dating from the Later Middle Ages, were still typically timber-framed and plastered, but their plinths (often now painted black) might be of brick—for strength and against damp. Similarly, brick was early used for the bases of timber belfries and arcades and then for supporting the trestles of postmills. There is a very close relationship between the employment of timber and of brick in our period. The two go along together, although to some extent brick was to displace timber—demoting it in the social scale. Brick-built manors were erected on the site of timber-framed ones, of which traces may survive —as in Faulkbourne Hall (Essex). Brick was also associated with the true domestication of the grander buildings, in this case replacing stone and genuine fortifications with brick and suspiciously-decorative battlements supported on trefoil-headed corbel-tables. Timber was retreating further down the scale, to help improve common living standards, when Leland said that brick was replacing it in the London area, for the great here had always employed stone—often Kentish rag, brought by river. By the Elizabethan and Jacobean eras so much timber had been cut—for houses and for the Royal Navy—without reaforestation that the lack of timber gave the greatest impetus to the use of brick generally and began to take it beyond the older brick areas. The reduction of woodlands may already have been significant in the early sixteenth century. With exceptions like the bare marshland area on the Norfolk–Cambridgeshire border, trees and brick-earth were found together. Indeed, although the town of Hull fired its brick kiln with turves, the Tattershall accounts of the 1450s record the cutting of *hundreds* of small trees and of 'underwood' (brushwood) for fuel. The amount of fuel needed per firing in the relatively inefficient mediaeval conditions is indicated by the Hull 'tilehouse'—admittedly only a wattle-and-daub construction—having needed 84,000 turves to fire about 35,000 bricks. Unusually some coal (brought by sea) was also used at Tattershall, and the 1437 commission for Vesey to find brickearth for the royal works also made him responsible for providing wood fuel and coal. Wood was the normal fuel. The amount needed, preferably cut on the builder's own land, added to the cost of the bricks.

The use of brick in Europe is associated with the growth of comparative political stability, after the absorption of the barbarians who had invaded from the East. It was used in the dark ages of the 'Barbarian West' only in Italy, and supposedly spread later to Flanders and North Europe via Venice. The Flemish and North German influence on England was dominant, but the connection with south-west France may also have been influential—particularly the brick buildings of the new towns ('Bastides') there and the fine stretcher bond brickwork of Toulouse and Albi. The concidence in England of the real growth in brick-making with the Wars of the Roses, and then the Early Tudor boom in brick building with renewed fighting with France and with the Reformation, only shows that the conflicts were fairly superficial or localized in impact. Lengthy building programmes were carried out despite political changes: Queens' College at Cambridge was continued through the Wars of York and Lancaster; the owner of Gainsborough Hall in Lincolnshire, prompted by destruction of his house in those wars, built himself a new and elegant one, mainly of brick—with an impressive and only partly serious gatehouse; the Howard family kept on in Norfolk and Suffolk, from the 1480s, building their brick houses despite periodic executions for treason or supposed treason and consequent sequestration of property. Since the material and then the 'green' bricks had to be cured for several months before they could be fired, and kilns (or clamps for lesser projects) had to be constructed for the firing, to choose to build in brick meant that patrons needed time and settled conditions for their investment from season to season to be worthwhile. Building with bricks made at the site was cheaper than having semi-dressed stone brought from distant good quarries and although a smaller proportion of skilled craftsmen was needed, the whole process was industrial in kind—even to economies of scale being possible. On the Continent, where sun-dried bricks were an impossibility, the making of brick belongs with the growth of states, with international trade and some specialization; in England the development or redevelopment of brick centuries after the departure of the Romans was delayed and can be seen as one response to economic growth (based on the wool trade), when higher standards found flint rubble, carstone, puddingstone, septaria, clunch and even the friable Kentish rag inadequate or too clumsy. In the early days brick was used to supplement these stones, often for quoins, archways and vaulting. This can often best be seen in the churches. At Cambridge, as at Magdalen, brick was used for a better facing on top of the traditional college clunch, a heavy chalk. The clunch-brick mix at Cambridge had decayed considerably by the eighteenth century. Solid brick was soon seen as impressive aesthetically as well as a practical or domesticated material. Sometimes a builder like Rotherham at Bishopsthorpe, near York, or Russell at the Chancery in Lincoln—where the town, despite all the neighbouring freestone, owned a kiln at the end of the fifteenth century—rejected the good local stone in favour of brick. The climax was when Henry VIII and Wolsey, who obviously could have afforded to build in stone all their numerous London and Home Counties palaces, used brick partly for speed but clearly also to impress—even the visiting French—though the fancy work was usually done in stone.

The mediaeval brickmakers used shallow deposits of clay, beginning perhaps with riverside or estuarine clay such as was used for the Norwich Cow Tower at the end of the fourteenth century. There is a record that tilers of Beverley in the 1380s were in trouble with the monks of Meaux Abbey for undermining the banks of the River Hull on abbey land by their diggings. At Beverley the town rented out land for brick-making, in contrast to the direct labour yard at Hull, and at both places all known names of workers are English. The 1548 Act which said that brickmakers and limeburners must be left to do their work indisturbed suggests that population growth had led to conflicts over land use. Stow's record that the clay digging in Moorfield in 1477 for the Mayor's repairs to the City of London walls had ruined the land for years shows this had been a strong grudge. The lawyers at Lincoln's Inn were able to make bricks on their 'coneygarth' next the site, and this seems to have been the normal practice. Commercial yards existed, though, like Beverley's from the fourteenth century. In the mid-fifteenth century Cromwell ran kilns for Tattershall Castle at Edlington Moor ten miles away and also, commercially, at Boston—supplying bricks for the Abbot of Bardney, for example. Kilns at Gestingthorpe in Essex supplied bricks for that parish church and for others nearby, bricks that are more purple than the usual Essex reds, and bricks continued to be made there into modern times. For his hall at Stoke-by-Nayland John Howard bought bricks at Ipswich; St John's College at Cambridge obtained some of its bricks from Wallington, Norfolk, where the Hall was brick-built too; Henry VIII obtained some bricks for Whitehall Palace from Kingston, Surrey.

During our period it was probably most common for production to be a temporary affair, of a brickfield that was worked for three or four seasons, for a big house or for additions to a church, though the patron might take the opportunity of selling extra bricks. Any shallow clay deposits were exploited: no one till modern times touched the deep Oxford clay that runs through Bedfordshire, and is so rich in oil and organic matter that it practically fires itself. In the eighteenth and nineteenth centuries hundreds of villages maintained regular small brickyards, but there were still itinerant brickmakers who worked a field for a period and left a few traces on the land or in place names. If a regular kiln was not set up, bricks could be fired in round clamps, possibly more common in the Middle Ages. The main items of equipment needed were only shovels and wheelbarrows, for the horse-operated pugmill for mixing clay was post-mediaeval. No doubt buildings of poor clays have disappeared, but there are buildings with bricks of extremely rough texture—like those of Fulham Palace, where chalk has weathered away to leave pits like stab marks. From the end of the fifteenth century diaper patterns with glazed dark bricks are common everywhere from Yorkshire to Hampshire (Norfolk's one wholly brick church of Shelton is diapered) except in the region of the Wash and Lincolnshire, where suitable clays for this one use were evidently lacking. The Firmans have pointed out the distorted, greenish bricks used for diaper at the Wainfleet School, (see 'A Geological Approach to the Study of Mediaeval Bricks', by R. J. and P. E. Firman in *The Mercian Geologist*, 1967). The Wainfleet diaper is significant—the patron had diapered his palaces at Esher and Farnham (Surrey)—but is an oddity, surrounded by good fabric bricks. Poor bricks must usually have resulted from failure to remove stones or break up chalk concentrations or from mistakes in firing. In 1427, for instance, the Hull workers—lacking a sufficiently skilled chief at the time—produced for St Mary's Church 10,000 bricks that proved completely useless. (The mediaeval fabric of this church, unlike Holy Trinity, is of stone, so perhaps plans were changed.) When brick was not very common people may have been suspicious of the innovation, as the will of John Baret of Bury St Edmunds shows: in 1467 he left money for the rebuilding of a town gate and advocated the use of brick and freestone, but thought his executors might believe the traditional flint rubble ('calyon') and mortar was 'more enduring'.

Many different types of clay were used, not just one ideal brick-earth. Deposits are irregular, discontinuous, and the search for them used to be called 'pot-holing'. Geologically they included jurassic clay—belonging with the younger, oolitic limestones that are often used for dressings when brick is the fabric material—cretaceous (chalky), glacial and alluvial. The main sites were river valleys, marshland and fenland. The varying colours of the finished bricks were produced both by the chemistry of the clays and by uneven puddling and firing. The contemporary term for the less well-baked bricks was 'samel', meaning salmon-coloured—or pinkish, instead of a 'well and sufficiently burned' red. Contracts might specify that only a certain proportion of samel bricks was acceptable. The pink and pale yellow bricks of the Isle of Thanet and the Colchester area are not less well-burned, though, but the products of clays with a higher proportion of chalk, which fires into lime, than usual. This is the composition of the light bricks of the thirteenth-century Little Wenham Hall, between the Orwell and the Stour in Suffolk, and of the still paler bricks of the sixteenth-century Hengrave Hall, near Bury St Edmunds, where 'Woolpit whites' became fashionable at the end of the eighteenth century. The gault clay belt in Kent, where Battle Abbey ran its tilery, and gault in Cambridgeshire have produced pale bricks. In Huntingdonshore and elsewhere the old term for digging clay was 'gaulting' and the word 'gault' itself is attributed to East Anglian brickmakers. There is also blue gault, which turns reddish or brownish purple in firing. The darkest bricks, of different clay or possibly just overburned, might be picked out for diaper work. Saltpetre in the clay produced a natural glaze, or one end of the plastic brick would be dipped in sand to vitrify during firing. A fair proportion of sand in the clay will produce a finer texture, as in the case of terracotta, while the Firmans believe that sand was added to the mix for the exceptionally early and sophisticated moulded bricks of Little Coggeshall Abbey.

If the clay is not fully puddled sand will leave creases on the surface, frequently found in mediaeval bricks. (If too much sand is present the brick will fragment in firing or gradually erode afterwards.) Sand naturally makes for paler colouring, including pale red, but is only one explanation of this. At Sutton Place in Surrey of the 1520s we find dark red brick, a small amount of rich red terracotta—used chiefly for the bulgy cherubs—and much pale terracotta varying casually between pink, yellow and grey. Redness, increased by hard firing, derives from iron oxides in the clay. Most brick of before and, still more, after 1550 is red. Hengrave Hall, with its old red brick that was cleaned when the new building was done in pale brick, went against the general trend. Not only were clays with iron more common than the lime clays, especially inland away from the estuaries, but it was red brick specifically that became fashionable and then popular. It is only Jesus College at Cambridge that has both yellowish bricks and red ones: Queens', Magdalen, St John's and Christ's (under its ashlar) are of red bricks with purplish diapering.

When the redness was thought inadequate for a certain task it might even be increased artificially. St John's College has the accounts of the building of a rich manor-house at Collyweston in Northamptonshire by its founder, Lady Margaret Beaufort: about 1505 the colour of bricks for chimneys was improved by a nasty-sounding mixture of ochre, the 'offalles' from glovers' leather and ale. Since, later, 4,300 'tunnelles' (shaft bricks, indubitably decorated) were brought from Peterborough at the high cost of 10*s.* a thousand, better work may have been wanted. At Hengrave Hall the new chimney-shafts were red, in contrast to the pale fabric—and pale stone dressings brought from Northamptonshire. The more regular or intense redness of chimneys which one often notices, surely resulted initially from having to use the harder-fired bricks to face the greatest exposure to weather. Aesthetic choices then belong with the makers' ability to shape ornament, culminating in the early sixteenth century. In its earlier incarnations the hardness of brick was appreciated just for taking the stress of angles and voids in rubble buildings and the bricks used were plain or with little more shaping than the chamfering of one corner. Choices about decoration or even colour were outside the capacity of the English makers in Hull in the fourteenth century and outside the expectations of their employers, the town chamberlains. The chamfered and specially named 'squynchontiell' used at Beverley North Bar in 1419 are a foretaste of the future.

While the early roll-moulded and segmental and other shaped bricks of Little Coggeshall are certainly of local manufacture, the makers must have come from North Europe. They shaped most of these dressings by moulding before firing, although the Chapel of St Nicholas has in its east window hollow-chamfered bricks which you can see were carved, because their less well-fired cores, dark with organic matter, are exposed. (In later buildings, incidentally, such cores may show that old fabric bricks have been cut in modern times for the repair of dressings, since most shaped bricks were now moulded.) Possibly these craftsmen made bricks for buildings, now lost, of other Cistercian houses in England: we know that Cistercians in Scotland and in Yorkshire and in southern places like Sawtry in Huntingdonshire (a few relics only are kept in the parish church) and Old Warden in Bedfordshire all had fine and early tile mosaic floors.

The exact sources of the clays used for particular houses are interesting questions, but the answers can usually be no more than good or incomplete guesses. Pebbles and other inclusions—such as shells—in the bricks can only suggest likely sources, not exact sites. The most common inclusions are small sharp flints and quartzite pebbles. The pebbles are very common, and have turned pink in the firing. These inclusions have been found by the Firmans in many, many buildings north of the Thames: they are also common in the south, as at Laughton Place in Sussex and Otford Place in Kent. H. A. Tipping, in the book on Tattershall Castle, expressed the belief that such inclusions proved the source of the bricks was local: in fact, the proof of local manufacture rests in the accounts and in the spoil heaps at Edlington Moor. Inclusions contribute to the uneven texture of early bricks. What the Firmans have deduced, though, that is particularly interesting is that mediaeval seekers for brick clay detected its likely presence from small surface flints, which made the layer of earth worth stripping off.

The number of brick buildings is sharply reduced not only in those areas where limestone and other good building stones were available, but also in the areas where the chalk forms outcrops lacking the clay deposit. In East Anglia brick supplements flint rather than takes over from it, at least in churches. In Essex brick did take over the churches. The spoil from digging a moat might be usable for bricks, as apparently at Hurstmonceux. At Kirby Muxloe the accounts fail to name the site of the kiln, but show very low transport costs. It was fairly unusual that the Tattershall bricks came from as far away as ten miles. If accounts do not name sources, the occasional survival of diggings and spoil heaps may do so. At Caister traces of brickworks were found in the Bure Marshes, but these evidently supplied only the earlier bricks used—not the bulk of the bricks, which are of a darker clay. The depressions of clay diggings can be seen beyond Thornton Abbey gatehouse (Lincolnshire).

There is no contemporary description of early brick-making (not before the seventeenth century) and what is known of it is pieced together from odd scraps of knowledge and a projection back of brick-making processes in more recent times, when bricks were still shaped by hand and mechanization was lacking—except for the pugmill, with horizontal beaters on a vertical shaft, used to mix the clay. The processes were seasonal, as the 1477 statute on roof tiles shows. The regulations this made would have been appropriate for bricks. One should note that, because of their thinness and greater exposed surface, to which frost was the great danger, tiles needed a finer mix and pebbles could not be tolerated. On the other hand clays suitable for making tiles were much more widespread than the brickearths: decorated floor tiles were made in stone-building areas from Scotland to Cornwall, and roof tiles were widespread and cheaper than wood shingles, slates or stone tiles. (Lead roofing was for the rich only and then usually only for the flat roofs of gatehouses.) The statute was probably more significant as an ideal than an effective instrument, for it tried to standardize the size of plain tiles—which varied widely. The 'earth' was to be dug up before the 1st of November: 'stirred and turned' before the 1st of February following; then 'wrought' after the 1st of March. 'Malm' or 'marle', stones and chalk were to be removed. The layer of soil—later known as 'callow'—was stripped off the ground and then the clay dug. (In the nineteenth century it was apparently common for a farmer to run a brickyard next to his agricultural land and use this callow on the farm.)

The clay was measured out and left standing in heaps to be 'cured' or broken down by frost and rain. In spring it was 'puddled' into a dough, that is 'tempered' with the aid of water. The Hull accounts mention 'waterpottz' for this purpose. The men worked the clay over with shovels. Stones, except for the small pebbles, were removed; chalk had to be removed or broken up and properly mixed in. If this was not done both stones and the quicklime formed by the chalk in firing would explode and break the bricks—and perhaps damage the kiln. There would be numerous 'wasters' after firing, as the extent of known spoil heaps shows, but broken bricks were usable if hard. As noted, sand might be added to the clay, but the sandier, coarser clays needed harder firing—perhaps needing coal, not just wood fuel. The 1430 contract between the two Germans and Bury St Edmunds Abbey said that the abbot must find a sufficient 'stramen' (strand or vein) of sand ('zabula' in the Latin; usually spelled 'sabula'), but this apparently means the brickearth itself. Sand was needed for mortar. This was made of sand and lime, and the lime was obtained by firing certain limestones. The Hull accounts calls it 'calce', the Latin term, but use English terms for much of the equipment. Thus, an oven for burning lime had to be operated when the kiln or clamp for the bricks was being used in the building season, apparently at the same site. The Caister Castle accounts mention burning of 'trays' of lime.

The puddled clay was left to stand for a couple of months to complete the curing of the material, but it was now protected from rain by stretching canvas over it from wood posts. Various accounts mention sailcloth, 'pakthred' and even needles used for this purpose. If the clay had not been properly pulverized the fired bricks would break up when exposed to weather: on the other hand, the strong early bricks that we see now are often very rough in texture. In particular, the 1380 bricks of the Cow Tower are formed of a half-stirred mix, which has fired red and pink or yellow and grey or green. Clays may vary every few yards. After the plastic 'green' bricks had been shaped they were stacked on 'hacks' or 'hacksteads' to stand again until firm. If they were fired when still quite plastic surfaces were marked with impressions where they touched. (In modern bricks the arrangement of the bricks, fired much more quickly, may show in small blocks of different colouring.)

Fabric bricks were shaped in two different ways and so were the bricks shaped for special dressings. Neither had 'frogs' or keys for the mortar till the eighteenth or nineteenth century. The earlier and more primitive way of shaping fabric bricks was to spread a layer of hay or straw on the ground to prevent sticking; roll out a layer of clay on this; cut the layer into rectangles. The products are known as 'place' bricks and were probably seldom made after 1350. They may be detected by their irregular sizes and, in use, made for irregular bonding. At the Cow Tower, for instance, the length has a four-inch variance and the width varies by two inches. Place bricks may also be detected by straw marks on the surface: the straw would stick to the plastic clay and burn away in the firing, leaving its impress. Bricks used in the flint and freestone church of St Margaret's at Lowestoft show such marks, and bricks at St Olave's Priory nearby at Herringfleet have such deep 'cuts' that they could have been made by reeds. A certain amount of straw may, however, have been used for other purposes and so straw marks cannot be taken as proof of the bricks having been cut in this way. The other way of shaping bricks was in a mould or 'form'. This was the established method. The form was an open rectangle or double rectangle of wood, placed on a table. The surplus clay was struck off the top of the mould with a piece of wood, 'the 'strike', or sliced off by a wire attached to two handles. In addition, later on, a piece of wood forming a loose base to the mould was used and was known as the 'stock': it made removal of the plastic brick easier. Moulds and forms are mentioned in various accounts, though the term 'form' may be used for a large pattern or building model. Oak moulds are mentioned in the Kirby Muxloe accounts, although many dressings were shaped by 'hewing' (cutting). The use of moulds meant that near regular brick sizes could be achieved and this made for regular bonding. The bond adopted was the 'English bond' of alternate rows of headers and stretchers, a bond used in North Europe: it is stronger than the modern Flemish bond. The size of bricks might, indeed, be specified in a building contract. The advantages of some standardization were soon realized, and it was the problem of building repairs which prompted the council of Colchester from 1425 or 1426 to keep in the Moot Hall a model 'fourme' for brickmakers to copy. This regulation shows the industry had really 'arrived', and the local bricks were now common in Colchester, where the earlier mediaeval buildings had absorbed hundreds of old Roman tiles. To prevent its sticking in the mould the clay might be lubricated with water—this wet moulding is known as 'slop'—and perhaps sanded later. From the mid-fifteenth century 'pallet' moulding was usual, using sand on the surface as the lubricant. This might fire into a rough glaze in firing. Wet-moulded bricks would have needed to stand longer after shaping, so they did not become distorted in firing.

Bricks for dressings were shaped either by moulding in the same way, but with special moulds, or by carving the bricks after firing.

The green bricks could be fired in a kiln ('kylne' or 'kyll') or in a clamp. The kiln may be called a 'tilehouse', as at Hull and as at Deptford in 1418. At Hull it was made of wattle-and-daub only and needed many repairs. Kilns were regular structures, which could be used and reused and so were appropriate for large projects and, commercially, when the industry was established. They must usually have been made of bricks, though perhaps started with unbaked bricks that hardened during the firings. The remains of ovens of soft, half-baked red bricks of the thirteenth century, found at Porchester (Hampshire) and at Carisbrooke (Isle of Wight), show brick used early in this type of context (information from S. E. Rigold). However, since there were no pumps, claypits would fill up with water and, on a confined site, this could cause the kiln to be abandoned.

The earliest known picture of brick-making in Europe was found by Salzman in the 'Nederlandische Bijbel' made at Utrecht about 1425 (and now in the British Museum). This shows simply the shaping of plain fabric bricks in a mould and the stacking of these still plastic bricks in criss-cross or herring-bone rows. The scene is theoretically of Jews making bricks in Egypt, where the bricks would in fact have been bonded with straw to dry in the sun, but these are the strawless European version made by workers wearing fifteenth-century costume. The yard is walled, but unfortunately the kiln is not shown. It is believed that the kilns were beehive-shaped, and there are surviving pictures of large domed industrial ovens—used for glass-making, for example—which must have been similar. Clamps were a temporary, once-only provision for firing bricks. The green bricks were stacked on the ground, presumably given a covering of daub or wattle-and-daub and then earthed over. Their use was appropriate for smaller projects or for limited uses, as when in 1525 'clampys' or loads of bricks were sent to Hunsdon House (Hertfordshire) for the chimneys. At Calais bricks brought from Flanders are recorded first, then clamps at Calais and then the town's own kilns. The terms 'clamps' and 'kilnsfulls' are used as measures of number. References to kilns are much more common, which is not surprising because they were used for the important works. In the Elizabethan period, however, 'clamp' and 'kiln' may be used interchangeably, so perhaps use of the terms was not rigid earlier either.

Both kiln and clamp needed some ventilation, and the green bricks and fuel were set out in the same way in both, in alternating rows. Hull had its turves and, as noted, a Lord Treasurer or King could afford coal, but the common fuel was wood cut into faggots. The use of wood fuel meant that firing was slow and very uneven, a matter of weeks. There are references in the Hull accounts to workers watching through the night during firing. The bricks at the base of the rows were fired hard or even too hard, while a proportion of those at the top and sides were too soft. Contracts demand well- and sufficiently-burned bricks. Bricks with black cores, where the heat from the wood has not penetrated strongly enough, are usually of before the eighteenth century. Irregular vitrification may also be a sign of early date, the saltpetre having been driven to the surface but failing to burn off there. Firing was probably no more scientific even in the booming Tudor period. The soft samel bricks would be rejected or accepted only in limited numbers. At Little Saxham Hall (Suffolk) about 1505 it was agreed that the fired bricks should measure 10 × 5 × 2½ inches, with no 'semel' or broken bricks though two half bricks could be counted as one whole. In 1530 Laurence Stubbs, Vicar at Kingston and once Wolsey's accountant at Hampton Court, supplied a load of bricks for the King's new Whitehall Palace. It comprised: 65,000 'samwelle bricke'; 24,000 'harde bricke'; 32,000 'in bricke battis'. These may have been the usual proportions achieved in firing, so that the relatively few hard bricks would have had to be kept chiefly for exterior facing.

Many different sizes of fabric bricks were used up to the Elizabethan period, when a rough standardization seems to have occurred, at about 9 × 4½ × 2 inches. This is a little shorter than what seems to be the typical later mediaeval or Early Tudor brick. The modern brick is squarer still, because thicker. This is a change, not a large one, that has been been attributed to the effect of the Brick Tax in the eighteenth century. The narrow early width of 2 or 2½ inches was probably the result of the amount of clay it is easy to tap down in the mould and also to do with economy. The wide mortar joints—seldom gauged, though Temple Newsam House at Leeds has some Early Tudor gauged brick—form about a quarter of the wall surface. The modern cement joints form a sixth or less of the wall surface. Using narrow bricks and narrow joints could employ a third more bricks. Good mediaeval mortar was extremely hard, much less quickly eroded by weather than cement is and making demolition difficult. Thus, the wide joints were practical, and the mortar was much cheaper than the bricks. On the other hand more buildings will have been lost through decay of the mortar than of bricks. In this context it is interesting to note a couple of uses of oyster shells to reinforce mortar in special jobs: of the mid-fifteenth century were the mortar and shells used between the *brick* core and the freestone facing of Norwich Cathedral spire; of the early sixteenth century are the shells driven into the mortar at Laughton Place (Sussex) in the arched vaulting of the stairs. The purpose of these shells may have been chiefly to keep the distances constant while the mortar was hardening.

Size is no real guide to the date of bricks. Date is better deduced from texture, from the ways in which the bricks are used and to what extent they are shaped for dressings and ornament. Sizes may be interesting, just because of their variety, sometimes prompted by functional reasons, and because of their aesthetic effect. The early wall tiles might be as thin as 1½ inches and be employed—like Roman tiles—for bonding, not for the main fabric. Bricks used for such tasks may be very long: the early thirteenth century Little

Coggeshall chapel has thin bricks, used for quoins, that are 20 inches long. The mediaeval 'great brick'—the term is used in the sixteenth century, when some of this type were still being used in East Anglia—might be a foot or 15 inches long, occasionally more. They tend to be unevenly sized place bricks. There are fourteenth-century examples at Waltham Abbey (Essex), used irregularly in rubble fabric. The early bricks of the Hull area are comparatively large, although moulded. Recent excavation has found bricks, used at the end of the fourteenth century for the town walls, that measure 11 × 5 × 2 inches. Thin bricks whose length is only 8 inches may be imports, as those of Horne's Place at Appledore (Kent), but the lining of the central tower of Canterbury Cathedral was done in the 1480s with local bricks about 8½ inches long, some only 1¼ inches thick. The patron at Canterbury was Archbishop John Morton, who erected brick buildings at Lambeth and at Croydon. These palaces are less than ten miles apart, but the Lambeth bricks are about 10 × 5 × 2¼ inches while Morton's bricks at Croydon are 9¼ × 4¾ × 1¾ inches. The underlying trends are to the disappearance of the longer bricks and to consistency in any one building programme, rather than to a common size. At Hampton Court, for instance, Wolsey's ranges are of bricks 9¼ × 4 × 2 (or 2¼) inches, while Henry VIII's are of 10 × 4 × 2½ inches. Wolsey's were made at the site; Henry VIII's were made elsewhere in the region as well as at the site.

The list of surviving buildings with brickwork of before 1450 takes us from Yorkshire to Kent. If the first buildings of Hull had survived the emphasis would have been northern not East Anglian. What most of the earlier buildings have in common is that the brick is only one material of several. Though Thornton Abbey gatehouse, however, has its elaborate stone carvings and facings it is basically a very considerable structure of long bricks. Even secondary walls there are five stretchers or three headers thick, in contrast to, say, the late fifteenth-century Someries' three stretchers or two headers (Bedfordshire). Brick appears as a main material regularly from the early fifteenth century. About the 1440s the shaping of dressings and then ornamental details is also established, and these finally reached the spectacular in East Anglia and Essex: tracery panels and arched corbel-tables with trefoil heads contribute some of the finest examples. It is interesting to see what a variety of unit bricks could be used to make up the same or very similar cusped heads of corbelling or blank panelling. Some forms are more common than others, but there is, neither early or late, a stereotyped method: the number of bricks needed for the cusped lobes varies as well as their shape. At Feering church (Essex), for instance, three different mouldings are used (in pairs) to make up the trefoils of a short arcaded plinth frieze. (See Figure 3, b–d.) The

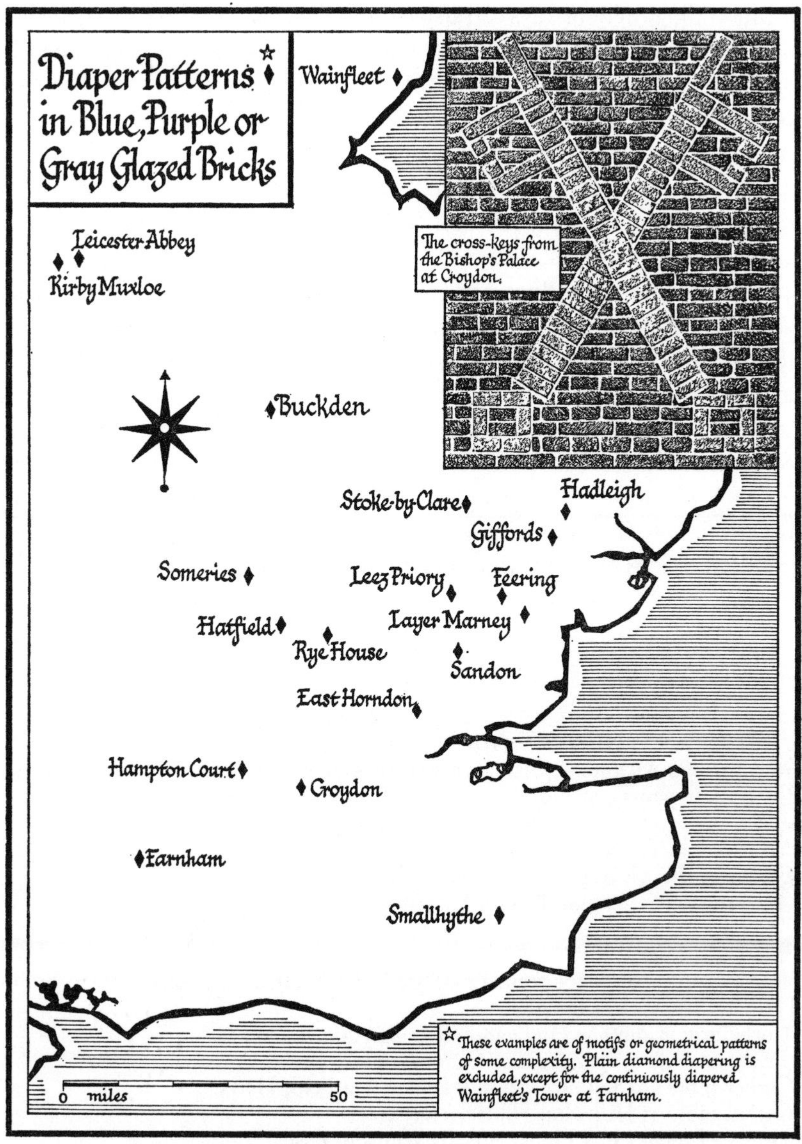
Diaper Patterns in Blue, Purple or Gray Glazed Bricks
Wainfleet
The cross-keys from the Bishop's Palace at Croydon.
Leicester Abbey
Kirby Muxloe
Buckden
Stoke-by-Clare
Hadleigh
Giffords
Someries
Leez Priory
Feering
Layer Marney
Hatfield
Rye House
Sandon
East Horndon
Hampton Court
Croydon
Farnham
Smallhythe
These examples are of motifs or geometrical patterns of some complexity. Plain diamond diapering is excluded, except for the continuously diapered Wainfleet's Tower at Farnham.
0 miles 50

2. DIAPER PATTERNS IN BLUE, PURPLE, OR GREY GLAZED BRICKS.

multi-mouldings of doorways can also be complex. In Yorkshire, Lincolnshire, the Home Counties and Hampshire stone dressings seem to have been the norm, though Kent has some late moulded brick—including the 'Flemish' tracery of Smallhythe Chapel.

The key decades in the development of brick in England are the 1430s to 1450s, which are marked by the records of Flemish or German craftsmen working in England. They are named in the Alien Subsidy Rolls or in individual building records. The 1436 Aliens roll includes 'Henry Henryson', 'born in Teutonic parts', living in Ipswich; 'Henry Mason', a South German at West Horndon in Essex, who was almost certainly a brickmaker and who could have worked on Heron Hall, East Horndon, at this date; William and John van Gildre, masons from the Lower Rhineland, living at Isleworth (Middlesex) and probably working on Syon Convent, from which a brick undercroft survives. Other names have certainly been lost. As Barnes and Simpson have shown, the strongest influence on the rare 90-foot tower and courtyard plan of Caister Castle is that of South German 'wasserburgen', water-sited castles, but the accounts do not give the mason's name. William

3. CUSPED BRICK DRESSINGS AND CORBELLING, EXAMPLES FROM THE MID-FIFTEENTH TO THE MID-SIXTEENTH CENTURIES. Cusped shapes or trefoils, formed with a surprising variety of unit bricks, were popular for corbel-tables, tracery panels, spandrels and other details of buildings.
(*a*) Black tracery at Prior Overton's Tower, Repton, Derbyshire.
(*b*) Cobelling at Rye House, Herts.
(*c*) Frieze at the Vicarage, Rickmansworth, Herts.
(*d*) Vaulting at Tattershall Castle, Lincolnshire.
(*e*) Intersecting archlets of corbel-table, with section of stair handrail, at Faulkbourne Hall, Essex.
(*f*) Decoration of fireplace from Prittlewell Guildhall, Essex, now in the Victoria and Albert Museum, London.
(*g*) Corbelling at Nether Hall gatehouse, Roydon, Essex.
(*h*) Frieze and door spandrels at Gifford's Hall, Stoke-by-Nayland, Suffolk.
(*i*) Corbel-table at the Old Bishop's Palace, Hatfield, Herts.
(*j*) Corbel table at Hunsdon House, Herts.
(*k*) Heads of niches in Chignal Smealy Church, Essex.
(*l*) Corbel-table at Meesden Church, Herts.
(*m*) Chimney base at Compton Wynyates, Warwickshire.
(*n*) Niche at chimney base at Sollershope Court Farm, Herefordshire.
(*o*) Black tracery panel at Leiston Abbey, Suffolk.
(*p*) Friezes in terracotta at Layer Marney Tower, Essex.
(*q*) Heads of blank panels at Snore Hall, Fordham, Norfolk.
(*r*) Quatrefoil panel at West Stow Hall, Suffolk.

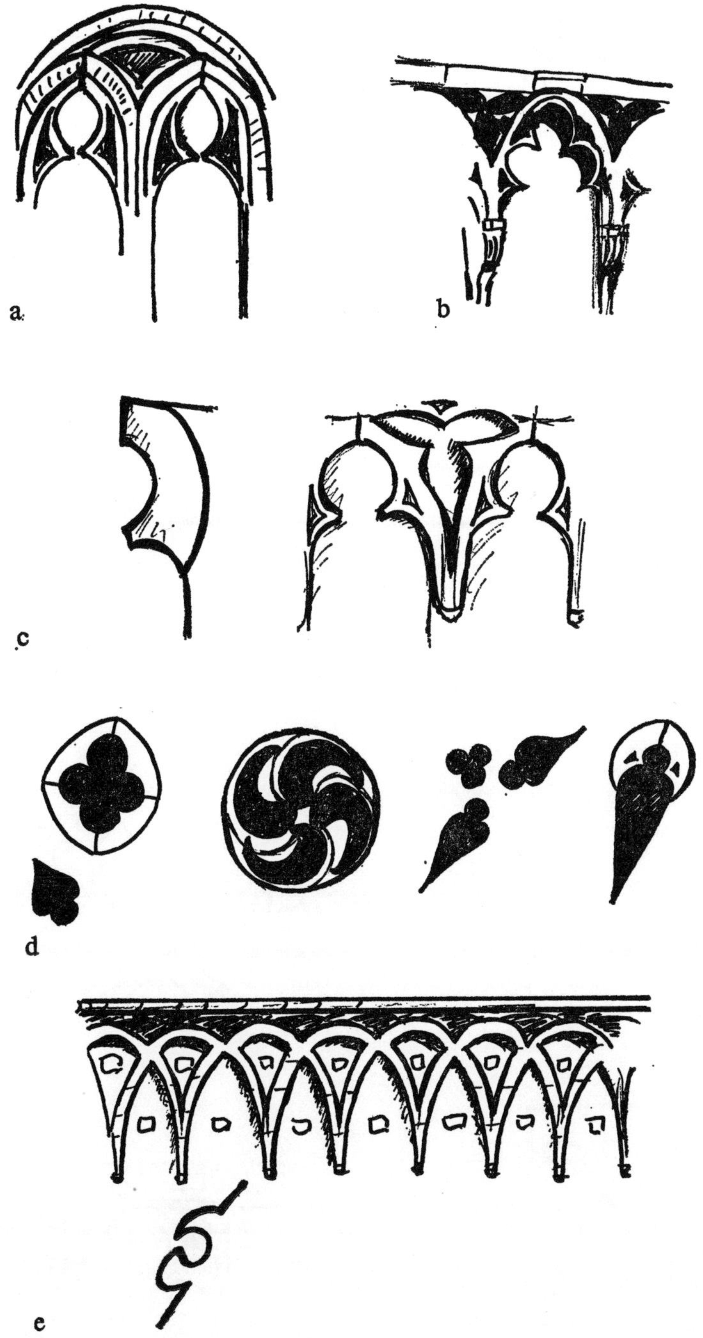
a
b
c
d
e

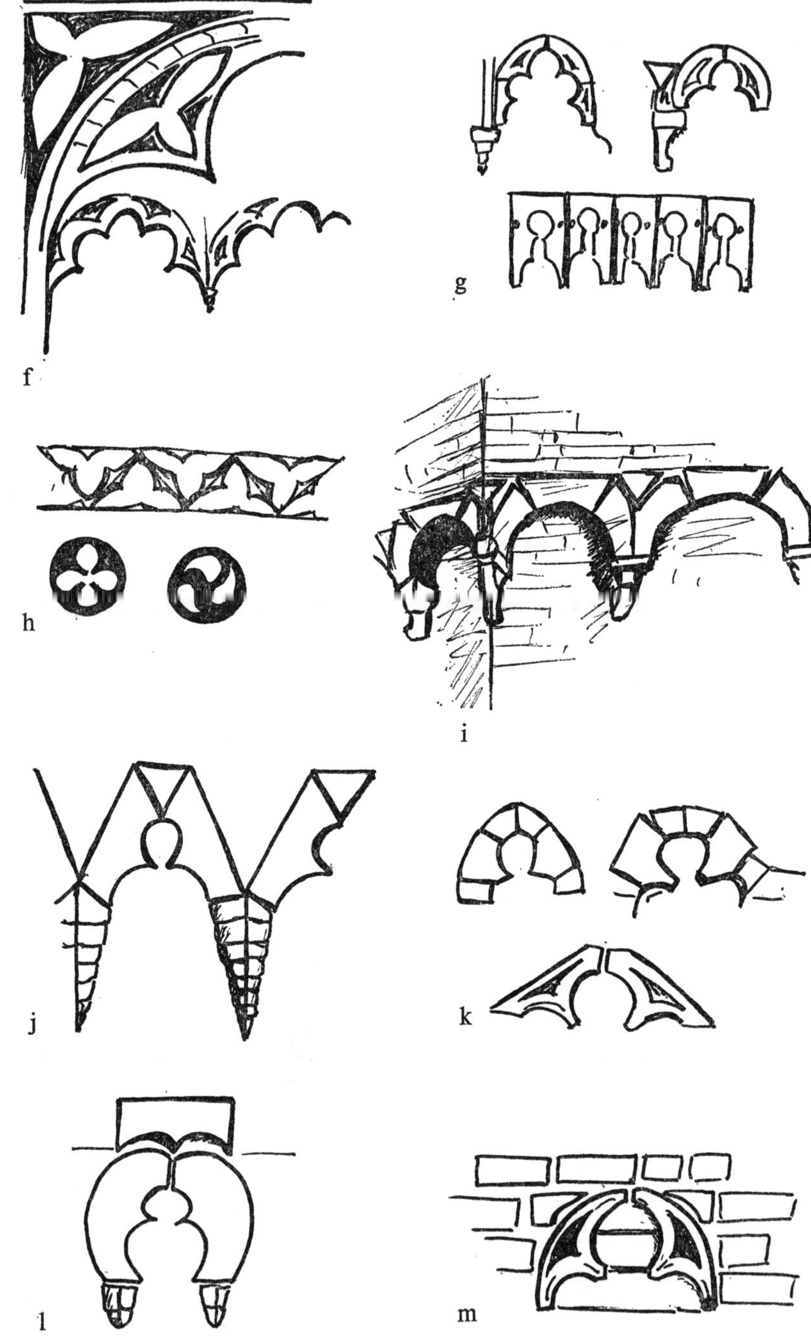
f
g
h
i
j
k
l
m

Vesey may have been responsible for Hurstmonceux Castle's Continental look.

By the end of the fifteenth century the leading brick-mason was John Cowper, an Englishman who built in a plain and heavily impressive style for Hastings at Kirby Muxloe and for Waynflete, Bishop of Winchester. In the Early Tudor period Henry Redman, whose ancestors were in Huntingdonshire, built for Henry VIII and was responsible for Wolsey's great West Gatehouse at Hampton Court, but the designs were not essentially based on brick: most of the dressed work was done in other materials. These climactic buildings, the dozens of palaces erected by Wolsey—who even built at Tournai between 1513 and 1518, as its bishop—and by Henry VIII demonstrate the convenience of brick. The makers were now able to supply thousands of fabric units that needed no further shaping; demanded a smaller proportion of highly-skilled workers; allowed building on a new scale and easy extensions. At Hampton Court there were as many as eighty-seven bricklayers working in 1537 and in 1538 the number rose to 113, headed by Christopher Dickenson. In 1539, though, he and the head carpenter and others were switched to the emergency building programme on the Downs forts, where brick was used only for inside work—including sinister 'murder-holes' over entrance passages. At Hampton Court work had been pressed on in the leisure and drinking time of the workers, with some work done by candlelight: in the hectic atmosphere of the invasion scare, there was a strike of common labourers for 6*d*. a day instead of 5*d*. (6*d*. had been the mason's rate before Tudor inflation) and the leaders or 'first beginners' were imprisoned.

In certain East Anglian halls and in the Essex churches dressings and ornament were shaped now with Tudor panache. The use of brick prompted some modifications in style, favouring a flattening of arches and a rather less complicated line than that of stone carving. Brick *was* carved sometimes, perhaps in shallow relief as at East Barsham (Norfolk), but most shaping was done by moulding—as in Flanders, whose step-gabled buildings had been the strongest influence. In England the stone-inspired crockets of arch finials and of the pinnacles of battlements and stepped gables are simplified into dumpy moulded knobs—as at Rayne and Feering in Essex—and are well short of the elegance that brick corbel-tables and archways and window dressings may achieve. Indoors, brickwork is usually obscured by plaster, though some moulded brick vaulting and the rarish brick lintels of fireplaces may appear unrendered. The late and short-lived fashion for terracotta ornament took fired clay to the ultimate in complexity, with details too fine to be seen close to. At Layer Marney the scallops and dolphins and initialled labels of the parapets of the eighth stage of the angle turrets blur, at a distance, into pale strawberry-leaf coronets. The main form of decoration that is limited to brickwork is simpler, the blue, purple or grey diapering. This varies from the frequent plain diamonds to crosses on stepped pedestals, grids, stars and zigzags and even, occasionally, initials and heraldic emblems. The glazed headers were also used in pairs to alternate decoratively with red stretchers for the voussoirs of doors and windows. The Early Tudor manor of Compton Wynyates has, besides notable decorated chimneys, diaper patterning—including on the not very stern gatehouse.

Early bonding of fabric brick is irregular. The cells of vaults, though, normally show stretchers only. During the fifteenth century English bond for fabric became the norm. Flemish bond belongs to the seventeenth century on, but houses are most commonly now faced with stretchers only. The rough texture of early bricks is the chief reason why surfaces are never monotonous,

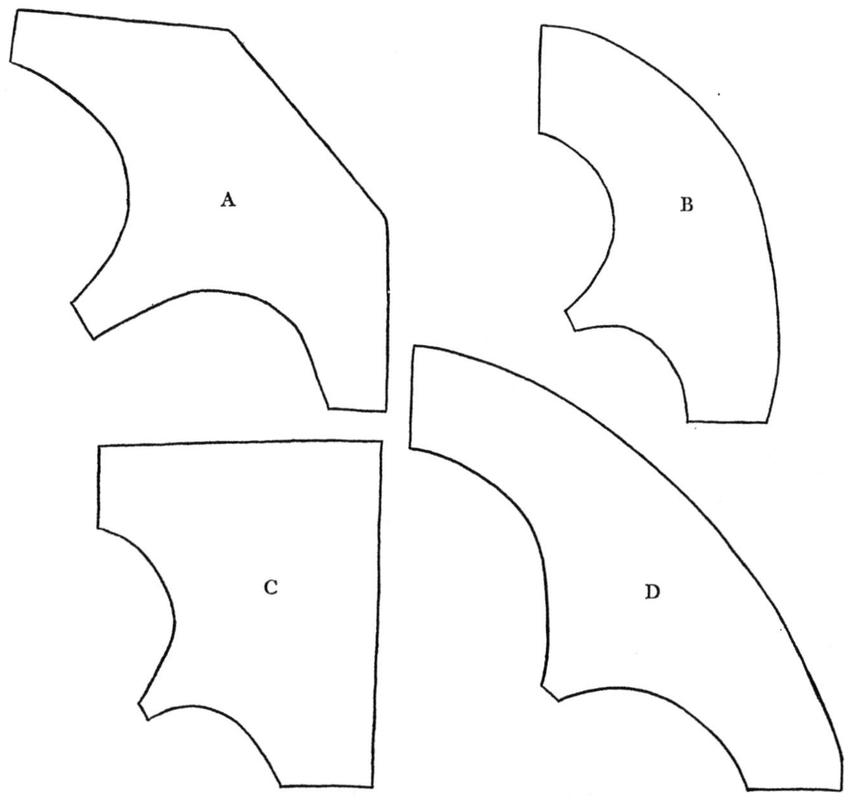

4. CUSPED BRICKS. (A) Cusped head of blank panelling of larger gatehouse of Leez Priory, Essex, of about 1536. (B, C, D) Cusped heads from south aisle freize of Feering Church, Essex, of about 1505. Tracings of *in situ* bricks, reduced by two-thirds.

although the English bond contributes to this. I think the one bond that with smooth mass-produced brick achieves a varied surface, actually because slightly restless, is the uncommon English Garden Wall or Sussex bond.

The surviving early buildings with brick fabric and fine dressings are predominately the church towers and porches and the detached angle-turreted gatehouses of great houses. Some of the houses themselves have disappeared, replaced by more modern ones (as at Lullingstone, Kent) or have been pulled down for building materials (as at Roydon). At Lullingstone, West Drayton (Middlesex), Rye House, Hodsock 'Priory' (Nottinghamshire), Kirtling (Cambridge) and Hadleigh (Suffolk) are fine gatehouses from lost brick mansions. The Beckingham Hall gate at Tolleshunt D'Arcy (Essex) is a small and wayward example, less grand than the tall ruins of Nether Hall at Roydon in the same county. In a sense the churches were grudgingly saved by the Reformation, because funds were long turned away from further ecclesiastical building. The gatehouses, however, were saved by their own strength and thick walls, if their beauty and swank was not appreciated. They proved too formidable to demolish economically. In an age when exterior brick walls were commonly three foot thick these gatehouse walls were made even stronger. Thus is preserved the decorative perversion in brick of defensive building, that was permitted by the increasing regularization of society both by London-oriented law and by the local Justices of the Peace.

5. Compton Wynyates, Warwickshire, main front with gatehouse, 1520.

Note 1: The shaping of brick by carving is further considered towards the end of the section on Chimneys in Chapter II.
Note 2: The influence of brick on architectural line is further considered towards the end of the section on Church Building in Chapter V.

2. *Holy Trinity Church and the lost buildings of Kingston upon Hull*

The concentration of brick in Hull made it the one brick-built town of the Middle Ages in England. Its only conceivable rival was nearby Beverley, though John Leland in the mid sixteenth century noted, perhaps surprisingly, large numbers of brick buildings in Southampton. Beverley, in the fourteenth century anyway, covered a larger area than Hull. Its brickworks, though they were not direct labour ones, have left records almost as early as Hull's. Yet Leland was to describe Beverley as built of wood. He did record several town gates of brick *or* stone, of which only the brick North Bar of 1409 remains, but could find no trace of town walls. The Minster was stone-built, with rendered brick used in some early vaulting, but Hull's main church as chiefly of brick.

It seems clear that Hull had many more conventual, municipal and commercial buildings of brick, though probably most dressings were of stone (unlike the even earlier Little Coggeshall Abbey, Essex).

Holy Trinity Church, sole survivor of Hull's early brickwork, was the focus of attention in the mediaeval town. It retains the only brickwork above ground in Hull, labelled by J. E. Morris (in *The East Riding of Yorkshire*) as 'the most important example of fourteenth century brick anywhere remaining in England', but, as at the much smaller church at Sutton-in-Holderness nearby, the dressings are of stone. The style is Decorated. The plain interior is largely plaster-rendered. Despite its great size and its institutional importance, shown by the twenty-five chaplains employed here in 1525, for example, Holy Trinity was erected just as a chapel-of-ease to Hessle, and it had this subordinate status till 1661. Both side aisles run the whole length of the building, and the centre aisle has its clerestory. Chancel, transepts and south porch, as well as the base of the square tower, are of brick; they were erected first, in the earlier fourteenth century, with local bricks. The nave and upper sections of the tower are stone-built and Perpendicular, dating from the early fifteenth century on. The brick parts have stone windows, quoins, battlements and pinnacles and stone-faced buttresses. Moulded brick is thus lacking. Though the exterior has been restored, the brickwork still dominates. The north side of the chancel and the north transept (especially its north face) are the best preserved.

Three main factors must have made for the use of brick: firstly, there was the absence of suitable stone, though smaller amounts could be brought in for dressings; secondly, there was the presence of brick earth—'unlimited quantities of excellent brick clays' (A. Clifton-Taylor)—cheaper anyway to work; thirdly, the subsoil was watery, making relative lightness vital. The church had to float on timber rafts. Shifts in these have caused the need for major repairs to the fabric. The desire to reduce weight also made for for the large windows and, inside, the disconcertingly thin piers. The chief cultural influences were evidently the expectations of the Hansa merchants and the experience of the English themselves of brick buildings in south-west France. The leading merchants concerned in building the church and in the whole development of Hull were the de la Poles (earlier 'Rotenherring'), whose money came from sheep and trade and who had their own brickworks. At first Holy Trinity was to provide in its Lady Chapel (later re-dedicated) their family chapel and burial place, but they later transferred their special patronage to the (lost) Charterhouse. In the mid fifteenth century, long after the body of the church was complete, John Alcock, later Bishop of Ely and builder in brick, lived at Hull: he set up, south-west of Holy Trinity, the Grammar School, which has lost its oldest buildings, and had a chantry chapel in Holy Trinity. The lesser mediaeval church of St Mary's, in Lowgate, is built of stone, although the town's brickyard records show that in the early fifteenth century St Mary's rejected as useless a complete firing. The concentration, however, on one great church, with a whole chequer of the grid plan to itself, was typical of the new towns ('bastides'), whether of Gascony or England. This accounts for the great size, making it difficult to see why Holy Trinity was left as a chapel. The few competitors in size include Boston Church and the lost St Michael's at Coventry, whose ruins are attached to the Cathedral. It has the breadth of churches of brick in North Germany, the Low Countries and the Baltic area, but lacks their brick piers, brick tracery or moulded vaulting.

Holy Trinity represents new stylistic and ecclesiastical developments, also expressed in St Thomas's Church at Winchelsea, another new and royally-established town. These were 'preaching churches', built for larger congregations and having a wide and open plan, unbroken by heavy screens and not splintering into big transepts or projecting chapels. John Harvey (in *English Mediaeval Architects*) explains the attribution to the mason Walter of Hereford of Holy Trinity, the smaller church at Winchelsea and the lost three hundred foot long church of the Greyfriars at Newgate in London, and sees Walter's as 'the principal influence, which formed the new type of preaching church destined to have so vital an effect on the Church design of the Later Middle Ages'. From the thirteenth century the friars were the leaders in popular preaching, more lively, travelled and often better educated than the parish priests, who thus became jealous of them. Congregations came to favour the less ritualistic approach, expressed in the vernacular, and responded to the wider spread of knowledge. Walter was chief mason at Caernarvon Castle, where he had a hundred masons to supervise in 1304–5. He worked for Queen Margaret at the Franciscans' (Greyfriars') Church. He evidently supplied the design of Holy Trinity about 1295 or 1300, though initial construction work was seemingly delayed or slow, and the rafts for the foundations had to be fixed. Harvey points out that the transepts are comparatively small projections, having 'a mere vestige' of the earlier significance of this part of a church.

Leland had seen that the fabric was 'for the most part of brike', but, as we have said, Bishop Lyttleton failed to see any old brick, by then disguised with 'compo' (T. Allen, 1828) or cement. A careful study was made by Carles Frost, who published in 1827 his *Notices concerning . . . Hull*, which included a whole chapter 'On the Restoration of the art of Brick-making in England, and the early use of Bricks in the town of Hull'. He obviously enjoyed debunking the influential Lyttleton, but realized his own sight of the brickwork was made possible by 'the present lamentable want of repair of the exterior'. He was also, incidentally, able to cite, from 'the testimony of persons now living within whose memory' the town walls were demolished, that these too were of brick, and he found some of their foundations. The whole church is 272 feet long. Nave and aisles are 72 feet wide, while the transepts, which are 28 feet across, add another 24 feet. John Bilson (in an article on Beverley North Bar, published in the *East Riding Antiquarian Society Transactions*, vol. IV, 1896) gave the dates for the brick parts of the church and showed that the earlier bricks were smaller than the later ones. Most are red, but some are blue (not used for diapering). The south and north transepts were of about 1315–20, the bricks of the former measuring $9 \times 4\frac{3}{8} \times 2\frac{1}{16}$ inches and those of the latter $9\frac{3}{4} \times 4\frac{3}{4} \times 2\frac{1}{8}$ inches. The chancel of five bays, with the choir, was of about 1340, with the larger bricks typical of the area. These here measure $10\frac{1}{4} \times 5 \times 2\frac{1}{16}$ inches. Alec Clifton-Taylor notes the 'broad mortar courses' and the regular sizing of the bricks, especially on the north side.

It is believed that the Black Death of 1349–50 stopped building, as it did St Nicholas's Church at Great Yarmouth. This plague severely attacked Hull's population and permanently ruined Meaux Abbey. Work on Holy Trinity was resumed towards the end of the century, but the 144 feet long stone nave, with eight bays, is of about 1425. The only other brick structure is the south porch, the main entry, but the tower base has early brick rising to about three feet above the sills of the lower windows. The two stone stages of the tower, much later still than the nave, have elegant windows like panels, which reduced the weight. The tower, indeed, looks like a huge square lantern over the crossing. The church was finished in Henry VIII's reign, nearly two and a half centuries after it had been begun. The careful brickwork is practical, devoid of mouldings and decoration, and yet the Perpendicular nave is, essentially, no more amibitious than the brick chancel. They make up, unchanged except for details, the great church that Leland saw and which showed itself as *the* landmark in Hollar's view of Hull.

There are records and sometimes pictures of early brick buildings that have disappeared, perhaps demolished in favour of new houses, as in the case of Stonor Park (Oxfordshire). One would like to see Andrew Ogard's Rye House, from which the gatehouse alone survives, and his other lost manor at Emneth in Norfolk. The brick house that his friend, Sir William Oldhall, built at nearby Hunsdon (Hertfordshire) was superseded by Henry VIII's, itself now reduced to a fragment attached to a later house. Sir John Fastolf's manor-house and lodge at Hellesdon (Norfolk) are lost. The mid-fifteenth-century de la Pole Manor at Ewelme (Oxfordshire) is lost apart from a small, inaccessible fragment. It is a great loss; so is Jesus College, built at Rotherham in the West Riding of Yorkshire by Archbishop Rotherham, a great brick builder; so is Bishop Vesey's Moor Hall, built in the early 1500s at Sutton Coldfield in Warwickshire where this bishop erected houses and public buildings (all stone, except for his own house). The lost Little Saxham Hall evidently rivalled the slightly later Westhorpe Hall, also in Suffolk and also demolished in the eighteenth century: the elaborate, much restored, East Barsham Hall (Norfolk) must do duty as souvenir of a group. Wolsey's lost house, the Manor of the More near Rickmansworth, apparently rivalled his Hampton Court. Much royal Tudor brick has disappeared from the Greenwich, Eltham and Richmond Palaces. Whitehall and Oatlands and other palaces are wholly gone.

All these losses are, though, small beer in comparison with the loss of mediaeval Kingston upon Hull, most of which was built of brick. The disappearance of this work has altered the whole picture, shifting the emphasis to the south geographically and to the Perpendicular and Tudor architectural periods. To remedy this I include this section on Hull, concentrating on the public buildings, with a postscript on the recent excavations.

Hull Corporation has some of the records of a municipal brickyard, administered by chamberlains from 1303 to 1433, which was called the 'Tilery'. Accounts were kept in Latin, but many of the technical terms, including names of tools, were written in English. The products were definitely bricks, though called 'walltieles' or 'walltyles' only from 1353 on, instead of the Latin 'tegulae' (tiles). Workers were employed by the corporation direct, and this was unique: at Beverley the tile-fields were rented out. F. W. Brooks said that Hull yard site was evidently near Prince's Dock. The highest annual production was just under 100,000 bricks. In the mid sixteenth century Leland saw another tilery, on the south side of the town outside the walls, and described it as the source of the materials for the town walls and most of the houses of 'Kingston'.

Mediaeval Hull was England's first brick-built town. It was the great brick-making centre of the area where Bilson noted that surviving mediaeval bricks were comparatively large. Leland was impressed, and gave a detailed description of the town. Wenceslas Hollar, after the Civil War, in which the town held out for the Royalists against a Puritan countryside, drew its plan: the layout was mediaeval and most of the buildings still seemingly unaltered.

Now only Holy Trinity remains. The mediaeval town (pls. 9, 10) is also known from a plan, apparently a sixteenth-century redrawing, now in the British Museum (*Cott. M.S. Aug. I i 83*).

Because Hull has continued as a great port into modern times it has been completely redeveloped. The old layout, by then with new buildings on the mediaeval plots, finally disintegrated under World War II bombing. It had survived so long because the modern dock concentration was against the Humber, not the Hull, and the railway was not brought into 'Old Town'. The 1377 Poll Tax returns showed that Hull was a smaller town than Beverley. Leland noted that there were no suburbs, and there were still none in the mid seventeenth century, and later changes were probably intensified by the constriction of the water boundaries.

This was a mediaeval 'new town', laid out on a coherent grid plan, most like the English town of Libourne near Bordeaux. The fortifications were like those of the Aquitainean 'bastides' generally. There is still magnificent early brick in south-west France—above all the thirteenth-century Albi Cathedral—where the bricks were laid in stretcher bond. The English long had territory round Bordeaux and imported much wine from the region. (Another cultural influence seems to have been the crossing of the legs of effigies, based on those of Toulouse.) The influence in England of the brick of Calais was later, being important in the fifteenth century. John Harvey has said that the mason Walter of Hereford 'must be suspected as the architect of Hull': Walter, who died in 1315, was architect of one of the greatest royal works under Edward I, Caernarvon Castle. Hull was established by that king in 1293—the first charter dating from 1299—on the site of a trading and fishing village called 'Wyke', itself established by the Cistercian monks of Meaux Abbey (sheep farmers and tile-makers). The earlier nearby port of Ravenser was declining, and Edward I persuaded its most important merchant, William de la Pole, to come to the new town of 'Kingston'. (Ravenser finally disappeared through erosion.) The King had obtained much of the old lordship of Holderness, in which Meaux Abbey held Wyke: he obtained the whole lordship, largely through exchange, and the monks, at least, complained they lost on the deal. The manor of Myton was granted to William de la Pole. By the end of the thirteenth century there was a Hanseatic merchants' establishment, a cultural influence and symptom of growth. There were several periods of growth, based first on fishing, then on ship-building and the wool trade (the de la Poles acting as distributors of Cistercian wool). In the mid fourteenth century de la Poles engaged in provisioning and money-lending to the Crown. Edward III reneged on his debts in 1350, which attacked the family's prosperity, but by this period their interests were shifting southwards to London and then to East Anglia, centred on Wingfield in Suffolk.

Construction work began in 1293, under the control of the founder, Edward I. The old houses of Wyke were initially retained and, though masons from Westminster Abbey were employed, the main work in the earliest period was in planning and road-making. Plots were laid out, but not all were rented at first. Use of brick must have been prompted both by lack of on-the-spot stone and by the marshiness of the site, which meant a relatively lightweight material was invaluable. Brick-making records are nearly coeval with the foundation: in 1303–4 54,350 bricks were made and in the next year 92,000.

A period of very great activity, with the rebuilding of dwellings in brick, and the erection of the town walls came when Michael de la Pole, Lord Chancellor of England, was head of the family. He was to die in 1389. Privileges were obtained from Richard II. 'The town waxid very rich' and 'was wonderfully augmentid in building'. Leland's accounts are invaluable because he often mentions building materials, though his history may be over-condensed. He says most of Hull's new buildings were brick. The greatest concentration was towards the River Hull, the merchants' houses lying along 'Hull Street' (now High Street), and round the churches of Holy Trinity and St Mary, with some open spaces beyond. De la Pole himself 'buildid a goodly house of brick again [against] the west end of S. Maries Chirch, lyke a palace, with goodly orchard and gardein at large, enclosid with brike'. Michael became Earl of Suffolk in 1385, and his Hull Street courtyard-plan mansion came to be known as 'Suffolk Palace'. The site is that of the Head Post Office. The de la Poles had their own brick kiln, north of the town at Trippett, from the fourteenth century.

Leland said Michael de la Pole 'buildid also 3. houses besides in the town, whereof every one hath a tour [tower] of brike'. Beyond the North Gate he established a Carthusian monastery, or charterhouse, with a linked hospital or almshouse. The monastery church, incidentally, replaced the de la Pole chapel in Holy Trinity as their burial place: Leland says their lead coffins were dug up at the recent suppression. 'Most part of this monastery was buildid in brike, as the residew of the buildings of Hulle for the most part be.' Hollar showed the town buildings as of two or three storeys, with steeply pitched gables.

Of the public buildings Leland mentioned the town hall (without specifying whether it was brick-built, which it probably was) and 'a tour of brik for a prison', both at the east end of Holy Trinity. The Chamberlains' accounts of the brickyard include bricks supplied for the prison ('gaolam'). Other municipal buildings erected or repaired in brick were the 'market stede' (covered market-stand), the 'fleshmarket' (meat market) and the 'weyhouse' (weigh-house), used mainly for wool.

The main public works were the walls. In 1317 the inhabitants first petitioned Parliament for permission to fortify the town with a wall, ditch and towers. In 1321 permission was granted, but possibly the first defences were simply the addition of a moat to landward. Two sides of the roughly triangular site were already outlined by the Rivers Humber and Hull (4,800 feet in all) and the third side was only a land boundary, of 4,800 feet. Wenceslas Hollar's picture of about 1665 shows the moat along this side, supplemented by the later wall. Hull was, thus, an island, with six bridges to the mainland. Only in the 1930s, when Queens Dock was filled in, did the 'Old Town' district cease to be an island. Some defences must have existed by the fourteenth century, Hull being the only major port between Newcastle and Lynn (Norfolk), but the battlemented walls and towers of Hollar's picture dated mainly from the end of that century. Leland observed: 'In Richard the secundes days . . . the toune . . . was enclosed with diches [ditches], and the waul [wall] begon, and yn continuance ended [completed] and made all of brike . . . In the walle be 4. principal gates of brike. Between the North Gate . . . and Beverley Gate be 12. touers of bryke, and yn one of them a postern. Ther be 5. toures of brikke and a postern yn one of them, as I remember, bytwixt Miton [Myton] Gate and Hasille [Hessle] . . . And from ther to the mouth of the Havin mouth be 5. toures of brick . . . From the mouth of the Hulle ryver into the Haven ther is no waulle, but every merchaunt hath his stairs even to the north gate.' This makes a total of twenty-one towers, but there were evidently more. At neighbouring Beverley Leland saw the surviving North Bar and some other town gates of brick (now lost), but could trace no wall circuit even though Beverley had been the larger town.

Hollar's picture shows the majority of Hull's towers as square and a few round. It shows clearly the arcade supporting the alure, for which compare Norwich and Great Yarmouth walls. Lynn also probably had a brick alure to the walls, but the remains of these are now very fragmentary. Leland's account mentions how the merchants' properties lined the bank of the Hull, where there was no castellated wall. In the 1540s, however, new defences were added along the opposite bank of the Hull. These consisted of a thick wall with three stout lobed forts, comparable to Henry VIII's main forts along the Kent Coast, at Deal for instance. The King was personally involved at Hull holding meetings of the Privy Council at the Suffolk Palace in 1541. In 1542 he was able to use stone from Meaux Abbey in the fortifications, so there was evidently the same mixture of materials, with some brick, as in the Kent and Sussex forts. The encouragement which the King at this time gave to the officers and pilots of Trinity House was part of his naval programme, just as the defences were.

Hull was able to withstand attack during the Civil War, but the walls had deteriorated by the eighteenth century and proved useless during the 1745 Rebellion. There are now no traces above ground. There is a postscript in the excavations carried out on the 'North Walls' area in 1969, which have given much information. The foundations were clay blocks. A clay rampart, perhaps later in date, backed the walls. The bricks were laid in English bond and they measured 'consistently' 11 × 5½ × 2 inches. Sections with twenty or thirty courses were found underground, including the base of a D-shaped interval tower, externally 23 feet 7 inches × 15 feet, with a batter to its front wall: the total height was perhaps originally 29 feet. The excavation made possible an estimate of the numbers of bricks used between 1321 (the excavation report takes it that building proper began as early as this, in which case Leland's attribution to the time of Richard II in the 1380s or 1390s would refer to a late acceleration of work) and the completion in 1400. For the *three* main gates [*sic*], *thirty* towers and 1,355 yards of curtain wall the estimate was 4,700 bricks. It is thought that the curtain was 14 feet high plus 6–8 foot battlements.

Note: For Bibliography see Hull entry in the Gazetteer.

3. *Early brick vocabulary*

It seems useful to give a short glossary of mediaeval and Early Tudor terms used for work in brick and tile. Tile, whether the Latin 'tegulae' or the English 'tile'—or 'tyle', 'tighel', 'tiel', 'till' (all plurals)—is ambiguous. Sometimes brick is meant, though, more often, floor or roofing tiles, though these might be of stone instead. Thus, if the term is used without qualification in a document and if the context is not informative, interpretation must be problematical. This ambiguity has been an important reason why the tradition has been allowed to continue that there was no brick building in England from the Romans to the fifteenth century. In his influential *History of Agriculture and Prices*, published in 1866, Thorold Rogers invariably translated 'tegulae' as roofing tiles, and mediaeval brick continued to be disbelieved in. Rogers thought that brick reappeared only just before the beginning of the fifteenth century. Related words, like 'tegulatores' (tile-layers) or 'tilehouse' and 'tilery', are with tile itself therefore also ambiguous.

The glossary includes early examples of these of of the unambiguous 'brick' itself, apparently always Anglicized from the French 'briche'. It is almost always used as a plural, though without a final s. Brick, however, is not the usual term till the end of our period of study. The terms for different craftsmen, too, are not consistently used, and the versatile fifteenth-century 'brickman' needs a context—to know if he is maker or bricklayer. We may note that the sixteenth-century terms for terracotta—the 'burnt pot earth' and 'burnt pit earth' lack one self-evident meaning. One might take these terms for pottery and brick respectively, 'earth' being the old term for clay, as in 'earthen ware'.

Latin 'tegulae' may be qualified by a Latin or Latinate adjective meaning wall—'murali' or 'muro'—when brick is meant. There are mixed language expressions, like 'tegulas de brike'. The English term 'tile' is qualified by 'wall'—as in 'walltyle' or 'waltighel'—or, more rarely, given as 'bricktile'. L. F. Salzman says the Latin 'latericio' is used for brickwork, but the term is not common and its basic meaning is just 'walling'. We also find, 'lateres' being walling blocks, the expression 'lateres vocatos le brike'.

The main documents are building accounts and contracts. Since Latin was mediaeval officialdom's language, that of accountancy as well as of the law and the Church, expenses were kept in Latin, even after English came to be the main language of the country. This was about the third decade of the fifteenth century. Henry V's reign seems to be the turning point, the King himself writing letters in English, but Latin accounts can still be found as late as the early sixteenth century. Wolsey's Hampton Court expenditure was largely recorded in Latin. Since boys trained by the Church sometimes became 'clerks' (in the modern sense), not clerics, it was natural for Latin to be used, at least until lay literacy became far more widespread. Outside the Church, only nobles and, later, merchants had become really literate. Norman-French does not normally feature because this was mainly the post-Conquest language of nobles' conversation and of their fashionable literature. The famous 'Chronicles' of France and England by Jean Froissart, written in the late fourteenth century, translated into French the *alias* of the main leader of the 1381 Peasants' Revolt, giving 'Waultre le tieulier' (Walter the tiler) for Wat Tyler. (One may note, though, that another eastern leader, Jack Straw, actually was a master-tiler.)

Sir John Fastolf of Caister Castle, Norfolk, who read Latin and French books, had his building accounts of 1432–5 kept for him in Latin. His secretary, William of Worcester, later wrote in Latin notes for an 'Itinerarium' of parts of England, concentrating on topography and on new buildings. Interestingly, though, at the end of the fifteenth century Sir John Howard of Stoke-by-Nayland (Duke of Norfolk from 1483) kept his 'Household Book' personally and in English. These include records of the new, now lost, brick house at Stoke, but mostly deal with the costs of equipment, wines, fuel, of rich cloths, music-making and of journeys. The building accounts of Kirby Muxloe Castle, Leicestershire, contemporary with these, are also in English. By the first half of the sixteenth century English was the norm, as in the records of Hengrave Hall, Suffolk, and those of Henry VIII's Hunsdon House, Hertfordshire.

The earlier and incomplete accounts of the building of Caister, Herstmonceux and Tattershall Castles, have been published by W. Douglas Simpson (see main bibliography). There are references to tiles and brickwork in the two 'History of the King's Works' volumes, edited by H. M. Colvin: they are more often in Latin than in English, since the books go up to the Later Middle Ages only. Most references are in the Exchequer Rolls. There are Latin and English references also given in L. F. Salzman's *History of Building*. Of accounts of later royal enterprises, those of Eton College (mid fifteenth century), Richmond Palace (mid and late fifteenth-century) and of Hampton Court (Henry VIII's accounts, of 1530–9) are particularly important for brick-building. These Hampton Court accounts, of the new buildings and their fitting out, are very full and nearly all in English, but have been quoted from rather than published. (Ernest Law's 1885 volume, the first of the three volumes on *The History of Hampton Court*, has an appendix of sample passages.) The Cambridge Colleges have some relevant building accounts among their archives. Little, however, is known of the costs of ecclesiastical building generally.

The other important sources in which brick is mentioned are official and institutional documents, in which English established itself earlier because of the lay readership. We may include municipal accounts in this group—such as those of Hull and Beverley, Yorkshire, both kept by 'chamberlains', and those of Norwich. In addition there are Parliamentary statutes and town or town guild regulations with some references to brick, in such contexts as these: fire protection, standardization of tile and brick sizes, the organization and conduct of craftsmen.

Known references of these types are scanty and scattered, with one notable exception: the chamberlains' accounts of the municipal (direct labour) brickyard at Kingston upon Hull. These begin in the fourteenth century, but are complete only for the major part of Henry VI's reign, 1422–1445. Initially the bricks were called 'tegulae', but from 1353 the term 'walltile' is normally used. In the mid sixteenth century Leland saw this tilery, 'where most part of the bricks, wherewitth the walls and houses of Kingston were built, was made'. Although the accounts were kept in Latin, large numbers of technical terms are given in English. Some sentences are only formally Latin, like one 1433 entry recording the cost of equipment: 'Willelmo Alcok pro ii pottes, iii troghes et uno rake xiiii d', that is, '(paid) to William Alcock for 2 pots, 3 troughs and a rake 14 pence'. At Hull, encased in Latin, we find records of materials and equipment—and of supplies sent out for the repair of town buildings, including the 'fleshmarket' (butchers' market-house) and the 'wey-house' (weigh-house). The works get in a 'carteful hay', a 'cachelful sande', 'cole', 'turves' (that is, turfs, these used for fuel as was the coal), 'wandys' (rods or poles) and 'saille thred' for 'nattys' (nets). Workers use 'shovells', 'colerakes', a 'barowe', 'scopes' (scoops), 'watterpottez' and 'formes' (moulds). They produced bricks by the 'kylneful'.

In other Latin documents also key words are sometimes given in Anglicized Latin or in English, either because they were the everyday terms—used by suppliers and workers—or because they were new words not derived from Latin or without easy Latin equivalents. The more detailed the records, the more English terms figure.

Note: The main book for further reading is L. F. Salzman's *Building in England down to 1540, a Documentary History*, in which most of the terms are indexed. (I have taken several references from the fullest version of the *Oxford English Dictionary*.)

GLOSSARY

Flanders tiles

1278: 202,500 'Quarellorum de Flandria'—also described as 'tegulae murali'—imported from Ypres (Exchequer Records) for Tower of London. Latin 'quarellorum' translates literally as 'squares'.

1283: Another Exchequer order for such tiles, also for use at the Tower of London, probably for floors.

1349: Flanders tiles imported for a fireplace at the Palace of Westminster.

1357: 1,000 'Flaunderstiell', supplied by Johanni Lovekyn and probably imported, for fireplaces at Palace of Westminster.

1365: 7,000 Flanders tiles, that is *bricks*, supplied by Henry Yevele, mason, for pavings and chimneys at Tower of London and Palace of Westminster, including the Jewel Tower.

1400: 5,000 'Flaunderstile' bought for three fireplaces at the Palace of Eltham (obviously for their flues also).

Latericio lateres

Salzman cites 'latericio' as term for brickwork. It is, literally, 'walling', with 'lateres' as walling blocks.

1430: 'Lateres vocatos le brike' (walling blocks called brick) feature in contract arranged by Bury St Edmunds Abbey for the burning of bricks at the manor of Chevington (Suffolk).

1586: William Camden, in his *Britannia*, described the walls of Hull as being of 'lateritio muro' (brick walling).

Tegulae

Latin term for 'tiles'. May be used for bricks, qualified by 'murali' (wall) or, alone, for bricks or any kind of tiles.

1189: London roofs to be made of slate or tile ('tegulae'), this fire precaution being reaffirmed in 1212 and later.

1278: Import of Flanders tiles (see above), also described as 'tegulae murali'.

1303: 'Tegulae', bricks, sold at Hull. They were made at the corporation brick-kiln, called 'tegularia'.

1321: William de la Pole had 'tegularia' (brick-kiln) at Hull.

1335: 'Tegularium muralium' made at Ely for the Abbey.

1344: 'Tegulae' made at Beverley.

1404: 'Tegulae' made at Beverley.

1418: 'Tegulas de brike' made at Deptford for London Bridge.

1437: William Vesey, King's serjeant, to search for brick-earth to make 'tegulae' for Sheen (Richmond) and other royal works.

1438: A property transfer describes William de la Pole, Duke of Suffolk, as having land at Hull bounded by 'muro tegular' (brick walls).

Tiles (the English term, when used for brick):

1418: 'Tilekylne' at Deptford, used for brick-making.

1422: Brick-kiln at Hull (originally known as 'tegularia') called 'tilery' or 'tile-house'.

1425: Hull brick-yard accounts list 'Item v (5) formes for makyng of tile'.

1426: Chelmsford regulations to standardize the size of 'tyle', that is bricks, for which a form (mould) was to be kept at the Moot Hall.

Wall Tiles

1307: From 1307 to 1327 'walltile' of English manufacture used for the Lodge Chapel of Ely Abbey.

1353: 'Walltyle'—or 'waltighel'—made at Hull.

1364: Exchequer records show plaster and 'walteghell' bought for the making of fireplaces at York Castle.

1391: Beverley town records of arrangement of rental of land for a brick-field, to make 'waltyle'.

1404: 'Walletiell' used at York Minster.
1409: 'Waltyle' used for construction of Beverley North Bar.
1440: Record of rental for making 'waltyle' at Beverley.
1440: From 1440s W. Douglas Simpson notes that the term 'wall tile' is used in the building accounts of Tattershall Castle, Lincolnshire for the *smaller* bricks.

Bricks

The word 'brick' is derived from the French 'brique' (Godefroy using the spelling 'briche' in 1264), in use on the Continent in the thirteenth century.

1340: A 'stayre' (stair) and 'dongon' (dungeon) built 'in petris et brikis' (of stone and brick) at Windsor Castle.
1390: The stores of the English-governed fortified town of Calais (France) included 626,000 'brikes'.
1416: During 1416–17 the papers of the Stonor family mention building work at their manorhouse at Stonor, Oxfordshire, for which bricks (made at Nettlebed) were used: the words used are 'brykes', 'brike' and 'de Bricke'.
1418: 'Henry Sondergyltes, brykeman', was employed by the Wardens of London Bridge to make 'bryktill' at Deptford, where his 'tilkylne for making bryke' was now enlarged. (Further records in later years too.)
1419: London fire precaution regulations stated chimneys were to be made of stone, tiles or brick.
1426: Licence to crenellate Moor Park, Rickmansworth (Herts.), with stones, lime and 'brik'.
1427: 2,000 'breke' for making chimneys purchased at Langley (Herts.), according to Exchequer records.
1430: 'Lateres vocatos le brike' feature in a building contract of Bury St. Edmunds Abbey.
1437: William Vesey, the King's 'brickmaker', was to search earth suitable for making 'tegulae' called 'brike'.
1440: Bokenham, in his translation of Ranulf Higden's 'Polychronicon', has a description: 'enviround abowte with bryke wallis'.
1441: 'Brekeston' used at Calais. Calais records also have 'lapides vocati brykkes' (stones called bricks).
1467: Worcester fire precaution regulations ordered that 'no chimneys of tre (wood) . . . be suffred . . . but that the owners make hem of bryke or stone'.
1535: Coverdale's translation of the Bible has: 'Come on, let vs bryck and burne it. And they bryck for stone' (Genesis, ch. XI, verse 3).
1535: Commissioners' survey of convent at Swine, near Hull, itemizes two chimneys of 'brikkes' (rare plural).

Makers and workers in brick

1334: Willelmus 'tegulator' (the tiler) made bricks at Ely.
1418: Deptford 'brykeman' (brickmaker).
1425: Hull 'camerariis' (Latin 'camera', a vault, related to Greek term for an arched construction) for kilners.

1430: Bury St Edmunds contract with 2 'breke brennerys' (brick-burners).
1432: Caister Castle accounts, in Latin, have 'tegulatores' for bricklayers.
1434: William Vesey, 'brikemaker', employed on King's Woks.
1436: Alien Subsidy Roll (tax record) lists Henry Henryson (name obviously Anglicized), of Teutonic origins, a 'brikemaker' living at Ipswich.
1440: In 1440s and 1450s the Tattershall Castle accounts have 'Bawdin Docheman' (Baldwin Dutchman) as the 'brekemaker'.
1442: William Vesey appointed to impress as many 'brikeleggers' (bricklayers) as he might need for Eton College.
1481–2: The Howard 'Household Book' has the entry: 'Item to the bryke-kyler of Eppswich viiij d.' (Item, to the brick-kilner—maker—of Ipswich 9*d.*) A later payment was made to the 'brykman' and his attendant for wages and board at Stoke-by-Nayland, where Sir John Howard (Duke of Norfolk 1483–5) was having a new house built. Here 'brickman' means bricklayer.
1481: Beverley ordinance on workmen's hours and methods has section beginning: 'No carpenter or tiler, viz. Tilethakker, Tilewaller and Plasterer . . .' The two types of 'tiler' named being roof-tilers and bricklayers.
1515: The underside of a reused brass memorial (palimpsest) in St Peter's Church at St. Albans has an English inscription to John Ball, 'brickemaker'.
1530: At this period, of Henry VIII's building works at Hampton Court Palace, the term 'bricklayer' is used.
1548: Act of Parliament (*temp.* Edward VI) ordains that 'No person . . . shal . . . disturb any . . . limeburner, brickmaker . . .'
1562: Act of Parliament (*temp.* Elizabeth I) concerns 'the Art or Occupation of a . . . Brick-maker, Bricklayer, Tiler . . .'
1568: Charter granted to London Company of 'Tylers and Bricklayers'. (This charter does not survive but its terms were reaffirmed in 1571.)
1598: Hull ordinance amalgamated into one company all the 'bricklayers, tilers, wallers, plasterers and paviours (layers of floor pavings)'.

Types of brick

'*Bakston*'*:* Another, but unusual, term for brick: in 1366 supplied by the master mason Henry Yevele for royal works at Gravesend.

Burnt pot earth: Contemporary term for terracotta (the Italian term, literally cooked earth and so burned clay), employed in 1520s to 1540s.

Great brick: Sixteenth-century term for the large mediaeval bricks (up to 15 or 20 inches long), such bricks having been used in East Anglia till the early part of the sixteenth century (as well as smaller ones): late fifteenth century and Tudor bricks generally were only 9 inches long.

Hard brick: The superior, hardest bricks, taken from the centre of the kiln.

'*Hewentile*'*:* Used in the 1440s to 1450s Tattershall Castle accounts, for specially shaped bricks. The derivation is from 'hew', that is to cut, but these particular bricks were apparently moulded.

Red brick: May be specified against the, usually earlier, white bricks. In 1535, though, the Hengrave Hall (Suffolk) accounts include payment for 'makyng clene the olde red bryke'.

Samel bricks (*or 'sammelle'*)*:* The softer and pinker bricks from the outside of the kiln. Salzman says they are sometimes rejected altogether, or they may be accepted as part of a load only.

'*Squynchon*'*:* Term used for chamfered or purpose-moulded bricks, in the 1409–10 accounts for the building of the North Bar at Beverley. (The modern term 'squinch' is limited to bricks or blocks supporting a join or projection from below.) The 1445–6 accounts of Beverley Minster include 'qwynschontille' and 'squynchontiell' for shaped bricks.

Miscellaneous terms, used in construction

Anchor: Wood anchor-plates used for reinforcement during building: for example, 'lez ankeres' mentioned in 1432–5 Caister Castle accounts.

Brickaxe: Tool for cutting brick, evidently shaped like a single or a double wedge. (Compare millbit, used for recutting grooves of millstones.) Brickaxes, and frequent records of their sharpening, feature on building accounts of Kirby Muxloe Castle, Leicestershire, in 1480s.

Brick earth: Term used for clay suitable for making bricks. In 1437, for example, William Vesey was to search for earth suitable for making 'tegulae called brick' for King's Works at Sheen (Richmond) and elsewhere. As late as 1667 diarist John Evelyn uses term: 'we went to search for brick earth'.

Brickends: Broken bricks used for filling in and for foundations. For example, in 1527 accounts of St John's Hospital (lost) at Canterbury is an item: 'a lode of brykendis xiiij d', a load of brickends 14 pence.

'*Calceria*' or '*calcifornium*'*:* Latin. Lime-kiln.

'*Cimentarius*'*:* Latin. Mason or architect.

Clamp: Some bricks made by firing them in a round earth clamp, not a kiln. Term used at Calais in 1441, 'clampe'. Exchequer records of 1525 have 'clampys' used as measure of number of bricks supplied for Hunsdon House, Hertfordshire, one of Henry VIII's palaces.

Form: The frame or open box used for making regularly-shaped bricks (contrast 'place bricks' cut on the ground) or dressings. In 1425 Hull brickyard accounts have 'Item v formes for makyng of tile' and in this year or 1426 the Chelmsford regulations for standardizing bricks said a model 'fourme' was to be kept in Moot Hall.

Frame: (1) As 'form' above.
(2) Building frame. For example, that of intended great hall of Wolsey's Esher Palace *c.* 1530, taken for Whitehall Palace of Henry VIII.
(3) Plan or model of building. For example, *c.* 1525 master craftsmen of Hengrave Hall, Suffolk, studied 'frame' of house of Duke of Buckingham.

Freemason: Master of craft of masonry, master-builder, designer or architect. Freemasons were a powerful group, theoretically banned in Late Middle Ages in favour of individual or specialist craftsmen not belonging to the 'mystery', but members continued to be employed even on royal works. Commonly abbreviated to *mason.*

Hackstead: Drying place for 'green' (unfired) bricks. Term used in fourteenth - and fifteenth-century Hull brickyard accounts.

Kiln: Variously spelled 'kiln', 'kill' or 'kele'. 'Kele' is used at Hull in 1398.

Kilnfull: Used as measure of number of bricks (compare 'clamp' above). In 1423 and 1433 Hull accounts have 'keleful' and 'kilneful' respectively.

Last: A load (usually that alternative is spelled 'lode') or measure of number of bricks. Caister Castle accounts apparently use 'last' for 10,000 bricks, but this seems to have been an unusually high figure.

'*Lathomus*': Latin. Freemason. Term still used in some Tudor documents.

Limeburner: Purifier of lime to be used in lime mortar. The Edward VI Act of 1548 commands that 'any . . . limeburner, Brick-maker . . .' should be left in peace to do his work, his yard undisturbed.

Mason: (1) Strictly freemason: master builder in stone or brick. (2) Rough mason. Skilled worker in stone masonry.

'*Molds*': Moulds for shaping bricks, including special mouldings, as listed in 1530s Hengrave Hall accounts (Suffolk).

Moulds: (1) Models for mouldings. (2) As 'molds' above.

'*Platts*': Templates or patterns. For example, item 'drawing of platts and making of moulds for the new hall', the great hall of Hampton Court Palace 1532, recorded by James Nedeham surveyor and carpenter.

Scaffolder: Constructor of large building frames and climbing frames for workers. 1530s accounts of royal palaces of Hampton Court and Oatlands list wages paid to numerous of scaffolders.

'*Tassis*': Stand for bricks or a load of bricks. Used in former sense in 1432–5 Caister Castle accounts (compare 'hackstead'). Latin.

'*Torale*': Kiln for brick or tile. 'Toralli' (plural) in Caister Castle accounts, 'my lord's kilns' being those of Sir John Fastolf. Latin.

Voussoirs: The blocks making up an arch, as present usage. An Early Tudor Anglicism is 'wousers', as used in a 1528 Balliol College contract.

'*Vowsyng*': Vaulting. Term related to *voussoirs.* Used by the Bury St Edmunds poet Lidgate, in the early fifteenth century, for the vaulting of a roof.

CHAPTER II

The manor-house complex

FIRED clay was used for certain structural and domestic improvements long before brick was regularly employed as a main building material. Tiles or bricks were first used for these jobs in castles or other great buildings of stone or, more commonly, of flint. Then, from say the second half of the fifteenth century, fired clay was also and commonly used in vernacular building, especially in timber-framed houses. It was used more often still, when relatively cheaper, in the sixteenth century. The geographical spread is much wider than the distribution of fabric brick. Tiles are found in many stone-building areas and they predated brick. The main categories—certainly the most common uses—are floor and roofing tiles, fireplaces and chimneys. There are, however, many other brick domestic fittings, as well as detached or semi-detached structures, the ancillary buildings of abbeys and great houses. It is possible to gather a series of images of fired clay contributing to convenience, to comfort and warmth and finally to luxury and display. As Sir Thomas More clearly did, when he wrote hopefully in his *Utopia* (1516) of a communal system of brick water pipes, one can see brick in these uses as putting some pleasanter flesh on the cold and stinking bones of mediaeval life.

In castles or houses built of other materials brick may be used for vaulting small rooms, the sidechambers off the main rooms, or for stairs. Indeed, the first time brick is named is in the 1340 record of a lost brick and stone stair constructed at Windsor Castle. Domestic stairs are matched by those in churches, leading to roodloft or porch-room, with brick used in flint rubble fabric. The vaulting of a charnel or tower passage or church porch may also remind us of domestic vaulting. Brick may be used for kitchens and about the great hall. As early as the mid fourteenth century Claxton Castle (Norfolk), a flint rubble structure with some brick, has a concentration of brick about the end wall of the lost great hall. This sort of usage continued into the Tudor period. The sixteenth-century Cowdray House (Sussex) is stone-faced, but has brick used for all sorts of coring tasks, for fireplaces and for the kitchen.

The ruined post-Dissolution great hall of St Osyth Priory (Essex), which is faced with a chequer of flint and stone, shows much brick coring, especially about the fireplaces.

The refinement and then ornamentation of these improvements belongs, though, mainly to brick building and is the most important part of the story of the development of brickwork. The general pattern seems the natural one: the more fired clay was used for fabric, the more it was also shaped for detail and decoration. Some of the finest details of the great brick houses are their moulded door jambs, arches, windows and battlement corbel-tables. These, too, may be matched by the late fifteenth-century or Early Tudor church dressings. In Essex the mouldings may even be duplicated between a church and a house. Finely shaped components are usually limited to brick buildings, the chief exceptions being these: early and late decorated floor tiles were laid wherever the money was available and the Early Tudor decorated brick chimney-shafts were attached to houses built of other materials as well as brick.

At the peak of development, in the Early Tudor period, we find both brick and stone dressings coupled with brick fabric. Wallington Hall in Norfolk and West Stow and the (lost) related Westhorpe Hall in Suffolk may have or have had their moulded figures and arcaded and trefoiled friezes of brick, but Thomas Kitson, the London merchant, had stone windows for his Hengrave Hall and full-bellied heraldry carved of Northamptonshire stone and for Elizabethan and Jacobean buildings one thinks of stone dressings as the norm. Even in the Early Tudor period stone dressings were evidently more common. Perhaps significantly, while the lesser gatehouse of Leez Priory (Essex) has brick dressings, the much grander and more fashionable great gatehouse is stone-dressed. One thinks of stone quoins, copings and the *larger* windows as typical of otherwise brick buildings, as at the royal palaces and St John's College at Cambridge and the Archbishop of Canterbury's Otford Palace. Indeed, the chief domestic improvement of this period, the projecting window, was typically built out or corbelled out in stone—for better engineering—from a brick fabric. Light-bringing bays gave the Eltham, Whitehall and Greenwich Palaces their modern, even luxurious, look in Early Tudor times. These were true domestic improvements, limited to domestic building. Projecting bays were polygonal or square, while the corbelled oriels were polygonal. The embrasures were provided with window seats.

Brick bay or oriel windows are uncommon, though there are two fine multi-moulded oriels at Rye House (Hertfordshire) and beautiful high thin bays of brick at Parham Old Hall (Suffolk). The Rye House oriels, not quite

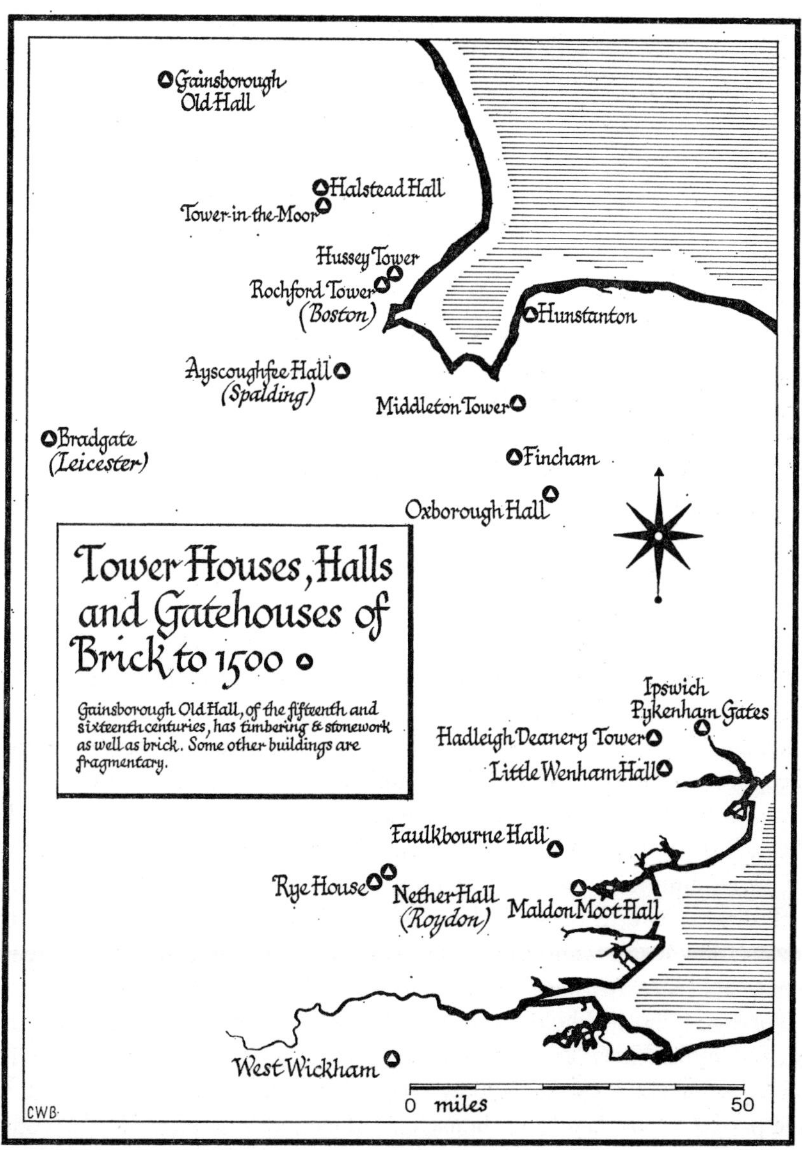
Gainsborough Old Hall
Halstead Hall
Tower-in-the-Moor
Hussey Tower
Rochford Tower (Boston)
Hunstanton
Ayscoughfee Hall (Spalding)
Middleton Tower
Bradgate (Leicester)
Fincham
Oxborough Hall
Tower Houses, Halls and Gatehouses of Brick to 1500
Gainsborough Old Hall, of the fifteenth and sixteenth centuries, has timbering & stonework as well as brick. Some other buildings are fragmentary.
Ipswich Pykenham Gates
Hadleigh Deanery Tower
Little Wenham Hall
Faulkbourne Hall
Rye House
Nether Hall (Roydon)
Maldon Moot Hall
West Wickham
0 miles 50
CWB

6. TOWER HOUSES, HALLS AND GATEHOUSES OF BRICK TO 1500.

a pair in size, are surprisingly early, being of about 1443. It is easier to think of stone windows projecting from brick fabric. Examples are: the Early Tudor oriel corbelled out from the late fourteenth century gatehouse of Thornton Abbey (Lincolnshire); the Early Tudor bays and oriels at the Beaufort foundations in Cambridge (Christ's College and St John's), at St Osyth's Priory and at Horham Hall in Essex. Hampton Court Palace had mostly stone bays, of which the Great Hall bay is the one survivor, but the Great Watching Chamber there has a bay window with brick fabric and stone mullions. That the period was a transitional one is suggested by the detailed accounts of the lost Little Saxham Hall, Suffolk, which itemize brick dressings and the moulds for making them at the site and also the employment of freestone, including dressings carved from Burwell stone brought from Cambridgeshire. One could, thinking of the dozens of chimney patterns, argue that the most elaborate work was still done in brick and, of course, the very finest ornament available was the rare and obviously expensive terracotta of the courtiers.

The surviving manor-houses stand in splendid isolation (an effect that was to be deliberately sought in the eighteenth century) and so give a misleading impression. They have outlasted their original cluster of domestic offices and farm buildings. This has happened everywhere, from the thirteenth-century Little Wenham Hall (Suffolk) to the ruins of the late fifteenth century Bradgate House, near Leicester, and to the early sixteenth century Sutton Place, near Guildford. Sutton Place, unlike the other two, is still used as a house, but has lost its gatehouse range and the kitchen and other recorded offices. More unusually, an ancillary building may have survived the destruction or modification out of recognition of its great house. Examples are the brick dovecotes of Stoke-by-Clare College (Suffolk) and of Belleau Manor House (Lincolnshire) and the barn at Ludham (Norfolk), which belonged to a house held first by the Abbots of St Benet's Holme and then by the Bishops of Norwich (who still hold the title of Abbot). The great brick barn and the low, incomplete ancillary ranges of Hales Court Farm, Loddon (Norfolk), survive while the great house they served has disappeared. Occasionally we have partial survivals of both house and offices. Examples, all Early Tudor, are: the cut-down ranges of Leez Priory with the fishing hut and two barns; the remnant of the manor-house at Great Snoring (Norfolk), now the Rectory, and its brick barn; the cut-down Ingatestone Hall (Essex) with the stables courtyard; and the domestic survivals of Layer Marney Tower (Essex) with the rather ornate stables block. Even Hampton Court Palace retains, despite the replacement of most of Henry VIII's new buildings by those of

Secular Gatehouses, Halls and Palaces of Brick from 1500 to 1550
CWB
Hodsock 'Priory' (Blyth)
East Barsham
Gt. Snoring
Lovell's Hall (Terrington St Clement)
Wallington
Upwell
Gt. Cressingham
Denver
Thorpland
Pooley Hall (Polesworth)
Plaish Hall (Longville)
Sheldon (Birmingham)
West Stow
Hengrave
Crows Hall (Debenham)
Parham
Papworth St Agnes
Kirtling
Gedding
Helmingham
Wells Hall (Brent Eleigh)
Compton Wynyates
Rickling
Giffords Hall (Stoke-by-Nayland)
Standon Lordship
Horham
Layer Marney
Beckingham Hall (Tolleshunt Major)
Chenies
Hunsdon
West Drayton
St James's Palace
Ockwells
Richmond Palace
Shurland (Sheppey)
The Vyne (Basingstoke)
Hampton Court
Lullingstone
Steventon
Sutton Place (Guildford)
Laughton Place
0 miles 50
Certain of the houses, like Gedding Hall (Suffolk) have been reduced to their gatehouses only. Ockwells Manor at Bray (Berkshire) is of timber-framed brick

7. SECULAR GATEHOUSES, HALLS AND PALACES OF BRICK FROM 1500 TO 1550.

Christopher Wren, one detached kitchen, stables, a water-supply tamkin in the park and, three miles away, the remains of Wolsey's conduit-houses at Kingston upon Thames (Surrey).

Dovecotes and barns have survived particularly well, because they needed no reform or modification of design. Dovecotes were used until modern times, especially in the eighteenth century. At Tattershall Castle, incidentally, one of the turret tops of the great tower was fitted out as a dovecote, with a timber-based clay partition wall, with square nesting places. Similarly-placed dovecotes were made at Oxborough Hall (Norfolk) and Kirby Muxloe Castle, but both are more recent than the 1480s brick fabric. Outside Kirby Muxloe moat, however, there is, besides a well, the base of a square dovecote contemporary with the Castle and set in the old garden and orchard area. The fifteenth-century Giffords Hall, Stoke-by-Nayland (Suffolk), still has its old dovecote, timber-framed on a brick sill. Mediaeval or Tudor may be in use, or partial use, today. Perhaps there are more timber-framed—though possibly brick-nogged—barns than ones with complete brick fabric, of before 1550, but both types have good, wide, tiled roofs. In the accounts of the lost Little Saxham Hall (Suffolk) the tiling of a barn is recorded. The alternative in East Anglia would have been thatch.

The manor-house complex must have been like a miniature town, perhaps even with the parish church in the park, as at Hengrave (Suffolk) and Layer Marney (Essex). The numbers of extra buildings at Hampton Court that partly survive on the north side of the Base and Fountain Courts —besides a tiltyard tower (converted into a restaurant) and the covered Tennis Court—were obviously on the grandest scale. This was not so much because of their size, apart from the great kitchens incorporated in the main building, as in their multiplicity. Every kind of processing—of linen, fuel, food, drink—had its own office there. Certain ancillary buildings would lie inside the curtain wall or moat; others, such as the barns, a water-mill (as at Mapledurham, Oxfordshire), walled gardens and orchards, lay just beyond the main site. Such buildings, now lost, lay outside the moated brick platform of Kirby Muxloe Castle in Leicestershire. As an old stone-built castle or house was enlarged or an institution developed additions and outbuildings might be erected in brick. This was done at the lost Castle Hedingham (Essex) home of the de Veres. At Watton Priory and Cawood Palace (both in Yorkshire) brick ranges were added to the older buildings. At Cakeham Manor House, West Wittering (Sussex), an Early Tudor lookout tower was added to a thirteenth-century stone range. Reformation conversions were made in this way too. Bisham Abbey (Berkshire) is a mixture of monastic stone and Elizabethan brick, including a brick lookout tower rather like that of Cakeham.

The use of brick for kitchens, exemplified by Cowdray House with its stone facings and contemporary brick kitchen, has been noted. The late fifteenth-century Gainsborough Old Hall (Lincolnshire), which is partly brick-built and partly timber-framed, has an impressive brick kitchen. It makes a square projection from the great hall range and is reached from the servery via the customary screens passage. In three corners are pairs of cells, or small rooms, set one above the other. These were for servants' quarters. The King's Kitchen at Hampton Court has a narrow ground-level cell, beside a fireplace, supposedly the master cook's. These open kitchens were based on the earlier stone-built ones with their central smoke-escape lanterns, like the Abbot's kitchen at Glastonbury in Somerset. Cooking was done on central hearths, like that of Penshurst in Kent, or, later, at wall cooking-places, like those of the Boston Guildhall in Lincolnshire. There were also two types of brick- or tile-lined ovens available: the large square wall ovens, like old bread ovens, and the big projecting ovens. Of the former there are several brick examples at Bragdate House, Leicester, and one at Downham Palace, near Ely. Both these houses are in ruins. Castleacre and Thetford Priories (Norfolk) have small ovens for sacred wafers, so there were probably also brick domestic ovens in these flint buildings. The larger ovens have an opening in the kitchen, but the bulk of their fabric projects beyond an outside wall. They are circular, with a domed top, like the detached ovens used for industrial purposes like glass-making. The earliest such ovens, or kilns, were only clay-lined: the later brick linings reduced fire-risk, as did placing the oven out of doors instead of in the main wall fabric. Brick examples are: the oven at Long Crendon Courthouse, a timber-framed building in Buckinghamshire; the oven projecting from the kitchen block at Gainsborough Old Hall; the sixteenth-century oven of The Brick House, Great Hormead, Hertfordshire.

At Castle Hedingham a seventeenth-century inventory and nineteenth-century excavation showed the domestic buildings, which were concentrated in the walled inner bailey of the mediaeval castle, much of which was replaced by brick building at the turn of the fifteenth century: ancillary buildings, their roofs tiled, included a domed well or conduit, detached kitchens, bakehouse, brewhouse, two brick stables (including the 'new stable'), barn, granary, tennis court (and archery-butts), with brick cellars, main sewer and moat bridge. The bridge alone survives. Round Henry VIII's revamped Palaces of Greenwich and Whitehall and his new St James's, room was made for gardens, tiltyards and bowling alleys. What, besides the encircling windmills, strike one in looking at old maps of London and Westminster are the great lay or ecclesiastical properties, each a walled estate. Fulham Palace, which has a section of Early Tudor garden wall remaining, was originally in the country, but Lambeth Palace also—across the river from the royal Palace of Westminster—had its garden and orchard enclave, described in the Parliamentary Commissioners' survey in the mid seventeenth century. The Castle Hedingham inventory has been mentioned. Lost buildings of Ingatestone Hall are likewise known from a plan made by the builder's own surveyor in 1566: Sir William Petre's new house had been completed by 1548. There was a partial brick curtain, brick boundary walls and 'dyvers houses builded of bryck'. The 1520s accounts of the building of Hengrave Hall mention kennels, 'mews' (stables), water supply and mill, a tiled barn and a bowling alley. The Hall remains, but these have gone.

The Parliamentary Commissioners' pre-sale survey of the Archbishop of Canterbury's Croydon Palace is almost lyrical as it lists the demesne buildings, the brick boundary walls and the streams dividing gardens, orchards and meadows. The property included: 'a granary, with all houses, outhouses, courtyards . . . a fruite house . . . pidgeon howse, waters, and three fish ponds . . . with a water which parteth the aforesaid gardens and the said meadows.' Much earlier, a real lyric by the Welsh poet Iolo Goch described the impressive surroundings of a great manor in the late fourteenth century. He praised the tiled roofs and non-smoking chimneys of the stone-built mansion of 'Sycharth', which had been erected for Owen Glendower. It was to be burned down in 1403, at the time of Glendower's campaign against the imperialistic English, in which Henry IV's son received his training for Agincourt and saw the Welsh long bows in action. (The poem, translated by Joseph P. Clancy, is printed in his *Mediaeval Welsh Lyrics*, 1965.) This is the ideal manor-house complex, described by Goch:

Each side full, each house at court,
Orchard, vineyard, white fortress;
The master's rabbit warren;
Ploughs and strong steeds of great fame;
Near the court, even finer
The deer park within that field.
Fresh green meadows and hayfields;
Neatly enclosed rows of grain;
Fine mill on smooth-flowing stream;

Dove-cote, a bright stone tower;
A fish-pond, enclosed and deep,
Where nets are cast when need be,
Abounding, no argument, . . .
His land a board where birds dwell,
Peacocks, high-stepping herons.

The early sixteenth century expansion in wealth showed both in the amount of new building and in the choice of brick for these manor-houses and their outhouses and then for their farm buildings too. Every manor was a farming manor and in addition to the lay demesnes there were, till the Dissolution, also ecclesiastical ones,—belonging to abbeys or, with a grange or palace, to a bishopric. Leland saw how brick was replacing timber for houses in the London region, and later in the sixteenth century William Harrison, rector of Radwinter in Essex, recorded that—whereas previously a few nobles only had stone houses and those of men of lower status were usually 'of strong timber'—'the manor and gentlemen's houses latelie builded are commonlie of brike or hard stone'. At Little Wenham in Suffolk the thirteenth-century yellow brick house was kept but a typical red Tudor brick barn was built for the farm. For farm buildings more stone was now used, instead of timber, in the areas where it was available; likewise, brick was used where suitable clay could be fired in clamps or regular kilns. Local growth was paradoxically spurred by the rudimentary state of roads but, if bricks were not made at the building site, they might be bought from a local works—as John Howard bought bricks in the 1480s from an Ipswich maker for his (lost) new house, Tendring Hall, at Stoke-by-Nayland. Hales Court in Norfolk exemplified individual industry, for its brickfield is traceable. The custom continued, and still in the eighteenth century many estates had their own brick kilns and so were independent of the commercial brickworks. This applied at Holkham Hall in Norfolk till about ten years ago.

If we come indoors we can find every sort of domestic provision made of brick. The one exception is, I think, lavatory seats, which were made of pierced wood or stone blocks. The shafts or 'vents' of garderobes might, however, be of brick. A record of about 1530 of work done for the Palace of Westminster (Whitehall) includes cut brick supplied for chimney-shafts and for the 'ventes for jaxys', that is 'jakes' or garderobes. The wider mortar joints of brickwork probably made it unsuitable also for washing places. We can find complete subsidiary structures, brick cellars or undercrofts, to stone or flint or brick houses. We can find domestic details, such as the brick window seats at Tattershall, which were useful in the relatively furniture-free Middle Ages —a domestic variant on 'the weakest go to the wall' in church. The great, of course had their own chairs, sometimes throne-like. There may be private religious details, like a tiny statue-niche (once blue-lined) in the master's quarters of Ewelme Almshouses (Oxfordshire).

At the underground level we may inspect brick drains and sewers and wells. As far as I know these are found only in brick buildings, and other examples must be lost, for most of those known date only from the reign of Henry VIII. At Kirby Muxloe Castle, however, pipes and drains of brick as well as of stone have been excavated, besides dams and sluices—including one 'vertical brick shaft'—for controlling the moat water level. These date from the early 1480s. As noted, Thomas More advocated a communal water-supply for the town of Utopia with water-pipes of brick. Presumably he chose brick for practicality in a sizeable scheme, but in towns till the nineteenth century small pipes were made of waterproof elm wood. Lead was too expensive: the lead pipes that conveyed water from Kingston to Hampton Court were quite exceptional, for a millionaire like Wolsey only. The Cardinal progressed well beyond the standards of his time, because the obvious water source was the River Thames. Into this the Palace drains and sewers were emptied. The sewers included a five foot high *cloaca* (the Latin term for sewer), large enough to be washed and brushed out by long-suffering servants. The household ordinances promulgated for Henry VIII by Wolsey refer to the forced periodical departures of the court from one palace to another, when the palace quitted was to be 'cleansed and sweetened'. Garderobes were flushed out at intervals with buckets of water, but only the greatest buildings of Henry VIII's time had scourable sewers. Small brick drains have been excavated under the Clock Court cobbles. A tall scourable brick sewer was found at the Nonsuch Palace site (Surrey), Henry's masterpiece. Henry also had new brick drains leading into the moat laid at Eltham Palace. This was similarly a country palace. The 1868 excavations of John de Vere's Castle Hedingham discovered the main sewer, described then as 'a beautful piece of brickwork, sufficiently large for a man to crawl some distance'. These sewers are round-arched, and so are the smaller kitchen and other drains of different sizes at Leez Priory (Essex). This was the mansion of Richard Rich, built up partly on monastic foundations. The Early Tudor kitchen drains, next the site of the great hall, are arched over with stretcher voussoirs and are three foot deep.

Garderobes normally discharged their sewage into the moat. (Collegiate Cambridge in the reign of Queen Victoria was still piping sewage into the

River Cam, though the river was already considered picturesque.) Garderobes were set in turrets, usually square projections of three or four stages, with outlets in the wall fabric at each level (rather than any more hygienic system of a sloping or vertical collecting drain fed from each level). At the brick-built Caister Castle, of the 1430s, the garderobe projection is a five-stage block with stone outlets at the different levels. The turret is built onto one side of the ninety-foot high great tower, in an angle of the moat, and is balanced by the taller stair turret at the other side. Among the ruins of the archiepiscopal palace of Otford, Kent, the big north-west turret, with its living rooms, has a square garderobe projection. Madingley Hall, near Cambridge, built in the 1540s, also has a square garderobe tower. Chenies in Buckinghamshire has a series of thin turrets for garderobes, built onto the back of a lodgings block and dating from the Early Tudor period. Excavation has revealed that, when Wolsey was modernizing the lost 'Manor of the More' (Rickmansworth, Herts.), he had a brick-lined garderobe constructed on the west side of the site, with outlets into three sides of the moat; and from the time of Henry VIII's possession a garderobe pit with a vaulted brick drain was discovered on the east side of the site (Martin Biddle *et al.*, 'The Excavation of The Manor of the More', *article* in *Archaeological Journal*, cxvi, 1959.) Some of the most attractive, though surely in use just as smelly as the others, are the series of garderobes built, next projecting chimney-stacks, on to the tall lodgings block at Gainsborough Old Hall: this, though, is Elizabethan.

No well has been found in the Kirby Muxloe platform, but moated brick platforms might be pierced for wells. This was done at Scadbury, where there are two wells. The survey of Castle Hedingham mentioned the well in the inner bailey. The sixteenth-century Brick House at Great Hormead has a contemporary well a few yards from the rear of the house. If a well was thought inadequate for the water-supply a conduit or well-house was a later development. There is a completely rebuilt conduit at the London Charterhouse. Nothing, however, can have rivalled Wolsey's Hampton Court scheme, with five or more conduits at Kingston and brick interval 'tamkins', which permitted the shutting off of the water supply while repairs were done. Little Walsingham village, Norfolk, has a communal conduit, evidently sixteenth century, built of brick but with an ashlar dome and stone brazier column above. There is an attractive private structure, dating from the early or mid sixteenth century, at Hales Place, Tenterden (Kent): it is a rectangular brick-built well-house, step-gabled like Wolsey's conduits. Hales Place belonged to an important trading family of this small town. Tenterden then had its port at Smallhythe, where the 1516 step-gabled, Flemish-influenced Chapel erected by Archbishop Warham still stands. Most of Hales Place, like Warham's palace at Otford, is now lost.

With the great buildings brick extends to the revetting of moats, as at Headstone Manor at Pinner, Middlesex. Where the moat was linked with a river, provision might be made for the reception of water-brought supplies. At Caister Castle (Norfolk) there is even an eight foot wide barge arch and, past this, the range wall by the moat has low square openings where, it is thought, goods were taken in. Rye House gatehouse has a low-arched opening at one side, leading into the passage, which may have been used for this purpose—for the moat linked up with the River Lea. In the ruins of 'Sopwell Nunnery', beside the River Ver at St Albans, there is apparently similar provision: a riverside opening leads into a sunk lobby or cellar of brick, that retains steps up to ground floor level. This post-Dissolution house was a mixture of flint and brick. In this watery context we should mention moat bridges, which gradually replaced the movable drawbridge, but the Early Tudor houses of Compton Wynyates (Warwickshire) and Helmingham Hall (Suffolk) still have drawbridges, although they also have the latest in decorated chimneys. East Anglia has some interesting examples of brick moat bridges. There are fifteenth-century ones at Pleshy Castle (Essex) and Castle Rising (Norfolk), both with a single low wide span. Castle Hedingham has its triple-arched moat bridge of the late fifteenth or early sixteenth century. Crows Hall, near Debenham, Suffolk, has a four-arched bridge. At Framlingham Castle, also in Suffolk, during the Early Tudor period the Howards renovated an older flint bridge with brick, building up the piers and parapet. They also employed brick for new fireplaces and chimneys at this centuries old flint castle, but they soon preferred to live at the new brick mansion of Kenninghall (Norfolk).

1. Vaulting and stairs

We find some of the best brickwork in the vaulting, without piers, of small rooms or passages. In Thornton Abbey gatehouse, Tattershall tower-house (both in Lincolnshire) and Oxborough Hall gatetower (Norfolk) the large rectangular main rooms have flat timber ceilings, but there are passages and side-chambers with attractive brick vaults. Sometimes such work is obscured by plaster, for interiors were normally plastered for warmth and against damp. Walls were also plastered, at least prior to Tudor wood panelling, which was to be used so extensively that it was sometimes even imported ready made from Holland. The details and texture of the brick can be seen where the lining has flaked away. Thornton Abbey gatehouse dates from about 1380 and

8. BRIDGES, VAULTING AND VAULTED 'UNDERCROFTS' OF BRICK TO 1550. The earlier examples belong to non-brick buildings. At Beverley Minster the nave vaulting is rendered. Norwich has five early brick undercrofts.

has both side-chambers and passages brick-vaulted. Oxborough, of about 1480, has good barrel vaults to the porter's lodges and really elegant pendant star-vaulting to the tiny polygonal rooms of the north-east turret (the south-west turret has the brick newel stair). This work at Oxborough is all plastered over. In the Tattershall tower, of about 1450, is some fine, unusually elaborate vaulting—which has lost most of the plaster coating, though this still obscures some *cavo relievo* detail. Some window embrasures are side room vaults are simple brickwork, but other embrasures and upstairs lobbies are rib-vaulted. The long narrow passages have brick ribs, whirlygigs and the curved so-called 'dagger' motif, only rarely found in brick. The finely carved heraldic bosses, like the ornate fireplace lintels, are of stone. It should be mentioned that, despite the other very limited uses of stone here, the stairs to first and second floors are of stone. There are good brick vaults to the polygonal side chambers of Lord Hastings's Kirby Muxloe gatehouse: corbels which were inserted in the walls to carry the wooden centering or frame on which the vaulting was built up (not the vault itself) remain. In the Early Tudor Rochford Tower at Boston (Lincolnshire) it is the main ground floor room that is vaulted in brick. At the slightly earlier Fincham Hall (Norfolk) only the entrance lobby has a brick vault. The ruinous Rye House gatehouse, of after 1443, has a plainish but very beautiful passage vault: the ribs are curved, very narrow, of dark red brick, but with simple shield bosses of stone. These are fine later vaults, built in brick structures, and utterly different from the heavy, simple, early undercroft vaulting more often found in non-brick buildings. The earliest brick vaulting in this country to a side chamber is plain, of the early thirteenth century, a prophetic minor use: this is the vaulting, with local gault bricks, of part of an interval tower at the stone-built Allington Castle in Kent.

If a vault has a large span it will be supported by central piers or, later, by two rows of piers like arcades. Some of the oldest vaults, which carried the bulk of the structure, are very impressive—in a plain, thickset or powerful way. These are the various East Anglian vaults. Some belonged to institutions, but others were built for storing goods below private houses. The oldest big brick undercroft is that of the comparatively poor St. Olave's Priory at Herringfleet (Suffolk). This dates from the thirteenth century and has brick piers, chamfered ribs and brick in-filling. Rather earlier is the small and narrow undercroft at Little Coggeshall Abbey (Essex), which was part of the domestic quarters. The Herringfleet buildings were of flint, and brick was obviously used in this stoneless region—close to the Broads—for its bonding and load-bearing capacities. The large pinky bricks were plastered over, but some texture shows, particularly of the thick polygonal piers. Of about 1308

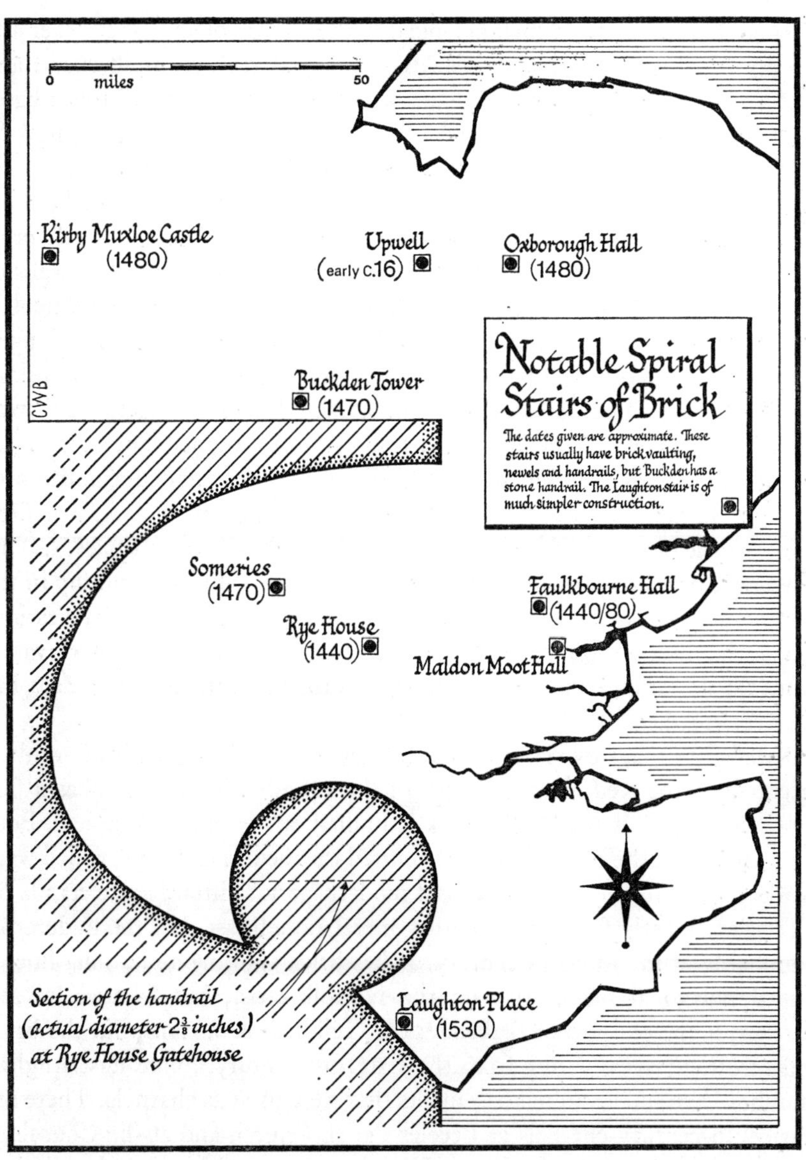
0 miles 50
Kirby Muxloe Castle
(1480)
Upwell
(early C.16)
Oxborough Hall
(1480)
Notable Spiral Stairs of Brick
The dates given are approximate. These stairs usually have brick vaulting, newels and handrails, but Buckden has a stone handrail. The Laughton stair is of much simpler construction.
Buckden Tower
(1470)
CWB
Someries
(1470)
Faulkbourne Hall
(1440/80)
Rye House
(1440)
Maldon Moot Hall
Section of the handrail
(actual diameter $2\frac{3}{8}$ inches)
at Rye House Gatehouse
Laughton Place
(1530)

9. NOTABLE SPIRAL STAIRS OF BRICK (see pl. 17).

is the lobby, now sunk, which belonged to the church of an earlier order and was absorbed by the Norwich Blackfriars. The Blackfriars built round and over this room, which is shaped like a small chapter-house: it forms a basement (and fuel store) on the north side of the Blackfriars' church, now St Andrew's Hall. It has a stone central pier, but the vaulting is of fairly big, light-coloured bricks. Another early fourteenth-century brick-vaulted undercroft in Norwich lies under the east end of the Guildhall, being the undercroft of the earlier Tolhouse. This has chamfered ribs, which die into the walls or meet at the top of low, octagonal piers. These two vaults are not domestic, but they have points in common with the other Norwich vaults, which belonged to merchants' houses. Still in use for commercial storage is a pierless vault in St Giles' Street. The undercrofts of the Bridewell and Strangers' Hall were private storage places, belonging to traders. Any original buildings above these vaults are of flint and stone, and the brick was intended as a fire precaution. These Norwich structures are rivalled only by the stone-vaulted cellars of the houses of Edward I's town of New Winchelsea in Sussex. This new town, based on a grid-plan like Kingston upon Hull, was built up in the thirteenth and early fourteenth centuries but suffered a Black Death recession. One of the most important functions of these New Winchelsea cellars was as stores for imported wines, for the town was then a port, though the sea has since retreated.

King's Lynn has two later mediaeval undercrofts, besides a brick-vaulted basement to the Red Mount Chapel of the 1480s. Clifton House has a fine big undercroft, but the St George's Guildhall one is now incomplete. Both these are beside the River Ouse and abutted the mediaeval quays, which were a little further inland than the closed modern port. Clifton House stands on the site of an early fourteenth century merchant's house, but the undercroft is probably of the fifteenth century. It has brick vaulting and a long line of central polygonal piers. Also on the Norfolk coast, but fronted by salt marshes, is the old port of Blakeney: the Guildhall is in ruins, but the brick undercroft survives, dating from the sixteenth century. Some East Anglian churches have small vaulted basements that were used as charnels. There are fourteenth-century charnels at Beccles Parish Church and at the Church of St Mary-the-Less at Cambridge. At Hitchin in Hertfordshire is an incomplete brick charnel of much later date, belonging to a flint and stone church.

To move into the Later Middle Ages is to find a much wider distribution of brick undercrofts or cellars. They are especially typical of the early sixteenth century, but the fifteenth century Crosby Hall in the City of London had one, that was built over earlier this century (though part of the house was moved to Chelsea). The excavation in Victorian times of Castle Hedingham in Essex discovered both stairs and a cellar of brick, with one surviving square pier, this below the (lost) brick great hall, all Early Tudor. Private mansions, such as Wyddial Hall in Hertfordshire, have brick cellars. There are several survivals from royal places. The remains of Greenwich Palace and of the lost Manor House of Henry VIII at Chelsea include brick cellars, while the related winecellars of Whitehall Palace and Hampton Court survive. These last two were only partly underground. Besides their plastered octopartite vaulting, with sharply chamfered ribs, both retain low brick platforms for the wine barrels. Hampton Court also has smaller and probably older cellars under Henry VIII's great hall, with the brick pier for the hearthstone above. The basically sixteenth-century Syon House at Isleworth (Middlesex) has a plastered brick undercroft, but this belonged to the convent which preceded Somerset's house on the site. Brick cellars are part of the expansion and improvement of domestic buildings, which now rivalled what the various religious orders had been able to erect earlier—though the accidents of survival may have given too unrealistically neat a pattern. Indeed, at Little Waldingfield in Suffolk a house retains groined cellar vaulting of brick, dated by P. G. M. Dickinson as fourteenth-century. Although this house is known as 'The Priory' no monastic establishment has been traced here: the cellar is thought to be that of an earlier manor-house and is, therefore, really unusual for its date in not having a town setting. We may contrast this with the other early house vaults, those of Lynn and Norwich. The usual difference between the older vaulting and that of the fifteenth-century or Early Tudor period is that the later vaults are much taller and have steeper, thinner ribs. They may also, but still with piers, span a wider area. The late piers are polygonal, with proper capitals, supporting octopartite rib vaulting.

Now to turn to a favourite subject—brick stairwells and their spiral stairs: these stairs can be more impressive than the finest ceiling vaulting, because so beautifully engineered and gauged. Most of our examples belong to ruined buildings, and nothing demonstrates their strength better than their being intact or virtually unscathed in roofless, long-deserted structures. They belong to brick buildings of the late fifteenth century on, though sometimes a brick stair turret has stone steps. This was surely so in the monastic Valpy Street turret at Reading (Berkshire), where, though the steps are modern replacements, the stone dressings of the exterior suggest that stone replaced stone inside. The steps of the ninety-eight foot Caister Castle stair turret were of stone. As noted, the Tattershall Castle stairs are of stone despite adjacent brick vaulting. Probably the Fawsley Dower House in Northamptonshire, which is partly brick and partly stone, had stone steps in the surviving brick stair turret. The stairwell is circular and of rendered brick, as is usual, though the exterior is polygonal. There is no plaster to the Laughton Place (Sussex) stairwell, and possibly, as some of the bricks are green-glazed, there never was any. Stairwells are usually faced with headers; the vaulting, if continuous, is faced with stretchers; the steps are formed of bricks laid on edge. A 1465 Farnham Castle (Surrey) record shows a new brick tower stair had proved faulty and another brick stair was built to replace it. In the main, though, the surviving stairs give an impression of remarkable power. The problems of stress must have been well understood for, in the 1530s, the stair turret of Leez Priory inner gatehouse was corbelled out on a squinch at first floor level (the steps are great wood triangles, which may not be the originals) and at Laughton Place the top stage of the stair was corbelled out on a squinch—this ornamented with red terracotta! It is true, though, that this top stage at Laughton is a few feet thinner, and therefore less heavy than the bulk of the stair which (taking a diagonal line) is about thirteen feet thick. The top stage gives access to the roof and, therefore, as is customary, rises well above the main parapets. This stair, all brick, is significant for its staying power: it is intact, surviving from a house pillaged for building materials and reduced to its main tower and stair and left to dereliction. Despite its late date, though, it is of an earlier type of construction from the beautiful fifteenth-century stairs at Maldon, Faulkbourne (Essex) and Oxborough. It has a rounded newel and steps formed of irregularly shaped brick slabs or tiles, which are carried on simple shallow arches of edgewise bricks. The triangular mortar joints between these supporting bricks were reinforced with oyster shells. There is no handrail. In the ruined Tower on the Moor, near Tattershall Castle, is another stair carried on ascending arches like this, but dating from the mid fifteenth century.

In the fourteenth-century city walls of Norwich, which were built of flint with some stone and brick dressings: bricks were used for lining slits and windows, for vaulting ceilings and for lining stairwells, but the surviving section of the Black Tower stair is of stone. The all-brick Cow Tower of 1380, however, has a round turret with brick spiral stair. Another mixture, just a detail, is for a brick structure to have brick stairs but a stone handrail sunk in the fabric of the well. This is the pattern at the episcopal Buckden Tower (Huntingdonshire) and at the Red Mount Chapel at King's Lynn, both late fifteenth century.

Our remaining examples are the *piéces de résistance*—brick newel stairs in brick mansions, fairly close to each other in location and date and with some common characteristics. The usual form is for the stairs to have deceptively plain edgewise brick steps, which rest on smoothly curving ploughshare vaults, with round newels of moulded brick. The earliest of these spirals is in the stair turret of about 1435 Moot Hall at Maldon (Essex). The origins of the Moot Hall were as a town house for the important D'Arcy family. The handrail is moulded brick. The latest is a spiral stair, early sixteenth century, in the ruins of Upwell Rectory (Norfolk), which has been compared with that of Oxborough, and thus with the Falkbourne Hall stair. Rye House gatehouse retains its brick stair: this is narrow, without a newel. It has a finely moulded brick handrail, with round grip about two and a half inches in diameter and a big scooped handguard. The section of grip and guard is much like that at Oxborough.

The stair of the Oxborough Hall gatehouse is contained in an eighty-foot high, seven-stage turret dating from about 1482. At the rather mysterious ruin of Someries (just outside Luton, Bedfordshire) there is a sunk handrail and guard, but plainer and much less finely moulded, to the stair, which may date from the 1470s. The stairs of Oxborough and Faulkbourne and the three stairs of 1483 at Kirby Muxloe have similar spiral vaulting. Of these only Kirby Muxloe, a 'castle by courtesy'—really a fortified manor-house—is in ruins. One stair there is in a square stair turret, which rises above an almost intact square angle tower; the other two are in the two rear turrets of the incomplete gatehouse. Faulkbourne and Oxborough are preserved and lived in. Oxborough is administered by the National Trust, and the stair has been carefully repointed. Its radiating ploughshare vaulting is more elaborate than that at Someries: it is as smooth, but the bonding is more complex and regular. The exact construction, the bonding under the facing of stretchers, is unknown. The stretchers fan out from the rounded newel in continuous triangular shapes, shell-like or like flattened, inverted spinnakers: if so hard to describe, how incredible was the concept, the brick by brick design. The vaulting was rubbed smooth, a gentle spiral covering perhaps two hundred feet.

2. *Chimneys and chimney-stacks*

Stone and brick or tile chimneys were initially developed against fire-risk and, in towns, under the stimulus of local government ordinances, though none of these as early as the 1189 London ordinances demanding the substitution of tiled roofs for thatch, or, indeed, as early as the legislation of other towns on roofing materials. Outside the major brick areas brick chimneys might constitute the only common or regular use of the material. This was true of York, for instance: though wall tiles were recorded as early as 1404 in the work on York Minster, even in Tudor times brick was generally used only for chimneys (Victoria County History of York). In the brick areas, starting with East Anglia about 1450, for the larger houses at least brick chimneys came to be 'regarded as a necessity' (A. Clifton-Taylor). For such houses in the early sixteenth century necessity came to partner a different sort of invention, and spectacular decorated chimney-shafts were erected. For such chimneys of Henry VIII's reign Professor Pevsner, speaking of Plaish Hall in Shropshire, uses the nice phrase 'gloriously overdecorated'. Appropriately, the great brick palace of Hampton Court has numerous ornate chimneys, the shafts about fourteen feet high, with numberous patterns. These, erected by both Wolsey, from about 1515, and by Henry VIII himself, have mostly needed restoration

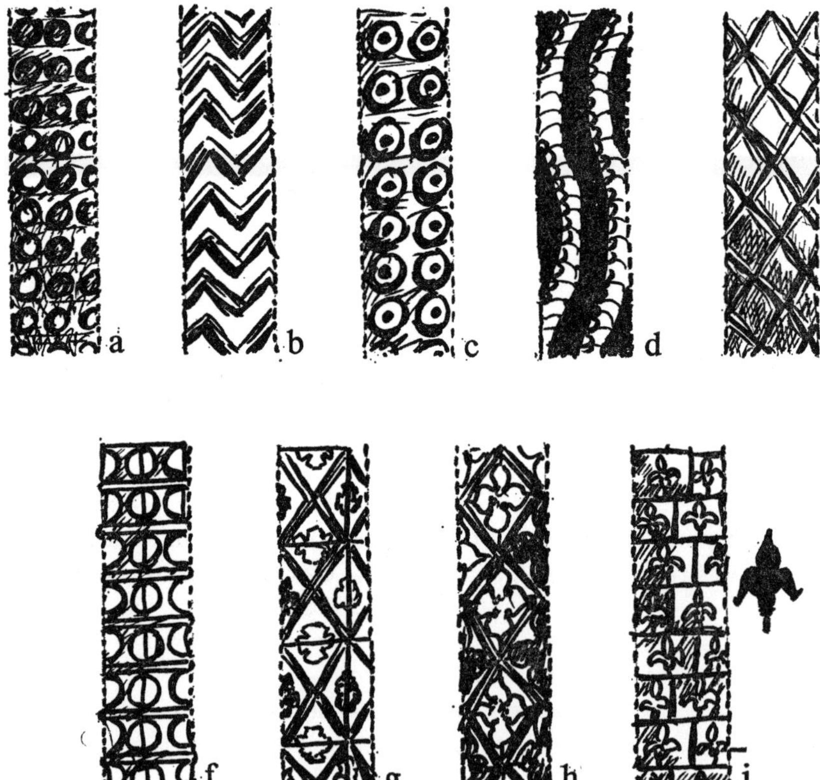

10. CHIMNEYS OF 1520–40. (*a*) Aston Bury, Herts. (*b*) Helmingham, Suffolk. (*c*) Hengrave, Suffolk. (*d*) Huddington, Worcs. (*e*) Chenies, Bucks. (*f*) Denver, Norfolk. (*g*) St Osyth's Priory, Essex. (*h*, *i*) East Barsham, Norfolk.

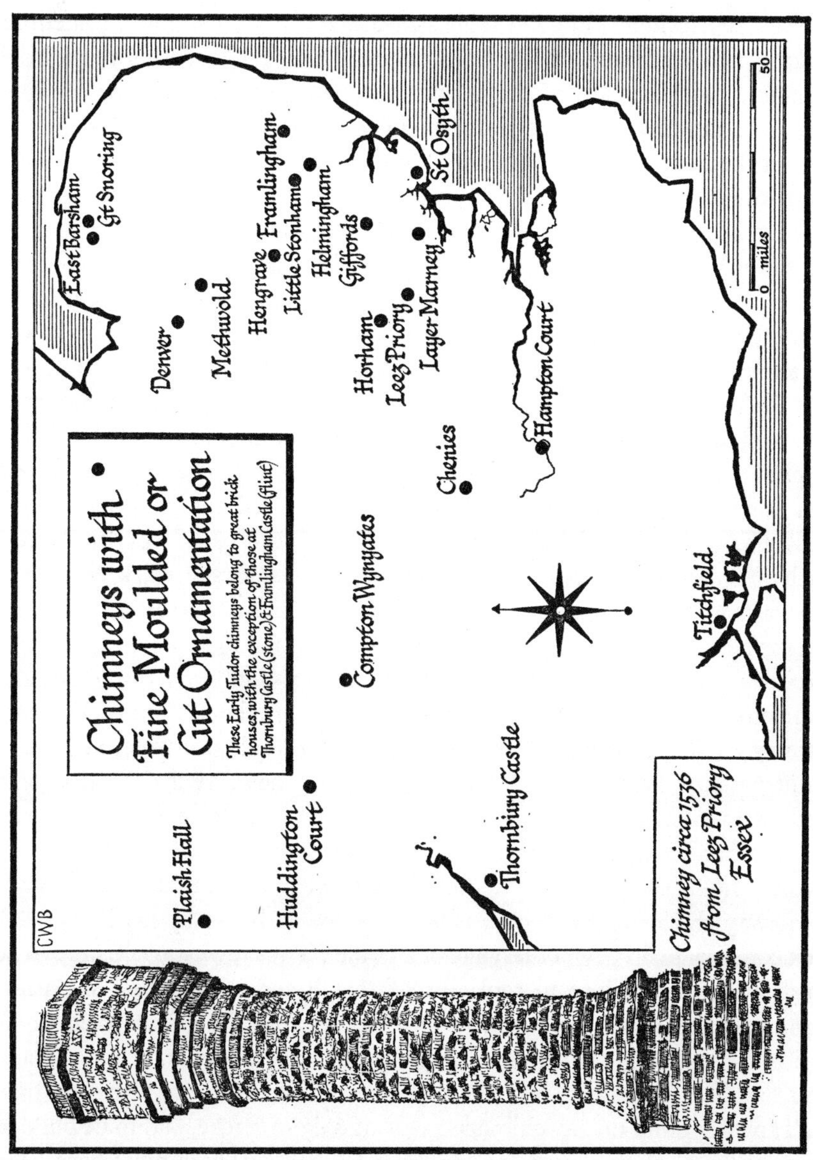
Chimneys with Fine Moulded or Cut Ornamentation
These Early Tudor chimneys belong to great brick houses, with the exception of those at Thornbury Castle (stone) & Framlingham Castle (flint)
East Barsham
Gt Snoring
Denver
Methwold
Hengrave
Framlingham
Little Stonham
Helmingham
Giffords
St Osyth
Horham
Leez Priory
Layer Marney
Chenies
Hampton Court
Compton Wynyates
Titchfield
Thornbury Castle
Huddington Court
Plaish Hall
0 miles 50
Chimney circa 1536 from Leez Priory Essex
CWB

11. CHIMNEYS WITH FINE MOULDED OR CUT ORNAMENTATION.

or even replacement, but the replicas are exact. Such chimneys sometimes make a rich contrast to plain brick fabric. During Elizabeth's reign brick chimneys, with unadorned shafts and buttress-like stacks, became common and were attached to quite ordinary houses. One advantage of shafts, as against the earlier shaftless masonry flues, was that the smaller flues reduced down-draught.

The riskier alternatives continued to be used, especially in villages, but the known ordinances show the spread of brick chimneys from town to country. The lateness of the date, 1621, when some borough headmen ruled on chimneys is interesting: it suggests that even in a brick-building region brick was still too expensive for small properties, though Jacobean Clare was, of course, well past the peak of wool trade prosperity. In the fourteenth century it had been ordained in the City of London that chimneys should be made of stone, tiles or plaster (and no longer of wood), and that fires were not to be sited near lath partition walls. In 1419, before brick was used for building proper, plaster was also rejected for chimneys, and the new ordinance was that 'henceforth no chimney shall be made except it be of stone, tiles or brick, and not of plaster or wood, under pain of being pulled down'. The Worcester Ordinance of 1467 belongs to a non-brick region, though floor tiles were made at Malvern, Droitwich and other places. Besides ruling on chimneys, the Worcester ordinance required the town chamberlains to keep firehooks for pulling down burning thatch, to prevent fire spreading. (Such firehooks were, at least in country places, kept in parish churches. There is one surviving at Eaton Bray Church in Bedfordshire: a very long pole with a thick rake-shaped metal head, rather like a dredging rake.) At Worcester in future: 'no chymneys of Tymber ne thacched houses be suffred wtyn the cyte but that the owners do hem away and make them cheymenys of stone or bryke by mydsomer day next commynge, in peyn of lesynge of a noble'. Thus townspeople were to be fined 6*s*. 8*d*. for failure to replace roof thatch and wood—that is, lath—chimneys: this was a large sum for ordinary people. To give a rough comparison: a thousand roof tiles, carriage not included, cost 4*s*. at Caversham, near Reading, Berkshire, in 1488. The 1621 Clare order was: 'that no man shall erect or build up any chimney . . . but only of bricke, and to be builded above the roof of the house fower feet and a halfe'. There must have been many other orders made in towns, earlier and later than this, demanding that roofs, be tiled and chimneys and stacks be made of stone or brick. Norwich's corporation condemned the use of thatch for roofs, naming it 'reddthak' (Norfolk reed), but not till 1509. Thus, the brick-building areas were not necessarily more forward.

Since the earliest 'fireplaces' were the floor hearths, what was needed for them was a smoke-escape hole in the roof and perhaps also some holes in the walls. The hearth of the great hall at Penshurst, being eight feet across, must have needed a sizeable escape for the smoke. The smoke-hole had to be protected from wind and rain, most satisfactorily by a lantern-style louver. Wells' Bishop's Palace has a specially beautiful traceried stone lantern. Pottery louvers as well as chimney-pots are known from the thirteenth century. Fairly recently an early pottery louver was found in Goosegate in Nottingham: it is green-glazed and shaped like a pagoda (Margaret Wood, *The English Mediaeval House*). Hearths and louvers were still employed at the end of the Middle Ages and in the early sixteenth century for great halls, the louvers then being small turrets or lead lanterns. Examples are those of the hall of Lincoln's Inn in London and of colleges at Cambridge. Henry VIII's great hall at Hampton Court has a lead lantern for its surprisingly late (1530) central hearth.

The early chimney-pots of pottery that were sometimes used were like later pierced brick copes in form. G. C. Dunning, in his chapter on 'Mediaeval Chimney-pots' in *Studies in Building History* (edited by E. M. Jope, 1961), stresses how early some of these pots were, although 'chimney-stacks or chimney-pots in the Middle Ages were usually made of stone, and it has been generally assumed that chimney-pots of baked clay were not introduced into England until later mediaeval times'. Clay chimney-pots, however, now known to archaeologists as the 'Sussex type', 'were in general use in south-eastern and southern England during the thirteenth century'. Several examples have been found at both Lewes and Chichester in Sussex, and one was found at Pleshey Castle in Essex. They are usually of unglazed pottery. the colour of the clay varying with the area, buff or grey or 'reddish brown', They are conical but tapering: from 8 to 10 inches across at the base and 4 or 5 inches at the top. The base would be set flush with the roof. These pots may be a foot or up to 18 inches high. G. C. Dunning notes different types of decoration, such as pin-pricks or stab-marks, which helped stop pots cracking during the firing. A form of decoration common on thirteenth- and fourteenth-century pottery jugs is also found—strips of clay pressed into the surface, like icing sugar. Pottery was, of course, universal. The southern counties also have comparatively early decorated floor tiles, such as those of Winchester Cathedral and Hailes Abbey, both early thirteenth century, but little early brick.

For stacks and shafts the traditional materials were, for the great buildings, stone or plaster of Paris or mortar and, for ordinary dwellings, wattle- or lath-

and-daub. The plaster chimneys were made in the same way as the wattle-and-daub ones, but were presumably rather less of a fire-risk. The flues were lined with plaster, mortar or clay daub and the chimneys were made of these materials moulded round wood—usually hazel—rods or laths. These were what the Worcester order of 1467 called chimneys 'of tymber', and, as we have seen, 'wood' chimneys had been rejected as early as the fourteenth century in London and plaster ones in 1419. The daub was baked hard by the heat of the fire, but these wood-based chimneys must easily have caught fire. L. F. Salzman, in his *Documentary History*, cites the 1370 contract for a row of eighteen shops (among the St Paul's Cathedral manuscripts), the shops to be stone-built with brick chimneys carried a foot above the roof. This contract shows fire-prevention in practice, clearly the sole reason for the clause about chimneys.

Reinforced plaster and mortar chimneys in these early days were not confined to the lesser dwellings, although stone was surely much more common for castles or other great buildings, such as the Exchequer at Abingdon Abbey, Berkshire, which has a thirteenth-century stone lantern-chimney. If the plaster used was plaster of Paris, this had to be imported. There is a 1368 record that four 'pipes', that is flues, of plaster of Paris were made for two fireplaces in Edward III's chamber at the palace of Sheen. The fourteenth-century poem of 'Sir Gawain and the Grene Knight' speaks of 'chalk whyt chymnees' at a castle. Much later, the extremely detailed descriptions made by Henry VIII's visitors of various small monasteries in Yorkshire mention different types of chimneys, attached to buildings of timber or stone with tiled or thatched roofs. Arthington near Leeds had 'a chymney dawbid'. Esholt near Bradford had 'a ffayre chymney of woode and morter', besides four stone chimneys to the 'parlours'. The small Cistercian convent of Swine, near Hull, rebuilt after a fire in 1308, in the mid sixteenth century had a mixture of materials in its buildings: roofs were tiled, thatched or of lead; walls were 'daubed' or of wood splints, of stone (the church at least) or of brick; there were at least two brick chimneys, one 'a fayre chymney of brikkes sheftes' (shafts).

The Latin, French and English forms of 'chimney' may be used in documents for the whole structure from fireplace to pot or shaft *or* for any of the parts. The French word is 'cheminée' and the earlier English spellings have that first 'e' rather than an 'i'. The Latin *caminum*, chimney, invariably or almost invariably meant the whole structure. The 1444 record of bricks imported from Calais for the walls and chimneys of the outer ward of the palace of Sheen has the qualification '*caminis exterioris*', exterior or outside chimneys, that is shafts and projecting stacks. The 1400 Exchequer record of the import of 5,000 Flanders tiles for only three fireplaces at Eltham Palace shows that firebacks, flues and shafts were all to be made of tile. The term 'pipe' is sometimes used for a flue, and 'reredos' may be used for the fireback only. There is a 1427 Exchequer record of 2,000 'breke pro chemeneys faciendis' (bricks for making chimneys) purchased at Langley in Hertfordshire. By Early Tudor times, though, it seems that 'chimney' is used for stack and shaft rather than for these plus the interior parts of a fireplace. The terms 'shaft' and 'shank' are found at this date for what we now call the chimney, the part projecting above the roofline, whether topping a projecting or a central stack. In 1535 the Hampton Court accounts recorded payment for chimneys at forty-five shillings each 'set up' on the Queen's new lodging: a bricklayer received £27 'for 12 chemney shaftes' with their caps and bases. The contract of 1525, between Sir Thomas Kitson and John Eastawe the mason of Hengrave Hall in Suffolk, included the clause that 'ye said Jhon (*sic*) must macke . . . of roubed (rubbed) bryck all the shank of the chymnies'. These shafts were decorated ones, their mouldings rubbed smooth. A certainly plainer 'chimne' for the general purposes domestic office called the 'back house' at Hengrave cost only 13*s*. 4*d*., a mediaeval mark.

Cylindrical chimneys, of which the ornate Early Tudor shafts were the ultimate development, had appeared by about the mid twelfth century. These chimneys initially capped flues constructed inside the thick walls of great buildings. The wall fireplaces provided not only heat but much better cooking facilities than the floor hearths. The flues were rectangular, often two to a fireplace, each with its own chimney. Some interesting examples at Framlingham Castle in Suffolk were taken over by the Howard family in Early Tudor times and absorbed into their brick improvements. The Castle, of which the shell remains, was built of flint with stone dressings in the twelfth century. The great hall lay against the curtain. Two stone hall chimneys remain, the earliest cylindrical ones known, of about 1150 or 1160, with round-headed slit openings. They probably had conical caps, removed when they were enlarged with decorated Tudor brick shafts. These Tudor shafts rise above the battlements and are part of a series placed at intervals round the curtain circuit. As well as the ones which are genuine chimneys, there are dummies used to complete the effect. Although one can think of decorative shafts the design of which was clearly based on chimney shafts, like the three twisted shafts which originally topped the surviving gateway of Wolsey's College at Ipswich, the dummy shafts at Framlingham appear to be unique in their pretence. As we have seen, once towns had ruled for stone, brick or tile chimneys, further improvements against fire-risk—specifically against sparks at roof level—became the ideal: the seventeenth-century Clare ruling was that the shafts should be at least four and a half feet tall. The 1370 St Paul's contract also quoted is interesting in that not only does it prefer brick to stone chimneys even in a stone-built range, but that it was agreed that the shafts should be one foot high. One may note that in Henry VIII's reign the shafts on great houses might be ten feet tall. The Great Fire of London in the seventeenth century was to demonstrate just how lethal the cramped, still mediaeval streets were. On the other hand, mediaeval London had many open spaces, such as St Bartholomew's and Lincoln's Inn Fields and the grounds of great houses, whether of lay lords or bishops, and of monasteries. It also had its open rivers, such as the lost Fleet (by Fleet Street), which must have helped contain outbreaks.

The next development, after chimney lanterns or shafts projecting at roof level and flues built up inside the walls, was the complete projecting chimney-stack of stone or brick. This was partly a response to changed building methods and partly the product of a demand for greater comfort, associated with the product of a demand for greater comfort, associated with the provision of separate kitchens and fireplaces for cooking only. These stacks were built out from the typically thinner late mediaeval walls of big houses and were also added as improvements to small houses, at least in the sixteenth century. Thick-walled defended structures (quoting brick examples only), like the Norwich Cow Tower of 1380 and Tattershall Castle of 1450, still had their flues inside the fabric of the walls, and so did the late gatehouses, like those of Lambeth Palace (1480), Hampton Court (1514), Layer Marney (1520) and Leez Priory (1536). Such gatehouses may have a line of chimney-shafts along one side, against the battlements. These carry the flues from a series of fireplaces—one to each floor, but with two flues to the lower, larger fireplaces. Besides the great hall, side-rooms now had fireplaces, as we can see even at a small manor house like Mannington in Norfolk, dating from 1450. These sidechambers and lobbies, with their relatively thin walls, demanded projecting stacks, and these took the flues from fireplaces on different floors. A range of small rooms, like the retainers' quarters surviving at Chenies in Buckinghamshire (1530), may have stacks set at intervals like particularly large buttresses. Similar provision is found in institutional buildings, each projecting stack carrying the flues of a pair of rooms or 'cells' one above the other. This can be seen at the Ewelme Almshouses in Oxfordshire (1430), Queens' College at Cambridge (1455—the Silver St frontage) and—impressive, for the chimneys are symmetrical and very tall—at St John's Hospital at Lichfield, Staffordshire (late fifteenth century). Sometimes the stack is stone-built while the chimney-shafts are of brick, as at Huddington Court in Worcestershire (of about 1500). This mixture signifies either that improved shafts were added to old stacks or, invariably in Tudor times and outside the brick-building areas, if the owners wanted decorated chimneys, which were more typically and inventively made of brick than of stone. Brick shafts were also used on non-brick buildings, of which the walls were still thick enough to carry flues. The example of Cowdray House, Sussex, has been mentioned. The most spectacular combination of stone-building and brick chimney-shafts is at the ruined Thornbury Castle in Gloucestershire. As at Thornbury and East Barsham (Norfolk) the linking of shafts is a sign of early date. Later shafts might be linked only at base and cap, probably to reduce wind pressure, or were completely detached although standing in groups as at Hampton Court Palace. A single flue from an upper room fireplace might be corbelled out in a stack, as in the porch of Tottenham Church, Middlesex.

Brick chimney-stacks are found attached to half-timbered buildings, whether or not the in-filling material is brick, and these are the most common because evidently within the means of many ordinary households. The big half-timbered farmhouse at Sollershope in Herefordshire, which is brick-infilled and has two brick chimney-stacks (though one pair only of shafts remains), was once the manor house, but dozens of vernacular buildings have their brick stacks. These lath-and-plaster infilled, timber-framed houses—in East Anglia, Kent, Sussex, the Home Counties and Warwickshire especially—belonged to yeomen, small farmers and weavers. The distribution of brick stacks, like that of roofing tiles, is wider than that of brick building. Strongly made examples may survive intact where the rest of the house has needed restoration. The rectangular (or sometimes square) stacks usually project from the centre of an end wall, and were often built on to old buildings as well as being an integral part of new ones. Sometimes, when the gable-ends are brick-built the flue may be contained in a central shaft-like stack rising from ground level. The Old Rectory at Methwold (Norfolk), which is early sixteenth century, has an extremely ornate stack of this type. A gable of about 1535 at Boughton Malherbe Manor House in Kent has a central chimney-shaft, but sometimes gables were headed by decorated brick shafts that only imitate chimneys, as at Denver Hall and a house at Castle Rising, both in Norfolk. In Early Tudor and Elizabethan times chimney-stacks might now be built up in the middle of the house against a partition wall, allowing more of the house to be warmed, so that the shafts project from the ridge of the roof. A house at Little Stonham in Suffolk has this arrangement, the ridge carrying a group of heavy and ornate chimney-shafts. Added or inserted stacks are fairly common in East Anglia, the Home Counties and Kent, though probably only a small number are pre-Elizabethan. The usual context is the conversion of a mediaeval building whose main component was the two-storey hall. To provide greater comfort and a more domestic way of life, the hall was now made into two chambers by the insertion of a first floor, and fires were provided for both. Pykerell's House at Norwich exemplifies this. Inserted central stacks are normally Elizabethan or Jacobean. The fifteenth-century brick-built Snore Hall at Fincham in Norfolk has a sixteenth-century central stack.

The earlier or the cheaper stacks have no real distinction between the stack and the shaft, which is just a continuation of the brick fabric reduced in size. The ultimate contrast is found at East Barsham Hall (Norfolk), where a rectangular stack projection (only the narrow end set against the battlements) carries ten flues and is itself decorated with moulded panels: the linked battery of thick circular shafts above is richly diapered with fleur-de-lis, quatrefoils and diamonds. These motifs are shared with the ornate angle shafts of the house, just as the decorative motifs on the stack are also used in friezes round the walls. After the Early Tudor extravagances, Elizabethan chimney-shafts to even great houses were typically plain, often octagonal or, set diagonally, square. They were angled rather than round and could thus be made with unmoulded bricks or bricks given no more shaping than a slight chamfer or dog-leg.

The famous passage in the *Description of England* of 1577 by William Harrison, the rector of Radwinter in Essex, speaks of 'the multitude of chimneys lately erected', showing that they were chiefly an Elizabethan phenonemon. It was one that he despised, for he idealized his youth when the smoke from central hearths—where the cooking was also done—apparently prevented the current nose and throat complaints of 'rewmes, catares and poses' (as people may argue a connection between colds and central heating). Harrison's notion was that people had been smoked into health. Previously, he implied, chimneys had been a feature of cities only and not of all the 'most uplandish towns'—outlandish or country places—where they were now appearing. Earlier, in the small towns 'there were not above two or three, if so many, . . . (the religious houses and manor places of their lords always excepted, and peradventure some great personages)'. Among recent chimneys, before they had become both general and demure, there had been an outbreak of extravagant Early Tudor decoration, which only the rich could afford. These ornate chimney-shafts were—contemporary with the individually moulded terracotta roundels and tomb panels—the most elaborate work done in brick and, in sum, infinitely more elaborate than patterned work in stone. They belong to the period when the chimneys of important houses were an architectural feature anyway and when, as A. Clifton-Taylor says, brick was well established as 'the leading material in Norfolk, Suffolk, Essex and Lincolnshire, and important in Kent, Surrey, Sussex, Middlesex, Hertfordshire and Cambridgeshire'. Some decorated shafts are also found in the West: ornate examples are the chimneys of Compton Wynyates (Warwickshire), Plaish Hall (Shropshire), Huddington Court (Worcestershire) and Thornbury Castle (Gloucestershire). There are also one or two survivors of the set of fine chimneys put up during the conversion of the monastery at Titchfield in Hampshire into a secular mansion. The majority are in East Anglia, with Essex as the chief manufacturing area, and at Hampton Court Palace. The Hampton Court records mention chimneys not only decorated but coloured red and green: this was surely exceptional, and sounds a bit much aesthetically. The record is from the Henry VIII period, not Wolsey's.

In 1482 Sir John Howard was himself writing the accounts of his household and of the new brick mansion he was having built at Stoke-by-Nayland in Suffolk, recording mainly in English the costs of that 'howshold at Stoke'. (The *Howard Household Book* of 1480–90 was edited by J. Payne Collier and published by the Roxburghe Club in 1844.) Howard was to be made Duke of Norfolk in 1483, but had his title removed on the defeat of Richard III in 1485 until 1489. He had a town house at Stepney and bought some materials in London, such as the Caen stone bought in August 1482 from the Prior of St Mary Overy in Southwark. The Stoke house has disappeared, but Howard made his contribution to Stoke-by-Nayland Church, which is partly brick-built. There are some traces of Howard occupation from then and later at Framlingham Castle, whose brick chimneys have already been mentioned, and at Kenninghall, Norfolk, where there was an Early Tudor brick mansion. In March 1481 John Howard had paid for bricks fired at Ipswich. In the late summer of 1482, as the Caen stone item also suggests, when Lady Margaret Howard was at the old house at Stoke and supervising the 'new building', the craftsmen must have been working on dressings. Howard also bought in London two 'aparaylls', separately, for chimneys. These 'apparels'—dress or equipment, like 'gear' in the modern usuage—must surely have been or included moulds for chimney-shaping or ornament. Howard would scarcely have needed to buy in London any sort of mere frame for a plain square or rectangular chimney, especially in an area where brick-building was now firmly established and where for the prosperous at least brick chimneys had been regarded as essential for at least the past thirty years. The exact meaning of 'aparaylls' here is important, because the earliest exactly dated brick chimneys are those of the stone-built Thornbury Castle, which was begun in the second decade of the sixteenth century and then perforcedly left unfinished by Edward Stafford, Duke of Buckingham.

The Thornbury chimneys are the most celebrated of England's decorated chimneys, just predating Wolsey's at Hampton Court and, unlike those, not replacements. They rise to twelve feet. The caps are mostly heavy and polygonal, but there are one or two of the old lantern-headed form. When the outlets of flues are close, the Thornbury chimney-shafts are joined. The ornament includes very delicate work, especially small heraldic shields with animals and the rounded knot badge of the Staffords done in fine moulded brick or terracotta. There is another, larger form of the badge which, repeated, makes more of a pattern. The three-shafted stack which has the fine heraldry carries, at its base, the inscription '1514'. As Nathaniel Lloyd rightly emphasized, this Thornbury work is too fine to be 'the first of its kind'. Such chimneys are peculiarly English: they are not imports, unlike the da Maiano terracotta roundels of Hampton Court Palace. Most of the decorated shafts are of the 1520s and later, but there is a solitary and unusual twisted shaft at Rye House, Hertfordshire, which is evidently very much earlier. Rye House proper, for which the licence to crenellate was dated 1443, is lost, but its gatehouse remains. The stone entrance arch bore the arms of Sir Andrew Ogard, who died in 1454. The brickwork was possibly erected under Danish influence, for Ogard's origins were Danish. The brick oriel windows are splendid, very sophisticated for their date. The one chimney-shaft rises above the battlements at the rear and its bricks appear to be of the same date as the rest of the building. The form is a four-fold twist, the twists coming directly from the base, which looks like elephant feet. The 'cap' has cusped lobes, like some of the Thornbury chimneys, but its quatrefoil section is little wider than that of the shaft itself. This chimney is about nine feet tall, in very bad condition and repaired with cement. Even in good condition, however, one imagines it had an unbalanced look, lacking proper base and cap—like an out-of-scale blank shaft. I think this Rye House chimney can be seen as a fifteenth-century example of what led to Thornbury or to any of the more attractive twists of Henry VIII's reign.

Early Tudor chimneys have moulded caps and bases, considerably wider than the shafts themselves which may be three or four feet in diameter (exterior). Bases may be crowstepped or even battlemented, or built up with a series of mouldings that take on the form of the shaft: round, hexagonal, octagonal or twisted. A base may be arcaded with blank niches. Caps are heavy, usually also rounded or polygonal and these perhaps battlemented. The most notable forms of cap, however, take little but their angles from the shaft: these are the scalloped, single and double star and spur caps, with points blunt or sharp and wild and spiky. The variety of the shafts is infinite, unmatched by stone, although there are stone twists, like the Ham stone ones of Barrington Court (Somerset) and, even less frequently, other designs, such as the zigzags and 'jug handles' of Sir William Sharrington's chimneys at Lacock Abbey in Wiltshire. The shafts alone of the four brick chimneys of the inner gatehouse of Leez Priory (Essex) are about ten feet high, but there are more examples that are stocky as well as being ornate. Such shorter chimneys may be found at relatively unimportant houses, like Little Stonham in Suffolk and Denver Hall in Norfolk.

The simplest forms of polygonal shaft are made with chamfered bricks. The twists or spirals are produced in several ways. When really deep the whole shaft looks as if it has been forcibly wrenched round—though with unlikely exactness—when the clay was still wet. The Old Manor House at Buckingham has just such a deep twist; and the Dower House at Fawsley in Northamptonshire has a less dramatic example. These twists are formed by laying concave-sided moulded bricks with a quarter- or half-inch turn to each new course. The ribbed or rounded twists can be produced by using bricks from one mould only, each brick having a round knob. The smooth finish would be given by rubbing. Such bricks could be used to make diamond and honeycomb patterns and even a hollow pattern that looks like diagonal courses of stretchers. (Hampton Court has a shaft of this type, but it is not unique.) Vertical or horizontal zigzags are formed in several ways and are of different depths. Another possibility is the staggered zigzag, with examples at Helmingham Hall in Suffolk and Huddington Court in Worcestershire. Then there are studs, rosettes, quatrefoils, diapers, lozenges, honeycomb cells, patterns geometrical or taken from plant forms or a mixture of both. All had to fit and use their frame of mortar joints. The very complex diapers found at East Barsham Hall are formed of six-inch square finely moulded panels and so are not true brick patterns. The best areas for examples of chimneys are Norfolk, Suffolk and Essex. Even a small building might have its decorated chimney. The complete domestication of an old military site, Old Buckenham Castle, Norfolk, where a Tudor house was built, may be symbolized by its 'circular chimney-shafts with geometrical decoration' (Pevsner). The Castle was Norman, built on a rectangular earthwork, but from the twelfth century to the Reformation there was an Augustinian priory here.

The finest and most varied chimneys are perhaps these, belonging to brick-built halls: East Barsham, Great Snoring and Denver in Norfolk; Hengrave, Helmingham and Gifford's Hall (which is partly timber-framed) at Stoke-by-Nayland in Suffolk; St Osyth's Priory, Leez Priory (of 1536) and Treasurer Cuttes' Horham Hall in Essex.

The grim little story of the patterned chimneys—they survive—of Plaish Hall at Longville in Shropshire illustrates the specialization of this work, but, of course, Shropshire was not a brick-building region. The lord of the manor, Sir William Leighton, about 1540 was building a grand house there; this house has notable plaster ceilings with Renaissance curlicues and royal badges, courtier's usage like the royal arms of the gatehouses of Compton Wynyates and East Barsham. Acting as judge at the assizes at Shrewsbury, he found he had condemned to death for sheep-stealing a craftsman who could make ornate chimney-shafts, reported to be the only man available locally who could do so. Leighton put off the execution, had the man make chimneys for Plaish Hall and then returned him to Shrewsbury for hanging. One wonders about the mentality of the judge: was he as keen to see his social rivals lacked fine chimneys as to impress? And did the craftsman, of whom more was required than the manipulation of extant moulds—skills in moulding, firing and carving—try to work slowly under guard or did he buoy himself up with false hopes of reprieve? Perhaps such a craftsman in East Anglia would have been found immediately dispensable. Even the most simply shaped bricks, however, had to to be laid very carefully by the workers, with joints gauged to keep both the pattern and a good bond between the decorative shell and the bricks outlining the flue.

How, apart from a final rubbing smooth *in situ*, when the shaft had been constructed and the mortar was hard, were the bricks normally shaped? Extra shaping of already moulded bricks could be done by rubbing, that is by filing. This is what the Hengrave contract means, 'a bargain made betwixt Thomas Kytson, Knight, and Jhon Eastawe. The said Jhon must macke . . . of roubed bryck all the shank of the chymnies'. Details could be added or a pattern sharpened up by carving. A chimney-shaft at Leez Priory exemplifies this, having ribbed diamonds of moulded brick each with an angled quatrefoil in its centre: the indentations, which turned a plain raised lozenge (made of two triangles) into four 'leaves', were cut. This is quite simple carving, like the cutting of spandrel decoration on the courtyard side arch of the outer gatehouse at Leez Priory, just more repetitive. The most detailed work—like the Thornbury heraldry and the East Barsham diapers—was clearly the product of moulds. The East Barsham blocks are more like terracotta, but almost everywhere else bricks of the usual nine- or ten-inch length were employed, each with an element of the pattern in relief or *cavo relievo* or with a fine motif in relief. If details were sometimes carved, so also twists and net patterns might be gouged out in the brickwork. Cut and moulded brick are found at the same places.

Modern writers speak as if carved brick was quite common, or as if the two methods of shaping Early Tudor chimneys were quantitatively equal at least. Nathaniel Lloyd in *The History of English Brickwork*, laid stress on brick-cutting. He illustrated modern brick-cutting tools, one type having the same basic form as the axes on the shield of the sixteenth-century London Company of 'Tylers and Bricklayers'. For Kirby Muxloe Castle in Leicestershire we know from the building accounts just how often the brick-axes needed sharpening, though most of the dressings there were stone. We know from the accounts that moulded bricks at Tattershall Castle were casually called 'hewentile' (literally, 'cut tiles'): chamfered edges and so on were probably cut, but the flaking plaster at Tattershall reveals the fine *moulded* brick of the vaulting of the passages, dating from the 1450s. Late fifteenth and early sixteenth century doors and windows also show the possibilities of moulded brick. To mould the elements of the patterns seems the more logical method for most purposes—despite the difficulties of achieving even firing—than gouging away deep into hard bricks. True, the big royal arms panel on the detached gatehouse at East Barsham is carved, but it is individual and figurative, not a pattern, and could be cut *in situ* in relatively soft brick. Such soft brick would have been impractical for chimneys, more exposed to weather. This work and, for example, the spandrels at Leez Priory and at Someries (Bedfordshire) are carved, but with shallow cuts. The accounts of Sir Thomas Lucas, for whom the (lost) Little Saxham Hall in Suffolk was built in the first decade of the sixteenth century, do, however, include expenditure on 'hewen' brick, used for the chimneys only.

Even though the accidents of survival may be misleading, so that we are left nearly everywhere with good-quality or at least strong bricks, it seems that mediaeval and Tudor brick was much harder than modern brick. This hard rough texture, with quite large pebbles to be eased out and the gaps filled in with mortar and brick dust, would have been more difficult to carve than modern brick, and the available iron tools would have been less strong than modern tools. The sharp edges we see in old buildings were not necessarily cut, but may result from the hard firing of unpulverized materials. Just because they were exposed to *every* wind, the detached Early Tudor shafts had to be of particularly hard brick for them and their patterns to last.

The unrestored chimneys (or the original bricks remaining in restored ones) have, of course, lasted out as much as four and a half centuries. Especially when a ribbed or twisted chimney face, or even a cusped design, could be produced by using bricks of only one shape—a unit brick—it seems more natural that these should be pre-moulded than that the background of the intended design be carved away from ordinary bricks. If there were wasters among such moulded bricks, so there were anyway with the fabric bricks. In 1427, for example, a whole load of 10,000 bricks from the town's yard, intended for St Mary's Church in Hull, proved useless, and accounts often mention a sizeable proportion of soft 'samel' bricks, which could be used for coring only.

From the single twisted shaft of the Rye House gatehouse to the Early Tudor shafts, most famously of Leez Priory and Hampton Court, and all of the Elizabethan plainer chimneys, the making up of patterns with one or two unit bricks was the normal method. The diaper blocks of East Barsham are apparently unique. Abbot Vyntoner's Early Tudor chimneys at St Osyth's Priory in Essex have larger blocks, also rare, that are used as pattern units. The post-Dissolution D'Arcy chimneys there are wide and stocky by comparison with Vyntoner's and are faced with normal-sized bricks with a section of rib or a stud. They have scalloped tops. The three chimneys of the ruined great hall are linked in a triangular group. The chimneys of the abbot's lodgings, twenty-five years earlier, are slim and dark red, with plain polygonal tops, pairs being linked at the cap only. Their shafts are formed of thick, slightly curved rectangular blocks, twelve inches high. Each block has a section of pattern, such as a ribbed hexagon with central flower, part of overall honeycomb; a ribbed diamond with quatrefoil flower or stud; a saltire with half flower studs at the edges between the arms, also part of diamond ribbing (with a whole stud to each diamond). The blocks are very hard-fired and are all the product of pre-moulding; even the flowers are sharply moulded.

The brick-axe was always available to improve the finish or, by adding detail, the design itself. One combination that seems quite common in chimneys, in vaulting ribs and in doorways was the sharpening up by carving of an angular order adjoining curved or hollow mouldings. The casual phrase 'cut and moulded brick chimneys' is, thus, misleading in its suggestion of parity. I would argue from envisaged practicality and from the appearance of surviving Early Tudor chimneys that their ornament was usually, or mainly, moulded and not carved.

Note: The chapter on Hampton Court Palace includes a section on chimneys.

CHAPTER III

Defence and the major castles

It is true that the increase in brick building in England is associated with the erection of numbers of relatively comfortable country houses, whether manor houses or palaces. Leland in the mid sixteenth century saw this; so did William Harrison of Radwinter, Essex, some years later. The association is so strong that, particularly with the virtual Reformation standstill in ecclesiastical building, we now think of the typical 'Tudor' building as a brick house. Second thoughts only are of the black-and-white houses of Cheshire and the stone ones of the West Country. More detailed knowledge adds to the association another typical image, from vernacular building, of a smaller house, timber-framed, possibly brick-nogged, possibly just with a brick chimney-stack. The context of these buildings is the falling away of the need for defences, whether from baronial armies or from less securely based groups of robbers or even, near the sea, from pirates or perennially from the French. From the Middle Ages we have an unforgettable picture, that of a correspondent of the Paston Letters, who wrote in 1450 that 'many enemys' were playing 'on Caster Sands, and in other plases, as homely as they were Englysch men'. The strong governmental policies, of which Edward III's J.P.s were a straw in the wind and which were helped on by Edward IV in the 1470s, were fulfilled under the Tudors. The main victory had been over the lords, now conceived of as disruptive forces in a society which had acquired centralized government. Moats, machicolations, the private manorial courts and then maintenance in the non-manorial courts and private armies belong to the mediaeval scene, when architecture was necessarily defensive—at least for the rich man in his castle, for the King, for the great abbeys and for the towns. We cannot, however, even attempt a tidy correlation of the replacement of the defensive by the domestic with the growth of brick building. If this is to some extent because it is impossible to categorize or categorize easily many late mediaeval and Early Tudor great houses, it is just as much because brick was sometimes used for true military building, in the English lands in France as well as in England. It should be noted that good-quality bricks and mortar were harder and stronger than modern bricks and cement. This was because they were denser and less easily pulverized. The harder firing and coarse, sometimes uneven, texture of mediaeval bricks accounts for this strength, but, of course, sections of brickwork would fall away more easily under attack than would stone blocks or even flint rubble.

That brick is not found more often in defended buildings in East Anglia—it is absent from post-Conquest Bury St Edmund's abbey's fortified precinct, Norwich Castle, Orford and Castle Hedingham's keeps—or in the later brick areas seems partly just to do with their comparatively early date. It was not so much that brick was rejected in favour of stone, but that brick was not available to be chosen. The Roman example was now centuries old, and anyway in their flint rubble defences the Romans had used big tiles just for bonding courses: at Colchester Castle and elsewhere this limited example was followed and the materials were reused. Brick fabric would have stood up less well to siege engines; when it does appear in fortified buildings the need for fortifications was no less serious but the style of attack had changed. Towards the end of the thirteenth century brick was thought appropriate for town defences in English Gascony, though the contemporary brick-built English settlement of Kingston upon Hull as yet lacked its full complement of walls and towers, being protected mainly by earth ramparts and river. If brick was thought suitable for the great fortified cathedral of Albi in the Languedoc, so it was for the small defended house of a knight, Little Wenham Hall in Suffolk. In the later Middle Ages the nature of warfare changed and great engines were not lumbered about the countryside and set up for sieges, but techniques of undermining, then explosives and finally cannon were adopted, inspired by the Crusaders' experience in the East. Brick was used in town defences, notably in the government-inspired Hull, whose walls dated from the late fourteenth century, and of Calais, where brick was used in the fortifications in the fourteenth, fifteenth and sixteenth centuries. Brick was used, incidentally, about 1382 for the great defensive gatehouse of Thornton Abbey, Lincolnshire, though the stern façade was mitigated by the statues of saints. At various dates in the fourteenth century, the towns of Norwich, Great Yarmouth and King's Lynn (then Bishop's Lynn) used some brick in their flint rubble walls. Norwich, however, has also the powerful detached Cow Tower of the 1380s, wholly brick-built, its lower walls eleven feet thick.

The fifteenth-century defended buildings of brick are those of lords, with an apparent lull in such royal enterprises in England, apart from Henry V's palace of Sheen (Richmond)—continued by Henry VI—and a lull in corporate fortification too. In the late 1470s the flint and stone London walls were

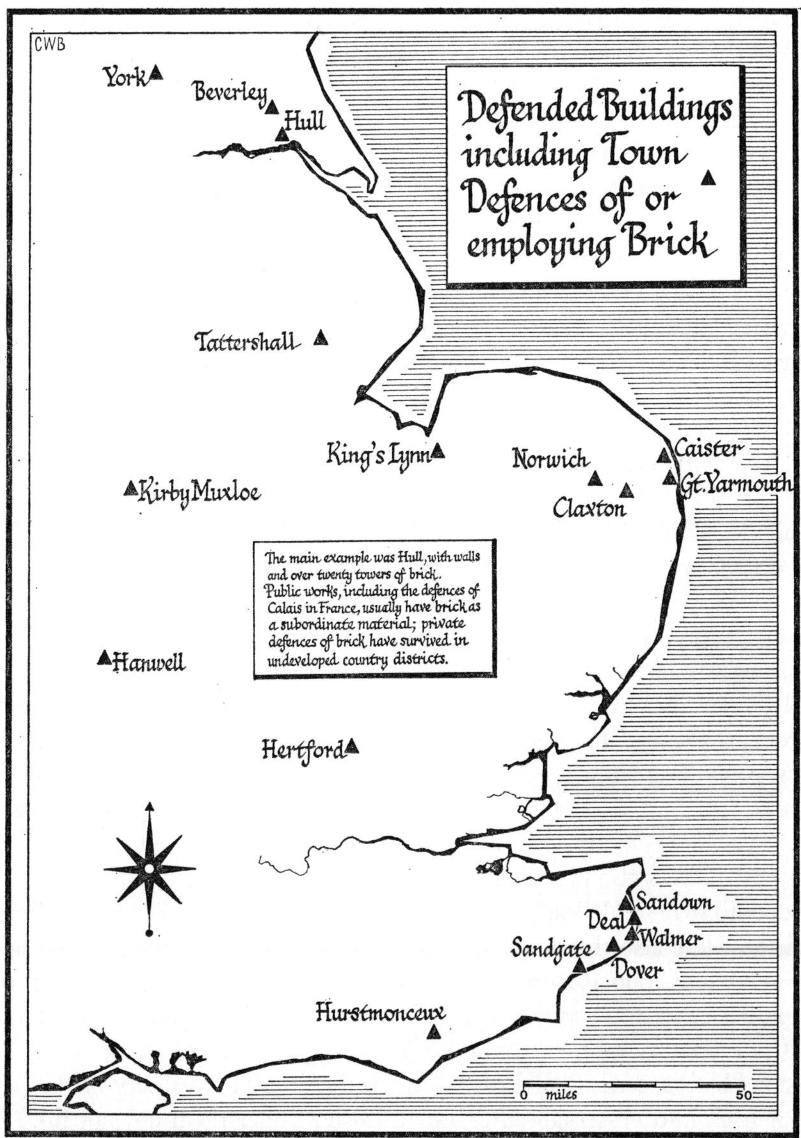
CWB
Defended Buildings including Town Defences of or employing Brick
York
Beverley
Hull
Tattershall
King's Lynn
Norwich
Caister
Gt. Yarmouth
Claxton
Kirby Muxloe
The main example was Hull, with walls and over twenty towers of brick. Public works, including the defences of Calais in France, usually have brick as a subordinate material; private defences of brick have survived in undeveloped country districts.
Hanwell
Hertford
Sandown
Deal
Walmer
Sandgate
Dover
Hurstmonceux
0 miles 50

12. DEFENDED BUILDINGS, INCLUDING TOWN DEFENCES, OF OR EMPLOYING BRICK.

patched, and the Mayor, Ralph Joceline, added a diapered brick alure. Edward IV used brick at the Tower of London. Then Henry VII used brick at Greenwich and Richmond Palaces, but domesticity was probably more important than defence at both, despite Richmond's tall towers. In the 1520s the French invasion scare led to the renewal of royal defensive work. Henry VIII's masons used stone as the main material for the long line of South Coast forts and gun emplacements, that ran from St Mawes in Cornwall to the North Foreland of Kent, because stone was locally available. For the three Sussex Downs forts stone already cut and worked was taken from the local dissolved monasteries, but even so bricks were made for inside work there. The added defences of Hull and Calais were built of their local brick, though siege by cannon, from land or sea, was to be expected.

On the Continent brick castles were built for great lords in the fifteenth and sixteenth centuries, particularly in the 'Low Countries' region, the Rhineland and France. There are spectacular examples, such as La Mota, in Spain. We do not know what possibilities of attack were in the mind of Ralph Lord Cromwell, who also built a more conventionally fortified stone house at South Wingfield in Derbyshire, when he used brick for the great moated tower-house of Tattershall, isolated in the Lincolnshire countryside—its lower walls twenty feet thick, its machicolations genuine. Hurstmonceux (Sussex) and Caister (Norfolk), however, were castles in areas open to invasion from abroad, at the least by pirates. Caister withstood a French attack when in the possession of its builder, Sir John Fastolf, but, with minute garrison and few weapons, fell after a siege in 1469 to John Howard, Duke of Norfolk, who employed heavy guns against it when numbers alone failed. At this date Howard's forces also literally undermined the so-called Hellesdon Lodge, the brick-built hall at Hellesdon which Fastolf had put up when he was building Caister. Here also the defender was a woman, Margaret Paston, who held Caister while John Paston tried to gain legal possession in London in the dispute over Fastolf's will. Sir John Fastolf had died in 1459, his long career that of a military captain, supplying his own force in the French wars. The Pastons had no such feudal force, but, maintaining the validity of the will, crept back into possession after 1469. Caister under them did not fulfil its 'wasserburg' function as a defended centre for the area: it was thought, and not just by the jealous and aggressive Dukes of Norfolk and Suffolk, that so important a castle should be in the hands of a lord.

Similar conditions shaped Hurstmonceux, with its moat, battered plinth, drawbridge and courtyards. Hurstmonceux is near Bodiam Castle, which was erected against expected French invasion sixty years earlier and is stone-built.

The history of Hurstmonceux, though, seems in fact to have been peaceful, at least after the 1450 Jack Cade rebellion. What this castle suggests is a strong home and base for estate administrators and armed retainers, as the stone-built Thornbury Castle, Gloucestershire, was anachronistically to be in the second decade of the sixteenth century. Thornbury survives, in ruins, with its splendid brick chimneys. Its builder, Edward Stafford, Duke of Buckingham, travelled about with a private army, against the fifteenth-century Livery statute that Henry VII's government had so strongly reinforced: Henry VIII had Stafford executed for treason in 1521. Whatever Stafford intended to do with this army, Thornbury's tiers of windows suggest that siege was not prepared for. Hurstmonceux looks more seriously fortified, but would have deterred a rabble better than an army. The same applies to the unfinished Kirby Muxloe Castle in Leicestershire, on its moated platform. Kirby Muxloe dates from the 1480s. Gunners firing from the gatehouse gunloops there would have hit the walls! Licence to crenellate was also needed for many buildings that appear to be just grand houses with some elements of the defensive. Their gatehouses, turrets and battlements begin to look first inadequate and then perhaps just decorative. Buildings like Faulkbourne Hall (Essex), Gainsborough Old Hall (Lincolnshire) and Middleton Tower (Norfolk) are difficult to type. Norwich corporation's Cow Tower was a stronger military building in its way than many large castellated structures of the late feudal, or 'bastard' feudal, epoch. That their defences were partly show is, however, little to do with brick as such. It was nothing to do with saving expense, either, in the case of the 'castles', since their builders were outstandingly wealthy. The factors were mainly politics and culture.

1. Town and royal defences

There was a political connection between town defences and those of the 'King's Works' that were primarily defensive, such as the Tower of London and Windsor Castle. The development of towns short-circuited the feudal system, making eventually for centralized government because they spoiled the theoretical pattern of graduated and distant loyalties to the King, owed only through the great lords and tenants-in-chief of the crown. The towns grew up literally as the strongholds of the middle classes—merchants, master craftsmen, lawyers—who sought independence from the lords, whether lay or ecclesiastical. The fourteenth century especially saw conflict between townsmen and ecclesiastical lords: in Norwich and Bury St Edmunds there was conflict with the great Benedictine abbeys and at Lynn with the Bishop of Norwich. Independence was gained through application to the King direct for charters of rights and privileges. Norwich, for instance, gained its free status, with a Mayor and corporation, in 1404; but there were already town defences. Towns might owe their dues, in exchange for charters, in goods instead of money: Great Yarmouth paid with ships and herrings. They were free of loyalty to any intervening lords and could charge customs at their gates and close those gates against attack. The Crown gave special grants of customs for 'murage', because it was in the royal interest to foster the building of town walls, since it gained from the towns' contribution to order—that is, to defence against marauding bands, disorderly lords or even attack from abroad. Equally, the Crown gained financially through trade, especially from exports. Always with the exception of Hull, brick was not a major material in the earlier, primarily military, town and royal architecture: when it appears in quantity, in Henry VII's and Henry VIII's reigns, it is used for royal palaces, not royal castles. Some important towns did not achieve walls. The port of Ipswich had its gates—some fifteenth-century brick was used—but apparently relied otherwise only on the old ditch and palisade. At Beverley, Yorkshire, Leland in the sixteenth century found town gates of brick and of stone, but no walls. He sounded surprised: Beverley was then a larger town than Hull. The Kings had their own fortresses for reasons similar to those of the town corporations for building their walls, but these reasons always had national significance.

The use of brick in English town defences parallels its general development. It is used in the non-stone areas, and at first for subsidiary tasks only. Much has been destroyed even in the East Anglian towns where parts of the mediaeval walls remain. Leland saw many brick buildings at Southampton, all now lost. Did they include any defences, one wonders? The all-brick walls of Hull have vanished, and were known only from records until the recent excavation of the base of a tower—one of the twenty or thirty that existed. At Yarmouth and Norwich we can see sections of wall and ruined circular towers, constructed of flint rubble with stone dressings and brick used for bonding work, for splays, vaulting, parapet walks. These structures belong to different dates in the fourteenth century. They were financed largely by grants of extra customs, as was also done to Lynn (Bishop's Lynn till the Reformation, then King's Lynn): the survivals there are much more fragmentary. The Norwich records show how sections of wall were maintained by the adjoining city wards. Lynn has patches of brick in the remains of the walls, besides late brick in the South Gate, which was remodelled in 1520: the front and sides are stone-faced, but the rear is brick. Norwich has one round tower wholly brick, a detached outlier at a bend of the River Wensum, the Cow Tower, erected about 1380. Norwich walls, angle towers and gates were complete and serious defences, facing not just traders who wanted to avoid paying customs, but jealous and disorderly lords and the rebels of the 1381 Peasants' Revolt, these last strong enough to capture the town. Two stretches of the river were used in the defences, as was done at Hull, and this explains the Cow Tower's site. It was an advance post, away from the main buildings. Even if this particular well-armed civil rebellion was not envisaged by the town officials, the Cow Tower—then seventy years old—had guns trained on it from nearby Mousehold Heath during the 1549 Kett Rebellion. It is possible that the damage done to the battlements then was not repaired. The present height of fifty feet is less than the original height. The Cow Tower has only a few stone dressings and a minute amount of moulded brick (just a narrow vault over the door). It has tiny voids only, with wide embrasures for firing the town's 'espringol' guns, and the one door is small and at the rear. The walls are eleven feet thick to the first stage. These elements make the tower a structure of Roman formidability.

In the north-east the losses are overwhelmingly more important than the survivals, though York does have its late mediaeval 'Red Tower' at one end of the white stone walls, and there is the North Bar of Beverley, a 1419 reconstruction. As noted, Leland saw more than one brick gate, but 'could not see that ever it (Beverley) was walled round'. The North Bar is an elegant structure, with crow-stepped battlements, not heavily defended. Hull was a port and its defences were real, though at first just earth ramparts, with (surely?) gates of brick. The brick circuit was erected in the late fourteenth century, and Henry VIII was to add harbour defences of brick and stone. In his reign, the Pilgrims of Grace, initially only unarmed, threatened the town in 1537 but could not take it. They were rebels against the Dissolution of the Monasteries. They held Beverley, though, for a short time. The Henrician defences at Hull were associated with the development of Trinity House and of the Royal Navy. In thinking of mediaeval Hull it is difficult to isolate its defences from the other buildings. The site was marshy and stoneless, the brick earth available at the site. Practically, this made for speed and cheapness and, conceivably more important, for structures lighter than if they had been made of stone. The site of the Holy Trinity Church in the mid fifteenth century was reinforced with timber 'mats' against subsidence through the action of the underlying water. The town's lost gridplan dated from the last years of the thirteenth century, modelled on the Gascon 'bastides'. The walls were erected a hundred years later and were described, with obvious admiration, by Leland in the mid sixteenth century. Hull had over twenty brick towers, most of them round, and square gatehouses, all linked by brick curtain walls with arcade-supported alures. The bricks were large, and lightish red. These brick defences withstood encirclement by Parliamentary supporters two and a half centuries later. Hollar's formal drawing of that date gives us the outlines of towers and battlement walks, and the layout of the buildings and streets, but it is difficult really to imagine the texture of this brick-fortified town.

One would like to *see* mediaeval Hull, closed, brick- and river-walled, smaller than Beverley; crowstepped warehouses lining the river bank; public buildings, the grand 'Suffolk Palace' of the de la Poles, most of the houses brick-built; Holy Trinity Church taking up its original complete chequer of the grid, like the great church of a 'villeneuve'. Defences, style, material would look continental to modern eyes. The settlement was subjected to French, Hanseatic (the first Hansa warehouses in England dated from Edward I's reign too) and South German influences. The Hull walls dated from the period of the marriage of Anne of Bohemia and Richard II, when English art also was influenced by South German. Yet the town council appointed from its number chamberlains to supervise the municipal brick-works, whose English-named workers supplied the building material from the very beginning—paradoxically long before the fashionable influx of Flemish and North German brickmakers in the mid fifteenth century. Hull was still European, predating separate national development.

Just as the towns needed governmental licence to fortify, so did individuals need the royal licence to crenellate. Perhaps the most important element of the anarchy of Stephen's reign (1135–54) was that great numbers of un-licensed or *adulterine* castles were erected by lords. These, though seemingly mainly just motte-and-bailey castles, with a keep and rampart defences (not full curtain walls), helped reduce Stephen virtually to the status of a baron himself. His successor, Henry II, cracked down on these castles, had them destroyed, and made the licence to crenellate again essential. Town defences were developed as a counterweight. In particularly disorderly regions new towns were actually planted in and around royal fortresses: through fortresses like Caernarvon and Harlech Edward I subdued North Wales and the Marches in the late twelfth century. Brick was not used then or till the late fourteenth century by the Kings, except for minor uses such as the tiling of floors or firebacks or, occasionally, bonding courses. True, Hull was brick-built under the direct patronage of Edward I, but the brick was used then only for the larger houses and for institutional buildings: the town had to wait for its brick walls till the end of the fourteenth century, when the chief mover was William de la Pole, Chancellor of Richard II. With this exception, and the work done at Calais, the royal works apparently employed little brick in a military context, though Edward III's lost Sheppey or Queenborough Castle (Isle of Sheppey, Kent) absorbed 37,800 flat tiles ('tegulis planis') or bricks in 1365, bought in 1365 from the mason and designer Henry Yevele at 3*s*. 4*d*. a thousand: they were used for inside partition walls ('parietibus'). The castle's circular plan gave some inspiration to the Henrician forts, where brick was also used in interiors.

Eltham Palace had some brick and Henry VI's lost Sheen (site of Richmond Palace) had much more, including imports from Calais. These, though, despite Sheen's brick curtain wall, were primarily domestic buildings. Henry VI's main project was indeed of brick, but this was a school, Eton College. The King's Serjeant, William Vesey, was commissioned to find suitable clays and make bricks for Windsor Castle as well as for Eton and Sheen, but again the context is domestic. The truly military parts of Windsor were long-established, built of stone and flint. There is an isolated reference of 1340 to a stair there, built of brick and stone, and Edward III used timber-framing with brick nogging for quarters for the chapel canons. Fifteenth-century work was probably for domestic improvements—rather as Henry III had early had decorated floor tiles in his palace of Clarendon in Wiltshire. Late in the fifteenth century Edward IV did use brick for a (lost) bulwark at the Tower of London, and the original 'Brick Tower' on the north side of the inner curtain there is attributed to him or to Richard III. It was in Edward's reign that the brick upper stage was added to the walls of London, of which a section remains in the old churchyard of St Alphege's, London Wall. Brick was now used for chimneys and fireplaces, domestic improvements at the old royal castle of Dover. The resurgence of royal building activity under Henry VII and Henry VIII at Greenwich, Eltham and Richmond, besides Henry VIII's country palaces, was all brick, but, despite gatehouses, towers and turrets, domestic. The tiltyard towers of Henry VIII at Greenwich and Hampton Court typify the fall of military seriousness. The chief gatehouse that the King built at Whitehall Palace (previously Wolsey's York Place) actually spanned a public right-of-way! St James's Palace gatehouse represents swagger and display, just as the lords' country towers had from the second half of the fifteenth century: it is like a Cambridge college gatehouse or Lupton's Tower at Eton (Buckinghamshire). Edward VI's government soon detected that Wolsey's and Henry VIII's Hampton Court Palace could not be defended against armed rebellion, and fell back on mediaeval Windsor.

When Henry had genuine defences erected brick was only a subordinate material, with the exception of the harbour defences and towers at Hull. Bricks were used in Kent, in the new forts of Deal, Walmer, Sandown, Sandgate, but only after the outer walls had been built. For these the stone came from many sources, from the local quarries, from the sea shore (compare use of septaria in East Anglia) and from several dissolved priories. The monastic stone included Caen earlier imported from France. At the peak of building activity there were five or six hundred workers at Sandgate, about which most is known because the ledgers of 1539–40 survive (in the British Museum). Sandgate survives, reconstructed as a Martello tower against Napoleonic invasion. These forts, contemporarily described as 'blockhouses or bulwarks', were the products of a crash building programme. The overseer was Sir Edward Ryngley, who had held this post at Calais, and he brought the Bohemian engineer, Stephen van Haschenberg, to work here too. Van Haschenberg was described as the 'deviser' of Sandgate, and he also designed Deal, Walmer and the now-eroded Sandown. These lobed forts, designed chiefly as gun emplacements, were new for England, but Sheppey Castle, erected in the 1360s, and with Henry Yevele as architect, was also circularly planned with much lower-walled lobes. By 1543, however, the Bohemian engineer was in unredeemable trouble with the English—dismissed because he had, it seemed, 'behaved lewdly and spent great treasure to no purpose'. When the numbers of bricklayers, as against stone masons, increased this indicates that the main walls were up. Bricks, certainly made locally, were used for inner walls, for lining window splays and—these survive at Deal and Walmer—the brick-vaulted entrance passages, between portcullis and inner door, that were pierced with 'meurtrières' or murder-holes. The best comparison seems to be with the flint town walls where brick had such tasks as lining loopholes. Camber Castle, Sussex, has the same construction: a stone tower with brick lining, but this dates from about 1511. The Sandgate ledger records the use of 44,000 tiles, mostly from the gault clay of Wye (where the monks of Battle Abbey had run a tile-works from the mid fourteenth century). Despite the military context the leading craftsmen were those of Hampton Court Palace. The master mason was John Moulton; the chief bricklayer was Christopher Dickenson; the chief carpenter William Clement, who had recently been working on the ornate ceiling of the Chapel Royal there. The invasion never came.

2. *Private fortifications*

The Norwich Cow Tower—and this is its unique importance—is the one extant brick building unambiguously intended for defence. If the walls and

1. MEDIEVAL BRICKMAKING: Illumination from the 'Nederlandische Bijbel', made at Utrecht about 1425, theoretically showing exiled Jews making bricks in Egypt but actually of contemporary practice. (Add. M.S. 38122 fol. 78v.)

2. ST. ALBANS ABBEY, HERTFORDSHIRE: Upper stages of central tower erected in the twelfth century and composed of re-used Roman tiles or bricks from Verulamium.

3. POLSTEAD CHURCH, SUFFOLK: Late twelfth-century brick arches to nave and clerestory.

4. LITTLE COGGESHALL ABBEY, ESSEX: Detail of interior of detached gatehouse, of about 1190, showing moulded brick in window splays and recesses.

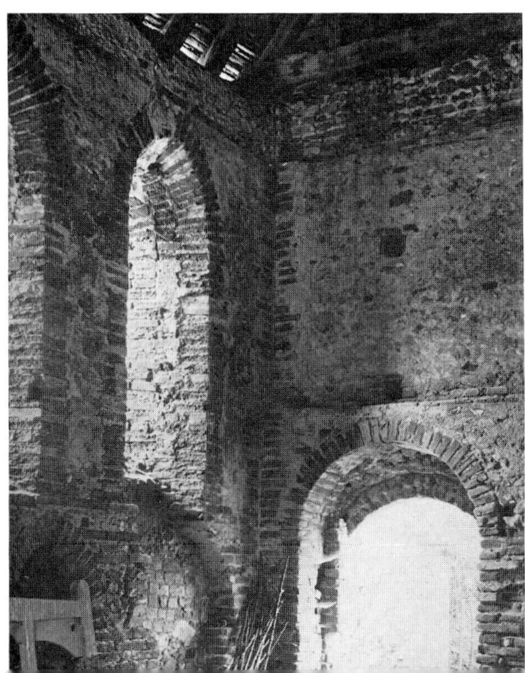

5. LITTLE COGGESHALL ABBEY, ESSEX: The early thirteenth-century Chapel (*capella extra portas*) from the south-east. The building is of flint rubble, with brick quoins and window dressings.

6. LITTLE WENHAM HALL, SUFFOLK: East side of building of 1270, or 1280. The three-light window is that of the chapel.

7. ST. OLAVE'S PRIORY, HERRINGFLEET, SUFFOLK: Brick-vaulted Undercroft of about 1300.

8. BRIDEWELL MUSEUM, NORWICH: Detail of early fourteenth-century brick vaulting of Undercroft.

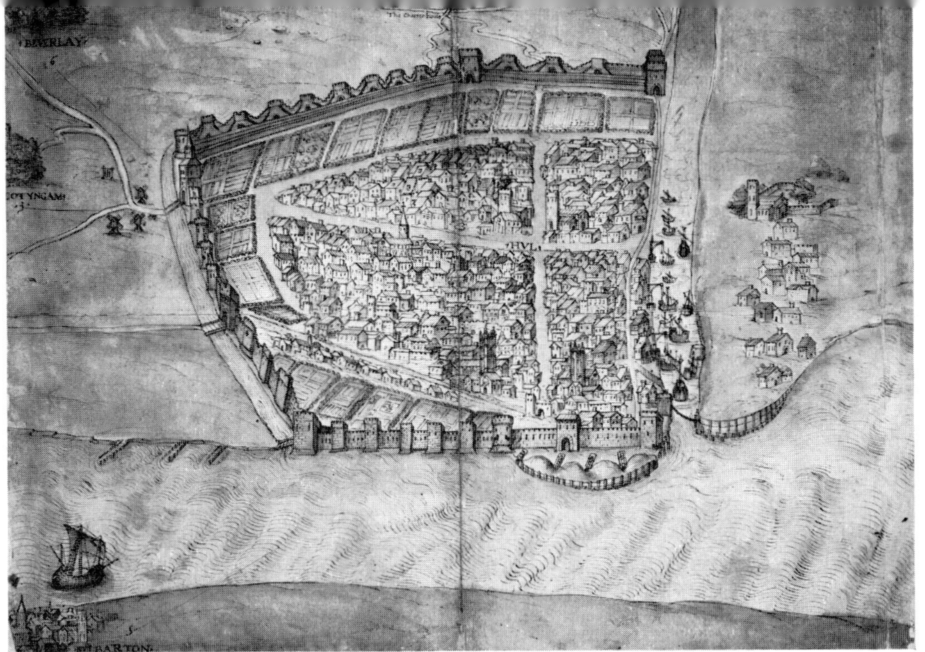

9. PLAN OF KINGSTON-UPON-HULL: Mid sixteenth-century redrawing of a mediaeval plan, showing the fourteenth-century town walls. In the foreground is the Humber, with a cannon emplacement; in the background, beyond the walls, is the Charterhouse monastery. (Cott. M. S. Aug. I, i, 83.)

10. PLAN AND VIEW OF KINGSTON-UPON-HULL: Mid seventeenth-century engraving by Wenceslas Hollar. The view looks inland from the Humber; the plan shows the Humber on the right and the Hull in the background, with the three forts (blockhouses) erected by Henry VIII.

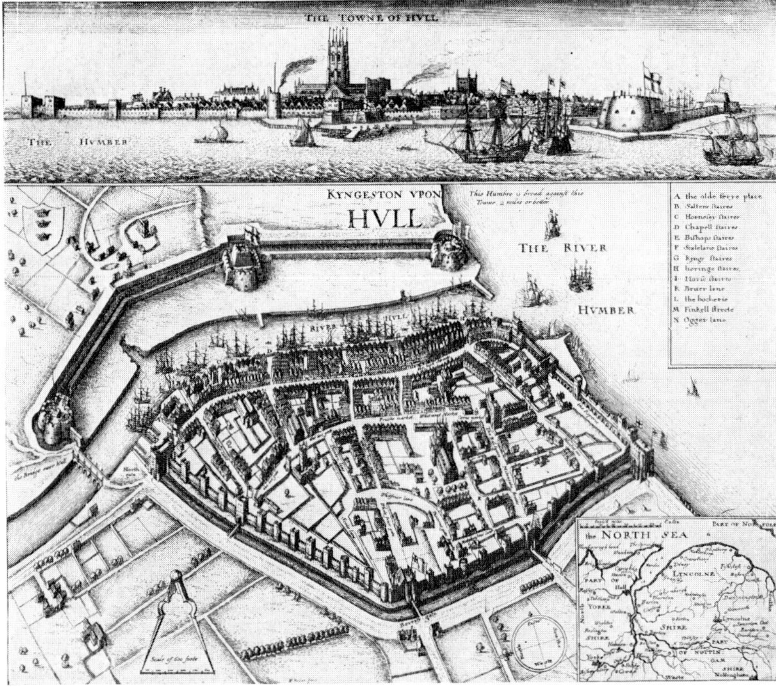

11. COW TOWER, NORWICH: Detached tower of about 1380, built as part of the Norwich defences.

12. COW TOWER, NORWICH: Detail of interior, late fourteenth-century work, showing fireplace and traces of vaulting of first floor.

13. COW TOWER, NORWICH: Part of upper stage of interior of late fourteenth-century round tower, showing deep splays to the defensive slit windows.

14. THORNTON ABBEY, LINCOLNSHIRE: Gatehouse of brick, partly ashlared, of 1382, with a section of the sixteenth century barbican wall.

15. THORNTON ABBEY, LINCOLNSHIRE: Section of gatehouse walling under repair, showing thickness of five stretchers or two-and-a-half headers.

16. THORNTON ABBEY, LINCOLNSHIRE: Interior of main room of gatehouse of 1382, of brick with stone dressings.

17. RYE HOUSE, HERTFORDSHIRE: Detail of top of hand rail of spiral stair, showing moulded brick handgrip (see Fig. 9).

18. RYE HOUSE, HERTFORDSHIRE: Part of front of the gatehouse (only surviving building) of about 1443, showing moulded brick corbel-tables and corbelled supports of oriel windows.

19. CAISTER CASTLE, NORFOLK: Built of brick with stone dressings in the early 1430s for Sir John Fastolf. The great tower, with its adjoining stair turret, is ninety feet high.

20. HURSTMONCEUX CASTLE, SUSSEX: Bridge leading to great gatehouse of the castle, about 1440. Machiolations and portcullis grooves are visible.

21. TATTERSHALL CASTLE, LINCOLNSHIRE: The great tower of about 1450, from the east. Note the deep machiolations and the traces, at the base, of the lost hall.

22. TATTERSHALL CASTLE, LINCOLNSHIRE: Detail of mid fifteenth-century vaulting, originally plastered, to a side-chamber on the third floor of the great tower.

23. QUEENS' COLLEGE, CAMBRIDGE: The gatehouse, erected in the 1450s, seen from the first court.

24. JESUS COLLEGE, CAMBRIDGE: Gatehouse erected at the end of the fifteenth century for Bishop John Alcock of Ely

25. FARNHAM CASTLE, SURREY: Aerial photograph showing, in foreground, the brick tower attributed to Bishop Waynflete (about 1470).

towers of Kingston-upon-Hull or of Calais, only twenty miles off the Kent coast, had survived, the balance would be different. In the main groups of buildings with military purpose brick is either non-existent or a secondary material only, or it may be the main material of structures where the military was not the sole purpose. As a secondary material brick might be structurally vital, as when it formed the alure, but the fortifications themselves were most often stone-faced flint. The early fourteenth-century castle of Claxton, Norfolk, has this combination. Its builder, Sir William Kerdeston, was also involved in the building of Norwich walls. A later example of major flint and minor brick is Baconsthorpe Castle, also in Norfolk. The growth, and therefore redevelopment, of towns has meant that most surviving defended buildings have country sites, though not all are as isolated as Claxton and Baconsthorpe, or Caister or Tattershall. The fourteenth-century Rotherfield Greys in Oxfordshire has some tiles (rather than bricks) in the flint rubble fabric, unusual for the early date. Baconsthorpe, of the fifteenth century and later, was the base of a gangster-like lawyer, Henry Heydon. The larger group consists of more or less fortified halls and castles, built of brick but usually with stone dressings. These are most often moated. There are some small tower-houses of brick. More commonly, part of the hall is fortified—a tower or gatehouse—and the rest is more domestic, of two storeys only, with large windows.

Licence to crenellate was necessary for any building to be embattled: the phrasing was 'to fortify and embattle', and the materials it was planned to use might be mentioned. The 1425 licence of the lost Manor of the More (Richmansworth, Hertfordshire) specified building with stones, lime and bricks: brick, it has been found by excavation, was a secondary material. This house was superseded by later work but the excavation has revealed early fifteenth-century tower bases. The 1443 licence of the lost Rye House (Stanstead Abbots, Hertfordshire) specifies lime and stone as materials for 'a castle with battlements and loopholes', but the surviving gatehouse is of brick, with fine moulded oriels: it is battlemented, but has no other defences. Halls that look to us domestic were erected under licence. As late as 1531 William Paulet, 1st Marquis of Winchester, had licence to crenellate his house at Basing in Hampshire. He built a turreted brick house on the site of, and utilized parts of, the mediaeval castle there. The new dwelling, Basing House, is lost, but linking walls and gatehouses remain. Paulet's was clearly not a castle, just an impressive Early Tudor mansion inside stone curtain walls. Various lords converted mediaeval castles to more comfortable living, just as they did abbey buildings at the Dissolution, using brick for fireplaces and chimney-stacks at least. The Howards did this at Framlingham Castle, Suffolk, and then built the virtually undefended mansion of Kenninghall in Norfolk. After the Battle of Bosworth John de Vere, Earl of Oxford, took over the ancestral stone keep at Castle Hedingham in Essex. He inserted modern fires in this, but also erected new (lost) castle buildings of red brick, including a great four-storey square tower, besides the bridge gatehouse, smaller towers, a great hall and new domestic offices. This work was contained in the mediaeval bailey, and the moat was now spanned by a brick-and-stone bridge (which survives). In some ways this castle layout was as anachronistic as the liveried retainers whose existence brought down on him a crushing fine, but it was an inherited layout. One should point out that maybe more castles and fortified dwellings might now survive if they had not, like Basing or Rotherfield Greys Castle, been 'slighted' by Cromwell's forces after they had been held by Royalists.

Decades, even centuries, earlier we notice the mixture of defence and the domestic. Little Wenham Hall, largely of yellow brick, has its thick walls pierced only by lancets for the ground floor, but the hall and chapel windows above are quite large, and safety would have been further spoiled by the lean-to domestic offices, now lost. In the mid fifteenth century Little Wenham was the home and base of Sir Gilbert Debenham, something of a gangster figure in local politics, one of whose crimes was smuggling. Later tower houses are Maldon Moot Hall, Essex—originally the house of the D'Arcys—and the early sixteenth-century Rochford and Hussey Towers at Boston, Lincolnshire, all three of red brick. The early fifteenth-century Faulkbourne Hall, Essex, has a most severe square tower, embattled, blank, thick-walled, but set at the angle of two large-windowed ranges. Gainsborough Old Hall, Lincolnshire, has fortified towers linked on to half-timbered work, even though it was erected during the Wars of the Roses. Gainsborough typifies the ambiguity over defence: it has both genuine machicolations and false machicolations, used for decoration. Hanwell Castle, Oxfordshire, has a surviving square brick tower, again at the angle of domestic ranges. There are Early Tudor towers of some size at Fincham Hall, Norfolk, and Pooley Hall, Polesworth, in Warwickshire.

The fifteenth-century Heron Hall (East Horndon) and Nether Hall in Essex had defensive elements: the ruins of Nether Hall, at Roydon, are of the gatehouse. If gatehouses were detached they were better protection. The Middleton Tower gatehouse, Norfolk, erected during the Wars of the Roses, has thick walls and small voids. It stands at the edge of a moated platform. We are reminded, however, of the elegant defensiveness of the Cambridge colleges. Oxborough Hall, Norfolk, also brings the Cambridge comparison to mind, but for its two-storey courtyard buildings. The great gatehouse of Oxborough is seven storeys high, but, though there are machicolations immediately over the entrance arch, the turrets and battlements of defence are now really just used for display. The Early Tudor great gatehouse took motifs from the towers of the past and has eight-stage turrets and terracotta dolphins on the battlements! The small, near-contemporary gatehouses at West Drayton (Middlesex) and Lullingstone Castle (Kent) are much more sober and strong, but led to country houses. Compton Wynyates, Warwickshire, has a gatehouse which even has a portcullis, but is flush with the north front. East Barsham has first—detached by a few yards only—and second gatehouses, of no defensive use at all. Sutton Place had a gatehouse in the lost range, but is terracotta-panelled outside and the epitome of grand domestic living. The Kirtling Tower, Cambridgeshire, is of about 1530, and elegance prevails. We see typical attenuated Tudor 'defences' at the ruined Beckingham Hall, Tolleshunt D'Arcy, Essex, of about 1546. Most gatehouses have loopholes, however, as at Leez Priory, where there was also a Guard Room, like that at Nether Hall (also in Essex).

The late castles described below actually exemplify the gradual run-down of defence and the intrusion of the new needs for regular living-accommodation for estate officers and armed retainers and the new desire for display. There is no one simple relationship with the use of brick, which for all four castles was made near the site. Tattershall tower may have twenty foot thick walling at the base, but it also has wide fireplaces and beautiful, ornate brick vaulting to its passages. Caister, though involved in coastal defence as well as local conflicts, was partly a vehicle for Sir John Fastolf's tapestries and painted glass. William of Worcester said Caister cost Fastolf £6,000, but mediaeval writers liked round firgures. It certainly cost more than the smaller Hurstmonceux, at £3,800. Fastolf also built turreted dwellings at Hellesdon (lost) and Drayton (surviving in ruins) at the same time. The Pastons lived here as middle-class interlopers, having obtained Caister possibly through over-influencing the last will of the old, ill Fastolf. They led an unfeudal existence, while the system decayed about them. They also had Paston and Oxnead and other farms, though they did not obtain any of Fastolf's property outside East Anglia. Finally the head of the family gained the title of Earl of Yarmouth. In the 1450s and 1460s physical attacks were made on them by the Dukes of Norfolk and Suffolk, and by their own lesser rivals, the knights or lawyers: Henry Heydon, Thomas Tuddenham, William Daniel, Gilbert Debenham. These attacks died out in the second, stronger part of Edward IV's rule. Like other late castles (stone-built) these four cover large moated areas with, usually, asymmetrical buildings. They do not present the tight fortress knot of building of the old castles, with their massively thick walls throughout. Kirby Muxloe, never finished according to the plan, is now reduced to patchy ruins at the edges of the completed moated platform. The ranges between the interval turrets seem to have been of two storeys only. Hurstmonceux alone is still used but is a revival—an elegant, clear-cut shell, comically housing the National Observatory. The interior is not open to the public. (Bibliographies for each are given in the main gazetteer.)

(i) *Caister Castle*, *Norfolk* *(Pl. 19)*

Caister Castle has been reopened to the public by the present owner, as a motor museum. It is situated near the ruins of the old church of West Caister. The site is low-lying and on clay. Now about one and a half miles from the eroded coast, it was probably once connected to the sea by a creek. The best access in mediaeval times was by water, Caister being linked by cuts and the River Bure with Great Yarmouth and Acle, which was then also a port. Acle was granted freedom from all tolls in the reign of Richard II. This watery setting is important, because the layout and architecture of Caister Castle has been compared with the mediaeval *wasserburgen*—water-girt fortresses—of the Lower Rhineland, especially Schloss Kempen. This comparison was made in the *Antiquaries' Journal* article by Barnes and Simpson. The surprising and dramatic great round tower is unrivalled in England, rising sheer from the water of the thirty foot wide moat to a height of ninety feet, with a further eight feet to the stair turret. The tower's diameter is just twenty-five feet. The date is about 1432. The building material is brick, as it was for the *wasserburgen*. This was appropriate for building in a marshy place, especially to exceptional height. All the bricks were made of the local sandy clay, fired at kilns next to or near the site. Limestone, used for most of the dressings, was imported along with plaster of Paris from France, via Great Yarmouth. The builder, Sir John Fastolf, gained permission from Henry VI to have extra sea-going ships to carry materials for the castle. Yarmouth, where brick had been used with flint in the town defences, recurs in the story of Sir John Fastolf. His grandfather was a Yarmouth sea-captain or small shipowner. The story of the castle-builder's rise to wealth and importance is known in detail, and its significance is both complex and interesting. In his personal French victory, 'The Battle of the Herrings' of 1426, he used provision carts with barrels of Yarmouth herrings as cover for his forces, rather in the manner of the Boer 'voortrekkers'.

The surviving buildings and fragments are the ruins of his not quite completed scheme. The building period was at the tail-end of the Hundred Years War, in which for forty years Fastolf was a great captain and from which he gained funds—though during his service he apparently lent to the Crown money that was not repaid. He was Deputy Constable of Bordeaux in 1412. He fought with distinction at Agincourt in 1415. Already a knight, he was made a banneret after the Normandy victory of Verneuil in 1424, when he said he won 20,000 marks in loot. He was made a Knight of the Garter in 1426, but this honour was taken from him at one time in France for reasons that are not clear. For a period he was Governor of Maine and Anjou (provinces given up on Henry VI's marriage with Margaret of Anjou, during the English retreat from France), but he was really more a professional soldier. He retired from France in 1439, with an associated office, the governship of Jersey and Guernsey. In England he was to hold neither local nor state offices. Caister was constructed with defence against possible invasion in mind, but was not government-inspired, unlike the earlier Bodiam Castle in Sussex. Caister Castle did in fact repel a serious French attack, though the fabric suffered serious damage. This was in 1458, when the eighty-year-old Fastolf's besieged forces 'shotte many gonnes' (presumably hand-guns). Incidentally, no cannon or hand-guns are mentioned in the inventory, but crossbows are. Fastolf was deeply involved in the Lancestrian government's effort to retain the English territories in France. The successes of Henry V and the smaller victories of the 1420s were followed by defeats and final withdrawal. Fastolf did not go back to France after 1439 or 1440. The continual expenses of the campaigns the government tried to cover by levying taxes: when this policy caused the Cade Rebellion in 1450 Fastolf was one of those threatened with assassination, unpopular because identified with the government by his past military career, although in England he was just a great landowner and farmer.

He is well documented, partly because his secretary William of Worcester, who had historical and topographical interests, collected material for an 'Acta Johannis Fastolf' (the deeds of John Fastolf). The 'Acta' itself is lost, but many of Worcester's records survive besides business documents. There is an inventory of Fastolf's goods, including his books, for he was a patron of literature. Earlier and incomplete are some accounts of the building of the Castle. Documents at Magdalen College, Oxford, came there through Bishop William Waynflete who, in 1474, finally acquired the endowments of Fastolf's proposed college for seven priests and poor men at Caister for his own foundation. The difficulties over Fastolf's college, caused by the need to have a 'mortmain' licence to put land permanently into the 'dead hand' of the Church, were the origin of the problem of settling the estate after Fastolf's death in 1459. In England grazier, farmer and trader, Fastolf showed himself awkward over money and prone to litigation. He was more friendly to John Paston, who was married to a cousin of his and acted as his legal agent in London, than to most of his own relatives. He is known also through *The Paston Letters*, the papers of his successors at Caister. His history shows an incredible accumulation of property, beginning with an income from land of £50 a year and ending with an income of £20,000, when the royal income was only £50,000 and had to be used for government expenses too; beginning with a little land in Norfolk and ending 'seized' of ninety-four manors, including the wealthy manor at Castlecombe in Wiltshire, acquired through his wife (the widow of Sir Stephen Scrope), where he had weavers' workshops. He took from these £100-worth of red and white cloth each year for his own contingent of soldiers in France. He sold corn and malt and wool (and conceivably bricks). He cut timber. He exploited the wardships of young people. He had his cargo-ships.

His lands were mainly in Norfolk, Suffolk and Essex, and their value may perhaps be compared with those of the de Veres of Castle Hedingham in Essex and Lavenham in Suffolk. Despite the Norman Conquest origins of the family, and the head of the family's title of Earl of Oxford, the de Veres did not own land on the greatest baronial scale, in contrast to, say, the Nevilles (the family of Warwick *the Kingmaker*). Unlike Fastolf, though, successive Earls of Oxford held offices of state. A closer comparison for Fastolf is with Sir John Pelham, one of the greatest landowners of Sussex, whose direct ancestor was one of Edward III's captains in France and brought war profits into the family. This exact contemporary of Fastolf's married, like him, a landed wife. Pelham's wife brought him land in Sussex, Suffolk and Cambridgeshire—and he continued accumulating more properties himself. Again, though, there is the great contrast with Fastolf: Pelham held regular offices, including those of J.P., M.P., Sheriff of Sussex. A colleague of Fastolf's in France and his friend in England was the Dane, Andrew Ogard, made a knight after the Battle of Verneuil: Ogard, based on his brick houses of Rye in Hertfordshire and of Emneth in Norfolk, held such offices as M.P. for Hertfordshire and J.P. in Norfolk. Fastolf had twenty years in England to put his energies, unaffected by official demands, into farming, trading and building and increasing his wealth. The inventory of Caister listed the rich contents of thirty-nine rooms, including 13,000 ounces of silver plate. Other plate was kept at St Benet's Abbey, Ludham, where Fastolf was buried in

1459 in the chapel he had built on the south side of the chancel of the abbey church. Besides Caister Castle, he built a mansion and lodge at Hellesdon and a lodge at Drayton, near Norwich. He built a great house in Norwich, which Blomefield saw in a state of decay in the eighteenth century, though it retained stained glass with classical legends, like the recorded tapestries of Caister. He built a mansion in Bermondsey, on the south bank of the Thames near where the Bishops of Winchester had a palace, and this was taken over by John Holland, Duke of Exeter, in 1459. The Castlecombe manor went back to the Scropes at this time.

Even without the documentation, however, the ninety-foot tower surviving at Caister would give some idea of the builder's unusual wealth. Fastolf was born at Caister in about 1378, in the earlier manorhouse. This was attacked and damaged during the 1381 Peasants' Revolt. In 1404, when he was in his twenties, his mother, Lady Mortimer, made over to him this Fastolf family house. He first applied for licence to crenellate a new building during Henry V's reign, but did not begin work till 1432. The accounts of 1432–5 survive, but the building period was evidently very much longer. Fastolf settled down here only towards the end of his life, not on his retirement from France. William of Worcester said the total cost of building was £6,000. This was surely exaggerated, since the contemporary Hurstmonceux Castle cost only £3,800. These limited accounts show receipts and expenditure equal at about £1,500. William Granere, or Granour, administered the work, being paid £3. 6*s*. 8*d*. a year. Unfortunately, the name of the master mason does not feature, but he was surely a foreigner? Granere wrote the items down in Latin, but with some English terms: 'tiel' and 'tielpynnes', 'lathes', 'freestone', 'plankes', 'stagyngtymber' for scaffolding, 'sparrys' of oak for repairing 'les waynes' (transport wains) and 'ankeres' (anchors for reinforcing building) are some of these terms. Two hundred and sixty-five trays of burnt chalk, for making mortar, cost £25. 14*s*. The brickmaker received £86 and cut his own peat turves for firing the kiln. Workers were boarded 'in the lord's hostel'. The bricklayers were still called 'tegulatores' (tilers). It is frustrating that the accounts are incomplete, but at least they confirm, from the lack of transport costs and the description of 'lasts' or 'lodes' of bricks as being made at 'Castre', that the bricks were not imported. The main material was local even if the style—especially of tower and corbelling—was foreign.

The historical background was anarchic. Not only did foreign enemies 'come up to the land and played them on Caister sands, as homely as if they were Englishmen', in the 1450 *Paston Letters* description, but there was also native lawlessness and violence. In fact, one vital objection to John Paston's taking over Caister after Fastolf's death in 1459 was that only a noble, with an army of retainers, could play a proper military or defensive role in the countryside. Fastolf died a testy eighty-year-old (it is recorded he swore by 'Whitebeard or Blackbeard' to obtain his way in some local dispute), a widower, heirless apart from his rather despised Scrope relatives. He was an asthmatic and now not well, though eighty was an exceptional age for a mediaeval man. John Paston was an executor, and saw to it that a last clause in the will gave him control of much of the property. The Paston claim to tenure probably rested, at best, on undue influence exerted in the last weeks of Fastolf's life or, at worst, on forgery. Through the clause, in return for a large sum paid to the other executors and a promise to establish the chantry college, John Paston gained the East Anglian lands. The family invented a fine family tree, while their detractors invented servile status a few generations back: they were just middle class, taking on property baronial in all but name. Disputes about the will followed: local lords were hostile and jealous, and Edward IV opposed the Paston claim. John Paston, who died in 1466, had spells in the Fleet prison in London. His wife Margaret bore the brunt of local, often violent, opposition. She and her sons maintained the claim. In 1469 a garrison of twenty-nine held off the army of John Mowbray, Duke of Norfolk, for a month before surrendering: the defenders had run out of missiles and powder and 'the place is being broken by guns', while Norfolk had brought up reinforcements. Norfolk held Caister till his death in 1476, when the Pastons returned. They were thereafter able to keep possession.

The family lived at Caister till 1599, when they moved to a newly built mansion at Oxnead. In 1659 Sir William Paston sold the Castle, scarred by attack and fire, to a London dealer called Crowe. Materials were removed. By the early nineteenth century, when painted by John Sell Cotman and Alfred Stannard of the Norwich School of artists, it was reduced almost to its present state, though Dawson Turner in 1842 recorded the barge-house, over the surviving eight-foot-wide barge arch at the south-west, as still standing. Blickling Hall has an ornate stone fireplace, bearing the arms of Fastolf and his wife. About 1782 a vandalistic parson called Trafford removed one-hundred-and-twenty-two stone steps from the great tower stair-turret, to make a parapet for his house at Wroxham! The L-shaped range to the south, Caister Hall, was remodelled in the eighteenth century, when it was given a fine Georgian porch. This Hall has been lived in in modern times by a succession of owners, who have admitted the public to the castle ruins. The Castle itself has been repaired and excavated. Pieces of red glass, bearing Fastolf's motto of 'Fault

Fayre' (one must be doing), were found in the moat. The plan of the lost buildings to the north used to be revealed in very dry weather, but the site has now been levelled.

The general outline was as follows. The moated platform, about three hundred feet long, was divided into two uneven rectangles by a now dry cross-cut. The east side of the moat is now also dry. The north part provided the entrance and a defensive forecourt, which was not heavily built up. At the east survives the buttressed curtain wall, now just twelve feet high. This wall is mainly of yellow or pink bricks, but with some flint. It is thought to be earlier than the other remains, and even, conceivably, belonged to the old manor house. It is pierced with brick-outlined arrow slits, whereas the tower group has circular stone gun ports.

The brickwork of the main court buildings is more varied in colour: besides yellow and pink bricks there are some dark purple ones, these used irregularly, not for diaper. Brick sizes are eight and a half (or nine and a half) by four by two and a half inches. The texture is uneven, but bricks are carefully laid with comparatively narrow mortar joints. The bond is English. String-courses, quoins, voids and gunports are of stone. Stone is also used for the large gargoyles, mainly surviving on the square south-east buttress, and for the newel of the stair-turret. As at Tattershall, however, there are deep machicolations of brick, with square 'meurtrières' and rounded archlets between the stepped brick corbels: these remain on the tower and the adjoining battlemented walls.

The great tower covers the south-west angle. There is the remnant of a gatehouse at the south, where a bridge has replaced the drawbridge, and opposite, to the north, is the base of the gatehouse that faced the lost cross-cut. By the south-west angle is a set of square rooms, which acts as the angle buttress and has heavy stone quoins. The great round tower has its stair-turret to the south-east, the lower section square and the upper hexagonal. On the north-east of the tower is the square garderobe block. The tower has five storeys, the rooms being roughly hexagonal inside. The small square windows, with brick relieving arches, and of course the gunports speak of defence, but the walls are not very thick and the tower's main function was as a look-out. The great hall, which William of Worcester, Fastolf's secretary, recorded as measuring forty-nine by twenty-eight feet and as being next to a separate dining-room, apparently lay behind the tower where a surviving gable-end rises above the north-west curtain. The large first-floor windows could be the hall's and there are the remains of a big fireplace here. The north-west curtain has some low square windows, where barge-brought goods might be delivered, the barges coming round the south-east range, under the barge-arch and past the great tower.

It is thought a further platform, bounded by an extension of the moat, was intended for the part of the site where Caister Hall stands. This house looks Georgian, but is basically mediaeval and has as its south-west angle a squat, round, three-storey tower. This, now rendered, is the only one remaining of the Castle's outer defensive towers. If plans had been completed, this range would have been matched by another L-shaped block. Fastolf founded at the castle a chantry college, for seven priests and seven poor men, and the history of the site is complicated by the possibility that buildings were begun for them—perhaps this block or perhaps in the forecourt. The resources he left for the college were, however, eventually diverted to Magdalen College, Oxford, in 1474 by Bishop William Waynflete, who was involved in the administration and distribution of Fastolf's property and himself acquired the surviving Lodge at Drayton. Waynflete, too, was Ralph Cromwell's executor, and responsible for finishing both castle and church buildings at Tattershall. The Paston family resources came mainly from agriculture, and would have run to repairs only. They did not obtain the mass of Fastolf's possessions.

The source of some of the castle bricks has been found. Lt.-Col. S. E. Glendenning about 1950 located this source, for the earlier bricks of the east curtain, one and a quarter miles to the south in Bure Marshes. A hillocky four-acre area, known as the 'Brick Pits', proved to include 'the usual debris of a brickyard' (see appendix to the Barnes and Simpson article in the *Antiquaries Journal*, 1952). Broken bricks found here matched brick at the Castle, and experiments in firing march clay produced the same colours and texture of brick. There are yellow streaks of sand in the bricks, with 'the remains of small estuarine shells'. Water transport, for two and a half miles to the Castle, was provided by the now-dry Pickerill Fleet. Thus, one of the 'lord's kilns' has been located, and all references to kilns in the accounts imply that they were near the Castle site. Bricks in the later parts of the Castle were made of similar clay. The absence of spoil heaps suggests that the clay dug out of the thirty-foot-wide moat could have been used for brick-making.

(ii) *Hurstmonceux Castle, Sussex* (*Pl. 20*)

The Castle has housed the Royal Observatory, transferred from Greenwich, since 1948. The grounds only are open to the public at limited times, but the Castle tends to be used for a mediaeval background to television films. The fabric is looked after by the Ministry of Public Building and Works. The Castle is still surrounded by its very wide moat.

It dates from the mid fifteenth century and was built by the elder brother of one of the most hated men of the Later Middle Ages. Their father, Sir William Fiennes of Hurstmonceux, had been a very unpopular Mayor of London. He died in 1405 and his brass remains in the parish church. The family could be accused of extortion but not, unlike many 'popular' mediaeval villains, of being parvenus. They had provided hereditary Constables of Dover and Wardens of the Cinque Ports since the Norman Conquest. Hurstmonceux they had acquired in the mid fourteenth century, John de Fiennes having married the heiress Maud de Monceaux. The prefix 'Herst', incidentally, derives from still earlier holders of the manor. A later heiress, who brought more property to the Fiennes family, was the daughter of Lord Say and Sele of Knole.

The Castle-builder was Sir Roger Fiennes, born in 1384, who died a natural death in 1450. He had fought at Agincourt in 1415. From 1439 to 1446 he was Treasurer of the Household of Henry VI. He was Keeper of Porchester Castle, Hampshire. This office he held from 1421 to his death. These posts were very profitable for their holders, especially under the corrupt and expensive government of Henry VI: 'Where the cat is a kitoun (kitten), the land is full eyling (ailing)' was a contemporary judgement. From 1447 Sir Roger Fiennes disappeared from his usual membership of Parliament: evidently his younger brother, James, had become more important in the state. It was the marriage of Roger's son Richard with the heiress of Sir Thomas Dacre which brought that property and name into the family. Roger Fiennes himself also built in brick at the parish church, which has the Dacre Chapel (described in the Gazetteer entry). Sir James held the great family property of Knole, later acquired by the Archbishopric of Canterbury. James gained his title of Lord Say and Sele (which may be abbreviated to 'Lord Say') in 1447, and became Lord Treasurer in 1449. His daughter was married to William Crowmer, Sheriff of Kent, an office which James himself had held in the past. Apart from local extortions, the main cause of James's unpopularity was that he had helped negotiate the marriage of the foreign Queen, Margaret of Anjou, with Henry VI, which involved the English giving up their French territories of Maine and Anjou. The end of the Hundred Years War was a story of heavy costs, taxation and losses of battles and lands. In the course of the Jack Cade Revolt in 1450, which was of Kentish origins, Lord Say and his son-in-law were 'executed' by beheading by the rebels in London. This diversion to the affairs of the builder's brother is a necessary counterbalance to Hurstmonceux's fairytale appearance, and even to its warm peach-coloured bricks, should brick suggest simply domesticity. Set unstrategically, though, at the end of a small valley, the moated castle floats like some Continental dream of feudalism. The strong batter may in fact have protected against damp rather than the siege engines of a still earlier period, but there was no chance of the mid fifteenth-century mob penetrating these defences.

The licence to crenellate was dated 5 February, 1441. Roger Fiennes was also permitted to enclose six hundred acres for his park. The Castle replaced an earlier manor house, which was destroyed. The building accounts survive, showing that the cost of building was £3,800! The money evidently came in part from Hundred Years War profits, such as ransoms, as at Caister Castle. W. Douglas Simpson suggests that the master mason was William Vesey, the King's Serjeant, employed by Henry VI at Eton College and Windsor. Indeed, provision for retainers led to certain similarities with a collegiate foundation: the original main court here, now part of the sole court and very much restored, was arcaded. In his *Castles in Britain* (1966) Simpson says: 'The Green Court, around which were grouped the state rooms, has clearly been modelled on contemporary collegiate buildings, such as Eton or Queens' College, Cambridge. It is interesting to note that the highly specialized, rigidly disciplined household of a great fifteenth-century landlord was demanding the same standard accommodation . . . A great baron's household in the later Middle Ages was in a very real sense a college.' As long ago as the eighteenth century Horace Walpole pointed out the likeness between the cloistered Green Court here and that of Eton. The comparison with Queens' College makes us think of the quadrangle buildings of Oxborough Hall in Norfolk which, despite its massive gate tower, is not well defended. Though fairly large, the Green Court was quite unlike a basecourt intended for military muster. Besides its servants and some craftsmen and clerics, such a community mainly consisted of estate administrators, clerks and armed retainers. As Treasurer of the Household, Fiennes would have been involved in the King's Works at Eton, for which there were brickworks at Slough, organized by Vesey. At Hurstmonceux the clay used must have come from close by: indeed, as A. Clifton-Taylor points out, even what was dug out for the moat could have been utilized. The hybrid nature of the building is emphasized by the comparisons—besides those with Eton—and contrasts made between it and the smaller, stone-built Bodiam Castle nearby (also in Sussex). Bodiam, which survives roofless, was a real military castle, unique in that it was licensed as part of the national defences, though belonging to and erected by a private citizen, Sir Edward Dalyngrigge. It was built from 1385 on, beside the River Rother which was then accessible to foreign invasion: the licence cites the danger of French raids. There was a rather smaller, more privateering, element of such danger in Henry VI's reign too, which could have marginally influenced Hurstmonceux. The danger of invasion was at its greatest when the Duke of Burgundy changed from the English to the French side in 1435, and a valuable neighbour and ally became hostile—effectively so, for this was one of the causes of the final French victory. Hurstmonceux was built on the plan of Bodiam, but with polygonal towers or turrets instead of round ones and, it seems, a more elaborate scheme of courts—the Green Court and three smaller ones. Bodiam has fewer but stronger towers. Despite the moat and the gatehouse, with its portcullis grooves and machicolations, and the battlements, Hurstmonceux's turrets are mainly for show. R. Allen Brown notes 'the thin walls and slender towers of this brick structure', which 'give the lie to [its] imposing appearance'. We can contrast these house-type walls with those of traditional castles, and even with the great brick tower-house of Tattershall.

The ground plan is a great square, about 219 by 208 feet externally. The walls incorporate the gatehouse, of about 1445, with its twin turrets, of which the two upper stages are round; four corner towers; eleven interval towers. The north entry is a single tower only. The whole shell of the Castle remains, restored in part, but the interior divisions and the courtyard buildings have disappeared. Despite the coherent appearance, some of the building was done later, in Henry VII's reign and even in the sixteenth century, still during Fiennes ownership, the head of the family now holding the title of 'Lord Dacre'. One section that was never completed was the (subsidiary) north barbican. In 1708 the Castle was sold for £38,215, but by the end of the eighteenth century deliberate destruction and decay had 'gutted' it, though some plans had been made as records. The greatest damage was done in 1777 by the second wife of Canon Hare, the first owner belonging to this family. She intended to stop the children of his first wife from inheriting it. Some materials were then used in building a house for her own children. The art collection she also disposed of, but as old-fashioned. The place was reduced to a shell, quite hollow. A 1900 photograph shows roofless towers, and thick ivy ramping up the gatehouse walls. Then, about 1910, Colonel Lowther began restoration, living in a house made out of the ruins on the south side. The great hall is mainly 1913 work. The major work of restoration, however, was done by Walter Godfrey, architect and historian, for Sir Paul Latham from 1933 to 1935. This was a most careful renewal, though there was no attempt to recreate the lost interior or courtyard buildings, and their detailed plan is unknown, not even revealed by excavation. A modern set of buildings was erected inside the mediaeval shell and new sets of rooms joined on to it. The original parts remaining, as well as the outside walls with their towers and the gatehouse, are these: circular staircase and ground floor, with stair lobby, of the great gatehouse; one wall of the chapel; one range wall; some other interior walling. The battlements were Godfrey's (restoration), and the moulded brick chimneys. So were the outer arches of the south bridge, but the inner arches and cutwaters are original, as Nairn and Pevsner confirm. The Astronomer Royal contributes a Union Jack, and there are Observatory telescope domes on the eastern slope beyond the moat.

The pinkish bricks are laid in English bond. There is some irregular diapering, with *paler* bricks, on the gatehouse turrets and between the interval towers. The bridge is also diapered. It is wholly brick, with shallow projections between the rounded arches. The dressings of the Castle are of stone, including the gatehouse's deep machicolations. These were a French-drived fashion, 'mâchicolis' with round arches—here with brick voussoirs—that link the stepped stone corbels. (See also Caister and Tattershall, where the corbels are brick nor stone.) The dressings at Hurstmonceux are of pale greensand stone. Above the tall moulded arch, with four-centred head, into which the portcullis fitted, is a rectangular stone panel with the Fiennes arms. There are stone capings to the plinth, the base of the Castle walls having a batter several feet high, and steeper on the towers, for strength and perhaps for defence. Nathaniel Lloyd pointed out small bricks in the batter of the south front as Dutch imports. Above the batter are two-storeyed sets of rooms throughout, though the angle towers and the central east and west towers rise fifteen feet from the main parapet level and are octagonal. The rounded gatehouse towers, in two sections—divided by the machicolations which circle the whole gatehouse—have an extra thirty feet. The symmetry is early and striking. It is that of a great mansion. There are even tall bay windows, though not on the south front. The details mix defence and display. There are the stone-coped battlements and cross-shaped arrow-slits and even, immediately below these, the round gunloops of a new age. Slits and loops are of stone: gunloops are also found at Kirby Muxloe, of the 1480s. Yet the square-headed windows are too big and the walls too thin for standing any type of siege except isolation.

The gatehouse turrets, polygonal to the second stage and rounded above that, have a topmost section recessed well behind the projecting battlements. There are flying steps up to this from the alure. The door has a four-centred arch and above it, between the portculis grooves, is a large square-headed window with twin arched lights; above that is the Fiennes arms panel between smaller windows. Inside, the ground floor of the gatehouse has its original lierne-vaulted ceiling, the springers rising direct from the walls, not from corbels. Nairn and Pevsner say this vault has the form of a Greek cross (like a multiplication sign). They note an original fireplace set, 'curiously', in the gatehouse passage. The hall, its bay window in the centre of the west wall, is a modern replacement: it was built in the usual position, in the north range of the court, over against the gatehouse. The lord's apartments were evidently concentrated against the east wall, with the chapel. Simpson says the state rooms and guest apartments were on the east and north of the Castle; on the west and south were the administrative rooms and domestic offices. The chapel, on the first floor, is partly original and a very interesting structure. The apse was canted out from the middle of the Castle's east wall, forming part of a polygonal turret, the topmost section, above the main battlements, being octagonal. The apse has tall thin windows, now with square heads, but A. Hamilton Thompson's *Military Architecture in England during the Middle Ages*, published in 1912 before restoration was begun, showed that the windows had round-arched lights. The chapel vault was of brick. Despite his military title, Thompson described Hurstmonceux as a castle 'only in name'.

The Castle is part of the mid fifteenth-century fashion for brick, and part also of the transition from defence to domesticity in the homes of great lords. The result is exotic, in spite of the mellow colouring of the bricks and the undramatic situation, *low* in an enclave.

(iii) *Tattershall Castle*, *Lincolnshire* (*Fig. 3(d); Pls. 21 and 22*)

The Castle is open to the public, and is administered by the National Trust. The keep or tower-house is alone virtually intact: it is 112 feet high to the top of the angle turrets and the exterior ground plan is 87 by 67 feet. Of deep red brick, it is visible for miles in the flat landscape of Lindsey. One high gable-end of the great stable and, complete though altered, the inner gatehouse, or 'Guard House', also remain. The Castle area is doubly moated and the tower has water lapping three sides. Nineteenth-century engravings show that the corner turrets were once roofed with lead-covered cones, which have not been replaced. Lord Curzon restored the tower fully, after rescuing the huge stone fireplaces then on their way to the United States. He bought the Castle in 1912, and later gave Bodiam, Sussex, and Tattershall Castle to the nation.

The builder, Ralph third Lord Cromwell, made some use of the extant castle of the de Tateshale family on this site, just as he made some use of the old parish church—but likewise completely transformed it. Cromwell was Treasurer to Henry VI. Cromwell's chief executor, who finished the church building, was a Chancellor of England, Bishop William Waynflete. It is suggested that the school at Tattershall was inspired by the royal foundation of Eton College, of which Waynflete was a chief executive, although here the parish church was also to serve the school, in contrast to the special chapel built at Eton. Remembering the (rebuilt) almshouses too, the scale of Cromwell's activities here can be seen as those of a multi-millionaire. He also built mansions at South Wingfield, Derby, and at Collyweston in Northamptonshire, besides Collyweston church. These were of stone (and Collyweston is famous for its slates). It was at Collyweston that he made his will in 1451, providing money for three thousand chantry masses for himself. With Cromwell scale must be the beginning of comprehension: it is known not just from looking at the surviving buildings, but from the contemporary records of the estate (which are among the manuscripts of Lord De l'Isle and Dudley at Penshurst in Kent) and from other sources, such as the 1436 tax records and the description of Tattershall by William of Worcester, secretary to Sir John Fastolf of Caister. Worcester said Cromwell's household of retainers totalled one hundred: this group excludes all servants and craftsmen, representing solely the type of liveried henchmen legislated against in 1377, 1450 and 1487. It was for the retention of such men that John de Vere, Earl of Oxford (of Castle Hedingham, Essex), was fined fifteen hundred marks at the end of the fifteenth century, after Henry VII had cracked down on livery and maintenance. Worcester also said that when Cromwell rode to London he normally took a suite of one hundred and twenty horsemen. In 1432 a worried government forbade certain lords to come to London with overlarge retinues: Cromwell was one of those named. The following year, however, he was made Lord Treasurer.

Cromwell's Tattershall Castle has been the subject of modern debate: was the great tower built for defence or as a luxurious tower-house, the administrative centre of great estates? The latter element is the stronger. W. D. Simpson (in the *Archaeological Journal*, 1939) stressed that the tower 'does not form a complete house by itself, but is simply a glorified solar block . . . Moreover, its martial garniture is largely for appearance sake; it is mere *appareil feodal*'. Elsewhere Simpson cites the architectural inspiration as being derived from 'such contemporary European parallels as the great tower of the *Palais de Justice* at Poitiers, or the palace of the Grand Master of the Teutonic Order at Marienburg'. This assessment comes partly from Cromwell's use of an old castle and its site and partly from the fact of the tower's being linked on to

Cromwell's previously built great hall. The holes for the connecting beams are still visible on the west face. Thus the tower did not stand in the present defensive isolation. Tattershall does, though, have its moats, and the tower does have deep machicolations. Simpson also mentions other North German or Hanseatic influences on the brickwork. At Boston, to the south, where Cromwell had brick kilns, there was an important Hansa office. Of this the great parish church has one souvenir, a Tournai marble slab of 1340, bearing the six-foot canopied effigy of Wissel Smalenburg, a Hanseatic merchant of Münster.

Cromwell also gave his mansion at South Wingfield a four-storey fortified tower, and there were two baileys, though this was certainly a house, not a castle. It survives, in ruins. He may have felt relatively secure in this more conservative part of the country. The government faced much more unrest in East Anglia and the South, the Home Counties, especially in Kent and Sussex. The economic causes of this trouble were often crystallized by taxation: just as the immediate stimulus of the 1381 Peasants' Revolt, when Sudbury the Chancellor and Hales the Treasurer were assassinated, was the regressive poll tax. After Cromwell had built most of Tattershall Castle, in one year (1450) these unpopular leading (or only recently discarded) government officers were murdered: Bishop Adam Moleyns (at Portsmouth), William de la Pole (on a ship in the Channel) and, when the Kent-centred Cade Rebellion broke out, Bishop William Ayscough and Lord Saye and Sele. Saye and Sele (James Fiennes of Knole) was the Treasurer and a successor of Cromwell's in this office. Cromwell was the King's Treasurer from 1433 to 1443. Latterly, however, towards the end of his life, his fears of the consequences of Henry VI's insecurity apparently made him something of a Yorkist. The brawl-begun first Battle of St Albans confirmed this tendency in him. Indeed, Richard Beauchamp, 'Warwick the Kingmaker', was to say that Cromwell had been the 'beginner of all that journey (trouble) at Seynt Albonez'. In 1453 he had been suspected of plotting a rising for York. It is significant that the Statutes against Livery and Maintenance, of fourteenth-century origin and being legislation against private armies in the main, had been repeated in 1450. This Battle of Saint Albans was the first of a series that escalated into the Wars of the Roses. Cromwell did not live on into the civil wars, but died on 4 January 1456.

Besides having married an heiress, fighting on the Continent in the Agincourt campaign had brought him a fortune. Cromwell thereafter accumulated wealth in two main ways, as official and as farmer of estates. His royal service culminated in its most profitable office, the treasurer-ship held from 1433 to

1443. His family origins were in Nottinghamshire, and his total inheritance of land was small in comparison with that of many nobles. To speculate about motivation may be rash, but his initial drive may have been determination to compensate for the two-thirds practical loss to that inheritance caused by the long survival of two dowagers (his mother and grandmother). In 1429, it has been calculated from the records, the annual income from the lands of Cromwell and his wife was £1,020. He had inherited Tattershall (ultimately from the 1367 marriage of his grandfather, Ralph Lord Cromwell, with the heiress of the then holders, the Driby family). In 1430 the estates were worth £1,364, including Lincolnshire estates worth £424 a year. By 1455 the worth of the Lincolnshire estates alone had risen to £1,140. In one year in the 1450s—the exact date is lost—the annual value of all the estates had risen to £2,263. About 1465, his executors valued the goods and cash he had left at £21,456, and calculated that he had given in his lifetime £2,666-odd in jewels and vestments to Tattershall College. He was, of course, one of England's very richest men, property interests being supplemented by mercantile enterprises.

For Tattershall, for which the main building period was 1435 to 1445, he organized brickworks at Edlington Moor (see the Gazetteer entry), but he had brick kilns at Boston used for commercial purposes too. In 1434/5, for example, 8,000 bricks from Boston were sold and delivered to the Abbot of Bardney, Lincolnshire, as part of an order for 20,000. In the same year bricks for the Castle were being made at both Boston and Edlington Moor. In 1445–6 Baldwin Dutchman made one million bricks at Edlington for the Castle. Apparently, for the great tower, 322,000 bricks were needed. The fabric bricks measure 8 or $8\frac{1}{2} \times 4 \times 2$ inches. Smaller shaped bricks were used for the parapets, turret corbel-tables and other details. In the accounts the term 'walltiles' is used for smaller bricks and the main fabric bricks are called 'brekes'. One of the factors the accounts show is the predominance of Flemish or North German workers, described as 'brekemasons'. The 'brekemaker' was 'Bawdwin Docheman' or Baldwin Dutchman, who organized the Edlington kilns. Interestingly, in 1458 his widow was paid £11. 13*s*. 4*d*. for the making and burning (firing) of 160,000 tiles. William of Worcester calculated that Tattershall had cost 'above 4,000 marks', which seems confirmation that his costing of Caister Castle at £6,000 was an overestimate.

This spectacular background shows that brick was a prestigious choice. Cromwell could obviously have used local stone, like the de Tateshales, but the Ancaster stone used is limited to quoins, stringcourses, voids and the splendidly carved fireplaces (though not for the firebacks). The inner moat is brick-revetted. Lost brick buildings can be seen in the detailed 1726 engraving by Samuel Buck, besides the two surviving low, round, stone towers of the de Tateshales. These were of thirteenth-century date, and between them Cromwell set his great rectangular tower. Tattershall Church, it should be remembered, is of Ancaster stone and is 186 foot long—completed in the 1480s by Waynflete, whose arms appear over the south porch. The Castle Guardhouse is fairly small and two-storeyed, with a steep roof and projecting chimney-stack. Stone is used for its doors and windows. The big solitary gable-end survives from the stables: records show that 'hewentiles', the term used here for moulded (not cut) bricks, were used for the windows and chimneys of this building.

The great tower has five storeys, including the basement where the walls are about twenty feet thick, adjoining the moat. The tower is not self-contained, having no kitchen—meals would have been served in the lost great hall—but constitutes luxurious living-rooms. There are forty-eight rooms in all, with garderobes on each floor, the polygonal angle turrets contributing many small rooms. The principal rooms are the great chambers on the first and second floors, with their fireplaces carved with Cromwell's fat purse emblem. Each of the four upper storeys has its fireplace, using the single chimney-stack that rises above the battlements. Externally, the tower is of red and red-brown bricks, with irregular diapering in blue. The main features are the deep triple courses of the machicolations, which have linking archlets: above is a parapet walk. On the second floor is a thirty-eight foot gallery. More unexpectedly, the second floor also has a large dovecote of timber and plaster, built like a partition wall.

The spiral stairs are wholly stone—steps, newels and handrails. They are not vaulted, because the steps are set directly in newel and walls. We may compare the wood steps at Old Warden Abbey in Bedfordshire. Otherwise, the elements of the interior are brick and often impressive, especially the narrow but elaborate vaulting of the passages, with lierne ribs that have cusped decoration. The window soffits are vaulted, for the embrasures are deep. In places the vaulting was plastered over and then white lines were painted on the plaster to imitate mortar joints! A. Clifton-Taylor singles out for praise 'the ribbed vaults of moulded brick' to some of the upstairs window recesses and lobbies and the high second-floor corridor. The cusping includes the curved 'dagger' motif.

Work, as noted, continued after Cromwell's death in 1456, though the Moor Tower at Woodhall (see Gazetteer) was allowed to decay. Besides the payment to Baldwin Dutchman's widow (not the only widow to continue her husband's business) in 1458, Peter Lyndon, another 'Docheman', was paid

£3. 5*s*. 10*d*. in the same year for building a square tower at the north-east corner of the site. Accounts were kept till 1472, by the executors. Cromwell had no son, but the estate did not escheat to the Crown because his niece, Maud, who was married to Sir Thomas Neville, took it over. Neville, however, was killed at the Battle of Wakefield in 1460, when his leader, Richard Duke of York, was also killed—following his abortive claim to the Crown. This brought Tattershall to Lancaster and finally to the house of Tudor. Henry VII's mother, Lady Margaret Beaufort, lived here for a time. Henry VIII granted the estate to Charles Brandon, Duke of Suffolk, after his impetuous marriage in 1520 to the Princess Mary. Lady Margaret Beaufort left money which was used for the brick-built colleges of Christ's and St. John's at Cambridge, and the Suffolks were to become brick-builders in Suffolk. In 1551 Edward VI granted Tattershall to the Earl of Lincoln and his heirs. In 1911 it was sold, and the dismantled fireplaces had already reached the London Docks, when George Nathaniel Curzon, Marquis of Kedleston, stepped in magnificently and, finally, munificently.

(iv) *Kirby Muxloe Castle, Leicestershire* (*Pls. 26 and 27*)

Kirby Muxloe lies four miles west of Leicester. The Castle is open to the public, being administered by the Ministry of Public Buildings and Works. The Castle is in ruins, but these are impressive. The full castle area of 175 × 245 feet is clearly defined by walls or foundations, including the brick platform. 'The internal measurements of the court were about 100 × 160 feet' (H.M.S.O. guide). The moat beyond, externally 100 × 120 yards, is a Ministry restoration. The Castle site was presented to the then 'Commissioners of Works' in 1911.

William Lord Hastings had the Castle erected from 1480 on, of red brick with stone dressings. He was a Yorkist leader and favourite of Edward IV. When that King died, Richard of Gloucester, soon afterwards Richard III, became suspicious of Hastings and executed him for treason. This was in June, 1483. Rather surprisingly the widow, Katherine, the daughter of Richard Neville (Earl of Salisbury), continued the building at Kirby Muxloe until 1484. She spent only £61 in the year, whereas Hastings had spent upwards of £1,000 in three years. He was one of the richest men in England at the period. He was no mere Yorkist partisan, but a man with a standing abroad. In 1474 he had gained licence to crenellate *three* houses in Leicestershire: Ashby, Bagworth and Kirby. The parks licences were for 3,000, 2,000 and 2,000 acres respectively! Bagworth was recorded by Leland in the mid sixteenth century as already being in ruins, but Ashby-de-la-Zouch and

Kirby Muxloe still have considerable buildings. (For Ashby see the entry in the Gazetteer.) The Kirby estate had been in the Hastings family hands from the fourteenth century, but Ashby was a recent, partisan gain: it was granted to William Hastings after its Lancastrian owner, James Butler, Earl of Ormond, had been executed following the Yorkist victory of Towton in 1460. Thus these crenellations had a Wars of the Roses context. At Ashby Hastings kept more of the earlier castle buildings and built his tower-house there and the parish church of stone. His finances need explaining. In his article, 'The Castles of Dudley and Ashby-de-la-Zouch' (in the *Archaeological Journal*, XCVI, 1939), W. Douglas Simpson lists some of Hastings's state offices: High Chamberlain of the Royal Household, Receiver of the royal Duchy of Lancaster (taken over by York), Master of the Mint, Chamberlain of North Wales, Lieutenant of Calais. Besides the incomes from these offices and his vast estates, Hastings even had a pension from the French King, Louis XI. To build both Ashby and Kirby, even unfinished, besides whatever buildings were erected at Bagworth, was an outstanding achievement—like that of Thomas Cromwell of Tattershall. Hastings, moreover, was building during the distractions of the era of the Wars of the Roses.

The building accounts of Kirby, apparently complete, survive. They go from the start of the work on 23 April 1480 to 6 December 1484, when the work was abandoned by Lady Hastings. There were the usual lulls for the winters. The accounts were written mainly in Latin, with some English and French wording too. The total cost recorded was £1,088. 17*s*. 6¾*d*., still a vast sum for the Middle Ages but comparatively low because the buildings were not finished. In the first season of work bricks were made and stacked by the thousand at the 'Breke house', the kiln run by John Eles *somewhere* (unknown) near Kirby. The firing—the contemporary term is burning—was supervised by an immigrant, 'Antony Docheman'. The transport costs from kiln to site are recorded. Flemish influence was apparently strong, but the master mason was John Cowper, who also worked at Tattershall.

Absorbed in the 800 foot square site was the earlier stone-built house, of which the foundations have been excavated. The plan of the fourteenth-century house has been marked out on the lawn inside. Hastings used the old great hall and its offices, though the walls were refaced with brick. The old gatehouse and other buildings were demolished. The moat was constructed by Hastings, and the brick platform built out to its edges. The Castle, quadrangular in plan, was given tall projecting angle towers linked by recessed rampart walls. There were (lost) interval towers in the centre of the east, south and west walls. The gatehouse, in the centre of the north range, is rectangular. The interior ranges of Hastings's buildings are now lost, but apparently they were two storeys high and set close to the ramparts. The gatehouse, though it was left unfinished and the walls just thatched over, survives. So does the west tower, complete. There are other, fragmentary, parts. Of the three other angle towers, all are traceable, but one only has a small section of walling (of an angle) standing.

The lower sections of the gatehouse turrets are blank except for stone gunports. These may give the impression of defensibility, especially when one remembers that gunports were an innovation at this date, intended for portable guns. These ones are, it seems, called in the accounts 'murder holes', but there are also real 'meurtrières' in the brick vaulting of the entrance passage. For these compare see also Deal and Walmer Castles, Kent. Then one looks at the line of fire from each gunport, and realizes that the other walls would have suffered. This misplacement occurs not only in the gatehouse, but 'the same thing would have happened on every rampart walk all round the castle' (Sir Charles Peers, in the Ministry guide). Indeed, W. G. Hoskins insists that Kirby Muxloe is a fortified house, not a castle at all. R. Allen Brown, too, (in *English Mediaeval Castles*) wrote: 'The structure itself is typical of the fortified manors of the Later Middle Ages, and though it is now referred to by common courtesy as a Castle, it is worth noticing that it is never so called in the surviving accounts.' On the other hand, despite the miscalculations, 'this castle seems to be the first example in England of a building systematically equipped for hand guns—though, to be sure, the provision made is sometimes naive enough' is the judgement of W. D. Simpson. As was typical of later castles or fortified halls, there was one focal point for defence, in this case the 'massive gatehouse, the strongest and most seriously intended part of the building' (R. Allen Brown). Unfortunately, the never-finished gatehouse is more ruinous than the west tower, rising only to the level of the first-floor window lintels. The portcullis was operated from the first floor, where the chamber was fitted out as two rooms with a wood partition, a non-defensive arrangement.

Despite the comparatively minor use of stone, which the accounts show to have come from several quarries, including Alton, there seems to be no moulded brick. The shaped bricks were cut, and we find the term 'hewen' (cut) in the accounts. Decoration is generally contributed by diamond diapering with black bricks, but there is more complex work on the gatehouse front: a ship, the initials 'W.H.' and the Hastings maunch (sleeve) badge. The maunch is formed of thin red bricks in a patch of dark bricks. More Hastings heraldry, incidentally, can be seen on the tomb and alabaster effigy of William

Lord Hastings, in his chantry chapel in St George's Chapel, Windsor. The Kirby gatehouse has stone stringcourses and square windows, and over the archway is a big stone panel. Inside are brick fireplaces and flues. The vaulting of the passage is mostly lost, but the ground-floor rooms have simple barrel vaults of brick. The front turrets had the garderobes; the rear turrets brick stairs.

The west, or more strictly north-west, angle tower is complete. It is of three storeys and square, with a projecting square stair turret of four stages. The brick is diamond-diapered. Sidney Toy in *The Castles of Great Britain*, (1953) describes the spiral stairs of the angle tower and of the gatehouse turrets. They are: 'constructed entirely of brick. The intricate curves and sweeps of the underside of the spiral vaults on which the treads are built are formed with remarkable skill and address; the treads are of specially selected bricks laid on edge.' The newels are made with horizontally laid bricks, one end rounded. As with other fifteenth-century stairs, this vaulting is the product of extremely careful gauging.

The accounts reveal such details as the existence of a forge on the site, the smith being paid on piecework, and the regular sharpening of the brick axes. In June 1481 the master mason's leading assistant was sent to Tattershall to study the work there, and in October John Cowper himself revisited Tattershall. In 1484 work was abandoned by Lady Hastings, and Kirby Muxloe Castle itself seems early to have been abandoned in favour of Ashby-de-la-Zouch, where new buildings of Tudor brick were to be erected. Kirby, though, was Hastings family property till 1630. By 1911 trees were sprouting where materials had been removed for buildings elsewhere. Only the strength of the brickwork saved the basic plan, the square tower and the great gatehouse. The major piece of restoration done between 1911 and 1913 was the replacement of a five-foot layer of brick above the moat's water-level, where the facing had cracked off through the action of damp and frost. The underwater brick was undamaged. Brick and stone pipes and drains were found, and sluices for the moat. Buildings outside the moat are mentioned in the accounts, but, apart from the foundations of a square dovecote and a well, all traces of these and the garden and orchard are lost. The consequent isolation of the castle, or fortified manor, perhaps emphasizes its rare and remarkable symmetry for its date. The plan shows up most strikingly in aerial photographs.

CHAPTER IV

Brick for the bishop's palace

WHEN John Leland recorded that brick and tile were replacing timber and thatch in the London region, he was writing of Early Tudor domestic building. Although the brick churches and added chapels or porches of Essex and its borders were many, such usage was unusual overall. It was for manor houses and even palaces that brick was the newly fashionable material. This was not just in and about London, but east of the line from Hampshire to Yorkshire, with East Anglia still predominant. This type of popularity was partly the result of certain lay or ecclesiastical lords having chosen this manufactured material, and partly the result of convenience and economics. The bricks, I believe, were normally made at or close to the building site. It was a fashion, though, that could only have developed strongly at a time when internal peace was the norm, since brick was far more suitable for domestic building than for genuine castles liable to be attacked by cannon. Besides, brick had new decorative possibilities with or, more rarely, without stone dressings. The Waynflete towers and Hatfield Old Bishop's Palace exemplify the combination of brick fabric and brick dressings. The specific period was the major part of Edward IV's reign, when the country had its first firm government for decades.

13. Hatfield Old Bishop's Palace, Herts. Diapered entrance tower to great hall range, 1480.

The earlier post-Roman brick is scattered and seemingly lacked any social pattern. The outstanding brick buildings of the mid fifteenth century, the castles—Caister, Hurstmonceux, Kirby Muxloe, Tattershall—are splendid but atypical. Later battlemented gatehouses and angle turrets, as well as moats, seem to have been just ornamental, status-full derivations. They were constructed for facing up to possible aggressive mobs rather than to military attack. The great houses with these motifs were just as much domestic architecture as were the less expensive timber-framed and brick-nogged homes, vernacular buildings the majority of which surely disappeared long ago, especially in towns.

There seems to be only one coherent, identifiable group of fifteenth-century people who stimulated the simultaneous fashions for brick, domestcity and comfort; that is the bishops. They form an 'establishment' group whose buildings can be linked with the numerous and undefended Tudor and Elizabethan brick houses, both grand and ordinary. Significantly, the bishops' houses more often than not lack even battlements.

True, there are the Cambridge colleges, with their two-storeyed ranges and courtyard plan, but these are not a type apart. Not only was education ecclesiastical still, but our bishops were deeply involved at Cambridge, and there are likenesses between the brick palaces and the college buildings. Rotherham of York contributed to Queens' College (brick), to the *old* King's College (stone, absorbed into Old Schools) and to Lincoln College at Oxford. Alcock of Ely founded Jesus College—the turretless gate of which is like the North Bar of his native Beverley (Yorkshire)—and endowed Peterhouse (stone with some brick). In the early sixteenth century John Fisher of Rochester was responsible for the brick-built first courts of Christ's and St John's Colleges, the Lady Margaret Beaufort foundations. These colleges have turreted gatehouses in a style Henry VIII himself followed at Trinity College. The Oxford college buildings, however, continued to be built of the local stones. They included Rotherham's Lincoln College gatehouse, Fox's Corpus Christi and Wolsey's Cardinal's College (later Christ Church). Everywhere else, though, Wolsey employed brick—in his own homes, the Ipswich school, and East Bergholt and Sandon churches.

Royal enterprises were generally too large to be comparable. They were backed by the resources of the chancellery and perhaps even the wardrobe or the privy purse. There is one set of educational buildings, however, which forms both an architectural and a political link between our bishops' palaces and the royal enterprises. These are the turrets and ranges of Eton College—but the contemporary chapel is of stone—on which work was begun in the late 1430s, accelerating in the next decade. The founder was Henry VI and the funds were largely royal: indeed the brick-built Eton and the stone-built King's College (new foundation) were extravagant projects against which the peasants and the discontented middle classes complained in the unsettled, and finally anarchic, years that led up to the Wars of the Roses. Expenditure in England itself was attacked, not just the larger resources wasted in France on the tail end of the Hundred Years War.

The King as patron was under fire. Four hundred years later Wordsworth could write: 'Tax not the royal saint with vain expense' on King's College Chapel. The Lancastrian government was under fire, and a leading member, Bishop William Waynflete of Winchester, had his chief palace of Wolvesey, at Winchester, attacked and looted during the 1450 Jack Cade rebellion. Now Waynflete, as Privy Councillor and involved in several royal building projects, was an understandable target for attack. His career illustrates the second half of the fifteenth century's extraordinary mixture of disorder and creativity. His creativity belonged to education, including his founding of an Oxford College which followed the example set earlier by William of Wykeham, Bishop of Winchester, founder of New College. Waynflete's was the stone-built Magdalen College. Already patron and headmaster of Wykeham's Winchester College, the school, Waynflete was to be made first headmaster and then provost of the new royal school at Eton and, finally, executor of the King's will there. In Henry VIII's reign a tall gatehouse, designed by the royal mason Henry Redman, would be added to the demurer ranges of Waynflete's Eton.

On his own behalf Waynflete was a builder in both brick and stone, the reasons for any particular choice apparently being simply geological. He was, too, involved in the disposition of the property of Sir John Fastolf of Caister Castle, who died in 1459, leaving incomplete the brick castle and the chantry or almshouse beside it. Still more interestingly, Waynflete was an executor of Ralph Lord Cromwell (died 1455), late Treasurer of England, was thus responsible for Tattershall Castle work and the completion of the Ancaster stone parish church nearby. Waynflete's origins were in Lincolnshire: he was born at Wainfleet. He went south, as a student, to Oxford. He became Bishop of Winchester in 1449. Apart from the school at Wainfleet, his own brick buildings were in the south: the brick tower added to the old stone castle at Farnham and and the palace at Esher, from which only the watergate tower survives, these being works of 1470 or 1480; the half-timbered, brick-nogged church at Mattingley. The Wainfleet school is a great hall with two formidable angle turrets, quite unlike the more gracious courtyard-plan schools and colleges.

Since he died in 1486, at the then incredible age of ninety-one, Waynflete can only have seen Henry VII as a new warlord, not as part maker of Tudor England's coming stability. The pious hopes expressed in the last speeches of Shakespeare's *Richard III* are anachronistically optimistic: the Battle of Bosworth was followed by years of rebellions. Although Waynflete was so deeply committed to the Lancastrians, and was a personal friend of Henry VI,

14. Eton College, Bucks, Lupton's Tower, 1516–20.

the Duke of York had found him acceptable as Chancellor. His behaviour in that office was as much a contribution to England as were his educational buildings. He was distinguished by his sense, fairness and lack of corruption. He was present as Chancellor at the Coventry Parliament of 1459, at which the Yorkist leaders—whose forces had just suffered heavily in battle at Ludlow—were attainted. He resigned the chancellorship, apparently at this vindictiveness. When the Yorkists succeeded in imprisoning Henry VI and making Edward King, Waynflete was not punished as a Lancastrian: his bishopric was confirmed in 1462, and he received a series of formal pardons. The last was in 1471, almost certainly because he had welcomed the released Henry VI at the beginning of the short Lancastrian revival.

His treatment by the Yorkists was a hopeful sign for the future, earned by his good administration. Lest, however, his career be misinterpreted, that is, understood in too modern or simple or tranquil a way, one should remember the events of the Cade rebellion. In 1450, when the rebels found themselves facing superior forces in London, Waynflete was sent with the then Chancellor, John Kemp, Archbishop of Canterbury, to negotiate with the leaders at St Margaret's Church, Southwark. Full pardon was promised in return for surrender—to men under whose auspices particularly hated government officials had been killed: Bishop Adam Moleyns of Chichester; Bishop William Ayscough at Salisbury, Clerk of the Privy Council; Lord Saye and Sele, the Lord Treasurer; William Crowmer, Sheriff of Kent, where the revolt began. Despite the sacking of his palace, Waynflete personally had not been a real target, which was a tribute to him. After the rebels' surrender Waynflete was appointed one of the Commissioners for their *trial*, which resulted in some death sentences, but many more pardons.

Apart from the buildings, there are other souvenirs of Waynflete. His chantry remains in Winchester Cathedral, but his other chantry chapel at Magdalen College was, strangely, moved to the choir of the church at Theale in Berkshire in 1830, to add tone to 'a wonderful Gothic revival structure, architect E. Garbett 1822' (*Berkshire Architectural Guide*, edited by John Betjeman and John Piper, 1949). Waynflete's Magdalen College chapel was was finished by 1483, but the interior was drastically remodelled in the ealry nineteenth century. The 'Founder's Tower' survives. The College has an authentic portrait of Waynflete, and also papers which passed through his hands when he partly solved the problem over Fastolf's property—by diverting Fastolf's funds for the Caister foundation for seven priests and seven poor men to Magdalen, along with the property of the alien priory of Sele (Sussex) and Selborne Priory (Hampshire), Selborne having been attacked years before by William of Wykeham for its abuses. Waynflete's beautiful coat of arms of lilies remains at the College and on the porch of Tattershall Church.

Waynflete's educational involvement at Winchester, Eton and Oxford (1448) predated his episcopal buildings at Farnham and Esher. The latter belong to the period of strong rule by Edward IV, during which were prefigured improvements in administration and its centralization that Henry VII was to adopt and expand. The Bishop's colleges were not threatened by the

Yorkist government, though there was considerable niggling and hostility over the royal foundation of Eton. His school at Wainfleet belongs to 1484, before Richard III's deterioration.

The comparative peace of the last three decades of the fifteenth century made worthwhile this domestic and institutional building. Many other bishops also provided themselves with combined homes and administrative quarters in their own sees, while their country homes punctuated the roads to London—to Convocation and to Parliament. Such building continued, seemingly with more spaciousness and splendour, into the sixteenth century. Between 1470 and 1520 southern and eastern bishops acted as fashion-leaders, the culmination being Wolsey's Hampton Court, York Place and the Manor of the More. The building of bishops' palaces ended, for decades, at the Dissolution of the Monasteries, when the sees also lost much land and wealth. The rumblings of the coming Reformation had already discouraged building, and the Reformation Parliaments' speeches and Acts drummed in the past 'waste' of resources by worldly prelates—not just abbots. The regular brick builders are not sixteenth-century men: they are John Alcock, John Morton (both died 1500), and Thomas Rotherham (died 1501). The surviving palaces of the Early Tudor period are usually more stately, remote even from the big secular houses and from vernacular building generally. They were erected by still richer men: William Warham (died 1533), Archbishop of Canterbury, and Cardinal Wolsey (died 1530).

The cost of Wolsey's Hampton Court was exceptional, but Warham's Otford Palace in Kent had a recorded cost of £33,000. Warham is a transitional figure: a patron of the New Learning and Chancellor of Oxford, but also—Archbishop and Lord Chancellor of England—a man who lived like a prince. William Lambarde (1536–1601) gave a harsh post-Reformation verdict on this building, which replaced a smaller one erected by Henry Deane, Warham's immediate predecessor only. Lambarde wrote: 'William Warham, wishing to leave to posteritie some glorious monument of his worldly wealth and misbegotten treasure, determined to have raised a glorious palace for himself' (this from the *Perambulation of Kent*, 1576). Indeed, Warham probably kept no more than Deane's chapel. His reformist successor, Thomas Cranmer, was embarrassed by Otford and soon handed it and the deer parks over to Henry VIII. Ironically, the King found the place damp and deserted it: by the mid 1540s the 'monument' of 'worldly wealth' was already dilapidated. Warham had called it his 'power house'. It was only three miles from the great stone house of Knole, which Thomas Bourchier had recently given to the see of Canterbury. Another way of looking at the scale of archiepiscopal building is to look at the number of palaces in a tiny area. There was Charing, too, just seven miles from Canterbury, and Bekesbourne close to Charing.

The remains of the Bekesbourne palace are slight, but they include a small brick range. This is dated, by style, to the early sixteenth century. It could be Warham's, for instance. It bears, however, stone panels with the arms of Cranmer, Archbishop from 1533 and executed in 1555, during the Marian reaction, and of Thomas Parker, Elizabeth I's Archbishop from 1559 to 1575. John Newman points out that the panels are re-set, and earlier dating is more plausible. Cranmer, Protestant reformer and scholar, was no builder, and, style apart, the Reformation discouraged any type of ecclesiastical building. Parker was just the son of a worsted weaver of Norwich, and not a rich man He was another scholar, and translator, who collected books and mediaeval manuscripts, and was a great benefactor to Corpus Christi College, Cambridge, which received many valuable gifts from him, and where he must have gone from the fourteenth-century college buildings to St Benet's Church through the brick gallery of about 1500. In Norwich and Cambridge brick was now an established, even ordinary, part of the environment. Before the Reformation, Parker had been last Dean of Stoke by Clare College in Suffolk, where at least one brick building was erected in the early sixteenth century: the fine surviving dovecote, which is sometimes taken for a gatehouse. Although the College was dissolved, its reputation was high, and Parker was given a good pension.

The mediaeval bishops were great political forces, at least those who held the most important sees. They counted as part of the mediaeval nobility, not only numbered among the lords meeting in Parliament but providing many officers of state. Their power was thus ecclesiastical and secular. They controlled large estates. The Bishop of Durham, indeed, was officially a 'Prince Bishop' with independent jurisdiction. Their willingness or unwillingness to let the Church be taxed by the King was an index of how strong the King was. Besides the two archbishoprics, the greatest sees were Durham, Lincoln, Ely and Winchester. Government office was virtually automatic for these prelates, while the Archbishop of York and the Bishop of Durham were often detailed to protect the English from the Scots. Office brought some bishops into the powerful Privy Council of the King. Often these men already belonged to the nobility by birth; the great William of Wykeham, Bishop of Winchester and Chancellor of England in the mid fourteenth century, was exceptional in his very humble birth, possibly the son of a serf. Later, John Morton, Archbishop of Canterbury, Cardinal, and Lord Chancellor of Henry VII, was another exception. Like those of the dreaded fiscal agents, Empson and

Dudley, Morton's origins were middle-class. Henry VII was, in fact, consciously rejecting the old nobility in favour of men whose loyalty would be personal. In doing this he went against the mediaeval tradition—whereby kings had allied themselves with the already propertied nobility, lay or ecclesiastical, such as the Nevilles, Despensers, Percies and Courtenays—and created his own 'new men'.

Thus it is interesting that the late mediaeval bishops, genuinely part of the power establishment, chose to build in brick, which so far had been more often than not a subsidiary material. The links between them are provable. However erratic the lay kingdom's affairs were, the bishops regularly met and talked in the Convocations of the clergy of the sees of Canterbury and York. This continuity, sometimes involving evasion of partisanship, contrasts with the battles and private wars of the lay nobility—'the kites and crows'. And, if the bishops had to take sides in the Wars of the Roses, it is perhaps fair to say that they also changed sides more successfully. Since bishops' sees were of different values and importance, promotions took place. Rotherham, Alcock and Russell held the see of Rochester in turn. Russell followed Rotherham at Lincoln, and both men built in brick at Buckden, Huntingdonshire, in that see. Alcock followed Morton at Ely. Thomas Bourchier and Morton, who both built in brick at the Croydon Palace, were successive Archbishops of Canterbury. Rotherham and Alcock were personal friends; from April to September 1474 they, uniquely, shared the Lord Chancellorship; Alcock took inspiration for his Jesus College at Cambridge (1496) from Rotherham's newly founded school, Jesus College, at Rotherham in Yorkshire (both brick-built).

Patterns recur at wider intervals. For example, Thomas Rotherham, once Bishop of Rochester, was Chancellor of the University of Cambridge and a founder of Queens' College. John Fisher, Bishop of Rochester, was Chancellor of Cambridge and organized the building of Christ's and St John's Colleges in the years after the death of the foundress, Lady Margaret Beaufort, in 1509. There can have been no other bishop so involved in the life of Cambridge—and all the colleges where Fisher worked had or then acquired brick buildings. As a student, his college was Michaelhouse. A brick-built lodgings block (of the fifteenth century) survives from Michaelhouse. The college was absorbed into Henry VIII's Trinity College after the Dissolution. From 1497 Fisher was Master of Michaelhouse. He became Chancellor of the University in the sixteenth century, fostering new ideas and new studies, and made his physical contribution in the two brick-built colleges of which Lady Margaret Beaufort, encouraged by Fisher, was financier and patron. Of St John's, this was posthumous patronage. At her funeral Fisher wonderfully described her, the mother of a successful usurper of the throne, as 'keeping always her straight measure and offending as little as any creature might'.

Fisher was Chancellor of Cambridge for thirty years, till he was arrested for his refusal to accept the Act of Supremacy. In 1535 he was executed, with Sir Thomas More. During his imprisonment the Pope made Fisher a cardinal. This act so enraged Henry VIII that he swore he should send Fisher's head to Rome, to save the Pope the trouble of sending the cardinal's hat to England. If the Reformation killed Fisher, it also threatened his University's life. The colleges might have been dissolved along with the monasteries. It was initially provided that they should be, and, if this had happened, the new Chancellor of Cambridge, Thomas Cromwell, would have been the experienced agent. There had been some secularization of both education and students, but the monastic connection was very strong, and, indeed, some secular education was provided away in new secular institutions like the legal Inns in London. Colleges like Magdalen and Peterhouse in some ways provided monastic extension courses. The dissolution of university colleges, along with colleges of secular canons and abbeys and priories, was definitely envisaged: even the New Learning was not an unambiguous life-saver. Fisher accepted Greek and Erasmus, even if he could not accept Royal Supremacy, and a man like Cromwell was inclined to view the new studies suspiciously, at best as a misguided distraction or sop and at worst as hypocrisy (rather like a communist viewing a social democrat). In St John's College chapel were stalls by the famous carpenter Thomas Loveday, for which the contract is extant. These were the gift of Fisher, and were carved with his rebus of a fish and an ear of wheat. Cromwell kept the stalls—they still survive—but had Fisher's badges struck away.

There is more to the comparison between Thomas Rotherham and John Fisher than Rochester and Cambridge. Fisher was yet another northerner and, like Alcock, born in Beverley. True, many links may also be found between men who employed the traditional materials for great buildings—stone and, to some extent, flint; the links are really significant in the case of a new material, especially an artifact. There are other, slighter links. Richard Fox, the blind Bishop of Winchester from 1500 to 1528 (when he was ousted by Wolsey), modified Waynflete's Tower at Farnham, and was perhaps also responsible for the odd patches of brickwork in the twelfth-century buildings—and was founder of the Holy Ghost Chapel at Basingstoke, which was built in brick. The other founder was Lord Sandys of the Vyne, the notable brick mansion nearby. Fox's Corpus Christi College at Oxford was, of course, stone-built.

Non-domestic buildings are cited to show how the same men tended to build in brick, but the great influences for the future were their palaces and granges. Episcopal palaces have, perhaps, been less prone to suffer 're-development' than buildings experiencing greater changes in the ways of those who inherit them. The likeliest fates seem to have been eighteenth- or nineteenth-century remodelling or abandonment. Bishopsthorpe was re-modelled. Downham, Esher and others were deserted when episcopal funds shrank after the Reformation. A second reason for abandoning old palaces was the immediate post-Reformation—and later—splitting off of smaller sees, with different centres, as happened to the vast mediaeval diocese of Ely, which had even included Hertfordshire, and to Lincoln. Country palaces especially were abandoned. Most surviving palaces are in ruins: the exceptions are Fulham, Lambeth and Bishopsthorpe, still inhabited, respectively, by the Bishop of London and the Archbishops of Canterbury and York. Fulham Palace illustrates both the growth of London and the shrinking of episcopal resources: it was once just a subordinate, country palace well outside London, built in the 1520s by Richard Fitzjames, Bishop of London. Hampton Court survives triumphantly, but it had ceased to belong to an officer of the church even before Wolsey's death. Like Fulham, it was built in the 1520s—as a home and a country retreat, as least so far as a compulsive statesman could retreat. Even Wolsey's Manor of the More received many official visitors and was the scene of treaty-making. Yet Wolsey did have smaller houses too, such as the brick-built Grange at North Crawley.

One total loss is the uncertainly dated palace at Scrooby, which Leland saw: 'a great manor place . . . (be)longging to tharchbishop of York, buildid yn to (two) courtes', with a great hall partly of brick. John Vesey (or Voysey, alias Harman) built a brick palace for himself at Sutton Coldfield in Warwickshire in the early sixteenth century, though his many benefactions to the town included buildings of stone only. Vesey, Bishop of Exeter 1519 to 1553, also held the office of Lord President of Wales, meaning that he was the King's deputy there. He died, a very old man, at his his own Moor Hall in Sutton Coldfield, his birthplace. Relevant to this context are two of the houses built on the newly bulldozed More Hall site near Rickmansworth. The earlier one is an outlier in date, for which licence to crenellate was obtained in 1426; brick and stone were the specified materials. Martin Biddle's excavations established that this house was of stone-faced brick. It was built as a house for a tenant, at a time when the manor had reverted to crown possession. The builders were Henry Beaufort, Henry VI's great-uncle, and Thomas Langley, Bishop of Durham from 1406 to 1438. Langley also built in brick at his palace of Howden in Yorkshire. (The brick at Beaufort's Holy Cross almshouse near Winchester long postdates him.) Beauforts' involvement at this Hertfordshire manor is easily explained. Bishop of Winchester from 1404 to 1447, he was the most influential prelate in England, deeply involved in state affairs, being Chancellor for both Henry V and the boy-king Henry VI, and lending these monarchs vast sums—£212,000 between 1417 and 1444. But why did the Bishops of Winchester and Durham co-operate in erecting a house in Hertfordshire for a *tenant*? The later house was built as a country palace for himself by Thomas Wolsey, wearing the hat of Abbot of St Albans—since he had acquired the manor through this office—and was all brick.

Here one might note one Abbot, John Penny, who built in brick at Leicester Abbey, before being promoted to the see of Bangor and then that of of Carlisle. The partly mediaeval Headstone Manor at Pinner, with its brick-lined moat, was a house of the archbishopric of Canterbury, but in-inhabited in the later Middle Ages by tenant farmers. Bricks from here dated 1501 would belong to the time of Henry Deane, who had also used brick at Otford. At Bishop's Waltham, Charing, Farnham, Lambeth, Cakeham, Croydon, Howden, Cawood, Bishopsthorpe, brick buildings were added to already established stone palaces. At Esher, though, Waynflete, was responsible for complete redevelopment, on a courtyard plan, in brick, but of this palace only a gatehouse survives—not in its original state, having been given 'Gothick' details in the eighteenth century.

Cross-references amount to a positive network, but the two archbishoprics and the sees of Winchester and Ely keep recurring, besides the chief names, Rotherham, Alcock, Morton and, later, Thomas Wolsey. Despite the southern bias in what survives, the northern origins of both Rotherham and Alcock seem the most important link because of their knowledge of the fourteenth-century town of Hull—its fortified walls and towers, Holy Trinity Church and municipal, mercantile and domestic buildings, all of brick. Hull uniquely showed the material's possibilities, in a region where stone was usually easily obtainable (though not at the marshy Hull site). Alcock's birthplace of Beverley neighbours Hull, where his father had been a burgess. The town of Rotherham is only fifty miles away—the birthplace of Rotherham, who later held the office of Provost of Beverley. Much new work had been done at Hull in the late fourteenth century, including the erection of Michael de la Pole's great house, which came to be known as 'Suffolk Palace' (from his title), and the improved town walls. All this was still intact for Leland to see forty years after the death of these two bishops.

Alcock had a stone chantry chapel built for himself in the brick Holy Trinity Church at Hull, and his nearby Grammar School buildings were of stone also. This choice perhaps partly derived from the decline of Hull's brick industry. To Leland was pointed out the *disused* municipal brickyard, but brick was employed here in Tudor times for Henry VIII's new fortifications. All in all, John Alcock was certainly the greatest builder in our group. He used brick for his own palaces and for the Cambridge College, but the traditional stone for work at Ely Cathedral, Great St Mary's Church at Cambridge and other Cambridgeshire churches, for Westbury Church in Shropshire and the beautiful Little Malvern Abbey Church in Worcestershire. His Ely chantry chapel is wildly ornate, fan-vaulted in clunch. Alcock was Comptroller of Works for Henry VII.

Many of the palaces are fragmentary, and we know there was more brick that has been destroyed, for example at Esher and at Bishop's Waltham. Warham's Malshanger is reduced to little more than a polygonal angle tower. Where, however, complete ranges survive we can see the episcopal style of impressive domesticity. Alcock's Ely is towering but domestic. Warham's Otford was deliberately built for this effect, but only the end tower is a good indication, the attached range being cut down and converted into a low row of cottages. Buckden's towers and part-ranges are domestic, but have a splendour aided by the very dark bricks—and the diapering—as well as the moulded details and the terracotta arms panel of John Russell. It was Russell's predecessor, Rotherham, though, who was the chief builder here. Russell built the brick part of the Chancery at Lincoln. Buckden has lost its courtyards. Hatfield Old Bishop's Palace, though reduced to two ranges only—from its original double courtyard plan—still makes the overriding impression of domesticity. At Hampton Court the splendour is more emphatic, and a contemporary found Wolsey's More Hall in Hertfordshire still grander.

Typical two-storeyed ranges are found at Croydon and Charing in the south, both in particularly complicated sites, where stone was employed before brick. Earlier two-storeyed buildings, each in a complex of different dates and materials, belong to the Yorkshire palaces of Bishopsthorpe and Cawood. Though Rotherham was more consistently a brick-builder than was his friend Alcock, not all the attributions to him are certain. The lost Jesus College at Rotherham, the Cambridge work, Buckden and the two diapered ranges at Bishopsthorpe are definitely his. The list might be augmented by these works: lost buildings in brick or brick with stone at York Place, London (replaced by Wolsey); brick buildings at Someries, outside Luton, which are attributed to either or both Sir John Wenlock and Rotherham, successive holders of the manor; two fifteenth-century brick ranges at Cawood (where Rotherham died of plague in 1501), which postdate the 1420s stone gatehouse erected by John Kemp, on to which these ranges were built. The remains of Cawood have for generations been used as a farmhouse and are somewhat eroded. The apparent absence of any diapering, though, seems an argument for a builder earlier than Rotherham. One regrets the loss of Jesus College, described by Leland as 'a very fair college', of courtyard plan, 'sumptuously buildid of brick'. Nor is the fragment of Wolsey's Ipswich College any guide to Rotherham's; and, anyway, it is thought that the unfinished College had an *irregular* courtyard plan.

The career of John Morton rounds off the Wars of the Roses period, in intervals of which he found time and peace enough to build. He chose brick for his own homes, but was also responsible for stonework at Wisbech Castle and at Oxford, where he was Chancellor, the Canon Law School and St Mary's Church. As Bishop of Ely Morton organized the digging of the twelve-mile drainage cut, still called 'Morton's Leam', from Peterborough to Guyhirn, where it ended at a now-lost brick tower. His rise to ecclesiastical power was aided by Thomas Bourchier, who preceded him at Canterbury. Morton was Bishop of Ely from 1478, gained the archbishopric in 1486 and was made a cardinal in 1493. He was always deeply involved in politics, and in the mid fifteenth century was the only bishop belonging to the Privy Council, which had only about nine members. He favoured the Lancastrians, but achieved pardon and trust from Edward IV, for whom he went on foreign embassies. The trust did not continue in Richard III's reign. Morton acted than as Henry of Richmond's agent, was arrested (like Thomas Rotherham) and imprisoned in Brecknock Castle, and prompted his gaoler, Henry Stafford, Duke of Buckingham, to a revolt—which proved abortive. Stafford was executed; Morton himself escaped to join Richmond in Flanders. When he returned to England after Henry VII's triumph, the new King made him Lord Chancellor, in succession to Alcock of Ely, and promoted his election as Archbishop of Canterbury. He was to serve Henry VII in developing the Tudor monarchy, towards which Edward IV's achievements contributed. Other bishops who similarly served the 'new monarchy' were Richard Fox of Winchester, and then William Warham and Thomas Wolsey. The marvellous casuistry of the 'Morton's Fork' argument, for taking money 'benevolences' from both sumptuous and simple livers, is traditionally credited to Morton, but is now thought to have been Fox's invention. Morton's participation in government is reflected in his being given a warrant in 1493, like a royal works officer, to impress workmen to repair the archbishopric's

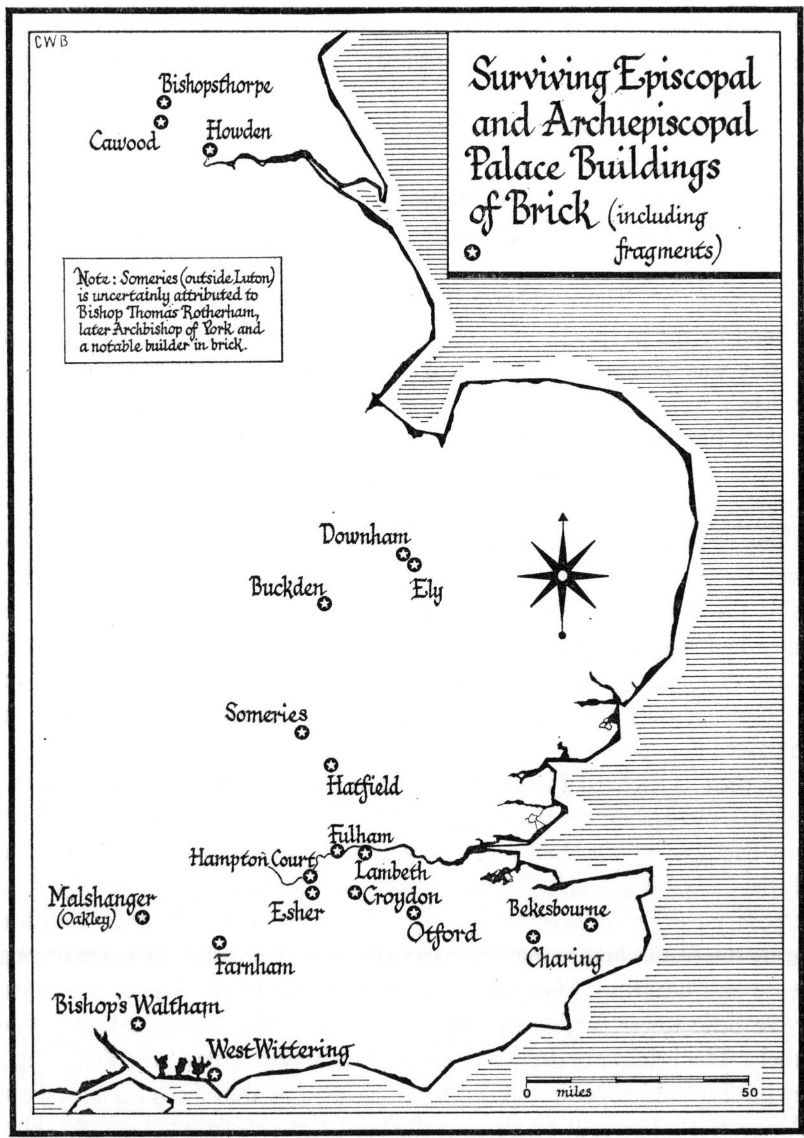

15. SURVIVING EPISCOPAL AND ARCHIEPISCOPAL PALACE BUILDINGS OF BRICK.

houses in Kent, Sussex and Surrey, and in his employment of a royal mason, John Westell, on the Canterbury Cathedral cross-tower, which, is brick-lined.

Despite this background of politics and even violence, Morton's Hatfield, Charing and Croydon ranges look peaceable enough. The brick dressings of Hatfield were not repeated at the post-Bosworth buildings, which included the Lambeth Palace gatehouse. Interestingly, Croydon and Lambeth, close though they are, have bricks of different size. Lambeth, in fact, spoils our main argument. The gatehouse is grim, once used as a prison, scarcely softened by the purple diaper decoration. It looks military, though the wide archway was obviously not practical for defence against true military attack and had a well-lit room over it. The towers and gatehouses of Otford, Malshanger, Farnham, Esher and even Buckden lack any trace of this ferocious character. The irregularly shaped tower of Cakeham Manor, near West Wittering in Sussex, was built as an outlook tower or as a landmark or both, nothing military: it is a country house tower, much like the Elizabethan brick tower Sir Thomas Hoby added to the stone-built former Abbey of Bisham beside the Thames in Berkshire. Adam Moleyns, as Bishop of Chichester, had gained a licence to crenellate—or really fortify—this house in the 1440s, though he apparently failed to use it, when the political background was one of mounting unrest against taxation levied to finance the last Lancastrian campaigns in France.

To turn to Richard Fitzjames's Fulham Palace is a relief, after looking at Morton's old-fashioned, para-military gatehouse. Fulham's low Early Tudor court exemplifies our theme perfectly. This is a purely domestic building, still recognizably a country palace—protected from London by trees. Contemporary garden walls remain. It was once moated, but the moat had been dug by the Danes before the Norman Conquest. You enter the court through a wide and beautiful Tudor archway of moulded brick. You face an unassertive little tower, with tiny decorative battlements supported on cusped corbels. The bricks are deep red, strong but heavily pitted; the diapering of grey bricks could never have been striking (contrast the all-over purple diaper of Waynflete's Tower at Farnham); the brick dressings are not ornate. There is nothing of the prodigious or boastful here. Fulham is as inward-looking as a Cambridge college. This is a practical building, derived from an episcopal tradition already a century old and having a long future of influence on domestic and farm building styles. Brick appears to us as the typical Elizabethan choice, though not yet for cottages, except in the great stone areas such as the Cotswolds and the West Country. Sometimes the full courtyard effect was to be elegantly dissipated by opening up the ground floor of one range as an arcade, as Somerset had done at Syon, or by building on the more complex 'E' or even 'H' plans. Even so, the simpler style might survive intact in forecourts and stables and in those large diapered barns. There is actually more in common between Fulham Palace and the lovely brick stables built by Sir Thomas Gresham at Syon than there was between Fulham and Protector Somerset's brick-built Syon House itself. For generations, too, stables retained the pierced gatehouse, perhaps an attenuated version with turret, clock and weathervane.

The dispersal of the Church properties in the 1530s and 1540s brought the episcopal granges onto the secular market, and the number of places that bishops held were sharply reduced. Many country houses like Cakeham, Malshanger, Charing and Otford, and Cawood in the see of York, came into lay possession at the Reformation. As with the monastic properties, they were either kept by the Crown or leased or sold through the Court of Augmentations. The Crown had already acquired Wolsey's Esher and York Place, Whitehall, in 1529, the former really belonging to the see of Winchester and the latter belonging to Wolsey as Archbishop of York. Thus, episcopal courtyard homes were used by Early Tudor laymen, just as the courtyard-plan colleges of Cambridge had come under secular control, with Thomas Cromwell following Bishop John Fisher as Chancellor.

SUMMARY LIST OF BRICK BUILDINGS ERECTED BY BISHOPS

Besides the references in the chapter, further details may be given in the Select Gazetteer.

BISHOPS' PALACES AND GRANGES	BISHOPS AND THEIR SEES
Bedfordshire	
(?) Someries, near Luton	(?) Thomas Rotherham of Ely
Buckinghamshire	
The Grange, North Crawley	Thomas Wolsey of York
Cambridgeshire and Ely	
Downham Palace	John Alcock of Ely
Ely Bishop's Palace	John Alcock of Ely, followed by Thomas Goodrich
Guyhirn Tower (Lost)	John Morton of Ely

Hampshire	
Bishop's Waltham Palace	Thomas Langton of Winchester, followed by Richard Fox
Malshanger House, Oakley	William Warham of Canterbury
Hertfordshire	
Hatfield Old Bishop's Palace	John Morton of Ely
The Manor of the More, near Rickmansworth	(1) Henry Beaufort of Winchester and Thomas Langley of Durham (1426); (2) Thomas Wolsey of York, as Abbot of St Albans
Huntingdonshire	
Buckden Towers	Thomas Rotherham of Ely, followed by John Russell
Kent	
Bekesbourne Palace	(?) (early C 16)
Charing Palace	John Morton of Canterbury
Otford Palace	Henry Deane of Canterbury, followed by William Warham
London	
Fulham Palace	Richard Fitzjames of London
Lambeth Palace	John Morton of Canterbury
York Place, Westminster (replaced by Palace of Whitehall)	Thomas Wolsey of York
Middlesex	
Hampton Court Palace (see chapter on Hampton Court)	Thomas Wolsey of York
Headstone Manor, Pinner	(?) Henry Deane of Canterbury ('1501' bricks)
Nottinghamshire	
Scrooby Palace (Lost)	(?) (date uncertain) Archbishopric of York
Surrey	
Croydon Palace	Thomas Bourchier of Canterbury, followed by John Morton
Waynflete's Tower, Esher	William Waynflete of Winchester
Waynflete's Tower, Farnham	William Waynflete of Winchester
Sussex	
Cakeham Manor House Tower (West Wittering)	Robert Sherburne, Bishop of Chichester
Warwickshire	
Old Moor Hall, Sutton Coldfield (Lost)	John Vesey of Exeter

Yorkshire	
Bishopsthorpe Palace	Thomas Rotherham of York
Cawood Palace	(?) (date uncertain) (after mid C 15—possibly by Thomas Rotherham)
Howden Palace	Thomas Langley of Durham

OTHER BRICK BUILDINGS BY BISHOPS

Buckinghamshire	
Eton College	William Waynflete of Winchester patron Henry VI)
Cambridge	
Christ's College	John Fisher of Rochester (patron Lady Margaret Beaufort)
Jesus College	John Alcock of Ely
Queens' College	Thomas Rotherham of York (patron Elizabeth, wife of Edward IV)
St John's College	John Fisher of Rochester (patron Lady Margaret Beaufort)
Essex	
Sandon Church (tower and porch)	Thomas Wolsey of York
Hampshire	
Chapel of the Holy Ghost, Basingstoke	Richard Fox of Winchester (with Lord Sandys of The Vyne)
Mattingley Church	William Waynflete of Winchester
Kent	
Canterbury Cathedral (lining of crossing tower)	John Morton of Canterbury
Smallhythe Church	William Warham of Canterbury
Lincolnshire	
The Chancery, Lincoln	John Russell of Lincoln
Wainfleet School	William Waynflete of Winchester
Staffordshire	
St John's Hospital, Lichfield	William Smyth of Lichfield
Suffolk	
East Bergholt Church (tower)	Thomas Wolsey of York
Ipswich College (Lost)	Thomas Wolsey of York
Yorkshire	
Jesus College, Rotherham (Lost)	Thomas Rotherham of York

CHAPTER V

Ecclesiastical buildings and the reformation conversions

IN the centuries before the Reformation in England there was no rigid distinction between domestic and ecclesiastical building. Important dwelling-houses had their chapels, as the bishop's palaces did. The late fourteenth-century Horne's Place Chapel at Appledore in Kent is a house chapel, but a detached one. Churches might have small houses attached for priests, and the parvise might have its fireplace and be used as a priest's room. The abbeys inextricably mixed domestic and ecclesiastical building, and the great Cistercian abbeys were also centres of farming. In the later Middle Ages the friars had their churches and living-quarters almost invariably in towns. There were colleges of secular canons, with lodgings for these priests, that were founded for chantry or educational purposes. The various guild buildings linked commercial and religious activities, though the normal pattern was for the guild to have its chapel in the parish church. The churches and these institutions, along with, first, castles, and then relatively undefended great houses, took up the bulk of the country's expenditure on building. In the eastern parts of England the monastic and institutional buildings can exemplify the spread of brick from minor to major roles, but the destruction or the partial redeployment of resources that the Reformation involved means that we are usually concerned with incomplete remains or ruins or mere fragments—with the exception of the parish churches. The survivals of Little Coggeshall Abbey in Essex now uniquely show the use of early moulded brick, for elsewhere shaped brick comes only with the use of fabric bricks. Was there more that is lost?

In Essex, and to a lesser extent in Norfolk and Suffolk, in the late fifteenth century and up to the Reformation, brick was used for the rebuilding of churches, made possible often by wool trade funds. Brick chapels, porches and towers of this period survive intact, but in the case of abbeys firstly brick-building postdated the expansion of most of them, and secondly the

Reformation losses may have unbalanced the picture—as they certainly did with the later friaries, colleges and guild buildings. Sometimes monastic or friary buildings were saved by conversion, even for industrial purposes. A town or parish might be allowed to buy an order's church to use as a church (as St Albans did the Benedictine Abbey church, now Cathedral) or as a hall (as Norwich did the Dominican friary church). Sometimes a lay lord set up house among monastic buildings—and used brick in the necessary conversion. A few surviving examples show that great abbots themselves might have been living like lay lords, with fine new quarters built of brick. Church-building can be a cool, impersonal, unpolitical subject; it is difficult, though, to look at the waste or the conversions and new buildings of the great secularization without awareness of the intrusive personalities and the nerve of the Tudor statesmen and officers involved.

1. *Church-building in brick*

Apart from the employment of brick for the main fabric of the church—nave, clerestory, aisle or tower—brick for uses or fittings absolutely limited to an ecclesiastical setting is rare, and examples are few. Obviously stairs, fireplaces, windows and doors have close similarities with such work in houses, palaces or institutional buildings. The typical narrow church stairs, though, whether to tower, parvise or roodloft, are much less ambitious than the finest domestic newel stairs. They are also very much more common, with numerous East Anglian examples. The movement in East Anglian and Essex churches from brick used only, in special jobs, to strengthen flint rubble is matched by a similar trend in houses. There is perhaps earlier brick building in the Perpendicular style among the churches than among the houses, though our view may be conditioned by the churches having survived better, for which, oddly, we have to give some thanks to the Reformation. The point is that the Acts of Parliament and the lurching changes of the Reformation, later unintentionally and ambiguously reinforced by Puritanism, virtually put a stop to ecclesiastical building for a couple of centuries. Then, although the towns often rebuilt their churches, population shifts left country churches—especially in East Anglia—intact. We may note, aside from the question of building materials, that of all the mediaeval churches left in the country one in thirteen belonged to the old diocese of Norwich, which encompassed Norfolk and Suffolk. Of 10,000 churches of mediaeval foundation in the United Kingdom over 600 are in Norfolk only (one in seventeen). The one truly coherent, closely related group of brick structures are among the

CWB
Pre-Reformation Churches & Chapels with major Brickwork
Besides the wholly brick-built churches marked thus: ■ churches with the typical tower-porch combination are included.
Copford and Polstead have brick aisle arcades.
Watton
Sutton
Hull
Roos
Theddlethorpe All Saints
Bardney
(Sutton St Nicholas) Lutton
Cowbit
Walpole St Peter
King's Lynn
Terrington St John
Wiggenhall St Mary
Wiggenhall St Mary Magdalene
Outwell
Shelton
Hopton
Kenton
Diddington
Charsfield
Waldringfield
Tilbury-juxta-Clare
Toppesfield
Polstead
Levington
Wyddial
Meesden
Pebmarsh
Colne Engaine
Copford
Gt. Horkesley
Berechurch
Hunsdon
Chignal Smealy
Feering
Layer Marney
St Osyth
South Mimms
Gt. Baddow
Sandon
Theydon Garnon
Tottenham
East Horndon
Basildon
Laleham
Littleton
Basing
Basingstoke
Smallhythe
Appledore
East Guldeford
Twineham
Herstmonceux
0 miles 50

16. PRE-REFORMATION CHURCHES AND CHAPELS WITH MAJOR BRICK-WORK.

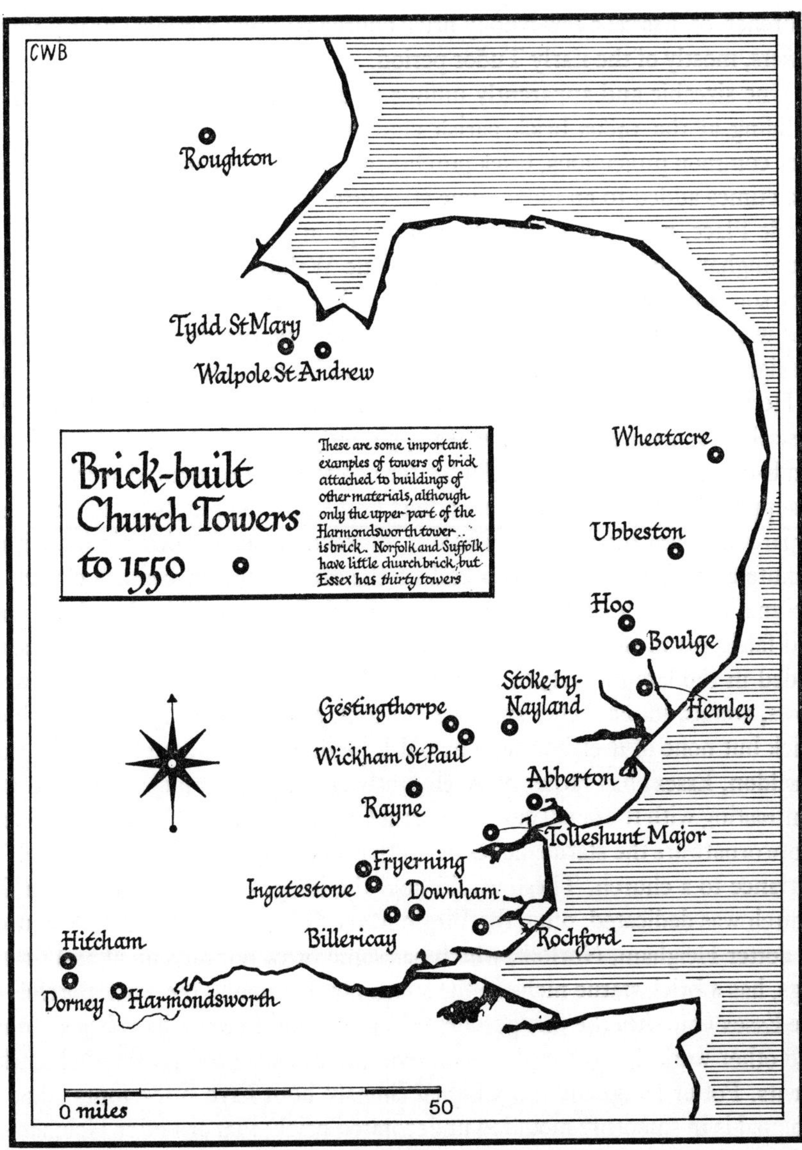

17. BRICK BUILT CHURCH TOWERS TO 1550.

churches of Essex: a few wholly brick churches; brick porches; nearly thirty towers, mostly of the Early Tudor period.

One sizeable and apparently unique structure in brick is the low sacristy building at the 1480s brick parish church of Shelton, Norfolk. The other very common projections, brick porches, are matched by house porches, these sometimes added to an older stone structure. We may compare the porch of Brede Place, near Rye (Sussex), with the plain brick porch at the church of Finningham and the two porches at Little Waldingfield church in Suffolk. The south porch of a church would be used as a meeting-place or even office and were thus more elaborate than house porches. Besides the side windows for light they had side benches, of which brick examples survive at Meesden in Hertfordshire and Feering in Essex. The other special church uses may be described as fittings, but there are apparently no early brick sedilia, altars, tomb-chests (until the Early Tudor terracotta ones) or figured work. There is supposed to be a brick piscina in East Guldeford church, Sussex, but it has apparently been blocked up. There is, however, a small brick piscina with a minute cusped arch at the west end of the early sixteenth-century church of Chignal Smealy in Essex, the so-called 'Brick Smealy'. This church is small and fairly plain, but all of a piece and all brick, with an imitative north aisle added in the late nineteenth century. Chignal Smealy has brick doors, windows, arches, statue niches and even the font, all this entailing much moulded brick but none of it elaborate. The old Langdon Hills church (absorbed into Basildon, Essex) has rather more elegantly shaped statue niches by the altar, contrasting with the small cusped ones at Chignal Smealy. More common and more ornate are the statue niches of south porches, over the main, or people's, entrance to a church. These would hold the image of the saint to whom the church was dedicated, often the Virgin Mary. The mainly flint rubble church of Potter Heigham, Norfolk, which has some brick reinforcement and dressings, has a brick statue niche in the south porch. Among the brick porches of the Essex churches the fine porches of Sandon and Feering have brick niches and other work that is simply decorative, besides stepped and arcaded battlements. Potter Heigham and Chignal Smealy both have brick fonts: that at Chignal is in smoothly moulded undecorated brick; that at Potter Heigham—evidently once plastered over—stands high on a Maltese cross base and has shields and saltires on the faces of its bowl. The only other surviving brick to a font is at Bradwell near Coggeshall, Essex, where an old stone bowl was re-set on a brick pedestal in the sixteenth century.

Another obvious church usage for brick was in the construction of tombs, though I have the impression that stone for tombs was hallowed by long usage and so was kept as the main material for those prosperous enough to have tombs anyway. Tombs might have an effigy, of wood or stone or alabaster, or a flat brass representation set in the altar-like top of the tomb-chest. The ornate East Anglian terracotta tomb-chests, described in the chapter on 'Terracotta', are extremely unusual. It is agreed, incidentally, that the so-called 'sedilia' of terracotta at Wymondham Abbey Church, Norfolk, is really made of re-set pieces from a tomb. There is a mid sixteenth-century brick tomb-chest—to a member of the de Vere family, the patrons—at Castle Hedingham in Essex, but I think there are few others until the cool and quietly grand ones of eighteenth-century churchyards. There was probably, however, much more brick used in this context of burial than is apparent, because examples have usually been found only during exacvations. In Kent, for example, some late fourteenth-century graves have been found to be lined with yellow bricks, like those that vault the 1366 undercroft of Horne's Place Chapel. These graves belong to the sites of mediaeval hospitals or almshouses, that of Saints Stephen and Thomas at New Romney and of St Mary at Strood (I owe this information to S. E. Rigold of the Ministry of Public Building and Works). In London the excavations among the badly bombed Charterhouse buildings in E.C.1 revealed both fourteenth and-fifteenth-century brick tomb-linings, including the tomb of Sir Walter Manny, founder of the Charterhouse, who died in 1372. This lining was wholly of stretchers. David Knowles and W. F. Grimes, reporting on the excavations, described the linings as being of 'soft red brick with yellow mortar'. The Charterhouse was a house of the Carthusian order, planned like the (ruined) Mountgrace in Yorkshire, with individual closed cottages and gardens for the religious. It was a strict order, and this London house provided the most notable martyrs of the Dissolution. The buildings survived through their secularization, conversion into a great house and then, early in the seventeenth century, into a school, but in a fragmentary way.

A 1964 discovery in the City of London was of a brick tomb-vault near St Clare Street, found during builder's excavations. The body inside was lead-shrouded, and mutilated writing scratched on the shroud gave a 1480s dating. Dr Francis Celoria of the London Museum showed that the body was not, as first assumed, that of a member of the Abbey of St Clare once on this site, but that of Anne Mowbray, child-bride of Edward IV's elder son, one of the two princes who disappeared in the confines of the Tower probably during Richard III's reign. We may note, concerning the site of this burial, that the entombment of secular persons in monastic or friary churches was common. There were two main reasons for this, though neither would probably have applied to a child: these people might be patrons or donors to the institution, as Manny was to Charterhouse, or they might have assumed membership of an order on their deathbed, in the hopes of dying in a more sanctified state. One of the most popular of such burial-places in London was the church of the Dominicans—the Blackfriars—whose rich house lay south of Ludgate Hill an typified the late accumulation of riches, only theoretically belonging to the Pope or a papal representative, by the Dominicans and Franciscans against their avowed strict poverty. It was this contradiction, with the abuses of their freedom to walk the world, that was the chief cause of pre-Reformation hatred of the friars. They had been the main targets of John Wyclif, as early as the fourteenth century, when he had prophetically desired to rid the country of friars, and even chantries, saying the possessions of the orders should be returned to the donors or be used by the King for the defence of the realm. In 1414 the property of the Alien Priories *was* used in part for financing the Hundred Years War effort, but the 1410 Parliament had proposed more drastically that all the religious houses be nationalized, to provide funds for foreign wars and for charity.

The use of bricks for voussoirs is also an ecclesiastical detail, but an engineering one. This usage is found in East Anglian churches too numerous to catalogue, a distinctive feature in the great grey Perpendicular churches of this region, built of local flint rubble. The bricks are found more often over doors and are not voussoirs in the sense of forming the arch, but constitute an outer arch, a sort of widely spaced relieving arch that exactly follows the line of the window's stonework from springer to springer. As the earliest examples are fourteenth-century these curve round a shallow point, and the latest ones follow the wider, increasingly flattened arches of Late Perpendicular and Early Tudor architecture. The bulk are probably of the turn of the fourteenth century to the late fifteenth century, quite often owing their existence to a wool-trade-financed rebuilding of a church, as at Cawston in Norfolk, though the contemporary and similarly financed church at Salle nearby is ashlared. One has the impression that these undressed flint churches are held together by the stone mouldings of their voids, especially those of the huge, close-set aisle windows, while the main and tracery lights of a great east window can take up nearly all the chancel's end wall above sill level. These wide brick outer arches are obviously vital for bonding and carrying the stress. Indeed, the top of the window splay inside the church may be brick too, and there may be bricks in the coring of the walls, so that the irregular flintwork is reinforced. Sometimes, too, stone dressings are supplemented by brick ones for the small voids, such as the louvers of the belfry. Such dressings are visible in the exterior fabric, but the inside of the church usually has its details obscured by the plaster rendering—with brick possibly visible in the stairwells only.

Outside, the cool whitey-grey of these massive structures has a warming contrast in the red stretchers of the voussoirs, the usual nine inches by two and a half, with narrow wedges of rubble between. It sometimes seems that these are the only bricks anywhere in the fabric, and they are oddly prominent—as at the marvellous landmark church of Blythburgh in Suffolk. There are a few variants on the pattern. At Wilby in Suffolk, for instance, the line of brick-end voussoirs to the clerestory windows is continued between the windows too, and there is a similar effect in the clerestory of March church in Cambridgeshire. At Norwich, the chief examples being at the Great Hospital (St Helen's, Bishopsgate), there are some heavy brick outer arches: the bricks are laid in continuous courses three stretchers deep, radiating out at right angles to the arch, so that the centre has a keystone effect made by a wedge of bricks. We may give some more examples of the usual type, the widely spaced brick voussoirs of church windows. They are found at North Walsham, St Peter Hungate Church in Norwich, Happisburgh, Blakeney, Worstead and Barton Turf (over door into tower) in Norfolk and at Fressingfield, Blythburgh, Botesdale (St Botolph's Chapel), Covehithe and Stratford St Mary in Suffolk. The largest number of examples are in the flint areas near the coast and the Thetford area of Norfolk.

This tentative use of brick is not typical of Essex, as we see from the later fifteenth-century brick-with-stone or brick dressings, following various mixtures including re-used Roman or mediaeval brick with flint in the Colchester area. Where in East Anglia in general dressed flint is used, especially where there is flushwork panelling, dressings and reinforcement are stone, and brick is usually lacking. This is so at Southwold in Suffolk, while at Lavenham there are stone voussoirs to the windows of the great square tower, which has also inset stone molets and 'TS' monograms—the marks of the de Vere and Spring donors.

Very occasionally flint is combined with brick in a deliberately decorative way, as in the south porch of Little Waldingfield, Suffolk, and in the unusual chequered Late Perpendicular tower of Wheatacre, Norfolk. More often a sort of chequered effect is given to a brick tower by the size of the stone quoins of the brick buttresses or even of the windows, as in the beautiful late fifteenth-century towers of Stoke-by-Nayland (Suffolk) and Walpole St Andrew (Norfolk). Smaller stone quoins are, however, still more common. The pleasing contrast with brick seems normally accidental, as at Tottenham in Middlesex, where the Tudor brick south porch was added to a stone church, or at Shelton in Norfolk, where the donor's executors failed to demolish the old flint tower and build a modern brick one to match the diapered brick body of the church. Very often in Norfolk, Suffolk, East Cambridgeshire and Essex the brickwork of a church constitutes a late addition or expansion, built in the now fashionable material onto a flint or roughly dressed stone nave. Sometimes a Perpendicular brick tower has survived, the rest of the church having been again rebuilt in Victorian times. Essex has about thirty brick towers, The churches quite often have a contemporary brick tower *and* porch, these sharing the same style of battlements and their supporting trefoil-headed and arcaded corbel tables. Of this combination the most impressive example is perhaps Sandon. There are brick towers in Norfolk and Suffolk too, in Middlesex (Dorney, Hitcham, Harmondsworth) and in Lincolnshire (Roughton, Tydd St Mary). Particularly good brick church towers in Essex are those of Colne Engaine, Downham, Fryerning, Gestingthorpe, Ingatestone, Rayne, Rochford, Tolleshunt Major and Wickham St Paul.

The geographical distribution of brickwork other than towers is much wider and the dating more varied, though Perpendicular and Early Tudor predominate. Great Baddow church in Essex has, besides its brick porch, a brick clerestory. Yorkshire has several brick clerestories—at Keyningham, Roos, Wawne and elsewhere—and some of them are fourteenth-century. The influential factor must have been the advantage of lighter weight than brick had over stone, in the risky business of adding a stage to an older fabric. Yorkshire has nearly complete brick churches, near each other, at Sutton and Kingston upon Hull. At Hull the great church of Holy Trinity had so marshy a site that floats were needed, as at Winchester Cathedral. The relative lightness of brick was obviously vital, and weight was further reduced by the size of the windows. The choice of brick cannot just have been a matter of using what could be made locally and so was cheaper: the argument of cheapness and convenience would never have been applied to an outstandingly important church, the main church of a new town. Nor can it be argued that the choice was fashion-following, since the first Holy Trinity bricks were laid as early as 1320. By 1514, when Archbishop William Warham built the new chapel at Smallhythe in Kent of brick, the material was fashionable, and the expensive, delicate brick window tracery there was even influenced by Flemish practices.

Among later mediaeval brick additions we might well expect to find brick side or chancel chapels, built for a guild or as the chantry of some great man or family. These, however, built on to a non-brick fabric, are uncommon. The few examples that come immediately to mind are these: the Crane chantry at

Chilton in Suffolk; the Fincham chapel at Outwell, Norfolk; the 1556 Petre chapel at Ingatestone in Essex, built on to the parish church during the Marian reaction. The Red Mount Chapel at King's Lynn, a detached building, was erected by a guild on the route to Walsingham Abbey and could be maintained by the pilgrims' donations. It is difficult to think of a convincing reason why added brick chapels are not common, but chantries were supported by small as well as great bequests, and might amount to little more than the cost of an inscribed tile or a few candles and masses. We may contrast the monastic benefactions of an earlier age, derived from rich men only. Perhaps the point is that guilds and chantries usually used part of an aisle, that aisle perhaps added in a larger scheme of church improvement. Thus, the north aisle of Wyddial church in Hertfordshire is all brick and includes a family chantry chapel at its east end, while the brick north aisle at South Mimms (Hertfordshire, transferred from Middlesex in 1965), includes the Frowyck family chapel. Freiston church, Lincolnshire, has an added north aisle the brick of which has been compared with that of Tattershall Castle. Unusually, Bardney church, also in Lincolnshire, has an early brick chancel. Hurstmonceux church, Sussex, has a brick north aisle contemporary with the castle and including the chantry of the Fiennes and related families.

A growth in population and in wool and shipping prosperity in late mediaeval Essex, which lacked good local stone, prompted the rebuilding of its churches. The clay for bricks was available, right at the site at Gestingthorpe for example, and the practical choice made the fashion. Essex has the great bulk of church brickwork, but not the earliest known post-Roman brick in England nor the monopoly of wholly brick churches or chapels (usually Early Tudor): there are brick churches or chapels at Smallhythe (Kent); Twineham and East Guldeford (Sussex); King's Lynn—the Red Mount Chapel—and Shelton (Norfolk); Sutton and Hull, Holy Trinity, both of early date (Yorkshire). Essex has several, the grandest being Layer Marney. Going centuries back, we find that Polstead in Suffolk has the earliest bricks, long and narrow and apparently locally made, set in the late twelfth-century rounded arches of the nave arcade and clerestory. Essex has arcade bricks of about 1300 at Copford and other dressings of the early thirteenth century in the flint fabric of St Nicholas Chapel at Little Coggeshall, which belonged to the abbey. There is a considerable amount of yellow fourteenth-century brick in Essex churches, as in Dengie and other churches in the Colchester area. Such brick is always only a small part of the fabric. It is similar to fourteenth-century yellow bricks, some possibly imported, in Kent, especially in the Isle of Thanet. The most striking early use is of 1366, when Horne's

Place Chapel, a private chapel, was erected at Appledore. Here some brick appears in the exterior fabric, but the chapel's undercroft is wholly vaulted in yellow brick.

These uses, like the quoins, lancets, voussoirs and stairs of non-brick churches, are predominantly engineering. In the Perpendicular period, however, the possibilities of decoration were seen. Brick fabric was diapered as Sandon (Essex) and Shelton (Norfolk), for example. The brick porches have their moulded trefoils, quatrefoils, stars, whirlygigs and other 'unnecessary' work, which are usually simpler, however, than contemporary stone carvings. This demonstrates the influence of the material on style, only terracotta in the Early Tudor period reaching the level of complexity of Gothic stone-carving. There is no particular difference between such mouldings in a church or a domestic setting. In the early sixteenth century, however, where there are brick dressings as well as fabric to a church, we may find a subtle relationship, even interaction, between structural engineering and style. To say this is to argue a case, or at least a significance, from a minute number of examples. Apart from Wheatacre church (Norfolk), which is situated in the Waveney Marshes, and Smallhythe's 1514 chapel (Kent), these examples are geographically close. All are close in date. The details of Smallhythe are not completely relevant to what is being said: this is firstly because the chapel is a very small, aisleless building, only administratively made a church, and secondly because the character of the window mullions and tracery, though a good example of the interrelation of material and style, derives from Flemish developments. The Flemish example, apart perhaps from the crowstepping of gables, was rarely followed in England, and the Smallhythe windows are best compared with a much older example—the 1436 blank cusped tracery over a doorway of Ewelme Almshouses in Oxfordshire.

In ecclesiastical building—as in the guildhalls and manor great halls of secular building—the combination of brick fabric and dressings is uncommon. It just does not belong typically to the big buildings of the fifteenth or sixteenth century, where we expect to find brick fabric and great windows of stone. The tall brick-mullioned windows of Parham Old Hall, Suffolk, are an exception, and their lights are very narrow. The relationship between style and material is seen in the making of arches, whether of large windows or of interior arcades that comment on but do not copy each other—as at Shelton church, with the nave arcades, wall arcading and aisle windows, though these are stonework. Brick is not used for large windows in a series, and evidently such a load would have been too much for it; but the problems posed by open arcades it could solve. Thus, the brick dressings of Sandon and Feering churches in Essex are unusual. So are the aisle windows of Wyddial church (Hertfordshire), but the aisle is not a tall one. The great height of St Osyth's church (Essex) demands stone voids, but the suave and marvellous arcades are of brick, which were plastered over till 1899.

The relationship is best seen in the churches, because it was a special response to the chief demand made by later mediaeval church architecture—the combined needs for unbroken space and for light inside the church. This demand produced wonderfully tall and wide Perpendicular windows to aisles and east ends. The consequent additional stresses of width and height in supporting the nave roof and clerestory of aisled churches needed wide, tall arcades. With brick, the lines of doors, windows and arcades could not be remotely fussy: deceptively simple, clear mouldings were technically possible, particularly roll mouldings and soft hollow chamfers. These contrast with the sharp-cut edges that still featured in contemporary stonework. Rubbing further smoothed the lines of four-centred or flattened curves, built up brick by careful brick on the frame.

Arcades and panel tracery windows apparently best demonstrate this subtle simplicity—a seeming inevitability that one knows is not inevitable at all. In domestic architecture, too, this character is shared by the widest and most beautiful brick entrance arches, including those of Fulham Palace, London, and of the smaller gatehouse of Leez Priory, Essex. It is seen in the panel tracery of the tower's west windows at Wheatacre church, Norfolk; of the east window of the Langdon Hills church at Basildon, Essex; of the east window of the north aisle of Wyddial church. It is also seen in the panache of Smallhythe's windows, with their heart-shaped tracery, whose curves are, and are essentially, of brick. At the village church of Chignal Smealy, Essex, the fabric and all dressings are brick: the unpretentious scale means that the voids—especially the south door and the two-light south aisle windows—are small and domestic-looking, but, inside the church, the high, narrow ogival arch at the west end and the fairly low, wide nave arcade demonstrate irresistibly the sweet lines brick may give, when unobscured by plaster. The arcades of the larger churches have their Perpendicular columns, of which 'fluted' is an inadequate description, because the effects may be achieved by mouldings with swelling lobes or fairly complex chamfers or small vertical cuspings. The capitals form an extension and expansion of these, when round brick piers have only rounded capitals and bases. We find the round piers in various chancel arcades that rise to no great height. The major brick arcades are at Chignal Smealy, Blackmore, Ingatestone (to Petre chapel) and St Osyth's, all in Essex, and at Wyddial church in Hertfordshire.

The double St Osyth's and single Wyddial arcades are closely related. They were originally plastered over to imitate stone, and Norman Scarfe points out that 'at least one' crossing arch at St Osyth's is of brick still plastered. All the early sixteenth-century work is of firm red or sour purplish brick, and we cannot now divorce the different effects of colour, of moulding and of the magnetic arched line: the engineering grips the texture. We are a world away from contemporary domestic architecture.

2. *The religious houses and the Reformation conversions*

It is impossible to tell how often brick was used for their buildings by the religious orders of monks and friars. What survives in the ruins and in the houses that were converted to secular use is rather sparse, but certain outstanding structures make one wonder about what may once have existed and, in particular, whether possibly the contacts between the different houses of an order in England and also on the Continent took brick into and beyond the Eastern Counties. There is the isolated case of the mid fifteenth century prior's lodgings, with its tracery and unique billet courses, at Repton in Derbyshire. There is the inaccessible site of Little Coggeshall Abbey in Essex, whose early thirteenth century moulded bricks—made at a kiln just a mile away—are matched only by bricks at another Cistercian Abbey, that of Coxyde in Belgium. The small, never rich, flint-built priory of St Olave's at Herringfleet in Suffolk has its surprising and big brick-vaulted undercroft. Was Thornton Abbey great gatehouse (Lincolnshire), beturreted and partly stone-faced, always as exceptional and without parallels as it now appears to us? What were the origins of the peaked 'mandorla' brick-vaulting of the early fourteenth century at Butley Priory (Suffolk and Westacre (Norfolk), both Augustinian houses? Their vaults are similar to the vault at the Blackfriars' site at Norwich. One surmises that the friars, town-dwellers, built their living-quarters normally in the vernacular style of their lay neighbours, as at King's Lynn, and that therefore they built in brick along the East Coast and inland in the brick areas. The Dissolution was so long ago and so drastic that we can only guess at the different groups of buldings and building practices. A certain amount of evidence from Yorkshire, though, suggests that the isolated and beautiful stone abbeys of the Cistercians in their sheep-pasturing valleys ceased to be the norm after the thirteenth century, when ecclesiastical building nearer the sea—at Hull, Beverley, Sutton,—was done in brick. Beverley, indeed, still has the partly brick-built Blackfriars' (in its enclosure wall a fine late mediaeval entrance arch of brick), which would be

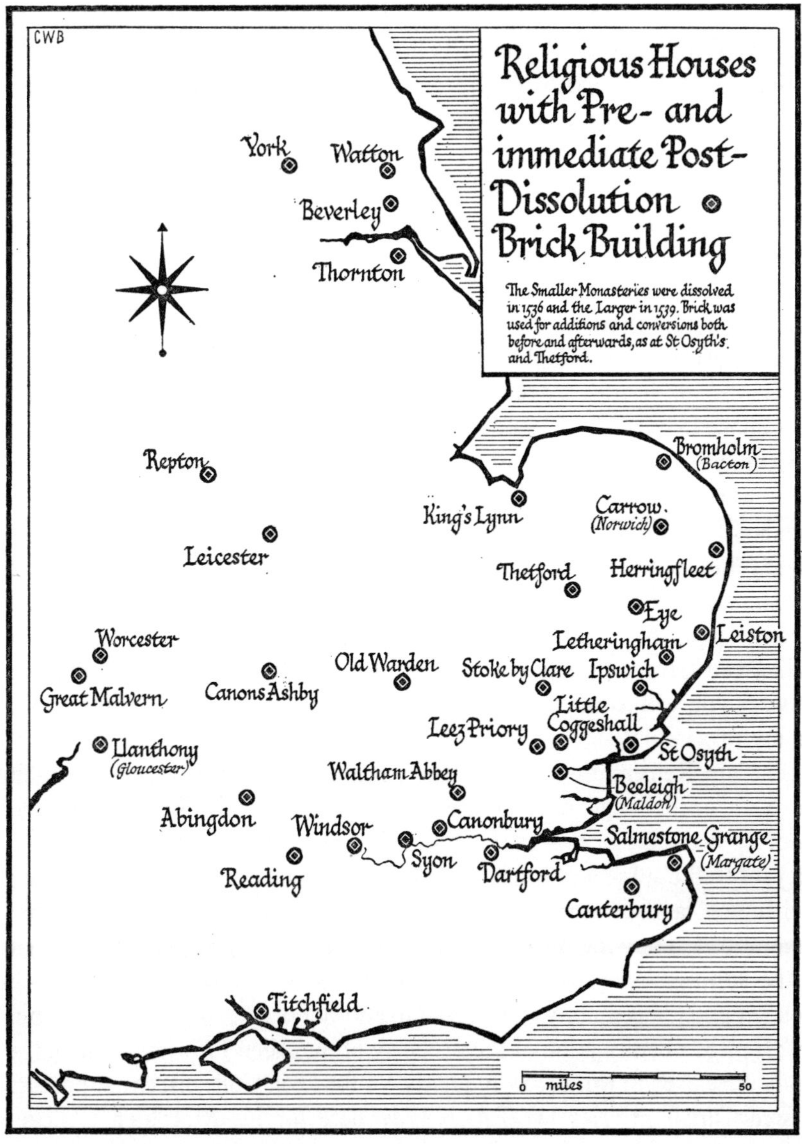

18. RELIGIOUS HOUSES WITH PRE- AND IMMEDIATE POST-DISSOLUTION BRICK BUILDING.

less unusual if the late fifteenth-century Jesus College buildings at Rotherham had survived or, above all, any early buildings of Hull.

Because of their mixture of church and domestic buildings the monasteries linked the ecclesiastical and the secular. This also applied to the friars' establishments, set up from the early thirteenth century on—whereas some of the monasteries dated back centuries before the Norman Conquest. Ideally, the friars were supposed to hold no property, but the Pope or some local nominee could be the theoretical landlord. By the Later Middle Ages some of the friaries were rich, and the more disliked for the contrast between ideal and actual than were the monastic orders or the secular clergy, where the ideal was often overlaid by generations of institutional pomp and secular power—except in the case of the poor parish clergy. The Dominicans' stone-built house in the City of London (Blackfriars' site) was particularly splendid. It is known from manuscript illumination. An important reason why the friars were so conspicuous was that they were town-dwellers as well as popular itinerant preachers. In this latter role they had the advantage of novelty and sometimes of better education and so incurred the jealousy of the seculars. All this was far from St Francis's passionate simplicity, from his negative reply to a young friar who had asked if he might have a psalter: 'When you have a psalter you will want a breviary, and when you have a breviary you will sit in your chair like a great prelate and say, "Brother, fetch me my breviary".'

The pre-Reformation ranks of the Church were not, thus, united against the State's challenge over power and over property. The struggle over property is the factor that influenced building and makes the Reformation so relevant to the subject of brick-building. The transfer of property, chiefly the exchange of lands, was more extensive than that of the Agrarian and Industrial Revolutions, if only because it was so swift. There were some precedents, such as the suppression of the Templars in the earlier fourteenth century—but their property was mainly transferred to another order, the Knights Hospitallers; the 1414 confiscation of the property of the Alien Priories (some of these funds were used in the 1440s by Henry VI for Eton College); the suppression of some small priories by Bishop Waynflete for his Magdalen College at Oxford, and of St Radegund's convent for Jesus College, Cambridge, by Bishop John Alcock of Ely; the early sixteenth-century suppressions of small houses by Wolsey and by Bishop John Fisher for their colleges. Successive statutes from the 1536 Act for the Dissolution of the Smaller Monasteries to the 1546 and 1547 suppression of the Chantries, Guilds and Collegiate foundations took the country through a ruthless redistribution of property, via the royal grant or more commonly sale, followed often by speculative resale. So complete was this process and so identified with it was the governing class that Mary Tudor and Cardinal Reginald Pole, who reversed all the doctrinal changes, could not touch this property revolution. They had to let all the new owners—including the members of the Privy Council itself—enjoy their gains 'without scruple of conscience' even.

Underlying these dramatic changes was a certain continuity, which the government of Henry VIII fostered to some extent. Some of the religious were allowed to reappear in new roles. The abbot of St Mary's at Thame was the first bishop of the new see of Oxford; the abbot of St Benet's Holme, Norfolk, became the new bishop of Norwich, and the Norwich prior became Dean of the cathedral. More important, the government, motivated by the needs of the national economy, ordered that secular households, and therefore demesne farming, were to replace the religious houses. This was achieved only in some cases, as is shown by the early records of destruction, the removal of lead and other useful building materials, or simply the abandonment of monastic buildings. The 'Weep, weep O Walsingham' poem, admittedly in romantic language, recorded the ruination within twenty years of England's second greatest shrine. The demolition of buildings continued during the reign of the boy king, Edward VI, when the severest doctrinal changes were made and when the government's promotion of iconoclasm—the destruction of religious images—was one of the causes of the Western Rebellion. Gilbert Thacker, son of Thomas Cromwell's steward and grantee of Repton Priory, Derbyshire, pulled down the priory church, although the townspeople wanted to keep it as a parish church. His justification, that he must 'destroy the nest for fear the birds should build again', was echoed at the highest level by Edward Seymour, the Protector: 'we must pull down the rooks' nests, lest the rooks should come back again.' Robert Aske, leading the 1536 Pilgrimage of Grace against the suppression of the religious houses of Yorkshire, was aware of their economic importance to this wide, under-populated area and spoke of the first Dissolution statute as the cutting down of a green tree. Yet, the *aim* of economic continuity was there and was significant, and its existence helps to explain the themes which link the monastic buildings with the post-Reformation conversions, for which brick might well be used.

The religious houses themselves now provide relatively few examples of brick-building, but the events of the Reformation four hundred years ago dealt out destruction to the institutions and more often than not to their buildings. The great majority of the monastic buildings probably dated from before the boom in brick-building in the second half of the fifteenth century, and in the fifteenth century funds apparently went more to non-monastic religious foundations. The typical monastic structures were certainly stone, combined with flint rubble in the flint-building areas. Brick thus came late to the monastic scene and at a time when the interest of prospective donors had largely shifted to the friaries, to schools, to colleges of secular canons, to guild chapels, to the Oxford or Cambridge colleges or to the endowment of chantries. Hundreds of people left money in their wills, so that masses might be sung for their souls, and the provision might range from the burning of a few candles to the building of a whole chapel. In the case of the friaries, though, their late date and urban location may have meant that in Eastern England there were more brick-built ones than is now detectable. If, as noted, all the friary buildings of King's Lynn (then Bishop's Lynn) in Norfolk had survived, this guess would certainly look more convincing. Even now, though, we can see brick in the Carmelites' gateway there and in the crossing tower of the Greyfriars' (Franciscans). As recently as the early nineteenth century the now-lost Blackfriars' (Dominican) site had a considerable amount of brickwork. The Red Mount Chapel, too, was established by a guild suppressed at the Reformation, and Thoresby College was built of brick as communal quarters for parish priests. Mediaeval Hull assuredly had religious houses built of brick. The most important was certainly the Carthusians' Charterhouse, to which the de la Poles were benefactors, situated on the landward side of the port near the de la Pole brickworks. At Norwich the Dominicans acquired a new site in the early fourteenth century and from that date used brick in various ways, but the main building materials were evidently flint and stone. The Blackfriars buildings, apart from the church (St Andrew's Hall), are now only fragmentary. They include a small and beautiful brick-vaulted undercroft—really a vestibule or ante-chapel—which shows brick in a load-bearing role, reminiscent of vaulting at Little Coggeshall Abbey in Essex. At Little Coggeshall the very important brickwork—quoins, window dressings, piers, vaulting ribs—'hold up' buildings of flint rubble, late twelfth and early thirteenth century in date. This work is exceptional because of its early date and because of the numbers of specially shaped bricks, for example segmental pier bricks. It is, though, comparable with the rather later brickwork in the East Anglian flint churches and also in some castles and houses, all dating from before the Early Tudor achievement of total brick construction. Brick was used in the same way in the early sixteenth-century abbess's lodging of Carrow Abbey, Norwich, and in post-Dissolution conversions at Thetford Abbey, Norfolk.

Among the later monastic buildings we can find themes that recur in the Early Tudor secular houses. Beeleigh Abbey, near Maldon in Essex, has both pre- and post-Dissolution brickwork, neither belonging to a really big house. St Osyth's Priory, Essex, has brickwork of both before and after the Dissolution, the former including grand brick-built stone-dressed lodgings for the abbot. Vyntoner's lodgings bring us to an important likeness between the late monastic improvements, and even display, and what was done sometimes to secularize and modernize a dissolved monastery—from little more than the running up of brick chimney-stacks to the addition of whole ranges built of brick. The fifteenth-century brick gatehouse of Letheringham Abbey and the more elaborate, but ruinous, early sixteenth-century brick gatehouse of Leiston Abbey (both in Suffolk) might both be used to illustrate secular developments in architecture. The diapered brick walling that alone remains from a sixteenth-century abbot's improvements at Leicester Abbey makes one think of the diapered brickwork of Leez Priory, Essex, which Richard Rich erected on the site of an Augustinian priory built of flint and stone. Rich replaced the church there with his great hall. His brick-built inner court followed the lines of the cloisters. Protector Somerset's Syon House was also brick-built and on a courtyard plan, though what appears now is the eighteenth-century remodelling and 1825 stone-facing. The site was that of the famous Brigettine convent, from which Somerset retained a brick-vaulted undercroft. Syon had a complex history in the Reformation decades. Somerset was followed by John Dudley, who managed to have him executed for 'felony', since the attempted impeachment failed: one clause in the indictment was that a riverside viewing platform—a triangular terrace—was the beginning of illicit fortifications for the new brick house, which neither had nor needed a licence to crenellate. Mary I executed Dudley, and re-established Syon as a convent. Elizabeth secularized the manor again.

The history of Syon was not typical of the church lands generally. Ownership of ex-church land was usually firmly settled by the 1550s, possibly after some quick speculative changes immediately following the Dissolution. The Syon changes were more a matter of politics than of economics. It was, however, typical that a big brick house was erected on ex-conventual land. Wolsey had done this at Hampton Court, legitimately acquiring a small house of the Knights Hospitallers long before the Dissolution. After it many built great houses for themselves on their grants and purchases, but not necessarily on the exact site of a monastery or monastic grange. Sir William Petre of Ingatestone in Essex was a monastic tenant who turned into the owner of land he had originally rented, from Barking Abbey, and built there a mansion of brick. Paget at West Drayton built a brick mansion, from which the gatehouse alone survives, on land that had belonged to St Paul's Cathedral. At Titchfield in Hampshire the monastic buildings, including the church, were used and the conversion work was done in brick and stone. At St Olave's Priory at Herringfleet in Suffolk, which had some early engineering brick already, brick was used in the secularization of flint-built structures. The same was done at Little Coggeshall Abbey, but for a farm not a mansion. Outside the brick-building areas, of course, stone was normally used in conversions—but see Canons Ashby in Nottinghamshire. Two notable examples of stone conversions are those of Lacock Abbey in Wiltshire and of Little Malvern Priory in Worcestershire, where monastic work is still linked to mid sixteenth century domestic buildings. William Stumpe, clothier, set up his looms in the great stone buildings of Osney Abbey, near Oxford, and of Malmesbury Abbey in Wiltshire. Hundreds of buildings, however, were evidently wasted or used as a source of materials.

Not even Mary I dared attempt the return of the monastic lands to the Church and the refoundation of Syon was the odd exception. Cardinal Reginald Pole, the papal representative, brought in from Italy as her chief ecclesiastical adviser and made Archbishop of Canterbury and Lord Chancellor, wanted to return the lands and failed to achieve this. Indeed, Clause IX of Mary's Second Statute of Repeal, 1554, confirmed and regularized the secularization of the lands. The First Statute of Repeal, passed in 1553, had removed from the statute book the legislation of Edward VI, the recent and more severe changes. The Second Statute of Repeal removed the Henrician legislation, with this shattering exception:

> And, finally, where certain acts and statutes have been made in the time of the late schism concerning the lands and hereditaments of archbishoprics and bishoprics, the suppression and dissolution of monasteries, abbeys, priories, chantries, colleges, and all other the goods and chattels of religious houses, since the which time the right and dominion of certain lands and hereditaments, goods and chattels belonging to the same be dispersed abroad and come to the hands and possessions of divers and sundry persons who by gift, purchase, exchange, and other means, according to the order of the laws and statutes of this realm for the time being, have the same: for the avoiding of all scruples that might grow by any the occasions aforesaid or by any other ways or means whatsoever, it may please your Majesties to be intercessors and mediators to the said most reverend Father Cardinal Pole, that all such causes and quarrels as by

> pretence of the said schism or by any other occasion or mean whatsoever might be moved, by the Pope's Holiness or See Apostolic or by any other jurisdiction ecclesiastical, may be utterly removed and taken away; so as all persons having sufficient conveyance of the said lands and hereditaments, goods and chattels, as is aforesaid by the common laws, acts, or statutes of this realm, may without scruple of conscience enjoy them, without impeachment or trouble by pretence of any General Council, canons, or ecclesiastical laws, and clear from all dangers of the censures of the Church.

(Clause IX is quoted from *The Reformation in England to the Accession of Elizabeth I*, A. G. Dickens and Dorothy Carr, 1967.)

The Crown had taken over perhaps an eighth of England's agricultural lands, had kept much of it and redistributed the rest through the Court of Augmentations, of which Richard Rich was Chancellor and John Williams of Thame the Treasurer. The 'Valor Ecclesiasticus' of 1535 had shown that the five greatest abbeys had an annual income each of over £2,000 a year, while another nineteen had over £1,000 a year. The total monastic income was £140,000, for which the Essex religious houses accounted for a high proportion. The most considerable economic activity of the religious houses was the sheep-farming of the Cistercians, especially in Yorkshire and Essex. The 1536 Act dissolving the 350 smaller monasteries, which were considered more generally corrupt, obliged grantees to keep 'an honest conventual house and household in the same site or precinct', but the 1539 Act removed that obligation and even the possibility, though farming continued. The 1539 Act ended 250 houses, including those of the Gilbertines (like Watton Abbey) and the friaries—187 houses—that had been exempt. The final surrenders, including that of Waltham Abbey, Essex, were taken in 1540. Even the swift and heavily prejudiced reports of the King's monastic commissioners—the commission lasting only four months, with a third only of the houses visited, sometimes at the rate of twenty a fortnight—acknowledged the importance of the hospitality given to travellers. The dispersal of about three and a half million religious, though some went abroad, and the acceleration of the enclosures of land, combined with other factors to leave a great social problem, the legacy of 'sturdy beggars' to Elizabeth.

Fisher had said the reformers wanted 'the goods, not the good of the Church', which was unfair to the religious theorists who had long seen the Church corrupted by its goods. In the redistribution, however, destruction appears paramount, for the resumption of farming under secular control is a less dramatic story. The promised spending on education and charitable purposes by the Crown was, in the event, limited to token spending and the setting up of six new bishoprics, including that of Oxford. The main funds went to defence, especially on the navy and the defensive forts of South England, which provided employment for hundreds of craftsmen. Henry VIII himself converted Dartford Priory, Kent, using brick there though this was painted over.

The first disposals of property were quick, and it has been calculated that the Crown could have made more money over a longer period, if it had not created a buyer's market. In 1539 Thomas Cromwell and Richard Rich were commissioned to sell £6,000 worth of land a year, at a minimum price of twenty times the normal rent. There was a further commission in 1543. By the end of Henry's reign two-thirds of the ex-monastic lands had been disposed of by the Crown. Few outright gifts were made, as the Patent Rolls show; there were some mixed transactions, part gift, part exchange and part sale, such as Henry VIII's transactions with William Lord Sandys (of The Vyne, Hampshire) over Sandys's Chelsea manor. The bulk of lands went in straight sales by the Crown, perhaps followed by speculative resales from which middlemen benefited. The early royal gifts went just to a few great lords and officials, the chief being Charles Brandon, Duke of Suffolk; Thomas Howard, Duke of Norfolk; Sir Thomas Audley, who held the great monastery near Saffron Walden but did not himself convert it; Thomas Cromwell, who, apart from gains in London and Essex, received the valuable Wimbledon Common area, which had belonged to the archbishopric of Canterbury; John Williams of Thame, who was to farm the Cistercian lands at Thame, where Abbot Robert King (the new Bishop of Oxford) had earlier built himself luxurious stone quarters, with fine wood panelling inside. John Williams was an archetypal Tudor 'new man', married to a relative of Thomas Cromwell, who managed to serve Henry VIII, Edward VI, Mary and Elizabeth. A mere conversion was obviously not grand enough for the Treasurer of the Court of Augmentations, and Williams built himself a grand mansion of brick at Rycote, three miles west of Thame Abbey. On the death of Edward VI, Williams proclaimed Mary I and raised 5,000 men in 1554 to suppress Wyatt's Rebellion against the coming Spanish marriage. The grant to him by Mary of the Barony of Thame was in part a reward for this support and in part compensation for the abolition of his profitable office with the Court of Augmentations! Incidentally, the last Chancellor of the Court, Edward North (builder of Kirtling Tower, Cambridgeshire)—who had converted London's Carthusian monastery or Charterhouse—was also made a baron by

Mary. Under Elizabeth, Williams gained the important office of Lord President of the Council of the Marches of Wales, though it was he who had taken her into restraint on the accession of Mary.

Williams died in 1559 and his heavy effigy still defiantly and oddly faces west in the centre of Thame Church. The carved armour is perhaps a representation of the suit he willed to Russell of Chenies and Woburn. Three sons died before him, satisfying the legend of the disappearance of those families who held monastic lands, which Henry Spelman's *History and Fate of Sacrilege* retailed. At the end of his life, he established a grammar school at Thame and refounded almshouses there, in what has been seen as a late bout of conscience.

Others who gained from the Court of Augmentations were Sir Richard Gresham of the City of London, father of the banker; Sir Richard Lee, courtier and military engineer, who converted Sopwell Priory near St Albans; Anthony Aucher, who built a brick house at Otterden in Kent, a courtier only, who gained most in Kent after the King himself; Sir Thomas Wriothesley, later Earl of Southampton, who built his stone gatehouse across the nave of the priory church at Titchfield in Hampshire, but who also employed brick in the conversion; Sir John Russell, who had a great brick house at Chenies in Buckinghamshire, and gained the important Cistercian farming abbey at Woburn in Bedfordshire; Sir John Gostwick of Willington in Bedfordshire, where he had already gained through his association with Wolsey, who used brick to convert Old Warden Abbey in the same county into a house; Sir William Petre, ex-monastic tenant, who replaced the 'Abbess Hall' at Ingatestone, a grange of the Barking convent, with a brick mansion. Petre was Secretary of State to Henry VIII, Edward VI, Mary I and Elizabeth. There were some conversions after Henry's reign, as we have seen from Somerset's at Syon between 1547 and 1549. Bisham Abbey in Berkshire is an example of an Elizabethan conversion: Sir Philip Hoby was granted the estate in 1552 or 1553 and worked on the conversion of the stone abbey buildings till his death in 1558, when his half-brother, Sir Thomas Hoby, built a notable brick outlook tower (1560). The tower at Canonbury, Islington, is also probably Elizabethan, added to an ex-monastic house where Prior Bolton of St Bartholomew's had built in brick before the Dissolution. The great brick mansion of Audley End, near Saffron Walden (Essex) is Jacobean, built on a monastic site by the grantee's grandson, the then Howard Duke of Norfolk.

The use of brick in church and abbey buildings and then in the post-Dissolution secular houses shows the progress of the material from minor bonding and engineering tasks to brick-building proper. The remains of

Waltham Abbey (Essex), Salmestone Grange (Margate, Kent) and Bromholm Abbey (Bacton, Norfolk) include early brick used with other materials. Thetford and Carrow Abbeys in Norfolk show flint combined with brick dressings: at Thetford there is pre- and post-Dissolution work of this type, while at Carrow Abbey (Norwich) there servive the lodgings built by the head of the convent, Isabel Wygun (and marked with her rebus), which were given to an ex-nun of Barking by her father after the Dissolution. It is a pity there are not more survivals, but there are strong similarities between late monastic work and the early sixteenth-century brick houses that replaced the monasteries in importance—and sometimes literally displaced them. Abbot Vyntoner's Early Tudor lodgings at St Osyth's in Essex and the Kirtling Tower in Cambridgeshire, both of brick fabric with Renaissance-influenced stone dressings, are close in style and spirit. The lost Manor of the More, which a contemporary said was as splendid as Hampton Court, was built by Wolsey as Abbot of St Albans. The secular interests of the richer abbots show at St Osyth's and, a little less strongly, in the brick and part-brick abbots' lodgings at Watton in Yorkshire and at St Mary's Abbey, York, the latter used after the Dissolution as the headquarters of the Council of the North and home of the President of that body. Brick was thus used to add comfortable lodgings to an older flint- or stone-built monastery. Another type of modern building, the gatehouse, illustrates the development of display. The ruined one at Leiston Abbey in Suffolk, built of rich red Early Tudor brick, has elaborate trefoil-headed panels like those of Hadleigh Deanery Tower, the Essex church porches and of the inner gatehouse of Rich's 'Leez Priory'. The practical thus combined with the fashionable in brick-dressed buildings, whether of Church or State.

DATELIST

THE REFORMATION PERIOD

(*Note:* Different dates for the same events may be found in different sources, because the year in our historical period was held to run from April to April. Thus, the Tudor dating 1 January 1537 we would label 1 January 1538.)

1529: Fall of Thomas Wolsey, Lord Chancellor, Cardinal Archbishop of York and papal 'Legate a latere'.
1532: Act of 'Annates' ('first fruits' of benefices: sharp reduction of papal income from English sources).
1532: Pregnancy of Anne Boleyn.
1533: Divorce of Katherine of Aragon. Marriage of Henry VIII and Anne Boleyn. Excommunication of Henry VIII.
1534: Act of Supremacy.
1535: Execution of Sir Thomas More and Bishop John Fisher.

1535: Thomas Cromwell appointed King's Vicar-General.
1535: 'Valor Ecclesiasticus' (survey of church property). Commissioners' Visitations of monastic houses.
1536: Dissolution of the Smaller Monasteries (with fewer than 400 members and income of under £200 p.a.: about 350 dissolved). Pilgrimage of Grace (1536–1537). Lincolnshire Rising.
1536: Execution of Anne Boleyn. Marriage of Henry VIII and Jane Seymour.
1537: Birth of Prince Edward and death of Jane Seymour.
1539: Dissolution of the Larger Monasteries (about 250 dissolved).
1540: Marriage of Henry VIII and Anne of Cleves.
Execution of Thomas Cromwell.
1546: Survey of Chantries.
1547: Accession of Edward VI. Formal possession of Guilds and Chantries by Crown.
1549: Suppression of Images. Western Rebellion.
1549: Kett's Rebellion.
1553: Death of Edward VI. Proclamation of Lady Jane Grey.
Accession of Mary I.
1553: Repeal of Legislation of Edward VI.
1553: Loss of Calais.
1554: Repeal of Legislation of Henry VIII (but no return of monastic lands). Marriage treaty of Mary I and Prince Philip of Spain. Wyatt's Rebellion.
1554: Marriage of Philip and Mary I.
1558: Death of Mary I. Accession of Elizabeth I.
1560: Proclamation against breaking of Images (mob iconoclasm had followed death of Mary I).
1588: Spanish Armada.

CHAPTER VI

Terracotta

TERRACOTTA in a study of brick is a subject inside a subject, specialized and yet in some ways difficult to isolate. The least elaborate description of its architectural role might be that it is unglazed pottery put to architectural or ornamental use, in which we might include tomb-chests and their canopies. This description as pottery suggests that terracotta is easily distinguishable from brick, which may not be the case: the dividing line between it and fine moulded brick is a wavering one, complicated by the use of both on the same buildings, examples being the chimneys of Thornbury Castle (Gloucestershire) and the decorative work at several of the Norfolk Halls. Thus, any description expresses trends rather than truly defining a category.

The term 'terracotta' is Italian, literally 'baked earth'. The word was first used in England in the eighteenth century, when this type of work was reintroduced. In the one earlier period of major use of the material, in the reign of Henry VIII, it was called 'burnt pot-earth' or 'burnt pit earth'. Although the adjective 'terracotta' is now used for brownish red, the Early Tudor terracotta in England ranges from darkish or pale red to biscuit or even cream. At Sutton Place both deep-red and pale biscuit-coloured terracotta is found. In contrast, yellow bricks, with rare exceptions like those of the late thirteenth century Little Wenham Hall (Suffolk), are a comparatively modern development.

For terracotta, the clay is baked very hard indeed and the resulting substance is dense and fine-grained, without the holes or pebbles, even, of mediaeval brick. It is invariably moulded, allowing the ornate Italianate Renaissance work that was fashionable under Henry VIII. Very much smaller and sharper detail is obtained than is usual with moulded brick. At Thornbury, for example, the knot badge of the Staffords appears in both moulded brick and terracotta, and the latter is much finer work. On the other hand, blocks making up part of the frieze at Great Snoring Rectory have little dogs under four inches long, greyhounds, theoretically moulded brick but not far removed from terracotta.

19. TERRACOTTA AND MOULDED BRICK DECORATIVE WORK AT GREAT HALLS OF 1520–40.

The combination of different techniques of shaping clay after as well as before firing is not unusual in domestic architecture, the supreme example being the Early Tudor extravagances of East Barsham Hall. Towards the end of the fifteenth century moulded brick was used at Someries (Bedfordshire) for the spandrels of a doorway: the points, however, were clearly finished by cutting. As the door has been exposed to the weathers for a few hundred years, this is an extraordinary demonstration of the staying power of fired clay, however shaped.

Terracotta receives its final shape in the mould and that shape can include the minutest detail. Looking at the tomb of Robert Jannys in St George Colegate Church, Norwich, I suddenly realized that what I had taken to be Renaissance-type foliage clustered round urns was, in fact—under the layers of time—and dust-darkened paint—pairs of small dolphins, each dolphin with a tiny ball in its mouth! At Sutton Place putti hold strings of beads. At Laughton Place the windows, inside and outside, have delicate feathery arabesques, some terminating in the profiles of fantastic fauna.

Moulded brick may have simple utilitarian functions, like the chamfered surrounds and the dripstones of doors and windows and even, however gracious the curves, the handrail and handguard to a stair (as at Rye House, Hertfordshire). Even in churches and tombs, though, terracotta is pure ornament. The religious significance of addorsed dolphins on Tudor tomb chests is elusive; the decorative element is so strong, and so slight is the connection with the ideal meaning. This I quote from *Signs and Symbols in Christian Art* by George Ferguson (1954): 'The dolphin is portrayed in Christian art more frequently than any other fish. Generally, it has come to symbolize resurrection and salvation. Considered to be the strongest and swiftest of the fishes, it was often shown bearing the souls of the dead across the waters to the world beyond.' On Layer Marney Tower dolphins figure on parapets and in window tracery; at Laughton Place on the plinth; at Sutton Place on a cornice.

The stylistic capacities of terracotta were, if the primary sources have been read right, fulfilled only in a period of twenty or twenty-five years in England, the 1520s to the 1540s, oddly exact dates for art history. There are only stray examples earlier, like a fifteenth-century angel in relief from a house in Little Walsingham, Norfolk (now in Room 141 of the Victoria and Albert Museum). This is characteristically mediaeval, with its feathered covering like a guild actor's costume, and comparable with contemporary work in alabaster or stone. Another angel, more elegant and maybe sixteenth century, is at the Whitlingham Hospital near Norwich. There are only stray examples after 1540, like the fine moulded brick or terracotta Hobart tomb recess in St Margaret's Church, Barking (Essex), of Elizabethan date. This (in the south wall of the chancel), with its uncomplicated section, rosettes and interlaces or fretty, is simple in comparison with the earlier canopies.

The Early Tudor Renaissance tombs in general, and much of the house decoration, represents an invasion of foreign ideas far more distinctive than the foreign influences, and sometimes workmen, involved in the resurgence of brick building in England in mediaeval times. There are eight Early Renaissance tombs of terracotta, some being incomplete. They could have been imported in pieces. The old belief that the workmen of Layer Marney were Italian lacks documentary backing, but the terracotta plaques or roundels belonging to the lost Whitehall Palace and to Hampton Court were the work of Giovanni da Maiano, a Florentine. The use of terracotta—employed by Greeks, Etruscans and Romans—had, in fact, been revived by North Italian artists in the fourteenth century.

It is not wise to play down the importance of foreign influences and craftsmen, as the coincidence of the Henrician Reformation with the abandonment of terracotta shows. This real break in fashions, when the profiteers of the Reformation took over, is intimately connected with religious and political nationalism; one product of this was the legislation forbidding, or levying fines on, the employment of foreign labour in certain trades. The Renaissance developments had temporarily swung the tide against the normal English xenophobia. The Field of the Cloth of Gold was atypical. So, too, was the employment of Pietro Torrigiano for the effigy of Henry VII in Westminster Abbey—and, incidentally, for the bronze portrait medallion (encircled by the ribbon of the Order of the Garter) of Sir Thomas Lovell, once at East Harling Hall, Norfolk, and now also in the Abbey. The European achievement and pretensions of Thomas Wolsey were unmatched by those of English 'nobles' in earlier times, in tune with his Renaissance-style patronage exercised at Hampton Court of large numbers of foreign craftsmen. Henry VIII, above all at Nonsuch, exercised similar patronage.

Patronage in the past had generally been insular, with exceptions such as the imported Flemish memoral brasses. There had been passing court fashions, like the stimulus to imitate foreign culture given by the marriages of Eleanor of Provence to Henry III and of Anne of Bohemia to Richard II. Above the Early Tudor roundels at Hampton Court and the panels with profile heads at East Barsham, we see what seems a more native development: moulded brick chimney-shafts. Though real terracotta on chimneys is rare, some mention of decorated chimneys is made where they are part of a complex including terracotta and would only be artificially divorced from the wall-decoration of the mansion. These *most* elaborate shafts are, like terracotta, a feature of Henry VIII's reign discontinued afterwards. They are, as Professor Pevsner says, 'gloriously overdecorated'. The phrase is from his *Shropshire* (1958) and refers specifically to Plaish Hall in that county. Such chimney-stacks may be studded with diamonds and rosettes, wreathed with roll mouldings, honeycombed or even twisted, and the tops are often wildly prickly 'stars'.

The chimneys are both more flamboyant and less elaborate than the terracotta parapets and windows of Layer Marney or the wall panels of Sutton Place or the da Maiano roundels of Hampton Court or the rare collection of terracotta tomb-chests and canopies in East Anglia. It is possible that the pagan quality of the tombs, their lack of Catholic symbolism, helped save them from destruction in Reformation or Commonwealth iconoclasm. The tombs cannot be taken as architectural features, though the pedimented canopies of Layer Marney and Oxborough have elements in common with the Layer Marney parapets. The Renaissance mode came in first through tombs Henry VII's in Westminster Abbey being by Torrigiano. The terracotta tombs are Italianate, though sometimes clumsily so. The moulded units may be two or three feet long, and Wymondham Abbey and Oxborough in Norfolk have spectacular tall drums over the canopies. We find Renaissance foliage, ferny and curling, including the acanthus leaves of the Corinthian order. We find columns, pilasters and balusters, egg-and-dart mouldings, cup-shaped flowers, vases and urns, scallops and lunettes, elegant cusped shields and plump inelegant cherubs. Most characteristically, there are large or small dolphins, in pairs, sometimes addorsed, with supple bodies, and open jaws. The work is often plastered over, notably the T-shaped tomb-chest and altar of John Marney. The stylistic connections are with Layer Marney Tower and the Shrubland windows, rather than with Sutton Place or any of the smaller halls.

A list may be useful. There are tomb fragments at Bracon Ash (Norfolk) and complete or near-complete tomb-chests with panelled sides at Barsham (Suffolk), St George's Colegate in Norwich, Wymondham Abbey, Oxborough and Layer Marney. The tomb at Wymondham is much mutilated and was later made into sedilia; its origins are rather mysterious, though it is traditionally said to have been that of Abbot Elisha Ferrers, last abbot, who became a landowner after the Dissolution. The work, though, is of the 1520s, like all the others. The tombs of the courtier Henry Lord Marney (died 1523) and his son (died 1525) were swan-song commissions which evidently directly inspired the canopied extravaganzas at Oxborough, tombs assumed to be those of Henry Marney's daughter, Grace, and her husband, Sir Edmund Bedingfield. (See the Oxborough Hall entry in the Select Gazetteer.) With the sole exception of Sutton Place, these tombs collectively have most of the country's Early Tudor terracotta, and demonstrate a rich and strange transformation of the possibilities of brick earth, hard-fired and with a high proportion of sand.

The subject of architectural terracotta is now best categorized. The material in England was only a passing, expensive fashion, not reappearing till the eighteenth century. If the number of examples, even so, seems rather sparse we must remember both the power of time and that a cold wind of deliberate destruction has blown at different times.

1. Halls and Mansions

We begin with an informative lament on destruction, the description chiming in with what has been said about the hard firing of terracotta and about the main style it was used to embody.

'I went to see the dismal ruins of Westhorpe Hall, formerly the seat of Charles Brandon, Duke of Suffolk. The workmen are now pulling it down as fast as may be, in a very careless and injudicious manner. The coping bricks, battlements, and many other ornamental pieces are made of earth, and burnt hard, and as fresh as when first built. They might, with care, have been taken down whole, but all the fine chimnies [*sic*] and ornaments were pulled down with ropes, and crushed to pieces, in a most shameful manner. There was a monstrous figure of Hercules sitting cross legged with his club, and a lion beside him, but all shattered to pieces.' I find the only implied invective of this last sentence very powerful. The passage is quoted in *Historic Sites of Suffolk* by John Wodderspoon (1841), where the source is given as Martin, 'the historian of Thetford'. This was Thomas Martin, 1697–1771.

Brandon had married Mary Tudor, sister of Henry VIII, and it is her coat of arms which remains over the door of the current, (Georgian) Westthorpe Hall. Luckily, West Stow Hall, also in Suffolk, still remains, even though it is far from complete. The house proper was originally quadrangular, but only one altered range on the north side was spared from demolition in 1795. This is linked with the gatehouse by an Elizabethan covered way, with a timber arcade carried on earlier, low, brick walls. The moat has long been filled in. The major part surviving is the gatehouse, which is essentially a long passage and half-timbered gallery above, with a stepped gable and a pair of polygonal turrets at each end. These ends are brick except for some dressings. What is of interest in the context of terracotta is the panel of quatrefoil decoration over the entrance arch and, more important, the finials crowning the turret cupolas and the highest points of the gables. The finials, six in all, consist of terracotta figures, mostly seated. The connection with the demolished Westhorpe is that this was the mansion of Sir John Crofts (or Croftes), Master of the Horse to Mary Tudor—and her arms appear again here, over the entrance in stone, with those of Charles Brandon. She predeceased Brandon, her second husband, in 1533. West Stow dates from about 1520.

With the main exception of terracotta medallions or plaques, which need not constitute exterior decoration, we can expect to find terracotta used architecturally with brickwork. Terracotta represents a refinement of moulded brick, not always easy to distinguish from it, as we have shown, and for technical reasons obviously belonging with brick building.

A group of neighbouring Norfolk halls again shows the combination, with terracotta used for Gothic *or* Renaissance detail (see also fragments and photographs at the Bridewell Museum, Norwich). Wallington Hall (Norfolk) is interesting, but perhaps the least coherent. It has one very unusual stepped gable of 1520 or 1525, of brick and rough Norfolk carstone in chequer pattern, plus terracotta ornament, being otherwise brick with a porch, which has terracotta friezes including blank tracery. Nearby Denver Hall, of about 1530, also has one striking gable, this with terracotta panels bearing the letters 'IWE' and 'WEN' (supposedly Willoughby family initials) and emblems. The ornate gable culminates in chimneys, as well as crow-stepping, and these are of moulded brick—with zigzags, round studs and other decoration. The appearance is provincial but not old-fashioned for its date.

Great Cressingham 'Priory' (Norfolk), with its largely mediaeval but rich motifs, is very impressive for all its long history of neglect and then dereliction, with the plaster flaking from the ground-floor brick. It is reduced to one range only. Fortunately it is now being restored. The upper storey and the turrets are wholly faced with blank mediaeval tracery in moulded brick, the tracery surrounding long thin panels of terracotta. These panels have emblems in relief, which alternate over the wall-surface—a fist-held hawk and the wreathed monogram of John Jenny. Jenny acquired the property in 1542, and the manor house dates from about 1545. (See Edwin Smith's excellent *colour photograph* in *The English House Through Seven Centuries* by Olice Cook, 1968).

North-east of Great Cressingham is Great Snoring Rectory, evidently once the manor house of Sir Ralph Shelton, builder of the lost Hall and the brick church at Shelton (Norfolk). Great Snoring's wall-decoration and chimney-shafts, with their diamonds and rosettes, are like the carved brickwork of neighbouring Thorpland Hall. The Rectory window bars are relatively plain. They are comparable with hollow-chamfered ones in terracotta, erected at the turn of the fifteenth century, in the abbot's lodging at the Benedictine Abbey of York. There are remains of this house, which was used after the Dissolution by the Lord President of the Council of the North, in the so-called 'King's Manor', York (information from Dr E. A. Gee, Royal Commission on Historic Monuments). Besides carved and moulded brick, Great Snoring has also, however, one Renaissance-style frieze in terracotta: between brick balusters are square terracotta panels with heads in profile. The date is probably about 1525, but might be earlier. The famous East Barsham Hall is still more elaborate, taking its motifs and techniques from several worlds, with a nod rather than a bow to defence in its gatehouse.

East Barsham Hall (Norfolk) presents serried ranks of turrets and chimneys—there is even a stack with ten shafts, impressive despite the loss of original tops—and the vigour is only accentuated by the gate-house being crowded in so close to the house. The builder was Sir William Fermor. The stone entrance arch has been dated about 1510, but the main dates are the mid-1520s for the house, including the porch and the tower next to it, and the mid-1530s for the detached gatehouse. This last is dated by changes in the royal arms of Henry VIII, and it features huge carved brick lion and griffin supporters. East Barsham has been much restored, particularly in 1919 and 1938, but the replacements—especially of chimneys, turrets and finials—constitute true restoration.

In the multiplicity of decoration, mainly brick but some ashlar, it is rather pedantic and perhaps unsuccessful to isolate terracotta from moulded brick, but it is important to our theme of Renaissance influence. Some of the finest work on the chimneys—the six-inch diapered squares with their fleurs-de-lis and roses—must be terracotta. The turret heads, rising above all the angles and wall buttresses, also have very fine work (mostly restored). The major Renaissance features are the decorative friezes at first-floor level and below the parapet, where there are sometimes two rows. The three-storey tower has a frieze at each level, the lowest outlined by hexagons. The friezes have panels or tablets, usually square, with devices in relief: roses, fleurs-de-lis, the profiles of a man and a woman—these last perhaps less sophisticated than the Great Snoring heads.

The Norfolk Halls, of which East Barsham is the most considerable and sumptuous, form a coherent group in their display of terracotta work. The remaining examples to be described do not form such a group; but, because the Renaissance Italianate influence is stronger, they are of national importance. We may take as a link an example of terracotta work at Thornbury Castle, Gloucestershire, that is otherwise rather difficult to place. The combination of stone building and moulded brick chimneys is not rare; fine consistency, hard-fired terracotta, though, normally goes with brick building. The exception is at Thornbury Castle, which was built by Edward Stafford, Duke of Buckingham, in the early years of the sixteenth century, with an ominously large household of armed retainers in mind. Thornbury is limestone, apart from the moulded brick chimneys, 11 feet 9 inches high, grouped in threes, and elaborately decorated! Some of the work is so fine that it must be identified as terracotta. This includes the repeated smaller version of the Stafford knot badge and some small heraldic shields, for example with the Beaufort yale (see these swivel-horned creatures in the heraldry of Lady Margaret Beaufort at Christchurch and St John's, Cambridge). One chimney in the south block actually has the date, 1514, at the base, applying to these luxurious chimneys only—not to the whole castle, which was begun about 1511 and was unfinished when Stafford was executed in 1521.

Considering other surviving dwellings outside East Anglia, we begin with tantalizing fragments in Sussex. Laughton Place, originally the mansion of the Pelhams, is now reduced virtually to one four-storeyed red brick tower which retains some elements of the eighteenth-century 'Gothick' house that was built round it. The tower was built was Sir William Pelham in 1534 and, despite its general plainness, it was given red Renaissance terracotta decoration. The family's wealth is shown by the appearance of the Pelham badge (a buckle, granted after the Battle of Poitiers in 1356) on several Sussex church towers, including that of the church of Laughton itself, marking large benefactions. It appears at Laughton Place, in terracotta, over a window.

The terracotta contributes two decorative elements at Laughton Place. Firstly, at parapet level—including the stair turret, rising a storey higher than the main tower—are friezes of cusped corbelling, with five lobes to each fairly shallow arch. Secondly, the windows, both inside and out, have elaborate decoration in terracotta: round the lights and in the spandrel of their arched heads wreathe arabesques of foliage, forming small semi-abstract patterns, controlled but obscure. There are tiny Pelham buckles; urns; birds; dolphins. The plinth coping has similar work. Little pilasters give some continuity and stress the verticals, as against the arabesques, which curve outwards, some lobed, some branching like candelabra. These are shapes the British probably know best from the work of Robert Adam and

'Athenian' Stuart in eighteenth-century interiors. In about 1595 the Pelhams built and moved on to another great house, again marked by the buckle, at Halland. This is now reduced in size and stature, as Halland Park Farm. It retains sections of a terracotta frieze of the early sixteenth century; Nairn and Pevsner (*Sussex*, 1965) date this as stylistically of about 1525—evidently removed from Laughton.

I hesitate whether to take next, or as the climax, Sutton Place (Surrey) or Layer Marney (Essex), both basically red brick with terracotta ornament. In sheer quantity of terracotta Sutton Place has the primacy, even though Layer Marney has both terracotta decoration to the great gatehouse and terracotta tombs in the parish church. For all the great wealth lavished on Sutton Place—the builder, Sir Richard Weston, was Treasurer to Henry VIII—it has odd but strong elements of conservatism, whereas Layer Marney is less mixed stylistically. Impressive or conspicuous waste of resources, Layer Marney is all of a piece as a building.

(i) *Sutton Place, Surrey* (*Fig. 19; Pls. 54–57*)

Sutton Place is paradoxical, a unique (in England) Janus of a structure, even though it provides a much more practical dwelling than Layer Marney. First impressions would probably be that it is forward-looking, and its symmetrical nature was certainly modern. The very ground-plan appears to be the 'E' shape (with a very short central projection) which was to become fashionable under Elizabeth, but this is delusory: Sutton Place was a court-yard house, and the fourth side, with gatehouse, was demolished in the late eighteenth century. Again, much of the wall surface between the larger windows of the courtyard is covered with creamy terracotta rectangles, but these, with their limited and repeated designs, seem simply mass-produced—stuck on, like modern tiles in a bed of 'Polyfilla'. There may be a big panel of twelve putti, inserted over a doorway, and non-mediaeval terracotta decoration to the window-frames and mullions—some of the forms remind one of plump 'water-boatmen' insects—but the window lights have the traditional mediaeval cusped heads. This may be the most Italian mansion of Tudor England, but it is stage Italian.

Layer Marney, though, is different. It may be rather mad in its ostentation—or is this just a moralistic reaction, following on knowledge that the son of the man who commissioned it died heirless only two years after his father?—but it is more genuine or original. At Sutton Place the translation shows, and this really explains why the work is nouveau-riche, though certain motifs, like the dolphin and tun cornice, are really beautiful. It is most unfortunate that Sutton Place is now normally unviewable: it is a revelation of one period, and has always been sought after.

Some more detail on the terracotta decoration of Sutton Place should be given. The mass of pale-coloured terracotta has the effect of making the brickwork look dark, though the bricks are actually quite a light, unaggressive red. It is interesting to see architectural terracotta clearly, without plaster: the sand content can be detected, almost to individual silica grains. The terracotta is mostly applied to the interior of the court, while now-traditional diapering and three crude brick crosses supplement the ornament elsewhere. The outside walls of the court, incidentally, are much less symmetrical, and have only a few putti and quatrefoils in terracotta apart from terracotta windows. The exterior east side is anyway much restored and the west side is obscured by later buildings.

As at Layer Marney, the involvement of Italian workmen has long been believed in, perhaps correctly but without documentary proof in either case. The same leading craftsman has been suggested for both aces: Girolamo da Trevizi (or Trevisano), who was employed by Henry VIII. The houses are dissimilar, though. Margaret Whinney (in *Sculpture in Britain*) stresses the inferiority of the Sutton Place putti, 'crude in design and execution', and deduces that the workers were not Italian even though they handled this 'un-English material, terracotta'. Weston himself was a visitor to France, but no visit to Italy is recorded. He also visited Flanders, whence he apparently derived the idea of locks on rivers and canals, applying this system to the River Wey. The mansion dates from about 1520–30, being visited by Henry VIII in 1533. Weston died in 1542, still in favour with the King though his son had been executed in 1536—under suspicion of being Anne Boleyn's lover.

Most of the terracotta is cream, so the continuous panelling of the central polygonal shafts and the walls produces large pale areas with relief decoration. Deep red terracotta, however, is used for the knobbly balusters dividing up the putti panel, which has two rows of six of these fashionable cherubs. Below roof level round the whole court is a continuous double frieze of quatrefoils and diamonds, but the south façade has most of the decoration, including the elaborate panel over the entry to the great hall. (This entry, directly into the hall, cannot be the original one.) Prominent motifs on the wall panels are Richard Weston's initials and his rebus of a tun and bunches of grapes. I do not know if the grapes belong to the rebus or not: they may emphasize that it is a wine tun, not just a barrel (R. Young). A concave moulded cornice of terracotta, at first-floor height and running right round the court, has the barrel rebus between pairs of curling dolphins.

The terracotta varies a great deal in colour, especially the light pieces: these are cream or yellow or pinkish or even grey. There is *no* moulded brick, except a couple of crosses, and the minimum of stone, almost confined to one very worn cornice with dolphins. In contrast, Layer Marney has much fine moulded brick and less terracotta. Terracotta at Sutton Place is used for pinnacles and quoins and even on the crowsteps of the east and west gables!

(ii) *Layer Marney Tower, Essex*

Layer Marney Tower has the place of honour in this section. The builder was Sir Henry Marney (Baron Marney from 1522) who died in 1523: the terracotta tombs in Layer Marney parish church are his and that of his son John (died 1525). Henry Marney was a Privy Councillor of both Henry VII and Henry VIII, also Captain of the King's Guard and, finally, Keeper of the Privy Seal, although Thomas Wolsey displaced him as chief adviser to Henry VIII. Locally he was Sheriff of Essex. He was rich enough also to rebuild the parish church of Layer Marney, in brick.

The mansion was not completed: the domestic offices, in particular, were not built. The main parts are the gate tower, with a range attached at either side, and the gallery range. The terracotta work belongs to the tower and to the west wing (the rebuilt east wing being plainer, with only moulded brick decoration). The tower was just servitors' quarters! Despite that, it is of unprecedented height for domestic architecture, with twin eight-storey turrets flanking the entrance, themselves flanked by slightly recessed and thinner seven-storey turrets.

In what was competition, rather than conflict, between Gothic and Renaissance forms, the Renaissance is seen to be winning. Marney as a courtier obviously had contacts with the foreign craftsmen Wolsey and Henry VIII employed: indeed, when Lady Margaret Beaufort died in 1509 (in that year Henry VIII had succeeded to the throne), Marney is named as an executor in the contract with the Florentine sculptor, Pietro Torrigiano, for her Westminster Abbey tomb. The scale of building activity at Layer Marney can be seen as a splendid swansong, for the Marneys had held the manor—and named the village—from the twelfth century. Sir Henry (born in the mid fifteenth century) was their first notable, but scarcely a 'new man' in the Early Tudor sense. The initial 'M' appears high up on the pediments of the gate tower, invisible to the naked eye.

References may usefully be given here. Besides the entry in Pevsner's *Essex*, see his lecture 'Mannerism and Elizabethan architecture—II' in *The Listener* for 5 March 1964. For photographs, see those by Edwin Smith in

The English House Through Seven Centuries, by Olive Cook (1968). For line drawings of the terracotta ornaments at Layer Marney—and also at Sutton Place—see *Early Renaissance Architecture in England* by J. Alfred Gotch (1901).

Clay, which formed the bricks of Layer Marney, was also moulded for the ornament into practically every classical moulding popularized by Renaissance activity. Here they constitute pale exotic trimmings, muddled but not bulky, even though the vocabulary is demanding. The colour of the material is buff rather than cream or biscuit.

The turret parapets are terracotta ornaments and these also top the central recessed section. This section, incidentally, rises only to the sixth stage of the turrets, creating a powerful imbalance. Here there are also two great windows one above the other, constructed with terracotta member, such as recur in the west range. The windows together thave the largest area of terracotta and they are show windows in more than one sense, for the secondary metal bars between the main terracotta mullions and transoms are fixed: the windows were not made to open. All the great windows are square-headed, each with a single transom, but the number of lights varies: the two windows of the central section over the door have five light seach. John Newman compares these pilaster mullions, with their candelabra ornament, to unique stonework in the Christ Church gateway at Canterbury, Kent.

In the ornamentation addorsed (back-to-back) dolphins are used repeatedly. Not only do they twist round the projecting semi-circles—which, like fans or scallop-shells, top the turrets (there are no battlements as such)—but they form the heads of the window-lights. This second use is particularly interesting because the distant impression given is that of traditional ogival arches with cusps. Similarly stylized dolphins are found in the tomb canopy in the church. The semicircles are 'antefixa', heading all the turret angles and the roof line in the central section, and having a fluted radiating pattern. A painting, which survives at Hampton Court Palace, ties this motif in firmly with the cultural vision of the court of Henry VIII. The subject is the Field of Cloth of Gold of 1520, showing the 'English Palace', or pavilion, with a scalloped pediment. The English contingent brought to France, besides 3000 horses, all their own furniture including the pavilions: the largest of these was over 300 feet square and made of wood and canvas, with glass window panels.

Besides dolphins, the terracotta bars of the Layer Marney windows—and all this decoration is repeated *inside*—have winged cherubs' heads and curling plants in calyx-shaped pots, which rise in series like balusters, and Corinthian capitals. A band of cusped trefoils in moulded brick mark the stages of the gate tower, but below the parapets are Renaissance tows of egg-and-dart and guilloche moulding. These are repeated on the west wing, immediately over a cusped Gothic corbel-table, also in terracotta! At Layer Marney, though, in the *close* view, it is the dolphins that dominate, their bodies curling like Renaissance foliage and their wide jaws gaping.

2. *The Shrubland Group of windows*

The title of 'The Shrubland Group, is given to some rather mysterious windows in West Suffolk, situated at and near Barham (south-east of Needham Market, near Ipswich). The windows of Shrubland Old Hall have some resemblance to those of Layer Marney, having dolphins at the head of the lights, but, instead of the curling ogival forms of Layer Marney, the heads of the lights have sharp lines and spandrels with Catherine wheels. Pevsner (*Suffolk*, 1961) says the whole Group is of about 1525 and suggests that the Layer Marney workmen moved on here. Directly related also to the Shrubland Group is the Renaissance-style tomb-chest of Sir Edward Eckingham (or Etchingham) at Barsham in Suffolk. Work which has been directly compared with Shrubland is the terracotta plaques situated on outbuildings of Crows Hall (near Debenham), again work of about 1525. It is, of course, suggested that the work at Layer Marney—and, therefore, at Shrubland—is linked with the terracotta tombs of Norfolk. Yet A. P. Baggs (of the Royal Commission on Historic Monuments) has suggested that the Shrubland windows date from earlier in the 1520s that all the tombs and are quite distinct from them.

Added to this uncertainty of origin is the odd distribution of the windows. At Barham there survives, in the grounds of the eighteenth- and nineteenth-century Shrubland Park, part of the Old Shrubland Hall with two terracotta windows. The parish church of Barham also has one such window, and so do the churches of nearby Barking and Henley. Some of the same moulds have been used for all the windows and, as at Layer Marney, the same motifs appear on both verticals and horizontals. Although documentation is lacking, it does seem more likely that one or more church windows result from a redistribution of Shrubland Old Hall fittings than the contemporary patronage provided a window a church. Possibly countering this is the fact that Barham Church have an Early Tudor clerestory of brick, showing improvement of the church about this period. It certainly has been traditionally said that the church windows came from Shrubland Old Hall. As has been noted, some of the same moulds have been used for all the windows, but there are differences in the number of lights. That the shapes of the heads of the lights also differ could constitute an argument that these windows are in their original sites. The Hall has just two terracotta windows, of three lights with triangular heads. Barham Church has a big window with four straight-headed lights, to the vestry. The window at Henley Church is large, because it belongs to the nave, with three lights: the heads are cusped with Renaissance, not Gothic, forms. Norman Scarfe in the *Shell Guide to Suffolk* (1960) just says: 'Terracotta window from old Shrubland Hall set in nave of church'.

3. Plaques and Maiano Roundels

An item of high fashion in Henry VIII's reign was the classical plaque, a roundel with the head of a god or emperor or a similarly exalted female. Occasionally, too, a mere Englishman might have his portrait constructed in this way: Sir Thomas Lovell commissioned Pietro Torrigiano to make his portrait bust. This, wreathed with the ribbon of the Order of the Garter (instead of laurel leaves, perhaps), was set in the front of his hall at East Harling, Norfolk. This bronze roundel is now in Westminster Abbey with Torrigiano's famous royal effigies, There has evidently been destruction as well as wastage, but that later generations sometimes recognized the artistic importance of these plaques, glosses on the English scene, is shown by their being salvaged on the destruction of their original settings. Their rescue may have been aided by the fact that they could be used for interior as well as exterior decoration. Sometimes they were evidently moved from building to building, like the rectangular terracotta plaques associated with Arminghall Old Hall, now at the Whitlingham Hospital (Norwich), Norfolk.

Fine Renaissance pieces in materials other than terracotta also became travellers. A telescoping of history produces the traditional statement that Renaissance wall-medallions at Salisbury Hall, just outside St Albans, came from the nearby Sopwell Nunnery. They include the head of Cleopatra, scarcely the decoration for a convent even just before the Reformation'. The Sopwell site and buildings acquired in 1540 by Sir Richard Lee, a courtier of Henry VIII's. Although Lee's will, with significant uncertainty, refers to the brick mansion he built as Lee Hall *or* Sopwell Hall, the terms 'Priory' and 'Nunnery' seem to have stuck better and are still wrongly used for the ruins of this Early Tudor mansion. Probably the medallions were Lee's, removed in the time of Charles II from Sopwell, which has long been ruinous. Although possession stayed with Lee's daughter's descendants, already by the late sixteenth century it had been let out to tenants.

The roundels at Salisbury Hall are not terracotta, but are carved in the notoriously soft, white Totternhoe clunch (from Bedfordshire) and are self-coloured, apart from the lettering and traces of colour on laurel leaves. One presumes that they were always indoors, as the lines are still so sharp. They are worth describing, both for comparison and contrast with our main surviving group, the terracotta medallions of Giovanni da Maiano. They form a wall-frieze, but were subjected to the insertion of later walls and panellings, so some are incomplete. Very large, with a diameter of well over two feet, they have borders with classical-style letters giving the names. The subjects are in full profile, with fillets fluttering at the back of the neck. They are Constantine, Julius Caesar, Marcus Aurelius and Vespasian (complete), with Marcus Antonius, Cleopatra and Zenobia (incomplete). Two more, lacking names and borders, remain outside the house. The artists—for the roundels look like the work of two different people—are unknown. If the Sopwell origin is myth, Cutte himself could have commissioned the roundels.

For all their size, these medallions are plain and undetailed in comparison with Giovanni da Maiano's work, in which the circular borders are wreaths composed of flowers, foliage and small heads, with further bands of egg-and-dart moulding. The clunch medallions have simple ridged edges, and it is plausibly suggested that the models were classical coins. Their size reveals the big ideas of Henry VIII's courtiers and ambassadors, with their Reformation-aided fortunes, and the foreign glamour they were temporarily prepared to pay for—in the period while Henry himself dreamed of finishing Nonsuch in Surrey. Think of Sandys, who had been Treasurer of Calais, with his continental (probably Flemish) glass for the chapel of The Vyne and the terracotta medallion there, most likely by da Maiano. Think of Sharrington, with his Italianate tiles for Lacock Abbey, that show his initials, dolphins and his own scorpion badge—the badge being most suitable for a notably fraudulent vice-treasurer of the Bristol Mint.

The great terracotta roundels are evidently all the work of the Florentine, da Maiano. Apart from Torrigiano's, they are the earliest Renaissance work in the country. Those at Hampton Court are his, with documentary proof. One stray, which does not fit in neatly with the group, is the large roundel over the fireplace in the Stone Gallery of The Vyne (Hampshire), the brick-built mansion, of about 1526 to 1540, of William Lord Sandys. Sandys could have introduced the roundel himself. The subject is the Emperor Probus, possibly chosen because he promoted the cultivation of vines in England. The name 'Vine' or 'Vyne' had belonged to the site at least from the fourteenth century. Still, Probus's achievement may be coincidental. Viniculture continued in England through the Middle Ages, though latterly much wine had been imported from the English territories round Bordeaux (lost as one result of the Hundred Years War). The border of the roundel is relatively plain: Pevsner and Lloyd (in *Hampshire and the Isle of Wight*, 1967) characterize the work as 'purely Tuscan', that is the simplest of the classical orders revived at the Renaissance. For the remainder of the group, see the photographs in the *Middlesex* volume of the Royal Commission on Historic Monuments and the relation of their chequered history in *Tudor Renaissance* by James Lees-Milne (1951) also.

There was once an important set of eight terracotta roundels at the Palace of Whitehall, a palace of the See of York taken over by Henry VIII in 1529, on Wolsey's fall. (The only part surviving now is the Henry VIII Winecellar, under the Air Ministry building: in fact, this structure was erected by Wolsey, but the vaulting is evidently Henry VIII's—very like that of his Hampton Court New Winecellar.) Henry's contributions included the three-storeyed dressed flint and stone gatehouse usually described as the Holbein Gate. This evidently derived its name from Hans Holbein's having lodged in it about 1536, when first employed by Henry VIII as a painter here, at St James's Palace and elsewhere.

Although Perpendicular in style, the Holbein Gate was decorated with Renaissance roundels of Roman emperors, indisputably da Maiano's work, and just like those Wolsey had earlier commissioned for Hampton Court. A painting of Whitehall by Canaletto shows the gate during the first half of the eighteenth century (the artist faces Charing Cross), with the four roundels in place on one side of the gatehouse. The thick wreaths show clearly. The roundels were set in the central recessed part of the gate, between the turrets, in pairs above each other (on either side of the central windows). At Hampton Court, though, they were set on the angle turrets. When the gate was demolished in 1759 the roundels were evidently nearly all saved. Wolsey's commission had been for eight roundels only for Hampton Court, besides 'three histories of Hercules', which have disappeared altogether: da Maiano's letter of 18 June 1521, shows that they had been made in London but were then installed at Hampton Court. Hampton Court, however, now has ten roundels instead of eight, and it appears that the extra two came from the Holbein Gate, although they were kept at Windsor Castle till about 1845.

The salvaging of the roundels, though it proves that the importance of da Maiano's work was recognized, was haphazard. There are two at Hanworth House, which lack their borders and seem, therefore, bald or pinched. Hanworth and Hampton Court account for four Whitehall roundels, but that others of similar form came from Whitehall is more speculative. At Stourhead House in Wiltshire—in the stable block—is one wreathless roundel.

Two others may be at St Donat's Castle (now Atlantic College) in Glamorgan, the subjects there being Caligula and an empress. The attribution to da Maiano is accepted, though the design of these roundels is somewhat different from those in Middlesex. The tradition at St Donat's is that the roundels were brought there in the early sixteenth century, which would rule out the Holbein Gate as their course, but the tradition could perhaps confuse the date of their arrival at the Castle with that of their manufacture.

The Hanworth roundels are at a fairly appropriate site, even though they are set in late eighteenth-century brickwork. Though 'Tudor Court' dates only from the mid-nineteenth century and the original Hanworth House was burned down in 1797, there are some relics from the latter: these are the moat and, long converted into flats, the old stables, which incorporate some Tudor brick walling and two huge fireplaces. Henry VIII took over the Hanworth estate, which provided him with deer-hunting, but he also granted it to several of his wives in turn, including Anne Boleyn, who was granted it in 1527. Thus, although the two terracotta roundels came from the Whitehall Palace and are exactly like da Maiano's work at Hampton Court, they are not inappropriate survivals at Hanworth. They are set in the pediments of two decorative features of the entrance court (now that of 'Tudor Court'). Each roundel is now reduced to the bust alone, without its separately moulded foliage border. One of the busts, the 'Minerva', can be identified in an old print of the Holbein Gate. She differs little from the anonymous emperor, the other bust, except in her long hair. The emperor has a ram's-head toga-brooch, identical with Hampton Court work, on his shoulder and trailing fillets at the back of his neck.

At Hampton Court Wolsey employed English architects, and the building was really only forward-looking in scale and in the abandonment of any pretence at fortification. The building was Gothic, but Wolsey filled it with Renaissance decoration. This must have been more conspicuous in the interior of the palace, for the architectural detail outside, like the diaperwork and the mouldings, had late mediaeval precedents. Wolsey's tapestries have disappeared, bar the odd border, but the woodwork of his suite remains, with its rough dolphin frieze. (The panelling, perhaps from his bed, in Hambleden Church has been mentioned.) He employed foreign craftsmen, contracting with Antonio Cavallari for his tomb, though what survives is by Benedetto da Rovezzano. This was not completed for Wolsey; was reserved, but not used, for Henry VIII; was broken up and sold during the Commonwealth in 1646; and ended up providing Nelson with a marble sarcophagus in the crypt of St Paul's Cathedral in 1805.

With the exception of Torrigiano's work, as noted, the da Maiano medallions are the earliest Italian Renaissance works surviving here. Henry VIII at Whitehall by 1536 simply followed Wolsey's example. It is sad that the three contemporary incidents, 'histories' from the story of Hercules, have disappeared: the 1521 letter to Wolsey claims payment for these and for the eight roundels (at £2. 6*s*. 8*d*. each), the total being £21. 13*s*. 4*d*., the work having been done five or six years earlier. The roundels are described as 'painted and gilded'—'*rotundas imagines ex terra depictas et deauratas*'—but the gold and the colours are lost. The roundels are forty inches in diameter, including the encircling wreaths, which are about eight inches wide.

William Tyndale said that, when Wolsey's cardinal's hat arrived from Rome in 1515, it was placed in an open cupboard for people to do it reverence. In the Commons Thomas More complained of Wolsey's fresh pomp. And, of this devotion to the hat, we have a terracotta souvenir at Hampton Court, the famous Italianate panel of Wolsey's arms, set on the inner side of Anne Boleyn's Gateway (or the Clock Tower Gateway). This is the only terracotta now at the palace, apart from the roundels. It has, below, Wolsey's 'DOMINVS MICHI ADIVTOR' motto, also found among the dolphins of the frieze in his rooms. Above is his monogram, with the date 'MD-XXV' (1525). The original surmounting lunette is lost. The panel proper is bordered by Corinthian columns.

James Lees-Milne, in *Tudor Renaissance*, says that Wolsey's panel was inspired by 'a panel, only in marble, of the altar rail to the Capella della Rovere, in St Maria del Popolo, Rome', which has Rovere's cardinals hat and arms and two putti—these similarly positioned, like supporters. The Hampton Court putti hold up Wolsey's shield, which has a cross and *the* hat above it, the twenty tassels swirling down to their feet. Besides lions' faces, repeated from the arms, the panel has acanthus decoration and lines of egg-and-dart moulding. It was probably also by da Maiano (Margaret Whinney, *Sculpture in Britain, 1530–1830*). Henry VIII, who rebuilt this gate of Wolsey's and initialled it for his new queen, Anne Boleyn, had the arms defaced with paint or plaster and his own substituted. Wolsey's were reinstated, in cement, in 1845. The cardinal's hat, however, survived above the royal arms, which the putti now supported—which was appropriate enough, with the 1534 Act of Supremacy declaring the King Head of the Church of England.

Returning to the roundels, the first pieces we see are on the exterior of Wolsey's Great Gateway (which lost two storeys in 1771–3). These two roundels came from Whitehall. They are labelled 'Tiberius' and 'Nero'. The labels are separate and rather suspect evidence of identity. Anne Boleyn's

Gateway has four heads in all, 'Trajan', 'Hadrian', 'Vitellius' and 'Augustus'. The pair on the inner face of the gate flank Wolsey's arms, that panel being set below the great astronomical clock. Facing are four roundels on the George II Gateway, 'Titus', 'Otho', 'Galba' and 'Julius Caesar'. The Augustus alone has a little colouring. Only details differ in design. Each bust has its complex wreath, much paler in colour: the outer border is of acanthus and the inner of egg-and-dart moulding; the wreath proper, between these, is composed of foliage and studded with lions' faces, rosettes and trophies—particularly hands. The busts of the emperors are fully sculpted, not just in relief, and individual, facing outwards. The fillets from their laurel leaves flicker across the medallion surfaces in shallow relief. Each emperor has an elaborate animal's head brooch, gathering the toga folds on one shoulder, most frequently a lion or an eagle or a dragon.

To make a subjective, and obviously anachronistic, comment, the loss of the original colouring perhaps need not be mourned. Many people, similarly, do not honestly regret the disappearance or diminution of mediaeval colouring in churches, suspecting that they would find it crowded and garish. The paint and gilding of these roundels must have been splendid, but the design alone comes over strongly, even sharply. With their fine detail and texture, and a grey-blue tone wholly absent from mellow surrounding brickwork, these terracottas now appear just as a superb and conscious refinement on brick.

CHAPTER VII

'Hampton Court hath the pre-eminence'

1. 'The Red Man': political context

POLITICALLY and as the owner of property Thomas Wolsey, son of an Ipswich cattle-dealer and butcher, developed into the overmighty subject of Henry VIII. This happened while he was acting as the King's chief adviser and officer of state—as Lord Chancellor (from 1515)—and European diplomat. Perhaps he was also culturally the overmighty subject of a man whose final architectural efforts, at the lost Nonsuch Palace (Surrey), have been labelled as megalomaniac. Indeed, James Lees-Milne (in *Tudor Renaissance*) speaks of Wolsey's desire to impress through 'an unparalleled patronage of the arts'. When, in July 1529, he fell so completely and frighteningly from the royal grace, the King stripped him of more than his powers. He appropriated his buildings and 'objets d'art', all his lands and property being officially declared forfeit in October 1529. Hampton Court, already the King's, was not included in the inquisitions of property.

There was, for instance, the (lost) Manor of the More, Rickmansworth, a house that Wolsey had floored with fine tiles imported from Flanders. For the King this mansion, with its deer-stocked estate, proved yet another palace conveniently near London. As the new patron he took over and refounded Wolsey's 'Cardinal College' at Oxford, though this, as Christ Church, was to need further re-establishment in 1546 after the Reforming Acts. True, Henry was also intermittently involved in the expansion of Trinity College at Cambridge, but Wolsey's Oxford College was probably particularly appealing because of its newness: the first buildings were erected on the site of the nave of the suppressed St Frideswide's Priory, beside which Wolsey planned a cloister, now the 264 × 261 foot Great Quadrangle. His Ipswich College, however, still unfinished, was allowed to disintegrate although Wolsey had intended it to supply students for the Oxford college.

The King took over York Place, the London home of Cardinal Wolsey as

Archbishop of York, renamed it 'Whitehall Palace' and added more buildings. By 1536 he had built the 'Holbein Gate' there, following Wolsey's example at Hampton Court by having this decorated with terracotta roundels by Giovanni da Maiano. He took from Wolsey's palace at Esher a great wooden building frame and used it in the construction of a gallery at Whitehall. He pressed on with the Hampton Court building works immediately after Wolsey's fall, when the Cardinal was banished to Esher. Anne Boleyn, the King's mistress and enemy of Wolsey, already had lodgings there. Theoretically, Wolsey—once 'my awne good cardinall'—had already given Hampton Court to the new jealous King, in June 1525, passing over the lease to him, but Wolsey's letters addressed to others had been sent still from 'my manor at Hampton Court'. His arms panel was now bodged up into the Royal arms. Henry even took his unfinished tomb (for all this see also the section on the da Maiano roundels in Chapter VI). In 1529 Wolsey was aged about fifty-six and Henry VIII was thirty-eight and ready to reject the power of a man once no grander than chaplain to his father, Henry VII.

Earlier in Henry's reign, about 1521, these were the questions and answers of a poet assessing the centres of power. Wolsey could scarcely be allowed to survive this greatness for ever. In fact, he died at Leicester Abbey on 29 November 1530, before his impeachment for treason could take place. The poet asked:

Why come yet not to court?
To whiche court?
To the kinges court,
Or to Hampton Court?
Nay, to the kinges court.

The kinges court
Should have the excellence,
But Hampton Court
Hath the pre-eminence.

The writer, John Skelton, once Henry's tutor, saw Hampton Court—along with York Place—as the magnet for all the ambassadors and petitioners.

That 'Hampton Court Hath the pre-eminence' was a political judgement, but we may read it also as an architectural truth. Wolsey's Hampton Court, measuring about 300 × 550 feet, was larger even than Francis I's new palace of Chambord. Wolsey as a domestic builder perhaps competed with the French King, whose greatest officers of state he entertained here, in a way that Henry VIII himself did not—that is, not until he built the small but highly ornate Nonsuch after Wolsey's death. This point must not be inflated, because during Henry's reign there were more royal building enterprises than ever before, of which a very important group were the modern polylobate forts of the South Coast. In domestic building, however, Henry made do with about twenty palaces in and around London, the great majority of which he inherited or appropriated: he usually added or remodelled, rather than clearing a site for a wholly new palace. St James's Palace, with its (surviving) tall gatehouse, is one exception and, of course, Henry's additions to extant buildings were on a grand scale. At Hampton Court Wolsey did not utilize the small manor house on the site; Henry was to use all Wolsey's buildings there, except that he built a larger hall, on the site of Wolsey's, and erected many more buildings. He did not innovate there, except in the tennis court and tiltyard.

Wolsey's competition with the French King was over size, not over architectural style. Francis I was the Renaissance fashion-leader in Northern Europe, the last employer of Leonardo da Vinci, who may have designed the double staircase at Chambord. Wolsey used no Renaissance architectural *elements*, despite the terracotta roundels and his Renaissance tapestries and plate. Nor did Henry VIII at this date, although a temporary structure, the main English pavilion in the Field of Cloth of Gold in 1520, carried classical scalloped pediments. It also, supported by round turrets painted to look like brick, had classical statuary on the parapets. These details are known from the painting at Hampton Court (possibly a copy), which uniquely shows the King and Wolsey side by side. Renaissance work emerged at Henry's unfinished Nonsuch, years later. Lees-Milne says: 'The earliest domestic building upon which the classical idiom was grafted in any measure is Hampton Court, whose first owner . . . shares with his royal master responsibility for introducing the Italian artists to this country.' The inserted roundels, like arms panels, are not integral to the building. The Italian craftsmen were employed at first mainly on such work as tomb-chests and interior fittings, not on architectural design.

Hampton Court's pre-eminence as a building was a mixture of old and new: old in its protective moat, new in its size; conservative in its stone dressings, new and English in the multiple decorations of its brick chimneys, new and foreign in the terracottas; conservative in style, but magnificently confirming the fashion for brick-building and employing bricks on a scale unprecedented for domestic building, the nearest rival probably being Henry VII's lost Richmond Palace, tall-towered but smaller than Wolsey's. Possible comparison with the military architecture of the mid fifteenth century courtyard castle of Caister (Norfolk) and Hurstmonceux (Sussex) fades—especially if one mentally rebuilds Wolsey's cut-down great gatehouse and thinks of the brick boundary walls of the park and, even, the Kingston (Surrey) conduit-houses for the water supply. For brick building, only the lost houses and fortifications, dating back to the fourteenth century, of distant Hull in Wolsey's unvisited see of York could make his enterprise look small—but that is to compare a palace with a town!

The playwright John Mortimer has convincingly credited Wolsey with wanting—illusively—'a palace that looks like a house'. What John Skelton was attacking was a prince and his key palace. That he was a churchman was essential to Wolsey's rise to power, and he had greater opportunities than any layman, apart from the King, for the accumulation of property. Much of his Hampton Court is left, and it seems impossible to divorce this from the builder's personality and pomp. You cannot approach it as just bricks, freestone and mortar—as a building without a context—although the colours of the rough-textured bricks are incredibly impressive. You were meant to marvel here. Skelton's marvelling at the phenonemon of Wolsey was sardonic and hostile. He describes people wanting to see Wolsey as having to 'dance attendaunce' for 'half a yere' on the leisure of a man with a countenance like a king's. He sees him—'set so high/In his hierarchy/Of frantic phrenesy (frenzy)/And foolish fantasy'—giving judgement in the Court of Star Chamber. The other justices are stunned to frightened silence. Wolsey, 'clapping his rod on the board', rhetorically demands: 'How say ye my Lords?/Is not my reason good?'

In the manuscript version of another poem, 'Speke Parot', Skelton presents Wolsey as a strange, luxurious creature, though when this poem was printed by Wynkyn de Worde, the attack was shifted mainly, and conservatively, to Greek studies. C. S. Lewis, in his *Oxford History of English Literature* volume, characterizes Skelton's as the 'voice of the mob' in his satirization of Wolsey. This may be accepted as a fair stylistic judgement, for these 1521–2 poems are traditional, that is mediaeval, in tongue. They do not, though, represent what the unlettered mob was saying about Wolsey. It is not just that Skelton could record what he had surely himself seen of the gold and blue (the word used is 'byse', perhaps sky-blue) roofs and of the fittings of Wolsey's rooms—the tapestries of the Triumphs of Caesar and Pompey, inaccessible and incomprehensible to the mob. Skelton was expressing not the people's hostility, but that of the nobles and sections of the middle class, especially the lawyers, whose position Wolsey threatened with his 'Is not my reason good?'

The Venetian ambassador, Giustinian, who complained at being kept waiting by Wolsey, was deeply impressed by his power in England and Europe and described him as 'of vast ability and indefatigable' and 'extremely just to the poor'. Giustinian recorded: 'he favours the people exceedingly, and especially the poor, hearing their suits and seeking to despatch them instantly. He also makes the lawyers plead gratis for all paupers'. This use, in the Court of Requests, of law against the propertied merely continued the policy of Henry VII (and before him to some extent of Edward IV). It contributed to the successful centralization of power under the monarch, and so to the eventual administration of the Reformation. Wolsey, like the hated Empson and Dudley (executed in 1509) in Henry VII's reign, 'knocked' the lords. Giustinian saw: 'All the power of the State is centred in him; he is, in fact, *ipse rex* (king himself) and no one in this realm dare aught in opposition to his interests.' Giustinian labelled Wolsey as 'seven times greater than the Pope himself'. Erasmus, writing to Cardinal Grimani, simply called him 'omnipotent'.

The poet Skelton fled to sanctuary in Westminster Abbey after his attacks—and then tried to make his peace through flattering dedications of new work to Wolsey. The mob the Cardinal *was* popular with. The pomp the butcher's son assumed—as Archbishop of York (1514) and Lord Chancellor (1515), as Cardinal (1515) and 'legate a latere' (the Pope's deputy in England) (1518), able to condemn the Archbishop of Canterbury himself for 'disobedience'—may have appealed to them like the sudden, uninvidious glitter of a pop star from the back streets.

The King's personal reason for rejecting Wolsey must have been that he looked like another king, while Hampton Court outdid Greenwich and St James's. The stated reasons were all diplomatic. Despite Wolsey's previous European achievements in ensuring a balance of power, he finally failed to prevent the 1529 Peace of Cambrai, which made an alliance between Charles V of Germany and Francis I. The immediate cause of friction with Henry VIII was that the Cardinal, who had himself aspired to the papal throne and failed, could not obtain the consent of Clement VII to Henry's hoped-for divorce from Katherine of Aragon. How could he have? Katherine was aunt of Charles, and the Imperial alliance was essential to the Pope. In any case, Wolsey had advocated that the King should marry next a French princess and not undynastic Anne Boleyn. The divorce was not in fact accomplished till 1533, made urgent by Anne Boleyn's pregnancy in 1532, and then only through England's defection from the Catholic Church, followed by the passing of the Act of Supremacy. One could describe Hampton Court as the supreme episcopal palace, and Henry took this property as well as 'York Place'. He later assumed also Wolsey's power in the Church, through acting as head of the Church 'as far as the law of Christ allows', though he made more institutional than doctrinal changes.

The particular charge that was used to demote Wolsey and take his property may be described as a significant excuse. His acceptance of legatine authority from Rome in 1518 was held to have offended against the fourteenth-century Statutes of 'Praemunire' (penalty being forfeiture of goods), which stated that royal permission was necessary for appeal to or acceptance of powers from a foreign (the papal) court. (Early in the fifteenth century another great statesman, Cardinal Beaufort, had been in trouble over 'Praemunire'.) Wolsey was left with the archbishopric plus an annual pension of 1,000 marks, a minute fraction of his previous income. He received a pardon, but then, in 1530, the charge of treason was revived after he had—hoping for aid—communicated 'treasonably' with Francis I of France, the enemy. The indictment was to be based on private notes made by John Palsgrave, tutor to Henry's children. The trial did not take place because of Wolsey's death at Leicester Abbey. The clergy, however, were fined £100,000 for having, against 'Praemunire', accepted Wolsey's legatine authority. Wolsey's successor as Lord Chancellor was Sir Thomas More, a layman whose modest way of life in no way competed with the King's. He was to be decapitated because he could not accept the Act of Supremacy. More's modesty strangely contrasts with Wolsey's ambitions. The topographer William Camden's verdict (translated) on Wolsey, in the context of the Ipswich College, was that his 'whole vast mind reached alwayes at things too high'. Wolsey was served by Thomas Cromwell, who supervised his building activities and was responsible for all his legal business. Cromwell, a blacksmith's son, who owed his rise initially to Wolsey—and was to become Henry VIII's Vicar-General and and Lord Chancellor after More—defended Wolsey in the Lords in 1529.

2. *Wolsey's Hampton Court*

The Knights of St John of Jerusalem, the Hospitallers, held the manor of Hampton for about three hundred years, from the early fourteenth century on. In 1514 Wolsey obtained the property. This transaction was part of an exchange whereby the Order gained land—now still known as St John's Wood—in the then Forest of Middlesex. Their London region properties already included another, but smaller, 'St John's Wood' in Highbury. The Grand Priory, the English Order's headquarters, was in Clerkenwell, where its stone gatehouse remains. Wolsey was to hold a ninety-nine year lease on Hampton at a rent of £50 a year (the document is in the British Museum). This arrangement was negotiated with the Prior of the Order, Sir Thomas Dowcra. The Knights were still to provide timber for maintaining the Hampton Weir. The lease Wolsey eventually passed over to Henry, and the property became the King's outright in 1540. In that year the Order's estates, with their forty-three houses, were surrendered by Prior William Weston at the end of the Henrician Dissolution, the English Order having refused to accept the royal supremacy. The Knights' Hampton manor was of 3,000 acres, the greater part of which, 2,000 acres, was demesne land. An early record, of 1338, shows that the Order had pastured 2,000 sheep here. The name 'court' was already attached to the demesne, which Wolsey enclosed for his park. The comparatively small dwelling-house of the Hospitallers he demolished.

The place he had chosen for its 'extraordinary salubrity'. It is low-lying, but the soil is well drained because gravelly. Wolsey, already middle-aged, was concerned about his health. His main complaint was the 'stone' and he was later given papal dispensation allowing him, for his digestion's sake, to eat meat during Lent. There is a story that Italian doctors from the great and ancient medical centre, the University of Padua, were consulted about the healthiness of the site. Wolsey's was to be 'the first great private house on the lower Thames above the immediate environs of London, chosen because it was at once easily accessible by water and far enough away to be outside the press of metropolitan business and the city's smoke and fogs' (Michael Robbins). The main 'road' to Hampton Court, twenty miles from London, was the River Thames—as it was to Richmond. The King and the great lords, especially those with houses on the Strand, kept their own barges, road travel being quite uncivilized by comparison. The traffic in supplies was well and long established: in the mid fifteenth century, for example, the Stonor Papers reveal, there was a precisely timed barge delivery every week from Queenhithe in the City of London to landing stages in Oxfordshire, of such goods as cloth, wine and oranges. The 1558 drawings of Anthonie van den Wyngaerde show that the relationship between palace and river was more important than it is now, when it has been toned down by the destruction of the immediate riverside buildings. Wyngaerde showed state barges on the river beside the palace, too. Wolsey's own red-painted barge Henry VIII commandeered and had re-painted.

The Thames water, however, Wolsey scorned to use for domestic supplies, and the arrangements he made were to be used by the Palace till the 1870s.

Possibly the scale and expense of the water supply provide the most significant and dramatic example of the whole building enterprise. Water was piped from Kingston upon Thames, 160 feet above the level of Hampton Court, for three and a half miles. This was pure but apparently, contrary to the Early Tudor belief, has no special properties. It was brought from the conduit-houses there (partly surviving), its course punctuated by brick 'tamkins'—chambers about nine by six feet—which allowed repairs to be carried out. One complete tamkin remains inside the Home Park boundaries, three-quarters of a mile north-east of the Palace. The pipes were of lead, which has always been an expensive material. Lengths of pipe were twenty-five feet long, and experiment has shown that half a dozen men were needed to carry one. Sections had to be laid under river—the Hogsmill as well as the Thames itself. These were much later replaced by iron pipes, because they had been fouling boats. The main pipes were three inches in diameter and the metal was normally three-eighths of an inch thick. The total metal used has been calculated at 250 tons and the cost at £50,000. Every part of the palace was carefully drained, and waste was carried into the Thames by brick sewers (*cloacae*) three feet wide and five feet high, which could be cleansed out. By about 1510 Wolsey had already an annual income of £100,000, but this rose sharply as, in addition to the Chancellorship, he accumulated church offices in plurality, multiple absenteeism, holding in turn or together the bishoprics of Lincoln, Durham, Bath and Wells and Winchester, the archbishopric of York and the abbacies of Tournai in France (the Public Record Office has accounts of the expenses of work at Tournai, kept with the York Place accounts) and of St Albans, the premier English abbey. It has been estimated that his income grew by 350 per cent in the last ten years before his fall. So the £50,000-worth of lead pipes may be set against a final annual income of upwards of £400,000.

To use bricks as the main building material was convenient, for they could be made of local clay, but obviously a man with Wolsey's finances would not have chosen a material simply for convenience and relative cheapness. Stone could have been brought by river, as it had been for the Tower of London. Wolsey's York Place, also of brick, was contemporary with Hampton Court. This was the deliberate choice of a material which in his eyes and those of Henry VIII was fashionable and pleasing. It is interesting that, evidently rather later, Sir William Gascoigne, Comptroller of Wolsey's Household, chose brick for his manor house at Cardington, near Bedford. The bricks were burned near the palace site and transport costs for them do not feature in the accounts kept for Wolsey. Apart from the elaborate chimney-shafts, purpose-moulded brick is not used. Dressings—gatehouse vaulting, doors, windows, courses and copings—are stone. Throughout the accounts the stone most frequently named is Reigate stone, but some Caen stone was imported from France. One may contrast the earlier Rye House (Stanstead Abbots, Hertfordshire) and the later Leez Priory (Essex), with their moulded brick windows and corbel-tables. Thus, in a sense, the brickwork is plain, although there is some diamond diapering with black or purplish brick in the First Court. The Clock Court has more complex diapering, including crossed inverted 'V's'. Apart from the terracotta roundels not much exterior decoration exists, although there are two much-restored stone gables to Wolsey's west front, which have dragons and such creatures climbing the copings. The variety comes from the lack of symmetry, the mixture of materials and from the irregular colouring of the bricks: russet, plum and damson. The fabric is fairly rough—including pebbles—in texture, with thick mortar joints. The bricks are just two or two and a quarter inches thick, nine and a quarter long and four inches across (smaller than Henry's). They are laid in the usual English bond. The impact comes more from colour and texture than from any adventurousness in detail, and it is correct to say that Wolsey's Hampton Court is a mediaeval building apart from its chimneys. The (restored) stone windows, for example, have fretted quatrefoils just like those of the early fifteenth century school, built by Archbishop Chichele, at Higham Ferrers or of numerous tombs.

Accounts for the Wolsey era between 1514 and 1529 have survived, but are far from complete. They, like the royal accounts of 1529 to 1539–40, are a mixture of Latin and English. Both sets are kept together in the Public Record Office (E 36/235). They were opened by Master Lawrence Stubbs, paymaster in 1515–16. The names of craftsmen and masons are given and are all English. In fact, the only documentation of a foreigner is da Maiano's letter of 1521.

Early work on the site was organized by John Bettes, described as 'Master of the Cardinal's Works'. The 2,000-acre demesne was converted into two parks, which were bounded mainly with brick walls, but partly with wood palings. Some of the walling survives: there are considerable stretches along the Kingston Road side of the park. The bricks here are very dark, with some still darker diamond diaper. The wall near the 'Paddock' (or Royal Paddocks, north-east of the palace) was marked with a big black cross. Compare Wolsey's work at Sandon Church in Essex and one Kingston conduit-house. The bond is English and the wall is reinforced with short buttresses. Beside, the palace gardens were made: as well as the gardeners' wages 'my Lorde's garthings' cost money for spades, shovels, barrows and plants. These items appear as early as building costs, as at York Place.

Immediately round the palace itself a moat was created, of which only the western section is now traceable. This was dug at a time when new moats were very rare indeed, though Hengrave Hall (Suffolk) had one made about 1525. Wolsey's was dried and filled in in the time of Charles II, but the section along the west front was restored—though left dry—in 1910 and 1911. Wolsey's moat was brick-revetted, but the new three-arched bridge built over it by Henry VIII is of freestone (with masons' marks) over a brick core. This, too, was buried in the seventeenth century. It is difficult to tell if the moat was intended as a serious defence or just for show. There are no other real elements of defensiveness, unless one counts the fact that the windows in the ranges erected by Wolsey are rather small. There was one abortive attempt to use Hampton Court as a fortress, instead of as a mansion, and to prepare it for attack. This was in 1549, when the Protector Somerset—in the seething economic and religious discontent of Edward VI's reign—expected general rebellion, when Edward and his court were here. The moat was filled up with water; cannon were set up; five hundred suits of armour were brought out for the servants. Then it was realized that thc palace could not stand a siege, and the court hurried off to the genuine royal castle at Windsor, falling back thus on the Middle Ages.

From 1514 on Bettes engaged hundreds of workers in different trades. The accounts name William Reynolds as warden of the masons. From 1515 the principal mason at both Hampton Court and York Place was Henry Redman. Redman also, with John Lebons (or Lovyns), designed Cardinal College. John Harvey points out that Redman at Wolsey's palaces was influenced by the 'simpler style' of John Cowper of Kirby Muxloe Castle (Leicestershire) and the other brick builders. The contrast is with the elaboration of late Gothic stonework. From 1519 Redman was the King's mason too, working at Greenwich Palace for example. He was not, however, dying in 1528 to work for the King at Hampton Court. (His and his wife's memorial brass survives, in St Lawrence's, Brentford, Middlesex. The brass is not complete. The name is spelled 'Redmayne'.) Redman was responsible for the First, Green or Base, Court, with the great West Gatetower that provides entry to it. This is the least altered part, though it has been much restored. The much-altered Clock Court, almost certainly earlier in date, was the core of the palace, in that Wolsey's own quarters were here. His great hall and the chapel, both of which may have owed something to the Knights' buildings, lay beyond (to the east). The kitchen and offices lay to the north-east. A great deal of work was done in the 1520s, but as early as 1516 Wolsey had been able to entertain the King with Queen Katherine of Aragon to dinner, not to stay, and in 1520 Wolsey himself began making long stays here. By 1523 the Base Court and the adjacent Master Carpenter' Court were apparently virtually complete.

Dating the parts of the palace is a complex business, especially as Henry VIII began making alterations and additions as early as 1528 and 1529. Edward VI was to stay here often. So did Elizabeth I, who had some comparatively minor works done, including erection of the stables at the west end of the palace area: there are a few inscriptions of the 1560s. Charles II spent £8,000 on repairs and alterations (1662). Drastic, though elegant, changes were made by Christopher Wren in the late seventeenth century. Restoration, including remodelling, was done by William Kent and others in the eighteenth century. In Victorian times restoration and careful remaking of details took place, but the wrong colour of the bricks normally shows this up. Repair work is continued now by the Maintenance Section of the Ministry of Public Building and Works. The best clues as to dates are found in the brickwork: after Wolsey's dark bricks, the bricks become progressively redder and smoother. It should be pointed out that sections of the palaces are private, providing apartments for the widows of royal servants. This 'grace and favour' usage dates back to 1760. It was the young Queen Victoria who opened the Palace to the public in 1837, soon after her accession.

3. Layout and fittings

The west front built for Wolsey measures four hundred feet across. Henry VIII enlarged it by adding the square projecting wings—on arches over the moat—at the north and south, but the same dark bricks were employed for this work. Redman's central gatehouse was massive, with polygonal angle turrets battered at the base. Brick shafts outline the central section, which has stone oriels carrying Henry VIII's arms, over-large and obviously replacing panels with Wolsey's heraldry. The gatehouse is still big, but its squat strength misrepresents the original work: in 1771–3 the proportion were spoiled when the two upper storeys were removed. The remainder was reconstructed, the central section now rising just three storeys. The four turrets were truncated and finished off with plain battlements, though the originals had high 'pepper-pot' superstructures, their ribbed lead cupolas bristling with spiky crockets and all topped by weathervanes. Instead, the chimneys have gained undue prominence. Some sense of the original proportions may be gained from Lupton's Tower at Eton College, also built by Redman (1517), but that is a much slimmer building with a pair of turrets at

26. KIRBY MUXLOE CASTLE, LEICESTERSHIRE: Detail of gatehouse of 1480–4, showing diaperwork.

27. KIRBY MUXLOE CASTLE, LEICESTERSHIRE: Angle tower and moat platform, 1480–4.

28. LAMBETH PALACE, LONDON: Gatehouse erected about 1485 for Archbishop John Morton. Brickwork and stone have been restored, the carriage and pedestrian arches accurately but the central window inaccurately.

29. LAMBETH PALACE, LONDON: Detail of interior of Morton's Gateway, of about 1485, showing stone dressings to archway and vaulting.

30. GREAT MALVERN PRIORY, WORCESTERSHIRE: Rear of Late Perpendicular gatehouse, of brick with stone dressings.

31. OLD BISHOP'S PALACE, CROYDON, SURREY: The west frontage, this part erected by Archbishop John Morton about 1485. Both gables have diapered motifs; that on the left belongs to the chapel.

32. TOTTENHAM PARISH CHURCH, MIDDLESEX: East side of south porch, built about 1500. The adjoining aisle is roughly contemporary and built of Kentish ragstone, which has worn badly. (The aisle plinth is brick.)

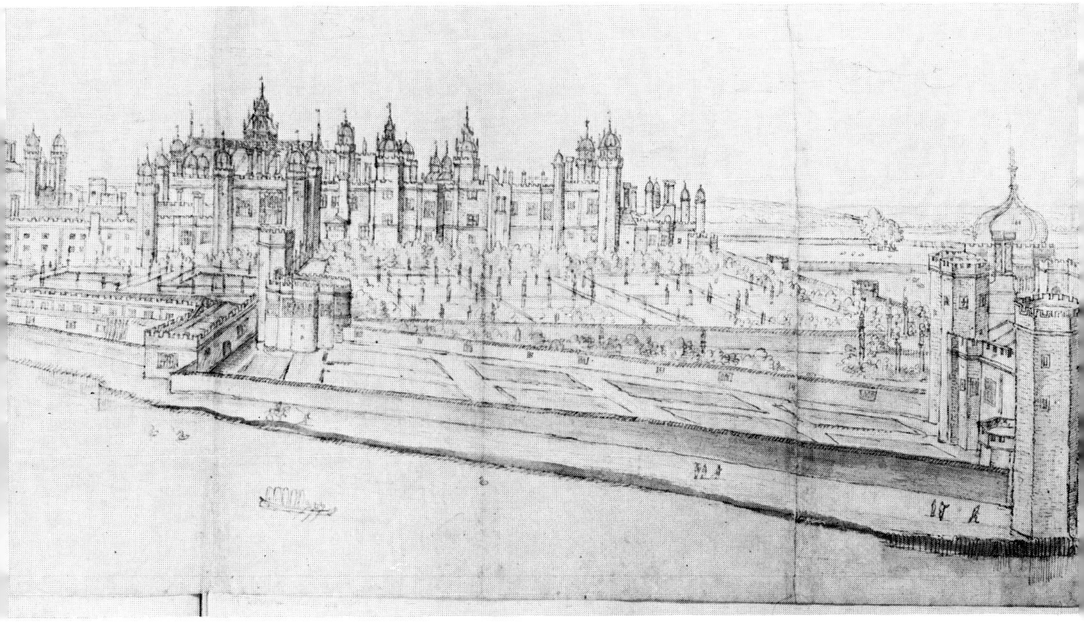

33. HAMPTON COURT PALACE: The major part of the river front, drawn in 1558 by Anthonie van den Wyngaerde. On the left is Wolsey's great gatehouse, later truncated; many of the other buildings have now disappeared, including those at the right. The pepperpot tops to the turrets are lost.

34. HAMPTON COURT PALACE: View of the Base Court, with Wolsey's second gatehouse and (left) part of west end of Henry VIII's great hall. (Note different texture of original brick and repairs.)

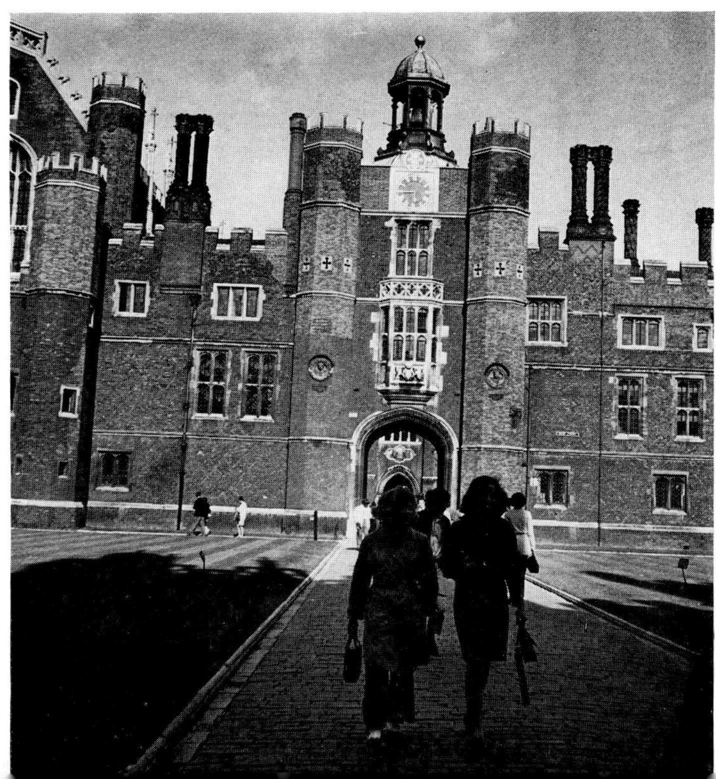

35. HAMPTON COURT PALACE: Detail of the west front, erected for Wolsey about 1514. The gable is restored but the dark, rough-textured brick below is original.

36. HAMPTON COURT PALACE: Group of four moulded brick chimneys (second court). Nearly all the Palace chimneys are exact replacements, but the shaft and base of the chimney on the left retains some original bricks.

37. HAMPTON COURT PALACE: Terracotta panel with the arms of Cardinal Wolsey.

38. HAMPTON COURT PALACE: Terracotta roundel of 1521 by Giovanni da Maiano. This is of the Emperor Hadrian and is set in original wide-jointed brickwork.

39. HAMPTON COURT PALACE: Terracotta roundel of 1521 by Giovanni da Maiano. This is labelled as the Emperor 'Otho' (or Otto), the only one of the series with a helmet, and is set in renewed brick.

40. SALISBURY HALL, HERTFORDSHIRE: Early Tudor roundel of clunch carved in bas-relief. The laurel wreath at least was once painted; the border is lost. To be compared with work in terracotta of the 1520s.

41. BRUCE CASTLE, TOTTENHAM, MIDDLESEX: Sole survivor of a great house erected from 1514 by William Compton, builder of Compton Wynyates (Warwicks.). Tower, of uncertain purpose, decorated with blank

42. SMALLHYTHE CHURCH, KENT: Chapel built about 1516, of brick with brick dressings.

43. SMALLHYTHE CHURCH, KENT: Side window of about 1516, with Flemish-style tracery of moulded brick.

44. FULHAM PALACE, LONDON: Inner side of main gateway of palace of Bishop of London, erected about 1520. The mouldings are hollow-chamfered.

45. FULHAM PALACE, LONDON: Courtyard of about 1520, of red brick with grey diapering. The porch forms the entry to the great hall.

46. SANDON CHURCH, ESSEX: Early sixteenth-century west tower.

47. SANDON CHURCH, ESSEX: Early sixteenth-century south porch, with stepped battlements on cusped corbel-table.

48. LAYER MARNEY TOWER, ESSEX: Terracotta window of about 1520, the bars decorated with urns and foliage and the tracery 'cusps' formed by dolphins.

49. OXBOROUGH CHURCH, NORFOLK: Canopied terracotta tomb of about 1525 forming entry to Bedingfield family chantry.

50. EAST BARSHAM HALL, NORFOLK: Front view of the Hall, with the detached gatehouse, built about 1525–1535.

51. EAST BARSHAM HALL, NORFOLK: Detached gatehouse of about 1525, bearing the arms of Henry VIII in cut brick.

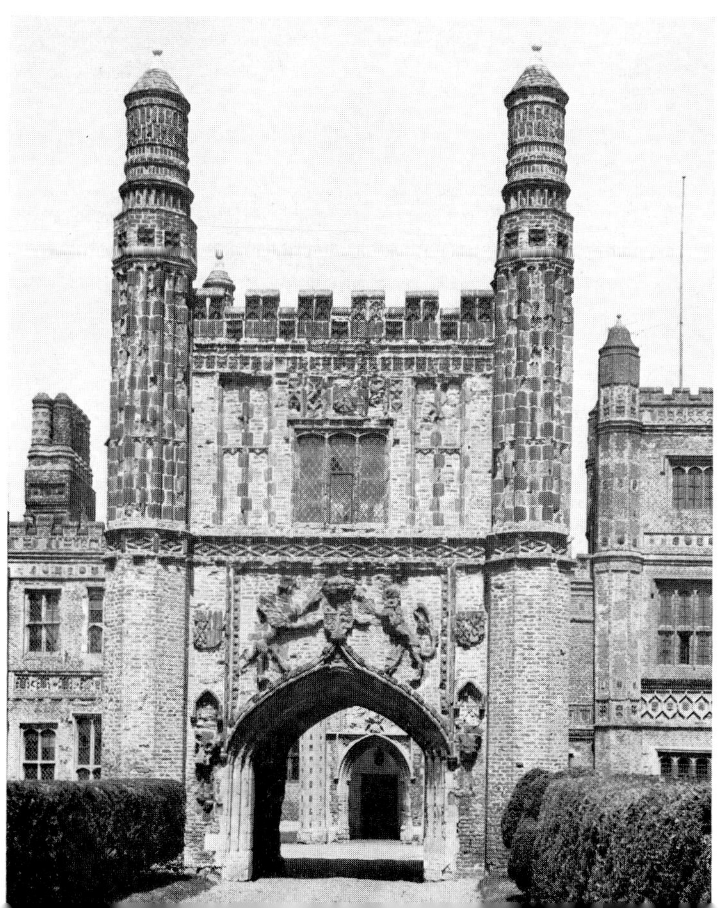

52. EAST BARSHAM HALL, NORFOLK: Detail of Early Tudor frieze, with heads and heraldic shields.

53. SUTTON PLACE, SURREY: Putti panel in cream and red terracotta, over rear door.

the front only. We can see from the drawings that Anthonie van den Wyngaerde made in 1558 that the great West Gatetower *dominated* the whole palace: not even the Clock Court Gate (Anne Boleyn's), reconstructed by Henry VIII, or his great hall was taller. In the nineteenth century Wolsey's gate tower was refaced with 'harsh' (Pevsner) red bricks, in Flemish (not the correct English) bond, that clash with the rest of the front. Only the north-west angle turret has its old bricks. The dating, as stated, is uncertain, but it is thought that the gate tower and Base Court were not part of the first plan, but were the products of Wolsey's increasing grandeur.

The two-storey Base Court buildings are battlemented and have stone copings. The battlements, like the narrow windows, echo the militaristic architecture of the past. Yet the irregularly diapered Base Court ranges look as domestic as the brick-built Cambridge colleges. The work is much grander than the contemporary Fulham Palace, but reminds us of it. The green measures one hundred and sixty-seven feet (north to south) by one hundred and forty-two feet. This was the second green, after the huge open green, beyond the moat, that formed the approach. The rooms for guests were concentrated in this court. The inventory of Wolsey's furnishings (in the British Museum) itemizes two hundred and eighty beds for guests.

To the north of the Base Court and the Clock Court were a series of ranges, punctuated by irregular courtyards, the location of the domestic offices. These have in part survived, though Henry's Great Kitchen, inserted east of Wolsey's Kitchen, meant some early demolition. The Tudor Kitchen, east of these, was Wolsey's Privy Kitchen (personal or private) and have a large chimney-stack. It is impossible to place all the offices known to have existed. The accounts kept for Wolsey list these provision rooms: great kitchens, privy kitchen, cellar, larder, pantry, buttery, scullery, saucery, wafery, ewery (where pitchers were filled) and bakehouse. Wolsey's household first numbered four hundred and twenty-nine and rose to five hundred. These five hundred retainers were sustained by perhaps eighty or more domestic servants and a hundred other servants, who staffed the laundry, the wood-yard and the stables for example. The stables remain, just west of the Great Gatehouse: in Wolsey's time the beasts to be looked after included his own white mules. Wolsey's personal attendants numbered one hundred and sixty. It was his 'gentleman usher', George Cavendish, who was to write a metrical life of Wolsey, that described the palace too. Cavendish's *The Negotiations of Thomas Woolsey, the great Cardinal containing his life and death . . .*' was not published till 1641. The Chapel had a staff of over a hundred, including the choir.

Probably the present palace, which has a thousand rooms and covers eight acres, is not much larger than Wolsey's, which had six courts, perhaps about five acres of buildings. The eastern section, however, is largely post-Tudor. The north side, despite some eighteenth-century sash windows and nineteenth-century replicas (especially at the east end), is largely Tudor. Its close complexity seems still 'a world within a world', which provisioned and warmed first Wolsey's and then Henry VIII's court. It even coped with the French ambassador's retinue for four hundred in 1527. The buildings are smaller and lower than those of the main courts, which are notable for their long galleries. As elsewhere, the stone windows (usually of Reigate stone) and four-centred doors have been restored, or—though this is less common than elsewhere in the palace—sashes have replaced the original rounded, cuspless lights. In places, though, the brickwork is untouched except for repointing. The Master Carpenter's Court—evidently the source of some palace furniture as well as wall-panelling—is just such an enclave. There is a certain amount of moulded brickwork among the domestic offices, such as the stepped bases of the chimney-stacks, corbelled out from second-floor level. The brick is a vehicle only (but what a vehicle) for dressings and fittings of other materials. It does, though, provide the character (in Robbins's words), 'peaceful, warm and comfortable'.

North-east of the Base Court Wolsey's main kitchen survives, sometimes known as the 'Great Tudor Kitchen'. This was cut short by a partition at a later date. The full length was forty-eight feet. There were three fireplaces. The one now visible is the largest, seventeen feet wide, set in the north wall, next to the cell for the master cook. It has a relieving arch of bricks above the stone lintel. These great fireplaces had twin rectangular flues. Inside this one is a later fireplace and oven. The Round Kitchen Court to the south was also Wolsey's, but takes its name from a later building.

If we return to the Base Court and face east we see the beginning of Henry VIII's work, though this range and gatehouse are basically Wolsey's. The range rises to three storeys, but the gatehouse, though considerably taller than them, is very slim in comparison with the great West Gate tower. The narrow polygonal angle turrets are set close to the archway. It is known as 'Anne Boleyn's Gateway' because of embellishment or even conversion by Henry in the 1530s, and the vaulting has her initials. Through the archway is Wolsey's main court, the Clock Court, though only its west side retains the exterior fabric of that period. In 1967, when a fire main was being laid here, the foundations of a range of Wolsey's was discovered, with 'extensive areas of Tudor brickwork', 'immediately below the cobbled surface of the courtyard'.

The drains of this range, apparently a lodgings block, were also found. The south side of Clock Court has a colonnade erected by Wren, but behind this is Tudor brickwork. This section of the south façade of the palace is original and has one stone bay window with four tiers of lights and the only surviving original lead cupola to a turret. Though the major part of Wolsey's quarters and his galleries have largely disappeared, there are important traces of his occupation indoors. On the south side of Clock Court is a pair of small upstairs rooms, known as 'Wolsey's Rooms', and there is 'Wolsey's Closet' east of the court behind the 'George II Gateway'. Even the Henrician accounts continued the references to 'my lord cardinal's lodgings' here.

The interior brick, supplemented by timber partition walls, carries floor-to-ceiling linenfold panelling, fine though slightly irregular. The main rooms, Wolsey's great hall, state apartments and, even, rooms in the Great Gate tower (1522 purchases for these last) would have been lined with tapestries. Part of his 'Triumph' series remains, and there are four Flemish tapestries of the Conflict of Virtues and Vices, dating from 1500, which could have been his. In the Great Hall are kept five strips of heraldic tapestry, once borders, with the royal arms and those of Wolsey and the see of York. The inventory records carpets both English and oriental, with great lists of utensils. Venetian visitors valued Wolsey's silver plate at 300,000 ducats (in 1519) and his gold plate at the same figure (1527). Wolsey's Closet has its ceiling ornamented with Tudor badges, and there is a rather rough panelled frieze with these badges, mermaids and Renaissance dolphins and vases. Wolsey's Rooms have ceilings of a type Henry VIII later had at Nonsuch: the decoration is strips of moulded lead set in blue-painted papier-mâché. The lead is gilt. The designs include dolphins and ecclesiastical cross-keys and a form like a 'caduceus' (Mercury's snake-twined rod) with a cherub's head at the top. These rooms, then, have Renaissance-style ornament complementing the da Maiano roundels set in the exterior brick. Wolsey's main personal rooms are likely to have been larger and grander, though. Most of his and Henry VIII's movables remaining then at Hampton Court were sold off by Parliament in 1649.

4. Chimneys

Throughout the palace the only elaborate brickwork is that of the chimney-shafts. These, *in their origins*, date from 1515 on. The largest numbers, including stacks with rows of six linked shafts, are on the west front, including the Great Gatehouse, and on the domestic offices on the north side of the palace. There are also groups of four shafts and pairs. Henry's chimneys were like Wolsey's, though any word that suggests sameness misleads: there are

20. Hampton Court Palace Chimneys, after designs of 1515 on.

dozens of different patterns. The nearest to duplication is to have the same type of twists curling up from left to right and from right to left. The shafts are virtually all exact Victorian copies, though one much-weathered shaft with cut-brick decoration seen from the Clock Court looks original. So do some in the kitchen area, especially by Henry's Great Kitchen. The tops are polygonal, with miniature battlements or shallow cusping. The bases are stepped, normally with roll moulding, below which may be repeated the battlement motif. Chimney-stacks may be diapered. Shafts are square—and these are set diagonally—or round or octagonal.

The patterns are made of both cut and moulded bricks. They include different twists, zigzags, cables, nets and honeycombs and nameless polygonal figures. There are studs and lozenges, recessed or in relief, and cusped quatrefoils. There are combinations of patterns, such as diamonds set between vertical cables. Ribs may be smooth roll-mouldings, or chamfered or canted. One particularly appealing design is like stretcher-bond brickwork set at an angle of forty-five degrees, the mortar joints represented by ribbing. It is, though, the multiplicity of designs that is exceptional, not the designs themselves. If, however, they can be matched by chimneys at East Barsham (Norfolk), St Osyth's and Leez Priories (Essex) and many smaller places, still, most of those are later in date. One may note here that the Hampton Court *fireplaces*—the surviving ones—are not ornate. They have just plain flat lintels of stone, however wide the four-centred arch that these form. This was typical of the 1520s and 1530s, and may be contrasted with the fine carvings of Tattershall Castle (Lincolnshire), dating from the 1450s. In one of Wolsey's Rooms, for example, the small plain fireplace is in strong contrast to the continuous carved wall-panelling.

The Wyngaerde drawings show the chimney-shafts as part of an irregular aerial frieze of dozens of shafts, crocketed cupolas and gilded weathervanes. The copies we see are dense hard-fired brick, very dark in colour. To give approximate measurements, the shafts, including cap and moulded base, are thirteen or fourteen feet high and up to three feet in diameter (exterior measurement), though many are quite slim. A detailed item in Henry's accounts shows that the chimneys were made locally, their parts premoulded. This says: 'paid to Robt. Burdges, of Hampton bryklayer for 12 12 chemney shaftes with their basys, geraundes and heddes reddy set up and fenysshed uppon the quenys (queen's) new lodgyng at 45s. the pece—£27.' Later items show that the patterns were not enough: there were bills for colourings for the chimneys, for 'verdy grese' (green) and 'redd lead'.

5. *Henry VIII's Hampton Court*

The Early Tudor chimneys and the courtyard plan are themes linking Wolsey's and Henry's work. So is the use of polygonal angle turrets, with the ornate cupolas that are now lost. Ian Nairn (in *Nairn's London*, 1966), however, stresses the great difference between the two: he sees it as a difference more impressive than that between Henry's work and the buildings of Christopher Wren. This perception is that of a refined eye. Henry used Wolsey's combination of brick with stone dressings, none of these stone dressings being forward-looking—not the arms panels set on the gatehouse nor the King's Beasts on their pinnacles round the Great Hall eaves, like those at St George's Chapel, Windsor. The buildings, however, are taller than Wolsey's; the windows are larger and placed symmetrically; there is more panache and, therefore, display in the architecture itself. The symmetry and display, achieved by style not ornament, suggest the Renaissance without being truly of it. Another difference is that the bricks used by the King are a paler red than Wolsey's. The two western blocks added about 1536 are partial exceptions, but, oddly, the joins between the old and new work are not properly bonded. In particular, the light-red facing bricks of the Great Hall were not locally made, but were burned at Taplow in Buckinghamshire in 1530–2, at a cost of four and sixpence a thousand. There was still a brick kiln in the park, but many bricks now came from Taplow, Bronxham and other places. These bricks of Henry's measure 10 × 4 × 2½ inches. Stone was brought from Reigate (Surrey), Barrington (Somerset) and Barnet (Hertfordshire), besides the imported Caen stone from North France. Another import from France was plaster of Paris, for interiors, for a load of which 'Richard Dyreck of Paris' was paid £5. 5*s.*

In the Public Record Office are a dozen folio volumes, (P.R.O. E 36/235–245) of eight hundred or a thousand pages each, beginning with the more patchy Wolsey accounts, and bound with accounts for some other places (for example, Wolsey's York Place and Henry's Oatlands). From 1529 to 1539 they constitute mainly the Exchequer accounts for Hampton Court, and these are very nearly complete. With them are some records of Henry's personal expenditure, the 'privy purse'. They were made up fortnightly. Henry spent more on this building and its fittings than on any other. Latterly, in the late 1530s, the accounts (elsewhere) lumped together Hampton Court, Oatlands Palace (Surrey) and Dover and Sandgate castles. The accounts have never been fully published and seem to have been only scrappily transcribed. By 1538 most of Henry's work here was done, though in 1537 John Lebons (or Lovyns) had been working on drawings for further extensions.

The second court, the Clock Court, belongs to the earlier 1530s. The chief masons were John Molton and James Needham. The Great Hall dates from 1531 to 1536. Buildings to the north and east of it—the Great Watching Chamber of 1535–6 and the Chapel Royal, fitted in the same year—followed. The lost buildings to the south and west were earlier, as was the King's Great Kitchen (1529 on) on the north. So anxious was the King to have the Great Hall finished that tallow candles were bought, so that work could go on at night, and overtime rates were paid to the craftsmen working 'in their own and drinking time'. From 1531 to 1533 Hampton Court cost £400 a month in Tudor money. Freemasons, who set the stone dressings, were paid 3*s.* a week, and the bricklayers 6*d.* a day. Significantly, the 1530–2 accounts are full of charges for heraldic panels, badges and carved beasts to label the King's work and what he had taken over as his. His palace was very much larger than the whole present palace, as can be seen from the early seventeenth-century painting by Danckerts (kept in one of Wolsey's rooms). G. H. Chettle says it was 'almost twice as large' before the period of Wren.

Henry VIII's part of the palace is entered through the Anne Boleyn Gateway, erected by Wolsey. As well as the usual stone dressings this has a small Tudor brick window, with triangular brick voussoirs. Under Henry the Gateway kept its terracotta roundels, though the terracotta arms panel on the inner face was altered. Along with the side ranges the gatehouse was revamped. One assumes that the top stage—the central section is of four storeys—was raised when Nicholas Oursian's astronomical clock was set up. 'The dial, 8 ft. in diameter, tells the hour, date and month, number of days since the beginning of the year, phases of the moon and the time of high water at London Bridge.' The arcaded bell-turret is eighteenth century, but has a 1480 bell inside. The small clock on the outer façade was brought from St James's Palace by William IV. Henry VIII installed himself with Anne Boleyn at Hampton Court in 1529. They were married four years later. After her execution in 1536 any devices like the Tudor rose with initials 'HA', which survives in St James's Palace gatehouse, were removed from this gatehouse. The vaulting is a replica. The (lost) lodgings begun for her were completed for her successor, Jane Seymour. Beside the west door of the Chapel Royal one can even detect how a lover's knot of 'A' and 'H' was converted into one for Henry and Jane Seymour: the 'I' (the old form of 'J'), replacing the 'A', does not fill its space properly. The pairs of angel supporters here, incidentally, may be Wolsey's, not Henry's, for whom one would expect King's Beast supporters. In the Great Hall ceiling, though, Anne's initials and the arms of Boleyn survive intact!

The Great Hall fills the north side of the Clock Court. Wolsey's hall was destroyed for it, but old foundations have been found below. In outline it is not unlike King's College Chapel at Cambridge, but has much shorter polygonal angle turrets and a hipped lead roof and is simpler in exterior detail. The stonework frames the warm red brick in tall symmetrical panels along the side, while the upper part of the west end is the vehicle for a great stone window of panel tracery (showing above the north-east corner of the Base Court). The tall square bay at the south-east angle is all stone, with forty-eight lights. The Great Hall is a splendid structure. The most sweeping of Wren's schemes for the rebuilding of the palace for William and Mary, who had been brought to the throne in the Glorious Revolution of 1688, was to destroy it all except for the Great Hall. It is reassuring that there was a limit.

The interior measurements are one hundred and six by forty feet, and the ceiling is sixty feet high at the apex. It is spanned by a single hammer-beam roof, painted and gilded. The dais for the high table is lit by the bay window, which alone is vaulted with stone—a fan-vault. The central arches of the roof are four-centred, echoed both in the tracery on the cross-beams above them and in the arch of the west window. Some aspects are old-fashioned. The hammers—besides their Tudor roses and portcullises—carry the busts of animated, behatted men and women, who peer down from false balconies on to the lost scene. This is a motif at least as old as Jacques Coeur's house at Bourges in France, begun in 1443. The Italian Renaissance, however, appears in the marvellous lantern pendants, carved and fretted, and the spandrel-shaped braces. These, besides the essential royal heraldry, bear the curling foliage and the cherubs of the future. This work is delicate, controlled and formal. It was done by Richard Rydge, a London carpenter.

It is an odd return to the mediaeval to note that the Hall was warmed in the old-fashioned way by a central hearth. The smoke rose to a louver (now blocked) in the roof. The *hearthstone* remains, near the dais, and is supported from the undercroft below by a thick brick column and vaulting ribs, all plastered. The hall floor is well above ground level.

If we penetrate the domestic substructure (entered from the north-east corner of the Base Court) we find a series of cellars. The main one, under the Great Hall, is the 'King's Beer Cellar', which has oak piers. A smaller cellar leads into the 'King's New Wine Cellar', which lies under the Great Watching Chamber. This cellar is attributed to Lawrence Williams, who had also worked for Wolsey. It is very like the Wine Cellar that survives in Whitehall. The Hampton Court 'New Wine Cellar' has stone piers, but the vaulting is wholly brick, though plastered over. The ribs are sharply chamfered. Built up from the tiled floor are shallow brick platforms, on which the wine barrels were stored. Members of the household had daily beer and wine allowances as part of their 'bouche' or keep. About 1498 John Skelton had written a satirical poem, 'The Bouge of Court', attacking the greedy-mouthed members of Henry VII's court. Interestingly, it was Wolsey who drew up the 'Ordinances of Eltham' (promulgated from Eltham Palace) in 1526, which regulated the household of Henry VIII, whether currently at Eltham or Greenwich or any other royal palace. Abuses were to be ended. There were limits to the provisions for the courtiers, according to their status. The Ordinances even detailed the cleaning arrangements. The inadequate sanitation of the old palaces encouraged the court to change its home frequently, servants cleaning up after each departure. Wolsey's substructure of large sewers—compare those of Henry VIII excavated at the Nonsuch site—was of more importance than his or Henry's cellars, for it enabled their households to use the palace as a regular, long-stay home. After 1529, of course, the Ordinances applied here too, and Hampton Court was to become 'the King's main residence in later years' (John Bowle); and all five post-Reformation queens lived here.

Set round the Great Hall on the north and east are the rooms whence it was provisioned and even protected. The most notable is the adjoining Great Watching Chamber, at right angles to it at the east end, next to the Round Kitchen Court. It was built in 1535–6, as the guard-room at the entrance to the King's lost Presence Chambers and State Rooms. It has a tall polygonal bay window, of brick though the mullions of the thirty-six lights are stone. Inside, the panelled roof has bosses with the arms of Jane Seymour and the badges of the King and his third Queen. In the north-east angle between Watching Chamber and Hall is the first-floor 'Horn Room': this was the serving-place for the dais table, linked by stair and the North Cloister Passage with cellars and kitchens. The larger 'Serving-Place', entered through two brick archways, was used to supply the lower end of the Hall through the screens passage. The original wood serving-hatches open on to the Kitchens area. All this work represents the enlargement of Wolsey's buildings. Since his forty-eight foot long kitchen was thought too small, the 'King's Great Kitchen' was built on to it, and also survives. It measures thirty-seven by twenty-seven feet and is nearly forty feet high at its apex. The flaking plaster reveals the English bond brick of the walls. Outside, incidentally, is one of the few Tudor doors with brick jambs and arch. The twin-flued fireplaces are seven feet high to the lintel. The two largest are sixteen and eighteen feet across. All have four-centred stone lintels, with deep brick relieving arches above. The largest fireplace (in the south wall) retains its original fittings—two sloping brick piers, like thin buttresses, with iron supports for the spits.

It is particularly difficult to understand and date the tight complex of tile-roofed offices on the north side of Clock Court and around and beyond the Round Kitchen Court. There are areas of original brickwork, areas of eighteenth-century and later remodelling or restoration and, linked on to these, the Wren ranges. In the main the east range of Clock Court is to be seen as Henrician improvements, but all remodelled by William Kent in 1732 when the state rooms were finished for George II. The Gateway has a patchy Tudor brick west face (all that is visible of the exterior) with Georgian windows and a 'Gothick' doorway. Just north-east of this is the Chapel Royal, with, on its north side, the irregular partly original Chapel Court.

It is not certain whether Wolsey's chapel utilized more of the Knights' chapel than its site, or how complete a renewal Henry's was. It is usually suggested that Henry kept the body of Wolsey's chapel, inserting the splendid timber ceiling and adding the three-aisled ante-chapel, over which is the Royal Pew. This work was done in 1535–6. The ceiling, with some lesser items, cost £451. It is a fan-vault, with gilded pendants like those of the Great Hall, and the vaulting cells are painted blue with gold stars: this woodwork now competes for effect with the ornate eighteenth-century altar canopy and wall-panelling. The brickwork of the low corridor at the west end of the chapel is plain and demure by comparison, though there are the two stone Royal arms panels at the west door. This cloister entrance provided a covered way for choir and procession. One imagines that Henry took over Wolsey's choir, which was famous, not that there was a complete change of personnel—whether ecclesiastical or domestic—on the fall of the Cardinal.

6. *Lost Henrician buildings*

Apart from the splendid gatehouse—now lost—that stood south of the palace and was linked to it by a long barbican, Henry's main extensions were to the east of Wolsey's buildings. The South or Water Gate and adjoining lost buildings can be seen in Anthonie van den Wyngaerde's drawings and in Danckerts's painting. It is Henry's work, rather than Wolsey's, that was demolished from 1689 on. A Water Gallery, near the river, had a temporary respite, for William and Mary lived there before any Wren buildings were ready. When they came to the throne in 1688 they found they liked the site of Hampton Court, a country palace with gardens round it—recently re-styled for Charles II—better than the Early Tudor ranges, widespread but mostly with rooms now considered small. The palace had been little altered since Henry's reign, apart from the addition of an Elizabethan wing on the south side. As noted, Christopher Wren at one time even proposed demolishing the whole Tudor palace apart from the Great Hall. What was desired in the late seventeenth century was galleries (wider and more impressive than those of Wolsey's innovations); more room for tapestries and pictures and china cabinets; state rooms, these including the royal bedrooms where levées were held while Royalty was dressed; wide stairs; the classical, late Renaissance style generally; formal gardens, inspired by the French. Wren was doyen of English architects, Surveyor-General in charge of the royal palaces for five reigns. His main secular building was done here. Demolition began at the east. Rebuilding went on till 1694, when it was abandoned for a period on Mary's death. When Whitehall burned down, and work was hastened and continued till William's death in 1702. This evidently saved the rest of the Tudor palace.

Wren, too, employed brick—light-red almost pink—with extensive Portland stone facings and dressings. His most beautiful work is the Fountain Court, a symmetrical four-storey secular cloister. The motifs—including the porthole windows and festoons of the third floor—echo the more widely spaced ones of the long south façade of the State Apartments. (For Wren's work see *Hampton Court Palace, 1689–1702*, published by the Oxford University Press in 1927.) Classical columns were also used for the colonnade on the south side of the Clock Court, for which some of Wolsey's work was demolished though the outer walls were left. The Fountain Court replaced the third court of the Tudor palace, Henry's Cloister Green Court. Work on the third court was begun in 1528, before Wolsey's fall, specifically on the range of 'Anne Bouillaynes lodginges', and went on into the 1530s, when the lodgings were completed but for Jane Seymour. Besides the building account references to 'the Lady Anne's lodgynges', the Privy Purse accounts were recording gifts to Anne, such as one hundred pounds at Christmas 1530. She was executed, having been condemned—this mother of the Virgin Queen, her rudimentary sixth finger an object of superstitious fear—in 1536 for unfaithfulness. Jane Seymour died of septicaemia after the birth of Prince Edward in 1537. These lodgings constituted the east range of the court, with close-set polygonal bays and turrets facing the park. The adjoining south range was built and fitted out as the King's own apartments. They overlooked the now lost brick-walled 'Privy Garden'. The Henrician accounts also mention a royal gallery and a library.

To the north, as we have seen, demolition was not wholesale. Enough remains of the Tudor courts and gabled ranges, running north to south between them, to give an impression of the rest. Henry added to the existing lodgings for officers and servants, and the accounts list numerous lost or untraceable domestic offices: flesh house; fish kitchen; pastry; confectionery; scullery; sellery (salt store); spicery; poultry; 'chawndry' (What was this? Perhaps the chandlery, for candle-making); scalding house; boiling house; washing house; pitcher house; still house (for distilling); coal house; feather house; hot house; jewel house; pay house; almonry; counting house; check house; victualling house; store house; and the 'squillery' and 'accatry', both mysterious to me.

7. *Royal recreation*

The immediate environs of the palace in Tudor times had elements now almost completely lacking—in what is the seventeenth-century setting. Charles II began the formalization of the old gardens, which was continued under William III. Indeed, old engravings show us that the formal gardens were once much larger and more elaborate than today's survivals, though the Tijou gates into the open parkland remain in place. The setting must have been less dramatic in Henry's time, for three main reasons. Firstly, the spacious parkland, which Wolsey had divided into two, Henry further divided with brick walls, now lost. Secondly, the gardens were not landscaped to lead the eye to wide vistas beyond. Thirdly, round the palace was an uneven fringe of recreational buildings.

The most spectacular provision for sport was the Tiltyard, for jousts and tournaments, on the north side of the palace. This was of seven acres or more. It had high brick walls, on which were five watching-towers for spectators. Wyngaerde's view from the north, in 1558, shows such careful provisions as two-storey bay windows and chimneys. The surviving gallery in the north-west angle of the palace also overlooks this area. One battlemented tower does remain: it is square, with one square projection and traces of two other lost projections, and of three storeys. The brickwork has diaper decoration—chevrons and a cross. This tower was converted into a tea-house in 1924. The others had been demolished in William III's reign, when the Tiltyard was made into kitchen gardens. There are fragments of the twenty-inch thick Tudor boundary walls, the bricks being very much pitted. When the 1527 French ambassador's party came, tents, pavilions and small wood houses had to be erected in the Tiltyard for some of the four hundred visitors. Henry had earlier had a tiltyard laid out at his own Greenwich Palace, where the watching-towers were built by Henry Redman.

Another recreational provision reminds us of Henry's contemporary additions to Wolsey's Palace at Whitehall, for Hampton Court had a covered bowling alley north-east of the palace. This is lost, but 'Tennis Court Lane' brings us to the surviving Royal Tennis Court of 1529–30. This is a long rectangular structure, the lower stage of which is solid Tudor brickwork, all the light being let in from the upper storey, which was altered in the late seventeenth century. It was described as the 'close tennys play', that is an enclosed, covered court for the extremely active indoor game, which may be loosely described as a mixture of squash and lawn tennis. The game is still played there. The Privy Purse accounts record payments for special tennis clothes for Henry VIII. He could play tennis, and bowl too, at both Whitehall and St James's Palaces and at Greenwich, where the court gave its name to one of the three open courtyards. There is an admiring contemporary account of how he looked, fair-skinned and flushed, as a young man playing tennis.

Out in the park, while he was still athletic, the King could shoot and hunt and hawk. The Exchequer accounts show that partridge (the common or grey partridge, a native bird), pheasant and deer were brought to stock the park. Like fallow deer, pheasants were probably introduced to this country by the Romans. Royal servants even dug holes for rabbits! Surprisingly, rabbits were not a native animal either, and were probably introduced after the Norman Conquest, in the eleventh or twelfth century. They were uncommon and localized in distribution till the sixteenth or seventeenth century, when warrening became extensive. In Tudor times great houses and institutions might have warrens: examples are those of the lawyers' Lincoln's Inn, London, and of Sir Richard Lee, courtier and royal officer, on his ex-monastic property at Sopwell, St Albans. The Privy Purse accounts mention 'angelyng rodds' (fishing rods) for the King.

These sporting activities were possible at most of his twenty palaces in the London region, but Hampton Court was the most favoured royal house. It was also, despite the free acquisition of Wolsey's buildings and fittings and utensils, the most expensive. Yet, for all its size, it was not a 'prodigy' house, unlike Henry's own Nonsuch or his courtier's Layer Marney (Essex). The comparatively low brick walls defined a practical entity, a dense, predominantly male village, with provision for courtly recreation, diplomatic entertaining, worship, and supportive domestic industry.

Note: See Gazetteer entry for bibliography on Hampton Court and for illustrations pls. 33–9.

Select Gazetteer

BUILDINGS are listed by counties, under the parishes in which they are situated, except occasionally by name when they are both famous and isolated. The notes concentrate on exteriors, because interior brick is usually plastered, though in ruins the plaster may now have disappeared. Halls, even ruined, received more attention than smaller houses, and timber-framed buildings are ignored unless particularly striking.

There are several justifications for playing down timber-framing with brick in-filling. Brick used in this way does not influence architecture or vernacular style much, and any individuality contributed by such brick is likely to be just a matter of diagonal or herringbone nogging. In addition, the brick often derives from a later improvement on lath-bonded plaster, and so is more modern than the main structure. This makes dating difficult, as does the practice of enlarging an old house with an overhanging first storey by building new walls of brick up to the overhang and then destroying the original ground-floor walls. The versatility of brick means it was often used for such alterations and enlargements in the sixteenth and seventeenth centuries, especially with the seventeenth-century population explosion.

Biographical references have been given *only* where the entries are especially dependent on the printed sources or where further details may be found from them. References to county books, listed under author or organization in the main bibliography, may just be assumed, or are given in abbreviated form. The 1965 boundary changes which produced the Greater London Council area and abolished Middlesex administratively are disregarded, except that a change of authority is noted by individual places, and places are listed under their old counties. This is done for convenience, to tie in with all the gazetteer-type sources. Most of the older or antiquarian county books and even books on architecture feature nowhere, for their usefulness to students is often vitiated by emphasis on style, without mention of materials, and by the blinding dogma that there was no brick building between the Romans and the Tudors.

An attempt is made to describe buildings and to give builders as well as dates. The total omission of any important buildings is regretted, but the distribution pattern, with the vast majority of buildings being sited in East Anglia, would not be affected.

I have usually shown (without opening times) what buildings are public property or, though private, are open regularly. Other buildings, especially institutional, may be open at limited times. For some isolated churches it may be necessary to borrow the key. The majority of other buildings are in private hands, and their inclusion does *not* imply that they can be visited. Because of the specialist interest, perhaps aided by my having concentrated on exteriors, I have been greeted with friendliness and help by owners, whether personally or by letter. I must record my gratitude to them here.

*With the exception of reused Roman brick, buildings wholly or in part of brick of before A.D. 1450 are marked with an asterisk.**

The further examples of brickwork listed at the end of each county are nearly all of the period 1450–1550.

ABBREVIATIONS OF PRINTED SOURCES

Organizations:

M.H.L.G. — the Ministry of Housing and Local Government list of 'buildings of architectural and historic interest'.

M.O.W. — Ministry of Works, later (1962) retitled:

M.P.B. & W. — Ministry of Public Building and Works, the official guidebook of both having been published by the Stationery Office (abbreviated to *H.M.S.O.*) Buildings controlled by the Ministry.

N.M.R. — National Monuments Record (originally, National Buildings Record, photographic collection).

R.C.H.M. — Royal Commission on Historic Monuments.

V.C.H. — Victoria County History.

W.E.A. — Workers' Educational Association. Any W.E.A. reference is to a local branch publication.

Authors (examples only):

Garner & Stratton—their *Domestic Architecture of the Tudor Period* (see main bibliography).

Pevsner—the relevant county volume in the Penguin *Buildings of England* series by Nikolaus Pevsner, (certain volumes having co-authors).

SURVIVING BUILDINGS WITH BRICKWORK OF BEFORE 1450

(The dates are approximate)

1160: Polstead, Suffolk: Parish Church (arches).
1190: Little Coggeshall, Essex: Abbot's Lodging.
1220: Little Coggeshall, Essex: Vaulting of Dorter of Abbey; St Nicholas's Chapel.
1270–80: Little Wenham, Suffolk: Little Wenham Hall.
C 13: Ashby, Suffolk: Parish Church.
late C 13: Copford, Essex: Parish Church.
late C 13: Allington, Kent: Allington Castle (vault).
late C 13
C 14: Great Yarmouth, Norfolk: Town Walls.
1300: Herringfleet, Suffolk: St Olave's Priory.
1300: Norwich, Norfolk: Guildhall Undercroft.
1307: Norwich, Norfolk: Blackfriars' Undercroft.
early C 14: Cowlinge, Suffolk: Parish Church.
early C 14: Norwich, Norfolk: City Walls.
1320: Butley, Suffolk: Butley Priory Gatehouse.
1320: Kingston upon Hull, Yorkshire: Holy Trinity Church.
1325: Norwich, Norfolk: Bridewell Undercroft; Strangers' Hall Undercroft.
1339: Claxton, Norfolk: Claxton Castle.
1346: Sutton, Yorkshire: Parish Church.
mid C 14: Cambridge: Church of St Mary-the-Less.
mid C 14: Roos, Yorkshire: Parish Church.
mid C 14: Wingfield, Suffolk: Parish Church.
C 14: Little Waldingfield, Suffolk: 'Priory' Undercroft.
C 14: Langley, Norfolk: Langley Abbey (vaulting).
C 14: Lincoln: Exchequer Gateway to Cathedral Close.
C 14: Dovercourt, Essex: Parish Church.
C 14: Dengie, Essex: Parish Church.
C 14: Letcombe Bassett, Berkshire: Parish Church.
C 14: Waltham St Lawrence, Berkshire: Parish Church.
1366: Appledore, Kent: Horne's Place Chapel.
1369: Beccles, Suffolk: Parish Church (charnel).
1370: Waltham, Essex: Waltham Abbey Gatehouse.
1378: Gillingham, Kent: Grench Manor.
1380: Norwich, Norfolk: Cow Tower.
1382: Thornton Curtis, Lincolnshire: Thornton Abbey Gatehouse.
1396: Ely (Cambridgeshire and Isle of Ely): Priory Gateway.
late C 14: Leiston-cum-Sizewell, Suffolk: Leiston Abbey.
late C 14: Brandesburton, Yorkshire: Parish Church.
late C 14: Stanway, Essex: All Saints Church Ruins.
late C 14: King's Lynn, Norfolk: Carmelites' Gateway.
late C 14: Levington, Suffolk: Parish Church.

C 14/C 15: Long Crendon, Buckinghamshire: Court House.
late C 14, 15: King's Lynn, Norfolk: Clifton House Undercroft.
1406: King's Lynn, Norfolk: Guildhall of St. George.
1419: Beverley, Yorkshire: North Bar.
1420: Spalding, Lincolnshire: Ayscoughee Hall.
1430: Cambridge: Old Schools; Magdalene College.
1430: Caister, Norfolk: Caister Castle.
1432: Drayton, Norfolk: Drayton Lodge.
1435: Bardney, Lincolnshire: Parish Church.
1435: Maldon, Essex: 'Moot Hall'.
1436–7: Ewelme, Oxfordshire: Almshouses; School.
1438: Cambridge: Peterhouse.
1439: Faulkbourne, Essex: Faulkbourne Hall.
early C 15: Boston, Lincolnshire: Guildhall.
early C 15: Margate, Kent: Dent-de-Lion Gatehouse.
1440: Isleworth, Middlesex: Syon Undercroft.
1440: Hurstmonceux, Sussex: Castle; Parish Church.
1440: Eton, Buckinghamshire: Eton College.
1440: Repton, Derbyshire: Prior Overton's Tower.
1443: Stanstead Abbots, Hertfordshire: Rye House.
mid C 15: Tattershall, Lincolnshire: Tattershall Castle; College.
mid C 15: Stixwould, Lincolnshire: Halstead Hall.
1448: Cambridge: Queens' College.
1449: Thanington, Kent: Tonford Hall.
1450: Baconsthorpe, Norfolk: Baconsthorpe Castle.

Select Gazetteer

BEDFORDSHIRE

CARDINGTON

Old Manor House: Compact but substantial Early Tudor house. In ruins. Two big ranges, with crow-stepped gables, form an L: angle filled in asymmetrically by smaller blocks. Brick-built, English bond, but later mainly pebble-dashed. Windows stone, but fancy crow-stepping and one original chimney, with deep twist and spurred top, brick. Attributable to Sir William Gascoigne, Comptroller of Wolsey's Household. Gascoigne's 1540 heraldic brass remains in parish church.

OLD WARDEN

The Abbey: Rich Cistercian foundation surrendered in 1537. Only remains above ground are materials incorporated in later house. (Excavations recently uncovered foundations and mosaic tiling.) House has brick, particularly on S side: twisted brick chimneys, buttresses with stone dressings, brick voussoirs to 2 archways. All mid C 16. This is an unpreserved ruin, described as 'dangerous', and a fragment only of mansion erected by Sir John Gostwick (d. 1545), M.P. Inside this so-called Abbey is spiral stair, with triangular wood steps resting loose in wall and newel. Property obtained at Dissolution by Gostwick, who at same date used stone for his main house, at Willington, also in Beds. (This is lost, but there remain contemporary stone stables and stylish dovecote with stepped gables.) At Dissolution was one of King's officers, dealing with monastic lands.

SOMERIES *Jacket photograph*

Known as '*Someries Castle*' or '*Manor House*'. In village of Hyde, 2 m. SE of Luton. Striking but mysterious building of last quarter of fifteenth century. Leland described it as 'very large and fair', 'of Brick', begun by Lord Wenlock in 1464. Wenlock was killed on Lancastrian side at Tewkesbury in 1471 (fine canopied stone tomb in Luton parish church). Edward IV granted his estates to Thomas Rotherham, later Archbishop of York. Wenlock and Rotherham were among the founders of *Queen's College, Cambridge*. Rotherham was notable brick builder. Manning argues Rotherham is likely builder of all Someries; Dyer says, reasonably, it is unlikely Leland was wrong so soon. Rotherham seems not to have lived here: probably only added to unfinished house.

Site is that of C 13 house of de Somery family. Next to it traces of lost village. Most of C 15 Someries is lost, for 1606 inventory listed 25 rooms. Now there is only gatehouse block, including chapel, originally just the N wing. 2 storeys. Of dark red brick with early blue-glazed diaperwork. Bricks about 9 × 4 × 2 in. Chapel was reduced from 49 × 18 ft to 34 × 18 when gatehouse added. This has carriage and pedestrian arches, the former 9 ft wide, and bays on either side. Elaborate work survives here: corbelling over entrance, squinch and stair to right. Other moulded bricks used for window and door arches and window slits of range. Pointed spandrels to one doorway. Style and structure of Someries must be compared with Bishop Morton's Palace at *Hatfield* (Herts).

Someries' best feature is spiral stair at rear, though this ruinous. Wholly brick, with handrail deeply inset, steps resting on vaulting bricks that radiate sideways from circular newel. Vault so beautifully laid it looks carved out of butter!

William H. Manning, 'Someries Castle, Luton', *article* in *The Bedfordshire Magazine*, Spring 1965; James Dyer in *The Story of Luton* by Dyer *et al.*, White Crescent Press, Luton, 1964.

BERKSHIRE

ABINGDON

**Abbey:* Benedictine foundation, with stone buildings. Exchequer building has chimney and fireplace of *c.* 1250: the famous chimney is of stone, with lancet openings to lantern; flue stone-lined, but fireback below rises 6 ft and is made of 10 or 11 in. long tiles set edgewise.

Also brickwork in C 15 or early C 16 Long Gallery, probably last building constructed—as clerks' lodgings. Brick firebacks to stone fireplaces inside. Building of 2 storeys, with notable timber roof to 1st floor. Much altered. Corridor runs along N side of upper floor and here wall is constructed of timber uprights with in-filling of thick red 'Tudor' bricks: these laid upright or flat.

BISHAM

Bisham Abbey: Now used by C.C.P.R. as National Recreation Centre. Thames-side site. Marvellous mixture of monastic remains of stone (including separate dovecote to N), reused masonry blocks and red brick of post-Dissolution conversion. Brick seemingly all post-1550. Too striking and significant to miss out, though.

Origins as preceptory, apparently on manor-house plan, of Templars. 1337 Augustinian priory established here. From 1536 to 1540 final Dissolution a Benedictine abbey, but under control of Margaret Countess of Salisbury and her husband, Sir Richard Pole. Trace of possession in impaled arms in *council chamber* glass. 1539 confiscation when Margaret, niece of Edward IV, was attainted, at end of Tudor purge of rival claimants and relatives. Aged 80, she was executed in 1541. See also *Warblington Castle*, Hampshire. The Poles apparently used buildings on S of site, the bulk of monastic buildings being to N (inside lost moat). By time of 1552 purchase from Edward VI by Sir Philip Hoby the monastic church had been demolished, but domestic and ancillary buildings survived, including the 'maltinge howse' (for brewing). The dovehouse was rented out. 1552 document shows that there was pre-Dissolution brick here: in the 'parcell of the possessions of Margaret, late Countess of Sarum (Salisbury), of high treason atteyntede', was 'the late monastery of Bustelisham Montegue', 'whereof is standing the late prior's lodgings buylded of tymber and brick and covered with tyles, sette betwene the Thamys and the Mancon house of the late Countess of Sarum, wherein is a lytell halle, a parloure . . . ketchyn . . . pantery'. This lodging sounds like late mediaeval or early C 16 improvements, the earlier buildings being all stone.

Sir Philip Hoby held manor till his death in 1558, when succeeded by his half-brother, Sir Thomas Hoby (died 1566). Demolition continued and both brothers put up new buildings, using brick, but more known of Philip's work for he left a diary. House not now as large as it was. E of pointed monastic door are Hoby additions, including stepped brick gables. Thomas Hoby demolished all but one range of Augustinian cloister and added on to that in brick, including polygonal brick bay window, with stone dressings and open base, to council chamber (1st floor hall). Behind this, more brickwork remains, above all tall, thin battlemented turret: its irregular shape may be compared with early C 16 episcopal tower of *Cakeham* (West Wittering), Sussex, though that rises really clear of other buildings. For 1560 Thomas Hoby's diary says: 'This yeere was the turret built in Bisham.' In 1561: 'this yere were the new lodgings finished.' Thomas Hoby was traveller and diplomat, visiting Italy and other parts of Europe. James Lees-Milne in *Tudor Renaissance* (1951) says 'he investigated the reason why brick used by the old Romans was so much more durable than those used by his contemporaries in England', but I have failed to find the reference. A 1553 entry on Munich, in the Duchy of Bavaria, shows him admiring brick: 'Not a house of tymber with in (the town walls), but all of freestone and bricke in such cumlie (comely) order . . .'

Sir Thomas Hoby, *A Book of the Travaile and Lief of Me*, published as *The Travels and Life of Sir Thomas Hoby, Kt. of Bisham Abbey, written by himself* 1547–1564, edited by Edgar Powell in Royal Historical Society's *Camden Miscellany*, vol. X, 1902; N. Pevsner, *Berkshire*, 1966.

BRADFIELD

Parish Church: Church subjected to alteration: interior is C 12, C 14 and Gilbert Scott. Tower, characterized as 'mysterious' as to date, is perp. in appearance and built of brick, with flint courses. Stone course and windows. Some of bricks appear mediaeval. Another mystery is small polygonal structure in churchyard, S of chancel. One-storeyed. Pevsner describes it as a rib-vaulted lobby, perhaps part of a gatehouse. Gatehouse to churchyard?

BRAY

Parish Church: C 15 timber-framed gatehouse to churchyard, brick infilled. *Ockwells Manor House:* ¾ m. WSW of Bray. A big house. Mainly half-timbered, brick infilled. Built for Sir John Norreys, from *c.* 1460. NE range was added in modern times. Very much a manor-house, without thought of defences. Strikingly large windows. Dressings stone and wood. Tudor stained glass, and appearance, despite mid C 15 date, is Tudor. Plan, however, asymmetrical courtyard. Dating problems: 1838 picture lacks the famous oriels of front, presumably a later 'restoration'. Pevsner calls it 'the most refined and sophisticated timber-framed mansion in England'. G. Holmes says it 'represents the aspirations of the richer gentry'. Interesting, then, that such vernacular style was thought suitable for a great house: the W and S sides, though, are wholly brick. Ockwells' bricks are thin, pale red.

COOKHAM-ON-THAMES

Parish Church: An interesting window (very like work at Tacolneston Church, Norfolk), to vestry—originally Lady Chapel established 1180. Window plain, Perp., with mullions of moulded brick. Thought to be of about 1465.

LETCOMBE BASSETT

**Parish Church:* Tower incorporates C 14 bricks. (*Murray's Berkshire*, 1949.)

READING

Abbey: Considerable stone and flint remains of Henry I's Cluniac foundation. Also, in Valpy St, C 15 octagonal brick turret, with stone quoins. 2 stages high, attached to what was first the monastic dormitory, then a grammar school, now part of municipal offices (all rebuilt, except it). Bricks pinky-red, fairly thick. Plinth is flint. Turret walls thick. Internal diameter about 10ft. (Spiral stair is modern stone.)

SHOTTESBROOKE

Shottesbrooke Park: Large-scale demolition has unified appearance of house. Difficult to date. A Tudor building, with possible *de Vere* connections, was revamped in C 18 and again about 1830. Square, 2-storeyed, battlemented. Pink brick, with continuous dark diaper. Polygonal angle buttresses. Some of this brickwork is Tudor and appearance is Tudor. Manor was that of Trussells (monuments in church). Putative builder, John de Vere, 15th Earl of Oxford (d. 1540), who married the Trussell heiress.

SUTTON COURTENAY

Parish Church: Stone church of all periods from Norman. Has really endearing S porch of mellow red brick: 2-storeyed, with parvise. C 16 Perp.

WALTHAM ST LAWRENCE

**Parish Church:* Flint and stone W tower: top evidently C 14 brickwork.

BUCKINGHAMSHIRE

BEACONSFIELD

Old Rectory: SW of parish church. Partly brick-built, partly timber-framed house, begun *c.* 1500. Terminal date, 1543. Restored 1901, still used by parish. Plan appears quadrangular, but E has only link wall between S and N gable-ends: modern stone gateway in original red brick, blue diamond diapered. Similar brickwork makes up lower storey of all 3 wings, including projecting S end of main (N–S) wing and the rounded stair turret on N side. In courtyard square brick chimney-stacks. Timber-framing, plaster-infilled, used for upper storey (over-hangs). Bricks, thin and red. C 16 spiral stair inside.
R.C.H.M.

CHENIES *Fig. 10(e)*

Manor House: On R. Chess. Russell family, of Dorset origins, acquired Chenies manor through marriage of John Russell with heiress, Anne Sapcoate (main property in this region, Woburn Abbey (Beds.), was a later, Reformation gain). This John Russell came of knightly family, unusual in having Continental connections through wine trade: Russell's consequent knowledge of Spanish brought him, aged 20, into court circle in 1504, when Archduke Philip of Austria & Burgundy and his Spanish bride were shipwrecked off Weymouth. Russell was brought to court as interpreter. Original Russell properties centred on lordship of Tavistock: Chenies marriage established him in Home Counties also. In early years of Reformation vastly added to West lands, when President of Council of York of the West and involved in building of Henrician fortresses along Kent and Sussex coasts. Became Baron Russell of Chenies; Lord High Admiral 1540–2; Lord Privy Seal 1542; executor of King himself (1547). Lived till 1555, aged 69, retaining ex-church lands *temp.* Mary I. In Russell Chapel in Chenies parish church are massed ranks of tombs of Earls and Dukes of Bedford.

Leland recorded how John Russell had largely rebuilt the old manor house at Chenies, using brick and timber: 'so translated by Mylord Russell that little or nothing of it in a manner remains untranslated'. Timber no longer apparent outside, the surviving old parts of Chenies being the S and W ranges, and their corridor-style link, all brick. Leland specifies: 'fine new lodgings be rected in the garden', these evidently the long S range: its windowless S façade has high chimney-stacks and big projections for garderobes and cabinets, gables of these being stepped. Range is 3-storeyed, corners marked by tall, thin polygonal buttresses with pepper-pot tops. W range, which may be a little earlier than 1530 date suggested for S range, has similar angle buttresses, besides stair tower rising above roof level.

Alterations and additions throughout, besides demolition, making complex plan. However, basic dull, blue-tinged red brick walling remains, with some grey or buff bricks too. Also 2 outstanding and repeated original features: (1) oriel windows projecting on brick corbels, (2) decorated chimney-shafts, with many different patterns. Twists, zigzags, network and honeycomb add an element of fantasy to the already complex roof line, with its crowstepped gables like those of *Horham Hall* (Essex). Chimneys are grouped in pairs or 4s. Building is solid, impressive. S façade, strictly the rear (but facing main road), suggests formidable tall barracks—and power of an Early Tudor 'new man' (this one having lacked an eye since the 1522 French campaign).

N. Pevsner, *Buckinghamshire*, 1960.

DORNEY

Dorney Court: Near church, Timber-framed with brick infilling. Particularly good vernacular building, of *c.* 1500.

Parish Church: W tower brick of *c.* 1530, with battlemented turrets. Plinth rubble, dressings stone. (Brick S porch is mid C 17.)

ETON *Fig. 14*

**Eton College:* 1440 charter established 'The King's College of our Lady of Eton beside Windsor', for 25 scholars. Already exceptional, this number soon enlarged to 70. No fees. Model available in Winchester College (Hants), founded by William of Wykeham 1394: Eton's 1st provost, Bishop William Waynflete, came from Winchester bringing 6 scholars with him. Almshouse was to be included, but this did not last into C 16. Very large funds (about £1,500 p.a.), including grant of 8 East Anglian alien priories. College led threatened existence *temp.* Edward IV and *temp.* Henry VIII (when forced exchange lost it valuable land in London, partly for St James's Palace), even being threatened with suppression 1546. Edward VI saved it. Earlier threats derived from Yorkist hostility to foundations associated with extravagant Henry VI. Apart from chantry elements, Henry's main motivation was anti-Lollard. Teachers swore 'not to favour the damnable heresies of John Wyclif or Reginald Pecock'. Eton was a school, with college of secular priests instructed (like those of Bishop Fleming's Lincoln College, Oxford, in 1427) to counter the pre-Reformation heresies.

Main building material was brick, but the high fine chapel (contemporary with *King's College Chapel*, Cambridge) is stone. Building accounts survive, showing that in 1442 field with brick earth was rented at Slough for 20*s.* p.a. and kiln was built there. Building operations controlled by William Vesey, 'brikemaker' and 'King's serjeant' (already commissioned for work at adjacent Windsor, 1437). (W. D. Simpson suggests Vesey was also architect of *Hurstmonceux Castle.*) In 1440s Slough supplied great numbers of bricks for the college, and work continued through 1450s. Between 1442 and 1451 2½ million bricks supplied—1 million in 1443–4 alone.

There were to be 2 courts of buildings, 2 gatehouses and a great tower. 1443 contract for cloisters cited 7 towers. Extant brick buildings of this date are 'Founder's Tower' and most of College Cloister (old, inner courtyard, behind Lupton's Tower), including arcades. Hall is of 1448–58, of stone though it has Early Tudor bricks at W end (Pevsner). As late as C 18 Caneletto painting (in National Gallery) shows the smallish, square, stone-dressed Founder's Tower standing in isolation. 2-storeyed Cloister is stone-dressed throughout; arches are stone with brick voussoirs; brick stair turrets at corners. Oldest parts N and E ranges, seemingly built before Henry's 1460 deposition, though these have attic storey of 1760. Diamond-diapered. Much modern restoration, including cleaning of bricks and repointing. Early records mention a kitchen, but the one surviving—with square ground plan and octagonal top—looks, says Pevsner, 'C 16 rather than C 15'.

Second important building period followed Lancastrian setback. Roger Lupton was donor and Provost 1503–35 (d. 1540). On N side of chapel is 'Lupton's Chapel' (with memorial brass bearing rebus of tun inscribed 'LUP'.) Thought to have erected the buildings on W side of Cloisters, including Library. Also probably completed *c.* 1443 Lower School (classroom) and Long Chamber (the 70 scholars' dormitory), both 2-storeyed and battlemented. There are here stacks of Early Tudor chimneys, mouldings including twists and counter-relief diamond patterning. Most conspicuous work was Lupton's Tower, the Provost's Lodge. This, set in diapered W range of about 1517–20, provides entry to old College Cloister. By Henry Redman, 'chief mason of the king's works'. Of rich red brick, diamond-diapered, with stone dressings (plinth, string courses, quoins, all voids). Main recessed section of 3 storeys. Great 2-stage oriel over entrance arch. 2 polygonal turrets at front (none at rear) have 5 stages, their pierced pepper-pot tops added in 1765, when clock also inserted. One rare feature in brickwork complements stone statue of the Virgin (in canopied niche at centre of oriel): over against this, on l. angle turret, is the Annunciation lilypot, formed of black bricks.

Pevsner, *Buckinghamshire*; B. J. W. Hill, *Pictorial History of Eton College*, Pitkin.

HITCHAM

Parish Church: Tudor brick W tower.

LONG CRENDON

**Court House:* National Trust. Timber-framed with brick infilling, on stone plinth. Long 2-storey range, upper floor corbelled out on wood beams. Possibly of C 14. Documented from C 15. Till C 19 known as 'Staple Hall'. Evidently erected as wool store, wool from this district being woven in East Anglia. At least from early C 15 also used as manorial courthouse. Panels between timber-framing of ground floor are of plastered brick. Upper floor had more uniform exterior: unplastered brick nogging, bricks laid flat. At E end rectangular Tudor chimney-stack: indoors, a brick fireplace. Round brick oven, projecting from S wall.

LOWER (or NETHER) WINCHENDON

Nether Winchendon House: Partly Early Tudor, of stone. Has moulded brick chimneys with ornamented round shafts. Heavy Gothic remodelling of house *c.* 1780, when battlements added.

NORTH CRAWLEY

The Grange: NE of parish church. Associated with Cardinal Wolsey. Date uncertain, conceivably Elizabethan, but R.C.H.M. volume on Buckinghamshire said: 'It was built probably in the first half of the 16th century.' Later additions. E-plan front, with 3-storeyed porch looks Elizabethan, but other elements earlier. Gables. Dressings stone, fabric brick.

CAMBRIDGESHIRE, WITH THE ISLE OF ELY

ARRINGTON

Parish Church: C. J. W. Messent cited C 15 brick in tower; R.C.H.M., however, describes it as rebuilt in C 16 partly of bricks.

BRINKLEY

Parish Church: Situated in extreme SE of county, has its one brick porch. C 15, Perp.

CAMBRIDGE

Note: The main sources for all buildings are Pevsner's *Cambridgeshire*, the 1959 R.C.H.M. volume on the town of Cambridge and Steegman's *Cambridge*.

**Church of St Mary-the-Less:* Below Perp. S chapel (vestry) is charnel evidently dating from rebuilding of church *c.* 1340–52. Though ribs clunch and springers stone, the cells are brick—about the earliest in Cambridge. Quadripartite vault. Bricks probably brought up R. Ouse, as some for Ely monastery.

**Old Schools:* In Trinity Lane. The early university teaching buildings, much later than the oldest colleges. Mainly of rubble, oldest part *c.* 1350 Divinity School. Second range of about 1430–60, has brick voussoirs. In 1457–70 S range built, as Schools of Civil Law and Philosophy with library on 1st floor, of brick. One contributor of funds was Sir John Fastolf of *Caister*, Norfolk. This range less changed than 1430–60 range (altered in C 18).

Colleges

Christ's College: One of 2 Cambridge colleges established by will of Lady Margaret Beaufort, mother of Henry VII (other is *St John's*). Christ's has an oratory room named for foundress, and still has her gift of plate. Work evidently begun before her death in 1509, inspired by her confessor or chaplain (from 1502), Bishop John Fisher, who continued the work. Fisher was Chancellor of University at this date. Lady Margaret also founded professorships of Divinity at Oxford and Cambridge. Besides Fisher, another of her executors was Sir Henry Marney of *Layer Marney*, Essex. Both Cambridge gatehouses are mediaeval, despite Tudor portcullis and rose badges. Both have stone-carved royal arms, supported by Beaufort yales—wonderful spotted beasts, with horns supposed to swivel, compounded of goat and antelope with elephants' tails—on a ground with clumps of borage and daisies (daisy, or marguerite, rebus of 'Margaret').

At first sight no brick apparent. Gatehouse and first range date from 1505–1511 and were built of brick, but ashlar-faced in 1714. Mason, William Swayn. First court also, ashlar-faced in C 18, early C 16. Some of original brick still shows in places. Chapel has brick turret, with 1772 top. On N outside wall of first range brick shows, with clunch, and there is one brick gable-end partly crow-stepped. Next to this, simple wholly brick gateway: head stepped and arch has brick mouldings, while recessed back has brick soffits. No sign of diapering. Bricks longish, deep-red. Some of adjoining wall looks contemporary.

Christ's records include impressment of bricklayers when building began.

Corpus Christi College: College founded 1352 by Guild of 'Corpus Christi and the Blessed Mary', to help increase number of clerks (clergy) after 1349 Black Death. Mary Bateson said of this rare guild enterprise: 'a remarkable event; not that this guild was the first of the last to take part in the endowment of education, for many founded or partly endowed grammar schools, but the foundation of a college was a more ambitious undertaking than is recorded of any similar society. It was further of peculiar interest as an effort made towards healing an old feud between town and university.' (Quoted in Rashdall's *Mediaeval Universities.*) Black Death also regarded as part of foundation motives for Gonville and Trinity Hall. Long known as 'Benet College', recording link with church of St Benet (Benedict), appropriated to college on foundation. Guild disappears from records at time of Peasants' Revolt riots in Cambridge, 1381. College continued, and so did connection with church, at least till later C 16.

L. F. Salzman (in *Building in England Down to* 1540) quotes contract of 1459 for a 'Bakhouse' (bakehouse), to be built of ragstone, clunch and brick. Walls partly brick; 4 'Wyndows of 'half the water-tabell'—projecting course —to be of the 'best endureing breke'. This lost.

First court of college is C 14 and stone-built. The one brick structure records link with church. Corpus Christi gallery survives intact. Of *c.* 1500 (terminal dates apparently 1487 and 1515). Of red brick, 2-storey, pierced by segmental archway with an oratory over. Upper floor connected with 2 chapels (overlooking chancel), used by master and students. College acquired own chapel only in C 16, allowing church to revert wholly to parish. At E end of church, across S aisle gable, is some old brickwork which looks possibly contemporary with gallery. Gallery has shallow pitched roof, with old tiles. Brick irregularly bonded, mainly headers, warm colouring. Dressings stone, including archway, the college entrance for a period. Stone-faced buttresses. Windows have plain arched lights, square heads. Empty canopied stone statue niche on courtyard side.

Jesus College: For John Alcock, founder, see also *Ely*, Bishop's Palace: he was bishop 1486–1501. College was founded in premises of dissolved nunnery, long before Wolsey's 27 suppressions for his colleges at Oxford and *Ipswich* (Suffolk). Inspiration for college derived from 1486 Jesus College or school established at Rotherham by Archbishop Rotherham (Yorkshire—see 'Lost Buildings'). Alcock himself came from *Beverley*. Two bishops were friends, shared office of Chancellor 1476. Alcock again Chancellor 1486, after Henry VII's take-over, also Comptroller of Works.

Cambridge college dates from 1496. Site, then outside town boundaries, that of Benedictine nunnery dedicated to St. Radegund (bad reputation for entertaining young scholars). In 1486 Alcock had labelled the remaining 11 nuns incompetent, extravagant and dissolute. Trouble possibly partly financial, as by 1459 buildings were in bad state and nuns so poor it was difficult to pay for food. By 1496 only 2 left, one described as 'infamis' (of ill-fame) and Alcock obtained papal bull for suppression of convent and necessary royal licence (1497). As Bishop of Ely had himself been overseer of convent.

A master and six fellows were now appointed. Despite retention of some conventional buildings, Alcock's style was so impressed on college that even in 1638 Stuart buildings, erected N side of 1st court, imitated his work. In 1718, when 3rd storey added to court, Perp. style kept and, even if contrast with gatehouse diminished, there was precedent in Alcock's 3-storey structures (unusual for date) in inner or cloister court. Bishop's statue in canopied niche over gatehouse arch; chapel bench-end of *c.* 1500 carved with bishop at prayer; arms, including 3 black cocks' heads with red combs feature on gatehouse; rebus of cock on globe ('Over all') appears in spandrels of ogee door to cloister court and elsewhere and in contemporary glass of library.

Gatehouse of brick was a model for later ones, but lacks their polygonal angle turrets: here is ogee decoration over depressed arch, with leafy finials rising up to base of founder's canopied statue; first use of brick with stone dressings. High narrow structure, completed *c.* 1500, of 3 storeys. Attached 2-storey ranges (3-storey from C 18) some time later. Alcock began building in red brick, and in gatehouse yellow gault brick used only for small continuous diamond diapering at top. Yellow or even cream bricks, however, were used for later buildings. Pevsner traces palaces where the 'conscious' changeover was made. Whole Jesus front is red brick (like rest of Cambridge brick, till Georgian times), but inner buildings yellow. Bond mainly English. Gatehouse dressings stone: arch, windows, thick string courses, quoins, copings to steep unusual stepped battlements, like those of Beverley North Bar. Brick voussoirs to round-arched upper windows. (Old-looking approach walls are C 16 and C 17 respectively.)

Gatehouse begun when Alcock otherwise was still just reconditioning convent buildings. New buildings were to follow old ground plan, and gatehouse perhaps stands on original entry. Even if convent lacked resources later, much wealth spent on it originally. (Incomplete) outer court includes W range of cloister, utilizing its stone arches, but walls refaced with brick. Cloister court, though altered and modernized, retains much of Alcock's work too. On E side survives beautiful early C 13 chapter-house entrance, but Alcock demolished chapter house itself. Traces of some domestic offices of convent. Chapel, in marvellous contrast to college brickwork, is nuns' stone cruciform chancel, with procession of high C 12 lancets and Norman transept: Alcock truncated church and demolished aisles. E end lancets are actually mid C 19 restoration by A. W. N. Pugin, since Alcock had inserted single great Perp. window. On N side of cloister Alcock's hall, most unusually on 2nd floor, with his library *above* it, linked from vestibule. Square stair turret. Furniture from chapel, marked with Alcock's badge, sold to Vicar of Landbeach in 1789 for £5 (survives there) and a door went to Ely Cathedral (in S transept). College is dark, quiet, inward, the early courts small. At rear later buildings, still imitative of Alcock's. *(Pl. 24)*

**Magdalene College:* Origins as hostel with cells for young monks from Benedictine abbeys of Croyland (or Crowland, Lincs.), Ramsey, Walden and Ely. In 1st form, as 'Buckingham College', Magdalene was built on site granted to Benedictines by Henry VI, 1428. 2nd (1460) and 3rd Stafford Dukes of Buckingham materially assisted building. (Henry was executed by Richard III after 1483 rebellion; Edward, builder of *Thornbury Castle*, Glos., executed 1521 by Henry VIII.) By Dissolution College had complete court, with hall and chapel, built of clunch faced with red brick. Much of this work survives (1st court).

Any monastic establishments were in greatest danger at Reformation, but Thomas Lord Audley obtained premises and re-established them as 'Magdalene Castle' 1542 (the 1st post-Dissolution foundation in Cambridge). Audley was Lord Chancellor, but even so the 1545 Act for Dissolution of Collegiate Foundations then threatened Magdalene along with rest of University: then Henry VIII was persuaded differently and himself issued foundation charter of *Trinity College*, 1546. Audley was important member of government, presided at trials of More and Fisher (in 1532 had replaced More as Chancellor). A promoter of Reformation who received much from it.

Magdalene's 1st court thus dates from *c.* 1430–1580, but is mainly C 15. Hall and butteries are of 1519, the bricks here $9 \times 4\frac{1}{2} \times 2$ in. (R.C.H.M.). Latest part is W range, with its plain chimneys, largely late C 16. Court was all brick-faced till plastered over—except chapel—in C 18 and C 19. Then submerged in ivy. In 1950s and 1960s creeper and plaster removed; brickwork repointed; repairs done, expecially on river frontage, which has chimney-stacks with diapering at base; stone windows inserted instead of original worn clunch; roof slates replaced with hand-made tiles, so restoring original uneven tile texture. This may sound drastic, but the *colour* is restored. Inside W range, with its largely C 16 shell, were found monastic cell partitions. Arms of patron abbeys are set over courtyard doors, once doors to groups of cells supported by Croyland and the rest.

M. E. Wood, *The English Mediaeval House*, 1965.

**Queens' College:* Rare Lancastrian-Yorkist foundation, where Elizabeth Woodville, wife of usurper Edward IV, followed Margaret of Anjou, wife of Henry VI. Several kings also involved: land and licence obtained from Henry VI; Edward IV gave very necessary permission for work to continue; Richard III gave grants, including one in 1477, when Duke of Gloucester, for 4 fellows (whose duties included praying for 'our sovereyne lady quene Elizabet fundress of the seyde college, of the prince and all the kynges childer', which children he is popularly believed to have murdered in 1483). Richard also fostered learning in other ways, including removing customs duty on imported books. He patronized Caxton (as had Edward IV), and in his reign Acts of Parliament were 1st printed.

True founder was Andrew Dokett, rector of St. Botolph's Church (Trumpington St.). History shows his persistence and tact. Conceiving a 'College of St Bernard', obtained licence and site in 1446: 1st establishment 4 fellows. 1448 moved to better site, to W, nearer river. Henry VI was building up *King's College*, and Dokett in 1448 interested young Queen, Margaret, in patronage of St Bernard's. She was just 18 (Henry VI, his instability already apparent, 26). Foundation stone laid by Sir John Wenlock (see *Someries*, Beds.), Margaret's Chamberlain. As his 'humble wif' she officially petitioned Henry that the college, called 'the Queen's College of St Margaret and St Bernard', proceed. 'In the which Universite is no college founded by eny Quene of England hidetoward' hers must be 'to laud and honneure of sexe feminine'. (1st women students admitted 1869; not allowed to sit degree exams till 1881; degrees withheld till 1922.) Margaret became extremely unpopular, and was a ferocious partisan in the Wars of the Roses. Dokett President till 1484 death, nursing colleges through chops and changes of the Wars. Obtained favour of Elizabeth Woodville, who re-established college in 1465, when name became 'Queens'. Elizabeth became 'foundress by right of succession' and tradition continued, involving her daughter Elizabeth of York, Henry VII's Queen, in college affairs too.

Much brickwork survives from C 15, but coring clunch. Only 2nd complete brick facing (after *Magdalene*). 1st court intact, with gatehouse in E range. Coherent plan. Surviving contracts covered front (Queens' Lane), N range and part of S frontage (Silver St), 1448, and next year remainder, including chapel. Thomas Rotherham, notable brick-builder, was involved in establishment. Vertical seams in brickwork inside court and on Silver St mark 1449 resumption of work. Court has been compared with domestic buildings of *Oxborough Hall* (Norfolk), 30 years later. It and gatehouse evidently by Reginald of Ely.

Castellated gatehouse, with polygonal angle turrets, is brick with stone quoins and clunch lierne vault to passage (bosses of SS Margaret and Bernard). Original wooden doors. Simple 4-centered arch. Niche with priest holding scroll, half-figure, evidently Dokett. Brick voussoirs. Round-arched stone windows. Proportions of turrets, marked by stone courses, 1:1:2. 1st court 2-storeyed, with same round-arched stone windows with brick voussoirs. 2-storey oriel of brick (compare *St John's*) may be later. Rectangular turrets at corners of court. One, seen from Silver St, with stone quoins and battlement copings, adjoins series of restored brick chimney-stacks. (In 1511 Erasmus had lodgings) on this Silver St side of Queens'; introduced study of Greek, and made annotated translation of New Testament here.) 1st court had original President's lodgings, in NW corner. Despite near-perfect C 15 form of court, some alterations. Hall remodelled in 1732 and C 19, and has fanciful late belfry; chapel demoted for sake of 1891 chapel; library extended along whole of S range (glass roundels in N side windows came from neighbours, Carmelite friars, expelled 1538). Pevsner says: 'Queens' College remains the most complete and compact example of a mediaeval college at Cambridge, although its architecture is neither specially early nor specially grand.' Another C 15 range, much restored, lies along river bank, W of 1st court, with W range of intervening 3-sided Cloister Court attached to it. Brickwork of this period uneven in texture. Colours, like the roof tiles, red, pink and brown.

Cloister Court unusual in Cambridge. Of different dates, more complex architecturally. Access from 1st court through rectangular tower, of which upper section of late even red brick. Most conspicuous feature, 2-storey block on N side, on brick-arcaded walk. This constitutes new President's lodgings, which were linked on to old ones. Elizabethan, including wooden gallery. Half-timbered, mostly with close timber uprights (painted black, but plastered over till 1911) and some braces. Hexagonal oriel windows. Infilling plaster. W cloisters thought to be of *c.* 1460: arcade has columns of chamfered bricks and depressed pointed arches, with 3 mouldings. S and E arcades supposedly of 1490/5, imitative but with only double-moulding. No E arcade: W range of 1st court makes the square.

Despite undramatic domesticity, 'Queens' has brickwork on considerable scale: all walls brick-faced till Elizabethan timber insertion (Pl. 23).

Edmund Vale, *Cambridge and its Colleges* (Methuen Little Guide), 1959.

St John's College: 2nd Beaufort foundation (see *Christ's College*). Established 1511 by executor John Fisher, 30 years Chancellor of University. Foundation difficult: site that of Augustinian hospital, and Fisher experienced both legal delays and opposition. This Hospital of St John finally suppressed 1509, through Margaret Beaufort's influence. Fisher had suggested college, dedicated to the Evangelist, to her (instead of Westminster Abbey bequest). Despite her retirement from public life, Lady Margaret fostered new ideas. 1511 Fisher endowed college with revenues of 2 nunneries (Bromhall and Higham) suppressed in his Rochester diocese.

Unlike *Christ's*, St John's still shows its early brickwork, and 2nd (1598–1602) and 3rd (*c.* 1669–71) courts are also brick. 1511 Beaufort gatehouse seems climax of Cambridge group, the grandest. (High turrets and defensive motifs—they *are* simply motifs—inspired 'Acanthus' (*Punch* May 29, 1968) to an image of student rebellion over looked by two smug old dons: 'Thank heaven we decided to preserve the battlements'.) Probably erected by William Swayn, master mason at King's College Chapel and Christ's. Decorated archway similar to Christ's, with Beaufort yales cavorting round ogee arch. Certain differences of style, though, and in placing of Tudor portcullis and rose badges. Ornate part of St John's taller and allows beasts more prancing attitude, with sharply arched backs and tails flung up high. Daisies and borage in great clumps. Frieze of roses and portcullises runs under St John's canopied statue (C 17 replacement). Gold-haired saint holds cup (whence he conjured poison in form of serpent).

Dressings, Barnack stone. Very large quoins. Brick contributes rich colour, slightly pinkish-red, and welcome irregular texture. Beaufort carvings have almost too great panche. Inside is stone fan-vault. Gatehouse windows at front still arched, as those of N range and most of court's. Central section quite narrow, with 2-light windows—brick voussoirs over—close to angles with polygonal turrets. 3 stages to turrets, unusual proportions: roughly 2:1:2. Height of top stage (taller than main section of gatehouse) accentuated by windowlessness. Small diamond diapering, in grey-blue, at top of gate. Attached ranges were diapered too (shows clearly in Loggan's engraving) but glaze now worn. Gate carefully reconstructed between Wars, deterioration probably hastened by traffic vibration.

College subjected to 'restoration' by G. G. Scott in C 19, involving such oddities as discarding early C 16 chapel screen (now in Whissendine church, Rutland). Chapel with N side of 1st court demolished for apsidal creation. David Loggan's engraving (in *Cantabrigia Illustrata*, 1688) shows original straight E end, with large Perp. window. Chapel and attached hall (once Infirmary) were still basically Early English, taken over from suppressed hospital. Some stalls by famous carpenter, Thomas Loveday—contract survives—remain in chapel. Have traces of Fisher's rebus—fish and ear of wheat—erased by Thomas Cromwell, following Fisher's execution in 1535 for rejecting Royal Supremacy.

Small 1st court is 2-storeyed, with square windows, plus dormers. Stone oriel, with Beaufort arms, as at Christ's. Court built 1511–16, with bricks from Coton, WNW of town. Later bricks, also pinky-red, from Fen country near *Wallington Hall* (Norfolk). Brickmaker Richard Reculver brought from

Greenwich 1511, and travelling expenses paid. Accounts 1511–16 kept by Robert Shorton, 1st Master. Reached total of £4,472. Some building afterwards, to 1520. Of blocks abutting gatehouse N is original, but S rebuilt 1772, when moulded brick used for some windows: Loggan engraving shows rebuilding exact in outline, with small square-headed windows to ground floor (where library was); larger round-headed windows to 1st floor; chimney-stacks. Brick relieving arches to square windows and brick voussoirs to rounded ones. Inside court, we see altered S range—made taller and ashlar-faced in C 18. As noted, N range C 19 replacement. E and W ranges show diaper.

Gatehouse is very much dominant building. Suitably, besides porter's lodge, treasury was established there.

R.C.H.M.; Pevsner.

Trinity College: Established by Henry VIII 1546. Partly amalgamation of C 13 colleges, Michaelhouse and King's Hall. Paradoxically, just when New Learning and royal (instead of ultimate papal) authority had been established at Cambridge—with Thomas Cromwell its Chancellor (from arrest of Fisher)—University's existence threatened by Reformation. Also, suppressed monasteries and friars had been main patrons and source of students. Roger Ascham spoke of 'this destitute and unhappy university'. (*Magdalene* was alone.) 1545 Act for Dissolution of Collegiate Foundations threatened Oxford and Cambridge, till exempted.

Apparently King had idea earlier of rebuilding King's Hall. Indeed, Great Gate belonged to it, and dates from 1519 to 1535. In 1519 William Burdon was mason. Upper stages finished 1528–35. (Statue of Henry VIII is C 17 work, apart from chair-leg sceptre.) All the King's Hall buildings reverted to crown in 1546. The mainly brick Great Gate *was* a free-standing structure. Brightish red bricks bought at Ely. 3 storeys, rather squat. Taller polygonal angle turrets, brick except for stone quoins and battlements. Outer face (E) conservative in style and stonefaced, with mediaeval arched lights, blank tracery panels, ogee arch to pedestrian entry. Rear more modern, with square-headed windows and moulded brick decoration in spandrels of single wide arch. Attached ranges are later: S from 1556 and N of late C 16. Stone-faced, but *c.* 1556 brickwork to part of S range, erected by Mary I.

Fronting Trinity Lane survive rooms and tall chimneys of lodgings block, originally of Michaelhouse, with purpley-red bricks and small windows, evidently C 15.

CARLTON

Parish Church: On border with W Suffolk. Pevsner cites 'castellated' (battlemented) bell-cote of brick. Church has 'nicely unrestored exterior', Perp. in main.

DOWNHAM (or LITTLE DOWNHAM) (ISLE OF ELY)

Tower Farm (Bishop's Palace): 3 m. NW of Ely, remains of favourite palace of bishops. Farm named after gatehouse tower built by John Alcock. Palace established long before his time: he is recorded as having made great improvements, and fragments remaining are from his work. Palace fell into decay in 2nd half of C 17 (after Bishop Wren died, 1667). 'Bishop Patrick in 1691 obtained an Act to lease out the mansion and other buildings, and to secure himself and his successors against dilapidations.'—J. C. Cox, (*Cambridgeshire*, Little Guide, 1914).

As at *Ely*, Alcock used brick—deep-red, with some blue diaper. Stone quoins and other dressings, including string courses. Absorbed in later farm buildings 2 late C 15 ranges and contemporary linking wall. Rectangular range is quite large, with arms of see over big stone entrance arch and stone windows. Stone groining inside, incomplete. Cox called this the chapel. Other range (W) used as barn, obviously less important. Has more brick detail: stepped gable, brick hoodmoulds to small windows of upper storey. Evidently a fireplace inside, and Cox, describing this as 'formerly the kitchen', recorded 'a large black oven'.

ELY

Bishop's Palace: Used by Red Cross for Palace School. Main palace of once vast diocese. Pre-Elizabethan buildings are by Alcock at end of C 15 and Thomas Goodrich about 1550. Careers of both of interest. Alcock a great builder in brick and a 'political bishop'. Cathedral has clunch-built chantry, fan-vaulted, elaborate, inscribed 'Johannes Alkoc epus Eliesis hanc fabricam fieri fecit MCCCC . . . .' (John Alcock Bishop of Ely had this structure erected 1500) and with cock rebus repeated. Alcock built in brick at *Downham*, too, and *Jesus College, Cambridge*, but in stone at more places. Conspicuous remnant of work survives here, fronting Palace Green (SW of Cathedral). He had found palace ruined, and built afresh. About 1670, however, Bishop Laney remodelled his palace, destroying most of Alcock's work. E tower is wholly Alcock's, of red brick with dark diamond diapering and stone dressings, including quoins. This was the gatehouse of 1490, oddly set very close to an angle of palace. Plain parapets, not battlemented (? original). Has square buttresses next corners, not stepped. Polygonal stair turret on W side. Triple stone niches between pair of windows on 1st floor N face. Imposing but domesticated.

Base of W tower, with rather larger ground plan, also Alcock's but finished in same style by Goodrich. Minus only diapering. Similar polygonal stair turret (E side). Goodrich also linked 2 towers by central range. Contains long gallery and has dormers. (The very much later doorway with curling half-pediments strikes an odd note.)This work about 1550. Goodrich was amazing political survivor, Bishop from 1533 to 1554! Accepted or favoured Reformation Acts; even, as Chancellor, attached Great Seal to declaration that Lady Jane Grey was Edward VI's heir. When Mary I gained control Goodrich's tenure was temporarily threatened by official dispossession, but convinced Mary of his reliability and kept see. Died not long after. His 1554 brass (in Cathedral) has full panoply of mediaeval and Marian reaction vestments, besides Great Seal that he had attached to acts abolishing images, chantries, Latin masses . . . . . .

KINGSTON

Wood Farm: Front misleads as late C 17 or early C 18 brick façade,) though it retains stone door with depressed Perp. arch (added cornice). One of 2 main manors of village, and house is mostly early C 16. Brick only one of materials: upper storey mainly timber-framed and remainder rubble or brick (and all later work brick). Early Tudor work includes diapered brick to S face and NE corner, a window and an inside door (latter plastered).

Pevsner; R.C.H.M. *West Cambridgeshire* (1968).

KIRTLING

Kirtling Tower: Edward North, a lawyer, was Chancellor of Court of Augmentations (distributed monastic property after Dissolution). Had friendship of Protector Somerset, Mary I and Elizabeth, and improved his finances thus. Mary gave him title of Baron.

He built the gatehouse, of *c.* 1530, which is sole relic of quadrangular mansion demolished 1801 (one wing had already been destroyed in 1752). C 19 diapered brick replacement just one range. Olive Cook cites drawing of about 1735 (in British Museum), recording original house. Site was moated, part of moat remaining, but impressive gatehouse is not defensive. 55 ft high. Of red brick, with stone quoins, courses and windows. Octagonal angle turrets, rising above central section. Outer ones very large, inner ones slimmer. Battlement copings stone. Battlement motif repeated, minutely, above upper oriel. 2-storey oriels of front are semicircular, taking up most of width of central section. Another window, flat, below was evidently substituted for original gateway arch. Oriels mix mediaeval motifs (quatrefoil frieze to upper oriel and individual rounded arches to 6 lights of both) with elements of Italianate Renaissance decoration—classical leaf ornament on corbelled-out base, on sills and on shields below top frieze. Surrounding brickwork has diaper decoration. So Tower (now covenanted to National Trust) is interesting in detail, as well as impressive in size and colour. House is to be mourned.

Pevsner; Olive Cook *The English House through Seven Centuries*, 1968.

Parish Church: Isolated from village, in grounds of Tower. C 15 and earlier church, to which North Chapel (at SE) added in early C 16 by Edward North as family chapel. Has his 1564 monument. Chapel brick-built, including windows with moulded cross-bars: 5 lights to E window, but 3 lights at S.

MADINGLEY

Madingley Hall: (University property from 1951—used by Extra-Mural Board.) Elizabethan appearances, resembling Long Melford Hall, Suffolk. Despite this (and later additions) basis is Early Tudor S range with some survivals in E front. House was L-shaped. E front was remodelled *c.* 1590.

Manor formally acquired 1543 by Sir John Hynde, then Serjeant-at-Law, by Act of Parliament. After 1545 Hynde became King's Serjeant and a Justice of Common Pleas. Believed, however, he had practical tenure before Act and had started building, despite interior and exterior carvings dated or dateable '1543'.

'The main range and the S wing were probably well advanced by the king's death in 1547' (R.C.H.M.). House probably finished by Hynde's own death in 1550. S porch carries initials 'KH' for Henry VIII and Katherine Parr (they married in 1543). More prominent carvings of clunch on bay window in reconstructed E front: Hynde's arms; initials and those of his wife, Ursula; royal arms; badge of Edward Prince of Wales (feathers and sun).

Chief building material brick, but dressings stone. Brick-facing hides core of various stones, clunch and rubble, as Cambridge colleges. Some diapering with black bricks. S range was stepped gable and octagonal stair turret next SE angle. Square garderobe turret at SW. Moulded brick chimneys, with horizontal zigzags.

Pevsner; R.C.H.M. *West Cambridgeshire*.

MARCH (ISLE OF ELY)

Parish Church: Dedicated to St Wendreda, local saint associated with Ely.

Perp. remodelling *c.* 1500, Part of great new work was including clerestory with 18 windows (9 a side). These have brick voussoirs set in flint flushwork. Also, N aisle has (lower) clerestory, with stone quatrefoil windows below which 'WENDREDA' is worked in flint. Brick voussoirs again, in continuous wavy line, with some moulding. Limited, rather fascinating, use of red brick with pale stone and dark dressed flint.

PAPWORTH ST AGNES

Manor House: 2 sections, E and W. E stone, apparently mediaeval in origin, remodelled in Elizabethan times. W brick-built, Pevsner saying 'clearly' *temp.* Henry VII or Henry VIII; R.C.H.M. says late C 16 only, and Sir William Mallory is sometimes cited as builder *c.* 1585. Star chimneys and blue diapering do, however, suggest Early Tudor period.

TYDD ST GILES (ISLE OF ELY)

Parish Church: Detached bell-tower has base, early C 13, of stone; upper part C 15 and brick, with stone dressings. 3 storeys in all, buttresses reaching 3rd stage. Buttresses, battlements, window voussoirs brick.

WITCHAM (ISLE OF ELY)

**Parish Church:* C 15 porch of brick added to C 13 and C 14 church, that has some brick in mainly rough stone fabric.

DERBYSHIRE

REPTON *Fig. 3(a)*

**Prior Overton's Tower:* Now part of headmaster's house Repton School. School site is that of Augustinian Priory, founded 1172. School instituted under testament of Sir John Port of Etwall 1557. At Dissolution priory had been granted to Thomas Thacker, steward of Thomas Cromwell (his son Gilbert pulled down the church to 'destroy the nest for fear the birds should build there again'). Priory ruins purchased by Port's executors. Thacker family's hall was built on to Prior Overton's Tower, both extant but altered.

Only N face of tower visible. Tower represents part of new lodgings for Prior John Overton, elected 1437, who despised old quarters. Notable piece of Perp. domestic architecture, described by Pevsner as having 'an importance considerably more than regional' and being 'one of the most ornate pieces of early domestic architecture in England'. Of brick, 2-storeyed, with 2 corbelled-out angle turrets. Inside is original ceiling to Overton's study, with oak beams (decorative bosses) dividing ceiling into 9 parts. In addition to turrets, notable features of façade are the top cornice ornamented with 'billets' (rows of small rectangles in relief) and blank cusping over pairs of windows on each floor. Similar work found at *Ewelme* (Oxfordshire), like Hanseatic architecture.

Pevsner, *Derbyshire*, 1953.

ESSEX

ABBERTON

Parish Church: Early C 16 red brick W tower.

ALTHORNE

Parish Church: Early Tudor red brick chancel. Benefactor perhaps William Hyklott, whose 1508 brass (with Crucifixion) survives. Part inscription says he 'paide for the werkemanship of the wall of this churche'. S side of nave has 2 Early Tudor windows.

ASHDON

Parish Church: Mainly C 14 ,with early C 16 clerestory.
Waltons: Tudor brick, built by Tyrells as manor-house. (Remodelled in C 18.)

BASILDON-CUM-LAINDON

Church of St Mary-the-Virgin and All Saints: Sit. Langdon Hills, Laindon (absorbed by Basildon). Not in good state, though flaking of plaster inside reveals brick detail (chancel and nave early C 16 brick, including windows). E window of 3 lights with 6 panel tracery. Ogee-arched niches beside altar: hooded, as exterior of windows, with boss-like label-stops.

BILLERICAY

Parish Church: Late C 15 red brick tower, with particularly fine mouldings to W façade.

BLACKMORE

Parish Church: Before Dissolution church of Augustinian priory, but S aisle belonged to parish. Norman, with later additions (including famous wood tower). S aisle Early C 16, brick-built. Perp. brick arcade, with octagonal piers; goes right to E end, for E part of S aisle provided chancel of 'parish church'.

BRADWELL-JUXTA-COGGESHALL

Parish Church: Stone font basin much earlier than octagonal pedestal of early C 16 brick. Simple moulded decoration, but also 8 quatrefoils carved in brick immediately under basin.

BRIGHTLINGSEA

'*Jacobes*' *House:* In High St of this little estuary port. Beautiful half-timbered and gabled house of Beriffes, outstanding in Tudor times as merchants and ship-builders. In 1513 hired 50- and 65-ton ships to Henry VIII, following Battle of Spurs. (Brasses in parish church, where donors.) In inner angle is small, battered stair-turret of brick. Trefoil ornament. Tiny crocketed cap. Brick stair inside. Appears to be Early Tudor addition.

BURNHAM-ON-CROUCH

Parish Church: Lesser porch, on N side, Early Tudor addition. Of brick with stepped gable.

CASTLE HEDINGHAM

Castle: Origins of de Veres, Earls of Oxford, Norman. Main building 100 ft high rectangular keep of stone, erected 1135–40 by Aubrey de Vere.

After Battle of Bosworth, John de Vere, 13th Earl, Henry VII's right-hand man at Bosworth, and then Lord Chamberlain, Lord High Admiral of England, &c., did some restoration and added almost a new castle, built of brick, including a 'great brick tower'. Early Tudor structures lost, except foundations and bridge.

Castle bridge is E of Norman keep. Crosses deep (but for long dry) moat to inner bailey. 3 tall 4-centred arches, with 'V'-shaped shafts up piers to flat coping. All brick. Little moulding, but voussoirs and soffits stepped. Date 1498–1500.

Parish Church: Mediaeval church with additions in red brick. Tower, S porch and clerestory Early Tudor. Patron evidently John de Vere, 13th Earl (d. 1513).

Tower, with taller stair turret topped by cupola and with diagonal buttresses, is brick but with stone dressings. De Vere badges in window heads. Clerestory has windows of brick and brick battlements; over windows a frieze with de Vere molet (work N. Scarfe compares with Sible Hedingham church).

CHIGNAL

Church of St James: S side, including chancel, has Early Tudor windows of brick with hood-moulds.

Church of St Nicholas: Body of church Early Tudor red brick. (N aisle, carefully imitative, added mid C 19.) Brick blue, diapered. Dressings of moulded brick. Not a big church, but impressive through unity of style and material. W tower not tall, but has diagonal buttresses and battlements, with pinnacles at four corners. Arched brick-mullioned windows. Whole S side retains original windows, but chancel window, with 3 arched lights, renewed. E end terminates in 3 gables: those of early C 16 chancel, low (lean-to style) N vestry and 1847 N aisle.

Inside church, also, brick predominates. N aisle plastered, but rest of interior stripped (N. Scarfe). Original brick flooring. Brick fittings: S door; cusped piscina niches in chancel and S wall of nave; cusped statue niches—arches single trefoils—at each side of altar at E end. W end has superb brick tower arch, like slim horseshoe, triple-chamfered. Arcade is early C 16 brick, of 2 bays with wide 4-centred arches.

Rarest feature, contemporary font. Rivalled only by more decorated one at *Potter Heigham*, Norfolk. 'Brick Smealy' font has brick stem and octagonal basin, with some moulding between these. Plainer than moulded brick niches for piscinas and statues (5 in all) in church (*Fig. 3(k); Pls. 58–62*).

CHINGFORD

(transferred to London Borough of Waltham Forest, 1965)

Parish Church: (All Saints): S porch *c.* 1500 red brick.

COLNE ENGAINE

Parish Church: Base of W tower mediaeval flint rubble, but upper stages are *temp.* Henry VIII red brick. Quite elaborate work, though tower stocky rather than tall. Carries molet badges of de Veres, patrons. Unusually placed buttresses have small statue niches high up and culminate in cone-shaped, crocketed pinnacles. Deep corbel table with cusped arcading. Tower windows brick. S porch contemporary brick, with crow-stepping over multi-moulded archway.

COPFORD

**Parish Church:* (Norman church famous for contemporary wall-paintings.) Late C 13 S aisle arcade—no later than 1300 (Pevsner)—utilized both Roman bricks and contemporary bricks for piers and pointed arches. One arch stripped of plaster rendering, showing mediaeval bricks in inner orders—which Norman Scarfe is convinced are 'products of very early revival of brick-making in this neighbourhood', rather than imports. Soffits and middle order chamfered. Compare *Polstead*, Suffolk.

DEDHAM

Parish Church: In Stour valley, mediaeval wool and cloth trade country, richest about turn of C 15. Church largely attributed to wool merchants Thomas and John Webbe. 131 ft W tower is pierced by a passage, vaulting of which carries the Webbes' merchant's marks and initials. Bulk of church about 1482, but N aisle added early in C 16 to provide chantries for clothiers also. Tower brick flint-faced. Norman Scarfe cites 'old brick tower-gallery-stair at the W end of nave'. Church walls brick and rubble and Caen stone.

DENGIE

**Parish Church:* Dengie has Blackwater estuary to N, Crouch estuary to the S, and marshes, mud flats and then sea to E. Chancel and nave, though restored, date from *temp.* Edward II. Walls are mixture of flint rubble, septaria and some of yellow C 14 bricks found in this region.

DOVERCOURT

**Parish Church:* (All Saints: absorbed into Harwich). Basically Norman church, but renovated when chancel added C 14. Exterior walls, rendered, rubble and brick.

DOWNHAM

Parish Church: W tower red brick, *c.* 1500. In chancel are tombs of Tyrell family, patrons at this date, who lived at Heron Hall, *East Horndon.*

EARL'S COLNE

Parish Church: Associated with de Veres of *Castle Hedingham.* W tower, (lavishly marked with molet badge,) dramatic and peculiar mixture of brick, stone and flint. Early Tudor. S face mostly red brick, however, with stone dressings. Big polygonal stair turret of brick, across angle, and side buttresses of brick. Battlements have numerous de Vere molets, in freestone, top of stair turret having 3 courses of them. Stone panels of de Vere arms, with supporters at sides and canopy over. Date inscription '1534'. Brickwork bond mainly English.

EAST HANNINGFIELD

Old Parish Church (All Saints): Abandoned to ruin since late C 19 fire. Has early C 16 brickwork, including chancel. Pevsner lists 4-light brick window in S wall of nave; octagonal brick pier supporting N arcade; 2-light brick windows on S side of chancel.

EAST HORNDON

Heron Hall Barn: A red brick barn survives, SE of house site, where Tyrells built C 15 brick mansion.

Parish Church: Church all red brick. Attributed to Tyrells of Heron Hall. Late C 15 and early C 16. (Exception W tower, originally *temp.* Henry VI, but rebuilt in the C 17.) Church has transepts, S being earlier than N, both of which have a rare feature: upper rooms, which possibly provided lodgings for chantry priests. S transept and chancel dated late C 15, remainder early C 16. S side has 2 projections—porch and S chapel, which has its own gable-end and was Tyrells' chantry. Exterior brickwork generally diapered, including cross on pedestal base. Inside brick details include recess with brick-panelled base in chancel's N wall.

FAULKBOURNE *Fig. 3(e)*

**Faulkbourne Hall:* 'Faulkbourne' means 'falcon's stream' (though 'lk' silent) and N front of house looks down to water.

In 3rd decade of C 15 a Welshman, Sir John Montgomery, acquired manor here with timber-framed house. He was a Hundred Years' War soldier, once Constable of Caen, perhaps influenced by brick-building on Continent. Licence to crenellate granted 1439 and use of stone or brick specified. Result was asymmetrical mixture of 2-storeyed house and castle. Montgomery willed Faulkbourne to his wife, who was still alive in 1462 when eldest son, John, was executed as Lancastrian by Edward IV's government. Building, though, was continued from mid 1460s by second son, Thomas, who died heirless in 1494, having shown, as Norman Scarfe puts it, 'all the political agility of the Howards, taking part in the governments of Edward IV, Richard III and Henry VII'.

Part of timber-framed house utilized by Sir John Montgomery, but given brick facing. N half of W wing basically timber. R.C.H.M. has recorded places inside, including kitchen, where timbers still visible. Exterior all brick: refaced older work, with added polygonal bay windows; wholly brick parts erected by Montgomery and son; late C 19 work, mainly restoration and extension of W front and addition of porch, in C 15 style. Most of windows modern casements, replacing single-transomed mullioned brick windows, such as survive on N front of main tower (NE corner), though only E bays keep original 4-centred arches to lights. Dressings brick. High great hall of 1430s remains (as dining-room), sit. in W half of N range. Ceiling original. 2-storeyed polygonal bay window projects by dais, brick lierne-vaulted at both levels. 4-light oriel window next bay rests on deep stepped corbels, and is supposed to date from 1489, when Henry VII arranged to visit Faulkbourne.

Square main tower, or 'donjon', unlike Tattershall's. Some arrow slits; machicolated tourelles projecting beyond angle shafts; battlements. Presents much blanker face than multi-windowed bulk of house, though whole battlemented. Polygonal stair turret, with tiny original windows, rises above main battlements. Notable brick stair inside, resting on 'a rising brick tunnel vault' (Pevsner), with circular brick handrail set in groove of complex section. Faulkbourne has other brick spiral stairs and handrails. Nathaniel Lloyd attributed stair to same workmen as *Oxborough's* (Norfolk), date 1494, but this seems mistake, whatever the similarities.

At NW angle of house thick polygonal tower of 2 storeys, topped by thin brick spire, with crockets up angles. Spire original (though there is another, C 19 imitation, above W front), and most unusual. If Lloyd linked tower stair, with Oxborough's of 1490s, Norman Scarfe points out that corbel-tables (mid-C 15) are 'more reminiscent of Hadleigh Deanery in Suffolk than anything anywhere else in England, but that was built *c.* 1495'. These corbel-friezes run right round older parts of Hall, supporting battlements, including those of towers and bay windows. Incorporating usual cusped (trefoil) heads, arcading finely designed: arches quite tall and seem to intersect in pairs, with hollow curved triangles above intersections.

See Pevsner and Scarfe volumes.

FEERING *Fig. 4 (B-D)*

Parish Church: Feering on R. Blackwater. S wall of nave of church red brick *c.* 1505. Includes great 5-light window between W tower—earlier and of flint rubble—and notable, ornate brick S porch. All details brick, including tall battlements and sharply sloping copings. No clerestory. Stepped buttresses, one big one adjoining SE tower buttress and lesser ones at porch angles. Windows have shallow 4-centred hoodmoulds and arched lights. Moulded brick mullions. Cusped corbel-table to battlements continued round porch: being deep stepped trefoil-headed arcading. Porch has crocketed pinnacles. Battlements over entry crow-stepped. 3 trefoils above round-headed statue-niche. Dark brick diapering, partly worn. Diamonds, crosses and 'V' patterns. Red brick itself complex in tone, mellow brownish-pink. Slightly darker roof tiles.

Inside porch also outstanding brickwork. 'Star-like' (Pevsner) tiercon-ribbed vault. Moulded corbels. Set in circle of radiating bricks; centre boss bears merchant's mark—shaped like a tent pole, with guys and pennons—on a shield with finely diapered ground. Unknown merchant, F. A. Girling (*English Merchant's Marks*, O.U.P., 1964) says 'presumably that of the donor. This appears to have been moulded in terra cotta or fine quality moulded brick, a material used for some heraldic devices of the same period'. Benches against porch walls also of Early Tudor brick, with little arcades along sides. Compare *Sandon*.

FREYERNING

Parish Church: ½ m. from *Ingatestone* church, and Freyerning has now been absorbed by Ingatestone. Not large church, but has fine late C 15 red brick tower of 3 stages. Diaper decoration. Battlements rest on deep corbel-table. At angles domed pinnacles, corbelled out on small arches. Stair turret at NE angle: its steps and newel are brick (Pevsner). Extravagant stepped battlements.

GESTINGTHORPE

Parish Church: Buttressed tower and stair turret red brick *c.* 1498. Angle pinnacles. Brick tower arch to nave. (Double hammerbeam roof contemporary, one of donors evidently being Thomas Loveday, carpenter of several Essex church ceilings.)

Norman Scarfe noted that Gestingthorpe's brick-field closed down as late as C 20, the village having been a brick-making centre for centuries, supplying, for example, bricks for *Wickham St Paul* church tower about 1505.

GREAT BADDOW

Parish Church: C 14 stone with early C 16 additions of red brick. Tower (lead spire) given plain brick battlements. Battlements added along S aisle (over fine Decorated windows) and chancel are stepped. So are those of clerestory, wholly Tudor brick. It has 5 2-light windows with rounded hoods. Battlements here carried on trefoil-headed corbel-table. Crenels of 2 sizes, larger ones being crowned with pinnacle shaped rather like small Early Tudor chimney. Some black diapering to walls. S porch also brick.

GREAT HORKESLEY

Chapel Cottage: Originally 'Chapel of Our Lady' or 'Chapel of St Mary'. Sit. Horkesley Causeway. Rectangular, 2-storey built of red brick. Tiny. Erected *c.* 1500 to provide chapel-of-ease, with priest's quarters, for people far from parish church (1 m. away to the S.), Secularized 1548, under Chantries Act. The 'front room', however, still has in S wall the chapel's piscina, with drain-holes between petals of a Tudor rose.

Exterior is largely unchanged. Walls are diamond-diapered. Dark bricks used in recesses of plinth: this about 3 ft 6 in deep, topped by moulded brick arcading (cusped). Straight twin buttresses at corners, rising to base of tall restored crow-stepped gables at E and W. At W end (priest's quarters) central twin-flued chimney-stack. At E end stone statue-niche, below which are 2 arched rows of bricks, the voussoirs of lost E window.

Norman Scarfe cites John Brewood, of nearby Brewood Hall, as builder. *c.* 1500 John Falcon 'put lands and tenements in feoffment to find a priest to sing in Our Lady Chapel . . . and to pray for the soul of the said John Falcon, during the term of 99 years and longer "if the laws of the nation will that permit"'. Falcon made other benefactions in parish. This one, at 1547 suppression, worth £5. 13*s*.

Article by H. Laver, in *Transactions of the Essex Archaeological Society*, vol. VI, N.S., 1898.

HORHAM HALL

In 1502 manor purchased by Sir John Cutte, Privy Councillor and Treasurer of Household of Henry VIII (see also *Salisbury Hall*, Herts). Moated house, of which he was main builder, sit. 2 m. SW of Thaxted, another Cutte manor. Cutte retained elements of earlier timber-framed house. For the new work, up to his death in 1520, used thin red bricks, with grey headers for relatively sparse diapering, and stone for majority of dressings, including windows. Decorated chimneys brick. Building continued by John Cutte, grandson, responsible for such important features as remodelled S wing, tall hexagonal tower of *c.* 1580 and plain square 'Hawking Tower'. C 17 additions and then some demolition, including destruction of gatehouse and chapel, further complicated the plan of a house which Treasurer Cutte erected without aiming at symmetry.

Main range (faces E), incorporating great hall, and N range off it are the Treasurer's and *c.* 1510–15. N range has English bond gable-ends with stone-coped steps. Great hall huge: 46 × 24 ft and 25 ft high. Screens passage remains, entered from outside through battlemented 2-storey porch. E façade dominated by stonework. Heavy stone battlements. Windows so big that diapered brick between them plays subordinate role, though providing vital contrast. 2 bays, smaller one having diapered brick-walling between its 2 sets of lights. Larger one, lighting dais inside, has continuous stonework from plinth to parapet, 4 rows of lights—in pairs at the sides and 6 across the front (40 in all). Thus, Hall's most splendid work is stone, though brick is the vehicle.

Garner & Stratton; R.C.H.M.; Pevsner.

INGATESTONE

Ingatestone Hall: Builder was William Petre, Doctor of Laws (1533) and Privy Councillor (1544), Tudor 'new man' of Devon origins, son of rich leather-tanner. Survived as councillor right through Mary I's reign, even though he and Richard Rich (*Leez Priory*) had forbidden her to celebrate mass before her accession. Secretary of State to Henry VIII, Edward VI, Mary and Elizabeth I. He died in 1572.

On Dissolution of Monasteries Petre bought many estates, including Ingatestone manor belonging to Benedictine Nunnery at Barking (Essex). Price was £849. 12*s.* 6*d.* (1536), but paid in instalments. Already living as tenant in conventual grange here, but this rejected as 'scant mete for a fermor (farmer) to dwell upon' and replaced by a brick mansion. Work still going on in 1550s, but apparently mostly on glass, chimneys and other fittings. Petre documents detain these building activities, but also go right back to conventual administration. They include transfer to Petre and later papal bull of absolution obtained during Marian reaction (1555).

In 1566 Thomas Larke, Petre's surveyor, wrote full description of new property, and drew a plan, using 'red lyne' for 'the brick walls round about the whole scituaction of the house, and in part, the very house yt self'. (Blue for drains and springs.) Described house as 'very fayr, lardge & sedately made of brick and imbateled', 'inclosed with a fayr brick wall', with 'dyvers howses of office bylded of brick' for gardener, poultry-keeper, &c. beyond this wall. Demesne 14 acres.

There were 3 courtyards to the house. Surviving domestic ranges are those of inner court. E wing of 2 storeys, but N and S wings have stepped gable-ends rising to 3 storeys. Lost W range, including the great hall, demolished turn of C 18. Dressings brick, including doors, windows and copings. Also some plain original chimneys. Polygonal turret in an inner angle a later addition. Pevsner points out that lack of symmetry makes the house *stylistically* pre-Elizabethan, but the 2-tier windows have straight—not arched—heads to lights—a relatively late development. These windows, however, largely restored, except on W side of E range (Pevsner). Lack of diaper may also be sign of the later date. Red roof tiles, and 'rose red' bricks.

There is a gatehouse range, that of lost outer court, but this completely reconstructed in C 18.

Of the 'dyvers howses' there survives one large *Barn*, brick-built, with stepped gables.

N. wing and Long Gallery leased to Essex County Council from 1953 and used for exhibitions.

Essex Record Office publication: *Introduction to Ingatestone Hall*, (1968 ed.).

Parish Church: Sir William Petre added a 'new ile' in 1556, where he was buried—alabaster and marble tomb—under an arch of brick S arcade. Octagonal brick arcade piers. This 'aisle', actually S chancel chapel, was to be used by inmates of almshouses established by Petre. E end of church also remodelled in Tudor brick, through Perp. E window of stone left, contrasting with brick mullions of Petre chapel windows, whose heads, though, are still arched.

The rare *post-Reformation* chapel is not main brick feature of church, which has 'the finest of the many brick towers in Essex' (Laurence King). Tall, straight, late C 15, built of very dark red bricks with shiny, glazed black headers for diaperwork. Angle buttresses and stepped battlements, all copings brick. Deep corbel-table. Across SE angle is polygonal stair turret, whose pyramidal cap reaches battlements. Round-headed windows to tower, but W face has 'a three-light brick window with Perp. panel tracery, and two-light windows in two tiers above it' (Pevsner).

KELVEDON

Parish Church: Early C 16 brick additions on N side, rarer than on S. N chapel has crow-stepped gable and big window with brick tracery.

LAWFORD

**Parish Church:* Mainly C 14 church, 'with at least three different shades of red brick' (N. Scarfe) in W tower. Tower a mixture of different stones, including septaria: brick is partly C 16 repairs and partly C 14 work. Tower arch early C 16 brick. Brick and flint chequer below window sill of mid C 14 chancel (R.C.H.M.).

LAYER MARNEY

Layer Marney Tower: Fantastic 7- and 8-storey turrets to gatehouse, which was erected as servitors' quarters of unfinished mansion. Wholly red brick, with terracotta ornament. Tower dominates 2 domestic ranges attached to it and the 'two-storeyed long gallery'. E range partly restoration. Builder was Sir Henry Marney, whose son John survived him only 2 years dying heirless in 1525.

Most notable element is Renaissance ornament to window bars of tower and W range and tower pediments. Grey headers used for diamonds on tower, and stables thickly covered with diamonds, chevrons, crosses and zig-zags. In contrast to *Hampton Court* and *Sutton Place* (Surrey), Layer Marney has numerous brick mouldings: trefoil friezes to tower; quatrefoils and arcading to stables; roll and cavetto mouldings to tower archway; all window jambs; smaller windows *in toto*, but perhaps originally rendered; square hood-moulds; plinth copings. Remains of decorated chimneys. Wall bricks laid in irregular bond, including courses of headers. For terracotta windows and pediments see section in chapter on 'Terracotta'.

Layer Marney may be viewed on Sunday and Bank Holiday afternoons (2–6 p.m.) from April to September.

J. A. Gotch (1901); James Lees-Milne (1951); *article* by N. Pevsner in *The Listener*, 5 March, 1964, and his *Essex*.

Parish Church : Inside, on N side of chancel, Marney chapel has the terracotta tombs of Henry and John Marney.

Of earlier church little remains, apart from foundations. Henry Marney replaced earlier church by a brick-built one *c.* 1520. John Marney left £250 in 1525 for the 'rebuilding'. Stone is limited to tower buttress quoins and a few stringcourses. Body of church had its brickwork plaster-rendered, in imitation of stone, now worn. Tower has tall 2- or 3-light windows with arched hood-moulds and voussoirs and blue diamond diapering; also rarer shapes like 'heart'. Windows 3 lights; E window of 5 lights. Mullions finely moulded. Heavy voussoirs, 2 bricks deep; S porch door has them too.

Three interesting projections from body of church:

(1) Square S porch, with stepped battlements, statue niches in square relief surround, elaborate mouldings to 4-centred archway. Otherwise comparatively plain.

(2) S chancel porch. Not so tall, but more ornate mouldings. Stepped battlements; '. . . an exceptionally rare porch, or priest's vestry' (Church Guide.)

(3) Priest's chamber, sit. at W end of N aisle. Retains chimney-stack, with octagonal shaft and moulded cap and base.

Interior of church: 'The arcade piers inside as well as the tower arch have semi-octagonal shafts and hollows in the diagonals' (Pevsner). All plastered brick. N chapel has terracotta tombs of Henry and John Marney.

LEEZ PRIORY *Figs. 4(A) & 11; Pls. 69–74*

Sit. at Hartford End, 1¾ m. from Little Leighs. Sometimes called Little Leighs Priory. Isolated house of Augustinian canons here, worth £114. 1*s*. 4*d*. a year ('Valor Ecclesiasticus'). Acquired 1536 by Richard Rich, first Chancellor of the Court of Augmentations, with much other monsatic property in Essex. He began building a mansion here in 1536–7, to which he retired from political affairs in 1551. Held title Lord Rich of Leighs from 1546. Built another house at *Rochford*. Died 1568 and buried at nearby Felsted, where his (completely rebuilt) Grammar School survives. Family kept Leez Priory till 1735, when it was sold to the governors of St. Bartholomew's Hospital, London, who demolished most of it. (Reasons unclear. Connection was that ex-monastic property of St Bartholomew's, also, was held by the Rich family till C 19.)

Of monastery some foundations survive, notably of *c*. 1280 church—with stone pier bases—and of frater. Rich razed the flint and stone buildings, but preserved elements of layout in new mansion; cloisters contributed to outer courtyard; 'the principal living rooms replaced refectory, dorter and frater' (Olive Cook); great hall was built on foundations of church. Rich's house was vast: he had perhaps 350 retainers. Red brick, with stone for a few dressings. Brick sizes about 10 × 4½ × 2½ in. Texture fairly rough, incorporating pebbles. Brick clay, presumably, came from some 2 dozen pits, afterwards turned into fishponds, dug along valley towards Felsted: 2 remain as ponds. Square moat now dry but traceable, as is layout of demolished ranges.

Remains belonged to out courtyard. L-shaped set of buildings constituted W side and part of S side of that court. Outer gatehouse is incorporated in S range, and at right angles to the great Inner Gatehouse, which how stands in isolation—except for fragments of walling, excavated foundations (monastic, but used by Rich) and a later stone circuit with domed top. To SE of Inner Gatehouse are Rich's drains, some 7 ft deep, all brick-lined and vaulted. 1730s engraving by Samuel & Nathaniel Bucks looks W, towards Inner Gatehouse, and shows lost angle turrets, half a dozen gables and hall lantern—like those of a lesser Hampton Court. Surviving domestic ranges are of 2 storeys, but only one room thick. Traces of diapering. Windows wholly brick, square-headed, usually of 3 round-arched lights without labels. Chamfered mullions. Moulded brick labels on outer façade of S range, including doorways. Remains of chimney-stacks here (S). Outer façade of W range plain and domestic-looking, with large and small gables. Bond here is irregular, as in all the buildings, but English bond seems predominant. These ranges without stone dressings, as in, smaller, Outer Gatehouse.

This Outer Gatehouse is battlemented, with polygonal angle turrets. Of 2 storeys only, not much taller than ranges, and squarish. Copings brick. Ribbed angles to turrets, with shallow trefoil-headed corbel-tables marking stages. Plain diamond diapering with blue bricks. Wide 4-centred archways have triple mouldings and are very fine. Stair in NE turret. Light (and friable) stone used for arms panel, under brick hood, above outer archway. Spandrels have cut brick shields (deviceless). Inner (N) face has different spandrel decoration; in shallow carved brick, in angled trefoil with globular centre.

Inner Gatehouse is more splendid and elaborate. Of 3 storeys, with polygonal angle turrets rising higher still. These battlemented, and so are sides, but top of recessed central section of W and E triangular pediments, progressive for date (1536 on), with decorative stone shaft in the centre. Central section comparatively narrow, with archways opening close to angle turrets and 2 tiers of windows taking up most of wall space. These windows are of 8 arched lights (4 across), with square heads. At the sides traces of lost adjoining buildings can be seen up to 2nd storey, including remains of aquinch on the S side. Chamber abutting on N side was guardroom, and there is decorative touch of defensiveness in cut brick loopholes in turrets (beside archways). Spiral stair is in SE turret: steps are great uneven wood triangles, conceivably replacements. Doorways inside have brick dressings, with triangular cut bricks at the angles. On both floors are great fireplaces, with 4-centred lintels: first-floor one is larger and of brick, with triangular pieces at turn of arch.

Different uses of brick and stone for Inner Gatehouse show stone was chosen for most important dressings, but decoration was supplemented by uniquely complex diapering in blue bricks. Archways have stone mouldings, and that on W has stone shields in spandrels and a stone arms panel. This, like the one on Outer Gatehouse, carries Rich's three crosses and a chevron, but is very worn: remarkably unsuitable motto inscription is 'Garde ta foy' (Keep faith). Great windows stone. Pediments stone-dressed. Battlements copings and courses stone. Doorway at base of stair turret is stone and so is that at head (leading on to roof).

Diaper even covers inner walls of archway, where it is pale blue and perfectly preserved. Exterior diapering well-preserved and covers all space between ribs of 1st and 2nd stages of turrets and round lower of central windows. Different sizes of diamonds are supplemented by zigzags, hearts, crosses, chequers, and shades like candelabra and Chinese lanterns. Blue and red bricks used alternately for voussoirs of archway on E side. Surprisingly, rest of brick fairly consistently laid in English bond. Panels between angle shafts have particularly fine corbelled heads, with cusped pieces like a mediaeval boat turned turtle. Archway on E has brick shields in spandrels.

Whereas Outer Gatehouse has lost its chimneys (except for base of one stack), Inner Gatehouse has marvellous battery of 4 ornate chimneys, their shafts alone 10 ft tall. They rise from battlements on S side. Tops octagonal and fairly plain. Shafts all different, octagonal or circular, with deep cut or roll-moulded ornament: one with zigzag ribs, the others with cut or roll-moulded diamonds and hollow quatrefoils or carved studs in the centres.

Three ancillary Early Tudor buildings remain, all brick-built. To NW small 2-storey structure, known as the '*Fisherman's Cottage*'. Rectangular plan, quite tall with peaked gables. Very much restored. To S are 2 *Barns*, both of 2 storeys, with later buildings attached. Roofs tiled, over original timber beams.

Stretches of thick contemporary boundary walls, mainly on N and W sides of site. Copings apparently mostly restored or replacements (? date of dentillated courses). Heavy original buttresses, square or diagonal. Some traces of diapering and a certain amount of moulded brick. Remains of one garden turret.

Nathaniel Lloyd; R.C.H.M.; Pevsner; Scarfe; Olive Cook (*The English House*), and information from N. Norman-Butler.

LEYTON

(transferred to London Borough of Waltham Forest, 1965).
Parish Church: C 16 tower of brick, including windows.

LISTON

Parish Church: Early Tudor red brick tower, not large. Trefoil-headed corble-table. Diaperwork.

LITTLE COGGESHALL

Pls. 4 & 5

**Abbey:* Not open to public, unfortunately. Buildings of this Cistercian abbey have practically earliest mediaeval brickwork, including moulded details. Rich red bricks, unlike later yellowish Colchester area bricks. Abbey founded 1140 by King Stephen for Savignac monks, but 1148 Cistercians took over.

Buildings, complete or ruinous, are late C 12 and early C 13. Of flint rubble with some brick in wall fabric and brick used for load-bearing jobs—such as vaulting and arches—and for dressings—such as labels and mullions. Bricks 'are of a warm red tone and generally from 1¾–2 in. thick; the fact that the majority of them are shaped to suit their present positions is an argument in favour of local manufacture' (R.C.H.M.). Norman Scarfe sees whole building design as based on brick. In 1845 (now lost) a kiln and wasters were found a mile away, including examples of abbey's mouldings. There are, apparently, similarly moulded bricks at the Cistercian abbey of Coxyde, Belgium. Bricks are up to 12 in long and 6 in deep, rather smaller than mediaeval 'great brick'. Datings not exact. Earliest possibility is *c.* 1160 for lost church (demolished after Dissolution): excavation has revealed segmental bricks used for columns. One circular column (capital is stone) of bricks of this type survives from *infirmary*. Then, dates from *c.* 1180 to 1220s for *cloisters* and adjoining domestic buildings. *Dorter* reduced to undercroft, of 1880, but with brick vaulting that was inserted in perhaps 1220. It is entered through a pointed brick doorway of 2 moulded orders. Lloyd showed that a fault in a mould can be traced in several bricks. He also noted 'roll-moulded' dressings of brick cut and then rubbed smooth. An early C 13 *corridor*, 'completely preserved' (Pevsner), was built on to the dorter. It is 40 ft long and 10 ft wide, of 2 storeys, with chamfered brick vaulting ribs. Exterior buttressed. Corridor links infirmary and *Abbot's Lodging*. Lodging is of *c.* 1190, with lancets and brick details. Upper storey was a chapel (piscina remaining).

Lodging also linked to house built in 1581.

The small detached building of *c.* 1190 was the *guesthouse*. It has flint rubble and brick walls, with brick lancets: inside, window arches are rounded (brick), with seating recesses of moulded brick below.

St Nicholas' Chapel: Interesting building stands well away from abbey premises, the '*Capella extra portas*'—chapel outside the gates: here just outside site of main gatehouse. Dedicated to St Nicholas. Date *c.* 1220/5. Separate chapel provided primarily for lay manual workers employed by regulars. Cistercians were farmers, and annual revenue here, despite their then elderly buildings, was £298. 8*s.* at Dissolution. Chapel apparently was or became parochial also, competing with church of Great Coggeshall across river. The (recorded) font is evidence of this. Chapel evidently survived Dissolution through usefulness as farm building. At restoration in 1897 long used as a barn. 1820 painting shows thatch being renewed, though E window then blocked and weed-grown. (Timber entry had been built on to S side and byre on to E end).

Fair-sized structure with rectangular ground plan, 43 × 20 ft. Gardner says these are proportions of other Cistercian outside chapels. Much brick throughout fabric. Brick quoins. Single-light windows with brick jambs and pointed arches: Pevsner notes those on N side 'quite regularly arranged'. Main feature E window, wholly brick, with 3 lights. Central lancet, taller than side ones, rises to 6 ft: all are set back under window arch proper, which is less sharply pointed. Similar windows at W end, but much more worn. Brick piscinas and 4-fold sedilia inside.

Lloyd; R.C.H.M.; Pevsner; Scarfe; *article*, 'Coggeshall Abbey and its Early Brickwork', by J. S. Gardner in *Journal of the British Archaeological Association* for 1955.

LITTLE LEEZ PRIORY: See *Leez Priory.*

LITTLE WARLEY

Little Warley Hall: Part of early red brick house of Tyrell family. Retains great hall and its Early Tudor chimney-stack (at front of house). Decorated chimney-shafts—'one spiral, one zigzag' (Norman Scarfe). Porch is notable feature, 2-storeyed with crow-stepped gable. Brickwork strongly diapered, including porch. English bond.

Parish Church: Brick chancel of early C 16.

MALDON

**Moot Hall:* Maldon sit. on R. Chelmer, which is linked with Blackwater estuary (clay area). Moot Hall is in High St. Tall, 3-storey red brick tower of C 15. Purchased 1575–6 by an alderman and given to town. Whole building 'much altered'. Other parts long demolished.

Tower is large, rectangular, with 'a small annexe at the NW angle'. Some small original windows remain. Groundfloor chamber has original ceiling-beams. Polygonal stair turret is at rear (NE angle), rising a stage higher than the tower itself. Newel stair brick with moulded and beautiful handrail. Attributed to Sir Robert D'Arcy. Built about 1435–40 as defensive tower house, providing town quarters for D'Arcy's of *Tolleshunt D'Arcy*, 6 m. away. At Maldon Robert D'Arcy made a family chapel in All Saints' Church. A man of more than local importance, M.P. for Maldon and Sheriff of Essex & Herts.

R.C.H.M.; Town Guide.

MANUDEN

Manuden Hall: Incorporates remains of gabled mid C 16 red brick house.

MARGARETTING

Killigrews (Older name Shenfield House): Killigrews was mansion of Sedge family. Moated. Of red brick, erected *c.* 1500, but much altered and added to from C 18 on. Remains of garden wall, rising from moat, more original. Two surviving polygonal angle turrets. Caps pyramidal, with moulded brick crockets to angles, and crenellated round base. Bricks of medium red tones.

MOUNT BURES

Parish Church: Brick S porch, with some flint in fabric. Moulded brick used for window tracery and doorway, but ornamented with cut brick. C 15.

NAZEING

Parish Church: Tower and its stair turret of C 15 brick.

NEWPORT

Parish Church: In Early Tudor times, when church was collegiate, chancel enlarged with clerestory of brick.

NORTH FAMBRIDGE

Parish Church: Wooden belfry, but church otherwise late C 15 brick. Not large.

NORTH WEALD BASSETT

Parish Church: Tall early C 16 brick tower. Diagonal buttresses. Battlements supported by cusped corbel-table. Large W window with brick mullions.

PEBMARSH

Parish Church: Early C 16 red brick ornamentation, including addition of battlements. W tower given diapered upper stage with battlements and dumpy crocketed pinnacles. S porch brick with stepped battlements and, at front, stepped gable: gable motif repeated in shallow relief above moulded archway. Two cinquefoils in cut brick. Tiny details: to r and l of the blank 'gable' a single header carved with a trefoil. Moulded brick statue niche projects.

PELDON

Parish Church: To stone nave in early C 16 added red brick buttresses and wholly brick clerestory with 2-light window.

PLESHEY

Castle: Low open ruins. Castle established C 12 by Geoffrey de Mandeville,

Essex-based 'warlord' in anarchic reign of Stephen. At S side moat spanned by long, sloping bridge of red brick, late C 14 or C 15. One high pointed arch, with brick voussoirs right round (compare *Castle Rising*, Norfolk). Possible argument for the earlier date is that castle began to decay some time after political murder in 1397 of Thomas Woodstock, Duke of Gloucester, who held it as Constable of England.

PURLEIGH

**Parish Church:* Perp. S porch of brick, with chamfered 4-centred arch. R.C.H.M. cited courses of C 14 bricks in tower and chancel.

RAMSEY

Parish Church: Tower of C 15 brick.

RAYLEIGH

Parish Church: N aisle of brick of C 15. S porch contemporary brick, battlemented, with moulded brick corbel-table and windows.

RAYNE

Parish Church: Body of church mid C 19, but red brick tower of *c.* 1510 survives. Blue diapering extends over buttresses. Other unusual features: 'a blank stepped gable above the W window with a finial at the apex, a castellated frieze below the bell-openings . . . and a curious stepped pinnacle as a roof to the stair turret' (Pevsner). Quatrefoil frieze with shields at tower base. Built by Sir William Capel of Rayne Hall.
Rayne Hall: Timber-framed and plastered house, dating back to C 14 but largely remodelled *c.* 1530 by Sir Giles Capel. Early Tudor garden wall of brick, with archway.

RICKLING

Rickling Hall: In moated site, where earlier a Norman castle. Oldest work showing is considerable amount of brick of *c.* 1500, which evidently hides older building. Quadrangular plan, this surviving except for loss of great hall—and relegation of one range to use as a barn. Gatehouse has stone archway, but other dressing brick. In Early Tudor times home of Langley family.

ROCHFORD

Rochford Hall: Ruin of brick mansion, which Norman Scarfe says was probably rebuilding by Richard Rich of *Leez Priory*. Also associated with Boleyn family. Built round 2 or more courtyards. 2-storeyed. Most walls much reduced, but gable-ends with Early Tudor chimney-shafts up centre remain. Some windows. Traces of angle towers and their spiral stairs. Brick dressings include window tracery and labels (see Pevsner).

Parish Church: Notable brick tower erected at turn of C 15; church generally late C 15 or early C 16. Blue diapering. Angle buttresses and stair turret all brick, as battlements with trefoil-headed corbel-table. Contemporary chapel, off chancel, also brick-built.

ROYDON *Fig. 3(g)*

Nether Hall: Reduced to ruined gatehouse and stretch of curtain wall which, despite picturesque decay, show fine details of brickwork. 'The romantic jagged fragment of the great 15th century red brick house of the Colts' (N. Scrafe). In late 1460s erected by Thomas Colt (or Colte), a Yorkist who had been an ambassador for Edward IV. His 1471 brass (in parish church) calls him 'Edwardi regis consul honorificus'. Big, quadrangular and moated. Demolished in 1773. Gatehouse apparently too expensive to destroy. Ruinous since early C 19, but 1784 print shows it intact—along with wall and squat polygonal angle turret.

Apart from stone entrance arch and window dressings, structure wholly brick. Apart from base of 2 turrets, covered with diamond diapering. Turrets, half-hexagonal, flank entrance. One complete, rising to 3 storeys and battlements. Remains of rooms at back, including guard-room. Chimneys had twisted shafts. Four-centred interior arches, including stair entrance, voussoirs single rows of stretchers. Garner and Stratton cited 'wide newel staircase with the sunk brick handrail'. Battlements and base of window over main entrance have fine corbelling; hollow trefoils, like pinhead figures with wide sloping shoulders. Similar but wider corbelling supports battlements of curtain wall. Cross-shaped loopholes in wall finished off with moulded bricks for the rounded ends. Remains of decorative blank niches.

Garner and Stratton; Pevsner.

ST OSYTH

Parish Church: Considerable amount of early C 16 light-red brick, inside and out. Fine work. S aisle and S porch brick. N aisle has brick about windows. Rood-loft stair turret wholly brick. Inside: both aisle arcades brick, with chamfered arches. Column beside chancel arch pierced with brick squint. For complex polylobate section of columns compare *Wyddial Church*, Herts. Three-course moulded capitals.

St Osyth's Priory: Augustinian priory established in 1127. Some buildings in ruins. Some in use. Complex building history. Briefly: stone used for monastic buildings until Vyntoner, in Early Tudor times, built in brick, but reversion to stone *temp.* Elizabeth. Masterpiece is 1475 freestone and dressed flint gatehouse. At rear of gatehouse block are some 2-light windows of brick, with chamfered mullions and cusped heads, perhaps belonging to Vyntoner's refurbishing of Priory in early C 16. Block also has decorated brick chimneys, I think of 1550 (Norman Davey said of 1475 and influenced by Hansa brick) or does Priory have ornate chimneys of 1475, 1527 and 1550s? (See also section on chimneys at end of Chapter II.)

Through Perp. gate, buildings and ruins irregularly grouped: directly opposite, at far side of site, 3 archways in a big brick range. Above main arch 2-tier oriel window of stone, its carvings having 2 main points of interest: along base initials 'J.V.' with frieze of bunches of grapes (a pun on 'vintner' for Abbot John Vyntoner 1523–33); at top, reliefs of naked figures and foliage in Renaissance style, which, as Pevsner points out, is lacking in the post-Reformation buildings. Window carries the date '1527'. What we have here is the remnant—this range and another at right angles to it—of luxurious quarters built for penultimate abbot (3rd block in group is C 19). Dressings mostly stone. Below flat stone-coped parapet, however, is brick frieze of cusped trefoils (compare *Giffords Hall*, Stoke-by-Nayland, Suffolk): trefoils, consisting of 2 large leaves and small one, are repeated and inverted. Brick voussoirs to windows. Elaborate brick chimney-shafts, with honeycomb and quatrefoil patterns and odd shape like a cottage loaf with 2 points at join. Wall fabric red brick, English bond, with continuous diamond diapering to parapet level. Brick fashionable choice; abbot was living like a lay lord.

Came the Dissolution, and Abbot Colchester accepted a pension of £100 a year, while his second-in-command, the prior, had only £10. The Crown kept property until Edward VI granted it, ironically, to the Princess Mary for life. Sir Thomas D'Arcy, K.G. (Lord D'Arcy from 1550) and his heirs held reversion, but managed to obtain property almost at once, in swap of lands, though he later paid £3,974 9*s.* 4½*d.* to Crown. His buildings just outside our period being of about 1553 to 1558 (death) delayed reaction to Reformation. D'Arcy was Master of Ordnance to Henry VIII and Vice-Chamberlain of Edward VI's household. (Son married daughter of Richard Rich of *Leez Priory.*) Building incomplete and partly ruinated, but including a great square angle tower with 6-storey turrets. Next this ruins of great hall. Facings of chequer of septaria and limestone, with stone for dressings. Brick used for subordinate roles only, but visible at some inner angles, as coring and inside chimney-stacks. Stack chequer-faced but shafts (on stone bases) are brick with star tops. Complex mouldings, including cusped network, diagonal staggered rectangles and diamonds with central stud (*Fig. 10(g)*).

Guide book by Somerset de Chair. (Priory open Easter weekend and May 1 to September 30.)

SANDON *Pls. 46 & 47*

Parish Church: Church dedicated to St Andrew. Body flint rubble, a C 14 rebuilding that re-utilized Roman bricks from Norman church—especially for quoins. Tower and S porch Early Tudor red brick, ornate. 1502 or 1505 date sometimes given; might instead by *c.* 1520, since attributed to Cardinal Wolsey, lord of manor. (About 1525 responsible for (unfinished) stone tower of East Bergholt church, Suffolk.) Brick is dark blue diapered, quite elaborately—although Scarfe notes 'an inept join at belfry stage' of W face of tower. E face has saltires and different sizes of diamond diapering; S face has different sizes of saltire (diagonal cross of St Andrew); W face has 2 big Latin (upright) crosses, which have been seen as processional crosses for Wolsey. Patterns, including saltires, carried across stepped angle buttresses.

Porch one-storey only, square. Its ceiling brick-vaulted—shafts, springers and ribs of moulded brick. Brick benches against walls. Compare *Feering*.

STANWAY

**All Saints Church Ruins:* Open ruins of small church, in grounds of Colchester Zoo. (Emus in roofless nave.) Late C 14. Apparently deteriorated after Reformation, but much repaired after 1601 by Sir John Swinterton. N porch is wholly his. Structure again deteriorated. N. Scarfe cites as C 14 and local the fairly pale red bricks in square tower, these laid in bands alternating with narrower bands of flint. Also brick through fabric of nave walls. Bricks large, thinnish and irregular. Much brick in now-incomplete stair turret. Slim diagonal buttresses. Dressings stone. Interior of tower about 7 ft square only. Vault to 1st stage very interesting and I think original (C 14). Slight remains of thin diagonal ribs of stone show these were structually unnecessary. Vault is all brick, palish pink (traces of plaster), and composed of perfect circular courses of stretchers rising to shallow dome.

STEEPLE BUMPSTEAD

Latchleys: Moated house. Timber-framed and plastered, with Early Tudor wing. Bridge across moat Early Tudor brick, with 2 wide arches.

Parish Church: Generally flint, but early C 16 additions in red brick. Chiefly S porch, aisle parapets, clerestory.

STOCK

**Parish Church:* Brick bases for posts of timber belfry, dated as early as end of C 13.

THAXTED

Mill End: Early C 16 brick house, (once forming part of now disused sweet factory), has blue diapering at front and back. At back, 'an ornamental brick corbel-table by trefoiled arches' (R.C.H.M.).

THEYDON GARNON

Parish Church: Inscription dates tower '1520'. Blue bricks used with red, but not for diapering.

THORPE-LE-SOKEN

Parish Church: Church rebuilt in C 19, but Early Tudor tower of deep red—'purple' (N. Scarfe)—brick. Bell-windows have moulded brick mullions and circular tracery. Diamond diapering, also zigzags.

THORRINGTON

**Parish Church:* Late C 14 S porch is a mixture of wall tiles, septaria and rubble. Tiles used for quoins and also jambs of the S doorway itself, depressed pointed arch of which is brick. Late C 15 tower has some brick to 2 windows.

TILBURY-JUXTA-CLARE

Parish Church: Church 1517–19 rebuilding in red brick. Diapered tower carries annulet (ring) badge, one of de Vere badges. Erected at cost of Elizabeth, Countess of Oxford.

TOLLESHUNT D'ARCY

Tolleshunt D'Arcy Hall: Some brick in *c.* 1500 wing of house of D'Arcy family (monuments in church). Some fine wood panelling inside worth mentioning for comparison with 1520–40s terracotta work: Renaissance foliage, vases, profiles in medallions, and initialled 'A.D.' for Anthony D'Arcy, sheriff of Essex 1512 (d. 1540).

TOLLESHUNT MAJOR

Beckingham Hall: Early Tudor mansion has almost completely disappeared, leaving traces of some foundations. Farmhouse on site. Part of red brick enclosure walls and the 2-storey gatehouse remain, both Ancient Monuments. Stephen Beckingham (of Kentish origins, i.e. Beckenham) obtained manor in 1540 from Henry VIII; besides extant house 'partly timber-framed and partly brick-built' (Pevsner), was absorbed in later rebuilding. Slightly dotty in style but fine work. Attributed to Robert Beckingham *c.* 1546 Square, battlemented, with small round angle-turrets—rear pair being even slimmer than front pair—apparently decorative only. Lloyd recorded 'the gateway towers are rendered with plaster in geometric patterns in black and white' (worn). 4-centred archway with 2-light window over. Dressings brick. Walling bricks $9\frac{1}{2}\times 4\frac{1}{2}\times$ about $2\frac{1}{4}$ in. Walls to E and W terminate in angle turrets: that at E mere shaft with pinnacle top; at W 2 canted circular turrets belonging to a lost gateway.

Date 1546 taken from inscription on fine wood panelling from Hall, now in Victoria and Albert Museum: besides portrait busts of Robert Beckingham and his son and daughter-in-law, this has Renaissance motifs—cusped shields, cherubs, birds, dolphins and foliage.

Parish Church: Buttressed and battlemented early C 16 brownish-red brick tower. Diapered: 'plum, brown, dark grey and other headers used for diapers' (Nathaniel Lloyd). Some moulded brick ornament. Windows brick. Attributed to Stephen Beckingham and dated *c.* 1540–45, middle of Reformation. N. Scarfe notes S and N walls of nave 'each have a small terracotta (or brick) canopied niche'.

WALTHAM ABBEY

**Abbey Gatehouse* (Parish church originally that of Augustinian Abbey; Last abbey to surrender, on 23 March 1540, under Act for Dissolution of Greater Monasteries): Ruined gatehouse, near W end of church, dates from about 1370. Of flint and stone. Contemporary wall on S side. Fabric of this wall includes mediaeval 'great bricks', up to 15 in in length, up to $7\frac{1}{2}$ in in width and 'correspondingly thick' (Norman Davey, *A History of Building Materials.*) Bricks laid irregularly in rubble fabric. M.O.W. administered.

WEELEY

Parish Church: Late C 19 church retaining buttressed and battlemented early C 16 tower of red brick. Norman Scarfe notes 'rosy Tudor bricks' as being 'remarkably big ($11\frac{1}{4}\times 5\frac{1}{4}$ in)' for period.

WEST HAM

(transferred to London Borough of Newham, 1965)

All Saints' Church: In Church St Chapel on N side of chancel of red brick, diapered. 4-centred heads to moulded brick windows. R.C.H.M. gives date as *c.* 1550.

WICKHAM ST PAUL

Parish Church: Tower Early Tudor red brick. Diapered. Dates from early years of C 16: 1505 testament willed £20 for building of tower. Moulded brick used for pinnacles, W door, window tracery. Norman Scarfe says these dull red bricks are from *Gestingthorpe.*

Other examples of buildings in Essex with early brickwork are:

Ashen Parish Church; *Ashingdon* Parish Church; *Audley End* Stables; Beeleigh Abbey (nr. Maldon); *Berechurch* Parish Church (Colchester); *Boreham* New Hall; *Boxted* Parish Church; *Broomfield* Parish Church; *Broxted* Parish Church; *Colchester* Churches of Holy Trinity, St Giles and St Peter; *Fingringhoe* Parish Church; *Fordham* Parish Church; *Frinton* Old St Mary's Church; *Gosfield* Gosfield Hall; *Great Bromley* Parish Church; *Great Coggeshall* Paycocke's; *Great Henny* Parish Church; *Great Holland* Parish Church; *Great Wigborough* Hyde Farm; *Greenstead-juxta-Ongar* Parish Church; *Helions Bumpstead* Parish Church; *Inworth* Parish Church; *Leigh-on-Sea* Parish Church; *Little Bentley* Parish Church; *Little Braxted* Little Braxted Hall; *Little Bromley* Parish Church; *Little Burstead* Parish Church; *Little Oakley* Parish Church; *Margaretting* Parish Church; *Mashbury* Parish Church; *Newport* Martin's Farm and Monk's Barn; *Panfield* Parish Church; *Rainham* Parish Church (in L. B. Havering, 1965); *Rickling* Parish Church; *Saffron Walden* St Aylotts; *Shenfield* Parish Church; *South Weald* Parish Church; *Stow Maries* Parish Church; *Toppesfield* Parish Church; *Ugley* Parish Church; *White Roothing* Colville Hall; *Wimbush* Broadoaks Farm.

GLOUCESTERSHIRE

HARTPURY

Tithe Barn: 50 yds long, later mediaeval, stone-built, but with huge area of fired roofing tiles. Majority are dark in colour. Light tiles used to form running patterns: horizontal bands, diamonds and zigzags. In no particular harmony with stone walls.

THORNBURY CASTLE

On Severn estuary. Stone castle begun 1511 by Edward Stafford, 3rd Duke of Buckingham, Lord Constable of England. Regarded as treasonable military danger, he never travelled without 300–400 armed retainers, and was executed by Henry VIII in 1521. Even unfinished, Thornbury with its two courts had room for an army. Also notable for a domestic luxury, decorated brick chimneys 11 ft 9 in high. Both design and ornament of chimney-stacks varies. Of the dated one Nathaniel Lloyd (*Building Craftsmanship*, 1929) said; 'probably the earliest and the richest brick chimney extant . . .' which is dated 1514, but it is impossible to believe that such a highly developed example was the first of its kind'. Chimney tops include lanterns with 2 rows of smoke outlets in moulded brick (to detached shafts) and caps of cusped lobes (to joined shafts). Carved as well as moulded brick used for ornament. Motifs include frets or knots (some cut, some moulded) (Stafford badge was a knot), dog-tooth, diamonds, quatrefoils, concave zigzags, roll mouldings and other spiral decoration. The Victoria and Albert Museum has some elaborate heraldic tiles from Thornbury, where brick too was used for paving floors.

HAMPSHIRE

BASING

Basing House: Most of Tudor house lost. William Paulet, 1st Marquis of Winchester, on site of and among remnant of mediaeval stone castle, did some rebuilding in brick and added a brick house—licence to crenellate 1531. House suffered siege in Civil War, 1645, and was 'slighted'. Present remains: some mid C 16 brick walls; diapered polygonal tower; 2 ruined gatehouses, each with 4 towers.

Parish Church: Large Perp. church, practically all brick of C 15 and 16 including tower. At E end N aisle 1519 inscription concerning 'hoc opus' (this work), associated with Paulet family. Brick mellow red. Dressings stone. Much restoration.

BASINGSTOKE

'Holy Ghost Chapel': A portmanteau name: to Holy Ghost Chapel (of which flint tower remains) Lord Sandys added Guild Chapel of brick, dedicated to Holy Trinity. For Sandys see *The Vyne* (stained glass from here now at that house). Co-founder was Bishop Fox (see *Bishop's Waltham* below). Brick chapel of 1524. Structure of half-hexagons.

BISHOP'S WALTHAM

Bishop's Palace: M.P.B. & W. site. Ruins. Complex and confusing architectural history, but much up-to-date information has been given me by S. E. Rigold of M.P.B. & W., who has supervised excavation there. Palace goes back to Henry of Blois, Bishop of Winchester 1129–71 (see also *Farnham Castle*, Surrey). Thomas Langton, Bishop 1493–1501, was 1st to use brick here. Some bays of his lodgings remain and brick chimneys incorporated in 'Dower House'.

Section of brick boundary walls remains. Walls have been called Langton's, but S. E. Rigold attributes them to Richard Fox, Bishop 1501–1528 and Lord Privy Seal 1487–1516 (see too *Farnham*, Surrey). Walls, fairly rich red, built in English bond, include near complete squat octagonal tower (sometimes called 'Guard House') (with one projection) and part of another, smaller turret.

OAKLEY

Malshanger House: One of many manors of Archbishops of Canterbury. Malshanger now only fragment, with early C 19 house attached, of house built by William Warham at beginning of C 16. Apart from a little walling, sole remains is polygonal brick tower.

ODIHAM

The Priory: House of different dates, earliest part being C 15 flint. Brick porch of *c.* 1530, 2-storeyed and buttresses. Compared by Pevsner and Lloyd with work in *Norfolk*, especially *Great Snoring* and *East Barsham.*

N. Pevsner and D. Lloyd, *Hampshire and the Isle of Wight*, 1967.

SHERBORNE ST JOHN

Parish Church: Brick S porch, dated by inscription 1533.

The Vyne: Situated 4 m. N of Basingstoke. This famous house now National Trust administered. Brick with stone quoins throughout, but of 3 different building periods: early C 16, C 17 and C 18.

First period includes 'E' plan S front—to which classical portico added 1634—and W front. Latter is of red brick blue-diapered as S front, but some work C 18: interior has Long Gallery (with linenfold panelling) of 1520s. E plan is early, but predated by Barrington Court, Somerset, a stone house of *c.* 1514. Lord Sandys was building from 1518 to 1527–8 (died 1540). Much is lost, for Leland *c.* 1530 cited a 'fair base court' or quadrangles. 2-storeyed house. S front has 2 gabled wings; W front has square 3-storey towers at NW and NE corners. Perhaps most spectacular feature is the Chapel, to be compared with Sandys's *Basingstoke* Chapel with its polygonal apse.

Pevsner and Lloyd; National Trust guide by James Lees-Milne.

TITCHFIELD

Place House: Administered by M.P.B. & W. Earlier 'Titchfield House'. Near Fareham. Ruins have typical post-Reformation features. Priory of White or Augustinian canons, with later mediaeval stone buildings, converted to domestic use by Thomas Wriothesley, later Earl of Southampton, to whom property granted at Dissolution. Work from 1540s (Wriothesley died in 1550) in stone and brick, exactly contemporary with similar *Cowdray House*, Sussex, whose builder had held Southampton title too. Here stone-faced gatehouse built across nave of abbey church! This retains one notable zigzag-moulded brick chimney, survival of more. It and a plain polygonal shaft have arcaded bases. Short range adjoining gatehouse has crow-stepped brick gable. Upper part of W front of house also brick 1542. C 18 Buck engraving shows lost ranges of house had much more brick.

H.M.S.O. guidebook by S. E. Rigold.

THE VYNE: see under *Sherborne St John*.

WARBLINGTON

Warblington Castle: Lost mansion was built by Margaret Pole. Countess was 'purged' by Henry VIII in 1541 because of York relations. In 1518 a total of £20 was paid for 3 'kyll' (kilnfuls) of bricks supplied for this courtyard plan house—'castle' is misnomer. The loads were of 70,000; 100,000; 40,000 bricks. Built on site of older house between 1514 and 1526. Building 'slighted' in C 17.

Part of the tall 3-storey early C 16 gatehouse remains, chiefly 4-stage octagonal stair turret. Stone dressings.

WINCHESTER

**Pilgrims' Hall:* Mid C 14, with early hammer-beam roof. Hall has brick ends and some brickwork in the piers.

Other buildings in Hampshire with early brickwork are:
Mattingley Parish Church; *Steventon* Steventon Manor; *Winchester* Pilgrims' Hall and St Cross Hospital; *Yateley* Parish Church.

HERTFORDSHIRE

BERKHAMSTED (strictly, GREAT BERKHAMSTED)
Berkhamsted School: Grammar School founded by John Incent (his half-timbered house also survives), Dean of St Paul's. Buildings from about 1544, still used and have been added to. Hall-style school room, with king-post roof, between 3-storey gable-ended sets of rooms. Elizabethan description says School was built 'all of brick and freestone very sumptiously.' Windows stone. Brick deep red, with blue diamond diapering.

FLAMSTEAD
**Parish Church:* Only a little brick, but interestingly used: in walls of C 14 flint-faced Sacristy 3 brick courses (one at level of first floor). Lean-up building at NE angle. Piscina inside. Upper chamber perhaps originally a priest's room.

GREAT HORMEAD
The Brick House: Style suggests pre-Elizabethan date and Pevsner says early C 16. V.C.H. cites 1579 grant of 'le New Brick House', suggesting Elizabethan. Lonely. 2-storeyed. Quite complex plan, with 5 crow-stepped gable-ends. Contemporary domed oven at rear, and a brick-lined well. Brick used throughout, but decoration lacking and even much moulded brick: exceptions found at some windows, plinth, chimneys, one wing join. Peepholes, made of 4 shaped bricks each. Crow-steps and some windows restored. Apparently once moated, this possible evidence of the earlier date. The Brick House is stark, oddly impressive, like Scottish lesser baronial architecture. Pinkish-red brick.

HATFIELD (originally BISHOP'S HATFIELD) *Figs. 3(i) & 13*
The Old Bishop's Palace: Situated in grounds of Hatfield House. Great hall used as refreshment room. Built about 1480–90 by John Morton, Bishop of Ely (later Archbishop of Canterbury—see *Lambeth*, London). Palace was a quadrangle, with further gatehouse range fronting the old London road. 3 wings of quadrangle demolished in early C 17 by Robert Cecil, who used materials for Hatfield House: their outline visible in sunk garden, forming 218-foot square. 2 surviving ranges slightly restored. Hall range has buttresses that were later additions. Heavily repointed in June 1970. (Why not tinted cement for such work?) Brick is warm red. Diapering in blue bricks (glaze worn) often quite elaborate: besides diamond and diamond variations, hall

towers have star, grid and inverted 'W'. Moulded brick used for corbels, stepped gables, dripstones over mullioned windows. Windows mostly square-headed, but S end of hall range has large round-headed window and gate-house range smaller ones. Round-arched doors, and wide 4-centred archways hollow-chamfered. One original twisted chimney to hall range. Gatehouse range is 2-storeyed less tall, also with stepped gable-ends.

Hall gable-ended sets of rooms taller than it. Hall ground plan about 230× 40 ft. At centre front and back square 3-storey towers or turrets. Larger one at front has octagonal stair turret attached. Besides their elaborate diapers, these towers have decorative corbel-tables. Inside hall, original brick fireplace with timber lintel. Great feature, supported on large and grotesque stone corbels, is chestnut and oak roof, with its rounded principals and ogee wind braces.

Palace was valued at £2,000 in 1538. Traded by Bishop Goodrich (see *Ely* Bishop's Palace) to Henry VIII.

R.C.H.M. *Hertfordshire*, 1910; 1966 W.E.A. publications, *A Short History of Hatfield and Its People*, with reproductions of 1832 drawings by J. C. Buckler.

HERTFORD

Castle: As well as damaged flint rubble walls there survives C 15 red brick gatehouse. This used as municipal offices. Clapham and Godfrey recorded fragment of concave brick handrail in a bastion tower in walls. Gatehouse recognizably mediaeval brick, with remains of small diamond diapering over entry but experienced 'Gothick' transformation *c.* 1800: windows, Gothick porch and wing added. Battlements also modern and corbel-table looks effective but suspect. Square plan with 4 angle turrets, one having stair. Crown property C 14—mid C 17.

HUNSDON *Fig. 3(j)*

Hunsdon House: What survives is odd but interesting. A quarter, perhaps, of great Tudor mansion given strange Italianate appearance after main and S wings demolished in 1804. Tudor plan was 'E'.

In mid C 15 Sir William Oldhall had built brick manor house here. In 1558 Elizabeth I created her cousin Henry Cary 1st Lord Hunsdon and gave him the manor. In interval house rebuilt by then-owner, Henry VIII. Salzman quotes Exchequer records of £199 10*s.* paid for burning 'xiiij clampys of brick' (at 20*d.* or 21*d.* the thousand) in 1525 and of brick chimneys purchased in 1528.

House, the original N wing, mostly altered. E façade, however, has much Tudor brickwork, with small diamond diapering in dark blue brick. Entry is high square tower, of 3 storeys, with hexagonal angle shafts rising as high as range. Brick has been plaster-rendered (worn), red-pointed and variously mistreated, but this E façade is impressive, rather grim. Both rear gateway tower and Tudor garden (or 'pleasance') tower on S side have moulded brick tracery (blocked). Garden tower shorter and thinner, octagonal, with plain stone string-course. Gate-tower, square, has elaborate (restored) corbel-table under battlements: corbels have triangular brick at top, with 2 shaped yellow stones below forming cusped head, resting on moulded brick supports. Loopholes partly stone, partly chamfered brick. Remains of diapering.

Hunsdon House lies about 1 m. SE of village. Obviously park would have been large, and I think, therefore, that some Tudor brickwork about one-third of a mile away (on village road) is remnant of boundary walls: diapered in large diamonds, constitutes part of wall following curve of road.

Parish Church: Perp. church, 1450 rebuilding with brick additions. Pevsner sees it as 'an appendix of the house', with Early Tudor brickwork. Chancel, N vestry—with small brick turret at end of N aisle—and 1610 S chapel all brick. Earlier bricks, perhaps more irregularly laid, are slightly thinner and include some worn blue-glazed bricks (no apparent diaper).

MEESDEN *Fig. 3(l)*

Parish Church: 1 m. E of isolated village, near Essex border. Small flint rubble church (much restored) with small elegant brick S porch of *c* 1530. Perhaps paid for by John Hagar of Clavering, Essex, lessee of Meesden from Abbey of St Mary Graces (London). Fairly rough-textured pinky-red bricks, $9\frac{1}{2} \times 4 \times 2\frac{1}{4}$ in, laid in stretcher bond. (Repairs in tinted cement.) Inside, one brick bench support remains. 2-light windows E and W with brick bars: heads rounded, but labels square. Diagonal angle buttresses, with shallow trefoil-headed niches. All dressings brick, S façade complex and even ornate. Arch depressed pointed, it and jambs consisting of tiny multiple roll-mouldings. Cusped corbel-table, its curves ogee, supporting stepped battlements (original copings lost). Central niche with star and other ornament. Corners terminate in polygonal shafts and brick ogee pepperpots (? finials missing). (Chancel has rare C 14 tile mosaic.)

REDBOURN

Parish Church: 1460 or earlier brick parapet and corbel-table to Lady Chapel and S aisle: moulded brick corbels forming trefoils.

RYE HOUSE: see under *Stanstead Abbots*.

ST ALBANS *Pl. 2*

St Albans Abbey Church (Cathedral): Belonged to rich Benedictine house, premier abbey of England. Most buildings destroyed, but church sold to town in 1551 for £400. Square central tower and the transepts (adjoining later work of stone and rubble) built in C 12 of russet red tiles from adjacent garrison town of Verulamium. Outstanding reuse of Roman tile, but originally rendered with plaster.

Sopwell 'Nunnery': Properly 'Lee Hall'. Ruins of post-Reformation conversion, by Sir Richard Lee, courtier and military engineer.

SHENLEY *Pl. 40*

Salisbury Hall: Bridge over moat is mainly a 1794 reconstruction, but vault itself—single round arch—largely of C 15 brick. Also some old brick revetting and buttresses left. Bridge to be attributed to Richard Neville (created Earl of Salisbury 1428).

Present house erected by Sir John Cutte, Treasurer of Henry VIII, of brick. Some Tudor work remains at rear and W side—mostly reused, thinnish bricks. House remodelled in C 17, and intermittent demolition of earlier work continued into C 19. For clunch medallions of Renaissance see chapter on 'Terracotta'. For Cutte see also *Horham Hall*, Essex.

STANDON

The Lordship: Remnants, including gatehouse, of 1546 brick mansion.

STANSTEAD ABBOTTS *Figs. 3(b) & 9; Pls. 17 & 18*

**Rye House*: 'Rye House' is gatehouse only of lost mansion. Tattered and isolated, among nettles in bend of River Lea. Traces of moat that completed encirclement. Building was used as farmhouse in C 18 and has long been uninhabited, but brickwork rich red and glazed blue bricks shine. 1443 licence to crenellate was granted to Sir Andrew Ogard (d. 1454), whose arms in stone were once visible over gatehouse entry (now too worn to be distinguished). Ogard could 'impark the manor of Rye' and 'erect thereon a castle with battlements and loopholes'. Use of lime and stone only specified. Gatehouse itself is of *c.* 1443. Ogardwas Danish, and gatehouse possibly influenced by Continental architecture. Stone used only for entrance, string-course with carved decoration, battlement copings. Bricks very deep, red thickish—$9 \times 4\frac{1}{2} \times 2\frac{1}{2}$ in—with rough pebbly content. Decorative work in blue brick: mainly continuous diamond diapering, in central part of front and on battlements, and some blue voussoirs. 2-storey building is practically square, except that there is more modern addition to W.

None of this conveys fascination of building, which rests on moulded brick of Tudor sophistication. Front (N) has 2 1st-floor oriel windows. Asymmetrical, for l is smaller with 2 lights, while r. has 3 lights. Wholly brick: square-headed, with layers of moulding at top and supported on deep-stepped moulded bases. Chamfered bricks also used. Below windows and over doorway are moulded brick corbel-tables, with cusped trefoil heads and smaller pointed trefoil decoration between. On E side is very low rounded arch, at ground level, perhaps used for reception of barge-brought goods. Rising above battlements on S side is one high twisted chimney with quadruple roll-mouldings. Next to it head of stair, top of turret square to outside but chamfered off at inside (so hexagonal) covers SE angle. Here is one great feature of 'Rye House': spiral stair, with brick newel, treads just over 3 ft wide. Beautifully, subtly curved ramped brick handrail. Section of rail shows circular grip ($2\frac{1}{2}$ in in diameter) in larger oval hand-guard cavity—like a ball-bearing resting in a small squashed tin. Entrance passage has fine brick vaulting, with slim ridge and diagonal ribs, but bosses stone shields. Building, roofless, ruinous, unsafe inside, is generally inaccessible.

Garner and Stratton; R.C.H.M. *Hertfordshire* volume—but this wrongly gives date of gatehouse as C 16.

WYDDIAL

Parish Church: N aisle and N chancel chapel added 1532 to Perp. flint church. Builder was George Canon, this recorded in brass inscription (apparently not kept at church). Canon was joint lord of manor. Pevsner says 'this triumphant entry of brick into chapel building is a significant sign of the Tudor age'. Suggested that same mason worked here and at nearby *Meesden* (Essex border), but Wyddial is grander. N wall of aisle and chapel continuous, but chapel narrower and line of arcade broken. Interior probably once plastered. Dramatic arcade has one big arch (restored) to chancel and 3 narrower ones to aisle proper (westernmost much the smallest). Arches triple-chamfered, middle order hollow, supported on similarly moulded columns. Strange, unfigured capitals curl over like fungus—more like formalized Early English stiff leaf than any Renaissance foliage. Columns technically half-octagonal with hollows between, more elaborate than this suggests. Much like fine contemporary arcade at *St Osyth* (Essex), which lacks complex capitals.

Exterior: bricks russet, roughish texture, English bond. Size, $9\frac{1}{4} \times 4\frac{1}{4} \times 2$ in. Traces of diapering at W end. Diagonal angle buttresses. Projecting plinth. 3-light windows with depressed pointed arches, but chapel's E window has 4-centred arch and *lovely* cusped panel tracery of rubbed brick. Unusual lozenge-shaped label-stops to all windows: some lozenges inside lozenges, others decorated with rosette, fleur-de-lis, and pair with caricature heads—tongues out—in cut and rubbed brick.

Wyddial Hall: In main postdating 1733 fire. R.C.H.M. found that 'the cellars are built of early 16th-century brick'.

Other buildings in Hertfordshire with early brickwork are:
Abbot's Langley Parish Church; *Aston* Aston Bury (1540s chimneys); *Bengeo* Parish Church; *Furneaux Pelham* Furneaux Pelham Hall; *King's Langley* 'Palace' and Parish Church; *Knebworth* Knebworth House; *Little Hadham* Clintons; *Sawbridgeworth* Parish Church; *Watton-at-Stone* Watton Hall (decorative panel).

HUNTINGDONSHIRE

BUCKDEN

Buckden Palace: Now school belonging to Claretian Missionaries; originally a palace of Bishops of Lincoln. Present survivals all late C 15, deep-red brick.

Leland in early C 16 recorded: 'Rotherham Bisshop of Lincoln buildid the new brike towr at Buckden. He clene translatid the haul (hall), and did much coste there beside.' This was Thomas Rotherham, 1472–80 Bishop of Lincoln, major brick builder and buildings by John Russell, 1480–96. followed. (See also Lincoln *Chancery*.)

Great Tower, probably Rotherham's, very distinguished building. Brickwork of this scale and date alone in county. A. Clifton-Taylor (*The Pattern of English Building*, 1962) says bricks 'may well have been brought up the Ouse from South-West Norfolk'. John Harvey (*English Mediaeval Architects*, 1954), having attributed the *Esher* and *Farnham* (Surrey) towers to John Cowper (who also worked at *Tattershall*, Lincs., and *Kirby Muxloe*, Leics.), says: 'another work with much resemblance to his style'. W. Douglas Simpson, comparing this 'fine brick tower' with Tattershall, describes it as 'smaller in scale and simpler in treatment, but likewise aiming at ostentation and privacy.

Ground plan 50×27 ft. Now a shell, the 5 storeys—including basement—once had a dozen rooms. 4 octagonal corner turrets a stage higher. Windows, string courses and copings to battlements—as well as remains of handrail in NE turret—of stone. Garderobes were in SE turret. S face has projecting chimney-stack. Certain amount of moulded brick. Dark blue or black bricks used for lozenges and for individual crosses on N and W walls.

Attribution of work between Rotherham and Russell confused, but other buildings carry Russell's arms. These buildings have more moulded brick, including slit windows. Small domestic range and 2 gatehouses, large and small. Larger gatehouse is inner, connected by wall with Great Tower. This wall has slit windows and an alure, carried on low moulded brick arcade. Inner gatehouse 3-storeyed, with stone dressings and black brick diapering. Stepped gable-end by connecting wall. On this, panel of arms: 3 white rosettes and a yellow chevron (inverted 'V'). Another panel with Russell arms (version of those of William of Wykeham, also native of Winchester) is over archway of outer gatehouse. Apparently also once appeared on Great Tower (but that does not make it Russell's). Emphasis given to arms, those on N gable-end panel being inserted under decorative ogee arch of moulded brick. The mediaeval buildings are isolated from street by old brick walls, incorporating part of embattled mediaeval enclosure wall.

Garner and Stratton; R.C.H.M., *Huntingdonshire*, 1926; Pevsner, *Bedfordshire and the County of Huntingdon and Peterborough*, 1968; *article* by W. Douglas Simpson in *Journal of the British Archaeological Association*, 3rd series, 1937.

DIDDINGTON

Parish Church: Church mainly stone, but with early C 16 tower and S porch of brick. Porch perhaps later than tower, and plastered. Some brick mouldings.

HINCHINGBROOKE

Classic post-Reformation history. Augustinian nunnery converted by Cromwell family. Granted to Sir Richard Cromwell (born Williams) a nephew of Thomas Cromwell. Main builder was his son, Henry. Post-Reformation work is in stone and brick, and dates are C 16, C 17, C 19.

Just inside gatehouse are parts of domestic offices, of diapered Early Tudor brick. Main conversion begun by Henry Cromwell after 1544, so Elizabethan work the most obvious, but P. G. M. Dickinson, County Archivist, says (1968) of the brickwork: 'there is plenty of dated work from 1541 onwards'. Main areas of earlier brick walling are centre and S sections of main (E) front, with black diapering. Recent finds of Tudor brick sandwiching priory stone walls. Now part of comprehensive school.

Pevsner.

Other buildings in Huntingdonshire with early brickwork are: *Huntingdon* All Saints Church; *King's Ripton* Parish Church; *Paston* Old Rectory (Early Tudor chimneys); *Southoe* Parish Church.

KENT

*ALLINGTON CASTLE

Moated castle (nr. Maidstone), beside R. Medway. Origins Norman, but oldest parts date from 1281 licence and rebuilding.

Building always done in ragstone, but in late C 13 work some subsidiary brick. Builder, Sir Stephen de Penchester, Warden of Cinque Ports. His curtain wall, with 4 D-shaped towers, remains, with 2 other towers, machicolated gatehouse, 2-storey W range (known as Penchester Lodgings) and part of great hall on E. Gault bricks, pale-yellow or pink, are used for vaulting and lining one of curtain towers and for window soffits in W range. Measurements $9 \times 4\frac{1}{2} \times 2$ in.

APPLEDORE

**Hornes Place Chapel:* Detached C 14 chapel with notable early brick. Open to public (M.P.B. & W.). Belonged to timber-framed home of Hornes (core of present house). Family held lands, as tenants of Cathedral Priory of Canterbury, C 13–C 15. Builder, Sir William Horne, became J.P. in 1378: this or church connection caused attack on house by Wat Tyler's rebels 1381. Descendants held such offices as Sheriff of Kent and M.P. Parish church, which had to be rebuilt after 1380 French raid, also had its 'Horne Chapel'.

1366 Archbishop gave licence for services as newly built domestic chapel (oratory). Fine carved detail includes clunch corbels with foliage and catherine-wheels. Dedicated, evidently, to St Catherine. Tall, 2-storey structure. 22×12 ft ground plan. Careful Ministry restoration 1955–57, following neglect. Crypt flooded by spring—electric pump now operates. Past cellar usage, when doors altered. Exterior fabric mainly ragstone blocks. Some, perhaps reused, yellow bricks, especially in N and S walls. Brick voussoirs to main door, S side of W wall. Stone dressings. Fine E, S and N windows to chapel proper. This, 23 ft at apex, has wood ceiling. Crypt, just 6 ft at apex, has ribless vault of brick. Its walls ragstone blocks for 3 ft. N and S walls then curve over to form slightly arched tunnel-vault. Brick part of E and W walls pierced by small rectangular windows, with deep splays.

Brick invariably stretcher bond. Bricks 8×4×2 in. Dull or straw yellow. Possibly imported (S. E. Rigold).

Information, Miss P. Harris; John Newman, *West Kent and the Weald*, 1970.

BOUGHTON ALUPH

Parish Church: Red brick used in repairs to flint church. Main brick structure a Tudor annexe or porch, thought to have been pre-Reformation provision for Canterbury pilgrims. Has chimney-stack and contemporary fireplace, this with wide 4-centred moulded brick lintel. Also smaller Tudor brick porch.

BOUGHTON MALHERBE

Manor House: Manor acquired by Wottons *temp.* Henry VI, when Sir Nicholas, Lord Mayor of London, married Corby heiress. In C 19 house became farmhouse.

Some demolition, but frontage with gables and great chimneys virtually intact. Fittings sold in America in 1923. Main building periods: Early Tudor, mainly stone; Elizabethan, mainly brick. Tudor red brick, however, includes big gable-end, its crow-stepping culminating in moulded chimney-shaft, *c.* 1535.

CANTERBURY

The Cathedral:

Central or 'Bell Harry' Tower: Cathedral church of archbishopric, founded 597. Became England's main place of pilgrimage from late C 12 murder by Henry II's knights of Thomas à Becket. His shrine, visited in 1520 by Henry VIII with the Emperor Charles V, was to be principal Reformation target. This was partly because Becket's martyrdom had humbled a king (Becket was labelled a traitor in 1438) and partly because of the accumulated offerings (26 cartloads of these were taken to London, including gold objects weighing nearly 5,000 ounces).

Stone, mainly imported Caen, used for Cathedral. When, at end of Middle Ages, central tower, over the crossing, was reconstructed, brick was used for lining. (Name 'Bell Harry' is said to come from (lost) original bell given by Prior Henry of Eastry.) Part of 'Angel Tower', erected by Lanfranc, Abbot of Caen, who became Archbishop in 1070, was absorbed into new tower. The supporting piers encased the old ones, and strainer arch reinforcements were added. Archbishop John Morton (1500 tomb in undercroft) employed Canterbury-born royal mason John Westell (or Wastell) on this from 1496. Facing of square, 4-turreted tower, 235 ft high, is Caen. Stair, in SW transept angle, has 287 steps. Brick lining visible in upper parts of stairwell, remainder rendered. Bricks mainly red, some pink. Some only $1\frac{1}{4}$ in thick, but majority (Lloyd's measurements) $8\frac{1}{2} \times 4 \times 2\frac{1}{2}$ or $2\frac{1}{4}$ in. Kestell Floyer cited record of 480,000 bricks made for lining (? accurate). Stone fan-vault bears arms of William Warham, Archbishop from 1503 when work was completed. (For Warham see *Otford*. His tomb (he died 1532), begun soon after his election, remains in Cathedral.)

Christ Church (Cathedral) Priory Buildings: Stone and flint were used for buildings, which suffered bomb damage in World War II. A smaller gatehouse of Tudor brick survives, but the main gate Christ Church Gate, which gives entry to Cathedral precinct at SW—is stone-faced. Gate dates from 1517 to 1522, but its stonework is very much restored. Impressive, and of particular interest because of panelling which John Newman points out is, uniquely for stone, like the Early Tudor terracotta at *Layer Marney Tower* (Essex). K. W. E. Gravett tells me that gate has a brick party wall, which is arcaded and can be seen in the adjoining restaurant.

Roper Gateway: In St Dunstan's St, opposite St Dunstan's Church, which has C 14 Roper Chapel (and Thomas More's head). Gateway is sole survivor of Place House, which belonged to Ropers, a local family who acquired trading and legal interests in London. (William married Sir Thomas More's daughter.) Elaborate red brick gatehouse, early C 16. Wide arch, stepped gable, window. Blue bricks for diamond diapering and relief decoration. 'Fussy'.

John Newman, *North East and East Kent.*

CAPEL

Badsell Manor House: Moated site with remains of Early Tudor diapered brick house, including chimneys. Plinth is of sandstone.

CHARING

Palace Farm: Among farmhouse and its outbuildings, fair-sized remains of important Canterbury palace, largely obscured with ivy. Main builder John Stratford in early C 14, using flint and stone. Leland said John Morton (see also *Canterbury*, *Lambeth* (London) and *Croydon* (Surrey) 'made great building at Charing'. This was at the end of the C 15, and Morton used largely brick. In 1545 Henry VIII took over palace from Cranmer (compare *Otford*). Crown property till 1629. 1586 panel on S side probably indicates renovation then.

Approach road (leading on to parish church) passes earlier stone buildings, including gatehouse, absorbed into row of cottages. Behind these, palace buildings in 3 groups surround irregular courtyard. (Stone great hall now used as barn.) Building history not clear, but Morton's main work was enlargement of private apartments. He built on E side of older apartments (now 'fragmentary'—Kipps) an L-shaped block, which later provided farmhouse. Longer wing measures 30×16 ft. Flint rubble to 2nd storey. 3rd storey brick, with diamond diapering composed of diagonally set headers. Dressings mostly stone, but brick jambs to window and stringcourse of moulded brick to chimney-stack. To N is a 2-storey structure, only 8½ ft wide, called on old plan 'Corridor': its S face has upper stage of brick, but N face wholly brick. This was Morton's, as also semi-octagonal turret built on to W side of great hall (set in angle with porch). Access from stair to upper storey of porch, which was then altered in brick. Upper part now lost, as is circular stair itself. Brick, with stone quoins.

Article by R. K. Kipps, 'The Palace of the Archbishops of Canterbury at Charing, Kent', in *Archaeological Journal*, XC, 1934.

CHISLEHURST

(in area transferred to Greater London Council, 1965):
Scadbury Park: Isolated site, on S side of Sidcup by-Pass. Private property, inaccessible. Manor once estate of Walsingham family (of Norfolk origins), acquired in C 13. Moated house site bramble-ridden, but conserved. Modern history of alternate dereliction and restoration of remaining structures. Building history uncertain: there seems to have been a late C 14 house of stone, lost except for re-erected timber hall roof; followed by large late mediaeval or Early Tudor house, said to have been half-timbered. House demolished in C 18.

Moat outlines rectangular (but nearly square) complete brick platform. Small square projections at intervals. Platform and footings made of 10×4×2 in pinkish-red bricks. Variously laid, including English and stretcher bonds. (No stone.) Cannot be earlier than mid C 15. Some footings carried on low and wide segmental arched passages, voussoirs alternating stretchers and pairs of half bats. Another part, filled with water, has wall pierced by 2 tiny arches—voussoirs simply pairs of diagonal stretchers—with relieving arch of stretchers only. Bases of 2 spiral stairs of brick remain. Also 2 circular wells, lined mainly with headers, the copings just radiating stretchers with triangular mortar joints.

Webb, Miller and Beckwith, *The History of Chislehurst*, 1899.

CUXTON

Whorns Place: On W bank of Medway. Brick building here in late C 15 by Sir William Whorne and, before 1550, by Levesons. All demolished, except C 16 gateway (incomplete) and one range. Range has crow-stepped gables. Originally an outbuilding only.

DARTFORD

Priory: Used as offices. Situated in Dartford Iron Works, off Hythe Road. Site that of 1346 Dominican nunnery, of which buildings lost, but in early 1540s Henry VIII had a brick courtyard house built here. The one remaining small range of this known as the 'Priory'. Has gateway, garderobe and chimneybreast. Newman says brick fabric of house was originally rendered and decorated.

John Newman, *West Kent and the Weald*.

DEAL

Castle: M.P.B. & W. One of 3 Downs forts built for Henry VIII when (after Field of Cloth of Gold euphoria had evaporated) traditional Anglo-French hostility reasserted itself and S coast invasion was feared. France and Germany were now allies and Pope Paul III had preached a crusade against Henry VIII, comparing him with the 'Turk'—the arch-infidel. Deal, *Sandown* and *Walmer* are close. Only part of long line of coastal forts, from Cornwall (St Mawes) to Kent and N to Hull, forts either specially built or reconstructed at this period. Kent coastline had altered, and some of old Cinque Ports had been silted up, but also coast partly eroded. Greatest activity on new defences *c.* 1539, when Sir John Russell, President of Council of the West, surveyed SW coast and Christopher Dickenson, mason, was appointed master bricklayer for the 'three Castles which keep the Downs', fronting the French or English Channel—and Calais, still English—and immediately protecting Goodwin Sands anchorage. Described as time as 'Blockhouses or Bulwarks', planned for cannon. With *Sandgate*, they were erected on a symmetrical plan by Bohemian engineer, Stephan van Haschenberg. English supervisor, Sir Edward Ryngley, also held position at Calais and had employed van Haschenberg there. Sandown and Walmer had 4 lobes to circular keep, but Deal's plan is much larger: a circular keep with 6 inner and 6 outer lobes.

As these were genuine defences, bricks used for minor purposes only. Main materials flint and stone, some reused from recently dissolved local monasteries. In 1540 Deal had 16 gunners. Castle still has its 145 gun ports (M.P.B. & W. figure). Original plan is complete. Most of fabric is C 16. Battlements modern.

Interior has much brick. Most ominous use is in tunnel-vaulted entrance passage: brick vaulting is pierced by 5 header-lined 'meurtrières' (murder holes for missiles). This dangerous passage, between portcullis and studded door, leads into hall (with contemporary flat timber ceiling). Hall walls of reused Caen stone, ragstone and brick. Bricks used at top of walls—though corbels stone—besides such uses as 3 orders of voussoirs (unmoulded) to a small door and round top of large stone archway. These examples show the bricklayers rallied later than stone masons on crash building programme, were involved in finishing work in castle interior—the murder holes are a different category! In June 1539 the common labourers struck for higher wages.

A. D. Saunders, *Deal and Walmer Castles*, H.M.S.O., 1963; section by B. H. St. J. O'Neil in *Deal Castle, Kent*, H.M.S.O., 1966.

For Sandown and Walmer Castles, now technically in Deal, see those entries.

DENT-DE-LION GATEHOUSE: see under *Margate*.

DOVER

Castle: M.P.B. & W. There was a Norman castle here, replaced in C 12 by Henry II. Called by Matthew Paris (C 13) 'the key of England'. Curtain wall once had 21 towers, for the manning of which Kent lords were responsible. Much new work evidently done in C 15: William Darell (*temp.* Elizabeth I) said Edward IV had spent £10,000 on the keep. Major additions by Henry VIII.

All parts stone-built and there are only odd pieces of brickwork. Late C 15 brick chimney flue, built inside older stone flue at period when Edward IV added fireplaces to the keep—these carved with Yorkist 'rose-en-soleil' badge (of a rose on a sun). Record that in 1481 William Elys, brickmaker, was paid £33. 6*s*. 8*d*., as small part payment for 20,000 bricks for repairs. Henrician invasion scare brought need for new defences: these, stone-built, included 'Tudor Bulwark' (this survives) and harbour works.

C. A. Ralegh Radford, *Dover Castle*, H.M.S.O., 1959; R. Allen Brown, *Dover Castle*, H.M.S.O., 1966.

EASTCHURCH (ISLE OF SHEPPEY)
Shurland Hall: see under *Sheppey.*

EAST PECKHAM
Roydon Hall: 1535 gabled red brick mansion of Twysdens (monuments in church). Completely modernized, and moulded brick chimneys are replacements, but W side has C 16 gables and windows. Wall at N front is remnant of range. In garden certain structures retain original appearance. Gateway, set in zigzag wall, has ogee arch of moulded brick. Wall ends with blunt octagonal towers (no parapets) at S and N, called 'Garden Houses'. Square base, upper parts octagonal. Square windows with brick mullions. S tower has projection.

ELTHAM PALACE: see under *London.*

GILLINGHAM
**Grench Manor:* In Grange (Grange Rd), Medway estuary, once a Cinque Port. 2 ragstone buildings remain, in ruins. One, with Early English lancets, was chapel built supposedly in 1378 by Sir John Phillpott, Lord Mayor of London. Other, with small rectangular windows, was secular. Window splays of yellow brick—fragmentary—brick surviving best at heads.

Information, K. W. E. Gravett; John Newman, *West Kent and the Weald.*

HEADCORN
Moatenden: Or Mottenden, hamlet 1½ m. NW of village. Farmhouse has some Early Tudor diapered brick—dressings stone—remaining from house of Trinitarian friars.

HERNE
Hawe Farm: Adjoining recent house, range or part of range of C 16. Believed to have belonged to big house built by Sir John Fyneux, lord of manor. (Parish church has small brass to Lady Elizabeth Fyneux, d. 1539.) John Newman says 'before 1525'. Façade half-timbered, but much more brick at rear, including buttress and 'chimneybreast with a moulded stack'.

John Newman, *North East and East Kent.*

LULLINGSTONE
Castle Gatehouse: Nr. Eynsford, in valley of R. Darenth. (Name 'castle' derived from lost mediaeval structure, of which a few relics are embodied in

farmhouse, 'Shoreham Castle'.) Lullingstone Castle (or Lullingstone Park) mainly C 18, Queen Anne, with some remains from Tudor house erected by Hart family. About 1500 Sir Percival Hart inherited manor from Sir John Peche, courtier of Henry VII. (tombs of both in parish church). Hart property to modern times.

Outer gateway, a perfect detached gatehouse, early or mid C 16, is wholly brick. Of curtain walls slight remains only. War damage necessitated careful repairs. Nathaniel Lloyd dated gatehouse about 1530, and gave brick measurements as $9\frac{1}{2}\times4\frac{1}{2}\times2\frac{3}{8}$ in. Symmetrical plan, but inner face of gatehouse looks more domestic than blank outer face. 2 pairs of polygonal turrets. Tall thin outer ones set fairly close to archway. Outer archway is narrower than inner one. Both 4-centred. 3-storey inner turrets adjoin archway and, lower and very much wider, are squared off into side walls. Simple recessed bridging chamber between turrets, with a big square window on both sides: below outer one an arms panel. The plan means inner skyline has 2 levels only, but outer skyline has 3—since turrets there much taller than rest of structure. Apart from central window and side door, only voids in outer face are rectangular peepholes and quatrefoils of moulded brick, accounting for closed appearance. Inner face has, besides central window and wider archway, arched turret entrances and large and small square window (wood window bars). Door mouldings brick, quite simple. Original gates, with linenfold carving. Gatehouse battlemented, copings brick. Battlements supported by shallow cut brick corbel-tables: uncusped, corbels stepped and archlets each formed of 2 plain bricks.

English bond. Bricks mostly lightish-red. Most attractive structure, especially more gracious inner façade. Of considerable size.

John Newman, (*West Kent and the Weald*, 1970) points out C 16 brickwork surviving in C 18 house, particularly at W and N.

MARGATE (THANET)

**Dent-de-Lion:* Ist half of C 15. S gate to big manor house, now lost. Situated near Canterbury road, in Carlinge ($1\frac{1}{2}$ m. SW of Margate, near Westgate). In parish of St John's—church of the old port.

Gate long in farmyard, and site of house now submerged by bungalows. In modern times, however, still an estate (in late C 18 owned by Charles James Fox). This tall gate variously called 'Dent-de-Lion', 'Daundelyon', 'Dandelion', as family established here from 2nd half of C 13. In St John's Church brass to Sir John de Dandelyon, died heirless 1445. (It says he imported a bell for the church 'on a mill cog' (ship).) Gate attributable to him or a recent predecessor, and certainly pre 1445, for family arms are carved on eroded stone panel over main archway and there are lions' heads on stone stringcourse.

Structure always impractical for military defence, despite cross-shaped arrow slits and the battlements. Now roofless, ruinous. Fragments only of curtain wall. One stumbles over description: 'gatehouse' too strong; 'gateway' indequate.

4 slim square angle towers, round recessed central section—little more than screen with archways. Odd, impressive building, with late mediaeval ambiguousness over defence. Battlemented throughout, but tower battlements evidently more shallow (now partly eroded) than central section's. Turrets rise perhaps three-eighths of their height above this. Outer faces sombre and blank, except for circular peepholes near base. In contrast, central section mainly open: arches abut turret walls, and their own meeting makes just a fairly thin double column—off centre, for pedestrian arch narrower. It has depressed pointed arch; main arch flatter (4-centred). Inside (N) one even taller archway, rising almost too parapets. No chamber over high passageway. Doors to alure from turrets. Chimney-stack between.

Gatehouse unusual in distribution of building materials, apart from stone: stone used for archways; battlements coping of central section: copings of turret plinths; peepholes; small windows, stringcourses to central section and carved panels on them; irregular quoins (found only in lowest quarter of turrets). Body, however, striped combination of dressed flint and brick. Turret battlements and turret tops *yellow* brick only. Rest of bricks—mixture of yellow and (more) *red*—laid in layers, alternating with flint. Flint 'squares' taller than bricks, so forming deeper layers, for each layer has 4 courses. Lloyd gave brick measurements as $8\frac{3}{4} \times 4\frac{1}{2} \times 2$ in. (He thought date late C 15.)

Nathaniel Lloyd, *A History of English Brickwork*; John Newman, *North East and East Kent*.

OLD ROMNEY

Midley Church (*Ruins*): Slight remains only—W end—dated *c.* 1500. Fabric mainly yellow bricks. There are several ruined mediaeval churches in Romney Marsh, much of which before the Dissolution belonged to and was farmed by the monks of *Christchurch Priory*, *Canterbury*, who would have helped provide churches for villages or hamlets—some of which likely to be cut off by floods at times (compare *Smallhythe*).

Information, K. W. E. Gravett; John Newman, *West Kent and the Weald*.

OTFORD

Archbishop's Palace: By R. Darenth. SW of parish church.) Palace part of farm, absorbed and built onto, but incomplete and mostly ruinous. Patches of renewed brickwork. There have been cows rather than ghosts in the ruined tower, but one range was reconstructed as cottages. Once a favourite among 16 palaces of archbishop. Otford had 2 parks—Great Park of several hundred acres, to S so hunting attractive. (Manor house known from *temp.* Becket, C 12.)

Despite takeover by Henry VIII, who stayed here on way to Field of Cloth of Gold, these buildings had comparatively short history. Between 1501 and 1503 Archbishop Henry Deane rebuilt earlier palace, but William Warham, successor, tore down nearly all new work—except chapel and hall—and built again on larger scale. Cost of Warham's work was £33,000. William Lambarde, post-Reformation historian of Kent, castigated primate as 'wishing to leave to posterite some glorious monument of his worldly wealth and misbegotten treasure' (*Perambulation of Kent*, 1576).

Thomas Cranmer became Archbishop in 1533: about 1536 surrendered Otford and Knole to Henry VIII, who envied the hunting land and who had been courting Anne Boleyn at Hever Castle, Kent. Henry, however, soon complained: 'The house standeth low and is rheumatik, like unto Croydon where I would never be without sickness, and I will live at Knole and most of household shall live at Otford'! (*Croydon*, Surrey ,was another archiepiscopal palace.) Diagnosis confirmed in 1596 survey: the ground at Otford was very wet and floors and walls in winter were 'hoary and mustie'. For a period Otford became a home for the Princess Mary, but decay began about 1545 and Edward VI's councillors, 1547, made a survey—but plundered the lead off the roofs. Site Crown property till early C 17. Some interest had continued in palace even during decline, and a 1573 survey—as one measure of decay—cited 200 missing door keys.

Principal remains—suggestive fragments—are a roofless tower of outer (N) court; arcaded round floor of range (the cottages); hexagonal building (sometimes said to be Deane's chapel, but wrongly oriented). Last, rather battered, has various diapers including zigzag and cross. Materials throughout lightish-red brick, mainly English bond, with purple diapering, and ragstone (worn) for dressings, including conspicuous pale quoins. Ground plan wax about 440 ft (N–S) by 220, the buildings set round N and S courts. Great gatehouse was in N range, and possibly lesser gatehouse too in S range (of which plan totally lost) entered from 'Privy Walk'. Great hall lay between the courts. S court had main living quarters. Surviving gallery, which provides ground floor of cottages, belonged to N court. At one end is NW angle tower, of 3 storeys. Main set of rooms 6-sided polygonal stair turret; another projection, largish and square, the garderobe. Fireplaces survive for main rooms, one to each floor, and top one wholly brick (others have stone lintels). Exterior mainly diamond-diapered, but also one big cross on diamond base.

NE tower site also traceable.

Chapter by Caroline C. Morewood in *English Episcopal Palaces* (*Province of Canterbury*), ed. R. S. Rait, 1910; Robert H. Goodsall, *The Ancient Road to Canterbury*, 1959.

OTTERDEN

Otterden Place: Present house is early C 19 'revivalist' or 'Regency Tudor' replacement and partial recasting of mid-Tudor and Elizabethan red brick house. 100 acre park. Manor held by Auchers from *temp.* Henry VI,when 'towards the end of Henry VIII's reign Sir Anthony Aucher, who had managed possibly through his comparative insignificance to retain that monarch's favour, built himself a large brick mansion round a courtyard' (James Lees-Milne). As Marshal of Calais was killed with his son John, in the successful siege of Calais by the French. Aucher was one of few recipients of outright grants of ex-monastic lands, his gains being in Kent and of high value. 1801 drawings of recently demolished house show it had pairs of Tudor chimneys, 2 storeys and a fine polygonal bay window (at E). At W end of N wing are remains of Early Tudor period. Projecting chimney-stack has 2 polygonal shafts, both with the same moulded brick network pattern in relief. (Indoors is one mid C 16 stone fireplace.) Beyond stack—its renewed, stone-coped battlements about level with caps of shafts—is polygonal turret of 3 stages. Windows are modern. Thin, bright-red bricks. English bond.

James Lees-Milne, *article* on 'Otterden Place, Kent' in *Country Life*, August 27, 1970; John Newman, *North East and East Kent*, 1970.

SANDGATE

Castle: Near Folkestone. One of the early C 16 forts, with 10 gunners in 1540. In 1806 reconstructed against another possible French invasion. Reduced by gale damage and neglect to 'little more than an enlarged Martello tower' (Ronald F. Jessup, 7th ed. of *Little Guide* to Kent). Building accounts for Sandgate were kept separately. Bricklayers joined stone masons later: 500 workers at peak of activity. 44,000 'wall tiles' used, mostly from Wye (NW). (Before Dissolution Wye tileworks had belonged to Battle Abbey (Sussex), records of production going back to mid. C 14.) As at *Deal* and *Walmer*, master bricklayer was Christopher Dickinson, active on royal works *c.* 1528–40. (he had come here from Hampton Court Palace). The designer—the contemporary term is 'deviser'—was Stephan van Haschenberg. Castle cost £5,543. 19*s.* 2¾*d.* Centrally planned keep had 3 lobed defences and gate-house.

A. D. Saunders, *Deal and Walmer Castles*, H.M.S.O., 1967.

SANDOWN CASTLE

Isolated. Almost completely eroded by gales. Most damage, 1864. One of 3 Downs Castles, stone-built in main. N of larger *Deal* (where subsidiary brickwork still visible). Not only have many forts been reduced like this, but the linking continuous earth defences and smaller bulwarks—and probably trenches too—have completely disappeared. There were 2 bulwarks between Sandown and Deal, and 2 more between Deal and *Walmer*.

SHEPPEY (ISLE OF SHEPPEY)

Shurland House (wrongly called 'Shurland Castle'): At Eastchurch. Shurland now pathetic ruined fragment of great brick courtyard house built by Sir Thomas Cheyney in Henry VIII's reign. Isle of Sheppey lies NE of Sittingbourne (mainland), where brickmaking was long major industry. One assumes bricks came from there, especially as Cheyney imported from mainland stone from Chilham Castle, demolished by him after 1529 grant by Henry VIII. In 1432 William Cheyney held manor *in capite* and successive lords held state offices, including membership of Privy Council. *Temp.* Edward IV William Cheyney was Constable of lost Queenborough Castle (Sheppey); Thomas, his son, held same office in early C 16 and was Sheriff of Kent, Governor of Rochester, Lord Warden of Cinque Ports and Treasurer of the Household. He had benefit, for a time, of relationship with Boleyn family of Hever. In 1530s Dissolution brought him convent of Minster. Part of his money came from export of wool, with special financial privileges.

Augustus Daly (who published history of Isle of Sheppey in 1904) discovered plan of Shurland in Public Record Office. Thomas Cheyney's replacement of old manor house was complete enough to receive Henry VIII in 1532. Plan showed original scale, now only guessable from wrecked house and remains and traces of stone boundary wall and moat. (House and land now have different owners. The P.R.O. plan has never been rediscovered.) In 1914–18 Shurland was requisitioned, and in 2nd World War it had as neighbour pioneer airfield of Eastchurch (bombarded in 1940): in interval lead off roof stolen. In C 17 Cromwellians had already demolished part, though this was not a castle to be 'slighted'.

Surviving parts are central block, with 2 tall polygonal turrets at sides of off-centre entrance arch; remains of another wing; a porch. 2 storeys. Thinnish, dark-red bricks main building material, but stone for all dressings apart from plain brick chimneys. Roughly dressed stone blocks form high plinth. Perp. main door has shields in spandrels, worn marks of ownership. Sash windows are replacements, of course, but turrets retain original small arched windows with square labels. All outward angles have stone quoins. Bricks laid English bond. Some diapering, glaze, worn. Some older bricks.

'Minor brick OUTBUILDINGS to NW' (—Newman).

Robert H. Goodsall, The *Widening Thames*, 1965; John Newman, *North East and East Kent*, 1970.

SMALLHYTHE *Pls. 42 & 43*

Church (or Chapel) of St. John the Baptist: Smallhythe is 2½ m. S of *Tenterden*, on Rye road. What is now creek below hamlet once held salt water, a branch of R. Rother connecting with estuary and sea, until Rother retreated from original course. This place provided 'hythe' (landing place) for Tenterden, its port and ship-building centre. Tenterden was then a Cinque Port. Chapel here was subordinate to Tenterden parish church.

Records show chapel here at latest from C 14, probably timber-built. An early C 16 'Priest's House' neighbours church, and this is half-timbered and plastered. An earlier half-timbered house of 1480 or 1490 (which brings Smallhythe its visitors, for it was Ellen Terry's house and is National Trust) was the mediaeval harbour-master's house, and a fortunate survival from the 1514 fire which devastated Smallhythe.

The chapel was destroyed, and replaced about 1516 by present brick building. Man responsible was William Warham, Archbishop (see *Otford*). Perhaps half-timber thought adequate for contemporary home for priest. At this date function of building as a chapel-of-ease was stressed, valley inhabitants sometimes being cut off from Tenterden by floods.

It is small and aisleless, all of a period. Carefully restored in 1900. Rather empty, but retains the old octagonal font and original screens. Deep window splays and plastered walls inside. Bricks rich red and have worn well. English bond. Style has been labelled 'Flemish', because of crow-stepped E and W gables and sharply moulded windows—particularly side windows, with most elaborate tracery forming different cusped shapes and daggers round a large heart (halved by central mullion). Moulded brick doorways. Small statue niche in W gable. (No tower, only tiny slatted wood belfry.) Low stepped W porch with big square label to door. Even plinth and buttress copings brick.

Blue diaper decoration: besides usual diamonds, other patterns like open irregular tents or sails. Stone E window appears replacement of wider original.

TENTERDEN

Brunger (*or Brunger's*) *Farm:* At Leigh Green (to E). 2-storeyed red brick building of *c.* 1540. Crow-stepped gable and porch. Simple label over rounded archway. Gable-end has 3-light brick mullioned window, but elsewhere casements inserted. Brick stringcourse. Contemporary tiled roof. (Tenterden has several tiled roofs of late mediaeval or early C 16, but to timber-framed not brick buildings.)

Nathaniel Lloyd;

M.H.L.G. list.

Hales Place: Off E side of High Street. Hales family long important in Tenterden, a port in Middle Ages (see *Smallhythe*). One of augmented Cinque Ports group, linked with Rye, with shipping, iron-founding and weaving industries. *Temp.* Edward III gained royal charter as brought: first Mayor, John Hales.

C 14 house on the Hales Place site was refashioned in C 16. Complete rebuilding by Sir Edward Hales in C 18. Subsidiary buildings of 1530 or 1540 remain: entrance gateway, 2 detached turrets; well-house. These are wholly red brick, no stone dressings. Lloyd gave brick sizes as varying round $9 \times 4 \times 2$ in. Gateway fairly plain, with triple mouldings to arch and outside and double mouldings on inside, the voussoirs stepped stretchers. Rear buttressed, Well-house (with contemporary well) also simple structure. A rectangular chamber with crow-stepped gable-ends, these having 2-light brick windows. Lloyd pointed it out as 'an excellent example of good architectural results achieved by simple means. Only two moulded bricks are used'—these for door and plinth coping.

Turrets more elaborate, providing 'Garden Pavilions'. Set on sloping ground, so partly one- and partly 2-storey. Doors at both levels. Windows blocked and weeds sprout from mouldings. Once plastered in imitation of stone—or was this just the doorways? Octagonal, with angled battlements. Battlements outlined by mouldings, copings vertical and horizontal stretchers in turn. Moulded brick window jambs, 4-centred doors, stringcourses. Tall pilasters of rounded bricks at side of doors of one turret, a Renaissance touch: John Newman (in *West Kent and the Weald*, 1970) therefore gives date as 'second half of the C 16'.

Nathaniel Lloyd, *A History of English Brickwork*, 1925.

THANINGTON

**Tonford Manor:* Moated site. Licence to crenellate 1449. Builder Sir Thomas Browne, Comptroller of Household and Treasurer to Henry VI. Striking gatehouse and turreted buttressed hall range remain, attached to C 18 house. Mainly flint, with stone dressings. Range, incomplete, has brick core. 2 of the 4 round interval turrets (on NW) have red brick headers used for chequer patterning in flint facing. Newman notes 'garderobes in the two r. towers'.

John Newman, *North East and East Kent.*

WALMER

Castle: M.P.B. & W. One of the 3 Downs forts, but better preserved than *Deal* and *Sandown*, which were once all linked by earth defences. 6 m. N of *Dover*. 1 m. S of *Deal Castle*, and now technically in Deal. Has (dry) moat. In good condition and still mainly C 16 fabric, but considerably altered. Open to public, but part residence of Lord Warden of Cinque Ports. 4 lobed bastions to circular keep—designed by van Haschenberg. Same workers recorded as at Deal, and same minor use of brick. The accounts (in Public Record Office) record costs of Downs Castles and Dover along with Hampton Court and the lost Oatlands Palace (Surrey) for 1539–40, only Sandgate being separately accounted. Records show 1,400 craftsmen on Downs works in May 1539.

Entrance passage at Walmer, like Deal's retains its murder holes. 8 of them, formed of headers in stretcher tunnel-vaulting. Walmer is recorded as having 11 gunners in 1540.

A. D. Saunders, *Deal and Walmer Castles*, H.M.S.O., 1963.

WEST WICKHAM

Wickham Court: Sir Henry Heydon *c.* 1470 rebuilt ragstone parish church and built nearby manor house of red brick stone-dressed. (Heydon arms in church and at house entry.) Has polygonal angle turrets, but all poshed up in C 19 with new windows, extra storey and battlements. Plan, single court: interior 'tiny' and timber-framed, Newman points out 'forceful' nature of architecture—including slits for defence in angle turrets, but no moat or gate-house—shrunk, however, to 'single family' size. (The court is now roofed over and contains a stair.)

John Newman, *West Kent and the Weald.*

Other buildings in Kent with early brickwork are:

Bekesbourne Old Palace; *Biddenden* Old Cloth Hall; *Boxley* Boxley Abbey (remains of Early Tudor arch); *Canterbury* Blackfriars (ribs of frater) and Greyfriars; *Fordwich* Town Hall; *Harrietsham* Lake Cottage; *Ightham* Ightham Mote; *Margate* Salmestone Grange; *Otham* Stoneacre (N.T.); *Penshurst* Penshurst Place (C 14 tiled hearth and pamments); *Tonge* Parish Church.

LEICESTERSHIRE

ASHBY-DE-LA-ZOUCH

Castle: In the main ruinous. William Lord Hastings, Chamberlain to Edward IV, added to existing stone buildings here. Had obtained property by royal grant, and licence to crenellate 1474. Exceptionally rich—probably built parish church also. His is most important and complete structure remaining, the stone 'Hastings Tower'. See also brick-built *Kirby Muxloe*. Was beheaded by Richard III, but family kept title and lands. Son fought for Henry at Bosworth. More building done in C 16. Brick structures remaining probably erected by Hastings's grandson, George, created Earl of Huntingdon 1529. 2-acre garden area, called 'The Wilderness', S of castle was enclosed with a brick wall, of which fragments remain on S, with SW and SE angle towers of brick with stone dressings. Square-headed stone windows. SW tower is the larger, with quatrefoil plan, of 3 storeys—spiral stair in N lobe. SE tower octagonal, 2 storeys, with projecting stair turret and traces of 'corbelled-out chimney stack from a fireplace on the first floor'.

T. L. Jones, M.O.W. guidebook, 1953.

BRADGATE HOUSE

In Bradgate Park, NW of Leicester. Belongs to Leicester Corporation. Builder was Thomas Grey, 1st Marquis of Dorset, who rose to further riches when his mother Elizabeth (née Woodville) married Edward IV as her 2nd husband. Grey was building Bradgate in 1490s. Largely complete on death in 1501, for family had already moved there from mansion at Gorby. Red brick, with stone quoins, fashionable for date and not a fortress: Hoskins labels it one of very first 'country houses'. Now ruin for bizarre reason (late C 17 lady of manor, describing country round as 'desert' and people as 'brutes', set fire to it). When 2nd Earl of Stamford (her husband, who had remarried) died in 1739 it was left to total ruin. Local builder allowed to take materials. More remained in Victorian times. Engraving of *c.* 1710 after Knyff shows house complete, with additions of 1630s made by Henry Grey (created Earl of Stamford 1628).

Brick came from site: clay-pit and drying floors traceable (S end of reservoir in park). Plan evidently 3 sides of quadrangle: centre portion, about 20 ft long, had great hall about 101 ft. long. Ruinous remains, mainly external walls, with octagonal angle turrets and 4-storey porch (held stair). Most of chapel survives: belonged to E wing, where private apartments were. Features are Renaissance tomb in chapel, large fireplace in kitchen and square ovens (deep, like old bread ovens). Stone used for quoins, conspicuously pale, and for square-headed windows. Part of garden wall remains, with dentillated coping and, seemingly original, arch with projecting keystone (brick). Brick-work is in good condition. *Kirby Muxloe*, only 4 m. away, looks like a castle; Bradgate, despite towers, a fine, dignified house. Tiltyard area to E, with more late C 15 walling. This and part of house diapered.

At Anstey, on route between Bradgate and Leicester, the stone packhorse bridge was possibly built by the Greys *c.* 1500.

City of Leicester guidebook to Bradgate Park, including article by W. G. Hoskins, n/d.

KIRBY MUXLOE

Kirby Muxloe Castle *Pls. 26 & 27*

Bibliography: M.O.W. guidebook by the last Sir Charles Peers, 2nd ed. 1957. *Articles* in *Transactions of the Leicester Archaeological Society*, XI, 1915–16, including one by A. Hamilton Thompson on 'The Building Accounts of Kirby Muxloe Castle, 1480–1484'.

R. Allen Brown, *English Mediaeval Castles*, 1954.

Pevsner, *Leicestershire and Rutland*, 1960.

See the chapter on 'Defence and the Major Castles'.

Castle is administered by M.P.B. & W. Open all year.

LEICESTER

Leicester Abbey: House of Augustinian canons, founded 1143, on N side of Leicester (near Abbey Gate). One of richest houses of order, with 20–30 canons. Now minimal, indecipherable remains, of stone, beside late Elizabethan Cavendish House (itself gutted by fire in 1645). About ½ m. of boundary wall on S and W survives. Of 1490 or 1500, red brick. Coping renewed. Blocked depressed pointed arch of brick has worn stone arms panel above. Niche at angle. Although work much weathered, wall shows notable and varied diapering, including 2 or 3 different versions of initials of builder: 'IP', for Abbot John Penny, sometimes with 'C'—evidently for 'construxit' (erected). Some diapering several courses thick. Designs largely geometrical:

horizontal zigzag, lozenges, squares, crossed chevrons, honeycomb, and also combinations of these (reminiscent of sampler patterns). One design like formalized Christmas tree. Several crosses, including St. Andrew's. Penny, who went on to be Bishop of Bangor (1504) and then of Carlisle (from 1508), was buried in 1521 in the alabaster tomb in St Margaret's Church, Leicester. Must once also have been brick among abbey buildings, for Leland—recording tomb—says: 'This Peny made the new bricke worke in Leicester Abbay, and muche of the bricke waulles (walls).' (In 1530 Wolsey came here to die.)

LINCOLNSHIRE

BARDNEY (LINDSEY)

**Parish Church:* When old church collapsed, 1434–35 *Tattershall* records show that Abbot of Bardney received 8,000 bricks for rebuilding, out of his total order for 20,000. Church mainly ashlar-faced, much restored in 1870s, but chancel all brick. Diapered. N side retains C 15 moulded brick door and window. Large resources of Abbot explained by Bardney Abbey's having been one of most important Benedictine houses in Lincs. (Holder of office always had major responsibilities over Fenland drainage.) Some relics of Abbey, adjacent, preserved in church.

BARTON-UPON-HUMBER (LINDSEY)

St. Mary's Church: Perp. brick clerestory.
St Peter's Church: Perp. brick clerestory.

BELLEAU (LINDSEY)

Manor House Outbuildings: Present Belleau Manor is of 1661 (M.H.L.G.) in main, but once-moated site retains some souvenirs of mansion of great Willoughby d'Eresby family (head was Earl of Lindsey). Another lost Willoughby mansion was at Spilsby: Leland (mid C 16) recorded of the then Lord Willoughby, 'I hear he intendeth to build sumptuously'. Spilsby church still has 7 family tombs, oldest of 1349. Another family mansion in Lincs is stone Grimthorpe Castle (at Edenham), partly C 13 but mostly mid-C 16 work of Charles Brandon, Duke of Suffolk, one of whose wives was Willoughby heiress. Another family mansion, but of brick was *Parham Old Hall*, Suffolk, which survives in part, (with statues of Willoughby wodehouse (wild man) by gateway.) At Belleau bust of wodehouse, once on a gatehouse, set in modern building.

Barn: Early C 16 red brick structure, once domestic. M.H.L.G. list says 'formerly great hall'. Contemporary windows, now blocked, of stone. Roof, C 20 restoration.

Dovecote: Also early C 16 red brick. Original roof replaced much later with slates. Octagonal, small, quite low. Locally called 'Guard House', perhaps from blank appearance: narrow windows, of moulded brick, and some walls blind. Inside, niches for nesting birds.

BOSTON (HOLLAND)

**Guildhall:* In South Street. Corporation property since 1546. Used partly as museum. Erected in 1st half of C 15 by then wealthy Guild of St Mary. Origins of guild (1260) wholly charitable, and Richard II ascertained, 1389, it still had no property; but after that date its character changed and many gifts were received. Among members, rich wool merchants, middlemen who sold Cistercian wool (from Revesby and Swineshead) to Flanders clothiers. New wealth used for hall and (lost) bedehouse beyond E end—reached by (surviving) passage along S side of hall. 1534 inventory of building and contents took both sides of 9 ft roll of parchment! 1545 Boston obtained royal charter as borough, and then town was able to take over guildhall on Dissolution of guilds. An upper room used as Council Chamber, till 1904, and other parts used for prison (1552 conversion) and administration of justice. Thus, interior altered, but exterior little changed, except for replacement of original side windows by sashes in 1772.

Building material brick—light-red, rough-textured, thinnish bricks. Stone dressings, including stringcourse, quoins and gable coping at W. E gable crow-stepped. Brick has weathered much better than the soft stone, but sides (N and S) largely C 18 rebuilding. W gable-end all Perp. Door leads to ground-level undercroft. At either side depressed pointed window. Above, fine W window, which lit great hall (musicians'gallery at E end). W window has statue niche incorporated in tracery, and retains some original figured glass. Other room on 1st floor subdivided, part being the 'Council Chamber'. On ground floor, E part has kitchen, still with spits and brick 'cooking places' along walls. Original rooms provided for guild included also parlour and buttery, and there was a chantry.

Guide published by the Borough of Boston.

Hussey Tower: Sit. near the Skirbeck Road, and outside old Boston boundary. Ruinous, incomplete. Tower was being dismantled as early as mid C 16, after

1536 Pilgrimage of Grace, when the then Lord Hussey, John (who had his main mansion at Sleaford), suffered attainder for involvement. Hussey Tower is one of group of brick houses not far from *Tattershall* (of mid C 15). Often described as C 15, but more exact date for Hussey Tower is *c.* 1510. Defensive and has battlements. Of red brick, with dressings of stone. 3-storeyed. Rectangular ground plan. Octagonal stair turret projecting at corner. Ground floor has rib vaulting. Thorold and Yates (in the Shell Guide) comment, it 'must have been quite a luxurious affair'.

Rochford Tower: Sometimes known as 'Kyme Tower'. In Skirbeck parish, S of Boston, and outside original Boston boundary. Square tower of *c.* 1510, defensive, of red brick with stone dressings. Taller than Hussey Tower. Embattled. Rochford Tower is in better condition, and even has remains of mural paintings on the 1st floor (subjects are Virgin and saints). Three main rooms, connected by stone spiral stair in turret. Octagonal turrets corbelled out at angles. Ground floor is brick-vaulted.

COWBIT (HOLLAND)

**Parish Church:* Sit. S of Spalding. Prior de Moulton of Spalding *c.* 1400 may have been responsible for centre part of church. (Priors of Spaldings incidentally, were among officers responsible for Fenland drainage.) Dating confused. Consecration ceremony in 1487 by Bishop John Russell of Lincoln (see *Lincoln* and *Buckden*, Hunts) must have followed new work. Tower is ashlar-faced and chancel of rubble, but nave is C 15 brick. Traces on tower show nave roof has been lowered.

EDLINGTON (LINDSEY)

**Edlington Moor:* Sit. 4 m. N of *Tattershall.* Main source of Castle bricks. W. Douglas Simpson described the still visible remains of brickworks as 'a tangled wilderness of pits and ponds and spoil-heaps' (*The Building Accounts of Tattershall Castle*, 1434–1472, published by Lincoln Record Society, 1960). Simpson cited 'a round dozen or so of ponds, including two large ones', so scale of Tattershall matched by scar on landscape here. For Halstead Hall, which may be connected with these brickworks, see *Stixwould.*

FREISTON (HOLLAND)

Parish Church: Priory origins. Has Norman and Early English work. Described by Thorold and Yates (Shell Guide) as 'immense and beautiful'. N aisle is C 15 brick, related by Pevsner and Harris to *Tattershall.*

GAINSBOROUGH (LINDSEY)

Gainsborough Old Hall: Architectural and historical medley. C 15 and C 16, plus *c.* 1600 E wing. Usually described as 'Tudor', though. Fell into industrial decline in C 18, but now rescued and a museum. De Burgh manor from 1375. House largely destroyed 1469 by supporters of Henry VI, since Sir Thomas de Burgh had rescued rival king, Edward IV, from captivity. De Burgh engaged on rebuilding in 1470s and 1480s, when Edward regained control.

Basic plan a courtyard: lost 4th side consisted of curtain wall with central gatehouse. Inner walls half-timber and plaster for 1st and 2nd floors, but ground floor brick. Great hall half-timbered, with notable octagonal 2-storey bay window of stone. Brick main material, but role quite complicated. Outer walls and domestic projections (apart from stone bay) are brick. One projection is complete brick wing, retaining some moulded brick windows—of 2 lights, with low rounded heads and square labels. Great hall wing has projecting brick chimney-stack and another tall bay window, again octagonal but of brick.

Between the 2 bays is a 2-storey tower with polygonal angle turrets, one rising to 4 storeys and apparently having garderobes. Windows of tower stone, but slit windows, elaborate cusped corbelling, battlements (copings stone), all of brick. Moulded brick chimneys at angles. Comparison has been made with ruins of *Nether Hall*, Roydon, Essex. Another brick projection is square kitchen, connected to great hall by servery arrangements: at 3 corners of kitchen are servants' rooms, each with another above it (6 in all).

All this work of about 1489. Apparently finished when Richard III visited Gainsborough Old Hall in 1484. Despite anarchic background to building and despite its intermittent battlements, domesticity—even luxury living—predominates. Surviving military features somewhat ambiguous. Corbelling of tower constitutes false machicolations, not even convincingly: had they been real, lower line of defenders would have had unpleasant time. There is a second, smaller tower.

Garner and Stratton; Pevsner and Harris.

LINCOLN (LINDSEY)

Cathedral Close:

The Chancery: Earlier known as 'Chancellor's House'. Situated in Minster Yard, on S side of Cathedral. Rear section stone and *c.* 1320. Front section dark red brick with stone dressings, dates from end of C 15, a gabled range. Main features are stone archway and large oriel window. Gables are restored. Builder evidently John Russell, Bishop of Lincoln from 1480 to 1494. His arms—a chevron and rosettes—carved on boss of timber ceiling of 1st floor room and stone lintel of fireplace. Chancery is souvenir of administration of vast mediaeval see. (Stone-built Tithe Barn of 1440 also survives.)

**Exchequer Gate:* Cathedral had licence to crenellate precinct 1285, with further licence to erect towers 1319. Exchequer Gate (strictly gatehouse) covers W entrance to precinct, of which buildings were almost without exception local stone. Principal gatehouse, name recording administration of see's estates. Of 3 storeys, but low and wide. Date C 14, Decorated in style. 3 archways. Over 3 passages quadripartite vaulting with stone ribs, the cells (in-filling) of brick.

LUTTON (HOLLAND)

Parish Church: Dedication St Nicholas. Lutton has another name—Sutton St Nicholas. Fenland church, SE of *Boston*. Exterior manily C 15 red brick. Stone W tower with spire rises to 160 ft. Inside, tower arch at W end of nave is stone, and so is Decorated and Perp. nave arcade. Main windows C 19. Brick constitutes walls and clerestory. Clerestory is sizeable. Can be seen from nave face of W tower that roof has been raised. Clerestory windows wholly cut brick, of 2 lights with cusped heads.

Pevsner and Harris.

ROUGHTON (LINDSEY)

Parish Church: Stone and brick church, brick belonging to C 15 or early C 16 remodelling, including upper section of W tower. Tower has contemporary greenstone base, incorporating church porch. Upper section has fairly elaborate bell-openings, with twin lights and square labels, of brick. Brick battlements.

SKIRBECK

Hussey and Rochford Towers: see under *Boston*.

SPALDING (HOLLAND)

**Ayscoughfee Hall:* Situated near parish church of Spalding. Now museum of ornithology. Building history quite complex, 1st parts being of 1420s. 1st builder Sir Richard Aldwyn (name derives from later owners, the Ayscoughs). Tudor parts have been overlaid with Elizabethan 'H' front and with general C 19 'Gothick' remodelling. House is built of stone as well as brick, but brick predominates in early parts. C 15 work includes tower; adjoining W wing; N wing, this with a brick-mullioned window and brick hood-mould.

STIXWOULD (LINDSEY)

**Halstead Hall:* 2-storeyed red brick house with stone dressings. Associated with Welby family (monuments at Allington and, later, at Denton which has C 17 Welby Almshouse). Often described as early C 16, and Pevsner and Harris think this the probable date, when Welbys would have been builders.

Hall neighbours *Edlington Moor* brickworks site and its bricks resemble those of *Tattershall*. Now a farmhouse, probably one range of large house. It is contained in a rectangular moat. There have been C 19 and C 20 alterations, but 4-light Perp. windows of Ancaster stone survive. Plinth, doors, gables also stone. Early C 16 dating queried by W. D. Simpson (in *The Building Accounts of Tattershall Castle*, 1960). Simpson says: 'I see no reason why it may not represent the residence of Baldwin Dutchman', the Tattershall brickmaker, who is also recorded as having his own farm at Edlington. This attribution gives Hall mid C 15 date.

SUTTON ST NICHOLAS: see *Lutton* above.

TATTERSHALL (LINDSEY)

**College:* Also known as Grammar or Choir School. Sit. E of Tattershall market place, where Ralph Lord Cromwell built market stance, of which cross survives. Cromwell's main buildings at Tattershall were Castle, Church and College, a complex perhaps only a Lord Treasurer could have afforded. What happened to College as institution unknown, but was evidently no longer functioning at Dissolution (when Henry VIII replanned Abbey at *Thornton Curtis* as college (school) for area.) Castle and College were brick, but Church stone—finished after Cromwell's death by his executor, Bishop Waynflete of Winchester, builder of *Wainfleet* School.

College building remnant only: 2-storeyed rectangular building almost entirely brick. Evidently one large room below and one above—same plan as Wainfleet School. Upper room still has impressive timber roof. Brickwork not diapered, but some dark bricks (red bricks also darkish). Windows frame stone and so are rounded door arches, but latter have double rows of brick voussoirs. Quoins are brick. Alterations, including blocking of windows, building having been used for agricultural/workshop purposes. Condition decayed: holes in walls, roof. In 1465 Cromwell's executors calculated he had given £2,666. 13*s*. 4*d*. in jewels and vestments to College.

Information, Canon Peter Binnall; National Monuments Record has black and white photographs taken in 1967.

**Tattershall Castle:* *Fig. 3(d); Pls. 21 & 22*

Bibliography: 1927, The late Marquis Curzon of Kedleston and H. Avray Tipping, *Tattershall Castle, Lincolnshire: A Historical and Descriptive Survey.*

1928, A. Hamilton Thompson, *Tattershall Castle*, guidebook published by National Trust and reprinted to date.

1935, W. Douglas Simpson, *article* 'The Affinities of Lord Cromwell's Tower-house at Tattershall', in *Journal of the British Archaeological Association*, New Series, XL.

1953, T. B. Hugh and C. D. Ross, *article* 'The English Baronage and the Income Tax of 1436', in *Bulletin of the Institute of Historical Research*, XXVI. Uses Historical Manuscripts Commission Report on MSS. of Lord De L'Isle and Dudley, at Penhurst (Kent), which include Cromwell Papers with Tattershall accounts.

1960, W. Douglas Simpson, *The Building Accounts of Tattershall Castle, 1434–1472*, published by the Lincoln Record Society.

For detailed description see chapter on 'Defence and the Major Castles'.

THORNTON CURTIS (LINDSEY) *Pls. 14–16*

**Thornton Abbey:* M.P.B. & W. Augustinian, founded 1139; under royal patronage from 1274. Valued at £591 at 1539 surrender, so considerable income despite isolation. Last abbot, John Moor, no longer in office because he had apparently aided with money the 1536 Lincolnshire rising against Henrician religious measures. Henry VIII, rarely, refounded Abbey as College of Secular Canons with school. This suppressed under Chantries Act.

Main remains the great gatehouse: Margaret Wood (*The English Mediaeval House*, 1965) calls it the 'most magnificent of the surviving Fourteenth Century monastic gateways'. Also notable example of early brickwork. Approach by 120 ft long raised barbican of C 16 red brick. This has 2 round towers, and walls 5 ft thick, but deep recesses of arcade make solidity more apparent than real. Fragments of alure. Perhaps erected before Dissolution; perhaps very late in C 16, for mansion. Precinct wall, too, of these later, darker bricks. In remnants of abbey domestic buildings some mediaeval brick, used for repairs, reconstruction and some added fireplaces: especially in E range—dorter and calefactory—and the refectory (S). (Part of C 13 stone Chapter House also survives.)

Despite its splendour, nature of gatehouse ambiguous. Licence for Abbot Thomas de Gretham to 'build and crenellate house over and beside the abbey gate' is dated 1382. Statement persists that gatehouse was fortified as response to 1381 Peasants' Revolt. Defensive elements are these: moat, staggered entry, portcullis grooves at entrance, battlements, inner turrets with small rectangular windows and outer turrets with arrow slits. Also, Stukeley's record (C 18) that there were stone imitation garrison figures (as remaining at Alnwick and Raby Castles and at York). The stone figures still extant, though, are finely carved figures of Saints, including St Augustine, with Christ and the Virgin. These, set in most of the canopied niches of the outer façade, scarcely conform with defensiveness. Nor, perhaps, does nature of timber-ceiled 1st floor great hall and the room above, these 48 × 20 ft spanning whole width of gatehouse. Interior plastered, but brick shows through. Big fireplaces, with stone lintels and brick relieving arches. Stone heads and figures decorate great hall and inside of entrance arch. Indeed, splendour of gatehouse has led to its being labelled 'the abbot's lodgings', but hall is served by only one narrow spiral stair—impractical for catering. Hall oriel, stone, corbelled out much later from inner façade (Early Tudor it appears).

Basically brick structure, thick-walled, tall and impressive: brick flanking walls rise to 40 ft and gatehouse proper is 68 ft high. Bricks pale red, large in size: $11 \times 5\frac{1}{2} \times 2$ in. Stone used for dressings, including all windows. Whole inner façade stone-faced, but at front upper parts—between turrets and niches—of brick. Ground plan not uniform either. Rear has 2 pairs of polygonal turrets, on either side of entrance arch, rising to high above 3rd (top) of gatehouse. Side walls, with put-log holes and small windows, re arcaded here. Front has 6 turrets: 2 polygonal stone-faced ones, corbelled out from 2nd stage, by entrances; 2 full-height stone-faced polygonal turrets; 2 round *brick* turrets, at extremities. Later precinct walls adjoin gatehouse at sides, and barbican walls adjoin stone entrance archways. Smaller arch is for pedestrians, whose path is diagonal. Inside, passageways wholly brick and some small rooms brick-vaulted. Garderobes remain.

Depressions near site may be the claypits.

Alfred Clapham and P. K. Baillie Reynolds, *Thornton Abbey*, *Lincolnshire*, M. P.B. & W. guidebook, 1956, reprinted 1961.

TYDD ST MARY (HOLLAND)

Parish Church: C 14 stone church, with C 15 additions mainly brick. W tower has stone base and spire, but otherwise brick with stone quoins. Brick voussoirs to windows. Clerestory also brick. Apparently contemporary brick at E end of nave, chancel roof being lower than C 15 remodelled nave roof. Inside, double arch of brick and stone.

WAINFLEET (LINDSEY)

Grammar School: One of lesser educational enterprises of Chancellor William Waynflete, Bishop of Winchester 1446–86, founder of Magdalen College (Oxford) and Headmaster of Winchester College (Hants) and of Henry VI'X *Eton College* (Bucks). As Cromwell's executor he finished building of stone Tattershall parish church. See also *Farnham* and *Esher*, Surrey, for his brick towers. Wainfleet was his birthplace. (Now 8 miles from sea, once a port.)

School dates from 1484. Probably designed by John Cowper (see *Kirby Muxloe Castle*, Leics). Roof was to imitate (lost) Esher gatetower's. Waynflete provided endowment, with £10 p.a. for schoolmaster-chantry priest. Schoolmaster's house has not survived complete. Main hall measures 76×26 ft. Used as school still. At one end are twin octagonal towers. At sides projecting chimney-stacks. Plan of this school building is of 2 large rooms, one over other. Upper incorporates chapel. Inside main hall small alcoves at side, formed by window embrasures.

Windows stone, including very large Perp. windows at each end. Some diamond and other diaper to exterior: Firmans mention distortion of dark bricks, evidently made of unsuitable clay. Main and unusual feature, the twin end turrets: although they rise one stage higher than main building, they are so wide and blank the appearance is strong and heavy, contributing to barrack-like impression.

Pevsner and Harris; R. J. and P. E. Firman, *article* 'A Geological Approach to the Study of Mediaeval Bricks', in *The Mercian Geologist*, 1967.

WOODHALL SPA (LINDSEY)

**Tower-on-the-Moor:* 4 miles from *Tattershall*. Leland (mid C 16) said: 'One of the Cromwelles builded a preaty Turret caullid the Tour of the Moore'. This was Ralph Lord Cromwell. The Tower on the Moor, situated on his manor of Whithall (or Whitehall), was evidently a hunting-lodge for Tattershall Castle. Cromwell died in 1456, however, and castle building accounts show that, as early as 1472, bricks were being taken from here for castle. Samuel Buck drawing of 1726 shows more remaining than now. Only a corner of tower, mainly the octagonal stair turret of about 60 ft. high, remains. Traces of 4 floors. Turret virtually windowless. Thus the 'preaty Turret' now odd tall relic.

Other buildings in Lincolnshire with early brickwork are:

Auborn (Kesteven) Auborn Hall; *Harrington* (Lindsey) Harrington Hall;

Lincoln High Bridge (in-filling of vault); *Theddlethorpe All Saints* (Lindsey) Parish Church.

LONDON

Note: I have kept to the pre-1965 London County Council boundaries for convenience. Buildings such as Fulham Palace and Canonbury Tower were originally *country* retreats.

CANONBURY TOWER

(London Borough of Islington, 1965)
Tower has basis of early C 16 brickwork. Chief remains of country house erected by William Bolton, Prior of St Bartholomew's at Smithfield. Priory church of St Bartholomew the Great has several versions of his rebus of 'bolt' (crossbow arrow) and 'ton' (barrel). Bolton prior 1509 to 1532. In 1570 this house acquired by John Spencer, Lord Mayor of London. About 1595 made major alterations, rebuilding and perhaps heightening Tower. Tower's appearance again altered in 1770 and 1907.

66 ft high. About 17 ft square. Wall thicknesses between 2 ft 6 in and 4 ft. Dark-red brick. Perhaps views were main justification. Bolton was 1st to realize possibilities of site for grand residence. (Tower sometimes attributed *wholly* to Spencer, in which case typeable, more neatly, as Elizabethan 'prospect' house. R.C.H.M. and Arthur Oswald, in *article* on 'Tudor Outlook Towers' in *Country Life Annual*, 1957). Adjoining gabled wing on W (plastered) and low brick wing on E, both part of Bolton's large quadrangular house.

Garden towers and wall: 1750 print shows house surrounded by brick walls with garden turrets. 2 of these turrets, octagonal and brick-built, survive as part of more modern houses. One is in Alwyne Place, turret being plastered and painted. Other is in Alwyne Villas, and retains original, rather dull-coloured, brick to 1st-floor level. Some grey diapering. Over door, stone panel with Bolton rebus. There also remains a broken strip of priory boundary wall, at rear of houses on N side of Canonbury Place, about 90 yards in all.

Richard Oakley, *Canonbury Tower, A brief history*' (Tower Theatre).

CHELSEA MANOR HOUSE

Remains of red brick mansion of Henry VIII, including cellars and boundary walls, at 18–26 Cheyne Walk.

CITY WALLS, E.C.2

Ralph Joceline, when Mayor for a 2nd time in 1476–7, repaired 'part of the wall about the city' of London, between Aldgate and Aldersgate, (Stow). Brick used for building up the battlements and for the alure where necessary. Context was Wars of Roses, when City's sympathies were Yorkist; City, however, avoided involvement is politics as far as possible (contrast Italian city states), but had attacks to fend off: in 1471 Thomas of Falconbridge, partisan of Lancaster, had invaded City itself, coming to Aldgate by river and destroying about 60 houses.

30 ft stretch survives, its base Roman stone and the upper stage, with battlements, of red brick. It lies N of London Wall, below High Walk of Barbican development. Forms N wall of small gardens formerly churchyard of St Alphege's (demolished 1853). Wall further exposed by bombing, 1940. Considerably built up with brick, the footings and base of alure also built up patchily. Irregular bond. Bricks purplish or rich red, rough-textured, with sand creases, 9½ in long and 2½ or 3 in thick. Diaper bricks, black headers on inside only (S) making diamonds. Chalk for lime for mortar was brought from Kent, to be burned at Moorfield. There the brick earth was dug and fired: 'by which means this field was made the worse for a long time' (Stow). Apparently surplus brick and lime were sold off afterwards, to partly reimburse Joceline, who had paid much of cost of work.

John Stow, *Survey of London* (1598), enlarged C 17 ed.; R.C.H.M. City volume.

ELTHAM PALACE

(London Borough of Greenwich, 1965; earlier included in Kent)

Buildings situated off Court Rd, London S.E.9. Moated site. Complex building history of growth. Remains now altered or fragmentary, apart from Great Hall (this opened to public by Ministry of Defence on Thursdays & Sundays). Excavation and restoration of moat walls and other parts begun 1951 by M.P.B. & W.

Royal estate permanently from 1st decade of C 14 to mid C 17, with buildings erected by different kings. Estate sold 1649 by Commonwealth. Building normally stone, with brickwork minor except in Tudor period.

Between 1295 and 1305 (or 1311) manor held by Anthony Bek, Prince Bishop of Durham and Patriarch of Jerusalem, who built new manor house. Parts of moat wall probably his. Excavation of Bek wall N of Great Hall showed it was of flint and stone squares, with bonding courses of light-coloured bricks.

Great Hall, near completion 1479, is Edward IV's. 101×36 ft., 55 ft. high at apex. 6 bays. Traditional form, with central hearth. Fine timber ceiling. Hall built of red brick, but N front faced with Reigate stone and S front has ragstone base. Big Perp. stone windows. Dais oriels at E end, where kitchen site was traceable. W wall base rubble, but gabled upper part brick. N of Hall brick and stone foundations—site of royal apartments—? date. Moat bridge (at N) contemporary with Hall. Stone-faced. Vaulting of brick, with stone ribs.

Circuit walls mainly C 14 stone, but brick bays *temp.* Henry VII traceable, as are brick and stone angle turrets *temp.* Henry VIII. (Pevsner notes 'tall brick wall with a brick gate a little S', which 'enclosed the Tiltyard', opposite No. 30 The Courtyard.) Eltham ended as 5-courtyard Tudor brick palace.

N. Pevsner, *London Except the Cities of London and Westminster*, 1952; D. E. Strong, *Eltham Palace*, H.M.S.O. guidebook, 1958; information, Libraries Dept., L.B. Greenwich.

FULHAM PALACE

(London Borough of Hammersmith, 1965) *Pls. 44 & 45*

Off Fulham Palace Rd, S.W.6, in Thames-side park. Tree-protected enclave. Now (from C 19) *the* Palace of Bishop of London; originally main *country* palace of see, one stage out of London. Till early C 19 Fulham was village 'famous for its market gardens and orchards'. In early C 20 palace still had 28-acre grounds. Bishops were lords of manor from about 691. Palace grounds not now literally riverside, for embankment built 1775. Palace moat, a mile round, has been partly converted into public gardens. Pevsner speaks of 'the Danish moat, filled in as late as 1921, although with its 1,200 by 1,300 ft it was the largest in the country'. This was remains of Danish 'sea-burh', moated permanent camp where ships might be laid up in winter or for repairs.

Oldest buildings early C 16: 'At this period herons and spoonbills are said to have built in the grounds of Fulham.' Buildings now much reduced: 'the meek old buildings' (Ian Nairn, *Nairn's London*, 1966). About 1510–20 they replaced Norman structures. Builder was Richard Fitzjames, previously Bishop of Rochester, who became Bishop of London in 1506. Fitzjames was to die of plague in 1522. Apart from manor house itself, his work included wall for kitchen garden—this marked with his arms, a dolphin between 3 molets.

Building material red brick, for walls and dressings. Grey brick, glaze now worn off, used for diamond diaper. Main courtyard, W part of palace, survives, with C 18 and 19 replacements and additions to E. Court is of 2 storeys.

Tiled roof levels irregular and perhaps altered, as the 2 plain gable-ends of the gate tower range seem to have been. In main original work; only W (strictly SW) range is a rebuilding. Low, flattened arch to entrance, with hollow chamfered mouldings. Original doors. Opposite, inside court, 3-storeyed porch, with modern parapet but original cusped corbel-table. Porch led into Great Hall, $50\frac{1}{2} \times 27$ ft, which Fitzjames erected. Courtyard windows are C 17 replacements, but one square-headed doorway looks untouched. Worn diapering is uneven, possibly made more prominent by blackening of fabric. Red bricks are deep in colour, brown rather than pink in tone, and pitted. Whole appearance, domestic.

Chapter by Valentina Hawtrey in *English Episcopal Palaces (Province of Canterbury)*, ed. R. S. Rait, 1910; F. R. Banks, *London* (Penguin), 1958; Pevsner.

GREENWICH

Greenwich Palace: Major royal palace from earlier in Middle Ages, remodelled on large scale and courtyard plan, in brick, by Henry VII and Henry VIII, when associated with dockyards nearby. In 1499 Henry VII bought 600,000 bricks for this palace. Henry Redman worked here. Tudor palace replaced by mainly C 18 Greenwich Hospital. Taken over by Royal Naval College, 1873. Slight early remains:

Undercroft: One major survival is undercroft, which lies in part under 'Queen Anne' block of Grand Square and in part under open courtyard. May have been great hall's cellar. Reduced in size: originally 70 × 30 ft with projecting bay. Retains a well. Pillars octagonal, stone, very short. Octopartite vaulting, with ridges and diagonals, has brick infilling and chamfered brick ribs. *Temp.* Henry VIII. (Photo and plan in R.C.H.M. vol.).

**Excavations:* Begun in August 1970. Have revealed Tudor brick foundations of palace waterfront, in Grand Square of Naval College. Brick foundations belonging to 'Bella Court' mansion of Humphrey Duke of Gloucester and probably of *c.* 1430 also found. (Information, Philip Dixon.)

The Vicarage: In Park Vista. ENE of St Alfege's Church. 2-storey building of irregular plan. Mostly C 18, but 'incorporates part of one of the outlying buildings of the old Palace' (R.C.H.M.). N side has early C 16 brick walling, with plinth. At 1st-floor level is small and worn stone arms panel 'of early Renaissance character'.

R.C.H.M., *East London*, 1930; N. Pevsner, *London Except the Cities of London and Westminster*, 1952.

LAMBETH PALACE *Pls. 28, 29*

(London Borough of Lambeth)

Across Lambeth Palace Rd, S.E.1, and the Thames, opposite Parliament. Palace once lay at water's edge (compare *Fulham*). Till mid C 18 palace lay in marshland.

Still London palace of Archbishops of Canterbury. First buildings erected 1197. In 1490s John Morton introduced brick.

Morton's Gateway: Morton, Archbishop from 1486, Cardinal of St Anastasia from 1493, holder of many state offices. Main power from 1485 on, for, as Bishop of Ely, had supported Henry Tudor against Richard III. Morton built in brick at *Hatfield* (Herts.) and, as Archbishop, also at *Croydon Surrey*) and *Charing* (Kent). See also *Canterbury Cathedral*, where he was buried in 1500. Deeply involved in Henry VII's administration, especially royal finances. Only bishop on Henry's Privy Council (of about 9 men). Learned, and 'eminently skilful in the law' (Thomas More). Of non-noble origins, like Henry VII's other most trusted officers of state.

Dating from 1490/95, gatehouse is very large and formidable structure. Red brick exterior much darkened by city conditions, while brick inside entrance passage still quite bright-red. Black diamond and some zigzag diapering—glaze worn. Dressings stone. Tall room over archway, lit by 4-light window as wide as entrance arch (top of this window incorrectly remodelled). Entrance flanked by 2 great rectangular towers, of 5 storeys.

Many small windows. Some side chambers were used as prison cells, since justice was not yet centralized. Much of primate's power was secular, so not surprising palace gatehouse has aura of barracks. Towers have several plain chimneys. At rear are 2 6-storey projections to the 5-storey towers: that on E is square, an extension to the rooms; that on W is polygonal, housing a stair. Archway stone-vaulted. One boss with Morton's tun rebus. Inside walls are brick. This irregular brick surround to deeply splayed Perp. archways—the bricks fitted in between corner columns and ribs of vault and archway quoins. English bond. Brick size about $10 \times 5 \times 2\frac{1}{4}$ in.

Chapter by Valentina Hawtrey in *English Episcopal Palaces*, ed. R. S. Rait, 1910.

LINCOLN'S INN

(County of the City of London)

Supposed founder of college of lawyers was Henry Lacy, Earl of Lincoln, royal justice. (Died 1311.) Lacy left own house for lawyer's use. Further land early obtained out of demesne lands of Bishops of Chichester. Clay of episcopal 'coney-garth' (source of rabbit-meat) was to provide bricks right through to modern times.

Lovell's Gateway: Also known as 'Old Gateway'. In Chancery Lane. Erected 1518. Of red bricks, diamond-diapered, with some stone dressings. Has square flanking turrets at both front and back, of 4 storeys. Carriage and pedestrian arches. Stone arms panel placed over 4-centred main arch, bearing arms of Lacy (founder), Henry VIII and Sir Thomas Lovell, then benefactor. Lovell had fought for Henry Tudor at Bosworth and, a lawyer, became M.P. for Northampton and Speaker of House of Commons. Had property in Norfolk. Stow said these 3 shields cost £16. 7*s*. 5*d*.

In 1967 a fire in adjoining buildings caused it to be labelled 'unsafe' and it has been very carefully rebuilt (but without need, according to S.P.A.B. and others). Inside gate N wall some deep-red Tudor brickwork. Discovery was made during demolition that entrance arch was of moulded brick heavily plastered.

Old Buildings: These erected about 1490–1520, including Hall of *temp.* Henry VII. Coneygarth bricks used. Bay-windowed Hall retains lights traces of Early Tudor work, despite 1926–8 reconstruction that used some old stone and red bricks in a rather jumbled way. Wall of an arcade of 4-centred arches of rich red moulded brick remains. Most of Old Buildings replacements, especially of C 17; smaller Tudor Court, less altered, has some early C 16 work, including polygonal stair turrets.

C. W. Heckethorn, *Lincoln's Inn Fields*, 1896; R.C.H.M., *London IV* (*The City*), 1929; Nikolaus Pevsner, *London I*, 1957.

ST JAMES'S PALACE

(London Borough of the City of Westminster) *Pl. 63*

In Pall Mall, London S.W.1. Thomas Cromwell in 1536, listing Henry VIII's building activities (he disapproved of the expense), noted 'St James's in the Fields, a magnificent goodly house'. Contiguous with lands of *Whitehall Palace*.

One great survival is the Gatehouse, built between 1536 and 1540. Tudor rose and initials 'HA', for Henry and Anne Boleyn, and original linenfold doors. Chief mason was John Molton, successor of Henry Redman. Gate tower brick with stone dressings. Fairly plain, but big: 4 storeys, with 7-stage polygonal angle turrets.

The palace had 4 courts, now just 3. First court has original stair turret, S wall and wall W of gatehouse (Pevsner). Chapel altered but retains 1540 ceiling. 'Tapestry' and 'Armoury' rooms also said to be original. Henry VIII's

2-storey buildings are diapered. Red brick itself now practically brown. (Sentries seem painful archaism, and stamp their boots at intervals.)

N. Pevsner, *London I*; N. Williams, *Royal Residences*.

2433 11-13-453
WHITEHALL PALACE (remains)
(London Borough of City of Westminster)

'*Henry VIII Winecellar*', *Whitehall:* Situated under part of Air Ministry building. In origins Cardinal Wolsey's wine-store. Belonged to York Place—London palace of Archbishops of York. 'Thomas Rotherham, Archbishop 1480–1500, undertook a considerable amount of rebuilding'. Revived by Wolsey, who became Archbishop in 1514. New buildings all lost except for this cut-down store, remodelled by Henry VIII, who took over palace in 1529, on Wolsey's fall. Henry built Whitehall Gate ornamented with terracotta roundels, but all his buildings likewise lost, through fire (1697) and demolition.

Store now 5 bays long and 2 wide. 24 × 62 ft and 20 ft at apex. Octopartite vaulting. Not an original site, since Wolsey built it at ground level, part of group of domestic buildings; became cellar to later building, 'Cromwell House', demolished 1951–2. At that date 800-ton 'cellar' shifted to one side, lowered and shifted back into 'a position almost directly below the original site', in stages of one-sixth of an inch, 'without a brick being disturbed'! Has 4 octagonal stone piers. Sharply chamfered vaulting ribs and cells are brick, disguised by plaster (flaking). Vaulting very like New Wine Cellar's at Hampton Court, and attributed to Henry VIII. Tudor brick walls are Wolsey's (his arms once visible in door spandrel), but the one stone wall is mediaeval.

George S. Dugdale, *Whitehall Through the Centuries*, 1950.

See my chapter on 'Terracotta' for the roundels.

Other buildings in London with early brickwork are:

The Charterhouse (Charterhouse Square, Finsbury); Sutton House (off Homerton High St, Hackney); The Tower of London (details only, including some in the Martin Tower).

MIDDLESEX

Note: The administrative abolition in 1965 of Middlesex—split between Greater London, Surrey and Hertfordshire—has been ignored for convenience and Middlesex treated as an entity in the gazetteer. There are R.C.H.M and Pevsner volumes on Middlesex.

HAMPTON COURT PALACE *Fig. 20; Pls. 33–9*

(London Borough of Richmond-upon-Thames, Surrey, transferred from Middlesex 1965)

For detailed description see chapter on Hampton Court. Palace is administered by Ministry of Public Building and Works. Open to public on weekdays from 9.30 to 4 (and 5 or 6 in the lighter months) and for shorter hours on Sundays. ½-million visitors in 1969. Most of Tudor parts open to public; the additions of about 1689 by Christopher Wren are more restricted. Great gateway and adjoining ranges erected for Cardinal Wolsey from about 1514 and buildings of second court for Henry VIII from about 1528. Kitchens and domestic offices survive. Brick used throughout, with stone for dressings. Numbers of highly ornate chimneys of moulded brick, now nearly all careful imitations of originals. Wolsey commissioned the 40-inch roundels of Roman emperors from da Maiano—see chapter on 'Terracotta'.

Bibliography:

1885, Ernest Law, *A History of Hampton Court* vol. I (*Tudor Times*).
1911, Victoria County History, *Middlesex*, vol. II.
1924, Ernest Law, *A Short History of Hampton Court*, new edition (of book first published 1897).
1935, Edward Yates, *Hampton Court.*
1937, Royal Commission on Historic Monuments, *Middlesex.*
1948, Philip Lindsay, *Hampton Court—a history.*
1951, Nikolaus Pevsner, *Middlesex.*
1951, James Lees-Milne, *Tudor Renaissance* (*passim*).
1953, Michael Robbins, *Middlesex.*
Guidebooks available:
1966, Marguerite D. Peacocke, *The Pictorial History of Hampton Court*, Pitkin Pictorials.
1967, G. H. Chettle, *Hampton Court*, Ministry of Public Buildings and Works guide, H.M.S.O., new edition, (first published 1950).

HANWORTH

(London Borough of Hounslow, 1965)

Hanworth House: This was a Tudor palace, used by Henry VIII as hunting-lodge—it had a deer park—and as a home for his consorts, from Anne Boleyn in 1527 to Katherine Parr. Burned down in 1797. New house nearby was built by 1st Duke of St. Albans, followed by present *Tudor Court* built in mid C 19 on palace site itself (S & SW of parish church). This retains square moat, and several fragmentary Tudor survivals. At front 2 terracotta roundels, reset in C 18 brickwork, that certainly came from lost *Whitehall Palace* and are by da Maiano—see chapter on 'Terracotta'. They are borderless: one an emperor, the other 'Minerva'. At back of Tudor Court, Tudor stables (known as 'Queen Elizabeth's', but dating from Henry VIII's reign) have long been converted into battlemented flats. Rear wall has some Tudor brick, but Martin S. Briggs wrote of 'this perplexing structure . . . Obviously it contains fragments of the past, perhaps substantial fragments, but as obviously it has been greatly altered and enlarged within the past hundred years' (*Middlesex Old and New*, 1934). Only clear remains, flush with rear wall, are 2 very large early C 16 fireplaces with 4-centred arches of brick.

HARMONDSWORTH

(London Borough of Hillingdon, 1965)

Parish Church: Square SW tower is brick for 2 storeys. Dressings of stone. 1853 restoration. NW angle has square stair turret. Bricks laid English bond. About 1500.

ISLEWORTH

(London Borough of Hounslow, 1965)

**Syon House:* Mixed house, of Bridgettine order, established here in early C 15. Suppressed 1534. Nuns brought back for short spell by Mary I, when, according to Spelman (*History of Sacrilege*), a gentleman rebuilt 2 of convent walls for them. Mansion followed convent ground-plan. Property remained in Crown's grant from 1534 to 1604, when finally made over to Henry Percy, Earl of Northumberland.

If Syon House were stripped of Bath stone facing—this renewed in 1825, when N wing built—mid C 16 brick would still be seen, constituting shell of quadrangular house. Interior remodelled by Robert Adam about 1762. Builder was Edward Seymour, Duke of Somerset, Lord Protector for Edward VI. 1547–9 imprisonment. (Executed through efforts of successor, John Dudley, who took over house.) Seymour's other mansion, Somerset House on the Strand (London), was stone-built, colonnaded (this demolished 1776). He followed Renaissance ideas in both houses, typified by arcades. Obtained Syon estate in 1547 only.

When attainted of felony (since treason charge failed to stick) one of charges was that he was fortifying Syon — misinterpretation of a viewing terrace SE of house, by river. Of course, house has traditional, if useless, battlements. Somerset's quadrangle is about 100 ft square, with small square corner turrets, all battlemented. (Robert Adam had plan for roofing court with rotunda.) All detail post-Tudor, but R.C.H.M. stated: 'the angle turrets, with the exception of that on the N.W., are all substantially of 16th-century brick and retain doorways with four-centred heads'. Their interior brickwork still evidently visible. 1752 painting by Canaletto shows house in original state, even to diapering of brick. Now only exterior brick appears in some *outbuildings*, notably an L-shaped structure (N of house) used as muniment room.

The monastic remains, dated about 1440 (convent still incomplete 1448), are 2 rooms in W range: 2 sections of original undercroft. One 2 bays long, the other 3. Octagonal piers are brick and so is vaulting, with ribs formed of chamfered bricks.

R.C.H.M.; Pevsner.

LALEHAM

(transferred to Surrey, 1965)

Parish Church: At E end of N aisle is Lucan (family) Chapel of Early Tudor brick. This has brick windows, diapering. Inside church C 16 brick used for chancel arch and arches of NE arcade.

LITTLETON

(transferred to Surrey, 1965)

Parish Church: Clerestory, embattled S porch, W tower, all of bright-red brick. About 1500. (Top stage of tower C 18 brick.) In clerestory 2 original brick windows: brick mullions, apparently cut, but square labels of moulded brick. Tower has stringcourses, door, round-headed and square-headed windows of brick. Pierced with decorative moulded brick quatrefoils.

R.C.H.M.

PINNER

(London Borough of Harrow, 1965)

Headstone Manor: 200-acre estate of Archbishops of Canterbury till 1543. Was rented out. House (council property) of different dates, with some early brickwork. Bricks with '1501' date stamp found. Remains of brick revetting of moat.

SOUTH MIMMS (or *South Mymms*)

(in Potters Bar U.D., transferred to Hertfordshire 1965)

Parish Church: From early C 13 to 1527 failure of heirs Frowykes held a South Mimms manor—about 300 years, 10 generations. Of fair importance.

Manor house lay on boundary of parish, 2¼ m. S of church. Lost. C 17 Old Fold Farmhouse, taken over by a golf club, is on site, 3 sides of moat still traceable.

Church has more considerable relics of family, especially tombs in 1526–7 chantry chapel at end of N aisle (beside chancel). Aisle windows retain some contemporary glass, with kneeling donors and date '1526'. Chapel has fine wood parclose screens, archways decorated with leopard's head badge of Frowykes.

Henry's 1523 will gave £20 'to the making of an Ile or chapel, if any be made or making, on the north part' of church. This N aisle built of red brick. With fittings represents considerable expenditure, and shows usual lack of inhibition in building on to existing structure in different material. (Stone arcade.) Stone used for square-headed windows. Plinth flint, interrupted by square brick buttresses. Sharply pitched roofs to aisle and chapel, (but near-flat ceiling timbers). Brickwork much restored. Texture of old bricks remains: very rough, rather creased-looking, with many pebbles. Colour, muted russet. Brick size 9 × 5/4½ × 2½ in. A few have strayed into flint walls of chancel.

R.C.H.M. *Middlesex* volume; History published by Potters Bar U.D.C., 1966.

TOTTENHAM

(London Borough of Haringey, 1965)

Bruce Castle Tower: Bruce Castle Park adjoins parish churchyard. Bruce Castle itself is C 17 and later house, now Borough Museum. Site was moated till C 20. Name derived from Robert the Bruce (*d.* 1329), who inherited land; on his revolt English Crown took it over. Henry VIII granted Bruce manor to Sir William Compton (knighted at Battle of Tournai, 1512). Compton evidently replaced extant house from about 1514 on. (His house replaced about 1630.) Favourite of Henry VIII (for time had rare privilege of keeping on his hat in royal presence). Died 'immensely rich', leaving property in 18 counties. In 1493, aged about 11, had inherited Warwickshire estate of *Compton Wynyates*.

His Bruce Castle evidently brick-built. The one relic is a mystery: detached circular tower of red brick, a few yards SW of C 17 house. Diameter of base about 20 ft. Walls 3 ft thick. 2 storeys, with basement. Battlements renewed, and octagonal lantern from top has disappeared. Tower's appearance strong, and even severe, but purpose unknown. Bricks mainly in English bond, but also courses of alternating pairs of headers and stretchers. 'The external face is in three arcaded stages' (R.C.H.M.) Corbels moulded: the unrestored ones have concave mouldings. Some glazed bricks, including stretchers (*Pl. 41*).

Parish Church: C 14 stone church has battlemented 2-storey brick porch of *c.* 1500. Stone dressings. In centre of W wall original chimney-stack corbelled out. Angle buttresses. 2-light windows with square labels. Patches of heavy black diaper (*Pl. 32*).

WEST DRAYTON

(London Borough of Hillingdon, 1965)

Gatehouse: Early Tudor red brick gatehouse, with contemporary enclosure wall by parish church. Bought by Middlesex County Council in 1930s against threatened demolition.

Only remains of great house (demolished *c.* 1750) built by Sir William Paget (born at Drayton in 1505) after 1547. Manor had belonged to St Paul's, London. Paget as royal officer had career of ironic ups and downs, including imprisonment in 1551 instigated by John Dudley of *Syon*.

In 1550 obtained Act of Parliament whereby he gave parish church a new piece of land for burials, and churchyard was then 'inclosed within sir William Paget's garden-wall, free ingress and egress being reserved to the vicar and inhabitants'. This surely followed on building of mansion. Large sections of garden-wall remain. Gatehouse long ruinous, its upper floors lost, but built up somewhat in modern times and given battlements—and windows were inserted at higher levels. Appearance squat, most likely historically inaccurate, and rather grim. Old oak doors, remarkably, survived. Archway flanked by stout octagonal turrets with stone quoins. Inner arch less elaborate, has 2 chamfered brick orders; outer arch has 3 moulded orders.

D. Lysons, *An Historical account of those parishes in the County of Middlesex, which are not described in the Environs of London*, 1800.

Further examples of buildings in Middlesex with early brickwork are: *Ickenham* Manor Farm and Parish Church; *Ruislip* Nos. 1 & 3 High St. (L.B. Hillingdon).

NORFOLK

BACONSTHORPE

**Castle:* M.P.B. & W. administered. Manor and dwelling acquired *c.* 1400 by William Heydon from Bacons. John Heydon began new house *c.* 1450.

Inner gatehouse and SW corner tower his work. Dating not precise, for no licence to crenellate was obtained (Kinross). John Heydon, with Sir Thomas Tuddenham of Oxborough and Thomas Daniel, had connections with corrupt court of Henry VI. All cited in Paston Letters as involved in shady practices and violence. John's son, Sir Henry Heydon, was lawyer (at one time Recorder of Norwich), useful profession for aspiring property-owner in county notorious for litigiousness. From late C 15 to 1503, built major part of Castle: his work mostly demolished. Used same materials as his father, big knapped flints with stone dressings and brick for some details.

In C 16 family built *Saxlingham Hall.* They grew in importance till Elizabeth's reign, and finally declined in mid C 17 through results of adherence to Royalist cause. After Civil War Sir John Heydon (Lieut.-General of the Ordinance to Charles I) had to sell off most of castle—then described as a 'spacious, sumptuous pile'—for building materials. Elizabethan outer gatehouse converted into a house and rest of site treated as walled garden. (This gatehouse follows the earlier pattern, being flint with brick fireplaces, splays.) Despite lack of licence, Baconsthorpe had moat—with lake for E side —curtain walls, square and semi-circular towers. SW corner tower has gunport. Ground-plan quadrangular, with 2 courts. '. . . a great semi-fortified house' (Harlech). Style seems more domestic, though impression helped by disappearance of battlements from ruined walls. As well as 3-storeyed rectangular inner gatehouse, there survive curtain walls to S, E and W and most of square SW and NE corner towers. (2 ranges on E Elizabethan).

Brick mostly used for inside dressings, rather than with exterior flintwork, but exception to this brick voussoirs to ground-floor windows of inner gatehouse (compare East Anglian churches). Internal dressings of gatehouse all brick: fireplaces, door arches, wall-cupboards, garderobes, and vaulting of the passage and its recesses (S. E. Rigold). SW tower has moulded brick dressings inside. NE tower, attributed to Henry Heydon, has brick quoins.

S. E. Rigold, Ministry of Works guidebook (1966); R. W. Ketton-Cremer, *Forty Norfolk Essays*, pp. 89–93 *passim*; John Kinross, *Discovering Castles in Eastern England* (Shire publication).

BARNHAM BROOM

Barnham Broom Hall: Early Tudor red brick house, perhaps of 1510, with later additions. Main feature step-gabled porch, with polygonal angle turrets. Moulded brick dressings. Range mainly contemporary. Blue diaper. Chimney base has cusped frieze.

Pevsner, *North-West and South Norfolk.*

BLAKENEY

Guildhall Undercroft: Ministry of Works administered. Situated on seafront of what was once important port, its prosperity aided by salt workings. Guildhall itself, possibly of 2 storeys, has disappeared. Undercroft wholly brick-vaulted, with quadripartite chamfered ribs and brick in-filling. Though often described as C 14, dates from turn of C 15, the guild acquiring its charter *temp.* Henry VII.

Information, Rachel M. Young.

CAISTER

**Caister Castle:* *Pl. 91*

Bibliography:

Edited by James Gardiner, *The Paston Letters*, 6 volume 'Library Edition', 1904.

Edited and translated by John Harvey, *William Worcestre: Itineraries*, 1968.

Entry on 'Sir John Fastolf' by S. L. Lee in *Dictionary of National Biography.*

Article by K. B. Macfarlane on 'The Investment of Sir John Fastolf's Profits of War', in *Translations of the Royal Historical Society*, 1957.

Dawson Turner, *Sketch of the History of Caister Castle*, 1842.

D. A. J. Buxton, *Caister Castle*, (leaflet history, 1957).

Article by H. D. Barnes and W. D. Simpson on 'Caister Castle', with appendix on origins of bricks by S. E. Glendenning, in *The Antiquaries' Journal*, XXXII, 1952.

Edited by Barnes and Simpson, *Building Accounts of Caister Castle A.D. 1432–1435*, published in *Norfolk Archaeology*, XXX, 1952.

Article by R. J. Kedney on 'The Changing Role of Caister Castle', in *East Anglian Magazine*, February 1968.

Pevsner, *North-East Norfolk and Norwich.*

For detailed description see chapter on 'Defence and the Major Castles'.

The Castle is open to the public, and now houses a motor museum.

CASTLEACRE

Priory: Great Cluniac Priory, established about 1900 by William de Warenne. Built of flint and ashlar, mostly Early English. 3 brick items. N of N transept of church survives *sacristy oven* (for sacred wafers), of brick and like the late C 15 one at *Thetford.* In C 15 diagonally buttressed flint-and-brick *gatehouse* was built to N, on higher ground than rest of valley-sited priory. Has carriage

54. SUTTON PLACE, SURREY: One of the great bay windows, of cream terracotta, of the court. Erected about 1530. Plinth, cornice and parapet are also of terracotta, some of it dark red.

55. SUTTON PLACE, SURREY: Section of cream terracotta panelling in courtyard. The motifs are barrels (ton) and the initials 'R.W.', forming the rebus of the builder, Richard Weston, and bunches of grapes. About 1530.

72. LEEZ PRIORY, ESSEX: Two-light window, with cut and moulded dressings, in range attached to outer gatehouse.

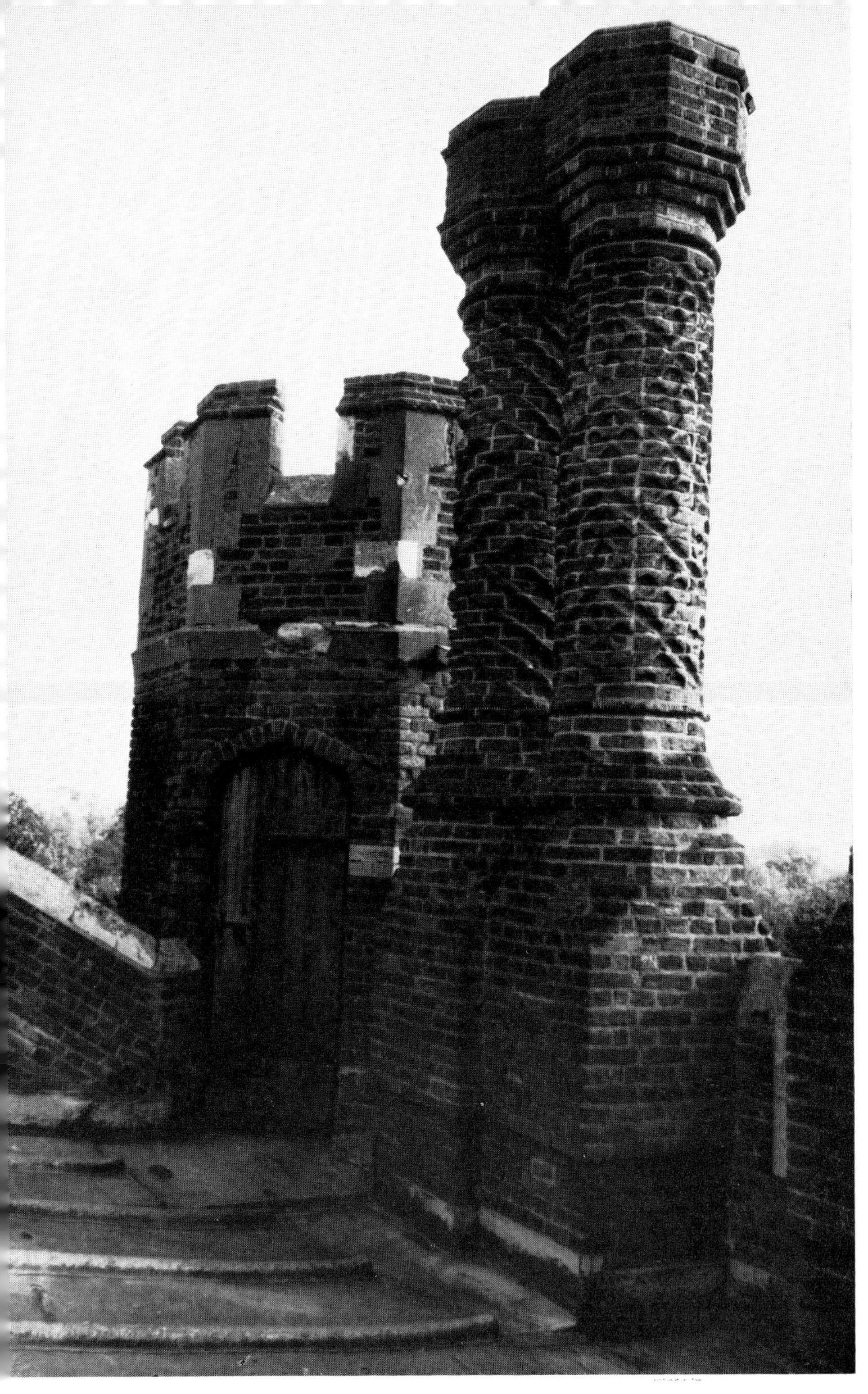

71. LEEZ PRIORY, ESSEX: Head of stair turret and pair of chimneys at roof level of inner gatehouse.

69. LEEZ PRIORY, ESSEX: The inner, larger gatehouse, erected in 1536.

70. LEEZ PRIORY, ESSEX: Carved brick loophole beside archway of inner gatehouse.

68. LAUGHTON PLACE, SUSSEX: Underside of steps of spiral stair, showing slightly arched rows of bricks. Their mortar joints are reinforced with oyster shells.

67. LAUGHTON PLACE, SUSSEX: Detail of inside of window in stair turret. Note Pelham family badge of buckle at base.

66. LAUGHTON PLACE, SUSSEX: Spiral stair, looking downwards. (Note imprint of dog's paw in slab near central newel.)

65. LAUGHTON PLACE, SUSSEX: Detail of red terracotta plinth. The coping pieces are taken from window moulds, set on their sides, as is shown by the pair of birds (right).

63. ST. JAMES'S PALACE, LONDON: Gatehouse of 1532–40 red brick, between traffic and tower blocks. The polygonal angle turrets are seven stages high.

64. LAUGHTON PLACE, SUSSEX: Square tower of 1534, only surviving part of mansion. The corbel-table is of Early Tudor red terracotta, but windows and door are eighteenth-century 'Gothick' replacements.

61. CHIGNAL SMEALY CHURCH, ESSEX: Detail of arch over small door on south side of chancel (interior), the arch being formed of single bricks.

62. CHIGNAL SMEALY CHURCH, ESSEX: Detail of tower arch of about 1530 at west end of church, slightly ogee in form and with triple chamfered mouldings.

60. CHIGNAL SMEALY CHURCH, ESSEX: South door.

58. CHIGNAL SMEALY CHURCH, ESSEX: Exterior of brick church of about 1530, from the east end.

59. CHIGNAL SMEALY CHURCH, ESSEX: Moulded brick nave window, about 1530.

56. (*Upper*) SUTTON PLACE, SURREY: Detail of cornice at first floor level of court, with ton and dolphins in terracotta.

57. (*Lower*) SUTTON PLACE, SURREY: Detail of window jamb and cusped head, with flower and foliage motifs.

73. LEEZ PRIORY, ESSEX: Great hall kitchen drain, 3 foot deep, 1536.

74. LEEZ PRIORY, ESSEX: Detail of inner side of rear archway of the smaller, outer gatehouse.

75. LOVELL'S HALL, TERRINGTON ST. CLEMENT: Of brick, but partly stone-faced. The porch carries the date '1543'.

and pedestrian entries. Some stone dressings, but windows brick (mullions lost). Fireplace inside. In early C 16 a new *lodging* was built for prior, with 2 beautiful stone oriels on N side: on W a stepped gable of brick, either contemporary with rest or belonging to post-Dissolution conversion.

The Tudor House (No. 61, SE of the parish church): In Dyke Hills area, part of castle site—but whole village lies inside castle's outer bailey. Fine house that has suffered some decay: 'grand proportions of interior suggest decline in status'. Restored 1968. Exact date, purpose are unknown: possibly connected with priory; possibly built after 1537 Dissolution for new steward of Castle acre estate of priory lands acquired by Thomas Howard, 3rd Duke of Norfolk (see *Framlingham*, Suffolk).

Certain likeness to post-Dissolution farm buildings at *Thetford Priory* but much finer work. Inside, the flat ceiling with 'fine moulded beams' confirms Tudor dating. Rectangular building of rough flints with brick dressings. Some of flint may have came from old castle of William de Warenne, deserted and decaying by 1400. Most of windows altered, but some old brick window-dressings remain. Brick used for quoins, windows, doorways. Main door (blocked) is pointed, with 3 rows of mouldings, the outer ones chamfered and the inner hollow. Notable brick feature is small, chimney-type finial topping one gable (pantiled roof and square central chimney-stack are later in date). It has layered polygonal base, shaft with vertical ribs and honeycombing (between them) and star-top.

Olive Cook and Edwin Smith, *English Cottages and Farmhouses.*

CASTLE RISING

Castle: Castle established *c.* 1150 by William de Albini. Gatehouse and keep are Norman, stone-built. In C 14 became Crown property and Constables were appointed: from mid C 15 they included brick-builders Ralph Lord Cromwell (*Tattershall*), Thomas Lord Scales (*Middleton Towers*), John de Vere (*Castle Hedingham*) and Henry Lord Marney (*Layer Marney*). In 1544 Thomas Howard, Duke of Norfolk, acquired property. Belonged to Howards till modern times. Now Ministry of Works administered.

Some bricks of 2 periods, Perp. and Early Tudor, none of work exactly dated. 60 ft deep main ditch (dry moat) is crossed by long Perp. bridge of brick. This replaced earlier drawbridge ('the grooves for working the portcullis may still be seen in the masonry of the gateway arch'—H. Bradfer-Lawrence) and utilized its stone piers. Bridge canted across moat and has shallow arch, nearly square. Coping stone. Also on top of inner earth rampart, remains of curtain wall of Tudor red brick with arched splays. In vestibule of great hall of keep a stone Norman arch was blocked in Tudor times and converted into a fireplace, with fireback of stretchers.

H. Bradfer-Lawrence, *Castle Rising*, 1954, (booklet); Pevsner, *North-West and South Norfolk*.

CLAXTON

**Castle:* In marshland area, near *Langley Abbey*, *Loddon* and Yare estuary (see *Caister* too). Kerdeston manor. Members of family held offices like Governor of Norwich Castle and Sheriff of Norfolk. Sir William de Kerdeston, the castle-builder, fought in Flanders (1340) and at Crécy (1345). Involved in Edward III's Scottish campaigns, and in city wall-building at *Norwich*. Claxton's important place then, for licence for fair obtained in 1340. Licence to crenellate castle obtained by William in 1339.

This castle is reduced mainly to the 130 ft long façade, with remains of 6 bastions, 3 round towers being almost complete—other parts evidently source of building materials when castle was abandoned. Mixture of flint rubble and large red bricks. Brick texture is very rough. Colour varies, but mostly *darkish*-red. Irregular bond. Bricks used for facing, especially of upper parts of exterior and whole interior (mainly stretchers here) and for arches. Some alteration. Major repairs done in C 16, according to Camden, by Judge Gawdy (see *Wallington*) for castle had become ruinous. A pier, now isolated, probably belonged to entrance, and portcullis grooves seemingly survive in brickwork. One side of great hall, staircase and upper rooms can be traced on inside of S wall, which, defensively, lacks windows (must have been lit from courtyard). Castle site was of 2 acres, bounded by moat—line traceable and there remains double moat on one side. To N was garth or pasture of 4 acres, with precinct wall also traceable.

Article by J. Wentworth Day in *East Anglian Magazine*, Sept. 1960; article, 'Some Norfolk Halls', by B. Cozens-Hardy in *Norfolk Archaeology*, 1960.

CRINGLEFORD

Bridge: About 1520, brick-and-stone bridge. 2 rounded arches. Sides and cutwaters ashlared. Arches stone, as are the parallel vaulting ribs (pair). Infilling brick. Replaced earlier bridge, destroyed by severe Norwich flood, 1519.

CROSTWICK

Parish Church: C 16 S porch brick, with brick doorway and statue niche. Also brick stair-turret.

DENVER *Fig. 10(f)*

Denver Hall: Early C 16 red brick house, with round decorated chimney-shafts and terracotta panels. See chapter on 'Terracotta'. (Small gatehouse dates from 1570).

DRAYTON

**Drayton Lodge:* On Costessey Road. Sir John Fastolf of *Caister* acquired manors of Hellesdon and Drayton near Norwich in 1432. Built lost manor house and lodge at Hellesdon, house being 'beaten down' in 1465 by John de la Pole, Duke of Suffolk, when in Pastons' possession. Built a lodge at Drayton which, although attacked also and partly undermined by de la Pole, survives as ruin. These buildings cost Fastolf £548. 13*s*. 4*d*. in 1437. Drayton Lodge has 4 round corner towers and was at least 2 storeys high. Ruinous. Small, undefended structure. Built in main of yellowish gault bricks, but some red. English bond.

Article by H. D. Barnes in *Norfolk Archaeology*, 1946.

EAST BARSHAM *Fig. 10(h, i); Pls. 50–2*

East Barsham Hall: Earlier known as 'Wolterton Manor House', as when Pugin made drawings. Red brick house of *c*. 1525–35, built by Sir William Fermor. Near and having similar motifs to *Great Snoring Rectory*. Interior has lost most original work, but 2 brick-vaulted ceilings in 3-storey tower next porch. Detached, but close to house and indefensible, gatehouse with cut brick arms of Henry VIII. Notable round decorated chimneys and terracotta panels with Early Tudor profiles and shields.

Many round finials, topping angle shafts. Upper part of gatehouse ashlar-faced and stone used for entrance arches and for dilapidated arms panel of porch. Remainder, including vaulting of gatehouse, brick or red terracotta. House much restored, but with careful replicas.

See also chapter on 'Terracotta'.

Nathaniel Lloyd; Pevsner.

FAKENHAM

Thorpland Hall: 2 m. NE of Fakenham church, on boundary with parish of *Great Snoring:* decorated brickwork, including chimneys, of Thorpland Hall and Great Snoring Rectory similar. Thorpland was manor house of Calthorpe family (associated with North Creake Abbey; North Creake church has 1500 brass of Sir William Calthorpe as founder). Early C 16 red brick, reduced to one range. Polygonal angle buttresses to this and central porch. Chimneys have round shafts with cut brick ornament and star tops. A little restoration throughout. 'One of the finest pieces of C 16 brick architecture in Norfolk' (Pevsner, *North-East Norfolk and Norwich*).

FELTWELL

St Nicholas Church: S porch is early C 16 and of brick.

FINCHAM

Fincham Hall: Finchams were in parish from *temp.* William II. Lords of manor from reign of John to that of Elizabeth (1572 sale). Early Tudor, red brick parts of the Hall are attributable to John (*d.* 1496) or Sir Nicholas (*d.* 1503). There are Elizabethan conversions and additions in stone. Once moated (traces on N and S sides). Pevsner notes that 'E wall has a big brick chimney-breast and S wall also has Tudor brickwork'.

Main feature is 2-storey octagonal tower at NE angle. Crow-stepped battlements—doubly stepped—above trefoil-headed corbel-table. Cornice over doorway. Steps inside lead into lobby (and an original entrance). Lobby has rib vaulting, with rounded ribs and central shield boss, work compared with *Oxborough's*. House was reduced to rectangular range and a NW turret was surely destroyed.

See also *Outwell* parish church.

Pevsner, *North-West and South Norfolk*; B. Cozens-Hardy, article on 'Some Norfolk Halls' in *Norfolk Archaeology*, 1960.

Parish Church: Flint rubble with some brick. Perp. Sir Nicholas Fincham (*d.* 1503) built 2-storey vestry. Brick paving.

FORDHAM *Fig. 3(q)*

Snore Hall: More modern range (parallel) added on N side, but bulk of hall is late C 15 rectangular, gable-ended house of red brick. English bond. All dressings brick. Contemporary cellar half length of block. Originally just 2 rooms on each floor, later subdivided. J. A. Gotch noted great thickness of walls of old block, which may mean core is older than projecting porch and oriel and, conceivably, the facing. Large, square chimney-stack is evidently Elizabethan or C 17 addition and windows of S side were remodelled (cusps removed) then. Corners of block diagonally reinforced with slim, square shafts, tops ornamented with small domed finials and cusped panels. Similar shaft up centre of W gable. Square 2-storey porch, unusually, attached to N half of this gable-end: it is battlemented, with slanting copings; upper windows single round-headed lights; lower windows of 2 lights with cusped heads; plain 4-centred entrance arch on S side. 2 windows to S of porch: lower one modernized; upper one a 3-light oriel carried on several mouldings and deep corbel-table. Main decoration of W end friezes round base and, shallower, at eaves level: they consist of blank panels with cusped heads.

Basil Oliver, *Old Houses and village buildings in East Anglia*; Pevsner, *North-West and South Norfolk*.

GREAT CRESSINGHAM

Priory: Sometimes, more correctly, called 'The Manor'. Part of *c.* 1545 red brick house, once moated. Has elaborate moulded brick panelling and 'rust-coloured' terracotta motifs. Motifs are: 2 versions of the falcon-and-hand crest of John Jenny, the builder, and monogram roundel of 2 crossed J's and an E (for Elizabeth Spring, wife) linked by a knot. This wreathed monogram sometimes set upside down (Olive Cook, *The English House Through Seven Centuries*). Friezes of Gothic archlets and Renaissance foliage.

See also chapter on 'Terracotta'.

GREAT SNORING

Rectory: Part of altered hexagonal manor house of Shelton family, lords of manor from mid C 14 to 1611 (sale): see also *Shelton*, their (lost) older home at other end of county. Great Snoring Manor built by Sir Ralph, *c.* 1525 or earlier. Red brick, diapered. Decorated chimneys (restored), traceried angle turrets, terracotta friezes and panels—Renaissance-style. One frieze of sacred monograms, 'IHC' and 'MR' (for Christ and Mary, Queen of Heaven). Window mullions, transoms elaborately moulded brick—polylobate, but inside edge straight. Hollowed jambs carry family rebus of scallop shells and tuns. Lights uncusped, which favours later dating.

See also chapter on 'Terracotta'.

Rectory Barn: Of uncertain date. Flint, but with slit windows of thin early bricks. When Rectory altered in 1685, and new block added, waste from demolished Early Tudor work was built into barn and extension wall: sections of windows and terracotta panels so employed. (Information from the Rev. A. R. B. Wylam.)

GREAT YARMOUTH

**Town Walls:* Yarmouth's exceptional wealth, from C 11 to C 17, came from herring-fishing. Town plan narrow strip, running N–S between sea and R. Yare. Town walls began at river bank and curved round to meet river again:

as at *Norwich*, river was part of defences. Wall circuit just under 2 miles, incorporating 16 towers and 10 gates (Pevsner). Remains 2 round towers and some sections of wall at SE end—in Blackfriars Road—and another tower, less complete, at NW—in Rampart Road. Flint rubble walls rise to 23 ft where battlements survive. Pierced with cross-shaped slits. Brick used, as at *Norwich*, for alure and windows, and some in fabric generally.

Walls begun after 1260, when Henry III granted licence. 'They were completed by the end of the 14th century. The outer face was of knapped flints, but the inner face was built up as brick arcading. The top of this arcade was finished off as a wall walk, and the flint facing continued a little higher as a parapet. In the early 16th century an earthen ramp was thrown up to back the walls on the inside. At the same time, the upper parts of the towers were finished in a decorative chequered pattern of alternate brick and knapped flint panels. The brick panels contain single courses of unknapped flint pebbles alternating with every two or three courses of bricks. The panels are separated from each other, horizontally and vertically by single courses of bricks (mainly headers) set edgeways which project a few inches out from the wall. There are some good stretches of brick arcading still remaining and there are two towers showing the brick and flint panelling.' (Information from the Tolhouse Museum.)

Pevsner, *North-East Norfolk and Norwich.*

HARDWICK

Parish Church: S porch of brick and flint chequer. N porch, early C 16, all brick: dressings cut, not moulded.

KENNINGHALL

Kenninghall Place: One range (now farmhouse) of great house situated about 1½ m. NE of village, near Saxon earthworks. Early mediaeval royal palace here. Then manor house called 'East Hall', which was demolished *c.* 1525 by Thomas Howard, 3rd Duke of Norfolk. He built new house, of red brick, a little to NE—in 700-acre park.

Framlingham Castle, Suffolk, abandoned in favour of this residence. In 1547, Howard, following his attainder, imprisoned (and his heir, Earl of Surrey, beheaded). Estate granted to Princess Mary, who made her claim to throne from here after Edward VI's death. As Mary I she released Howard, who lived at Kenninghall till death in 1554. Estate still Howard property.

Despite early Tudor date, Kenninghall Place had 2 features normally thought of as Elizabethan: ground plan was an 'H', with 'stately' E and W façades, and angles had thin polygonal shafts, some of which remain, instead of buttresses (Pevsner, *North-West and South Norfolk*). Known as the 'new palace': 'this magnificent palace contained apartments for the Duke and Duchess of Norfolk, the Earl and Countess of Surrey, the children, the Master of the Children, . . . the children of the Chapel, the Almoners, the Master of the Horse', the controller of the household and so on (A.D. Bayne, *c.* 1872, *History of the Eastern Counties*). Continued as Howard residence till Commonwealth when major part demolished, materials sold. In C 19 'vestiges' of moulded brickwork noted locally: 'the arms of Arundel and Hereford' (family alliances) 'which appear upon the bricks, scattered remains of the ornamental brickwork are to be seen in the houses of the neighbouring villages' (1872). These have apparently disappeared, but still believed in village that bricks from palace were used as building materials there.

Remnant of house still standing, red brick with blue diapering, known as 'Place Farm.' Has the angle shafts noted, and one stepped gable. In 1968 farmer discovered foundations when ploughing small field adjacent.

KING'S LYNN

**Carmelites' Gateway* Monastery situated between R. Ouse and Nar tributary, in South Lynn (separately governed, but walled in with then Bishop's Lynn). Carmelites—or Whitefriars—like all Lynn friars, had house close inside walls. Sole remains entrance gateway in Southgate St. Small, late C 14 structure, of red brick. Stone dressings, including quoins. Shallow arch, with 3 statue niches over.

**Clifton House:* In Queen St. House entered through 1708 doorway (with marvellous barley-sugar columns), but behind is much older work. In 1960 2-tiled *c.* 1325 floors (blue tiles patterned with yellow) discovered. They have hearths with moulded brick surrounds. Belonged to original merchant's house, which has additions of different periods and was modernized in 1708 by Henry Bell. Undercroft apparently absorbed (with another, once detached, building). Late C 14 or C 15, of rectangular plan, brick-vaulted. Low. 'Four by two bays with short octagonal piers and broad, flat brick ribs' (Pevsner). Rib edges chamfered. Ouse-brought goods must have been stored here. (Outside our period, but red brick and most dramatic feature of house: square 5-storey Elizabethan tower (with 6-storey stair-turret), evidently look-out. Like Tower House, Bracondale, Norwich.)

Pevsner, *North-West and South Norfolk*.

**Greyfriars:* Off St James St. Early Franciscan house established 1230–5. Church built C 13, on usual Franciscan cruciform plan with relatively narrow crossing between nave and chancel. In late C 14 lantern tower—sole remains of friary—was built up from this crossing on a gabled base. Vaulting is tiercon, with in-filling of brick. Fabric materials: stone, for dressings, and red, plum and brown bricks about 9 in long and 2 in deep. Mainly stretcher bond. Tower is hexagonal, thin.

**Guildhall of St George:* In King St. National Trust property. Now used as theatre, etc. L-shaped building, with thick short range along King St and long thin range stretching out behind towards R. Ouse. 'The largest ancient Guildhall in England to survive intact'—Marshall Sisson. St George's Guild was merchant, not craft. Mediaeval warehouses at W end of Guildhall, reaching quay, and—but this post-mediaeval (perhaps C 17)—a wine-cellar linking undercroft and quay. Rounded arch to quay in brick wall.

Guild was established in 1376. Present building dates from 1406, when charter obtained from Henry IV. Tall rectangular building, constructed of thin red bricks laid in irregular bond. Surface uneven. Dressings stone. S side has passage from street to original landing-space at rear. W gable-end is plain. E gable-end shows signs of renovation at different dates: gable straight and stone-coped (this clearly new). Great stone-dressed window (restored), 6 lights across, probably early C 16. It and the 2 stone doors have radiating brick voussoirs, 2 and 3 bricks deep. SE and NE angle shafts, but not in original form.

Undercroft, once used for storage, mainly coincides with street level. Part has original brick vaulting—'segmental tunnel-vault' (Pevsner, *North-West and South Norfolk*)—but major part has instead wood beams, dating probably from before 1500, supporting timber floor of hall. This early alteration resulted from pressure on side walls, displacement perhaps accelerated by subsidence of riverside ground. 5 stepped buttresses then built on N wall: base of each buttress is pierced by small round-headed arch, to relieve weight, with brick voussoirs.

Booklet history of the Guildhall by Marshall Sisson, F.S.A., R.F.I.B.A.; *article* by W. A. Pantin, 'The merchants' houses and warehouses of King's Lynn', in *Mediaeval Archaeology*, VI–VII, 1962–3.

**Hampton Court:* In Nelson St. S-storeyed building of different dates, forming quadrangle. Now administered (as dwellings) by King's Lynn Preservation Trust. Property continuously occupied and altered, main post-mediaeval development being erection of N range *c.* 1600—perhaps replacing earlier range. Oldest part is S range, complete merchant's house of C 14, built in brick and stone on narrow piece of land between Benedictine Priory (St Margaret's) and river, then much closer inland. In E half was hall, initially open to roof, with traditional triple screens passage to pantry, buttery. This copybook early mediaeval house is a large one, whose 1st occupants are unknown—but 'they were probably people of some substance' (Vanessa Parker). Courtyard side least altered. Other walls hidden by later buildings.

Occupation by merchants continued, and major new buildings added apparently in last quarter of C 15. Attributed to Richard Amfles, whose brewer father transferred property to him in 1482. At this date added 2 completely commercial ranges: Nelson St. range and quayside range. Nelson St façade has square-headed entrance of chamfered bricks with timber archway and Amfles' merchant's mark carved in spandrel. Ground floor wholly brick, but projecting timber-framed upper floor, with diagonal nogging between close uprights. This range divided into shops. Quayside range provided warehouse at water's edge. Effect of most dramatic feature muffled: open quayside arcade of lower storey was later blocked, while ground level considerably raised. Building wholly red brick. Irregular bond, largely of headers. Arcade had 4-centred chamfered arches, carried on 6 round columns. Only small part of arcading now visible, but shows as very fine work.

King's Lynn Preservation Trust booklet on Thoresby College and Hampton Court, with *articles* by W. A. Pantin and Vanessa Parker.

Hanseatic Steelyard Buildings: St Margaret's Lane. Remains of premises of Lynn depot of Hansa, North European merchant league initiated by towns of Hamburg and Lubeck in 1266. House, or 'steelyard', for agents at Lynn established 1271, but so-called 'Hanseatic Warehouse'—strictly group of brick warehouses—now surviving is C 15 in date. Pantin says *c.* 1475. Building fronting street is S range of steelyard quadrangle and looks as if always at least partly domestic. Ground floor all brick but renewed. Upper floor overhangs on timber beams, has horizontal and diagonal nogging, between timber uprights. Contemporary tiled roof. Other 3-storeyed warehouse behind, at right-angles to quay, and adjacent C 16 brick warehouse.

Hansa actually kept this property until 1751, though did not continue trading so late in Lynn. In 1751 'Burgomasters of Hamburg, Bremen and Lubeck' sold 'stillyard' to local merchant, Edward Everard, for large sum of £800.

W. A. Pantin has stressed contrast between long merchant tenements of Lynn (200 or 300 ft), of which steelyard was one, and the more cramped sites in the Hansa towns themselves where dwellings, offices and warehouses 'had to be piled up one on top of the other in lofty buildings', as in the Low Countries too.

Red Mount Chapel: Off Broad Walk, near fragments of Town Wall. Unique octagonal chapel on small earth platform. Said to have replaced earlier structure, perhaps wooden, belonging to 1329 Gild of Our Lady. Chapel dedicated to Virgin Mary, and built to house relic. Has been called 'Lady Mount Chapel' and 'St Mary on the Hill': 'Red Mount' may be corruption of 'Rood Mount'—1783 engraving by Hooper shows lost shaft on top of building that could have carried crucifix. Corporation on 29 September 1482, 'agreed that Robert Curraunce shall have licence to bilde a chapel upon the mount called the Lady hylle, with sech (such) grounde as shall be leful (lawful), nothing neyying (denying) the Comons of their necessaries . . .' Chapel built 1483 on. On pilgrim route to *Walsingham* (shrine of European stature) from such places as Cambridge and Northampton and for anyone landing at port. Fabric red brick, exterior mostly stretcher bond. 2 stone staircases spiral round inside thick brick shell, allowing pilgrims to circulate in one direction: going up, through upper chapel, and down again. 3 squints through wall into chapel.

Lower windows staggered, following stairs: above these a row of regular 4-light windows. Dressings stone. Sides of octagon irregular. Angles have stepped diagonal buttresses, of brick stone-faced, several pierced with small niche. Building of 3 storeys, crowned by strange cruciform structure, ashlared, pierced by quatrefoils: this roofs over upper chapel. Cruciform plan right through building. Middle chamber thought to have been priest's living quarters. Tall basement chamber was another chapel, with priest's room in N wall. Lower chapel entered via separate passage on W, down brick steps. Vaulted simply, with stretchers laid parallel with side walls. Another use of brick evidently for stair handrails, but only one section remains (on stair up to chapel). Finest work is in upper chapel, and this stone. Room itself tiny—17ft 7 in E–W, 14 ft N–S, 13 ft high—with great stone altar slab. Rare and beautiful fan-vaulting (only other one in Norfolk is in S porch of St Giles', Norwich, while one intended for porch of brick church at *Shelton* was not finished (Pevsner)). In 1509 income of tiny chapel was 4 times total of those of the 3 Lynn churches (St Margaret's, St James' and St Nicholas' Chapel), but Reformation put chapel out of use. In C 17 had odd employment: as water store, gunpowder store, fort in the 1643 Civil War siege, as plague house in 1665. When restored 1828, had been used as stables and store. In 1968 reconsecrated as Chapel of Unity.

William Taylor, *The Antiquities of Lynn*, 1844.

South Gate: Only surviving town gate, belonging originally to South Lynn, which was walled in with Lynn but separately governed. A 1520 rebuilding, instituted by Thomas Thoresby, of a 1437–40 structure, itself a rebuilding. Gate rectangular, of 3 stages, with taller angle turrets. S façade wholly ashlared, but side and rear walls show this is a brick building. Thin, dark-red bricks, in English bond. All dressings, including those of angle buttresses and battlement copings, stone. Ashlaring of just main façade unusual for period.

Thoresby College: Queen St. Founded 1500 by Thomas Thoresby, merchant, Member of Holy Trinity Guild and Mayor of Lynn. A college—with a Master—for 13 chantry priests of his merchant guild, but complement extended to include chantry priests of Lynn churches.

College buildings not finished at death in 1510, when he left more funds: 'of my goods, the sum of Five Hundred Marks if it shall so need or more'. Establishment, protecting priests from disadvantages of odd lodgings, and courtyard layout of the buildings was similar to contemporary colleges at Oxford and *Cambridge* (except that there was no chapel). Dissolved in 1547 (Chantries Act). Buildings, of 2 storeys, of dark-red brick, with tiled roofs. Ornate wood door in Queen St is Thoresby's and carries (mutilated) inscription. Vanessa Parker describes entrance as 'four centred cut brick arches', but these plastered. Though brickwork of the Queen St façade looks old (? some reused), 5 Dutch gables of attic storey most likely of *c.* 1589 and brickwork below them could have replaced a brick-and-timber front like *Hampton Court*'s in Nelson St. Inside of court has more original work. Present conversion of College into youth centre and homes for old people has revealed more C 16 brickwork. Most dramatic part is W range; includes great hall of the College, open to (surviving) hammer-beam roof.

Booklet on Thoresby College and Hampton Court, with *articles* by W. A. Pantin and Vanessa Parker, issued by King's Lynn Preservation Trust.

**Town Walls:* Scattered and battered fragments, apparently mid C 14 in date. Engraving in William Taylor's *The Antiquities of Lynn* (1844) shows inner side of impressive stretch of wall, with square and polygonal towers and arcaded alure, demolished 1800. Remains situated in St Ann's St and along

Kettlewell Lane to the Walks. Materials flint rubble and stone, with red brick. This used irregularly through fabric and for some small voids. Most brick in Kettlewell Lane section. One assumes alures were brick-built, as at *Norwich* and *Great Yarmouth*.

Pevsner, *North-West and South Norfolk*.

LANGLEY

**Abbey:* Small house of Premonstratensian canons, founded 1198. Parts of several monastic buildings remain, mostly absorbed into later farm buildings. C 13 range, now barn, has section revaulted, apparently in C 14, with quadripartite ribs (Pevsner) and brick infilling. (Sketched by Cotman in 1813.)

C. J. W. Messent, *The Monastic Remains of Norfolk and Suffolk*, 1934.

**Parish Church:* E window is brick: has Early English 'Y' tracery.

LITTLE HAUTBOIS

Bridge: Over R. Bure (no-longer navigable). Brick bridge of C 15 or early C 16, with 2 sharpish arches. Cutwaters. Curved parapet. Voussoirs alternately stretchers and pairs of headers. At both ends a cubicle with a seat. (Little Hautbois Hall: Red brick house with pointed finials, Elizabethan, perhaps 1555).

LODDON

Hales Court Farm: Hobart family held 11 manors in Norfolk and Suffolk, when Sir James Hobart erected great brick house on main manor at Loddon. Chief Justice and then Attorney-General of Henry VII. House, Hales Court, has disappeared, but square moated site visible, with base of one octagonal angle turret and traces of foundations. Outside moat depressions survives large outer courtyard, mainly of Early Tudor ancillary brick buildings, where Farm now sited. Alterations, including of some windows. Tiles replaced by pantiles.

Lesser gateway facing house site remains. Also, at right-angles 2-storey gatehouse with room over 4-centred archway. This gabled, with niche. Polygonal angle shafts. Very plain shaped brick spandrels. Inner arch has only timber head. Gatehouse set in 'one room thick' range, where strengthening timbers traceable. Part of range is 2-storeyed and part, retaining some small original windows, one-storeyed. Red brick is very warm colour—'poppy coloured'. Irregular bond. Patches of dark diapering, with large and small diamonds. Decorated chimneys, including pair with raised network patterns.

Opposite range an 'enormous barn, said to be the largest in Norfolk', built of same red brick, with 'immense red stepped gable, and another 2-storeyed block attached. Inside barn notable timber roof of 14 bays. 13 steps to gable, and wall-ends themselves slightly stepped. Loopholes for ventilation (some blocked) in 3s, and in 2s above eaves level.

¼ m. from rear of house unexcavated brick kilns, which most probably supplied bricks for house. (Information, A. P. Baggs, R.C.H.M., Cambridge.)

Olive Cook & Edwin Smith, *English Cottages and Farmhouses*, 1960 reprint.

Parish Church: Brick voussoirs over clerestory windows. Bricks outlining stone-coped parapets. Church built *c.* 1480 by Sir James Hobart (1496 painting of him, as donor, and wife kept in church).

MANNINGTON

Mannington Hall: Late C 15 moated house. Brick with stone dressings, but brick windows details plastered over. Manor property of Lumners from mid C 14. Licence to crenellate obtained by William Lumner (or Lumnor) 1460. Described in *Paston Letters* as 'of Mannington', and was a Paston agent.

House a rectangular block, with polygonal angle towers, no higher than eaves—Pevsner queries whether 3rd storey is original—and a W wing. Additions, especially at rear, made mid C 19 by 2nd Earl of Orford. Orford may have augmented mediaeval detail. (Also added black-letter inscriptions on unreliability and beastliness of women.) Windows a mixture: 2 or 4 lights, cusped or uncusped, with pointed or square labels, and probably also mixture of dates. Plan not symmetrical: at S end smaller angle tower has stairs and larger one rooms. Further polygonal projection at SE has twisted finial, apparently C 16 like some other details. Inside, great hall fireplace is original, with timber lintel, and there are 2 stone fireplaces in parlour off hall. Details of fittings known from 1504–5 will of Margaret Paston, who had apparently been living at 'the manor place of Mannington': she calls Lumner her 'son', and he was her executor. She itemizes 'all the hangings' of hall, parlour and other rooms, 2 beds and cooking vessels.

E. P. Willins, *Some of the Old Halls and Manor-houses in the County of Norfolk*, 1890; *Paston Letters*, ed. J. Gairdner; Pevsner, *North-East Norfolk and Norwich*.

METHWOLD

Old Vicarage: Cotman made engraving of spectacular gable-end in 1812. It faces street, and adjoins contemporary 2-storeyed house—half-timbered and plastered and much lower than gable. Origins of building unknown. Date early C 16. Gable wholly brick: projecting plinth, wall-ends irregularly stepped, crowstepping at head. 6 square-headed windows in 3 tiers, all with deep chamfered surrounds. Lowest pair retain original cable-twist labels, but windows are Georgian sashes—like pair above. Top pair much smaller, set closer in to centre: of 2 depressed pointed lights, with original brick mullions. Great feature is 5-stage polygonal chimney-stack, rising like massive pilaster, up centre. Has lost its 3-flue shaft. Top and bottom stages plain, but 3 stages between ornate. They have (rising): tall tracery panels, trefoil heads of which Olive Cook says are terracotta; cut brick network; vertical zigzags, also cut brick. Old Vicarage was derelict, but now restored.

Parish Church: Perp. Flint walls, but brick and stone parapets. Firmans say brick dates from 1st half of C 16.

MIDDLETON

Middleton Towers: Our concern is with just one brick tower, but house is called 'Towers' from it and imitative castellated wings (with 'Early Tudor' chimneys) added in Victorian times. These form an L, one end built on to W wall of then isolated and roofless original gate tower. This stands at edge of rectangular moated platform, of about an acre, moat itself being modern revival (crossed by modern bridge).

Middleton Towers' site that of old Scales family Hall. Suggested that Thomas Scales began building on to timber-farmed house, planning great quadrangular, fortified mansion. Evidently *began* gate tower and (lost) W wing attached to it. His heirless daughter, Baroness Scales, in 1460 married Sir Anthony Woodville, who completed tower at least. Project again interrupted, probably for good, in 1483 when Woodville—by this date 2nd Earl Rivers—was murdered at Pontefract by Richard III (in purge of relatives of Elizabeth Woodville, late Edward IV's Queen).

Not known what buildings were completed. Francis Speer notes one 'very small isolated fragment' at rear. C 15 brick-built W wing was, however, still traceable in 1812 and 1817, when Cotman drew gate tower and showed crumbling walls at W. Tower derelict then, though retaining gabled ends of roof (E and W) with their square central chimney-shafts. Shell structurally sound. Victorian restoration—apart from what was involved in putting in floors and roof—comparatively minor work, such as renewal of battlements and insertion of one flight of wood steps, replacing lost section of stone newel stair in NW turret.

Red brick 3-storey gate tower is 54 ft high, octagonal angle turrets rising to about 60 ft. Rectangular plan, 51 (E–W) × 27 ft. Defensive, battlemented, but like Cambridge gatehouse. Stone used for quoins of turrets and for pointed arch and windows. Steer notes relative lack of shaped/moulded brick decoration, which is confined to arched corbelling of turrets. 'The brickwork is superb' (S. Mottram). Entrance (S) flanked by 2-light windows, with oriels above. Stone heraldic panel combines scallop shells—punning arms of Scales family—with arms of Anthony Woodville. (Note: Woodville was brother of Edward IV's Queen, who herself built in brick at *Queens' College, Cambridge.*)

Middleton Tower, Norfolk, booklet by Francis W. Steer, 1961.

NEEDHAM

Parish Church: Near *Shelton*. Perp. church except for Norman round tower, which was given octagonal top stage with brick quoins in late C 15. Late C 15 also brick S porch, with polygonal angle shafts. Cut brick quatrefoil decoration round archway and under crow-steps. Brick statue niche.

NORWICH

**Blackfriars Monastery:* Remains situated N of St Andrew St. Monastic church is now *St Andrews Hall*, town having acquired the property for £80 in 1540. Site has complex history. Some brick, but wall fabric flint. Hall consists of nave and chancel of Perp. church. On N side of chancel, is small remarkable 'undercroft'. Used as fuel store and boiler room. Dominicans acquired this site when Order of Friars of the Sack was suppressed in 1307. Sack Friars had built church or chapel. (dedicated to St Thomas à Becket). To this Dominicans contributed vestibule, but they soon built their own first church, raising ground level of site by 11 or 12 ft so vestibule became an undercroft. Vaulting supported by central stone pier, the sharply arched ribs springing from the 4 corners. Ribs chamfered brick and cells brick. In-filling bricks laid, roughly, at right-angles to ribs, in courses forming irregular ovals. Very pale in colour—'golden pink'. 2-storey C 14 cloister buildings have been much altered, and arcading, where it survives, is filled in. Depressed-pointed arches of dark-red brick with 4 or 5 'orders' of bullnose (double-chamfered) bricks.

**Bridewell Museum:* Bridewell Alley. Museum of Local Industries and Rural Crafts, with section on building materials: exhibits include mediaeval 'place' bricks; bricks from early C 14 *Blackfriars* undercroft and late C 15 *Cathedral* spire lining; moulded brick from *Great Snoring*; terracotta from *Oxborough* church and from the lost Arminghall Old Hall.

Geoffrey de Salle bought up and demolished old property on site, and built new courtyard house *c.* 1325. From this survive N range, hall (at right-angles) and undercrofts.

N range has original flintwork; some shaped pink bricks over pointed doorways and providing coping course for plinth. Clay perhaps estuarine, as that of undercroft vaults supposed to be. These wholly brick-vaulted undercrofts may be in part later than 1325, because floor levels are different. They form an L, below N and E ranges. E undercroft of 6 quadripartite bays, with middle piers; N undercroft of 5 bays, without piers, and with 6 or 8 ribs to a bay. (M. E. Wood says brick-vaulted undercrofts were long employed in towns for fireproof storage; but ribs more usually stone.) Ribs double-chamfered, reaching low down the flint rubble walls. At corners meet floor. Cells courses of bricks laid roughly at right-angles to ribs. Some brickwork disguised by plaster. Bricks lightish-red and thin (*Pl. 8*).

Information, Rachel M. Young.

Carrow Abbey: In Bracondale, just inside mediaeval city boundary. Benedictine nunnery foundations traceable in garden. Convent had good revenues. Latterly, a fashionable convent providing home for aristocratic young ladies—like Jane Scrope, for whom John Skelton wrote a poem of lament on the death of her pet sparrow (early C 16). At Dissolution convent bought by Sir John Shelton, who treated it as a private house, installing here his daughter who had been a nun at Barking, Essex. Last Prioress, Isabel Wygun, had built herself luxurious new quarters, her 'Lodging' being the only surviving building. Still a house, but restored and added to in early C 20. Inside are early C 16 beams. Hall has huge fireplace. Various places, including spandrels of main doorway, bear prioress' rebus, the letter 'Y' and a hand-gun. Fabric un-dressed flint. Brick dressings include quoins and jambs of sqaure-headed windows. 3 decorated brick chimney-shafts (restoration).

**Cathedral:* Established 1096. Basically Norman and of stone. 2 interesting pieces of C 15 brickwork found recently, neither normally visible.

*(1) In Bauchun Chapel, S of S aisle of apse. This established by William Bauchun, keeper of monastic granary (this survives), *c.* 1300. Chapel remodelled *c.* 1450 (has Perp. S window) and vaulted ceiling inserted. Apparently given by William Sekyngton, 'corrector of crimes' to Bishop Alnwick. 'Of remarkable construction' (Gilbert Thurlow) previously—and now again—hidden by plaster. Ribs stone. At junctions 47 bosses, bearing story of falsely

accused empress. In-filling brick, 4½ in deep, but only main ribs set in brick: subsidiary ribs independent, and gaps filled in with plaster.
(2) In the 315 ft octagonal spire. This built up from square Norman crossing tower by Bishop Walter Lyhart (1446–72). Lyhart was also responsible for new nave vaulting. Replaced post-1362 timber-framed spire (itself replacement), struck by lightning 1462. Construction of final spire discovered by restorers in 1963. Spire has thin Caen facing laid on rough stone shell 9 in thick. Then there was a layer of lime mortar, which had shrunk and shaken right down the spire. This mortar was full of oyster shells, apparently used for strength and to keep blocks of stone and the inner bricks in place—with correct slope—while mortar joints hardened. The central core of the spire is a great hollow cone of bricks. Cone mainly 4½ in thick. but at base 14 in and the 8 angle buttresses here are of brick stone-faced. Thought that brick cone and stone shell were built up together, in 'lifts' of 12–15 ft from internal scaffolding (apart from top stage, for which external scaffolding necessary). Also thought bricks were an economy, in contrast to imported stone, but relative lightness surely main argument for use: 1362 fall of stone spire caused much damage.

Friends of Norwich Cathedral annual reports.

Churches:
Note: Norwich has over 30 mediaeval parish churches, some abandoned. Usually built of flint, with stone dressings, and sometimes stone facings too. Bricks used, as in dozens of late mediaeval East Anglian churches, in limited ways such as voussoirs to windows and, sometimes, doors, besides quoins, especially in alterations. These churches given as main examples.

St George's: Tombland. In Princes St. Perp. (but some C 17 work on tower and chequered brick clerestory is also late). Flint with some dressings. Single brick voussoirs to windows, except that chancel has continuous triple voussoirs—like some at the *Great Hospital.*

**St Gregory's:* Pottergate. Chancel rebuilt 1394, work being paid for by Benedictine Cathedral Priory. Fair amount of brick used in its flint fabric, some of bricks as large as 10×2½ in. N and S windows have brick voussoirs. Base of chancel (beneath the altar) pierced by round-vaulted passageway, and this is brick-lined, with stretcher courses laid N–S. E end of church, visible from the garden of *Strangers' Hall,* has brick-lined statue niche and signs of brick arcading.

St James' : Cowgate. Top stage of Perp. tower is brick 'showing all headers' (Pevsner, *North-East Norfolk and Norwich*).

St John Maddermarket : Brick voussoirs to windows and doorways. W tower pierced by arched passage, with brick at head of arch and flint and red brick chequering above.

**City Walls :*

A report on 'The City Walls of Norwich' was issued by 2 local societies in 1964. Relevant documents printed in *Records of the City of Norwich*, edited by W. Hudson and J. C. Tingey, 1910. Licence to erect defensive walls obtained 1294. Special taxes on goods entering city were levied in 1297, 1305, 1317 and 1337. City circuits (larger than City of London) was nearly 4 miles: about 2¼ m. of walls plus a long and a short section of R. Wensum. By mid C 14 much of work had been done, but expense was punishing, and Richard Spynk finished it largely at own cost: was responsible for long stretch of wall and 4 towers between St Augustine's and Magdalen Gates, for Bishop's Gate and even for providing stone-throwers, crossbows and stone balls to be kept at different gates and towers. 1343 document freed him and heirs of taxes for ever. In 1345 a general tax was taken for maintenance of walls and outside ditches. In 1386 city records deal with upkeep of walls, gates. Parishes were responsible for sections of wall, measured by battlements—these totalling 1,630. Extensive damage was done in 1549 Kett Rebellion. Complete repairs done *temp*. Elizabeth I. Decline from C 16 on, and demolition—of gatehouses especially—in C 18.

There were 12 gates and 40 round towers. Walls rose to 12 or 20 ft. Wall thicknesses varied between 3 and 5½ ft. Stretches of wall survive, not to their full height, and some towers or remains or towers. Sections of parapet walk remain, carried on arcading, so inside of wall has series of deep recesses. Building material is flint, set in lime mortar. Walls were faced with dressed flint, but this all lost. Dressings brick: archways, windows, arrow slits, peep-holes, vaulting (some remains), stair wells and alure arcading. Dates as shown, between 1294 and 1343. Towers listed here (alphabetically, by usual name) are given as the most important examples.

**Black Tower :* On Carrow Hill, Bracondale. Has also been called 'Governor's Tower'. Built *c.* 1300. Largest and best-preserved of towers, though walls patched, top straightened off, interior gutted. It is a circular angle tower, set on sloping ground at top of hill. Has rounded stair turret, with doorway on to

alure of surviving Carrow Hill section of wall. Diameter of tower at base 30 ft. 40 ft high at S side. At level of alure 3 quite large pointed windows (N, S & E). Cross-shaped arrow slits and square peepholes, these formed of 4 bricks each. All voids brick, no special shaping. Bricks long and thin. Fair number throughout fabric (but some introduced during restoration). Stair turret brick-lined, but newel stair stone (now reaching alure only).
Carrow Hill section of wall has lost some of height but is still impressive—completest part of circuit. Has arrow slits *c.* 3 ft. tall with a brick-lined embrasures. Good sections of brick alure arcading. Brick doorways, including one just W of Black Tower.

**Bullclose Road Tower:* At junction of Bullclose Rd and Barrack St Section of wall, with brick arches, and 2-storey tower rising nearly to original height. Brick quoins to exterior flintwork, tower being partly round and partly octagonal. Exceptionally retains brick-vaulted ceiling of first floor: vault rounded, with ribs 2 stretchers wide. (Tower rather messed about by repairs at some date.)

**Queens Road Tower:* S end of Surrey St. Semicircular tower, its walls between 10 and 20 ft high. Brick lower floor vault remains. Brick voids include doorway to alure (W) and 2 gunports. (Recently uncovered and repaired by city council and M.P.B. & W.)

**St Stephen's Street Tower:* Found 1963. Groined vault of brick.

**Cow Tower:* Ancient Monument. Always open. In Hospital Meadow, beside sharp bend of R. Wensum. Erected at end of C 14 as part of city defences, but outlier not linked with walls. Also distinct because wholly brick. Replaced—and utilized foundations of—stone tower that had belonged to Cathedral Priory. 1378 record shows corporation acquired land, with old tower in ruinous condition. New tower constituted advanced post or watch tower E of city. East Wymer district responsible for its upkeep. Believed top was damaged during Kett's Rebellion (1549) by rebel gunner Myles (rebel camp was on Mousehold Heath, to NE). Structure still military-looking, despite cracks in fabric and largely ruinous battlements. Plain and formidable. City records include treasurer's account for purchase of bricks and making of the cross-shaped (stone) arrow slits. Recorded as complete by 1398–9, when the mason Robert Snape was paid 9*s.* for making 12 shotholes. He was also made a freeman of Norwich. Most strongly built of towers. Circular. Strong batter: diameter for major part 29/30 ft. but at base 36 ft. Height 50 ft. Taller if once stone-coped battlements complete. Projecting round stair turret at WSW (landward). Put-log holes visible inside and out. Small stone door at W, otherwise voids only above 1st stage: these small square-headed windows (staggered), some brick, some stone. Flint in plinth; plinth coping stone. No moulded bricks. Bricks vary in size, colour, texture. Apparently place bricks, not evenly mixed or always flat, but strong. 2 in thick only, but length varying from 9 to 12 in (10 in perhaps most common) and width from 4 to 7 in. Colours: *dull straw*, *dark-red*, red, pink, orange, bright yellow, green, grey. Courses not true horizontal, but rising especially round stair turret. Largely stretcher bond. Some header courses, especially in turret.

Interior gutted. Diameter 25 ft. Mainly header bond. Mortar joints seemingly a little thicker than exterior's. No moulding more complex than a chamfer. Traces of 1st floor vaulting (uneven zigzag of missing springer courses). Big round-headed window splays (some skewed), bricks at right-angles to rest. Ground floor fireplace (NW) with shaped lintel, herringbone fireback, twin flues. Smaller fireplace at 3rd stage (SW). In 1809 spiral stair was complete, now fragment only. Depressed pointed archways to different levels (stone). Vaulting evidently continuous spiral; steps bricks set edgewise; newel stone; no handrail; wall about 2 ft thick only. Tower walls, though, 11 ft thick at base and 6 ft above (*Pls. 11–13*).

**Guildhall:* Market Place. Revamped in Victorian times, but largely 1407 building. Site that of older 'Tolhouse', of *c.* 1300, but remodelled later in C 14 (*temp.* Edward III). New building ('gild' originally meant payment) also used for collection of city dues. E part, with linenfold-panelled 'Council Chamber', was built in early C 16 after a collapse. Undercroft below that is of *c.* 1300 and belonged to first toll house. Brick-lined stairwell at SW corner, apparently largely contemporary (but steps modern), with slim brick newel. Undercroft ground plan about 15×20 ft (E–W). 12–13 ft at highest. Some alterations and patching. Vaulting wholly brick, with flat wide chamfered ribs that end fairly low down walls. Carried on 2 thick ($3\frac{1}{2}$ ft) low octagonal piers, only 5 ft high to springers. Irregular bays. Cells of different sizes and depths, their bricks usually at right-angles to ribs. Vaulting heavily plastered, but bricks show lightish-red in places. $11\frac{1}{2}$ in long. $4\frac{1}{4}$ in wide and, seemingly, 4 in deep; bigger still are the double chamfered rib bricks, 13 ins. at longest. Whole effect rough and weighty—yet think of the rebuilding that went on over it.

**St Giles St, No. 35:* Premises of W. J. Boddy & Son Ltd (dairy and electrical engineers and ironmongers). House C 18, but below survives L-shaped mediaeval brick undercroft. Presumed C 14. Brick ribs, 6 to a bay, chamfered, narrow and irregularly placed. In-filling bricks at right-angles to ribs. Bricks pink with straw-marks, but heavily plastered.

**Strangers' Hall:* Now Museum. Charing Cross front mediaeval but remodelled C 17. Through courtyard is mid C 15 merchant's house, which superseded one of *c.* 1325 attributed to Ralph de Middleton. Of this rectangular (N–S) undercroft survives, W of hall. Of 3 bays. Stone ribs springing from short wall piers; cells are brick.

OLD BUCKENHAM

Manor House: Built inside earthwork of Norman castle which was converted into Augustinian priory in mid C 12. Tudor, brick-built house, with 'a W gable of brick, diapered, polygonal angle-shafts, and circular chimney shafts with geometrical decoration'—N. Pevsner, (*North-West and South Norfolk*).

OLD HUNSTANTON

Old Hunstanton Hall: Manor Le Strange property for 900 years. (Monuments in nearby parish church.) Hall was greatly damaged by fire in mid C 19 and again in mid C 20: till 1960s oldest part only was a shell, but now mid C 19 range—built as replacement—also gutted. Rectangular site is moated. Present house had origins in late C 15, with important additions in early C 16 and C 17. Courtyard plan. Brick, with stone dressings: this combination used at later dates too, when Perp. style also imitated—including battlements and tall chimneys.

Core of NW angle late C 15 apparently. Main Tudor structure is rectangular 2-storey gatehouse, in centre of E front. This attributed to Sir Roger Le Strange (died 1506: canopied brass remains on tomb-chest in church, the figure loaded with plate and heraldry). Gatehouse originally detached, but in 2nd decade of C 17, when inner quadrangle formed, wings built on to it. Gatehouse brick mainly English bond. Stone quoins, battlement copings and windows.

Bridge across moat also Tudor, abutting sides of doorway. Single round arch and bottom half of bridge stone: remainder brick, with dentillated course under coping. Condition bad, with one side bulging outwards.

Information, M. Power.

OUTWELL

Beaupré Hall Gatehouse: In Marshland area, near *Downham Market* and the *Walpoles*. Only gatehouse remains from originally moated brick and stone Hall—erected from 1500 onwards—for other surviving parts were demolished in 1966. Gatehouse attributed to Nicholas Beaupré in early C 16: described by Pevsner as a 'domestic showpiece'. In Outwell church tomb of Nicholas (d. 1512) incorporated into elaborate Elizabethan wall monument to his son Edmund (d. 1568), who continued building.

Front of house was predominantly brick-built (English bond) and Elizabethan. Gatehouse dressings stone: big quoins, fine 4-centred doorway and square-labelled window above, smaller windows, slits, courses and copings. Main fabric brick. English bond, except in irregular patches between quoins of turrets.

Geoffrey Hastings, article in *East Anglian Magazine*, June 1966.

Parish Church: Sir John Fincham (see entry for *Fincham* nearby) added *c.* 1527 N chapel of brick, bearing his arms on stone corbels of ceiling. Chapel 'in a transeptal position'.

N. Pevsner, *North-West and South Norfolk.*

OXBOROUGH

Oxborough Hall: Given to the National Trust in 1952 by Dowager Lady Bedingfield.

Manor owned by Sir Thomas Tuddenham, a disorderly force locally (according to *Paston Letters*), involved in unpopular and corrupt government of Henry VI. Tuddenham executed in 1461, on Yorkist takeover. Heir was great nephew, Edmund Bedingfield. Bedingfield's 1st wife Alice, daughter of Sir Ralph Shelton (see *Shelton*); 2nd wife, Grace, daughter of Henry Lord Marney (see *Layer Marney*, Essex). In July 1482 Bedingfield obtained licence from Edward IV to crenellate manor house and to hold market in the small town, which had port or hythe 1 m. to SW. Bedingfield knighted *temp.* Edward IV, and given fetterlock arms.

Built mansion wholly of pink-red brick, though licence to crenellate mentioned only 'stone, lime and sand.' Almost only stone dressings are battlement copings of gatehouse and its big windows and front archway. Sited moated, nearly square. Walls rise from still wet moat about 50 ft wide. This was the real defence. Despite grandeur of embattled great gatehouse, keynote is not defensibility. When Oxborough *was* besieged in the Civil War, in 1647, great damage was done, especially to E range. Parliament sequestered Bedingfield estates till 1660 (Restoration of Charles II), when Hall was repaired.

(Family had stayed Catholic since Reformation, though Spelman's *History of Sacrilege* cited them as holders of ex-monastic land.) Plan was symmetrical: 2-storeyed courtyard house (compared with *Queens' College*, Cambridge), with gate tower in centre of N range. Green Court was 118×82 ft. Ranges up to 170 ft long. No angle towers (except C 19 one at SE). Present bridge across moat built 1710.

Symmetry spoiled in 1776, when 4th baronet demolished most of S range, including great hall (oak hammerbeam roof) and kitchen. Major restoration done in early C 19, virtual rebuilding of ranges being necessary. Old materials used, but roofs pantiled. Passageway built along S side to replace range, and square tower added at SE angle. Plan made 1774 confirms symmetry of interior plan too, though S range was more complex than remainder. Crow-stepped gables and gable-ends evidently original, but corbelled battlements to ranges and decorated chimneys renewal or invention. In 1813 Cotman drew gate tower and part of Hall, before the 'Tudor' oriel at W of E range had been added.

Gate tower alone not revamped. A. N. W. Pugin, Gothic revivalist architect, called it 'one of the noblest specimens of the domestic architecture of the fifteenth century'. Foundations 10 ft down in moat. Above water level gate tower rises 70 ft and polygonal angle turrets a further 10 ft. These turrets are of 7 stages, ornamented by tracery-headed panels between ribbed angles. False machicolations to battlements. Eaves of adjoining buildings do not reach to 3rd stage of turrets. Magnificently disproportionate height shown up by comparison with full length of S front, turrets being nearly half as high as that is long. Olive Cook sees gate-tower as 'an exaggerated allusion' to recent need for defence, this converted to advertisment of 'power and status'. Between turrets, at 6th stage, crow-stepped battlements supported on moulded connecting arch with *genuine* machicolation. Below this, windows of 2 rooms: higher 'Queen's Chamber' and lower 'King's Chamber', apparently reference to 1497 stay of Henry VII. 4-centred stone entrance arch.

Passageway is 22 ft long × 13 ft. Unusual vaulting, wagon-type in woodwork sense: infilling brick between rounded brick ribs (these plastered), effect that of canvas stretched over angled bars of travelling carriage cover. Indented billet-type course below springers. Narrow rooms for porters, to l, and r., have same type of vaulting, wholly plastered. Plan of rear differs, though triple-stepped battlements are carried right round tower. At angles, small, fractionally projecting angle turrets above parapet level only. Main turrets, thin and polygonal, are set in from angles and rise only to parapet. Extra space allows pair of windows at 2nd and 3rd stages of central section. Archway brick, hollow-moulded, Chimney-stack on E side.

NW turret (front) has spiral stair, lit by quatrefoil peepholes. Steps brick, supported on continuous 'ploughshare' vaulting. Elaborately moulded brick handrail—with handgrip and guard like those at *Rye House* (Stanstead Abbots, Herts.). Mouldings at base of round newel. NE turret divided into 4 small octagonal rooms, top room being fitted out as dovecote. Turret lit by peepholes at base, and then round-headed windows with square brick labels. Some small upper rooms have unusual vaulted ceilings, of brick but plastered and painted over: ribs form stars, cells are concave (occasionally, wrongly, described as fan-vaulting). Main chambers have flat wood ceilings. Although stone is used for some windows and fireplaces, the King's Chamber has not only herringbone fireback but chamfered brick surround to fireplace. Floor of original 'small fine bricks' survives. The pair of big windows facing courtyard are set in narrow recesses. Recesses framed by wide and beautiful 4-centred brick arches, faintly ogee, with triple hollow mouldings.

Beauties of England and Wales—Norfolk, 1809; J. A. Gotch, *Early Renaissance Architecture in England*; Olive Cook, *The English House Through Seven Centuries*; Pevsner, *North-West and South Norfolk*; National Trust guidebooks: (1) by F. de Zulueta, 1953; (2) by A. L. Bedingfield, 1968, (both have spelling 'Oxburgh').

Parish Church: For early C 16 screens of Bedingfield Chantry see chapter on 'Terracotta' and Pl. 49.

POTTER HEIGHAM

**Parish Church:* Considerable amount of red brick, of C 14 and C 15, throughout flint rubble church. Much brick in Perp. S porch, including dressings.

Inside church a brick font, rivalled only by one at *Chignal Smealy*, Essex. Tall, but relatively narrow. Date C 15. Wholly brick, perhaps with some terracotta, seemingly once plaster-rendered. Base and stem much restored, bowl not at all. Base shaped like Maltese cross, remaining at ends of 2 arms. One shield has St Andrews cross. Round stem has mouldings at head and foot and with small buttresses. Octagonal bowl no wider than stem. Rounded lip. Faces have, alternately, St Andrews cross and pair of tiny blank niches. Bricks pink, small, still partly obscured by plaster.

RANWORTH

Parish Church: Brick-lined stairwell of spiral tower in exceptionally high (flint flushwork) tower.

SAXLINGHAM

Old Hall: NW of their *Baconsthorpe* Castle, branch of Heydon family built quadrangular manor house, of which considerable, but completely ruinous, remains. Late C 15 or, more likely, early C 16. Main building material undressed flint, with knobbly effect of cottage building. Some brick. Main part surviving is a long range, with plain square gatehouse projecting at centre. Gatehouse has 3 rectangular stone panels, with beautifully cusped shields bearing Heydon arms. Most dressings stone, but bricks used for quoins and, evidently, inside joints—for example in gatehouse (plastering is worn). Segmental stone arch of inside doorway outlined with headers. Gable has brick crow-steps, with copings like sloping cottage loaves; brick quoins in long and short pattern; 3-deep brick courses at eaves level, midpoint and plinth. Bricks thin, darkish-red.

SEETHING

'*1614*' *House:* SW of church. Pevsner says 2 small windows 'are blocked with moulded brick panels', these 'probably of the time of Henry VIII'. They have blank tracery, fleurs-de-lis, swans, double-headed eagles (see *Shotesham* nearby).

N. Pevsner, *North-West and South Norfolk.*

SHELTON

Parish Church: Small parish (population only 230): splendid church. Mainly brick, with stone dressings. Mainly attributable to Sir Ralph Shelton, lord of the manor (d. 1497; see also *Great Snoring* Rectory). Brick dates from *c.* 1480. Shelton evidently intended to rebuild whole church, generously, and left instructions in will for continuation. Executors, including his son John, failed him. Work was skimped: founder's tomb (N of altar, brass has disappeared) left without canopy planned; S porch vaulting not finished, so no parvise; roof (now C 18 replacement) probably was utilitarian only, not employing the angel corbels; above all, small early C 15 tower not replaced. This tower is square, narrow and of un-dressed flint. Besides early C 15 East Anglian lion font, another survival from earlier church is Decorated window incorporated in W side of S porch. Masons employed by Shelton are known to have gone on from here to rebuild St Andrews Church, Norwich (ashlared, finished 1506).

Body of church rectangular, with small projecting Sacristy at E end. S and N aisles end flush with chancel. Nave and chancel have tall 9-windowed clerestory, on N and S stone-faced. Church has suffered from lack of care, though bricks must to some extent have protected it from damp, but during recent summers volunteers have worked on restoration. Still coherent memorial to Ralph Shelton, who had roof corbels initialled 'RAF' and ornamented with rebus. This rebus, scallop shell on tun, repeated along base of E window of S aisle and in tracery lights of aisle windows. Shelton arms, yellow (for gold) cross on blue ground, figure in glass here; also in spandrels of S doorway. E windows of chancel and S aisle have donor figures in Early Tudor costume. Interestingly, E window of N aisle, partly made up of fragments, includes painted glass version of strip of brickwork.

Church has 'a very familiar and formal 15th-century East Anglian design' (C. L. S. Linnell), despite unusual material. Brick inside church has been rendered or lime-washed. Dressings stone. Church very light and seems tall because of relative heights of chancel and narrow E window: this part attributed to executors, whereas nave was Shelton's work. Aisle walls arcaded, with arches lower and considerably wider than those of nave arcades. Canopied empty niches in clerestory. Rood screen extended right across church. Stair (on N side, and brickwork here shows through plaster) D-shaped and brick-lined, with 9½ in deep splays for small square windows (blocked). Top steps are original, lower ones repairs: treads bricks laid edgewise, supported on stretchers. Chamfered brick in recess behind and above stone door. Exterior of stair turret polygonal, with brick copings to dentillated stone course.

Brick of S porch interior is not rendered and construction is fascinating. Put-log holes, 1 brick deep, in walls of '2nd storey'. Chamfered bricks for door from non-existent stair in centre of walls and groove in brickwork. Angle piers and springers of proposed fan-vaulting were constructed, but vault never inserted (in Norfolk compare only *Red Mount Chapel* at King's Lynn and S porch of St Giles', Norwich). This work stone. Porch high, square and thin. Stone-coped, not battlemented (nor are aisles) with stone copings and quoins. Dressings stone, but porch windows have brick voussoirs—alternating stretchers and pairs of headers—as do 2 windows in N aisle and the priest's door. Brick statue niche between 2-light windows. Brick of porch diapered with darker headers, once glazed: lower level has diamonds, with red header in centre; upper level has small diamonds inside large ones. Aisle walls also continuously diapered, mainly with large diamonds (header in centre), sometimes skewed. Voussoirs to 3-light windows brick alternating with dressed flint or stone.

Some oddities. N door cuts into base of NW window. On W side of the porch, where C 14 work adapted, Decorated window partly obscured and, W end of S aisle upper storey cantilevered out on wide stone arch. Thus, W end of church appears mixed and patchy in detail, but survival of small flint tower actually provides good contrast to rich red brick. Bond mainly English, but made irregular by voids and diapering. Brick texture very rough, with many large pebbles. Bricks measure about $10 \times 4\frac{1}{4} \times 2\frac{1}{4}$ in.

Besides intended porch vaulting church has another rare feature: the sacristy at E end, compared by H. M. Cautley to those at St Peter Mancroft (carried on vaulted passage) and St Peter Parmentergate churches in Norwich, though Shelton's is smaller. Brick-built, of one storey. E wall diapered, S and N walls not. Dressings stone: 3-light window, with square label, and canopied statue niches at either side, with deep square labels. Large stone gargoyle, lion's head, presides at centre of flat parapet. SE door perhaps not original. Sacristy entered through door in chancel wall, r. of altar (chancel raised). Whole E end of church elegant, of complex texture. E wall of chancel not diapered, but aisle E walls are. Mixture of brick and stone in buttresses, and radiating brick voussoirs of 3 E windows add more variety.

The Sheltons' courtyard plan hall is lost.

H. M. Cautley; C. J. W. Messent; Harrod and Linnell; Pevsner, *North-West and South Norfolk*; *Norfolk*, in Travellers' Guides series ed. Seán Jennet (Darton, Longman and Todd).

SHOTESHAM

St Mary's Church: Dressed flint tower has brick louvers. Perp. brickwork in top parts of nave. Pevsner mentions the moulded brick panels, probably Early Tudor, set round chancel piscina, with 'a swan, double eagle and a lion'.

TERRINGTON ST CLEMENT *Pl. 75*

Lovell's Hall: Gabled structure, with high 2-storey porch. Remnant of larger house erected by Lovell family, who held manor from C 15. Porch carries date '1543', later inscription 'on what authority is not known for its erection or rebuilding'. That 'the walls are in places 5 ft. thick' could argue for this as rebuilding date. Lower parts of porch Barnack stone, brought by R. Welland. Rest brick, 'characteristic yellowish pink brick' (Harrod & Linnell) of area. Unusual hybrid in materials.

B. Cozens-Hardy, *article* in *Norfolk Archaeology*, 1960.

TERRINGTON ST JOHN

Parish Church: Till 1530 Terrington St John just chapel-of-ease to Terring-to St Clement's, erected in response to conditions of wide marshland region.

Church has small 2-storey 'priest's house', for parochial chaplain, visiting or chantry priests. Structure related to church in complex way. Of brick with stone dressings, whereas rest of church ashlared or plastered. Uncertainty over dating of thin SW tower, which is 15 ft. from nave; priest's house section partly off-centre (S) fills gap between the two. Usually argued that tower was originally detached (as at Terrington St Clement), but Pevsner points out there is no trace of stair in lower part of tower. Nave is C 14 and C 15. Tower, Pevsner says, has C 13, C 14 and C 15 work, though H. M. Cautley describes it as 'plain' C 15.

Spiral stair, entered from lower room of priest's house or from W end of S aisle, is in the 4-stage linking section: at different levels gives access to tower, upper priest's room and, via passages, belfry and nave roof, at level of Decorated clerestory. 2 rooms, flush with S wall of tower and nave, form the house. Their fabric plastered over. 2 much narrower stages above contain passages with reddish brick infilling. Priest's room (upper chamber), 9 × 12 ft. is stone-dressed, but lower chamber has brick vault. Cautley fairly calls house 'a curious erection'.

THETFORD

**Cluniac Priory:* Ministry of Works administered. Mowbrays and then Howard Dukes of Norfolk were benefactors, whose burial-place the church was. *Valor Ecclesiasticus* showed priory had lands in 125 parishes in East Anglia. At Dissolution 3rd Howard Duke (see *Framlingham*, Suffolk) tried vainly to save priory by seeking permission to convert it into college of secular canons. Gained possession of priory buildings.

Layout of this smaller priory compares with *Castleacre*, also Cluniac. (C 14 heraldic tiles of same designs here and at Castleacre.) Surviving buildings late mediaeval. Ruinous, except for gatehouse—walls intact, though floorless and roofless. Building materials flint, the local material (Thetford is close to old flint-knapping centre, Brandon), and stone. Bricks used mostly for domestic arrangements and alterations. Buttery (later kitchen) has early C 15 brick fireplace. Very late C 15 brick fireplace and oven for wafers in Sacristy. By site of high altar of church remains of great tomb of 2nd Howard Duke, died 1524: this has brick vault (protected now by concrete slab). (Coffin removed to Lambeth Parish Church after Dissolution.)

In SW of site is a long 2-storey building known as the 'Prior's Lodging', retaining some original C 15 one- and two-light windows. At some date, perhaps C 18, when there was interest in picturesque ruins. fargments of monastic work—including 2 C 12 arches—set in walls. Immediately after

Dissolution, however, Lodging converted into secular dwelling, and brick was used in this work, including big fireplace. 'Large rectangular windows with plastered brick heads and jambs were inserted on both floors' (Raby & Baillie Reynolds). (These brick windows later blocked, partly replaced by small wood windows.) NW of site a flint-and-brick farm building, which looks old enough to be associated with abbey or with post-Dissolution conversion. Possibly reused materials. Best structure is late C 14 NW gatehouse. Of 3 storeys, with polygonal turrets at inner angles. SE turret has newel stair and SW garderobe with ribbed vault. Knapped flint with stone dressings, with a little red brick in fabric. Main (segmental) arches of stone, but brick arch at W side, which led to adjoining range (gable of this shows). Interior of gatehouse mainly brick. Brick fireplaces (W wall).

Ministry of Works guidebook by F. J. Raby and P. K. Baillie Reynolds, 1960 reprint.

THORPE ABBOTS

Parish Church: S porch Early Tudor brick, including dressings.

THORPLAND HALL: see under 'Fakenham'.

UPWELL

(Section of long village, adjoining *Outwell*, on E bank of old River Nene, and so in Norfolk not Cambs.)

Rectory: Remains, partly ruinous, of early C 16 brick house. Entrance range reduced to isolated angle turrets, but main range more complete, with stepped gables including one to porch. Brick buttresses. Decorative cusped friezes (trefoils). Brick dressings include those of a doorway and 'several original brick windows'. Rectory noted for brick-vaulted stairs, comparable with those of *Oxborough* and *Faulkbourne* (Essex): one stair in angle turret of old entrance range; another in larger turret, projecting from rear of main range. Door inside porch has blank tracery.

N. Pevsner, *North-West and South Norfolk*.

WALLINGTON

Wallington Hall: Brick-built hall of *c.* 1525, with later additions. Attributed to Christopher de Coningsby. Later owner and builder, Judge Gawdy (d. 1588) (see *Claxton*). Gawdy depopulated village. Reddish-pink bricks came from nearby Brick Kiln Wood (also a source for *St John's College Cambridge*). Dressings brick. Ornament, concentrated on E gable and N porch, includes cusped friezes. Embattled porch has polygonal angle shafts, with black tracery panels between, and crocketed finials. Smaller, but wider, cusped and crocketed panels and lozenges over moulded 4-centred archway. Battlemented Early Tudor oriel has cusped frieze at base. Most windows later replacements. See also chapter on 'Terracotta'.

Pevsner, *North-West and South Norfolk*; Harrod and Linnell; A. Clifton-Taylor, *The Pattern of English Building*.

WALPOLE ST. ANDREW

Parish Church: W tower of red brick, but none showing in rest of C 14 and C 15 church. Tower square, Perp., C 15. Dressings stone: windows, quoins, battlement copings, pinnacles, outer facings of otherwise brick pairs of stepped angle buttresses. Bond largely English, but not regular. Polygonal stair turret at SE angle, with slim turret top of brick and stone set back at parapet level. At base of S buttress a tiny brick chamber, with own exterior doorway and small windows. This was a priest's room, perhaps used at time of flood. (Church of nearby Tilney All Saints has similar room—of stone, in one of double buttresses of detached C 13 and C 14 tower—said to have been provided for priests when village or church was cut off by floods.)

WALPOLE ST. PETER

**Parish Church:* W tower of stone, *c.* 1300. Built on to probably Norman church, which was destroyed in great flood of 1337. Body of church then rebuilt, with stone dressings and facings evidently from Northamptonshire quarries (compare *Lovell's Hall, Terrington St. Clement*) and considerable amount of pinkish-red local brick in fabric. Nave (built as nave and chancel) of *c.* 1360. Perp. chancel is extension of *c.* 1425. Underneath high altar, which is raised 10 steps, runs a passage known as the 'Bolt Hole'. Passage sometimes explained as constructed o preserve old right-of-way, but could have been to allow processions to circle church without leaving churchyard: in addition, evidently used as shelter for parishioners' horses (still iron rings set in the wall). Vaulting ribs stone, but infilling and thick passage walls brick. Exterior S and N ashlared, but whole wall below great 7-light stone E window just brick, English bond, with 3 small stone niches.

Church guide.

WATLINGTON

Parish Church: Perp, brick stair turret added on S side of tower.

WESTACRE

**Priory:* Augustinian priory founded early C 11 by Ralph de Toni, Earl of Warwick. Toni family benefited by grants of land—including 22 Norfolk lordships, among them Westacre—after Conquest. Priory site was a little larger even than nearby *Castleacre*. Priory's main structure is gatehouse (N), but there are ruins on both sides of R. Nar. Rectangular gatehouse is C 14, of flint with stone dressings. Stone shields, over rounded entrance arch, bear arms of Toni and later Beauchamp Earls of Warwick. Vaulted passage ceiling has stone ribs with early brick infilling like *Butley Priory*, Suffolk. Cells are small oval domes, bricks laid in oval courses.

WEST DEREHAM
Parish Church: Round tower Norman carstone, but in early C 16 new belfry stage added: 'very pretty octagonal brick top with brick bell-openings and a frieze of little round arches'—Pevsner (*North-West and South Norfolk*).

WHEATACRE
Parish Church: Body of church older, flint rubble. Tall W tower of early C 16 brick chequered with un-dressed flintwork. Tall plinth (rises almost to arch of W door) wholly brick, English bond. Best feature is large Perp. W window, which has deep brick voussoirs, an only slightly arched head and panel and tracery: 3 tall lights with 6 small ones for tracery, mullions being of moulded brick.

WIGGENHALL ST GERMANS
Parish Church (St Germaine): Early C 16 brick S porch.

WIGGENHALL ST MARY MAGDALENE
Parish Church: Perp. Nave largely brick and some brick in chancel. Dressings stone. (Earlier tower is stone.)

WIGGENHALL ST MARY THE VIRGIN
St Mary's Hall: Most of house is Victorian, castellated Gothic. Origins, however, late C 15 house—*temp*. Henry VII—built of reddish Fenland brick. Section of original battlemented gateway survives: it has 2 polygonal turrets. Pevsner notes detached stable block of *c.* 1540–50. House erected by Kervil family, lords of manor.

WORSTEAD
**Parish Church:* Spectacular late C 14 flint church with 109 ft tower. Wealth

necessary for its erection derived from wool trade: Worstead gave name to 'worsted' cloth. Dressings stone, but window voussoirs of brick. These especially prominent 2–3 bricks deep, round arch of the great 5-light E window of chancel (tracery reticulated): this work may predate nave, which was begun 1379.

YARMOUTH: see under *Great Yarmouth*.

Further examples of buildings in Norfolk with early brickwork are:
Ashwellthorpe Parish Church; *Ashwicken* Parish Church; *Bacton* Bromholm Priory; *Bressingham* Valley Farm; *Burgh St Peter* Parish Church (base of tower); *Carleton St Peter* Parish Church; *Cawston* Parish Church; *Cley* Parish Church; *Downham Market* Parish Church; *Fritton* Fritton Hall; *Great Witchingham* Parish Church; *Great Yarmouth* Tolhouse; *Heckingham* Parish Church; *Hindringham* Old Hall; *Little Walsingham* Abbey Gateway (C 15) and Common Place Conduit (probably C 16); *Ludham* Barn and St Benet's Abbey, Holme; *Narborough* Narborough Hall; *Newton Flotman* Parish Church; *Old Catton* Parish Church; *Poringland* Parish Church; *Raveningham* Castell Farmhouse; *Salle* Parish Church; *Sharrington* Sharrington Hall; *Surlingham* St Saviour's Church; *Sustead* Parish Church; *Swardeston* Gowthorpe Hall; *Tacolneston* Old Manor Farmhouse and Parish Church; *Thurne* Parish Church; *Trowse Newton* Newton Hall; *Upwell* Parish Church; *Wiggenhall St Mary the Virgin* Parish Church; *Yelverton* Parish Church
and at NORWICH:
All Saints' Church, Bishop's Bridge, Gate to Bishop's Palace (Bp. Alnwick 1426–1436), Great Hospital and St Helen's Church, Pykerell House (Pitt St), St Giles's Church, St Peter Hungate (Church Museum), Suckling House.

NORTHAMPTONSHIRE

FAWSLEY

Fawsley Park Dower House: Fawsley Park has buildings, mainly stone, which belonged to Knightley family from Later Middle Ages or Early Renaissance to modern times. Church retains many Knightley monuments. Hall, C 16 with Victorian addition, has been timber works for many years. Dower House, despite its 'Ancient Monument' notice, is ivy-covered. Early C 16.

It stands alone, ¾ m. NE of Hall. Builder probably the same, Sir Edmund

Knightley, whose brass is in church (died 1542). Believed to be a little earlier than Hall, and 'is the earliest example of brick building in the county' (Pevsner). In Middle Ages customary for dowager to have one-third of estate for life: this house was lived in by Knightley dowagers till 1702. Continued to be inhabited till end of C 18, but then became progressively ruinous. In *The Old Halls and Manor Houses of Northanptomshire* (1936) J. Alfred Gotch published photograph of house: ivy rampant, but 4 brick chimney-shafts visible—with 2 types of twisted decoration, zigzag and 'honeycomb' pattern (alternate rows of small diamonds and long hexagons). Now only one topless twisted chimney rears above ruins and ivy (and only eye of faith believes others still there).

Rectangular building, about two-thirds ironstone and remainder brick. Seemingly once roofed with tiles. Stone windows mostly have arched lights and square labels, but square-headed lights in ironstone section give delusory later appearance. Brick used for hexagonal stair turret, which projects from W side of house, and for partition wall which incorporates (partly blocked) fireplaces and double chimney-stacks. State of chimneys already noted: the one visible, deeply twisted shaft, is made of canted bricks.

These practical domestic uses suggest brick was admitted to ironstone house on value of convenience, but there are decorative elements too. Besides the chimneys, there is diamond diapering in dark purpley-blue bricks to the stair turret, which has an odd decorative course of scooped bricks at 1st-floor level. This turret, of 3 stages against the house's 2, has stone-coped battlements. The spiral stairs have disappeared except for traces in plaster of stairwell. Brick part of house has stone quoins.

NOTTINGHAMSHIRE

BLYTH

Hodsock 'Priory': Present house was erected in C 19, on still-moated site of mediaeval manor house of Cressys and then Cliftons. ('Priory' is later romanticizing: no records of a religious house here.) The one survival is early C 16 gatehouse, built of red brick, inside moat. Has pair of polygonal angle turrets. 'Two flat projections' at other angles simulate turrets and have 'a nice corbel table as the crowning motif' between them. The Cliftons, builders of gatehouse, were very important family in region: their mediaeval base was Clifton (Notts), where parish church has C 15 Clifton monuments.

Pevsner, *Nottinghamshire*, 1951.

CANONS ASHBY

Canons Ashby House: Canons who gave name to place belonged to Augustinian priory, founded *c.* 1150. After Dissolution Sir John Cope made house out of priory buildings, lying S of lost church. In 1551 his son-in-law, John Dryden (died 1584), inherited and replaced these buildings with courtyard house of brick and ironstone—much brick in E face expecially. Further alterations in Jacobean times. Major additions in early C 18. Thus house appears to be too late for us, but parts look late mediaeval (mullioned windows with arched lights) and reminiscent of conversion of monastic property, for which brick was one of materials used. Indeed, J. Alfred Gotch, the architect, was convinced that surviving big tower belongs to immediate post-Dissolution period (not to John Dryden's new building). In 1535 monastic visitors had reported priory was 'in ruin and decay'.

EDWALTON

Parish Church: Dedication, the Holy Rood. W tower of brick and, through date uncertain, deserves to be included for 2 reasons: firstly, local tradition is that it goes back to reign of Mary Tudor (1553–58), which makes it a rarity, and, secondly, style is extremely conservative. Added to earlier nave, tower has buttresses across angles. Brick still laid English bond. Black brick diapering. Pevsner, finding tower 'sumptuously covered with ivy' about 1951, stated: 'the top windows are still pointed and of such early detail that one is tempted to suppose mid- C 16 origin'.

OXFORDSHIRE

EWELME

**Almshouses:* Date about 1436–46. Founded by William de la Pole (assassinated 1450) and wife, Alice Chaucer, who continued work. De la Pole, Dame Alice's 3rd husband, had wealth based on merchant origins in *Hull*, Yorks; wool trade; lands in East Anglia (gained through *Wingfield* alliance, Suffolk); his own royal offices—finally that of Chancellor. Alice was daughter of Thomas Chaucer, wine-merchant and Speaker of the Commons. Charity survived Dissolution as King himself was patron. 13 bedesmen.

Almshouses are red brick, but with timber uprights to (brick-infilled) inside walls and timber-constructed cloisters or ambulatory (largely herringbone nogged). Stone dressings. At rear are brick chimney-stacks. Most notable feature is exterior archway (N side), compared by Nathaniel Lloyd with

Flemish work: arch is of moulded brick with crow-stepping above and, between these two parts, a recessed panel with blank cusping. Similar, plainer arch to main door. Steps up from cloister to church, brick walls of this passageway having worn pale blue diapering. 1970 alterations to almshouses, including addition of dormers.

**School:* Soon after Almshouses had been begun, School was built at their W side, established jointly. Foundations date 1437. Of red brick. No timber. Only the main windows stone. Porch, which leads into lobby, has small moulded brick windows. Dimensions of main school room 28 ft 6 in × 18 ft 3 in. 2-storeyed structure, tall and impressive, with brick chimney-stacks and angle buttresses. Has kept its first purpose (like *Wainfleet* School, Lincs). Brick deep, rich red. Tiled roof.

Sidney Heath, *Old English Houses of Alms*, 1910; *Guide to St Mary's Church, Ewelme* and *to the Almshouse and School*, 1967, based on earlier guide by Arthur Bolton.

HANWELL

Hanwell Castle: Near Banbury. Part of late mediaeval castle of brick and stone, converted into country house: in Tudor times home of Cope family. Leland recorded how Anthony Cope finished off building in mid C 16. It was a square, mainly brick castle with 4 towers, erected *c.* 1490. Surviving tower (SW) is 3-storeyed with 2 projecting turrets of 5 stages. Other towers pulled down 1790. Quoins and parapet copings stone. Brickwork strongly diapered. Of the 2 wings adjoining tower—castle now L-shaped—one is stone-faced and the other brick (also diapered). Windows throughout stone, with brick relieving arches over square-headed windows at front of tower.

ROTHERFIELD GREYS

**Rotherfield Greys Castle:* Built by Sir John de Grey, a favourite of Edward III's. Licence to crenellate 1348. Castle was rectangular, built round court, with 4 corner towers. Slighted by Parliamentarians mid C 17. There remain: 2 small octagonal towers (SW and SE); curtain wall linking SE tower with NE; square NE tower, much larger than others. (Small C 17 brick house attached to SW tower.) Of mediaeval work, quoins stone but towers built mainly of brick and flint. Bricks, exceptionally thin, laid flat and herringbone-wise.

RYCOTE

Rycote House: John Williams—Lord Williams of Thame, ironically from *temp.* Mary I—built great brick mansion here, of which fragmentary remains. As commissioner for Dissolution of Monasteries obtained best church lands in Oxfordshire (including Thame Abbey). Made Treasurer of Court of Augmentations in 1533, receiving compensation on 1553 abolition. Died in his 60s in 1559, preceded by 3 sons. Latterly founded almshouses and grammar school at Thame, 3 m. to E, where his armoured alabaster effigy is in parish church. Had worked for Henry VIII, Edward VI, Mary I—whom he proclaimed—and for Elizabeth, whose favour he had obtained when escorting her to gaol at Woodstock!

Began building 1539. New house quadrangular, 'with turrets at the angles and two large towers at either side of the main entrance'. Burned down 1745. A house was later made on S side of site, by restoring Elizabethan brick stable block and extending it in Tudor style. Some Early Tudor fragments incorporated in this, and one turreted angle tower of red brick remains complete.

E. Carleton Williams, *Companion into Oxfordshire*, 1935.

STONOR PARK

*Large Elizabethan brick house, which has lost forebuildings and gained Gothick work of *c.* 1795, but earlier work also included brick. Manor in Stonor family hands from Middle Ages. Oldest surviving building is C 14 flint-and-stone chapel: has square tower, mainly of brick, some of which is probably C 14 according to M.H.L.G. list. (Upper part altered in C 18.)

The 'Stonor Papers' include 1416–17 accounts of building of a new manor-house and of the making of bricks near Nettlebed, both by *Flemish* workers.

Further examples of buildings in Oxfordshire with early brickwork are: *Mapledurham* Old Manor House and *Whitchurch* Hardwick House.

SHROPSHIRE

CRESSAGE

Belswardine Hall: Isolated and fragmentary. 2 diapered chimney-stacks. Recorded date, 1542.

LONGVILLE

Plaish Hall: John Leighton (or Loton) changed sides at Battle of Bosworth (1485) and victor, Henry VII, granted him manor at Alberbury (Shropshire) —where there is still 'Loton Park', and 'Loton Chapel' in parish church.

Henry VIII knighted son, Sir William Leighton, who took over old house 2 m. from Longville and built Plaish Hall on site. Inside survives painted ceiling with emblems of political and cultural significance: initials 'HR' for King, Tudor portcullis, 3 lions of England, Prince of Wales' feathers—with curly Renaissance shields and scrolls and dolphins' heads. About 1540. House of red brick, with blue brick diapering and dressings of stone, the fashionable combination as Pevsner points out. Window lights arched, not cusped. Later alterations and additions, but, of 'the gloriously overdecorated chimney-stacks of the Early Tudor age', zigzag, diaper and diamond-patterned shafts survive, with wild star tops and niches and billet mouldings at base of shafts. These erected by a man condemned to death for sheepstealing—by Leighton, as Judge at Shrewsbury assize—and afterwards returned for hanging. Reputed to be the only craftsman available for such fine work.

Pevsner, *Shropshire*, 1958.

UPTON CRESSET

Upton Hall: Entry through Elizabethan gatehouse of brick and stone, which has recorded date of 1580. Hall, however, evidently incorporates earlier brickwork, notably in windows and twisted chimneys. Blue brick diapering. (Newel stair of solid oak blocks survives, as at *Old Warden* Abbey, Beds.)

STAFFORDSHIRE

LICHFIELD

St John's Hospital: Re-endowment and rebuilding by Bishop William Smyth, Bishop of Lichfield from 1493 (but soon translated to Lincoln, died 1514). These brick almshouses have stone chapel. Most notable 8 tall brick chimneys, projecting from St John St wall, which rise well above roof level of 2-storey living quarters. Some dressed stone, but there are brick oriel windows—including 2-storey oriels to each set of rooms (on other side from chimneys); brick buttresses, doors, other windows. Appearance domestic and simple, perhaps more C 15 than C 16.

SUFFOLK

ASHBOCKING

Parish Church: Built on to Decorated nave, early C 16 brick W tower. Lower stages diapered in blue brick.

ASHBY

**Parish Church:* Round W tower. Constructed of flint rubble for bottom third; above that octagonal (tapering) and of brick, with brick quoins and lancets. C 13.

BARDWELL

Bardwell Hall: Mixed materials and periods, considerably restored, but mainly early C 16 timber-framed house. Brick nogging. N and S gables brick, crow-stepped. S gable culminates in chimney, shaft having moulding slike a taut bow.

BARHAM

Parish Church: Church refaced in Victorian times except for early C 16 brick clerestory. Also, in chapel N of nave, 3-light terracotta window possibly from Shrubland Old Hall. See chapter on 'Terracotta'.

BECCLES

**Parish Church:* Brick-vaulted charnel (bone-hole) at W end of S aisle. Probably 1369. Brick voussoirs to C 14 and C 15 windows of flint church.

BLYTHBURGH

Parish Church: Huge Perp. church included as most splendid example of East Anglian combination: flint fabric, stone dressings, brick voussoirs. Plain square 83 ft high tower of *c.* 1330. Body of church completely rebuilt from mid C 15. 128 ft long, with only slightly shorter N and S aisles. Un-dressed flint fabric but careful work, with flint flushwork to buttresses and at E end. Most elaborate stonework fretted parapet of 7-bay S aisle—where windows depressed pointed. All windows have reinforcing brick voussoirs, including great E window and (blocked) N and S windows of chancel. Clerestory is spectacular, having 18 4-centred windows separated only by flat stone shafts, so the 288 bricks to a side—outward sign of rubble and brick splays—form strong undulating line.

Necessary wealth came from wool trade and other commerce, Blythburgh having been port from early C 14.

Pevsner; Scarfe.

BOULGE

St Michael's Church: In grounds of demolished Boulge Hall. Victorian church retaining early C 16 brick tower.

BOXFORD

Old School House: Built as Tudor Grammar School, timber-framed (plastered) Big brick chimney-stack on Flemish-bond battlemented base. 'Stack' not divided into separate shafts. Formed of unmoulded bricks laid in zigzags.

BRANDON

Bridge: Dilapidated, by-passed mediaeval stone-and-brick bridge.

BRENT ELEIGH

Wells Hall: Near Milden. Moated. Retains C 16 red brick gatehouse with round arch of moulded brick, square buttresses and thin turrets. Set in contemporary wall. Really just gateway. Battlements decorative.

BURES

Parish Church: S porch, early C 16, of dark red brick with *cut* and moulded dressings. Seemingly later S chapel was chantry of Sir William Waldegrave, *d.* 1528 (monument inside): fabric red brick, much paler, with stone dressings. (Also associations with de Vere family, whose arms appear on C 15 font.)

BUTLEY

**Butley Priory*: Beside ancient Staverton Forest and sea (near Orford). Augustinian Priory founded 1171 by Ranulf Glanville, who also founded *Leiston*. He became Henry II's Treasurer and Justiciar of England. Priory came to own over 50 manors. Income £318. 17*s*. 2¾*d*. in 1534. Voluntary surrender 1539, and following year granted to Thomas Howard, Duke of Norfolk.

Samuel and Nathaniel Buck engraving of 1738 shows gatehouse—the only remains—as completely ruinous. A house was built round this later. Entrance passage and pedestrian entry turned into room 33×24 ft. Gatehouse is flint, with stone dressings including flushwork. Front decorated with most fabulous collection of heraldic shields (stone). Erected about 1320 by William de Geyton (tomb now in Hollesley church), prior 1311–32. Entrance passages stone-vaulted but tall rectangular chambers on sides—one originally porter's room—have peaked vaulting cells of brick. Vaults quadripartite, with chamfered stone ribs. Cells rise in dome shapes, the (unmoulded) bricks being laid in oval courses. Plastered. Compare brick vaulting in *West Acre* Priory gatehouse (Norfolk) and St Andrew's vault in *Norwich*, though cells of latter flatter and ribs are also brick.

J. N. L. Myers, 'Butley Priory, Suffolk', in *Archaeological Journal*, XC, 1934.

CHARSFIELD

Parish Church: 'A steep, light building consisting of nave and chancel in one, an extravagant tower built of narrow orange-coloured bricks during the reign of Henry VII and a pinnacled Tudor Porch' (Ronald Blythe). Tower and S porch diapered, and both built on older flint base with flushwork frieze (plinth), that of tower having elaborate symbols and inscription and that of porch only stars and patterns. Tower has diagonal buttresses and porch polygonal ones. Brickwork exceptionally good.

CHILTON

Chilton Hall: Remnant of brick mansion begun by Crane family about 1430 and added to till mid C 17. Oldest part now tall E wing with polygonal angle buttress and turret at SE corner, evidently *c.* 1550. House still has moat, crossed by brick bridge—thought to be a C 18 reconstruction.
Parish Church: Tower brick, evidently C 16. Church has Crane chapel (NE) and alabaster effigies of family who built Hall, ¼ m. away. Chapel brick-built. Pevsner notes 2-light window in N wall of nave, again Tudor brick. Church otherwise flint. Neglected. Village has disappeared.

COVEHITHE

Parish Church: Great mid C 15 church in ruins except for section of W end, reconstructed about 1672 to serve as parish church. Original church 3-aisled, with square W tower. Not church of large community which later shrank, for apparently never more than 300 inhabitants. Building attributed to wealthy priest, William Yarmouth, from 1459. Mainly flint rubble with flint facing and stone dressings, but considerable amount of brick also used—this showing more clearly perhaps in ruins. Brick appears throughout exterior fabric, especially of chancel, and used to reinforce interior walls. Niches and other details brick-lined. Brick voussoirs to nave window. E end has brick and flint courses, with scaffolding holes remaining in brick. Inside church 2 brick-lined stairwells; that in N wall of nave apparently led to clerestory; that in N wall of chancel apparently led *up* to rood and *down* to crypt. Stone steps, supported by brickwork. Remains of brick vaulting of crypt under old sanctuary.

COWLINGE

**Parish Church:* Early C 14 church of septaria and brick. (Brick tower, 1733.)

CROWS HALL

Near Debenham. Moated. Brick bridge with 4 arches. Fragment of gatehouse.

House is N wing of 1508 red brick mansion, itself incorporating part of early C 14 house. Brick is blue diapered. Terracotta plaques, *c.* 1525, in outbuildings.

DENSTON

Denston Hall: Remains of early C 16 brick house given C 18 front. Moated. What is lost includes turreted gatehouse. Rear part of house is Tudor range, brick, including windows and labels.

EAST BERGHOLT

Parish Church: In Dedham valley. Late Perp. church of brick and flint. E end brick. N aisle largely brick, including polygonal turret at E end. Tower likewise partly brick, on stone base; begun 1525 but never completed. Attributed to Cardinal Wolsey, who was also builder of *Sandon* church (Essex).

EYE

Parish Church: C 16 porch with courses of red brick and stone (stone dressings too).

Priory: Eye had Benedictine priory, founded after Norman Conquest. Now C 18 house on site, known as Priory or Abbey Farm. To NW long 2-storey range, which has been used as barn and is incorrectly known as the 'Chapel', probably the guest-house. This wholly brick, early C 16. Walls stepped in 3 stages above shallow plinth. Copings brick. Narrow, 4-centred door (blocked) with chamfered mouldings. Upper windows of one light only; lower windows 2 lights, though mullions mainly broken away. Shallow pointed heads. Brickwork English bond. (Modern roof.)

FRAMLINGHAM

Castle: Central ward of late C 12 castle of Bigods encircled by 44 ft wall with 13 projecting towers, tall and square. Flint with stone dressings. Wall surrounded by old inner moat. In 1476 acquired through inheritance by Howard family, of whom John Howard of Stoke-by-Nayland became Duke of Norfolk in 1483 (killed fighting for Richard III at Bosworth that year). Castle remained in their possession till mid C 16, though not regularly lived in from time Thomas, 3rd Howard Duke, built brick mansion at *Kenninghall* (Norfolk). Early Tudor brick additions to castle attributed to Thomas Howard, Earl of Surrey (created Duke of Norfolk by Henry VIII in 1513 after victory at Flodden), or to 3rd Duke, who succeeded him 1524. Earlier date seems more likely historically, but later date of 1530 or '40 is accepted by Ministry of Works. Additions are bridge over moat and modernizing domestic work—chimneys, fireplaces, door jambs and recess linings: 'copious use of the thin

Tudor bricks' (M.O.W.). Bridge has C 18 parapets, but is largely Tudor brick including piers. Adjacent brick-faced buttresses. Entrance gateway was rebuilt at this period, with the Howard arms inset above and one of famous chimneys above that. These early Tudor chimney-shafts top battlements of C 12 towers and have elaborate cut or moulded decoration—deep twists or fretwork, for example. Some real, being extensions of C 12 stone chimneys, but majority ornamental dummies. Definitely odd, but have become essential to skyline, even though castle is ruined—its inner buildings demolished about 1636 in favour of poorhouse. (Most heads of Howard family had been executed by Henry VIII or Elizabeth,)

M.O.W. guide by Raby and Baillie Reynolds, 1966 ed.

GEDDING

Gedding Hall: Moated, with deep plinth. Consists mainly of very tall red brick gatehouse, Henry VIII, 1897 tower extension. High 4-centred arch between ribbed polygonal turrets. Front decorated with globular friezes of moulded brick. One stepped gable. Work of Chamberlayne family, who took over from Geddings in late C 15. Arms of both appear. Has been compared with *Layer Marney* gate tower (Essex).

GREAT BRADLEY

Parish Church: For exceptionally good S porch bricks 'said to have been made by the King's own brickmaker' (Norman Scarfe). Porch has crow-stepped gable with 6 brick statue niches. G. Ewart Evans, in *The Pattern Under the Plough*, points out that decoration includes moulded brick horses' heads (rendered) and compares them with horses' heads found in Tudor houses in Suffolk, often on chimney-stack. They were charms, of pagan origin.

HADLEIGH

Deanery Tower: Built as free-standing tower, gatehouse to original deanery, W of parish church. Parish of Hadleigh was rare 'peculiar', that is, not subjec to local bishop (then of Norwich) but directly to Archbishop of Canterbury, who appointed rector and *dean*. Tower dates from 1489–90. Built by Dean William Pykenham (see also *Ipswich* and *Stoke-by-Clare*), who held several church offices simultaneously. At Hadleigh he also built Almshouses and endowed them (will dated 1497); they were rebuilt 1887, though chapel is largely original. Deanery Tower very like the *Oxborough* gatehouse (Norfolk), of which it is just two-thirds the size, having 6 storeys, not 9. Has also been compared with *Faulkbourne* Hall, Essex (N. Scarfe), and with

Sassenport (gateway) at Zwolle in Holland (Nathaniel Lloyd). Wholly brick. Exceptionally fine, elaborate work. At front 6-storey polygonal angle turrets. At back small turrets across angles corbelled out from top storey. Only mouldings of 4-centred entrance fairly plain. Moulded brick used for crow-stepped main parapets, supported on cusped corbel-tables—motifs also used above oriel window. Turrets have deep stepped parapets and are decorated with series of panels, heads of these being trefoils each formed of 2 moulded bricks. In addition, Tower is diapered, mostly with diamonds though there are 2 triangles over archway. Between tops of turrets twisted chimney-shafts. Inside turret, brick-vaulted rooms, including oratory with original brick vaulting—with central boss and 'Ave Maria' inscription. In SW turret brick-vaulted spiral stair, with quatrefoil lights.

Toppesfield Bridge: Some restoration, plastering and cutwaters evidently altered, but in main mediaeval brick bridge. Curved coping to parapet and dentillated course below. Three arches, shallow-pointed, with mouldings, voussoirs, vaulting ribs.

HARGRAVE

Parish Church: Tower Tudor brick. Buttressed.

HAWKEDON

Langley's Farmhouse: Retains 4 Tudor chimneys, with elaborate mouldings. About 1520. A John Langley was rector in the 1540s. Inside house original fireplaces, with vine decoration in plaster.

Parish Church: Trefoil-headed corbel table of brick to S porch (Pevsner). C 15 church.

HELMINGHAM

Fig. 10(b)

Helmingham Hall: Built on quadrangular base, with buttressed plinth rising from moat. Still has drawbridge. Tollemache family home—they hold manor from late C 15—probably partly financed through land grants at time of Reformation. Fairly uniform appearance, but this house of 4 building periods (Pevsner), starting with half-timbered and brick-nogging of about 1500. Dominant work *temp.* Henry VIII: much of N and S ranges, including open-sided entrance. Despite stepped gables, ornamented with brick pinnacles and diaperwork, Tudor building rather plain. There are, however, stacks of decorated chimneys, with different twists and zigzags. Battlements added by Nash in C 18. Considerable later imitation and restoration.

Articles by Arthur Oswald in *Country Life* from 9 August 1956.

HEMLEY

Parish Church: Big C 16 W tower of red brick with dark blue diamond diaper. Moulded brick used for voids—W window and louvers. (Church proper largely rebuilt in late C 19.)

HENGRAVE *Fig. 10(c)*

Hengrave Hall: Rare, harmonious, mid C 16 merchant's house, built of pale stone and pale brick, with swaggeringly ornamented, pinnacled entrance. Three m. NW of Bury St Edmunds. Now Convent School (but can be seen by appointment). Once moated. The light-yellow or so-called 'white' bricks were made of local gault clay, with comparatively high proportion of chalk. Some bricks made at site, others from Bury St Edmunds Abbey kilns, from Ickworth and elsewhere. This clay then little used till late C 17, when kilns at nearby village began producing famous 'Woolpit Whites' (made till C 20). Olive Cook describes Hengrave bricks as 'blanched, silvery', matching limestone brought from King's Cliffe, Northamptonshire (S of Stamford). House superseded earlier one: Hengrave accounts show payment made in 1535 'for makyng clene the old red brycke'. Some red brick used in new work, for chimney-shafts decorated with roll mouldings or studs. 1525 contract with John Eastawe specified chimneys of 'roubed (rubbed) bryck'. Fair amount known about new work at Hengrave, from accounts. One of themes in describing it must be mixing of late mediaeval and Renaissance elements. Contemporary record of 'Kyston the Merchant' as owner: Sir Thomas Kitson (d. 1552), whose tomb—'six-poster with stubby Tuscan columns' (Pevsner) —is in his mid C 16 family chapel, built onto parish church (in grounds). Gage said portrait of him at Hall was by Holbein. Thought to have been richest cloth merchant in England, trading at Antwerp and in Flanders generally, but put arms of his London livery company over front door (under Royal Arms), and this was the Fishmongers' Company. Sheriff of London, 1533. Bought land in Dorset, Devon, Somerset and Nottinghamshire. Gained some of Bury Abbey land in Suffolk.

House built about 1523–38, chief mason and bricklayer being John Eastawe. He 'and all his company yt (that) he settes a worcke for ye said house' were to be boarded out at the same house for 16*d.* a week. Eastawe was to make all the mortar needed. Kitson would supply timber and roughly cut wood for the carpenters. Eastawe was to follow a 'frame' (that is, model) which he had seen in possession of Duke of Buckingham. This thought to have been of Stafford's *Thornbury Castle* (Glos), left unfinished when he was executed in 1521. Thornbury characterized by courtyards, tall rows of windows, galleries and largely symmetrical plan. Another mason was John Sparke, responsible for ashlar work and carvings of entrance, which has inscription '1538'. Fittings, including surviving panelling, made by Thomas Dyricke, joiner, and Davey, 'carver' or carpenter, while Thomas Neker was paid £116 for woodwork, including fitting up 16 1st-floor 'lodgings'. Finest work is contemporary stained glass in chapel in S range, of national importance and possibly by King's Glazier (Pevsner); 'twenty-one scenes from Creation to Crucifixion' (Scarfe).

Hengrave Hall is quadrangular, S front original in detail, except for late C 18 remodelling of some of gabled parapets into plain battlements, and removal then of bay window. House subjected to rebuilding in late C 19, especially N and E wings. Projecting kitchen range was demolished, so house smaller than originally: inventory listed 40 bedrooms, and all sorts of domestic provision, for catering and for dealing with linen. Great hall is not in first state, but once typically mediaeval with screens passage. Non-mediaeval elements of the house are its exterior symmetry and the entry from courtyard corridor. Gatehouse incorporated in S range. With rounded oriel between polygonal turrets, gatehouse has something in common with 1530 *Kirtling* Tower (Cambs), but turrets with their domed crocketed caps are comparatively low and triple-lobed oriel uniquely ornate—all pinnacles, Renaissance acanthus mouldings and putti supporters, either nude or absurdly overdressed in Roman armour. This work all limestone, and stone facings extend over central section of gatehouse, crocketed pepperpot tops of turrets, similar tops of corner towers and over parapets of house itself. Windows stone, with square labels and slightly arched lights. Role of brick limited in one sense, but contribution extremely important (besides, structurally, stone is only ashlar). Turrets brick, and so are exterior walls generally; walls of court are stone-faced. Nathaniel Lloyd pointed out that, in the 'rare but effective association' of brick and ashlar, 'nearly the same colour' effect was gained by contrast between small rough-textured brick and smooth ashlar. The brick can be said to 'carry' the stone.

The accounts run from 1525 to 1538, and there are records of plate, jewels and 'household stuffe'. One latish item is this: 'pd. to Wm. Daye for making iij payer (pairs) of bryck molds (moulds) xij d.' Another item details 'barres for ij windows of brycke' for the tower. Lime-burning for mortar recorded. Also making of moat and stocking it with fish. There were waterworks and (water) mill. The separate offices lay E and W of house, including barn (with tiled roof), kennels, mews (stables) and a bowling alley. John Gage, using records in hands of Gage family, the then owners, published *The History and*

Antiquities of Hengrave in 1822, and there is further material, including the accounts, in his *History and Antiquities of Suffolk: Thingoe Hundred* of 1838.

The 2 Gage volumes; N. Lloyd, *History of English Brickwork*; John Harvey, *English Mediaeval Architects*; Olive Cook, *The English House Through Seven Centuries*; N. Pevsner, *Suffolk.*

HERRINGFLEET *Pl. 7*

St Olave's Priory: Brick of 2 periods: *c.* 1300 vaulting of refectory undercroft, and mid C 16 domestic conversion of property. Augustinian priory sited near crossing of R. Waveney, which had long-established ferry. Property supposed to have covered 10 acres. Despite this, St Olave's was small house, rather poor. Suppressed 1537 with lesser monasteries, after which leased to Sir Henry Jernegan (Jerningham), the patron. Ten years later he bought it for £92. 8*s*. 6*d*. He built 3-storey house on N side of cloister. This continued as a Jerningham house (later plans for almshouse, based on priory, having evaporated) till sold 1604. Almost completely destroyed, along with priory buildings, at end of C 18. Remains of house in adjacent farm buildings, and also a big barn.

Of priory buildings only refectory undercroft survived with a 'roof'. This used for cottages from early C 19 to early C 20. Remains odd and confusing, except for splendid vault, and whole place smells overwhelmingly of pigs. Priory established in early C 13 by local landowner, Roger FitzOsbert. Marriage to FitzOsbert heiress brought in Jernegans in early C 14. Buildings were flint. Fragments of cloister and church held to be contemporary, early C 13. Farm lane, incidentally, cuts across E end of both. Cloister piers were evidently brick-faced. Brick in peepholes and drains, possibly C 15.

Refectory vault is 'an exceptionally early example of English mediaeval brickwork, dating from the end of the thirteenth or the early years of the fourteenth century' (Harlech). Walls flint rubble, and 5 surviving octagonal central piers Purbeck marble, but polygonal wall shafts, vaulting ribs and cells are all brick. E bay destroyed, and there is partition wall of C 15 or C 16 and C 16 stair turret (both contain brick) which spoil original plan. Bricks were covered with plaster, but much has fortunately fallen away showing pinkish-red colour of bricks and their rough texture. Vaulting quadripartite, but irregular. Ribs form fairly shallow arches. Soffits of chamfered bricks and wall piers also chamfered bricks. Perhaps, despite import of Purbeck columns, bricks were used just because they were cheaper than stone vaulting: in 1291 priory's income was only £26. 17*s*. 4½*d*. One column stands on a Roman millstone, evidently salvaged from Burgh Castle nearby. However, this low vault

—about 11 ft. at apex—is very impressive. Undercroft would have been used for stores.

Remains of upper part, the refectory, now mostly of C 16 brick, including fireplaces. For these moulded brick used, as for square-headed windows and big 4-centred archway in ruins of the house on N side. These bricks much darker red and have 'place' marks so deep it seems likely reeds, not staw, were used. More Tudor brick shows at N end of Abbey Farm buildings. There is also the large red brick barn, surely built after Dissolution as a hall? Until early C 19 it had 'a fine carved timber roof with bosses and pendants'. Tudor bricks reused haphazardly in boundary wall along E side of lane.

H.M.S.O. guidebook by H. Rutherford Davis.

HOO

Parish Church: Early C 16 red brick W tower (parapet later).

HOPTON (WEST SUFFOLK)

All Saints' Church: Clerestory Early Tudor brick. Inside, brick shafts, with seated figures against them (Pevsner), up to hammerbeam roof.

IPSWICH

Christchurch Mansion: In Christchurch Park. Basically red brick 2-storey E-plan house, built about 1548–50. On site of Augustinian priory (then outside town's lost boundary walls), purchased by Paul Withipoll, rich merchant tailor of London. Builder was his son, Edmund, whose inscriptions record building stages: '1548' in hall, '1549' on porch and '1550' on E wing. W wing an extension dated '1564'. Apart from hall, house consists mostly of small rooms. Mansion appears later in date, mainly because of remodelling after fire in late C 17: whole upper storey rebuilt and given curved Dutch gables with dormer windows; central porch rebuilt and given tall classical columns at angles; except for most of ground floor, original windows were replaced by casements. Further altered in C 18. Tudor windows are stone, not brick. House is diamond-diapered. (On N side part of Tudor house, salvaged from demolition, re-erected in C 20.)

Pykenham Gates

'Pykenham Gateway': In Northgate St (near site of lost town gate). The larger gateway to Archdeaconry (Pykenham House), which was rebuilt by William Pykenham, canon lawyer, who became Archdeacon of Suffolk in 1471. House survived but much altered, and is timbered and plastered. Pykenham was pluralist, also holding offices of Dean of *Stoke-by-Clare*

College and Rector and Dean of *Hadleigh*, from 1472, where he also built in brick. This gateway is of 2 storeys with restored crow-stepped top and (plastered) square buttresses. Brick mouldings to pointed archway and, to room above, 2-light window of moulded brick with shallower arch and label. Other side of gateway, however, timber-framed, and even doorway is wood: this had initials 'W.P.' but now retains only Pykenham's rebus, a fish (pike), carved in one spandrel. On one side some old brick walling.
Smaller Gateway: To S of main gate, in garden wall of Pykenham House. Considerably altered and top plastered over, but archway itself of red brick with fine and complex mouldings, some concave.

(There was a boundary wall (lost) built round property by Pykenham, known later as 'Archdeacon Pykenham's wall'.)

Lilian J. Redstone, *Ipswich through the Ages*, 1948.

Wolsey's Gateway: In College St Wolsey's foundation charter of 28 July 1528 was for 'Cardinal College of St Mary', the buildings of which had already been started. College dedicated to the Virgin Mary. Run by secular canons. Left unfinished when Cardinal Wolsey fell from King's grace in 1529. Wolsey was born in Ipswich, son of a butcher. College was intended as a great grammar school, to supply Cardinal College (now Christ Church) at Oxford with students, just as Henry VI had established *Eton* to supply King's College, Cambridge. Wolsey's charter shows Ipswich school had slightly larger body of clergy and masters than Eton had in 1441. Records are of building with Caen stone, but gateway—the only structure remaining—is of brick. Dr William Capon, Dean of College, wrote to Wolsey in September 1528 and 121 tons of Caen stone had already arrived and 1,000 tons were expected by Easter 1529.

Money and endowments came from suppression of small priories in East Anglia, and Wolsey appropriated St Peter's Church (W of gateway) as his college's. When college was suppressed in 1531, parishioners regained church. Part of brick-and-rubble wall, built between college and churchyard of St Peter's, survives. College had site of 6 acres, so gateway is a very small relic. Other buildings destroyed, and stone taken for King's works in Westminster, and site soon used as rubbish dump. School itself, however, was allowed to continue in a small way, with royal grant and using old school buildings Wolsey had taken over (where he had gone to school himself). He had also established printing press at Ipswich, and that survived him too.

Brick gateway is small; evidently led to a wing only. Of rich red brick, with stepped polygonal angle buttresses abutting mouldings of 4-centred archway. Five rows of mouldings. Above, 2 statue niches with cusped heads and, between them, square stone panel with arms of Henry VIII (worn). Above these, row of large moulded brick quatrefoils. Buttresses (now flat-topped) originally culminated in pinnacles and there was 3rd, central, pinnacle. C 18 print shows these pinnacles, already incomplete, as shafts with deeply grooved twists.

IXWORTH THORPE

Parish Church: C 16 red brick tower with crocketed pinnacles in brick. S porch has remains of crocketed pinnacles in brick, besides step gables. Early Tudor, like tower. Some flint also used in decoration of porch, which is mainly of diapered brickwork.

KENTON

Kenton Hall: A part of Garneys family mansion built of red brick. Two storeys. Buttressed. Pediments to ground floor windows though windows above much simpler (Pevsner; Scarfe). Perhaps mid, rather than early, C 16.
Parish Church: S aisle Perp., brick-built. Unusual entry direct through E wall of porch (also Perp. but flint). Windows brick. Inside, octagonal brick piers and chamfered brick arches. Incorporates chapel of Garneys family (with 1524 Garneys brass).

Pevsner.

LAVENHAM

Guildhall: Used as meeting place of Gild of Corpus Christi founded in 1529, though building might be a little older. Angle post has figure perhaps of 15th Earl of Oxford, who was patron. Very big timber-framed structure, with much carved woodwork—especially oriels and 18 in overhang of upper floor. Plastered, but has sharply sloping plinth of brick with moulded copings; brick jambs to some windows; rectangular chimney-shaft. Inside, cellars have thick walls of rubble and brick. After guild was suppressed, building became successively Town Hall, prison, workhouse and store for wool and grain.

F. H. Crossley, *Timber Building in England*, 1951.

LEISTON (LEISTON-CUM-SIZEWELL) *Fig. 3(o)*

**Leiston Abbey:* Premonstratensian abbey founded 1182 by Ranulf de Glanville (see *Butley*) in Minsmere marshes, but in mid C 14 moved a mile inland to better site by Robert de Ufford, Earl of Suffolk. In 1389, new buildings burned down and abbey again rebuilt. Annual value in 1535 quite high,

£182. Suppressed with lesser monasteries. Granted to Charles Brandon, Duke of Suffolk. Site devolved into a farm, and abbey church used as barn. Most of buildings left roofless. Sizeable sections of mediaeval flint rubble walls remain. Certain amount of brick used, particularly for voussoirs to stone windows, in late C 14.

Early in C 16, entirely brick gatehouse was added on to W range of cloister, making elaborate entry. Two octogonal turrets, of which only one survives, nearly complete. This has chamfered angle shafts with elaborately cusped blank panels between. Also rows of ogival corbels to each of 3 stages. Apart from mouldings, exterior mostly stretchers. Red brick.

Min. of Works guide.

LETHERINGHAM

Abbey: Small Augustinian abbey here, of which only few remains. These include partially restored gatehouse, with polygonal angle buttresses, which is C 15 in date and of brick.

LEVINGTON

**Parish Church:* Sit. in Orwell valley. Described by C. J. W. Messent as late C 14 and built largely of local bricks. These red in colour. Brick window tracery.

LINSTEAD PARVA

Parish Church: Quite a lot of brick in fabric. Nave windows early C 16 brick (Pevsner).

LITTLE STONHAM

Clock House: Of mediaeval origins, but plastered front much later in date. (Inside, C 14 woodwork, Elizabethan ceilings.) Central chimney-stack Early Tudor, about 1525, partly restored: round shafts with moulded brick decoration, including double roses and fleur-de-lis.

LITTLE WALDINGFIELD

Parish Church: S porch late C 15, of brick and flint in alternate courses. N porch, with stepped gable, is 'good Tudor brick' (H. M. Cautley), marked with de Vere molet badge.

*'*The Priory*': P. G. M. Dickinson has investigated cellar of this post-mediaeval house. Has very early vaulting of brick. Groined, evidently C 14. Apparently not monastic.

LITTLE WENHAM *Pl. 6*

**Little Wenham Hall:* Near Capel St Mary, about 8 miles from Ipswich and Orwell estuary. First domestic building in England built of brick—or very largely of brick. From 1720 to 1280. Good condition, though uninhabited. Once believed bricks must have been imported—via Ipswich, a major port—from Flanders. Certainly, Flemish influence may be detected in small size of bricks, and Flemish immigrant craftsmen could have made them. (Flemings began to settle in East Anglia as early as C 12, though peaks were later, in mid C14 and C 15.) Overwhelmingly probable these yellow bricks were made of local comparatively chalky clay (gault). Hall may be seen by written appointment (it is in grounds of modern Hall Farm). Important architecturally, as well as for use of brick.

Plan an 'L', with rectangular stair turret in inner angle. No destruction except of one projection from hall range, probably garderobe, and of a C 16 wing. Entry at first floor via wooden stair evidently replacement. Hall erected as house of a knight, not as castle keep. Coeval with great red stone Bishop's Palace at Acton Burnell (Shropshire), but more like the Norman Boothby Pagnell Manor House, Grantham (Lincs). Despite moat, thick walls—with more narrow lancets to ground floor—and battlements, essentially small *dwelling*. Protected, but only battlements have any semblance of the aggressive. (One recorded attack on Little Wenham Hall, though, took place during Wars of Roses. Then owner, Gilbert Debenham, 'Lord of Little Wenham', was notorious lawbreaker and extortioner. Debenhams had held manor from C 14.)

Davey, on subject of architectural detail (mouldings, vaulting, windows) says Hall is 'illustration of the way in which architectural features normally associated with church building were also introduced into secular buildings'. Detailed likeness between windows at Hall and in parish church: both have, besides lancets, the 'Y' form and circles for tracery. At Hall ground floor, stair turret and top level windows are lancets, while more ornate windows—of 2 lights, except for chapel's 3-light E window, which has circular tracery—light first and second floors. Dressings stone. Buttresses ashlared (restored). Quoins, stringcourse and battlement copings also ashlar.

Ground floor consists of quadripartite vaulted undercrofts, of 3 bays and 1 bay, with hollow chamfered brick vaulting ribs. These used for stores. Interior generally plastered, except for lining of stairwell where brick unrendered. Spiral stair itself is stone. Slim rectangular stair turret is much the tallest part of building. Gives entry to all rooms, including chapel. Longer range of 'L' is that of the hall proper, which is comparatively wide—16 ft 9 in

× 37 ft—and has no 3rd storey. Its ceiling is a flat C 16 one. Other C 16 work, including brick fire-backing and octagonal chimney-shafts.

Other wing much smaller in ground area, but rises to 3 storeys. Second floor has chapel, which has stone rib-vaulted ceiling, with brick cells, resting on stone corbels (E.E.). Stonework fine, especially E window, piscina and voids beside doorway up from hall. Above chapel another room, the solar. There were presumably detached wooden kitchens and outhouses, which have left no trace. Central boss of chapel vault represents St Petronilla, apocryphal 'little daughter' of St Peter. This dedication extremely rare, but Whepstead Church (Suffolk) also has it. Little Wenham Hall attributed to Sir John de Vallibus, but manor inherited in 1287 by Petronilla of Nerford (or Narford), and chapel dedication suggests the work was not complete by that date.

Now for wall fabric. Ashlared buttresses already noted: they rise just to 2nd stage, with small ones in centre of walls and thicker, double ones at angles. Walls of mixed stone for about 1st 5 ft and then brick: changeover can be detected inside too. Stone wall bases consist of large and small pieces of flint and septaria, roughish work. Septaria is fairly light in colour, being layered shale ('fossilized mud') found on the East Anglian coast—'lumps of soldified mud dug from the seashore' (A. Clifton-Taylor). Brick makes more uniform wall surface, but still irregular by later standards. No systemmatic bonding. Bricks vary in size between 8–9¾ × 3¾–4¾ × 1¾–2½ in (N. Davey). Colours vary too, though pale brick—'mostly cream and muddy greenish-yellows' (N. Lloyd)—predominates. Otherwise, touches of pink, light-red or orange. Remarkable survival, and a reproach to repeaters of legend of dearth of mediaeval brick in England.

Nathaniel Lloyd; Norman Davey, *Buildings in England*; A. Clifton-Taylor, *The Pattern of English Building*; Margaret Wood, *The English Medaeval House*; Olive Cook, *The English House Through Seven Centuries*; Scarfe; Pevsner; illustrated article by W. I. Haward in *East Anglian Magazine*, Sept. 1951.

Hall Farm Barn: C 16 timber-framed with red brick in-filling.

Parish Church: Bulk of church late C 13, like old Hall, or perhaps *c.* 1300. Flint structure, with E.E. 'Y' tracery to some windows and a lancet (as in Hall). W tower mediaeval flint, but top stage red Tudor brick—probably *temp.* Henry VIII, when Brewse family held manor (1514 brass to Thomas Brewse 'armiger', knight, inside).

LITTLE WHELNETHAM

Chapel Hill Farm: Group of Crutched Friars established themselves here,

late in C 13, and built a flint house of which there are some remains. After Dissolution this apparently converted into secular dwelling. Brick was main building material for conversions, though there is a Tudor half-timbered court with arcade. Two stepped gables of brick, chimneys and 'pretty ornamental brick panels' (Pevsner).
Parish Church: Porch, with stepped gable, of brick. Perp.

LOWESTOFT

Parish Church (St Margaret's): Long red 'place' bricks of C 15 used with main building material, flint rubble. Appear mainly in chancel walls, N aisle exterior and stair turret of S porch. Also used for voussoirs, for junctions of buttresses and, sometimes, for quoins. Brick appears to be lining material of walls; can be seen clearly in rood-loft stair in N wall. Typical East Anglian Perp. (Dressings stone.)

NEWBOURN

Parish Church: Nave mainly red brick. S aisle has dark blue diapering. Early C 16. Doorway to chancel also brick of this date (Pevsner).

PARHAM

Moat Hall: Sometimes called Moat Farm. Entrance, across ornamental moat, through simple cut-down Tudor brick archway. This set in crumbling boundary wall, dark bricks forming big diamonds. Stone jambs, but brick voussoirs to 4-centred arch. To l. and r. large brick niches with rectangular stone panels inside, each carved with shaggy club-bearing wodehouse (wildman) in relief. House belonged to Willoughbys (who were still there during Civil War): for them and wodehouses, see *Belleau Hall* (Lincs) entry. There was a more elaborate, main gateway, with half a dozen stone shields with Willoughby arms and those of Uffords (Earls of Suffolk), predecessors at manor. This sold and taken to the United States in 1926.

House partly timber-framed, partly red brick, early C 16 in date. Now reduced to T-shape, of which bar of T mostly brick-built, but S range plastered and later in date (including elaborate brick chimney). No defences. S side of older part retains brick window like those on N. E and W sides (altered) have timber-framed gable-ends, with diagonal brick nogging in herringbones or lozenges. Where brick is used without timber uprights, it is decorated with smallish diamond diapers, with single header in middle of each diamond.

Most notable brickwork that of N façade. This has 3 large projections, all diapered (worn): rectangular chimney-stack and 2 polygonal bay windows, 2 storeys high. Base of chimney-shaft ornamented with cusped arcading. Windows moulded brick, rectangular but lights having arched heads. Only a few of lights are in original state: of the others, some have been blocked up with daub and some have had moulded mullions knocked out and casements inserted. Thus, not much trace of original cusping of heads, though spandrels mostly visible. Despite this destruction, main lines of brick bays are clear enough: central windows at both levels had 3 lights and side windows 2 lights. Ground-floor windows not large (and are the most altered), but those of first floor—divided into 2 sets of lights, 14 in all to each bay—are 12 ft high. House may be attributed to Sir Christopher Willoughby, who was at Parham from 1498 to 1527. A 'creation of Tudor romanticism, . . . ghostly and faded' (Olive Cook).

Olive Cook and Edwin Smith, *English Cottages and Farmhouses* (1960 reprint), and *The English House Through Seven Centuries.*

POLSTEAD *Pl. 3*

**Parish Church:* Roman bricks were re-used at Brixworth (Northants) in Saxon times, for arches, and the thin bricks employed for large Norman arches at Polstead have something of the same effect. Several authorities—including H. M. Cautley (*Suffolk Churches and their Treasurers*)—are convinced Polstead bricks are English-made. Date is late C 12, perhaps 1160, and so earlier than those at *Little Coggeshall* (Essex). Some brick quoins to remodelled exterior of church, which Cautley thinks the same date as those inside. Brick arches are the chancel arch, the triple arcades of nave and also clerestory window heads. Clerestory is blocked. Stepped, round arches, rising from stone capitals. Surrounds are semicircles of stretchers and soffits $1\frac{1}{2}$ stretchers deep. Pevsner gives brick measurements at 10–11 by 5–7 in, in contrast to Roman-time size of 18 by 12. Thickness is $1\frac{3}{4}$ in, Roman thickness being not much more than an inch. In fact, difference and irregularity of size virtually proves Polstead bricks native. Besides the bricks, largish square blocks of tufa—dark, pitted stone (? of volcanic origin)—are used in the arches, normally just near capitals. Also some bricks in square nave columns.

POSLINGFORD

Parish Church: S porch brick, evidently early C 16. (H. M. Cautley noted exterior holy-water stoup, which would give pre-Reformation date.) Three niches of brick over entrance, and windows brick too.

REDLINGFIELD

Parish Church: Red brick chancel, and brick shows through plaster of nave (Scarfe). W tower also red brick, with blue diapering, but this has been truncated. Brick window on N side. Perp. Early C 16.

SHELLEY

Parish Church: N. Chapel (of chancel) brick-built, evidently in Early Tudor times, as Tilney chantry. Pevsner cites brick windows, and, inside, 'a fine square panel with the Tylney arms, *c.* 1540–50'.

Shelley Hall: Part of mansion built by Sir Philip Tilney (or Tylney), who died 1533. Red brick, blue-diapered. Demolition and alterations have left little but brick buttresses showing, but gatehouse remains although now blocked up. This has polygonal buttresses, decorated with blank cusped panels.

Pevsner.

SHIPMEADOW

Parish Church: Some brick in flint fabric, particularly in region of N porch, which has brick hood to entrance, brick parapet copings and brick in angle buttresses. W tower, early C 16, also brick and flint, with brick parapet copings: it is small and has no battlements.

STOKE-BY-CLARE

College Dovecote: Benedictine priory, first established at Clare itself, was transferred here early in C 12. In 1415 (priory was cell of Abbey of Bec, France, and at this date 'alien' priories in England were suppressed) Edmund Mortimer, Earl of March, converted it into a college of secular canons. There was to be a dean and several priests. Provision of food, clothing and tuition for 5 choristers. At end of C 15 William Pykenham (see *Ipswich* entry) was Dean. Last Dean, when college with school was suppressed in 1548, was Matthew Parker, later Archbishop of Canterbury. College had accumulated considerable wealth (and had various East Anglian rectories in its gift). In 1526 Bishop Nykke of Norwich had fended off attempt of Wolsey to suppress Stoke and use funds for his Ipswich or Oxford college. In 1535 worth £324. 4*s.* 1½*d.* p.a. Not dissolved by *temp.* Edward VI. Buildings, and there are still remains of them, were converted into Elwes family residence, itself altered in C 18 (and now a school). Entry through what seems, at first sight, a tall, square gatehouse: actually this rich college's dovecote, built of brick in early C 16. Base open, with wide, flattish arches of chamfered brick. Moulded brick used for small upper window. Birds' entry was through projection in tiled roof. Quite elaborate blue diapers, including portcullis. No stone used. Length of old garden wall adjacent. Canons' activities included gardening, dove-breeding and forestry.

STOKE-BY-NAYLAND

Giffords Hall: 2 m. E of Nayland Church. Name 'Giffords' derives from earlier owners. Builders were Mannock family, who held property from 1482 and, by mid C 16, held land in Essex also. After this period, prosperity fell away because of continual heavy fines levied in Elizabeth's reign for 're-cusancy' (keeping to old Catholic faith). Yet this was Mannock property till late C 19.

Giffords Hall mainly Early Tudor, erected from about 1500, and largely brick. Plan quadrangular. One range incorporates hall with its double hammerbeam roof (has been lowered). Most striking and ornate feature is brick gatehouse—Norman Scarfe says this has flint interior, apparently earlier and matched by work in one range, evidently *temp.* Henry VIII. Multi-moulded depressed pointed arch between polygonal angle turrets, these with ribbed angles and tracery-headed blank panels. Pinnacles (compare *Faulkbourne*, Essex) and battlements, all brick. Every type of brick dressing to brick parts of Hall. Polygonal chimneys with moulded decoration and star tops. Scarfe says one cusped tracery frieze is identical with a frieze at *Layer Marney* (Essex). Over gateway arch is panel with cusped trefoils. Big cusped trefoils in spandrels. Labels end in brick rosettes. Gatehouse projects from end of brick range. Diapers—to 1st floor only—include various diamonds and vertical and horizontal zigzags. As Pevsner points out, the windows are all brick but jambs and mullions plaster-covered in imitation of stone. Inside courtyard a small porch: this partly timber-framed with brick nogging, like courtyard walls *Fig. 3(h)*.

In garden is square dovehouse, probably C 16: of lath-and-plaster, but tiled roof and brick base.

Pevsner; Scarfe.

Parish Church: In Stour Valley, which enjoyed wool trade prosperity in Later Middle Ages. Great Perp. church, retaining only C 14 S porch with Tendring and Howard arms from earlier structure, dates from mid C 15 on. Erected by local merchants and gentry, including Howard family which was gaining lands and importance (in 1483 John Howard of Stoke was made Duke of Norfolk). Church flint rubble, with stone dressings including big quoins, but considerable amount of brick used. Later still in C 15 more brick than stone was used for W tower. Finally, in early C 16, N porch was built: all brick, except for stone copings. Porch is not very elaborate, but front has stepped battlements with cusped corbel-table of moulded brick, and side windows have fine brick mullions and tracery. Red bricks laid in English bond.

The 120 ft high tower, however, is truly elaborate. Complex mixture of brick fabric and stone dressings having effect of patterns. The more conscious decoration—such as crocketed pinnacles and quatrefoil panels of parapets and the heraldry (including Howard arms) over W door—is stone. Moulded brick not used. Two particularly effective combinations of stone and brick are these: (1) stepped diagonal buttresses of brick, which reach to top of tower, have usual stone quoins but also brick-lined statue niches (empty), with stone pedestals and canopies; (2) incredibly deep window splays brick, outlined by stone quoins and jambs, but from level of tracery window arches fan out in series of stone mouldings. C 15 brick pink rather than red.

SUDBURY

St Gregory's Church: First of Sudbury's 3 parish churches. Fabric, mainly that of 1480s remodelling financed by wool trade money, is flint rubble with stone dressings. Considerable amount of brick in tower and walls. Brick battlements (restored). Despite late date, bricks have straw marks ('place' bricks). On N side of chancel early C 16 vestry of brick.

St Gregory's College: College of secular canons, established *c.* 1370/75 by Simon of Sudbury, Archbishop of Canterbury, was attached to St Gregory's (which he rebuilt). Simon was born in Sudbury, and his head was returned here after he had been 'executed' in Peasants' Revolt, 1381 (skull displayed in church). College buildings, which were on N side of church, have disappeared, except for C 15 brick gateway with stone arch.

THORINGTON

Parish Church: Round Norman tower of flint was given octagonal top of C 16 brick. Stepped parapets.

TRIMLEY ST MARTIN

**Parish Church:* N chapel early C 15 brick, built by Roger Cavendish, testament 1405 (cited by N. Scarfe).

UBBESTON

Parish Church: W tower Early Tudor brick. Diapered. Also S porch of brick.

WALDRINGFIELD

Parish Church: Early C 16 stepped brick tower, one of number in Deben estuary. Diapered with worn blue headers.

WATTISFIELD

Parish Church: S porch, of flint and stone, has 'a poor brick top containing in brick the arms of de-la-Pole' (H. M. Cautley).

WESTHORPE

Westhorpe Hall: Mansion of Charles Brandon, Duke of Suffolk, and Mary Tudor (d. 1533), largely demolished in C 18, when Thomas Martin recorded destruction of moulded brick or terracotta ornament. New house then erected. Mary Tudor was widow of Louis XII of France. Brandon secretly married her in 1516, being fined £24,000 by her brother Henry VIII, whose favourite he was and a regular and continuing recipient of land grants. Westhorpe Hall retains a little Tudor work, but main relic is brick bridge with 3 arches crossing moat. See also chapter on 'Terracotta'.

WEST STOW

West Stow Hall: Built about 1520–33 by Sir John Croftes (or Crofts), Master of Horse to Mary Tudor (sister of Henry VIII and wife of Charles Brandon). Her arms, in compliment, remain on front of gatehouse. Land had belonged to Bury St Edmunds Abbey, apparently without buildings (no conversion, therefore, and not a Dissolution gain). Croftes's son married daughter of Kitson, builder of *Hengrave Hall.* Croftes built a quadrangular house, now largely demolished and part remodelled. Gatehouse—extended in Elizabethan times by arcaded corridor to house—is fine Tudor brick. Four polygonal angle turrets, with domed cupolas. A pinnacle, shaped rather like the cupolas but just capped, at each end of roof ridge. Cupolas and pinnacles have quite elaborate terracotta finials, figures, including cross-legged man blowing a pipe, a seated lion with man's face (bearded) and a sitting dog (? heraldic). Of moulded brickwork, most striking part is a rectangular panel over entrance arch: this has rows of diamonds in relief, alternately plain and cusped. Angle turrets have, for 2 stages, blank panels with cusped (trefoil) heads.

John Gage, *History and Antiquities of Suffolk: Thingoe Hundred*, 1838; N. Lloyd, *A History of English Brickwork*, 1925.

See also chapter on 'Terracotta' and *Fig. 3(r)*.

WINGFIELD

Wingfield Castle: Moated castle is really 2 buildings. S front, incorporating gatehouse and 2 angle towers, is C 14 flint with stone dressings. Derives from licence to crenellate granted to Michael de la Pole at time of 1381 Peasants' Revolt. A little mediaeval brick, especially in voussoirs and vaulting of arch, but this seems to belong to remodelling of *c.* 1490. Curtain wall battlements are brick, but still later: those to W are Tudor and those of gatehouse and E are 1826 replacements.

Adjoining gatehouse range is 2nd building: 2-storey house, attributed to Charles Brandon, Duke of Suffolk, or his tenant, Richard Catelyn. Built in early 1530s. By this date Henry VIII had destroyed rest of castle, the estates of the de la Poles having been forfeited to the Crown in 1525, as a consequence of the King's purge of possible rivals. Wingfield was granted to Charles Brandon. It is, perhaps, more likely that the landlord built the house. He let it to Catelyn, Sheriff of Norwich, in 1531–2. House is plastered and stands on flint rubble plinth, presumably that of destroyed W range of castle. Exterior has a big Tudor chimney-stack of brick, projecting up from the moat, culminating in 4 shafts with multiple star tops. Rear pair plain polygonal shafts, but front pair have rounded shafts with moulded brick diamonds and interlaced hexagons in alternate rows.

(Peasants still held at bay: the only private property where permission to view has been refused (1967).)

S. W. H. Aldwell, *Wingfield: Its Church, Castle and College*, 1925.

**Parish Church:* Wingfield family heiress married to Michael, who became 1st de la Pole Earl of Suffolk, in mid C 14. From this period church considerably enlarged. Tombs of both families in chancel, notably that of Michael, 2nd Earl of Suffolk, and his Stafford wife, which has badges in canpopy mouldings: pair of wings (for Wingfield), leopard's head (for de la Pole) and knot (for Stafford). Church mainly flint rubble, with stone dressings, but much brick in the external fabric (though some later repair work) and usual brick voussoirs. Inside, in N and S walls—rood screen stretched across the 3 aisles—can be seen brick lining and steps of 2 rood stairs.

Farm S of church has some relics of chantry college established by Sir John Wingfield (will, 1361) which was linked with church.

WINSTON

Parish Church: Some brick in tower. Buttressed S porch Early Tudor brick, with quite elaborate mouldings to entrance archway and 3 niches above that.

YOXFORD

Cockfield Hall: N wing and gatehouse range survive from red brick mansion erected by Sir Owen Hoton in mid-C 16. Also range of contemporary outbuildings. Remainder C 18 reconstruction. Gatehouse and N wing have stepped gables and decorated chimney-shafts. Gatehouse regarded as definitely of *c.* 1540 and N wing is most likely contemporary. In entrance passage (gatehouse) a *terracotta* relief of bust of man in Tudor costume—possibly a Hopton portrait. Brought to Cockfield Hall only in 1950, but came from an associated Blythburgh property (information, M. Blois).

Further examples of buildings in Suffolk with early brickwork are: *Ashbocking* Hall; *Badingham* Parish Church; *Blaxhall* Parish Church; *Botesdale* Chapel of St Botolph; Bredfield *Parish* Church; *Bromeswell* Parish Church; *Bures* Bevills; *Buxhall* Maypole Farm; *Campsey Ash* Parish Church; *Finningham* Parish Church; *Fornham St Martin* Parish Church; *Framsden* Parish Church; *Fritton* Parish Church; *Great Ashfield* Parish Church; *Great Barton* Parish Church; *Great Bealings* Parish Church; *Great Cornard* Parish Church; *Great Wenham* Wenham Place; *Heveningham* Parish Church; *Hitcham* Brick House Farm; *Holbrook* Parish Church; *Hoxne* Abbey Farmhouse; *Ipswich* St Lawrence's, St Mary-at-Elms' and St Stephen's Churches; *Kesgrave* Parish Church; *Lakenheath* Parish Church; *Lawshall* Parish Church; *Laxfield* Guildhall; *Lidgate* Suffolk House; *Lindsey* St James's Chapel; *Little Bealings* Parish Church; *Long Melford* Long Melford Hall (begun 1545); *Shadingfield* Parish Church; *South Elmham St Cross* Parish Church and C 15 building on Bishop's Palace site; *Stoke Ash* Parish Church; *Thorpe Morieux* Hall; *Thwaite* Parish Church; *Tuddenham St Martin* Parish Church; *Uggeshall* Parish Church; *Wickham Market* Parish Church.

SURREY

CROYDON

(Greater London Borough of Croydon, 1965)

The Old Palace: SE of Croydon parish church. Once palace of Archbishops of Canterbury, who held land here from before Conquest. One stage out from London—10 m. from Lambeth. Main function was as summer palace. Convent school from 1887 (*Fig. 2; Pl. 31*).

During Commonwealth taken over by state and sold (buyer turned chapel into a kitchen). 1646 inventory, assessing annual value at £40, makes it sound a prosperous, delightful property: 'with a chapel wainscotted, a granary, and all houses, outhouses, courtyards, and other yards and stables thereunto belonging, encompassed with a faire court yard on the north, a small running water east and south, and the church yard west, and of all that great garden and fruite house, with all other gardens, orchards, pidgeon howse, waters, and three fish ponds fenced on the west with a brick wall on the south, with a small running water and a hedge on the east, with another hedge belonging to the howse keepers meadowe, on the north, with a water which parteth the aforesaid gardens and the said meadows'. These mentions of streams, though, indicate one past disadvantage of Croydon Palace. It was low-lying and, until early C 19, on an island. Church was also on this island, though a small stream ran between it and the palace. Henry VIII complained he was always ill when he stayed at Croydon.

See sold property as late as 1780, but it had been allowed to decay from mid C 18. Act of Parliament, needed for sale or demolition of palace, complained of 'so low and unwholesome a situation, and in many respects so unfit to be the habitation of an Archbishop of Canterbury'. In first years of C 19 many buildings demolished. Calico-printing and linen-bleaching works run here. Remaining buildings are being carefully restored, and cut-down palace is an impressive enclave despite total disappearance of its green belt.

As at *Charing Palace* (Kent), stone and flint rubble were used for earlier buildings and brick for later ones. Alterations and refacing in C 17, particularly by Laud and Juxon, and in C 18. Thus history of buildings is very complex. The later buildings have main rooms on 1st floor: this including brick chapel. Chapel attributed in main to Thomas Bourchier, Archbishop 1454–86. From 1480 he also worked on Knole (Kent), but in stone. He was a great-grandson of Edward III, so emphatically one of landowning nobility; his successor Morton, Chancellor (1487), Cardinal (1493), deeply involved in politics, was not a noble. Bourchier's E chapel window has 7 lights. Chapel is 24 ft wide, 70 ft long. W section, or ante-chapel, evidently work of Morton, who built it out as part of new gabled W front, adding (surviving) inside stair up from an annexe to the W end. As Oswald points out, there is no documentation proving this work was Morton's, but details of fine brickwork are like those of *Lambeth Palace* gatehouse, and wood W screen has carved tun on cornice: this tun most likely had painted inscription 'MOR', making up Morton's rebus, as on a Lambeth boss. Late C 15 part of W front is diapered with grey bricks: beside the usual diamonds, there are cross keys (emblem of St Peter) and a cross on small pedestal. Brick size here: $9\frac{1}{2} \times 4\frac{3}{8} \times 1\frac{3}{4}$ ins.

Domestic buildings rather confusing, but include other work attributed to Morton. 'Guard Room' (really solar) was built in brick and stone by Arundel

(1396–1414), and extended westwards by Morton with private dining-room—to gable-end in W front. Dining-room, which has original ceiling, shows contemporary withdrawing of great lords away from communal living. It has brick fireplace in N wall.

Palace brickwork is normally English bond. Dressings stone, except for a few voussoirs. Despite quality and quantity of rich red C 15 bricks, remarkable lack of moulded brick.

The Old Palace is open at certain times in the summer. Guidebook available; also, with photographs and very detailed information on buildings, 2 articles by Arthur Oswald, reprinted from *Country Life* for 8 and 15 April 1965. See also entry in Nairn and Pevsner's *Surrey*.

ESHER

Waynflete's Tower: Beside R. Mole. In grounds of Esher Place, mansion built in mid C 18 for Prime Minister, Hon. Henry Pelham, replacing late mediaeval palace of Bishops of Winchester. Water gate tower is sole remains of palace, which was comparatively small house of great see, a country posting house on London route. Bishop William Waynflete built his house here, apparently on courtyard plan and of brick, about 1470 or 1480.

Pelham employed William Kent on new mansion, retaining gate tower but giving it a 'Gothick' transformation. (Same was done to *Laughton Place*, Sussex, also Pelham property.) Waynflete had apparently employed John Cowper (later master mason at *Kirby Muxloe*, Leics.,) here and at *Farnham Castle*. (John Harvey says Cowper was perhaps also designer of *Buckden Tower*, Hunts.) Gate tower is firm, square, 3-storeyed, with 4-stage polygonal angle turrets. Stair at NW corner. Red brick, irregularly bonded with blue diaper to central section. Battlemented. Cusped corbel-tables of moulded brick. Other dressings, including plinth and stringcourses, of stone. Kent's 'Gothick' facelift gave a slightly oriental look. Built one-storey porch here, with ogee mouldings. Left the original square labels, but inserted new windows below: either (a few only) large quatrefoil openings or ogee-arched windows. Inside, evidently stuccoed rib-vaulting of entrance (Nairn and Pevsner). Mixture is much more attractive than facts suggest.

FARNHAM

The Castle *Pl. 25*

Waynflete's Tower: Brick was considerable innovation at Farnham Castle, and this tower remarkable in design too. Earlier parts of castle, including C 12 keept set in triangular bailey, are M.P.B. & W. controlled. Stone-built.

Tower is in mostly later section, belonging to Oversea Service College, on S side of site. Originally castle of Bishops of Winchester.

Waynflete's Tower dates from 1470 or 1475. A timber-framed gallery range was erected in Tudor times, for visitors' lodgings: this survives, but refaced. All early buildings stone or heavy chalk, but area has much clay—evinced by modern brickworks and potteries—and Waynflete was notable builder in brick. Held see from 1447 to 1486. In 1450s William Burgess was paid for making brick stair in a new tower, £1. 11*s*. 8*d*. Waynflete's 4-storey tower, which is not free-standing, was erected as entry to earlier Great Hall. Of deep red brick, with very dark purplish diaperwork of continuous diamonds all over surface. No stone, except battlement copings. C 18 sash windows have replaced originals. Polygonal angle turrets at front, rising a little higher than bulk of tower; also, high up on E side, a squinch-supported turret projection carrying top of stairs. Turrets have few windows: original windows throughout tower either replaced or blocked up (outlines visible). Entrance has 4-centred arch of moulded brick, not in centre of wall but uniquely placed to side—set into base of SE turret.

With 2 exceptions there is miniature cusped corbelling round top of tower, with second line of corbelling to turrets. Exceptions constitute most notable feature of tower: on S and W sides, stretching in layers of mouldings down from projecting parapets, are extremely deep *false* machicolations (capable of casting still deeper indented shadows). Tower is powerful structure—with tall W and S faces and E face made squarer by projections (N hidden)—but defensibility sham. Elements treated as motifs alone. Mason thought to have been John Cowper (see *Esher* entry above). Nairn and Pevsner stress 'subtle asymmetry' as Renaissance refinement, lacking in simpler Esher tower.

Sometimes called 'Fox's Tower' after Richard Fox, Bishop of Winchester from 1500 to 1528—who became blind during this period, so special regular steps were constructed for him up to castle keep (replacing drawbridge). He worked for Henry VII and then Henry VIII, holding office of Lord Privy Seal, but was removed from real power by Wolsey, who, in 1528, also removed him from bishopric. Fox repaired and altered tower and adjoining buildings. Another brick building connected with him is Holy Ghost Chapel at *Basingstoke*, and he built in brick at *Bishop's Waltham* (Hants).

Nairn & Pevsner, *Surrey*, 1962; Oversea Service College's booklet history of Farnham Castle.

KINGSTON UPON THAMES

Wolsey's Conduit-Houses: In 1516 Wolsey had pure water for Hampton

Court Palace channelled in lead pipes, for $3\frac{1}{2}$ m., from Kingston Hill and Coombe Hill. Three conduit-houses remain here, 2 of them pairs (so 5 structures in all). Wolsey most probably never saw these conduits, for he had superstitious fear of name 'Kingston' and avoided the place, even though on the direct route between Hampton Court and Westminster. ('Kingston' proved to be a man, Sir William Kingston, Constable of the Tower, sent to take him into custody in 1530.)

Gallows Conduit, in grounds of 'Wolsey Spring', George Rd, best-preserved. About 14 ft square, with 'pitched roof' of tile. Has some diapering —thought to be Wolsey's monogram—on plinth. Ivy Conduit, short distance to E, in grounds of Convent of Holy Family. Coombe Conduit is off Coombe Lane West (in grounds of 'recently demolished' 'Coombe Springs'). Retains underground passage connecting its 2 buildings. All are built of red brick, with some stone dressings.

At intervals along pipes were 'tamkins', small buildings where water supply might be temporarily plugged. Gallows Tamkin is complete, with gabled ends.

Nairn & Pevsner; *article* by J. W. Lindus Forge, in *Surrey Archaeological Collections* vol. 56, 1959.

NONSUCH PARK

Nonsuch Park: Site of great Tudor Palace, recently excavated. Brick was only subsidiary material.

RICHMOND

(London Borough of Richmond-upon-Thames, 1965)

Richmond Palace: In Old Palace Yard remains of brick palace built by Henry VII from about 1499. Given new name of 'Richmond' from his title of Earl of Richmond (Yorks). Older name was Sheen (or Shene). As early as 1125 Henry I held manor. Old Palace Yard was once base court, still entered through Early Tudor brick Gatehouse.

Building records always seem to involve brick. In mid C 14 Edward III converted then manor house into palace: record of *c.* 1365 that 'wall tiles' were bought, at 5*s.* 6*d.* to 10*s.* a thousand, for royal manors of *Eltham* (London) and 'Shene'. Then Richard II had part of palace razed, because his Queen, Anne of Bohemia, had died there, and palace was abandoned. Henry V rebuilt, a London chronicler in 1414 noting 'the kynges grete werk begonne at Sheen'; 1413–14 Chancery records show collection of materials, including bricks from Calais; in 1422 Treasurer of Calais supplied 114,000 bricks, used for walls and chimneys of outer ward. Brick-building continued for Henry VI.

Bricks were also made locally, at Petersham. In 1440, Henry VI's 'Sergeant', William Vesey, supplied 9,500 'breke' at 4*s*. 6*d*. a thousand. In 1444 there were more supplied from Calais.

In 1498 Henry VII had planned to spend Christmas at the palace, when it was gutted by fire. He rebuilt, in his turn, with rare extravagance. Looking at old engravings, Nairn and Pevsner see 'a forest of towers with bulbous tops . . . and hints at elevations like Henry VII's Chapel or Thornbury Castle, using mannered, exaggerated vertical strips of windows'. Privy Lodging, where Henry VII died, had 14 turrets. Great chapel is identifiable from engravings, a structure comparable to King's College Chapel, Cambridge. After Civil War—it was sold in 1649—palace declined. And, despite residence by Georges I, II and III, in C 18 most of buildings were demolished. The mainly brick palace of Henry VII was a controlled Renaissance fantasy, fairly symmetrical, built round 3-storey inner court and 2-storey base court. Latter evidently had galleries like Thornbury Castle's, round yard 200 ft square. 'Fantasy' surely fair word, though Richmond was not a Nonsuch. Turrets were 6 storeys high—one can count a dozen in one C 17 riverside view—while main tower had 120 steps. Complete brick curtain, with interval towers.

What remains? There is the Gatehouse and some buildings, known as 'Wardrobe Court', at right-angles to it. In C 18 partial rebuilding, but so-called 'Old Palace', adjoining Gatehouse and Wardrobe, also retains or has reused Tudor brick. 'The house attached on the l. of the Gateway, called the OLD PALACE, is a symmetrical castellated brick house . . . partly made up of Tudor material, but in its appearance essentially C 18 Gothic' (Nairn and Pevsner). Three 3-storey oriels at front: Gatehouse adjoins one of them. Entrance arch is wide, with stone dressings. Above it a worn stone panel with shield and supporters of Henry VII. Single line of renewed windows. Through gateway, with its taller inner arch, we find the Wardbrobe has much Tudor brick, including diamond diapering. This was once part of S side of inner court. Gap between engravings and present reality is immense.

Nairn and Pevsner; Neville Williams, *The Royal Residence of Great Britain*; ed. H. M. Colvin, *The History of the King's Works*, vol. 2.

SUTTON PLACE *Fig. 19*; *Pls. 54–57*

In parish of Send, but isolated. Built in 1520s. One of great houses of England, but can be described as 'way out', untypical. Originally quadrangle, with N range or screen set back a few feet. No angle towers. Renaissance ornament in cream terracotta on courtyard walls and S façade. Quadrangle broken in 1786 through demolition of N range, including gatehouse. Gatehouse was 70 ft high, but hardly fortified. 1782 drawing of this survives. Builder, Sir Richard Weston (died 1542), granted estate in 1521. He held such offices as Under-Treasurer, Treasurer of Calais, Privy Councillor.

Weston's rebus features among repeated terracotta motifs. James Lees-Milne cites 'some forty or fifty different moulds'. Windows have Renaissance decoration but cusped Gothic form, rather like *Layer Marney* (Essex). Square labels to windows and doors. Two-storey house of red brick, diamond-diapered where continuous terracotta panelling is absent. Decorative friezes of moulded brick at parapet level. Some of terracotta also red, particularly knobbly balusters dividing up panels of Italianate cherubs. Despite much Gothic detail mansion notable for exterior symmetry, major examples being in courtyard face of S wing where great hall is: for matching purposes, tall one-storey great hall has 2 separate rows of windows, while of twin bay windows here one lights great hall itself and the other (quite out of interior scale) lights only a small passage. Round outside of house plain polygonal chimneys. Simple indented dog tooth courses at eaves. Crow-stepped gables to N end of W and E wings. Real defenceless mansion—'prospect house' built beside R. Wey. (Not open to public.)

For the decoration see the chapter on 'Terracotta'.

Nairn and Pevsner, *Surrey*, 1962; *articles* by H. Avray Tipping in *Country Life* 7 and 14 February 1914; James Lees-Milne, *Tudor Renaissance*, 1951.

WEST HORSLEY

The Place: House of mixed dates and materials, mainly brick. Major work by Sir A. Browne, Henry VIII's Master of the Horse, in early years of C 16: this visible at rear and sides, but front mainly Georgian. Browne later grantee of great Battle Abbey, Sussex, where stone buildings converted for mansion.

Further examples of buildings in Surrey with early brickwork are:
Albury Church of SS Peter and Paul; *Lingfield* Pollard House; *Old Woking* Old Hall Barn (relic of palace of Henry VIII); *Send* Church of St Mary (Studgrove); *Weybridge* Oatlands Palace enclosure wall (Thames St).

SUSSEX

BODIAM

**Bodiam Castle:* National Trust. Of 1380s, stone-built. Several firebacks of horizontally laid tiles; big brick kitchen fireplace and tile-lined oven.

CAMBER CASTLE

On Rother estuary. Defences reduced 1642, during Civil War. Though castle is ruin, its ground-plan still clear: in main one of Henry VIII's lobed coastal fortresses, erected against French invasion scare. Exchequer rolls show £23,000 spent here between 1539 and 1543. Incorporated in new fortress, with linking covered way, was an earlier fortified tower. For this Sir Edward Guldeford had been responsible, receiving £1,000 in payment from the Exchequer about 1511. Exterior stone, interior yellowish brick.

Nairn and Pevsner.

COWDRAY HOUSE

Near Midhurst. Erected from 1539. Known as 'Buck Hall'. Work still continuing in Elizabethan period but in Early Tudor style. Ruined by 1793 fire. Main survivals, gatehouse, hall and chapel. Parts of mediaeval house on site had been used. Cowdray is monument to one of Tudor 'new men', a favourite of Henry VIII: Sir William Fitzwilliam, later Earl of Southampton (next holder of title was Wriothesley of *Titchfield*) and Lord High Admiral of England (1539). Hall porch, despite Gothic exterior, has fan-vault decorated with cherubs' heads, initials 'WS' (William Southampton) and anchor badges. Exterior of house stone, but brick had useful structural and domestic roles. Some brick walling remains and brick was used as coring. Shows in interior fabric of great hall, particularly in window recesses—as in chapel—and in 2 fireplaces with herringbone fire-backs. Five square brick chimneys remain, shafts set diagonally in Late Tudor manner.

EAST GULDEFORD

St Mary's Church: Built after reclamation of salt land in Romney Marsh. Faculty, giving permission to establish new church, dated 1499 (Nairn and Pevsner). Church consecrated 1505. Builder Sir Harry Guldeford, local lord. There survive panels with his arms. Exterior was altered about 1820, and original timber aisle arcades have been removed. Church has double-peaked tiled roof and slatted belfry in 'V' of roof at W end (no tower). Despite changes, very much of piece and period. Early Tudor brick walls, brick floor, simple brick piscina (plastered over). This last a rarity: see also *Chignal Smealy*, Essex. Buttresses have stone copings. Most of brick window jambs survive, the stone mullions looking like replacements. Flattened arch of brick to big W door, with pointed arch over. Wide, squarish church, not pretty. Virtually abandoned, interior in poor repair.

HARTFIELD

Bolebrooke: C 16 gatehouse and part of gabled brick house. Both irregular in plan. Early Tudor date most likely. Gatehouse has turrets at front; polygonal angle shafts facing house; brick windows.

Nairn and Pevsner.

HURSTMONCEUX *Pl. 20*

**Hurstmonceux Castle:* (Other spellings are Hurstmonceaux and Herstmonceux.) Home of Royal Greenwich Observatory. Grounds only open to public: 2–5 p.m. Mondays, Wednesdays and Thursday (but not public holidays) from April to end of October. For detailed description see section in chapter on 'Defence and the Major Castles'.

Bibliography:

W. Douglas Simpson, 'Herstmonceux Castle', *article* in *Archaeological Journal*, XCIX, 1942.

R. Allen Brown, *English Mediaeval Castles*, 1954 (for context rather than detail).

Ian Nairn and Nikolaus Pevsner, *Sussex*, 1965.

A. Hamilton Thompson, *Military Architecture in England during the Middle Ages*, 1912.

J. C. Wedgwood, *History of Parliament . . . 1439–1509* (the vol. of *Biographies*), 1936—for Fiennes family.

**Parish Church:* Exterior presents striking contrasts of materials and styles. Body of church and squat NW tower of sandstone, ashlar and some plaster facing, with slate roof, of very late C 12. About 1440, during building of Castle, Roger Fiennes altered and added to church in red brick, using tiles of darker red for roofs. New chancel built up from stone base of old, but to lower roof level. On N side added family chapel, all brick except for thin stone plinth: the 'Dacre Chapel', from Roger's son Richard having married heiress of Sir Thomas Dacre and himself later gaining hereditary title of 'Lord Dacre'. Chancel and chapel have big Perp. windows of stone. Square brick buttresses across angles and at junction of chancel and chapel (E).

LAUGHTON *Pls. 64–68*

Laughton Place: Terracotta frieze at Halland Park Farm assuredly came from here: for it and details of Renaissance terracotta remaining at Laughton Place see chapter on 'Terracotta'.

Remnant of house at first sight both unpromising and rather odd. Till

Halland Park was built in 1595 this was main home of Pelham family, whose buckle badge in terracotta still shows above a window. Sole relic of house is ruinous tall square tower of brick. Set well inside moat. This tower was later incorporated in C 18 'Gothick' farmhouse, of which now little trace except triangular stone pediment. Some quatrefoil windows also look like later insertions (compare *Esher* tower, Surrey), but the original square brick labels and relieving arches remain.

Builder of mansion was Sir William Pelham. Date, 1534. Mainly red brick, with some black, but no regular diapering. Topless octagonal stair turret rises one stage higher than tower. Inside, stairs less well developed, as Nathaniel Lloyd pointed out, than late C 15 vaulted stairs at *Faulkbourne* (Essex) and elsewhere. Steps are rows of stretchers, resting on simple slightly curved arches of stretchers. Scallop shells embedded in mortar. Immensely thick and strong. Traditional appearance of tower almost masks surprising Renaissance terracotta details: (1) multi-cusped corbelling below parapets of tower and stair turret; (2) curling largely abstract decoration of some windows, inside and out; (3) oddity, window jamb blocks used for plinth (on sides). Delicate, surprising work, in dark red terracotta.

Pelhams were not a newly-rich family. They were long and well established in Sussex, having held government offices in county from Later Middle Ages. One basis of wealth had been monies gained by Sir John Pelham in mid C 14 fighting in France as one of Edward III's captains. Thus contrast between Sir William Pelham and some of the brick-building Early Tudor courtiers influenced by Renaissance style.

Nathaniel Lloyd, *A History of English Brickwork*, 1924.

TWINEHAM

Parish Church: Like *East Guldeford*, of Early Tudor brick, but more intact. Timber used for S porch and spire of brick tower. Much brick detail, including windows with 4-centred arches and quoins of tower. Fabric mainly English bond.

WEST WITTERING

Cakeham Manor House: Seaside site, 1 m SE of West Wittering. House of different periods: C 13, C 14, Early Tudor and Georgian (*c.* 1800). Was manor or palace of Bishops of Chichester. Oldest parts undefended, stone-built.

1447 licence to crenellate was seemingly taken up only in early C 16 by Roger Sherburne (or Sherborn), Bishop 1508–36. Revived manor, restoring and adding. Of about 1520 are the high brick tower and small 2-storey range built on to SW end of C 13 range. Tower's dressings brick, including moulded stringcourses and small square-headed windows, but no ornament. Straight parapets. May have been built simply for the views, but possibly meant as landmark for ships making for Chichester Harbour to NW (Chichester itself is 5 m. to NE, by estuary). This function might explain odd, complex shape of tower, which makes its silhouette different at every angle: it can appear, for example, almost squat *or* thin and irregular. Tower proper is 5-sided, the sides uneven, and of 3 stages: attached is the rather taller octagonal stair turret.

Arthur Oswald, *article* on 'Tudor Outlook Towers' in *Country Life Annual*, 1957; Nairn and Pevsner, *Sussex*, 1965.

Further examples of buildings in Sussex with early brickwork are:
Angmering New Place Farm; *Brede* Brede Place; *Ditchling* 'Anne of Cleves' House'; *Halnaker* Halnaker House; Hickstead House (near Twineham); *Itchingfield* Priest's House.

WARWICKSHIRE

COMPTON WYNYATES (or WYNGATES) *Fig.3(m) & 5*

Isolated great house at Compton-in-the-Hole, Tysoe. Main building material brick and that mainly of *c.* 1520. Exceptions: some earlier stone walls 4 ft thick, slate and stone roofs, stone windows. Despite harmony of colour, a complicated building with C 18 additions and C 19 repairs. Moat and other features—as well as history, the Civil War siege when neighbouring church was destroyed—remind us this was a fortified manor house, but general appearance domestic. The 1520 gatehouse bears marks of drawbridge chains, but is flush with house front and flanked by half-timbered gable-ends.

Replaced earlier house, Comptons having held site from early C 13. They still do (with Northampton title), but surprisingly it was uninhabited from 1770 to 1884, and contents auctioned 1774: the agent ignored Lord Northampton's orders to destroy Compton. Some repairs done 1835.

The earliest work dates from time of Edmund Compton, 1481–93, but main builder was his son William. Succeeded him aged 11, became favourite of Henry VIII and knighted at Tournai in 1512. Was given augmentation of royal lion, and Henry's coat-of-arms features on stone panel over gatehouse arch. Main part of house is courtyard of 4 ranges. Brickwork rose-red, with dark brick diapering in some parts, especially the front. Numerous brick chimneys with decorative mouldings. All other dressings—doors, windows, battlement copings—are stone. Sir William's resources were vast: he died holding land in 18 counties. (See also Bruce Castle, *Tottenham*, Middx.) This is rightly one of the most famous houses in England.

MAPPLEBOROUGH GREEN

Gorcott Hall: Some timber-framing and later alterations, but brickwork includes projecting chimney-stack and a porch, which is diapered. About 1540.

POLESWORTH

Pooley Hall: Originally courtyard house, but W wing with great hall destroyed. Quite sizeable tower at E end of N range and a contemporary chapel. Built in red brick, irregularly diapered. Dressings stone, except on S front which is wholly brick. There was building done late in Henry VII's reign by Cockaynes (originally Derbyshire family), but this house is apparently the major rebuilding done by Sir Thomas Cockayne from 1509.

Garner and Stratton; N. Pevsner and A. Wedgwood, *Warwickshire*, 1966.

SHELDON (BIRMINGHAM)

Sheldon Hall: Early C 16 manor house, originally in village. Diapered brick, but quoins and windows stone. Later additions, including the brick chimney-stacks (late C 16 or early C 17).

WORMLEIGHTON

Manor House: Remnant of brick mansion erected with wool trade wealth by John Spencer, grazier, about 1512. Had bought manor in 1506. Moved here from nearby old manor house in its 'lost' village, where sheep displaced houses and crop-farming. The one wing remaining has windows with square labels, but stylistically early arched lights (no cusps). (Early C 17 stone gatehouse.)

Pevsner and Wedgwood.

WILTSHIRE

CHILTON FOLIAT

Littlecote: Brick mansion, stone dressings. Mainly Elizabethan but also some early C 16 work. Pevsner (*Wiltshire*, 1963) says NW wing is C 15. Manor belonged to Darells, or Dayrells, from 1415 to 1589 (infanticide).

SALISBURY

56 The Cathedral Close: 2-storey house with some C 15 work. Fabric of this mixture of flint rubble and herringbone wall-tiling, with stone dressings and large irregular quoins. Wall tiles were concealed by plaster at beginning of century. They constitute some of few examples of genuine wall tiles, i.e. thin tiles used like bricks. Herringbone inconsistent, with a few horizontal courses. Nathaniel Lloyd compared this to early firebacks.

WEST DEAN

Tithe Barn: Near Salisbury. Barn now attached to Church Farm. Was apparently property of Mottisfont Abbey, Hants. Red brick, of early 1500s. Buttressed and large—of 13 bays.

WORCESTERSHIRE

GREAT MALVERN *Pl. 30*

Priory Gatehouse: Malvern priory was Benedictine, established late C 11. Rich, receiving benefactions from Crown and great families. Church largely mid C 15 rebuilding, vehicle for wonderful glass (*c.* 1440–1506) and local wall tiles (1,200 of them, with 90 designs). Cloisters and most monastic buildings lay S of church, but single survival is gatehouse at NW. Gabled rectangular structure, of brick. Late Perp. (C 15). The front (N face) faced with lightish local stone, with blank panel decoration, heavily restored 1891. Pevsner points out motifs those of N porch of church too, also restored. Rear (S face) English bond bricks of different reds, fairly light in tone. Square-headed windows, stone-dressed, restored.

HUDDINGTON *Fig. 10(d)*

Huddington Court: Near Droitwich (mediaeval tile-making centre). Huddington family had moated manorhouse here, obtained in mid C 15 by Wintours, who then held property till mid C 17. Moat remains. Timber-framed house erected on old site in early C 16, but later altered. Some losses. Inner angle has projecting stone chimney-stack with decorated Early Tudor moulded brick shafts. Most ornate: battlemented spur top; trefoil-headed blank niches at base; zigzags to shaft—smallest curve having shape and power of taut longbow.

KEMPSEY

The Nash: Basically red brick house of *c.* 1540–50, with C 17 and C 18 fittings. 'Much pulled about *c.* 1900' (Pevsner). Stepped gables and diapering with blue brick. Cellar with octagonal brick piers. Pevsner compares The Nash with Madresfield Court, to the SW, which is a brick Elizabethan house built for the Lygones; Madresfield retains part of S wing and layout of mid C 16.

N. Pevsner, *Worcestershire*, 1968.

WORCESTER

**Cathedral Priory Reredorter Sub-vault:* On S side of Cathedral there are remains of Benedictine monastery, including (by W range of cloisters) late C 12 dormitory and reredorter. Below reredorter (privies—'hardly a very satisfactory idea', Pevsner) was part of infirmary. The stone-walled sub-vault of this survives, but smaller than original 123 × 63 ft. Has round stone piers and 'single chamfered ribs between cells made of very large bricks'. In-filling mainly stretchers; a *little* brick among stone dressings of ribs too. Floor brick. Exact date uncertain, but C 14: probably belonging to reconstruction work done here in mid/late C 14.

Harold Brakspear, 'On the Dorter Range of Worcester Priory', *Archaeologia*, LXVII, 1916; N. Pevsner, *Worcestershire*, 1968.

YORKSHIRE

BEVERLEY (EAST RIDING)

The Friary: In Friars' Lane, NE of Minster. Remains of Dominicans' house. Founded C 13. Surrendered 1539 with about 4½ acres of land. One range survives, part stone and part Early Tudor red brick—latter mainly short projecting 3-storey wing, with some moulded brick and flattish arch with 2 rows of brick voussoirs. In Friars' Lane and East Gate parts of brick boundary walls, incorporating 2 gateways, again with brick voussoirs. Main gateway has 3 orders of mouldings, quite complex design: above, square label and stepped rounded gable, compared with Flemish or Hansa architecture.

**The Minster:* After chancel built, nave begun in 1308. Roof is plastered, but between limestone ribs of quadripartite vaulting is brick in-filling. Lloyd gave date as about 1335 and size of bricks as 10½ × 5¼ × 2 in, same as later North Bar. (Minister fabric rolls for 1445–6 itemize 'squynschontiell', chamfered bricks.)

***North Bar:** *North Bar:* Leland in early C 16 recorded: 'The toune is not waullid: But yet be there these many fair Gates of Brike, North Barre, Newbigyn Bar by West and Kellegate Barre by West also.' Instead of walls presumably earth ramparts and ditch. Town generally was timber-built, Leland says. Of the gates only North Bar survives, and so do its building accounts of 1409. Was complete rebuilding, apparently prompted by Percy rebellion against Henry IV. Cost was £96. 9*s.* 11½*d.* About 125,000 bricks used. Local source. Restored 1867.

Gate is 3-storeyed: arch carefully labelled '10 ft. 9 in.' Headroom, just enough for special local double-decker buses. (As King's Lynn South Gate, takes only one line of traffic.) Practically square ground plan, buttressed N face at 23 ft 6 in being some 2 ft wider than S face. Modern-looking stone sills and window heads, but otherwise dressings brick. Accounts mention 'squynchons', moulded chamfered bricks used for jambs and arches. Three blank niches on S front. Dentillated string-courses of unmoulded bricks. Vaulting has brick ribs and cells, but latter now plastered. Corporation still holds accounts.

Articles by Arthur Leach and John Bilson in *East Riding Antiquarian Society Transactions*, vol. IV, 1896.

BISHOPSTHORPE (WEST RIDING)

Archbishop's Palace: Still inhabited. Buildings range from mid C 13 stone chapel of Archbishop Walter de Grey to mid C 18 'Gothick' work commissioned by Archbishop Drummond. Also survive, with some later alterations, 2 late C 15 diapered brick ranges erected for Thomas Rotherham. Dark diaper patterns. Rotherham held see from 1480 to 1500–1. (See also *Buckden* (Hunts.)

BRANDESBURTON (EAST RIDING)

**Parish Church:* Clerestory late C 14 brick.

CAWOOD (WEST RIDING)

Archbishop's Palace: Also known as 'Cawood Castle'. Most demolished 1646, as had been held for Charles I. Remains long a farmhouse. Stone gatehouse attributed to Archbishop John Kempe (1426–51), but on either side are mid C 15 brick ranges. Work includes brick voussoirs to windows and brick buttresses 2 stages high. (In 1500 Rotherham died here (see Bishopsthorpe). In 1530 Wolsey was arrested here.)

EASINGTON (EAST RIDING)
**Tithe Barn:* 'Grand thatched red brick tithe-barn, in farmyard SW of church, which is said to be 14th cent.' (J. E. Morris, *Little Guide* to the East Riding).

FOSTON-ON-THE-WOLDS (EAST RIDING)
Parish Church: Clerestory C 15 brick.

HOWDEN (EAST RIDING)
**Bishop's Palace:* Relics of palace of prince-bishops of Durham, which Walter Skirlaw reconstructed (in stone) in late C 14. Palace building, much altered, now part of house. Leland in mid C 16 saw palace of stone, timber and brick. In Vicarage grounds is gateway and part of brick curtain wall, built by Cardinal Thomas Langley between 1406 and 1437. N face of the 4-centred archway is complete. Worn panel with Langley's arms. (In 1426 Langley and Henry Beaufort of Winchester see obtained licence to crenellate in brick and stone a lost building on the Manor of the More site, Rickmansworth, Herts.)

HULL (EAST RIDING)
Strictly 'Kingston upon Hull'. Mediaeval 'new town', with records of municipal brickworks beginning in 1303, but only Holy Trinity Church surviving. See Chapter I, section 2, and *Plates 9 and 10*.

Bibliography:

The Itinerary of John Leland In or About the Years 1535–1543 edited by Lucy Toulmin Smith, 1964.

F. W. Brooks, 'A Mediaeval Brick-yard at Hull', *article* in *Journal of the British Archaeological Association*, 1939.

T. F. Tout, *Mediaeval Town Planning*, Manchester University Press, reprinted 1948.

Maurice Beresford, *New Towns of the Middle Ages*, 1967.

K. J. Allison, ed., V.C.H. volume on Kingston upon Hull, 1969.

John Bartlett, *article* reporting on excavation of walls, in Hull *Museums Bulletin*, No. 4, March 1970.

Official Guide to Kingston upon Hull.

KEYNINGHAM (EAST RIDING)
Parish Church: Late Perp. clerestory of brick to chancel and nave.

ROOS (EAST RIDING)

**Parish Church:* Due E of Hull. Hull bricks used in 2nd half of C 14 for clerestory of considerable size. Windows stone.

SUTTON (EAST RIDING)

**Parish Church:* Just N of Hull. Originally chapel-of-ease to Wawne. About 1346 Sir John de Sutton, who fought at Crécy, obtained Edward III's permission to make it a collegiate church. Effigy of knight wearing 1340s armour and bearing Sutton arms, on tomb-chest on S side of chancel, is surely founder's (d. 1356). College was to have 6 priests. In 1535 worth just £13. 18*s*. 8*d*. a year. Dissolved under Chantries Act, 1546. Church was rebuilt when college founded, nave and chancel dating from this period, and aisles and tower rather later. Set inside W end, tower is supported at E by Perp. panelled, piers. All red bricks, a major building.

J. E. Morris, *The East Riding of Yorkshire*.

TEMPLEHIRST (WEST RIDING)

Temple Farm: Establishment of Order of Templars here, from which C 13 archway in porch survives. On suppression of Order in 1308, Edward III granted this 200-acre estate and *Temple Newsam* to Sir John Darcy. Thomas Lord Darcy was living in house built on site (using remains of Templars' buildings), when he led 1536 Pilgrimage of Grace against suppression of the monasteries and against other 'Protestant' measures of Henry VIII's government—for which Darcy later executed. All family property then confiscated. Interesting irony, therefore, that his estate derived from earlier suppression and sequestration. Temple Farm is mainly C 16, having red brick 2-storeyed S front with brick porch. Octagonal tower with stair, taller than main building. Pevsner (in *Yorkshire: the West Riding*, 1959) says: 'The building does not seem to have been studied in detail.' Ministry of Housing and Local Government listing officers not allowed inside (1964), 'so that its exact importance is not easy to assess'.

TEMPLE NEWSAM (WEST RIDING)

Temple Newsam House: In outer Leeds. Darcy property from 1308 suppression but forfeited 1536 (see *Templehirst* above). In reign of James I then owner, Sir Arthur Ingram, demolished major part of house and built present mansion (owned by Leeds Corporation, used as museum) with its parapet inscriptions and balusters. Thomas Lord Darcy (executed 1536) built earlier house about 1520, which was square with central courtyard: 'Ingram made an

'E'-plan house. Early Tudor survivals are W wing and a little of adjacent N and S wings, though most windows later. Stone dressings. Brick diapered with dark blue bricks. Inside, one great beam with Darcy's crest. Upper floor of W wing has small Early Tudor brick doorways. (2 floors to Ingram's 3.)

In 1521 Darcy built hospital and school at Whitkirk, adjoining Temple Newsam Park, but no remains. Also associated with Dominican *Priory* at *Beverley*.

WATTON (EAST RIDING)
Parish Church: Late Perp. and mainly brick built.

Watton Priory: Gilbertine priory, belonging to only English order, which was founded by St Gilbert of Sempringham (Lincs.). Order notable for having mixed houses. Watton was founded 1148/9 for 13 canons and 36 nuns, by Eustace Fitzjohn who gave the manor of Watton. Order did attract benefactions like this, and survived till Henrician Reformation. At Watton canons' and nuns' quarters were divided by a wall, but there were accusations of immorality. Establishment had increased. After surrender, convent stone and Tudor brick were used to convert house into secular dwelling. What survives now is still in part inhabited and partly ruinous. In C 17 much stone removed.

What is notable in brickwork is pre-Reformation: the early C 16 Prior's Lodging. Of good size, and had kitchen wing (now lost) projecting from S end. Lodging has 2 halls, of which larger is known as the 'New Hall'. Two-storeyed. Held public meeting-place and prior's private solar (dining room) and sleeping quarters. Apart from stone quoins and windows—including 2-storey oriel on W side—main part of lodging (SW block) is brick. Octagonal brick corner turrets, stage higher. Morris noted tunnel for stream.

WAWNE (EAST RIDING)
Parish Church: Perp. clerestory of brick.

WHITGIFT (WEST RIDING)
Parish Church: Church is small, mainly C 14, but W tower Perp: upper parts lined with brick.

YORK
**Merchant Adventurers' Hall:* In Walmgate, but entrance from Fossgate has stone archway with worn panel of arms of Merchants of the State. Site has complex architectural and institutional history, but great hall and undercroft

erected by charitable guild in later C 14. Taken over, with the hospital in undercroft, by merchants in early C 15. Some rebuilding then and at later dates. Apparently late mediaeval brick in ground floor, with chamfered brick window jambs on Walmgate side, though V.C.H. stresses its rarity in York before Tudors. W end of undercroft has 8 windows with 5-sided jambs. The red brick firestead with quadruple set of fireplaces seemingly dates from *c.* 1420, pierced with passages perhaps for drying wood or to reduce fire risk from concentration of heat. Rounded arches. Used for cooking for feasts, but must have benefited charity cases too.

V.C.H. *The City of York*, ed. P. M. Tillott, 1961; guidebooks by Maud Sellers.

The Red Tower: An oddity in date and material in York's 2¾ miles of stone walls. In Walmgate area, on S bank of R. Foss. As at Hull and Norwich, river made part of defences. Here faced only marshland. At one end of walls was lost Layerthorpe postern; at other end was Red Tower, possibly replacing earlier structure. On stone base, which could be derived from an older tower. Red Tower is early C 16, of red brick, known by this name at least from 1511. Small defensive structure, renovated in 1957–8 but having been altered at various dates before. Roof lowered in C 18. Square, now of 2 storeys only, with first-floor projection perhaps for stair. Windows have brick or stone dressings.

St Mary's Abbey and Abbot's Lodging (*The King's Manor*)*:* In Bootham, next York Art Gallery. Abbey was Benedictine, established after Norman Conquest. Became 'the richest and most influential Benedictine house in the north' (V.C.H.), which means a great deal if one thinks of the importance of the monasteries to the Yorkshire economy and then the strength of the anti-Reformation Pilgrimage of Grace. St Mary's surrendered in 1539, with the greater monasteries. Buildings lay between Bootham and R. Ouse.

This house was begun by Thomas Boothe after 1483, but major work that of Abbot William Sever (1485–1502) *temp.* Henry VII. Some of older abbey buildings were cleared away at this period. Sever largely used brick, still visible in NE range of King's Manor. Rest of building is post-Dissolution. Converted into headquarters of Council of the North, home of Lord President of the Council, which had delegated powers from the King to oversee order and defence in the region. At end of C 16 the then Lord President, Earl of Huntingdon (d. 1595), made considerable alterations and added buildings on NW, using brick and stone. Again remodelled in C 17.

Part attributed to Abbot Sever retains its timber ceilings and brick walls, with 2 complete brick and terracotta windows (to 1st floor) and remains of others: 'a relieving arch, a turned-off label, or a bit of terracotta' (information, E.A. Gee of the R.C.H.M.). Windows not large, usually of 3 arched lights, under brick relieving arch of alternate stretchers and pairs of headers. Mullions and transoms plainish, terracotta, hollow-chamfered. Square labels quite elaborately moulded brick.

Bibliographical section: *Historical background*

BASKERVILLE, GEOFFREY. *English Monks and the Suppression of the Monasteries*, 1st publ. 1937 (current Cape paperback).

BENNETT, H. S. *The Pastons and their England*, 1922.

BINDOFF, S. T. *Tudor England*, Penguin, 1950.

BOWLE, JOHN. *Henry VIII*, 1964.

DARBY, H. C. *Historical Geography of England Before A.D. 1800*, 1936.

DICKENS, A. G. *The English Reformation*, 1964.

and CARR, DOROTHY. *The Reformation in England to the Accession of Elizabeth I*, in series *Documents of Modern History*, Arnold paperback, 1967.

Dictionary of National Biography.

FLETCHER, ANTHONY. *Tudor Rebellions*, 1968.

GAIRDNER, JAMES, ed., *The Paston Letters*, 6 vols, 1904.

GREEN, V. H. H. *The Later Plantagenets*, 1955.

JACOB, E. F. *The Fifteenth Century*, Oxford, 1961.

KINGSFORD, C. L., ed., *The Stonor Letters and Papers*, 2 vols, Camden Series of the Royal Historical Society, 1919.

Prejudice and Promise in Fifteenth Century England, 1925.

KNOWLES, DAVID. *The Religious Orders*, Vol. II: *The End of the Middle Ages*, 1955.

LIPSON, E. *The Economic History of England*, Vol. I: *The Middle Ages*, 11th. ed., 1956.

LOCKYER, ROGER. *Henry VII*, 1968.

LYLE, HELEN M. *The Rebellion of Jack Cade, 1450*, Historical Association booklet, 1950.

MACFARLANE, K. B. 'Bastard Feudalism', *article* in *Bulletin of the Institute of Historical Research*, 1945.

MYERS, A. R. *England in the Later Middle Ages*, Penguin, 1952.

POWICKE, F. M. *The Reformation in England*, 1st publ. 1941 (current Oxford paperback).

SPELMAN, HENRY. *The History and Fate of Sacrilege Discover'd by Examples.* 'Wrote in the year 1632' and printed by John Hartley, 1698. 4th modern edition, 1895.

STEEL, A. B. 'Financial Background to the Wars of the Roses', *article* in *History*, 1955.

TAWNEY, R. H. *The Agrarian Revolution in the Sixteenth Century*, 1912.

WEDGWOOD, JOSIAH C. (First volume of) *History of Parliament: Biographies of Members of the Commons House 1439–1809*, H.M.S.O., 1936.

WOODWARD, G. W. O. *The Dissolution of the Monasteries*, 1966.

Main bibliography: *Architecture*

THE main book used was the major work by Nathaniel Lloyd, *A History of English Brickwork*, first published in 1925. General books most helpfully supplementing this were Alec Clifton-Taylor's *The Pattern of English Building*; Norman Davey's *A History of Building Materials*; Margaret E. Wood's *The English Mediaeval House*. W. Douglas Simpson's articles on the later mediaeval brick-built castles were essential. For houses, *The Domestic Architecture of England during the Tudor Period*, by Garner and Stratton, liberally illustrated the late fifteenth and sixteenth centuries. The 1913 article by the Rev. J. Kestell Floyer, although outdated in its thesis of overriding French influence on the architectural plans of nobles returning from the wars, was a useful grouping. The sources for churches built of brick are more scattered. Fortunately for students Professor Nikolaus Pevsner's *Buildings of England* series has covered most of the Eastern Counties. The East Riding of Yorkshire, however, still lacks an inventory (no R.C.H.M. or Pevsner and the V.C.H. incomplete). The literature on Kent was also inadequate for our purposes, but two *Buildings of England* series volumes, by John Newman, appeared in May 1970.

The works cited in the bibliography are listed alphabetically under author, including the Ministry of Works (or, now, Ministry of Public Buildings and Works) pamphlet guidebooks. Articles are likewise listed under author's name. In addition, some main references are given in the gazetteer. It proved impracticable to group the sources by place, as they were such an uneven mixture of guides, articles, entries in topographical books and some detailed sections in general architectural books. For some interesting buildings there is virtually no guide but the eye.

ANDREWS, FRANCIS B. *The Mediaeval Builder and His Methods*, Oxford, 1925.

ATKINSON, THOMAS DINHAM. *The Local Style in English Architecture*, Batsford, 1947.

BARNES, H. D., and SIMPSON, W. DOUGLAS, ed. 'The Building Accounts of Caister Castle A.D. 1432–1435', *article* in *Norfolk Archaeology*, XXX, 1952. 'Caister Castle', *article* in *Antiquaries Journal*, XXXII, Jan.–April 1952.

BEDINGFIELD, A. L. *Oxburgh Hall, Norfolk*, booklet published by the National Trust, 1968.

BIDDLE, MARTIN, *et al.* 'The Excavation of the Manor of The More', *article* in *Archaeological Journal*, CXVI, 1959.

BILSON, JOHN. 'The North Bar, Beverley', *article* in *East Riding Antiquarian Society Transactions*, IV, 1896 (publ. Hull). The same volume has an article by Arthur Leach, 'The Building of Beverley Bar', giving the complete accounts of 1408–9.

BROOKS, F. W. 'A Mediaeval Brick-yard at Hull', *article* in *Journal of the British Archaeological Association*, 3rd series, vol. IV, 1939.

BROWN, R. ALLEN. *British Mediaeval Castles*, Batsford, 1954.

CAUTLEY, H. MUNRO. *Norfolk Churches*, 1949.
Suffolk Churches and their Treasures, 1937.

CHETTLE, G. H. *Hampton Court Palace*, H.M.S.O. guide, 1950–5.

CLAPHAM, ALFRED, and REYNOLDS, P. K. B. *Thornton Abbey, Lincolnshire*, Ministry of Works guide, 1961.

CLIFTON-TAYLOR, ALEC. *The Pattern of English Building*, 1952.

COLLIER, J. P., ed. *Howard Household Book*, 1844.

COLVIN, H. M., ed. *The History of the King's Works*, vols 1 and 2, *The Middle Ages*, by R. Allen Brown, H. M. Colvin and A. J. Taylor, Ministry of Works, 1963.

COOK, OLIVE. *The English House through Seven Centuries*, with photographs by Edwin Smith, Nelson, 1968.

CURZON, THE LATE MARQUIS OF KEDLESTON, and TIPPING, H. AVRAY. *Tattershall Castle, Lincolnshire: a historical and descriptive survey*, 1929.

DAVEY, NORMAN. *Building in Britain*, 1964.
A History of Building Materials, Phoenix, 1961.

DAVIS, K. RUTHERFORD. *St Olave's Priory, Herringfleet*, (Suffolk), Ministry of Works guide, 1949.

DENT, JOHN. *The Quest for Nonsuch*, 1962.

DUGDALE, GEORGE S. *Whitehall Through the Centuries*, 1950.

EVANS, JOAN. *English Art 1307–1461*, Oxford, 1949.

FIRMAN, RONALD JOHN and PATRICIA ELEANOR. 'A Geological Approach to the Study of Mediaeval Bricks', *article* in *The Mercian Geologist*, vol. 2, no. 3, 1967.

FLOYER, J. KESTELL. 'English Brick Buildings of the Fifteenth Century', *article* in *Archaeological Journal*, LXX, 1913.

GAGE, JOHN. *The History and Antiquities of Hengrave*, 1822.
The History and Antiquities of Suffolk; Thingoe Hundred, 1838.

GARNER, T., and STRATTON, A. *The Domestic Architecture of England during the Tudor Period*, 2 vols, 2nd ed., 1929.

GOTCH, J. ALFRED. *Early Renaissance Architecture in England*, 1901.

HARLECH, LORD. *East Anglia and the Midlands*, H.M.S.O., 2nd ed., 1955.

HARROD, W., and LINNELL, C. L. S. *Norfolk: A Shell Guide*, Faber & Faber, 1957.

HARVEY, JOHN. *English Mediaeval Architects*, 1954.
Gothic England, 1948.
William Worcestre: Itineraries, Oxford, 1969.

HEATH, SIDNEY. *Old English Houses of Alms*, 1910.

HUGHES, PENNETHORNE. *Kent: A Shell Guide*, Faber & Faber, 1969.

JACOB, E. F. *The Fifteenth Century*, Oxford, 1961.

JAMES, M. R. *Norfolk and Suffolk*, 1930.

JESSUP, RONALD A. *Kent* in the *Little Guides* series, 7th ed., based on the original guide by J. Charles Cox, 1950.

JONES, T. L. *Ashby de la Zouch Castle, Leicestershire*, Ministry of Works guide, 1953.

KELLY, ALISON. *The Book of English Fireplaces*, 1968.

KNOOP, D. and JONES, G. P. *The Mediaeval Mason: An Economic History of Stone Building*, Manchester University Press, 1931 (3rd ed., 1967).

LAW, ERNEST. *A Short History of Hampton Court*, new ed., 1924.

LEES-MILNE, JAMES. *Tudor Renaissance*, Batsford, 1951.

LLOYD, NATHANIEL. *A History of English Brickwork, with Examples and Notes of the Architectural Use and Manipulation of Brick from Mediaeval Times to the end of the Georgian Period*, published by H. G. Montgomery, 1925; New Edition, 1935.
A History of the English House, Architectural Press, 1931/reprint, 1951.

LONDON COUNTY COUNCIL. *Survey of London* volumes, published from 1900 on.

MAJENDIE, S. A. *Some Account of the Family of de Vere, the Earls of Oxford, and of Castle Hedingham in Essex*, 1904.

MESSENT, C. J. W. *The Monastic Remains of Norfolk and Suffolk*, 1934.

Parish Churches of Norfolk and Norwich, 1936.

Suffolk and Cambridgeshire, Penguin Guide, 1949.

NAIRN, IAN, and PEVSNER, NIKOLAUS. *Surrey*, Penguin *Buildings of England* series, 1962.

Sussex, Penguin *Buildings of England* series, 1965.

NEWMAN, JOHN. *North East Kent and East Kent*, Penguin *Buildings of England* series, 1970.

West Kent and the Weald, Penguin *Buildings of England* series, 1970.

OLIVER, BASIL. *Old Houses and Village Buildings in East Anglia*, 1912.

OSWALD, ARTHUR. 'The Old Palace, Croydon', *articles* in *Country Life*, 8 and 15 April, 1965.

'Tudor Outlook Towers', *article* in *Country Life Annual*, 1957 (pp. 84–7).

PEERS, CHARLES. *Kirby Muxloe Castle, Leicestershire*, Ministry of Works guide, 1957.

PEVSNER, NIKOLAUS. *Bedfordshire, Huntingdon and Peterborough*, Penguin *Buildings of England* series, 1968.

Buckinghamshire, Penguin, 1960.

Cambridgeshire, Penguin, 1954.

Hertfordshire, Penguin, 1953.

Leicestershire and Rutland, Penguin, 1960.

Middlesex, Penguin, 1951.

North-East Norfolk and Norwich, Penguin, 1962.

North-West and South Norfolk, Penguin, 1962.

Suffolk, Penguin, 1961.

Yorkshire: the West Riding, Penguin, 1959.

'Mannerism and Elizabethan Architecture II', *article* in *The Listener*, 5 March 1964 (for Layer Marney).

with HARRIS, JOHN. *Lincolnshire*, Penguin *Buildings of England* series, 1964.

and RADCLIFFE, ENID. *Essex*, Penguin, 2nd ed., revised by Enid Radcliffe, 1965.

POLRUAN A. M. 'The Art of the Local Brickermaker', *article* in *Country Life*, 27 Sept. 1956.

RAIT, R. S., ed. *English Episcopal Palaces: Province of Canterbury*, 1910.

ROBBINS, MICHAEL. *Middlesex*, Collins, 1953.

ROYAL COMMISSION ON HISTORIC MONUMENTS:

1. The most relevant volumes published by the R.C.H.M.:
   Cambridge (town only), I & II, 1959.
   Essex, I–IV, 1916–23.
   Hertfordshire, 1910.
   London, II, IV & V, 1925–30.
   Middlesex, 1937.
2. Facilities:
   The NATIONAL MONUMENTS RECORD, consisting of '600,000 items', linked with the Ministry of Housing and Local Government Historic Buildings listing section. The M.H.L.G. lists cover over 100,000 buildings of 'special architectural or historic interest' in England and Wales (incomplete for rural areas).

SALZMAN, L. F. *Building in England Down to 1540: A Documentary History*, Oxford, 1952.

English Industries of the Middle Ages, 1923.

SCARFE, NORMAN. *Essex: A Shell Guide*, Faber & Faber, 1968.

Suffolk: A Shell Guide, 1960.

SIMPSON, W. DOUGLAS. *Castles in England and Wales*, 1969.

' "Bastard Feudalism" and the later Castles', *article* in *Antiquaries' Journal*, vol. XXVI, 1946.

'Buckden Palace', *article* in *Journal of the British Archaeological Association*, 3rd series, 1937.

'Herstmonceux Castle', *article* in *Archaeological Journal*, vol. XCIX, 1942.

The Building Accounts of Tattershall Castle 1434–1472, published by the Lincoln Record Society (Lincoln), 1960.

'The Affinities of Lord Cromwell's Towerhouse at Tattershall', *article* in *Journal of the British Archaeological Association*, New Series, XL, 1935.

SMALL, TUNSTALL, and WOODBRIDGE, CHRISTOPHER. *English Brickwork Details 1450–1750, A Portfolio of full-size Mouldings*, The Architectural Press, n/d.

SMITH, LUCY TOULMIN, ed., *The Itinerary of John Leland*, 5 vols, Centuar Press, London, 1964.

THOMPSON, A. HAMILTON. *Military Architecture in England during the Middle Ages*, 1912.

'The Building Accounts of Kirby Muxloe Castle, 1480–4', *article* in *Transactions of the Leicester Archaeological Society*, vol. XI, 1915–16 (other articles on Kirby Muxloe in same issue).

Tattershall Castle, guide published by the National Trust, 1946.

THOROLD, HENRY, and YATES, JACK. *Lincolnshire: A Shell Guide*, Faber & Faber, 1965.

TIPPING, H. AVRAY. *Articles* on 'Sutton Place, near Guildford', in *Country Life*, 7 and 14 February 1914.

TURNER, HENRY HUDSON, and PARKER, HENRY. *Some Accounts of the Domestic Architecture in England*, 3 vols, 1851–9. Especially vol. iii (published in 2 parts, separately bound) on the period of Richard II–Henry VIII.

VALE, EDMUND. *Cambridge and its Colleges*, Methuen *Little Guide*, 1959.

WEBB, GEOFFREY. *Architecture in Britain: the Middle Ages*, Pelican History of Art, 1956.

WHINNEY, MARGARET. *Sculpture in Britain, 1530–1830*, Pelican *History of Art*, 1964.

WILLIAMS, NEVILLE. *The Royal Residences of Great Britain*, 1960.

WOOD, MARGARET E. *The English Mediaeval House*, Phoenix, 1965.

YARWOOD, DOREEN. *The Architecture of England*, Batsford, 1963.

Glossary: Technical terms and background notes

THE majority of the technical terms are architectural. Further reference should be made to *The Penguin Dictionary of Architecture*, by Fleming, Honour and Pevsner, or a similar work. Other technical terms concern decoration, heraldry and relevant geology. The background notes are historical, mainly concerning institutions of the Later Middle Ages and the Early Tudor period, with certain events such as rebellions.

Details are usually given under the main term, rather than under any qualification: for example, types of *Arches* and *Vaulting* are given under those headings, and parts of chimneys under *Chimneys*. *Machicolation* and false machicolation appear under the former. On the other hand, particularly with the historical terms, an established phrase may be given under the first word in the phrase. Examples of such phrases are *Court* of Augmentations and *Order* of the Garter. In addition to dynasties of the royal family, the *de Vere* and *de la Pole* families are included (under 'D').

Cross-references are indicated by italics.

ABBEY: Monastic establishment headed by Abbot. Superior to, and so tending to be larger than priory. Organized under a particular set of rules: see *Orders*.

ACANTHUS: Used with *Corinthian* column in particular, for the capital. Plant with thick, fleshy, scalloped leaves. Formalized for classical and Renaissance decoration.

ACROTERION: Plural, *acroteria*. A block carved with foliage or with the formalized version of the honeysuckle flower, used on the end or at the top of a classical pediment. (An alternative term is archifix.)

ACT OF SUPREMACY: Legislation of 1534, which made the monarch head of the church in England, 'as far as the law of Christ allows'.

ADDORSED: Mainly heraldic term, of pairs of animals or birds placed back to back.

ADULTERINE: Unlicensed castles, particularly of twelfth century in the anarchic reign of Stephen. See *Licence to crenellate.*

AISLE: Side section or passages of a church.

ALURE: Cat-walk, supported on arches, behind parapet of *curtain-wall.*

AMORINI: Or, *putti.* Italianate cherubs.

ANCASTER STONE: Quarried south-west of Sleaford, in Lincolnshire. Geologically, old limestone. Light-coloured.

ANCHORITE: Person not in holy orders or a monastic order, but living an enclosed life in a cell attached to the wall of the chancel of a church.

ANGLE: Corner of a building or meeting of two walls.

ARABESQUE: Non-realistic interlacing of leaves—or scrollwork. Italianate Renaissance motifs.

ARCADE: Row of arches, either free-standing or blank (against a wall). Free-standing arcade divides nave and aisles of church. Arcading in relief may be used for wall-decoration.

ARCHES: The shape of the arch is one of the chief guides to the date of a building. After the pointed arches of *Early English* and *Gothic* building, the arch became flatter, and this is characteristic of Late Perpendicular and Early Tudor building. These are the later types: *Four-centred*: Very shallow pitch. Four-centred means being formed of two pairs of arcs taken from centres on and below the springers. A slight point.

Tudor Arch: The typical archway for large doors. A *depressed* or *dropped* arch (alternative terms), being a flattened *four-centred* arch. Has a shallow point. Slightly ogival above the curved springers.

Segmental Arch: Segment-headed, being flattish arch, without true springers.

ASHLAR-FACED: Any continuous stone facing, that is thin slabs of stone worked to dress some other material, such as rough stone, flint.

ATTAINDER: Sentence passed by Parliament on a person accused of treason.

AUGMENTATION: Heraldic term. Addition to coat of arms. Royal mark of honour; for example, the royal lion granted by Henry VIII to Sir William Compton of Compton Wynyates.

AUGUSTINIAN: Sometimes abbreviated to *Austin. Order* of regular canons, influenced by the *Cistercians.*

BADGE: Heraldic badge. Usually crest of coat of arms, utilized for marking livery or parts of a building erected by the owner of the badge.

BAILEY: Castle enclosure. Might be double, giving inner and outer baileys. Origin defensive, but might be used also for outbuildings.

BALUSTER: Short post or pillar supporting horizontal rail or moulding in a series. May be carved in relief.

BAR: Town gate.

BARBICAN: Outwork protecting gateway.

BARGE-ARCH: Low or basement arch used for reception of goods brought by water.

BARNACK STONE: Derived from Barnack (this original quarry exhausted by mid C 14), Northamptonshire, a major source of stone for mediaeval building and facings. Geologically, oolitic limestone. Quarries situated between Peterborough and Stamford. Stone transported by River Welland, etc., to East Anglia.

BASE: (1) Bottom part of a shield, heraldic.
(2) Outer courtyard (mediaeval term).

'BASTARD FEUDALISM': Developed from the late thirteenth century, basically retainers linked to lords by indentures, with a diminution of connection with land and with the King (as overall feudal lord). Particularly associated with the private armies of lords in the Later Middle Ages, in contrast to the feudal army of the king, which could be called for wartime service only and that limited to forty days. Compare *Feudalism.*

BATTER: Sloping face of wall at base of building, for strength or defence.

BATTLEMENTS: Parapet with alternate raised sections, allowing shelter for defenders. Mediaeval term, *crenellation.* Used also for decoration as the need for defence fell away.

BAY: (1) *Arcade:* in a free-standing arcade each section is described as a bay.
(2) Bay window: projecting window, semicircular or polygonal, rising from ground level.

BEAUFORT: Family derived from affair of John of Gaunt, Duke of Lancaster (son of Edward III and uncle of Richard II) with Katherine Swinford or Roet. Legitimization shaky, but the relationship was one of the claims of Henry VII to the throne, his mother being Lady Margaret Beaufort.

BEDEHOUSE: Almshouses (or hospitals).

BELL-OPENINGS: Or louvers. Small, sometimes slatted, openings to the bell-chambers of church towers.

BENEDICTINE: *Order* following rule of St Benedict (about 550).

BENEVOLENCES: Forced loans taken by the crown, one of Henry VII's sources of income.

BILLET MOULDING: Bands of short cylinders, rectangles or squares at regular intervals, in relief, decorative. This ornament appears on Prior Overton's Tower at Repton (Derybshire).

BISHOPRIC: Or 'see'. Jurisdiction of a particular bishop, overseeing churches and those monasteries subject to his visitation. A bishop would have feudal or manorial jurisdiction in certain places.

BLACK DEATH: General outbreak of bubonic plague in Europe, reaching England in 1349, with further outbreaks in 1361 and afterwards. A fairly *conservative* estimate is that one-third of population died in 1349. Caused some '*lost villages*'. Demand for labour afterwards gave some freedom to labourers to move and to ask higher wages, which the Statute of Labourers attempted to keep down. These changes ultimately led to 1381 *Peasants' Revolt*.

BLACKFRIARS: See *Dominicans*.

BLANK: Blank, or blind, work is relief work used decoratively: architectural features set in a wall, without any function except decoration.

'BLUE' BRICKS: Colour may be added to bricks, but the dark bricks used for late mediaeval and Early Tudor diaperwork were normally of blue clay or were harder fired.

BOND: The way in which bricks are laid. If only the ends of the bricks showed, this would be *Header Bond*; if only the sides showed this would be *Stretcher Bond*. More usually, a combination is used, for greater strength. The regular bond of thd pre-Elizabethan period is English.

English Bond: This bond had become firmly established by the mid sixteenth century and was used till the eighteenth century, when commonly replaced by Flemish Bond. The bond consists of alternate rows of headers and stretchers, giving a more varied wall surface than Flemish bond.

Flemish Bond: Used early seventeenth century and typical of eighteenth century. It is now the standard bond, and is therefore thought of as modern. It consists of headers and stretchers laid alternately in each row.

BOSS: Projection at join of vaulting ribs.

BRICK-AXE: Used for shaping bricks at the building site. See also *Cut brick*.

BRICK-EARTH: Alternative term for clay suitable for brick-making.

BULLNOSE: Shaped bricks coming to a blunted point, used for the mouldings of arches, vaulting ribs or *quoins*.

BUTTRESS: Slanting projection, strengthening building, typical of late mediaeval and Early Tudor church towers and gatehouses and the side walls of long ranges.

Angle buttresses: pairs of buttresses meeting at the angle of a building, meeting each other at 90 degrees.

Diagonal buttresses: placed across angle, at 45 degrees to the walls of the main structure.

CADE'S REBELLION: 1450. Concentrated in Kent and South-East. Leader, Jack Cade. Caused by economic changes such as rising prices and taxation. Preceded by political murders, of government officials associated with taxation for the French war.

CAEN STONE: Imported from Normandy for much South-East architecture. Economical for facings.

CANTED: Skewed joints, such as those of the bricks used for polygonal chimney-shafts. The face is bevelled (oblique).

CANTERBURY, SEE OF: One of the two archbishoprics. Often provided royal officers—especially Lords Chancellor.

CAPITAL: Head of column.

CARMELITES: Whitefriars. First established about 1154 in Palestine, retaining missionary emphasis.

CARSTONE: Dark rough stone found in North-West and North Norfolk, a type of ragstone. Not malleable, so not used for fine work.

CARTHUSIAN: Strict monastic *order* founded by St Bruno of Chartreux. A few houses in England, the first in 1180, known as 'charterhouses'.

CARVING: Some brick carved, or *cut*.

CAVETTO: Hollow or concave mouldings. With Gothic architecture, applied to shallow mouldings about one-quarter of a circle in section.

'CAVO RELIEVO': Opposite of relief. Carving sunk below the surface. Cut away.

CELL: (1) in vaulting: the in-filling between the ribs;
(2) a small room, such as a monastic cell or a side-chamber off the main rooms of a tower-house;
(3) small 'house' subordinate to any abbey or priory elsewhere.

CHAMFER: Strictly an edge shaved off at an angle of 45 degrees.
Hollow chamfer: The edge scooped away further, instead of flat surface.
Double-chamfered: Projection, such as moulding, chamfered off at both sides.

CHANCEL: Eastern part of church, containing choir and sanctuary. Divided from nave (the congregation) by the chancel arch which, in the Middle Ages, invariably had a screen below.

CHANCELLOR: Chief royal official, but closer to state than king in that the chancellor was not an *intimate* official.

CHANTRY: Chantries were foundations of different types, all involving the saying of masses for the soul of the dead founder. A chantry priest had a 'sinecure', being without care of living souls—unlike the parish priest of the church where these masses would be said or, literally, chanted. Funds were left by the founder's will (testament). A table-top tomb would be used as altar, perhaps in a side-chapel of its own. Attached, by a rich founder, might be a college or almhouse. One of the credos of Protestantism was that God was not to be bribed in his judgement by prayers for the dead, and this was one justification for the Act of 1547, at the beginning of the reign of Edward VI, which suppressed all forms of chantry. One that escaped was the de la Pole almshouse at Ewelme, Oxfordshire, because this was partly under royal patronage.

CHAPEL-OF-EASE: These chapels are now either abandoned or have the status of parish churches. They may be recognizable visually, from their having no real division between the nave and the chancel. Originally inferior in status to a parish church, being built to serve some isolated area inside the parish boundary, such as one liable to be cut off by floods. The 'ease' means easing the burden of travel.

CHARNEL: Or bone-house. Bones stored after period of burial, allowing reuse of churchyard space. Typically a vaulted room under the chancel.

CHARTERHOUSE: House of *Carthusian* order.

CHEQUER: Alternate checks or squares of light and dark colouring, used in several different ways.

(1) In architecture, squares of different building materials.

(2) In heraldry, a shield may have a chequer pattern.

CHEVRON: An inverted 'V' shape, used in several different ways. In architecture, such uses as decorating Norman arches and, much later, zigzagging diaperwork in brick walls. In heraldry the chevron is a familiar heraldic *charge*.

CHIMNEYS: The parts of the chimney are:

Chimney-breast: Sole part of chimney projecting *inside* the building, supported by a bar or lintel, though the chimney-breast may be flush with the wall. Contains the flue, which will split higher up if there is more than one shaft.

Chimney-shaft: When the chimney rises high above the roof line, a single flue (contained in a detached column) is called a shaft.

Chimney-stack: (1) Several flues in a group, a number of shafts rising from one stack. (2) Whole projecting chimney-stack, built out from the wall of the building. Common both to cottage and great house, though in latter may be supplement to central hearth.

Moulded and cut brick chimneys typical of the Early Tudor period, being described by Pevsner as 'gloriously over-decorated', which expands the vocabulary needed to describe them. Unornamented shafts of this period were typically round but, being made of unmoulded short bricks, have a knobbly appearance. Other shafts polygonal, utilizing *canted* bricks, also needed for the various *twists*.

Continuous patterning of the shafts, with shapes such as squares, diamonds or hexagons, may be called *diaper* work. The tops or heads of the shafts may also be ornate: *star-tops* having one or two stars; *spur-tops* having blunted points with *scallops* between.

The *lantern-type* of chimney is usually earlier in date, but an example of 1514 is found at Thornbury Castle (Glos): the flue is hooded, with vents round the top of the shaft.

CILL: Base for timber arcade.

CISTERCIAN: Monastic *order* founded in 1098. Strict *Benedictine*. Secluded houses, with emphasis on manual labour, which combination encouraged the development of sheep farming by the Yorkshire monasteries.

CLASSICAL: Elements of Greek or Roman structures, revived in Renaissance.

CLAYPIT: Source of clay for brick-making and site where bricks made. Normally close to the building site.

CLERESTORY: Upper section of main (nave) walls of church, pierced with smallish close windows—introduced to increase the light in the church.

CLERK: Person in holy orders. Related to the modern use because these people had a monopoly of literacy till towards the end of thc Middle Ages, supplying the necessary skills in lay as well as ecclesiastical administration.

CLOISTER: Covered way round courtyard, arcaded.

CLUNCH: Heavy chalk used as a rough building material, typically used for vernacular building in East Anglia and Cambridgeshire, where it is found. Might be faced, or come to need facing.

CLUNIAC: Order founded 910 in France. Strict *Benedictine*. Sometimes appropriated by the Crown as alien houses, though there was little real control from Cluny. In England, at the Dissolution, 8 greater and 30 lesser houses.

COAT OF ARMS: Heraldic devices on shield. *Supporters* for the shields were usually only granted to the great lords.

COLLEGE: Term used for various religious institutions as well as educational ones, including (1) the Colleges at Oxford and Cambridge; (2) institutions with religious, educational and/or chantry purposes.

COMMONS: Lower house of Parliament called by King, which began towards the end of the Middle Ages, to balance the Lords (lay lords and the bishops), the main royal officers in advising the king. The Commons, though, met in the Chapter House of Westminster Abbey, being excluded from the Palace of Westminster, where the Lords met.

CONDUIT: Pipe for water-supply.

CONVENT: In the Middle Ages 'convent' and 'conventual' were used for both male and female enclosed institutions.

COPING: Facing stones or bricks, usually sloping, protecting the top of a wall or other structure, such as parapets, battlements, buttresses.

CORBEL: Projecting support, for example for a roof beam.

CORBEL-TABLE: A row of corbels, providing support for a projection from a building, such as parapets or machicolations. Term used particularly when the corbels are linked up with each other, so that the structure is continuous.

CORBELLING: Continuous support for a projection, that is corbelled out, usually a series of mouldings (without individual corbels).

CORE: Or, coring. Inside layer of solid structure.

CORINTHIAN: One of the classical *orders*, revived in the Renaissance. Distinguished by column heads formed of acanthus leaves. The leaves curl over away from the column.

CORNICE: Projecting moulding at top of building. Non-mediaeval.

COUNTER-REFORMATION: European Catholic movement, only pursued in England in the reign of Mary I (and by secret Jesuit missionaries afterwards). During Mary's reign the old Catholic doctrines and to some extent institutions were restored, but property was not restored. The laymen who had obtained church land kept it.

COUNTER-RELIEF: Carving sunk below the surface.

COURSE: Layer of building material. See also *String-course*.

COURT OF AUGMENTATIONS: Set up in 1530s to deal with monastic property. (Lesser monasteries dissolved 1536.) The aim was to gain as much profit for the Crown as possible from sales, against the popular pressure favouring immediate, cheap distribution.

CRENELLATE: To crenellate, or fortify, licence had to be obtained from the central government.

CRENELLATION: Alternative term for *battlements*.

CRESTING: Small projections above top moulding of structure.

CROCKET: Foliage decoration at the pinnacle of an arch, a crocketed arch being one with foliage decoration at regular intervals up its sides with a single crocket—or finial—at the top. This was often a fleur-de-lis.

CROSSING: Part of church where nave, chancel and transepts meet. May have tower over, or a lantern.

CROW-STEPS: The tops of walls shaped like a series of steps. Most frequently applied to gable-ends. Common in sixteenth century.

CUPOLA: Domed top to a small projection, such as a circular or polygonal turret.
CURTAIN-WALL: Outer wall, linking different buildings, (contrast free-standing *enclosure-wall*).
CUSPED: Decorative work with projecting points between rounded lobes, making, for example, trefoils and quatrefoils. Used in window tracery and, sometimes, in corbel-tables. Although cusped decoration is frequent in both Perpendicular and Tudor tombs and architecture, the change-over from arched lights to cusped lights in windows did not take place till the end of Henry VIII's reign.
CUT BRICK: Brick shaped by carving after firing, in contrast to moulded brick. Tool used was the 'brick axe', comparable to a chisel rather than a modern axe.

DAUB: Dried mud used in building. See *Wattle*.
DECORATED: Style of architecture, from late thirteenth century to mid fourteenth century, characterized by ogee tracery and arches.
DE LA POLE: Important late mediaeval family. Origins, Hull merchants. From late fourteenth century head of family held title of Earl of Suffolk, and later, at times, Duke of Suffolk. Notable rise to power of family prompted baronial jealousies. Family obtained great wealth and high state offices. Royal (York) blood-relationship led to their suppression in the sixteenth century by the Tudors.

Three brickwork contexts: (1) Involved in C 14 brick-making at Hull. (2) Later, built in flint with some brickwork at Wingfield (Suffolk). (3) In mid fifteenth century William de la Pole, with Alice Chaucer, established the brick-built school and almshouses at Ewelme (Oxon).
DEMESNE: The lord's domain. Lands belonging to lord of manor, including equivalent of home farm.
DENTILLATED: Literally 'toothed'. Spaced decorative blocks or projecting headers.
DETAIL: Apart from the more finely worked parts of a sculpture or painting, 'detail' has architectural use for the smaller elements of a building—for example, loopholes, spandrels.
DE VERE: Important family. Norman Conquest nobility who survived into Tudor times and beyond. Title, Earl of Oxford. Lands mainly in East Anglia, especially in Essex, including Castle Hedingham. Suffolk lands concentrated round Lavenham. More noted for their survival powers, aided by steady line of male heirs, than for very great wealth. Sometimes endangered by providing unpopular royal favourites, especially Robert de Vere, favourite of Richard

II. Otherwise, main interests in landowning. Survived but hard pressed by the fine for keeping retainers levied by Henry VII.

DIAPER or DIAPERING: (1) All-over surface decoration composed of a small repeated pattern, such as squares or lozenges, for example with a quatrefoil flower inside. For example, Early Tudor ornamentation for chimney-shafts. (2) Brickwork patterns made by using a different-coloured brick from the main wall surface. Usually 'blue' bricks made of gault clay—including grey, mauve, purple, blackish bricks—and glazed, or 'vitrified'. In photographs, the glaze tends to catch the light, making these bricks look light. Normally only headers used. Became fashionable from the end of the fifteenth century, apparently inspired by French use. The simplest and most common pattern is continuous, or near-continuous, diamond diapering. Sometimes much more elaborate work.

DIOCESE: Or, *See*. Area of a bishop's jurisdiction.

DISSOLUTION OF THE MONASTERIES: Or, *Suppression*. The activity of Henry VIII's government, when the monastic *orders* were disposed of and their property redistributed. Such activity was not unprecedented: earlier suppressions and confiscations include that of the Order of the Knights of the Temple (Templars) in 1308 and of the Alien Priories (that is, houses subject to control from mother houses abroad) in 1411.

DOLPHIN: Part of fashionable Italianate decoration in Early Tudor times, shown in highly formalized style.

DOMINICAN: *Order* of friars, popularly 'Blackfriars' from habit. Founded early in thirteenth century by St Dominic. Emphasis on study and scholarship.

DORMITORY: Sleeping-quarters in a monastery.

DOVECOTE: By law, only the lord of the manor could have a dovecote, the doves enjoying the tenants' corn—a considerable grievance (like that against the doves kept by the miller, who was a monopolist anyway). Ventilation holes in barns might be used by doves. Doves used for food.

DRESSED: Flint or stone shaped by cutting and used for details. Brick would usually be moulded to shape before firing.

DRESSED FLINT: Split and shaped flint, typical of East Anglian churches, used for fine work and for decoration. Inside of flint shows grey, blackish brown or blue but, when combined with dressed stone panels, this is described as 'black and white' *flushwork*.

DRESSINGS: All shaped materials, including brick, used for windows, doorways, *quoins* and so on.

DRIPSTONE: A projecting moulding above a doorway, window or niche, intended to deflect rain. Above a lintel or square-headed window the dripstone will be flat (horizontal). The ends have a *label-stop* at right-angles.

EARLY ENGLISH: Post-Norman architecture, typified by pointed arches, lancet (pointed, thin) windows and 'stiff' leaf decoration to capitals.

EARLY TUDOR: Used for the period of the rule of Henry VII and Henry VIII, and sometimes including the reigns of Edward VI and Mary I was well (1558); *Tudor* can include the last of Henry VIII's children, Elizabeth I, but 'Elizabethan' seems preferable.

EGG-AND-DART MOULDING: Alternate ovals—strictly 'ovolo', convex, quarter-round—and 'arrowheads'. Found in Renaissance-style decoration.

EMBATTLED: Descriptive of defensive walls, with *battlements*: the mediaeval term was to *crenellate*.

EMBRACERY: Corrupting or putting pressure on a jury Statute against his in 1450, reinforced by Henry VII's legislation.

EMBRASURE: Opening in wall, usually for a window, or in an *alure*.

ENCLOSURE: Term used for fencing off of land for pasture, prompted in the Later Middle Ages by the growth of the wool and cloth trades. This produced wealth for the sheep-farmers, but impoverished the labourers, as fewer were needed and as they might have lost common land. The greatest outcry against this was in the sixteenth century, but the process had been going on through the fifteenth century (as William of Worcester records). A contemporary saying was: 'Sheep eat men.'

ENFIEF: To grant land for duration of a vassal's life, or for the duration of the family or ecclesiastical office.

ESCHEAT: Lands of the tenants-in-chief were held from the crown: if a tenant-in-chief died without heirs, the land would escheat to the crown.

ESTUARINE CLAY: Clay found in river banks and the surrounding marshland. This was the first clay used by the mediaevals for brick-making; later supplemented by inland claypits. The expert sees a difference in the texture of the bricks.

EXCHEQUER: (1) Office dealing with royal (government) finances, which had its own law court (one of the three royal courts, the others being King's Bench and Common Pleas). The king's personal finances were dealt with by the Household, which had a treasurer. (2) Any organization's financial office, the centre of its fee-collecting and administration.

EXECUTORS: As today, overseers of a will, charged with carrying out its provisions. The scale of executors' activity that was possible is shown by the continuing work at Tattershall (Lincs.) after the death of Ralph Lord Cromwell.

FACADE: Exterior walling of building, often used for the 'front'.
FACED: Layer of different material applied to exterior of wall, the facing. *Ashlar-faced*, covering of thin stone slabs.
FESTOON: Suspended carved garland of foliage with fruit and/or flowers, revived at the Renaissance.
FEUDALISM: Chief characteristic was that only the great lords owed direct loyalty to the Crown, all land in theory belonging to the Crown and being granted out in exchange for loyalty and services; the lords' tenants owed loyalty to the lords, and so only indirectly to the Crown. In England the near-disintegration of the feudal system towards the end of the Middle Ages is associated with anarchic conditions, while the rise of the middle class, especially in the towns, which had some independence from the system, challenged the power of the lords. At this time the lords themselves acquired the regular services of paid retainers, held by money contract not loyalty.
FIEF: Land held from the king or from a lord.
FIELD OF CLOTH OF GOLD: 1520 meeting of Francis I of France and Henry VIII of England, near Guines, France. Treaty-making was secondary to Renaissance-style display of splendid clothes and fittings by two young kings. Short interlude in endemic hostility of France and England.
FINIAL: Ornament at top of pinnacle, canopy, gable and so on. (Similar projection at base may be a *corbel.*)
FIREBACK: Lining of fireplace, usually of bricks or tiles—even if fireplace itself stone.
FIRESTEAD: Free-standing fireplace or fireplaces.
FIRING: Bricks hardened by firing, in kilns. Difficulties of obtaining even firing must have been considerable.
FLAMBOYANT: Literally, flamelike. *Decorated* period of architecture included work of this type, with free foliage ornament. Not typically in brick.
FLEUR-DE-LIS: Usually described as 'lily', but really a formalized iris. Used for decorative moulded brick, for example as *finial.*
FLINT: Form of silica, found in nodules in chalk. White or brown on outside; inside, black or dark grey, which may turn blue with weathering. *Dressed flint* is flint split and shaped, usually into rough squares.
Flint flushwork: Dressed flint combined with stone, imitating tracery panels and so on, giving a 'black and white' effect. Typical or late mediaeval churches in East Anglia, built mainly of flint. Role of brick may be limited to providing voussoirs to doors and windows.

Flint rubble: Usually, strictly, flint and rubble. May be used for coring or as facing material as well, where stone was expensive.

FLUTING: Column mouldings in Renaissance (classical) work, the shaft being grooved.

FOLIATED: Work of Decorated period, running foliage carvings.

FORFEITURE: Confiscation of property following *Attainder*.

FORM: (More archaic spellings include 'fourme'.) Term used for the frame, or open box, used in brick-making.

FRANCISCAN: Or, Greyfriars. Order founded in early thirteenth century by St Francis. Not *enclosed* order. Emphasis on poverty, but soon houses were being held (in trust) for these friars. Provided popular travelling preachers and aroused jealousy of secular clergy.

FREESTONE: Stone used decoratively, for example in panels of *flushwork*. Term also used, from mediaeval times, for all dressed stone.

FRET: A *knot* or single interlace.

FRETTY: Series of *knots*, either rounded or formalized with angled corners, used in decoration or heraldry.

FRIAR: Men in orders, neither enclosed nor secular clergy. Earliest orders, *Franciscan* and *Dominican*. Function chiefly to be travelling preachers, living by alms. Theoretically held no property, houses in towns being held in trust by Pope or local representative.

FRIEZE: Running decoration, for example at top of panelling or in terracotta work. A *corbel-table* may have such effect.

GABLE: Top part of end wall carrying roof, so normally triangular. May be *stepped*. *Gable-end* means whole end wall.

GARDEROBE: Mediaeval or Early Tudor latrine—contemporary term. Usually stone seat, with hole, contained in projection of building, for example in angle turret of tower.

GATE: Term used for entry to town, usually strictly a *gatehouse*.

GATEHOUSE: Fortified entry, of at least two storeys, to large house, castle, college or town. *Gate tower* may be used for structure of three or more storeys.

GAUGED BRICKWORK: Precisely laid bricks, with measured bonding and *mortar joints*. Seldom applicable to early brick, except to some high-quality work with wide mortar joints.

GAULT: Name's origin uncertain: ? French, ? brickmaker's term. *Gault bricks:* Of two types: (1) White or yellow bricks, produced from clay with relatively high proportion of chalk. (2) Blue, mauve, grey or black bricks, often used for *diaper* decoration. Colour derived from phosphates. *Gault clay:*

Found particularly south of chalk downs—the Wye area (East Kent)—and in Essex and Thames basin. Used for pottery as well as bricks. Light-coloured after firing. *Blue gault clay:* Stiff blue clay which includes nodules of grey substance (phosphates). Dark colours after firing.

GILBERTINES: Rare mixed monastic *order*, founded by St Gilbert of Sempringham (died 1189). Cistercian model, but had sections for monks and nuns.

GILD: Alternative, older spelling of *Guild.* Originally meant payment.

GLAZE: Glassy-surfaced bricks used for *diaper* decoration.

GOTHIC: General term for later mediaeval architecture and style, chiefly characterized by pointed arch.

GOTHICK: Eighteenth-century spelling, usefully distinct from *Gothic.* Reintroduction and transformation of mediaeval forms. Mediaeval buildings might be given 'Gothick' touch.

GRANITE: Hardest rock, in most rugged parts of country. Used for major building, but seldom finely carved.

GREAT BRICK: Term, used from early sixteenth century, for older unstandardized bricks. Up to 20 in long. Fifteen more common. Fairly thick. About 7½ in across.

GREAT HALL: Main room of mansions, continuing into Tudor period. Two-storey open hall, with central hearth. At one end screens, with three doors leading to kitchen, etc. Thirteenth century on.

GREENSAND: Sandstone, weathering to yellow or orange (iron). In southern England, including Kent and part of Norfolk. *Gault clay* is found between upper and lower layers.

GREENSTONE: Old term for some types of limestone, with dark or greenish tinge. Combined with brick, sometimes, in Lincs.

GROINS: Romanesque (pre-*Gothic*) ceiling structure, the vaulting having no ribs but ridges where the different vaults meet. Not brickwork.

GROUND-PLAN: The arrangement of the ranges of a building. Examples: 'L' plan (two wings at right-angles to each other, mediaeval and later); 'E' plan (like the letter, including short central wing or porch, typically Elizabethan); 'H' plan (no pre-Elizabethan examples and typically of that date).

GUILD: Various types of guild developed in towns, largest being the craft guilds. These included employers and employees in a certain craft or, since the eventual trend was to amalgamation, certain related crafts. They were concerned with prices, wages, conditions and quality of work (the secular skill was their 'mystery'). They were also concerned with social welfare of group, including provision of funerals, and would have an altar in the local church. (This religious link was the 'fraternity'.)

GUILLOCHE: Classical (Renaissance) moulding with two or more interlacing bands forming a plait, with rounded curves to twist.

HALF-TIMBER: Building with wooden frame of uprights and cross-pieces, panels between timbers being filled with plaster or brick. See *Nogging*.

HAMMER-BEAM ROOF: Introduced in fifteenth century. Typical of great building in reign of Henry VIII. Allowed wide roof-span of beams on projecting horizontal brackets.

HANDRAIL: Type used with brick spiral stair. Sunk in wall, ramped, with projecting moulding for grip and concave hand-shield.

HANSA: Adjective, Hanseatic. Mediaeval North German and Scandinavian trading organization, which had offices in ports in other countries.

HEADER: Brick-end.

HEARTH: Normally used for open fireplace, such as flat space for fire in floor of great hall. Escape-hole in roof for smoke.

HERRINGBONE: Materials laid in zigzag, or series of 'V's. Used for early tiled firebacks, walling (rarely) with tiles and, later, for brick *nogging*.

HOODMOULD: Projecting moulding over void, arched, to protect from rain. Also called *dripstone* or *label*.

HOSPITAL: Mediaeval term for foundation of almshouse type. Might also be called '*Bedehouse*', term being derived from rosary beads (prayers). Chantry-type foundations, inmates being supposed to pray for founders.

HUNDRED YEARS WAR: Running conflict between France and England, from reign of Edward III (mid fourteenth century) till Henry VI's withdrawal in mid fifteenth century. Originally stimulated by conflict over English provinces in south-west France, developed into war over English king's claim to French crown. English rulers continued to use French royal arms of *fleurs-de-lis* on blue ground, as part of their arms, long after loss of Calais in reign of Mary I.

ICONOCLASM: Destruction of religious images.

IMPALE: Term used when two *coats of arms* are combined, for example to show a marriage. The shields were each halved, to form a complete new shield (this now known as 'dimidiation'). Imitated by merchants, who would 'impale' *merchant's mark* with arms of a merchant company.

IMPEACH: Treason trial by Parliament, penalty death.

IN-FILLING: Filling between vaulting ribs or timber-framing.

IONIC: Classical *order* revived at *Renaissance*. Columns are fluted and column head (capital) has 'volutes', which curl round and downwards like a scroll.

IRONSTONE: Iron found in irregular layers in lower *Greensand* and in nodules (clay ironstones) in coalfields and elsewhere, producing dark marks in stone.

JACOBEAN: Of reign of James I, 1603–25.
JOINTS: Used for *mortar* joints, the layers of mortar between stones or bricks. See also *gauged.*
J.P.S: Justices of the Peace. Local law officers, first established in 1361 (reign of Edward III) and strengthened by Tudor monarchs.

KEEP: Main defensive tower of castle.
KETT'S REBELLION: 1549. Concentrated in Norfolk. Included siege of Norwich. Main leader, Robert Kett of Wymondham, tanner and landowner. Causes, rising prices and *Enclosure.* Some sympathy from the Lord Protector, Somerset, but put down by his successor-to-be, Warwick (later Northumberland).
KNIGHTS OF ST JOHN: Also called the 'Hospitallers'. Eleventh-century foundation in Jerusalem, as military *order* caring for pilgrims and then for sick also. By suppression in England had forty-three English establishments, comparable to monasteries, and were large-scale farmers.
KNIGHTS TEMPLAR: Founded in 1118 in Jerusalem. *Order* rose to great power, lands, houses and influence in Europe. Suppressed in France and, soon after in 1308, in England—where property granted to Knights of St John and others.
KNOT: Heraldic badge of Stafford family, rather like a single rounded *fret.*

LABEL: Term used for flat or arched moulding over door or window, to deflect rain. See *Hoodmould* and *Dripstone.* Form imitated for niches indoors.
LABEL-STOP: Small moulding, perhaps decorated with a *boss.* Attached to base of *label,* usually set horizontally.
LANCASTER: Family. Title of head, Duke of Lancaster. Royal status acquired by deposition of Richard II in 1399 by Henry Bolingbroke, who became Henry IV. Duchy of Lancaster gave fund base for Henry IV, Henry V and Henry VI, and continued in royal possession after end of Lancastrian dynastry.
LANCET: Small pointed window. Typical of *Early English* style, but used later too.
LANTERN: Polygonal pierced tower or turret. For example, lantern over *crossing* of church.

LANTERN-TYPE-CHIMNEY: Strictly refers to top, not whole shaft: lantern is pierced for smoke outlets at sides, top being covered.

LATH-AND-PLASTER: Wood strips with fine clay, used in vernacular building for filling in panels between timbers. Improvement on earlier *wattle-and-daub*.

LEGATE: Papal representative. This office gave Wolsey unprecedented powers, just before Reformation in England. Earlier legates usually foreigners.

LELAND, JOHN: Mid sixteenth century writer. Took topographical and other notes intended for a 'Description of England', dedicated to Henry VIII, but did not complete work. Notes published later as Leland's *Itinerary*. Had particular interest in buildings and their materials.

LICENCE TO CRENELLATE: Organized system dates from reign of Edward I (late thirteenth century). Royal permission needed for erection of a castle or for fortifying an existing house. Adulterine (unlicensed) castle of Stephen's reign (twelfth century) had been major contribution to anarchy, and later kings realized importance of control. Could apply to fairly small buildings. By Later Middle Ages licence to crenellate was only symbol of power and status.

LIERNE: See under *Vaulting*.

LIGHTS: Term used for sections of a window, with separate heads, divided by *mullions*. Arched lights may feature under square *labels* in Perpendicular and Early Tudor architecture, allowing decoration in *spandrels*.

LIMESTONE: Yellow or grey stone, often light in colour, found in many parts of England. Recent (geologically) limestones lie next to clays, including brick earth, so limestone often used for dressings in brick buildings. Also burned and used in *mortar*.

LINCOLNSHIRE RISING: 1536. Prompted by religious measures of Henry VIII and rumours of further measures. A main factor was fear of people of Louth for new, expensive parish church.

LINENFOLD PANELLING: Early Tudor wood panelling for walls and sides of chests, stiffly imitating folded material.

LINTEL: Horizontal cross-piece or beam at head of void—for example, over window, doorway, fireplace—taking strain of walling above.

LIVERY: Institution of keeping retainers (not servants), who were distinguished by a uniform or badges. This 'livery', by derivation, the lord's colours taken from *coat of arms*. These retainers were armed. Institution banned by 1377 statute, this repeated 1450, and finally successfully enforced by Henry VII.

LOAD-BEARING: Part of building taking structural strain, for example *lintel.* (Contrast *in-filling* panels which, like glass panels in modern steel frames, do not take load.)

LOLLARDY: Religious beliefs developed in Later Middle Ages, and bearing some similarity to later *Protestantism.*

LORDS: Mediaeval House of Lords, predating *Commons.* 'Magnum concilium' of kings (the great council). Met in royal Palace of Westminster. Consisted of the magnates, that is the *tenants-in-chief* and the bishops.

LOUVER: Various mediaeval and modern spellings, apparently derived from French 'ouvert' (open). (1) Bell opening in church tower. (2) Hall lantern.

LUNETTE: Semicircular shape, such as *pediment.* May be used in relief decoration.

MACHICOLATIONS: Defences *corbelled* out, providing holes down which to project missiles. Term derived from French, and perhaps use in England French-inspired too.

False machicolations: These have appearance of machicolations, but are blind and useless, built as decorative feature.

MAINTENANCE: Term used for maintaining a lord's interests in a lawsuit, illegally influencing the verdict. First statute against this 1327, repeated 1450 and enforced by Henry VII. Associated with later mediaeval custom of keeping *retainers*, who might exert such pressure.

MANOR: Mediaeval estate, which had own law court (till fifteenth century at latest) and administration. Estate could be that of layman or ecclesiastic.

MARK: Mediaeval coin, value 13*s.* 4*d.* For present real value multiply by 60, though very rough gauge.

MAYOR: Office of mayor developed in Later Middle Ages, showing independence of town from any lord, enshrined in royal charter.

MERCER: Originally dealer in small goods, then textiles especially. Mercers were one of the London companies.

MERCHANT'S MARK: Origin might be from marking goods. Used later as substitute for *coat of arms.* Marks have similar design often, utilizing a cross or arrow shape. Minor changes made for different members of family. May be used to mark parts of building to which a merchant contributed: compare *rebus.*

MOAT: Water defences, out of fashion by 1540s. Normally round or rectangular. Protected castles and also manor houses.

MOLET: Heraldic charge. Star, with 5 or 6 points. (Another spelling is 'mullet'.)

MONOGRAM: Decorative combination of initials, especially found in Early Tudor and Renaissance ornament. May be used to mark responsibility for building.

MORTAR: Bonding materials. Lime, sand and water mixture, used with stone or brick. We still speak of 'bricks and mortar' (but modern cement is calcinated lime and clay). Mortar *joints* of early brick comparatively wide.

MOTTE: Literally, a mound. 'Motte and Bailey' castles of Earlier Middle Ages (earlier than the brick-building period) had a keep on the mound surrounded by an enclosure.

MOULDED BRICK: Brick clay pre-shaped by firing in mould, used for special purposes or decoration.

MOULDING: Shaped work. For example, round archway. Rows or *orders* give *relief* and *counter-relief* ornament.

MULLION: Window upright, the vertical bars dividing a window into separate *lights*.

MURDER HOLES: French 'meurtrières'. Pierced in ceiling of castle entry, allowing attack on intruders as through *machicolations*.

NEWEL: Central column of spiral staircase.

NEWEL STAIRCASE: Spiral stair, with central post taking points of the triangular steps, with the wide ends embedded in the wall. Such stairs in early buildings contained in a projecting stair turret.

'NEW LEARNING': Study of classical literature, especially of Greek, associated with a critical attitude to texts and with certain humanistic ideas.

NOBLE: Mediaeval coin, value 6*s* 8*d*. (Multiply by about 60 for modern worth.)

NOGGING: Horizontally or diagonally laid bricks between timbers of *timber-framed* building. Typically, vernacular building.

NORMAN: Post-Conquest English architectural style, sometimes called 'Romanesque'. Mainly characterized by round arches.

OGEE: Doubly curved arch, found especially in *Decorated* work: curves in below point of arch and then swells out again (so concave-convex).

OGIVAL: Adjective from 'ogee'. Practically, with a double curve.

ORATORY: Small private chapel, usually in a house.

ORDER: (1) *Architectural:* Combination of elements making up the different classical orders. These were revived in the Renaissance, regularized by the work of Serlio (published 1540) based on Vitruvius's *De Architectura* of 1st century B.C. (Vitruvius *flor.* 46–30 B.C.) Elements mainly parts of columns and pediments. (2) *Historical:* Belonging to an order, that is ruled by certain special regulations. Applied to both the enclosed monks and the unenclosed friars. The rules were those of the original founder.

ORDER OF THE GARTER: 1348 foundation by Edward III at time of campaign against France; chivalric order intended to unite peers involved. Membership in gift of monarch. Chapel of order, St George's Windsor. The emblem, a ribbon-like garter.

ORIEL WINDOW: Window projecting only from upper floor level.

OVERHANG: With an overhung house, the first floor is cantilevered out. Typical of timber-framed, vernacular building. Later, a house might be enlarged by building new ground-floor walls up to the overhang and then demolishing the original ones now inside: this work was normally brick.

OVOLO: Oval moulding or beading, with ovals placed at intervals. Typical Renaissance ornament. When between the ovals there are pointed shapes, like spearheads, the combined moulding is known as *egg-and-dart*.

PALACE: Mansion, really defined by status of owner—in this study, home of a king or of a *bishop*, really seen as administrative centres. Contemporaneously, tendency to describe any outstanding mansion as a palace.

PANEL: Individual square or rectangle. Or, section in a series of panels, such as on the side of a tomb-chest or a wall frieze of wood.

PANEL TRACERY: Comparatively simple heads to windows, with the upper lights simply following the line of the arch without further decoration.

PANTILE. Double-curved roof tile. In our pre-Elizabethan context a pantiled roof usually indicates that the tiles are replacements of the original flat tiles. Pantiles made in England only from seventeenth century on, but some had evidently been imported from Flanders in sixteenth century.

PARAPET: Low walls, sometimes battlemented or pierced, at the top of a flat-roofed building. A walk behind parapets is an 'alure'.

PARVISE: Upper chamber of church porch.

PASTON LETTERS: Collection of documents, mainly letters, of late mediaeval Norfolk family which obtained possession of Caister Castle (Norfolk).

PEASANTS' REVOLT: 1381. Immediate cause the Poll Tax. General causes economic, resulting from recent past improvements in the position of labourers following the 1349 Black Death—improvements which were now felt to be threatened. Widespread rising, certainly involving the whole of south-east England and not at once repressed. Several leaders in the different localities.

PEDIMENT: Renaissance pediments over windows, porch doors and so on. Possibly semicircular in shape (see *Lunette*). Usually Elizabethan or later.

PENDANT: Hanging decoration, based on a boss, usually in roof vaulting—especially *Fan-vaulting* (always stone, not brick).

PERPENDICULAR: English version of late *Gothic* style, from about 1360 to 1540 or 1550. Characterized by straight lines, vertical and horizontal, by very large window areas and by panel decoration (in tracery or blank). The abbreviation 'Perp.' is used in the Gazetteer.

PILASTER: Part of early Renaissance decoration. Rectangular columns, not free-standing and with shallow relief carving only.

PILGRIMAGE OF GRACE: 1536–7. Initially peaceful demonstration against the *Reformation* changes, especially the *Dissolution* of the Smaller Monasteries. Centre, Yorkshire. Leaders included D'Arcy of Temple Newsam. Brutally suppressed by government (300 hangings). The monasteries in Yorkshire, with its scattered population and comparative poverty, were important in the local economy.

PINNACLE: Tall ornament on top of angle turret or buttress and so on. May be topped by a *finial.* Typically stone rather than brick.

PISCINA: Drain for holy water, set in niche in church wall beside altar.

PLACE BRICKS: Those early bricks shaped by the wet clay being cut on the ground on a layer of straw. The straw stuck to the clay and then burned away in the firing, meaning that very distinct straw marks can be seen on the brick surface. Size uneven.

PLASTER: Lime-sand mixture used for coating inside walls. For exterior use see *Lath-and-plaster.*

PLINTH: Base of building, ground level projection. Typically found with vernacular building, such as a brick base to half-timbered and plastered houses.

PLOUGHSHARE VAULTING: See *Vaulting.*

PORTCULLIS: (1) Large vertical grid, which could be lowered to close entry of castle or defended manor. The portcullis grooves survive at Compton Wynyates (War.). (2) Heraldic badge of Tudors.

POSTERN: Subordinate gateway, giving entrance to castle or in town wall. Not part of the main defences.

PREMONSTRATENSIAN: Regular canons, following Augustinian *order.* Founded in France in 1120. Houses of the order in England were rare.

PRIEST'S HOUSE: Quarters for a local or visiting priest might be provided at an isolated church or *chapel-of-ease.* Attached to the church by lean-to construction or a cell in the tower set aside for such use.

PRIORY: Monastic establishment headed by prior. Lower status than abbey. Example, Thornton (Lincs.), founded as priory in 1139, was promoted to abbey in 1148.

PRIVY SEAL: Personal seal or authorization for documents of king. Kept by

Lord Privy Seal, his office in Early Tudor times being more intimate with the king than the old Chamber, which it was supplanting.

PROFILES: Decorative profile heads, usually on small panels, characteristic of Early Tudor architecture, and ultimately the product of Renaissance influence.

PROTESTANTISM: Beliefs which supplanted the Catholic Church in some European countries, an essential condition being that authority in the church was local and not that of the Pope in Rome. In England the institutional changes were mainly made in the reign of Henry VIII, but doctrine was scarcely touched till that of Edward VI when *chantries* and images and the use of Latin were rejected.

PUTTI: Italianate cherubs appearing in England with the Renaissance. Singular = 'putto'. Also called amorini. Naked and winged.

QUADRANGLE: Interior courtyard to building, which may include a covered walk, as in the cloisters of a monastery. May be found in a late castle, contributing to defences and to the castle's autonomy (room for workshops and so on).

QUARTERED: Shield of arms divided into four parts. Such divisions may be part of a family's arms, such as those of the *de Veres*—quarterly *gules* and *or* (red and gold) with a *molet* argent (silver star) in the 1st quarter (top left).

QUATREFOIL: Four-leaved, a common form of decoration in Perpendicular and Early Tudor work, quatrefoils usually having a small point like a clover leaf. Found in moulded brick, though trefoils more common.

QUOIN: Angle, or corner, stone or brick. Usually laid to give an alternating long-short pattern, the purpose being to strengthen the corners of the building. In late fifteenth-century and Early Tudor work a frequent combination is brick building with stone quoins.

RAGSTONE: Type of stone, such as Kentish rag (used, for example, for Lambeth parish church). Much used in Middle Ages, though it cannot be chiselled or finely shaped.

RAMPED: Curving upwards, as the handrail of a spiral staircase.

RANGE: Term may be used for linked building, or wing, or for a free-standing structure of some length.

REBUS: Punning device on a mediaeval or Tudor name, which may be used as a badge to mark parts of a building as the donor's.

REGULAR: Clerk in monastic and other orders, that is living under certain rules. Contrast *secular*.

RELIEF: Carving standing out, but not free-standing.

RELIEVING ARCH: Shallow arch relieving pressure, especially over square voids. In brickwork found most often when a stone lintel is used. These arches are flush with the wall surface; contrast *Squinch*.

REPOINTING: Brickwork repaired by filling in worn mortar joints with new cement.

RESPOND: Support for an arch, consisting of a short column projecting from a wall about eye-level.

RESTORED: Used for repair of whole building, unless specifically said of a part only—e.g. chimneys.

RETAINER: Dependent or follower of a person of rank and possessions, linked to him by indenture. In the Later Middle Ages such men constituted the barons' private armies. There were later mediaeval statutes passed against such men, but they were not really suppressed until enforcement by Henry VII—particularly through the so-called 'Star Chamber' Act of 1487.

REVET: To face, with masonry or brick, e.g. moat linings.

RIBS: Projecting supports of vaulting. Even when the cells between the ribs are brick, the ribs themselves are often stone.

RISER: Vertical part of a step in a stair. May be formed of brick ends, with the stretcher for the tread.

ROMAN BRICKS: Hard-burned, fairly pale in colour, thin (like tiles). Size about 12 × 6 × 12 in. Reused examples in mediaeval churches.

ROOD: The rood itself was a crucifix with the Virgin and St John, particularly that above the chancel arch of a church. To give access to this several structures were needed:

Rood loft: The cross-beam, on which the rood was fixed, with a catwalk behind.

Rood stair: Stair from north or south (or both) side of arch.

Rood stair turret: If the rood stair projected beyond the walls of the church a stair turret was needed—normally polygonal, and of the same height and plan as a porch turret.

ROSE, TUDOR: Double rose adopted to symbolize the union of York and Lancaster under Henry VII. Prominent in decoration in time of Henry VIII, for example as a roof boss.

RUBBED BRICK: Moulded decoration completed by on-the-site work.

RUBBLE: (1) Rough and irregular walling, consisting of quite large pieces of stone or of flints. (2) This used for the core of the wall only, the exterior being faced with dressed stone or flint.

SACRISTY: Repository for vestments, vessels, etc., of a church.

SANCTUARY: (1) Section of church, the east part of the chancel, with the altar. Often provided site for founder's or benefactor's tomb. (2) The church as a sanctuary for criminals or the pursued, allowing temporary respite, after which the criminal had to make his way into exile.

SANDSTONE: Stone of varying colour. Red or brownish shade indicates presence of iron. May be white, yellow or greenish also. Fairly soft stone.

SARCOPHAGUS: Ornate coffin.

SCALLOP: Fluted semicircular decoration, as for Layer Marney (Essex) pediments, or scooped, as for Early Tudor chimney tops.

SCREENS: (1) Church screen, dividing chancel from nave. (2) Domestic screens: the traditional plan of the mediaeval hall house included a screens passage connecting the hall with buttery, kitchen and pantry, with separate arched doors.

SECULAR: Basically, in or of the world. (1) The parish church clergy, as opposed to the *regulars*. The income of these priests was often low, while the monasteries could be richly endowed and, latterly, the *friars* attracted popularity and donations, so there was often jealousy between seculars and regulars. (2) lay, as opposed to church, including state as opposed to church jurisdiction.

SEDILIA: Seats on south of chancel, used regularly in the Middle Ages for the attendant clergy. Usually triple.

SEE: Area of jurisdiction of a bishop. See also *bishopric*.

SEPTARIA: A yellowish, layered shale or stone, with minerals in cracks. Includes clay ironstones. Used as a building material in some, especially coastal, East Anglian churches.

SEQUESTRATION: Take-over of property by the Crown.

SHAFT: (1) Upright. Attached column (columnette) used structurally—for example, buttressing angle shafts—or decoratively—for example, dividing panels of tomb-chests. (2) *Chimney-shaft:* Column-like section of chimney, carrying flue between the chimney-stack and the head or top. Main decorated part of chimney in late fifteenth century and Early Tudor times.

SHIELD: Apart from its defensive use, a shield provided the main display of heraldic achievements. Changes in the shape of shields help date effigies and brasses, when the inscription has disappeared. Roughly, the simple 'heater-shaped' shield—like an old smoothing-iron—is a sign of early date. Later a 'bouche' was cut as a lance-hole. This features in shields of the Renaissance period, possibly only as one of a series of cuspings, and the base of the shield is also shaped (like an inverted ogee arch).

SILL: Base of window.

SKEWED: Oblique or slanting. Examples, sloping top of buttress, gable copings, chimney-shaft decoration.

SOFFIT: Underside of a structure such as a lintel, arch, stair.

SOLAR: Mediaeval term for room comparable to parlour. Upper room, traditionally private quarters of lord.

SPANDREL: Triangle formed at top and side of arch, between curve of arch and a square *label* in Perpendicular and Early Tudor buildings. Often filled with cusped decoration.

SPLAY: Window recess, splayed out so that the interior opening is wider than window itself. Exterior brick *voussoirs* in rubble fabric may signify brick splays (esp. in East Anglia).

SPRINGER: Lowest section of vaulting, support projecting from side wall and forming the arch base.

SPUR: Decorated chimney tops may have spurs, a series of sharp projections.

SQUINCH: The mediaeval term 'squynchon' was used, as in the accounts for Beverley North Bar in 1409, for any shaped brick. The modern use is more specialized, a squinch being an arch or group of arches carrying a projection above ground level—e.g. stair turret.

STAPLE: From Fourteenth Century Company of Staplers employed by Crown to organize the police wool and cloth trade with Continental buyers. From 1363 the headquarters, the Staple, was at Calais. A limited number of English ports had monopoly of wool exports and part of the customs duties. See *Wool Trade* below.

STAR CHAMBER: The Court of Star Chamber (the name came from its painted ceiling decoration) at the Palace of Westminster was used under Henry VII to enforce laws against the powers of the lords. This made the court popular with the common people. (Its ominous reputation derives from the Stuart period, when the court was used to defend resented royal prerogatives.) In reign of Henry VII chosen punishment was fining, which reinforced royal power, in preference to earlier mutilation or imprisonment. An Act of Parliament of 1487 has been called the '*Star Chamber Act*': this grouped and reinforced the mediaeval statutes against *livery* and *maintenance*.

STAR TOP: Pointed decoration at head of *chimney*.

STATUTE: Mediaeval Act of Parliament, really royal law pronounced in and publicized through the *Commons*.

STEPPED: Or *crow-stepped*. Rising parts of a structure squared off at different levels. Examples, gable-ends and chimney bases.

STRETCHER: Side, or longest face, of brick.

STRINGCOURSE: Stage of building marked by a horizontal strip, which may be moulded. Early brick building often has stone *dressings*, including courses.
SUPPORTERS: A pair of heraldic beasts, or sometimes people, in a coat of arms. Their function is to hold up the shield. They are usually found only in the coats of arms of the really great.
SUPPRESSION: Alternative term for the *Dissolution of the Monasteries*. Confiscation of property and dispersal of the *regulars*.
SWAG: Or, *festoon*. Looped garland.

TABLE-TOP TOMB: Or, tomb-chest. Flat-topped tomb, which might have brass effigies inset; usable as an altar.
TEMPLARS: See *Knights Templar*.
TENANTS-IN-CAPITE: Or, Tenants-in-chief. Direct vassals of the king, alone subject to the royal feudal *incidents*, which had become very unpopular by the later Middle Ages (including *wardship*). If a tenant-in-chief died heirless, his lands returned to crown ownership. It was because Sir John Fastolf of Caister (Norfolk), though a great lord, was not actually a tenant-in-chief that the Paston family was finally able to obtain Caister which was supposedly left them.
TERRACOTTA: Hard-fired pottery used for fine ornament in buildings and for small-scale statuary. Moulded. Unglazed. Used mainly for wall ornamentation and tomb-chests in the 1520–40 period, part of fashionable Renaissance work.
TIMBER-FRAMED: Building formed of wood uprights and crossbeams, the panels between these being filled with another material—*wattle-and-daub*, *lath-and-plaster* or brick.
TIMBER-HANGING: Exterior of building faced with overlapping wood slats.
TITHE BARN: Term has been used casually of any very large old barn, but strictly a barn for the storing of church or monastic tithes—a tenth part of agricultural produce taken as a local religious tax.
TOMB-CHEST: Large stone or brick coffin. See *Table-top Tomb*.
TOURELLE: Turret corbelled out from a main wall.
TRACERY: Usually windows where lights are decorated at the top. May be used as motif in other decoration. *Blank* tracery used as wall decoration.
TRANSEPT: Side arm of church, projecting from meeting-place (crossing) of nave and chancel. Transepts used as chapels.
TRANSOM: Horizontal window bar.
TREAD: Flat part of step. With brick spiral stairs treads normally stretchers.
TREASURER: Official in charge of royal household, an intimate of the king's of the Later Middle Ages and the Tudor period.

TUDOR: Family name of monarchs from Henry VII to Elizabeth, that is 1485 to 1603, from the Welsh parentage of Henry VII, his father being a Welsh gentleman of this name and his claim to the throne being through his mother and grandmother. 'Tudor' is also used for the architectural style of the period from 1485 (approximately), sometimes to the mid sixteenth century and sometimes on until the end of Elizabeth's reign. This second use covers too great a period and diversity of style: Tudor or *Early Tudor* here applied only to the period up to the end of Henry VIII's reign, about 1547.
TUDOR ROSE: See *Rose*.
TUN: Wine-barrel. Used in several *rebuses* for names ending in 'ton'.
TWIST: Decorative skewed and twisted chimney-shafts, using canted bricks, especially Early Tudor. Barley-sugar style.

UN-DRESSED FLINT: Unshaped flint. May be combined with stone dressings and brick voussoirs in East Anglian churches (especially).
UNDERCROFT: Usually a cellar or basement, but may not be wholly below ground. Vaulting main feature.
URN: Calyx- or cup-shaped classical vase, in Renaissance ornament usually filled with foliage.

VALOR ECCLESIASTICUS: 1535 government survey of church property, which formed a useful inventory for the later confiscations. Showed total church revenue of £300,000 a year.
VAULTING: Curved ceilings, sectionalized to distribute the stresses. The different types listed below are in rough chronological order. Brick was used only for the later types.
Groined vaulting: Roof having edges (groins) formed by the meeting of two or more vaults. Found in Romanesque building only. (Gothic, from about the end of the thirteenth century, is invariably ribbed.) Co-eval with:
Barrel or tunnel vaulting: Simple early form of vaulting, formed with a series of single semicircular ribs, allowing a comparatively low vault only.
Rib vaulting: Any form of vaulting with single ribs meeting at central point, so that ceiling is arched, not rounded. Rectangular ground plan, the main ribs being diagonal.
Quadripartite vaulting: Vaulting ribs from four triangular cells, the form being repeated in a series of bays.
Lierne vaulting: Rib-vault which has additional lesser ribs at angles to and linking the main ribs. This produces large numbers of rib junctions, which may be ornamented with decorative bosses, typical of late mediaeval vaulting.

Ploughshare vaulting: (1) Term may also be applied to the vaulting of a spiral stair, when stretchers are laid in series of rough triangles. (2) Staggered vaulting used for small areas. Initially, to increase light in a clerestory, the wall ribs rose from *springers* higher than those of the diagonal ribs, producing a surface rather like that of a ploughshare (also known as 'stilted vaulting').

Fan-vaulting: Late and very ornate type of ceiling, always of stone throughout, the fans being squat, pierced and with pendant cones.

VERNACULAR: (1) Use of English. (2) Local or domestic building, using local materials and workers. Examples, all cottages and small houses, 'industrial' buildings—such as warehouses.

VISITATIONS: Inspection of monasteries, usually by the bishop of the diocese in which they were situated.

VISITORS: (1) Monastic visitors, as above. (2) Imitative title used for the mid sixteenth century survey of the monasteries instituted by the government of Henry VIII, prior to the *Dissolution*. The chief post was Thomas Cromwell's, and visitors such as Legh and Layton reported to him the moral condition of the religious houses (at the same period the *Valor Ecclesiasticus* listed plate and sources of income), usually in the blackest terms. These reports eventually justified the Dissolution, first of the Lesser Monasteries and then of the Greater, and more respectable, Monasteries.

VITRIFIED: Glazed finish given to brick used for *diaper* work.

VOID: Any opening in wall of building, such as window or door.

VOUSSOIRS: (Irresistibly spelled 'wousers' in a 1528 document.) Series of blocks used to form or strengthen an arch. In stone work they are wedge-shaped. In brickwork there are wedge-shaped mortar joints between the bricks, at least with early brickwork. In dozens of East Anglian churches bricks are used for voussoirs—like low relieving arches, except that the bricks are quite widely spaced—to bond the flint rubble above window arches.

WARS OF THE ROSES: Began with the 1455 1st Battle of St Albans, an attack on the party of Henry VI, and in fact resolved by the Battle of Bosworth in 1485, after which Henry VII married the York heiress. Yorkist and Lancastrian parties among the barons were deeply involved and the baronage suffered many losses, although the mass of the people were only indirectly affected by military action occasionally and, more regularly, by failures in law and order.

WASTERS: Bricks rejected after firing because of faults.

WATTLE-AND-DAUB: Withies woven and 'plastered' over with daub (clay), used between the relatively few timbers of early vernacular building.

WESTERN RISING: 1547 and later. Prompted by opposition to the *Chantries*' Act and the *iconoclasm* of Edward VI's government.

WIND-BRACE: Curved or straight timbers in roof, reinforcing main timbers against thrust.

WOOL TRADE: Most paying later mediaeval English trade. At first wool was sent abroad for weaving; later the English cloth trade was developed, with the immigration of foreign skilled workers encouraged as government policy. Cloth was the result of seven processes, and finally became such big business that in the fifteenth century 'Jack of Newbury' (John Winchcombe) had a virtual factory of looms, and in the sixteenth century William Stumpe filled the dissolved abbeys of Osney and Malmesbury with looms. Churches are sometimes described as 'wool churches', when the source of the funds for their building was donations by wool merchants.

WORCESTER, WILLIAM: William of Worcester, or Botoner, mid fifteenth century secretary of Sir John Fastolf of Caister (Norfolk). He visited various parts of England, including his native Bristol, taking topographical notes which are a useful source of information. He talks of contemporary *enclosures*, long before the sixteenth-century outbursts against their effects. (Notes published as *Itinerary*.)

WYATT'S REBELLION: 1554. Led by Sir Thomas Wyatt of Allington, Kent, against the proposed marriage of Mary I with Philip of Spain, feared as a powerful foreign monarch and a Roman Catholic. Wyatt was executed when revolt suppressed.

YALE: Swivel-horned, deer-like beast. Mythical and heraldic. Arms of the *Beaufort* family.

YORK: Family headed by Duke of York. Acquired royal status in 1461, following attacks on Henry VI from 1455 on (the first Yorkist claim on the throne was by Richard Duke of York), in person of Edward IV. Despite 1471 return of Henry VI, Edward IV ruled again and was followed by his brother, Richard III.

ZIGZAG: Motif in decoration from end of fifteenth century: (1) on moulded brick chimney-shafts; (2) in diaper decoration in brickwork. Normally zigzag is vertical, except for some moulded brick chimney-shafts with close horizontal zigzagging.

Index

Refers to pages 17–221